A PLUME BOOK

THE SIGN

THOMAS DE WESSELOW is an art historian experienced at tackling "unsolvable" problems. He studied art history at Edinburgh University and at the Courtauld Institute of Art in London, where he worked successfully on the Guidoriccio problem, one of the great mysteries of Italian art. Later, he became a scholar at the British School at Rome, researching an even more complex puzzle, the so-called Assisi problem. In 2002, he was appointed a postdoctoral research associate at King's College, Cambridge University. Since 2007 he has been researching the Shroud full-time. He lives in Cambridge.

Praise for *The Sign*

"Some people will dismiss [*The Sign*]. Some people will be intrigued by it. And some people may change their attitudes on one thing or another by it."
—Harold Attridge, dean of Yale Divinity School,
as told to CBS *Sunday Morning*

"Fascinating . . . startling."   —*Telegraph* (London)

"A fresh insight into the Easter story."   —*Financial Times*

"Thorough, well-researched, and fair-minded . . . Persuasive . . . much more than just an addition to the canon of Shroud literature."
—*The Irish Times*

THOMAS DE WESSELOW

The Sign

*The Shroud of Turin and the Birth
of Christianity*

A PLUME BOOK

PLUME

Published by the Penguin Group
Penguin Group (USA) Inc., 375 Hudson Street,
New York, New York 10014, USA

USA | Canada | UK | Ireland | Australia | New Zealand | India | South Africa | China
Penguin Books Ltd, Registered Offices: 80 Strand, London WC2R 0RL, England
For more information about the Penguin Group visit penguin.com

First published in the United States of America by Dutton, a member of Penguin Group (USA)
Inc., 2012
First Plume Printing 2013

REGISTERED TRADEMARK—MARCA REGISTRADA

CIP data is available.

ISBN 978-0-452-29903-0

Printed in the United States of America
10 9 8 7 6 5 4 3 2 1

Original hardcover design by Palimpset Book Production Limited, Falkirk, Stirlingshire

While the author has made every effort to provide accurate telephone numbers, Internet addresses, and other contact information at the time of publication, neither the publisher nor
the author assumes any responsibility for errors or for changes that occur after publication.
Further, publisher does not have any control over and does not assume any responsibility for
author or third-party Web sites or their content.

For my mother
Who encouraged me to work things out for myself
With love

Contents

PART 4
Seeing through the Shroud

PART 5
Easter

PART 6
The Birth of the Church

PART 7
Conclusion

Figures

Every effort has been made to locate and contact the copyright holders of these images. Readers able to supply any missing relevant information are invited to contact the publisher.

The Holy Land at the Time of Easter

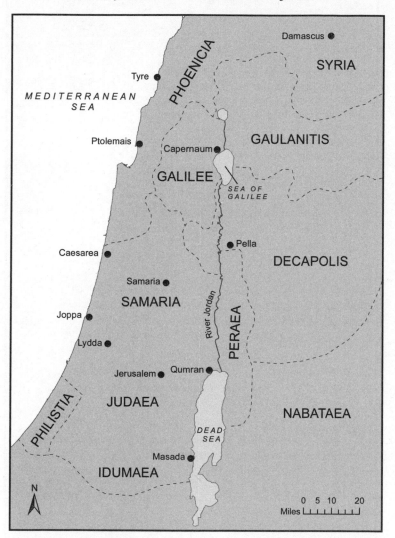

Damascus

SYRIA

Tyre

PHOENICIA

MEDITERRANEAN SEA

GAULANITIS

Ptolemais

Capernaum

GALILEE

SEA OF GALILEE

Caesarea

Pella

DECAPOLIS

Samaria

SAMARIA

River Jordan

PERAEA

Joppa

Lydda

Jerusalem

Qumran

JUDAEA

DEAD SEA

NABATAEA

PHILISTIA

Masada

IDUMAEA

N

0 5 10 20
Miles

Locations of the Shroud/Mandylion

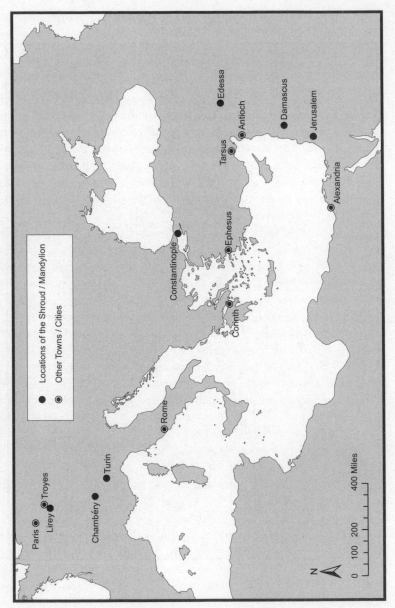

Legend:
- Locations of the Shroud / Mandylion
- Other Towns / Cities

Edessa
Antioch
Tarsus
Damascus
Jerusalem
Alexandria
Constantinople
Ephesus
Corinth
Rome
Turin
Chambéry
Paris
Lirey
Troyes

0   100 200   400 Miles

N

Preface

This book is about two of the world's greatest mysteries. The first—which scholars long ago grew weary of debating without ever resolving—is the mystery of Easter, concerning the alleged resurrection of Jesus soon after his crucifixion. The second—which scholars have avoided discussing altogether—is that of the world's most famous relic, the Shroud of Turin, in which Jesus is supposed to have been buried. It is my contention that these two mysteries are interconnected and that to resolve the first, we have to discuss the second.

This is not an academic book. It can be read by anyone interested in how Christianity began or in the Shroud; no prior knowledge of either subject is assumed. My aim is to set out, as clearly as possible, a revolutionary new way of understanding the birth of Christianity. Much more could have been said at every stage of the argument, but, in the interests of clarity, discussion of all side-issues has been postponed till another time.

Some may be concerned that, in entering the debate about Christian origins, I am trespassing on the territory of theologians and New Testament scholars. While I respect these scholars' expertise, I believe ideas matter more than credentials, and it is surely about time more outsiders weighed into the debate. As an art historian, I can approach the problem from an entirely new angle. I am as qualified as anyone to speak about the Shroud, and it is this relic, I believe, that holds the key to solving the historical puzzle of Easter. Moreover, experience in the art of analysing visual imagery is surprisingly useful when considering those most complex of representations—the Gospels.

My argument is bound to be controversial, since it casts fresh doubt on the reality of the Resurrection, the linchpin of traditional Christian belief. It is important to stress, therefore, that what I write is not intended in any way as an attack upon Christianity. My aim is simply to illuminate one of the most important and obscure episodes in human history. The conclusion I reach regarding the Resurrection is perfectly compatible with progressive Christian thinking and is no more skeptical, in fact, than many a Christian theologian's. If it seems more radical, it is because it is based on study of a controversial relic, rather than a philosophical proposition.

This book, then, is about rethinking both the Resurrection and the

Shroud of Turin. The plan is straightforward. Having introduced the twin
subjects of the book in Part 1, I consider the historical evidence about the
Resurrection in Part 2. Then, in Part 3, I take a close look at the Shroud
and the various scientific and historical arguments that surround it. In Part
4 I explain how the Shroud and the Resurrection may well be intimately
related, though not in the way believers in the relic currently assume. The
rest of the book is essentially a narrative, an attempt to retell the founding
events of Christianity in accordance with the book's central idea.

By the end, I hope, Easter and the Shroud will seem a little less mysterious, the whole of history a little more marvellous.

PART I

Introductions

I

The Resurrection

Nearly 2,000 years ago, in the reign of Emperor Tiberius, in a peripheral, troublesome province of the Roman Empire, an episode took place that would change the world more profoundly than any other event in history. A spark was struck amid the religious kindling of ancient Israel, a spark that led, within a short space of time, to a spiritual fire-storm threatening the entire Mediterranean world. Real flames soon accompanied this metaphorical fire. A generation after the Church was founded, Roman followers of "the light shining in the darkness" were being turned by Nero into human torches—"to be ignited after dark as substitutes for daylight," as Tacitus coolly informs us.[1] Three centuries later, following Emperor Constantine's adoption of Christianity as the state religion in AD 325, the flames were being lit by Christians themselves, as bishops and their mobs set about razing pagan temples and sanctuaries, including the famous library of Alexandria, the greatest center of learning in the ancient world. From the end of the fourth century on, the triumph of the Church was assured. In Europe, it has taken the best part of two millennia for this religious inferno to die down; elsewhere, notably in Africa and America, it is still blazing.

What, then, was the spark? What ignited Christianity? This is surely one of the most important historical questions we can ask. Yet the answer is still radically uncertain. We can be confident that it had something to do with a Jewish man called Jesus, who was executed as a revolutionary leader by the prefect of Judaea, Pontius Pilate, around AD 30. But how this relatively obscure individual, whose activities are not mentioned in a single contemporary source,[2] came to have such an extraordinary posthumous career is a historical mystery of truly epic proportions. It is this mystery that I here set out to solve.

Christians themselves have always explained the origin of their religion via a divine mystery, the Resurrection, by which is meant (roughly speaking)

God's miraculous restoration of Jesus to new life after a brief spell among the dead.

In the "Acts of the Apostles," the legendary history of the early Church contained in the New Testament, the Risen Jesus appears to his disciples forty days after Easter (the occasion of his Resurrection) and tells them of their preordained mission: "you shall receive power when the Holy Spirit has come upon you; and you shall be my witnesses in Jerusalem and in all Judaea and Samaria and to the end of the earth."[3] And we then read how the eleven remaining disciples elected a replacement for the treacherous Judas to become with them "a witness to his resurrection" and how Peter gave a great speech to the assembled crowd on the day of Pentecost, climaxing with the words: "This Jesus God raised up, and of that we are all witnesses."[4] Whatever Jesus did or said before his death, Acts is clear that the early Church was dedicated, above all, to proclaiming his Resurrection.

The book of Acts is not a particularly reliable source, but in this respect, at least, it is perfectly historical. Testimony to the Resurrection is at the heart of the earliest Christian writings we possess: the letters (or epistles) of the apostle Paul. These were all written in the 50s, half a century or so before Acts. Famously, Paul nowhere shows the slightest interest in the life and career of Jesus. Instead, he is fixated on the death and Resurrection of the man he exultantly calls "the Lord." He even states that the Resurrection is at the heart of everything he preaches: "if Christ has not been raised, then our preaching is in vain and your faith is in vain."[5] Paul's focus on the Resurrection is sometimes considered eccentric, but it agrees with the picture presented in Acts, and the same focus is evident in the Church creeds he recites. The opening of Paul's letter to the Romans, for instance, proclaims that Jesus was "designated Son of God in power according to the Spirit of holiness by his resurrection from the dead."[6] This creedal statement, which must have been devised within a quarter of a century of Jesus' death, testifies to the pivotal significance of the Resurrection in earliest Christian thought.

The doctrine of the Resurrection, then, goes back to the very foundation of the Church and has always been considered central to the Christian faith. Asking what sparked Christianity, therefore, is equivalent to asking what caused belief in the Resurrection. The questions are the same, because the Church was founded, after the death of Jesus, on belief in the Risen Christ. Had nothing happened at Easter, Jesus' bereaved, disillusioned followers would never have been inspired to launch a religious movement in his name.

It would help, of course, if we could say for certain what the first Christians understood by the concept of resurrection—especially those who claimed (as did Paul) to have seen the Risen Jesus. As yet, scholars have been unable to agree on this issue, mainly because it is inextricably linked to the contentious interpretation of the Resurrection itself. Did the apostles think that Jesus had been revivified in his flesh-and-blood body? Did they think that he had assumed a purely spiritual existence in heaven? Or did they, perhaps, just use the language of resurrection to express a feeling or conviction about his continued "presence" among them? All three possibilities (and others) are currently entertained by New Testament researchers, reflecting a variety of religious and anti-religious attitudes.

What is not in doubt is that, by the end of the first century, many Christians understood the Resurrection in physical terms: Jesus' mortal body was put back on its feet and exited the grave. This "flesh-and-blood" interpretation conditions the way the Resurrection is narrated in the four Gospels (Matthew, Mark, Luke and John), texts generally reckoned to have been written sometime between 70 and 100 by anonymous second- or third-generation Christians. As described in the Gospels, the Resurrection of Jesus was demonstrated by three phenomena: an empty tomb, implying the revivification of the body that was buried; an angelic witness (or witnesses) at the tomb; and various appearances of the Risen Jesus to his close followers, during which he ate and was touched (in addition, apparently, to passing through solid walls and vanishing into thin air).

If the flesh-and-blood interpretation of the Resurrection was not already dominant when the Gospels were written, it certainly became so in the period following their distribution. By the end of the second century the Gospels were well on the way to becoming canonical and their fleshly portrayal of the Resurrection was claimed as the traditional Christian view. From then on, all other interpretations were deemed heretical by the self-appointed leaders of the "universal" (catholic) Church, the powerful bishops who led congregations in the major centers of early Christianity.

The traditional notion of a flesh-and-blood resurrection remained unquestioned in Christendom for more than a millennium and a half. In retrospect, it is rather astonishing that such an improbable dogma could have dominated the minds of so many for such a long time. It stands as testimony to the imperialistic power of the Church and its sustained stranglehold on intellectual endeavor, a grip that only began to loosen during the period of the Renaissance and the Reformation. Even then, it was another 200 years before religious skeptics began to challenge the very basis of Christian faith, reviving voices that had been silenced since antiquity.

Disbelief in the Resurrection goes back to the time when it was first proclaimed on the streets of Jerusalem. Some first-century Jews regarded the whole idea of resurrection as wrong-headed; others accepted it in principle, but were not convinced that Jesus had been raised from the dead. According to Matthew, even some of the disciples had doubts about the Resurrection.[7] Matthew also furnishes us with evidence of the first alternative explanation for the claimed emptiness of the tomb. Apparently, at the time Matthew was composed there were Jews who said that Jesus' disciples had stolen his body away by night.[8] On this view, Christianity was founded on a fraud.

Gentiles (non-Jews), too, were generally skeptical of the idea that someone could come back from the dead, and many an ancient writer derided the Christian notion of resurrection. Most notable was Porphyry, a philosopher of the third century, who wrote a lost fifteen-volume refutation of Christianity, deriding the Gospel evidence and ridiculing the idea of the Resurrection.[9] Similarly, in *The True Doctrine*, a work of the late second century, a philosopher named Celsus poured scorn on the "nauseating and impossible" concept of resurrection, asking "what sort of a body is it that could return to its original nature or become the same as it was before it rotted away?"[10] Tertullian, a contemporary Christian apologist, disarmed such rational objections by simply asserting, "the fact is certain, because it is impossible."[11] Needless to say, Tertullian's heirs made sure that the works of Celsus and Porphyry perished in the pious book-burnings of the fourth and fifth centuries. We know about their arguments only because confident Christian authors quoted them extensively in order to refute them.[12]

Once Christianity was established as the Roman state religion, the Gospels and Acts were enshrined in the New Testament as Holy Scripture, and it became dangerous, as a subject of Rome, to question their version of events. The sea of faith gradually swamped the empire, and the spirit of rational inquiry was washed away.

It was not until the eighteenth-century Enlightenment that the tide began to turn. Inspired by the scientific revolution, philosophers began, once again, to pour cold water on the Christian faith in miracles, a faith that ran counter to their own passionate belief in a rational universe. At the same time, Enlightenment historians reinvented their subject as a "human science"; that is to say, history became a discipline dedicated to explaining the civilized past purely in terms of human behavior, attempting to discover laws of human nature and eschewing any notion of Providence or divine intervention. Gradually, God was marginalized in academic discussion and by the end of the nineteenth century was confined to theology departments.[13] In this new climate the traditional Christian story of the birth of the Church—the story told in Acts of a mission launched by the Risen Christ—no longer carried conviction. Belief in the Resurrection, the most egregious miracle of all, began to seem increasingly implausible.

But this meant that rationalists had to explain the birth of the Church some other way. They were left, as it were, with a Resurrection-shaped hole in history.

How could this hole be filled? One of the first writers to take up the challenge was the eighteenth-century philosopher and linguist Hermann Samuel Reimarus, who took his cue from the Jewish rumor reported in Matthew, that the disciples had stolen Jesus' body from its tomb. Reimarus argued that, enamored of the leisurely lifestyle they had enjoyed while helping Jesus spread his gospel and unwilling to lose their status as wise and holy men, the disciples concocted a cynical plot to relaunch their preaching careers by staging the empty tomb and claiming that Jesus had appeared to them in a resurrected form.[14] Few were convinced by this irreverent theory, which was published posthumously and anonymously to protect the author's reputation, but the genie of speculation was now out of the bottle. Reimarus had reinvented Easter as an ordinary historical episode that could be investigated and debated, like any other event of the past, using the methods and assumptions of academic history.

Rationalists soon developed another theory to fill the hole. Instead of being resurrected, they argued, Jesus had merely been resuscitated: he had lost consciousness on the cross, had revived (with or without help) in the cool of the tomb-chamber, left the tomb secretly and then been reunited briefly with his disciples.[15] Several different versions of this "swoon theory" were proposed, but in 1865 it was dealt a devastating blow by David Friedrich Strauss, who famously pointed out that "a being who had stolen half-dead out of the sepulchre, who crept about weak and ill, wanting medical treatment, who required bandaging, strengthening and indulgence, and who still, at last, yielded to his sufferings" could hardly have given his disciples "the impression that he was a Conqueror over death and the grave, the Prince of Life."[16] Strauss, though, was no conservative. He dismissed the empty tomb as an unhistorical legend and interpreted the appearances as a series of "subjective visions" (hallucinations) induced in the minds of the disciples by their intense grief at the death of Jesus. The disciples were not charlatans or fools, in Strauss's view, but naive visionaries, an idea that soon became popular with rationalists.[17]

Though the hallucination theory was open to numerous objections, Strauss's argument forced more conservative theologians—those unwilling to abandon the notion of divine intervention—to rethink Easter for themselves. A new interpretation that had (and has) a strong appeal for many was that, rather than being mere hallucinations, the Resurrection appearances were "objective visions," i.e. real, mental perceptions of the spiritually resurrected Jesus. This theory was popularized by Theodor Keim in a book published in 1872, in which he likened the appearances to a series of "telegrams" sent from heaven.[18] The analogy proved persuasive. Although it involved abandoning the idea that Jesus rose physically, leaving behind an empty tomb, Keim's theory seemed to rescue the Resurrection from Godless psychologism.

By the end of the nineteenth century, then, the traditional Christian view of the Resurrection had been overturned. Rationalists and conservatives alike were reinterpreting Easter as a series of visions—either illusory or real—and relegating the empty tomb to the netherworld of pious legend. Having cast aside the ecclesiastical myth, scholars seemed poised to reveal the historical truth of the Resurrection. But the revelation never came.

Over the course of the last 150 years the failure to solve the "Resurrection problem" has become chronic. Innumerable scholars have followed in the footsteps of the eighteenth- and nineteenth-century pioneers, proposing many weird and wonderful ways of understanding the birth of Christianity, but there are major difficulties with every solution so far proposed, and none is generally accepted. Confounding the intellectual optimism of the Enlightenment, the secret of the Resurrection has turned out to be as elusive as the Snark, the mysterious quarry in Lewis Carroll's glorious nonsense poem. There seems to be something about the episode that defies common sense.

It would help if there was agreement about some of the basic facts to be explained, but, such is the depth of the problem, not a single point is uncontested. After all these years, there is no consensus as to whether the tomb was found empty or not, whether the disciples saw anything or not, even whether anything happened or not. Different scholars see significance in different elements of the New Testament tradition and dismiss different reports as nothing but myths. Some think that the tomb really was found empty but theorize that the Romans or Jewish leaders removed the body surreptitiously, in order to prevent it becoming the focus of a martyr-cult;[19]

others, reckoning the accounts of the empty tomb to be fictitious, regard such speculation as misguided and irrelevant. Some say that the appearances were meetings with Jesus or someone who looked like him—perhaps his twin brother; others say they were just illusory sensations brought on by grief, disappointment or post-hypnotic suggestion.

The result is that now, at the beginning of the twenty-first century, in addition to the "fraud theory," "swoon theory," "subjective vision theory" and "objective vision theory," all of which are still on the table, we have to reckon with the "cognitive dissonance theory," the "mistaken identity theory," the "body-snatching theory," the "bereavement experience theory," and various others.[20] This extraordinary scholarly confusion regarding the most influential episode in world history is unnerving, to say the least.

One response to this situation has been to deny that the Resurrection has any basis in history whatsoever, that the Church was not "born" in response to anything that happened after the death of Jesus but began as a widespread and complex social movement, with various groups of "Jesus-people" gradually coalescing and developing their beliefs from both Jewish and pagan roots. The Resurrection, these scholars say, was an idea derived from ancient myths of dying and rising gods (Osiris, Attis, Adonis and Tammuz), an idea appropriated by the early Christians to help explain the origin of their new religious community.[21] The problem of Christian origins is thus transferred from the realm of events to the realm of ideas: there is no historical hole to be filled, just intellectual rubble to be cleared away.

This "mythicist" approach has its merits. Apart from anything else, it forces us to clarify the nature of the historical mystery that confronts us. What, precisely, is in need of explanation? How can we be sure that something happened to kick-start the Church and that it didn't just gradually evolve? How do we know that the Resurrection did not originate as a pure myth, later transposed onto history by the Gospel writers? It is important to ask these questions, to be sure that we are dealing with a real historical problem, not just an illusion produced by the literary activity of a few early Christians. Ultimately, though, the argument is unconvincing. Jesus cannot be completely erased from history, and a range of historical evidence points to something extraordinary having happened in the wake of his death. The Resurrection-shaped hole in history cannot simply be dismissed as a mirage.

Several centuries ago, Enlightenment rationalists challenged traditionalists to a debate about the Resurrection, a debate right at the heart of the contest between faith and reason. They could never have anticipated how long, complex and inconclusive the debate would turn out to be. As the influence of Christianity declined in the later nineteenth century, rationalists lost interest in the topic, inscrutable as it was, and theologians were left to please themselves. The great debate became an academic sideshow.

This wouldn't matter if the Resurrection was just another miracle-story, like the stilling of the storm on the Sea of Galilee or the healing of the blind Bartimaeus. But it is far more than that: it is an issue of fundamental importance, both historical and religious. Unsure of what happened at Easter, Christianity lacks its own birth certificate. It is as if modern Americans were unsure of how European settlers had first arrived in the New World or as if physical anthropologists had no idea how or where human beings evolved. And because Christianity has been so extraordinarily influential throughout the last two millennia, the whole of the modern world shares, to a significant extent, in its identity crisis. As long as the events of Easter remain obscure, we will not know how the Christian era—the Common Era—came to be. The birth of Christianity is a marginal issue for no one.

Nevertheless, the collective failure to understand the Resurrection goes largely unnoticed and unacknowledged. Historians have grown so accustomed to ignoring the Resurrection problem—and the whole question of Christian origins—that they rarely attempt to investigate it for themselves.[22] Instead they pass the buck to theologians and the specialized guild of New Testament scholars (whose work is all too often theologically motivated).

Ironically, many liberal theologians of the last century have appeared almost as skeptical about Easter as the mythicists. For one reason or another they have declined to speculate about the historical cause of the Resurrection belief or have argued that it arose in the absence of any special event.[23] These sophisticates are opposed by others who insist, even now, on the reality of the flesh-and-blood Resurrection. This traditional doctrine is still espoused by vast numbers of Christians and is increasingly championed by conservative theologians.[24] This trend has more to do with the successful institutionalization of evangelical scholarship and postmodern open-mindedness than with the inherent worth of the idea itself, but it serves as a potent reminder that mainstream historians have not yet managed to account for Easter.

The weightiest recent work on the founding event of Christianity is a spirited defense of the traditional doctrine by an Anglican bishop, Tom Wright, who makes hay out of the ongoing failure of secularists to come up with a convincing theory of their own. Wright recognizes the possibility that someone might one day "come up with the skeptical critic's dream," an entirely naturalistic explanation for the genesis of Christianity which "causes no fluttering in the critical dovecotes." But he takes comfort from the thought that, "despite the somewhat desperate attempts of many scholars over the last 200 years (not to mention critics since at least Celsus), no such explanation has been found."[25] It is a striking thought—critics have been seeking a rational explanation for the Resurrection almost as long as Christians have been awaiting the Second Coming.

Emboldened, Wright issues historians with a challenge: "what alternative account can be offered which will explain the data just as well, which can provide an alternative *sufficient* explanation for all the evidence and so challenge the right of the bodily resurrection to be regarded as the *necessary* one?"[26] Nearly a decade on, the gauntlet remains untouched.[27] The current attitude of historians is typified by Charles Freeman, who concedes pessimistically, "It is probable that no 'alternative account which will explain the data for all the evidence' can ever be offered."[28] Reimarus might as well never have taken up his pen.

We are at an impasse: "human science" is unable to show the way forward; traditional faith can only point backward. How can we extricate ourselves from this centuries-old dilemma? The only way is to try a new approach, one unfettered by the usual modes of historical and theological thought. I believe that there really is a way to understand the Resurrection rationally, a way that enables us to reconstruct the events of Easter in remarkable detail, transforming it from a historical blank into one of the most thoroughly knowable episodes of ancient history. But it is not a way that will avoid fluttering in the critical dovecotes. For it means taking seriously an object that has long been banished to the outermost fringes of academic debate. That object is the Shroud of Turin.

2

The Shroud of Turin

The Shroud of Turin is a large linen cloth imbued with a mysterious image of a tortured, crucified man. According to tradition, it was used, along with other cloths, to wrap the dead body of Jesus, and its image, so believers say, is a miraculous imprint of the crucified Lord. Still cherished by many Catholics as one of the holiest relics of Christianity, the Shroud is regarded by nearly everyone else as a medieval fake, largely on the basis of a carbon-dating test carried out in 1988. Sacred and contentious in equal measure, the relic is exhibited very rarely and is generally kept locked away in a shrine in the Royal Chapel of Turin Cathedral, where it has been housed since the seventeenth century.[1] There it rests, like a lethargic ghost, occasionally disturbing the intellectual complacency of the modern world, but, for the most part, unseen, discredited and ignored.

Most people have at least heard of the Shroud and are vaguely aware that it bears what appears to be an imprint of a man's face, an image reproduced around the world as the true face of Christ. Fewer realize the full extent of the image. The cloth is over 14 feet long and is marked not just with a face but with two complete impressions, front and back, of a man's flogged and crucified body (Figure 1). Of the two figures, it is the frontal one, inevitably, that grabs the attention (Figure 2). Here we see the well-known face, a bearded mask housing a pair of glowing, owlish eyes, the hair and forehead flecked with blood (Figure 3). The body appears physically robust. A major wound is visible below the chest on the right-hand side, which seems to match the report that, as Jesus hung on the cross, a soldier pierced his side with a spear. Lower down, rivulets of blood traverse the forearms, stemming apparently from nail wounds in the wrists, only one of which can be seen. The arms are crossed. The rather spindly hands are placed decorously over the groin. The whole figure is clearly legible, except for the feet, which disappear into bloodstained nothingness.

Relatively misshapen and formless, the dorsal figure is perhaps even more expressive of physical torment (Figure 4). The marks of the scourge are seen more clearly here, covering every part of the body from the shoulders to the calves. The scalp is ringed by minor blood flows, recalling the crown of thorns. The feet, which appear to overlap, bear the bloody traces of nail wounds. The most peculiar features are two messy pools of watery blood, which run into each other across the small of the back (Figure 5). These bring to mind John's strange report that, when the soldier thrust his spear into Jesus' side, "there came out blood and water."[2]

Though clearly discernible, the figures are extremely faint and are not now the most prominent marks visible on the sheet. Framing them is a set of large burn marks, holes and scorches, strung out along two parallel lines. This damage occurred in the sixteenth century, when the relic was caught in a devastating fire. It was rescued just as its silver casket began to melt and drip onto the cloth within.[3] Along the same lines is another smaller set of burn marks, known as the "poker-holes," made on an earlier occasion: four clusters of holes, each resembling a knight's move in chess (Figure 6). A set of diamond-shaped water stains mark the cloth as well, visible most clearly around the knees of the frontal figure. All these stains, holes and markings are symmetrical, having been made when the cloth was folded (in different ways on different occasions).

Otherwise, the cloth is in reasonably good condition, although it shows its age in its color: originally it would have been bleached pure white, but the gradual oxidization of the linen fibers has caused it to darken, so that it now has the color of old ivory.[4]

Could this extraordinary artifact really be the burial cloth of Jesus?

The very idea strikes most people as preposterous, an offense to common sense. The Shroud is generally lumped in with silly-season subjects such as Atlantis, yetis and UFOs. Among scholars, the Shroud is perceived as the plaything of "pseudo-historians" who play fast and loose with historical reality, exploiting the gullibility of certain sections of the reading public with imaginative accounts of Templar plots, Masonic secrets and Holy Bloodlines. Yet, unlike such Grail-oriented conspiracies (and Atlantis, yetis and UFOs), the Shroud very definitely exists. Peculiar it may be, but it is a real phenomenon and demands explanation—not glib dismissal.

There is nothing inherently improbable in the idea of a shroud surviving from first-century Palestine. Plenty of ancient shrouds still exist, including numerous examples from Egypt, Palestine's southern neighbor (e.g. Figures 7 and 8). None of these examples, however, bears an image anything like the haunting figures emblazoned across the Shroud of Turin. It is its image that makes the Shroud seem so incredible. It corresponds to no

other image, artificial or natural, currently known. Despite decades of trying, no modern experimenter has yet been able to reproduce it; despite
decades of investigation, no scientist has been able to say conclusively how
it was created.[5] The Shroud is a complete anomaly. That does not make it
miraculous, but it does make it very difficult to understand.

Indeed, the Shroud is as difficult to understand, in its way, as the Resurrection. This should give us pause for thought, for it points to a remarkable
coincidence. However we are inclined to view it, the Shroud can surely
claim to be one of the most puzzling artifacts in the world, and it is linked,
via the burial of Jesus, which it represents, to the most puzzling episode in
human history, the Resurrection. Two supremely inscrutable subjects, both
associated, either directly or indirectly, with the same historical incident:
there is something uncanny about this, something that hints at an unreal-
ized connection. Conventional wisdom, mindful of the need to separate
science and religion, demands that the Shroud and the Resurrection be
treated as separate issues. But deciding, on principle, to deny any relation
between them is hardly rational. As twin mysteries, they could well have a
bearing on each other. It may be that the Shroud and the Resurrection
remain mysterious precisely because they have been kept apart.

To understand why the issue of the Shroud has, until now, been divorced
from that of the Resurrection, we need to trace the history of the relic since
the Middle Ages and follow the twists and turns in its perception over the
course of the last six and a half centuries. The divorce, we will discover,
was neither accidental nor inevitable, but the result of historical contingen-
cies and fears about what the marriage might mean.

The Shroud made its European debut, as it were, in the mid fourteenth
century in the village of Lirey, near the city of Troyes in northeastern
France.[6] In the early 1350s the lord of Lirey, a poor but prominent knight
called Geoffrey I de Charny, founded a church in the village, a modest
foundation which he soon adorned with an astonishing treasure—the
Shroud. This relic, which, if authentic, would have outshone any other in
Christendom, was exhibited in the Lirey church c.1355–6, attracting
hordes of pilgrims. A badge worn by one of them provides an invaluable
record of the cloth's fourteenth-century display (Figure 9).

Contemporary documents indicate that the cult was approved by a
council of bishops at the papal court and by the bishop of Troyes, Henry
of Poitiers. According to a later report, however, the exhibition of the
Shroud was considered a scandal by Bishop Henry, who inquired into its
origin and pronounced it to be a painted forgery. It is difficult to know

what to make of these contradictory signals. But whatever happened between the local bishop and the custodians of the Shroud, the public displays soon ceased, and the cloth was returned to Geoffrey's widow, Jeanne de Vergy, Geoffrey having died heroically at the battle of Poitiers in 1356.[7]

It was over thirty years before the Shroud was exhibited in Lirey again. After Geoffrey I's death, his son, Geoffrey II, became lord of Lirey, and in 1389 he decided that the time had come to try to revive the cult. He was vigorously opposed by the new bishop of Troyes, a man named Pierre d'Arcis, who was convinced that his predecessor, Henry of Poitiers, had proven it to be "a work of human skill and not miraculously wrought or bestowed"—in other words, a damnable fraud.[8] Having tried unsuccessfully to ban the display himself, he appealed for support to both the king of France and the Pope. A high-level diplomatic tussle ensued, Geoffrey II de Charny making representations of his own, and in 1390 the Pope, Clement VII, issued his verdict: the custodians of the Shroud were allowed to continue with the exhibitions, as long as they referred to it and treated it as a *figure or representation* of Christ's burial cloth, not a true relic; and d'Arcis was forbidden ever to raise the topic again on pain of excommunication. With this strangely ambivalent ruling, the fourteenth-century controversy was closed.

For the next three decades or so the Shroud was kept in the treasury of the church at Lirey, in a casket bearing the de Charny coat of arms. Presumably, it continued to be exhibited occasionally, but, given the conditions attached to its display, it cannot have drawn much interest. Then, in 1418, when the village was threatened by English marauders, the dean and canons of the church decided to hand over the Shroud for safe keeping to Humbert de Villersexel, husband of Geoffrey II de Charny's daughter, Margaret. It was a costly mistake: the Shroud would never be seen in Lirey again. Twenty years after becoming its temporary guardian, Humbert died, leaving the relic in the possession of his widow. If the Lirey canons thought they would now be able to reclaim the cloth, they were sorely mistaken. Having regained her family heirloom, Margaret was determined not to relinquish it. From 1443 until 1459, the year before her death, she was engaged in a constant legal battle with the Lirey canons and was even briefly excommunicated for her refusal to return the cloth. Eventually, her prosecutors agreed to accept compensation for their loss. By then Margaret was no longer the Shroud's possessor. It seems that, childless and growing old, she resolved to seek out an heir able to promote the cause of her precious relic and give it a suitable home. Her choice fell on Duke Louis I of Savoy, whose family would own the Shroud for the next 530 years.

The gift was apparently made in 1453. In March of that year Margaret received from Duke Louis a castle and the income from one of his estates in return for "valuable services," which can only refer to the gift of the Shroud. The first official record of Savoy ownership of the cloth dates from 1464, when Duke Louis made a settlement of his own with the Lirey canons. The Savoys' devotion to the Shroud is beautifully illustrated in a miniature of the "Man of Sorrows" decorating a famous manuscript known as the *Très Riches Heures* (Figure 10). The picture shows Duke Louis's grandson, Charles I, and his wife, Blanche, praying before a gently swaying figure of Christ, whose wounded body clearly reflects the Shroud's image.[9]

Was Margaret de Charny able to tell Louis something of the origin of the relic, something that convinced him and his family that it was more than just a cleverly painted copy? All we know for sure is that the Shroud's new owners regarded it as the real thing, and from the 1460s onward high-ranking ecclesiastics concurred.[10]

During the latter half of the fifteenth century the Shroud accompanied the Savoys on their travels around the duchy. In 1502 it was decided to house the relic permanently in the Holy Chapel at Chambéry, the Savoys' capital in southern France. Placed in a silver casket in a niche behind the high altar of the chapel, the newly enshrined relic began, for the first time, to acquire an international reputation. Four years later Pope Julius II instituted the Feast of the Holy Shroud, to be celebrated locally every May 4, and by 1516 the cult was well enough established for King Francis I of France to visit Chambéry as a pilgrim. The first full-length copy of the Shroud was painted in the same year (Figure 11).

Then, in 1532, disaster struck. A fire caught hold in the Holy Chapel and, having consumed the rich furnishings round about, threatened to destroy the precious relic as well. By the time a blacksmith managed to prise away its protective grille, the silver casket had begun to melt and liquid metal had dropped onto the folded Shroud within. Fortunately, the fire was doused before the damage spread too far, but the cloth was now badly disfigured by burns.[11] After the fire, the Shroud was patched and relined by local nuns, and then, during a period of war with the French, it resumed its travels. It was displayed in Turin for the first time on May 4, 1535, but it was not until 1578, following a return to Chambéry, that the Shroud was permanently transferred to the Italian city.

Installed as a palladium—a divine protector—in the new capital of the Savoy domains, vaunted as the talisman of one of the most powerful families in Europe, the Shroud now embarked on the most glittering phase of its checkered career. When it was held aloft in Turin's Piazza del Castello on October 12, 1578, 40,000 people were there to witness the spectacle, including bishops, archbishops and cardinals. Over the course of the next century the Shroud was exhibited in public sixteen times, often to celebrate a royal marriage or to give thanks for the passing of a plague. It was made the subject of numerous copies and commemorative prints, disseminating its image throughout the Catholic world (e.g. Figure 12). In the seventeenth century the Shroud was more visible and more venerated than ever before. In 1694 it was transferred from Turin Cathedral's presbytery, where it had been kept for over a century, into the splendid new Chapel of the Holy Shroud, in between the cathedral and the Ducal Palace.[12] It has remained there ever since, bar removal for temporary exhibitions, restoration programs and a six-year interlude during the Second World War, when it was transferred to a monastery near Naples.

During the Counter-Reformation, when Catholics were at war—physically and intellectually—with Protestant "heretics," the Shroud was considered a fit subject for Catholic scholarship. Alfonso Paleotto, Archbishop of Bologna, wrote a lengthy treatise on it in 1598. He was followed by Jean-Jacques Chifflet, who published a history of Christ's burial-linens in 1624. Chifflet did not regard the Shroud as a shroud per se, but as a cloth used to enfold Christ's body at the base of the cross and transport it to the tomb (cf. Figure 13), other cloths having been used for the actual entombment.[13] He interpreted the image, as did others, as a sort of miraculous stain produced by the body's blood and sweat before it was cleaned and anointed for burial—that is, as an image of the dead Christ, not the Risen Christ. This may help explain why, when the debate about the Resurrection kicked off in the eighteenth century, no Catholic thought to adduce the Shroud as evidence of a miracle occurring in Christ's tomb.

It would not have availed them much if they had. The cult of relics was by then in decline, and the Shroud was beginning to lose its intellectual respectability, even among Catholics. The chief problem was its dubious provenance: no one knew where it had come from. During the Counter-Reformation this problem could be ignored; the cloth was felt to stand as "testimony to its own authenticity," as one observer put it.[14] As the Enlightenment took hold, however, doubts about the Shroud—as about relics in general—began to increase. It was still exhibited fairly regularly (nine times in the eighteenth century), and its appeal to the faithful remained strong, but as an object of scholarly interest it was now decidedly suspect. There was no particular reason to think that it was anything more than a clever forgery, one of the many false relics cluttering the altars of the Catholic Church. So, when German scholars began to debate the issue of the

Resurrection, they naturally left it out of account. Images and artifacts were not widely used as historical sources at that time, in any case, and nothing would have been gained by citing the evidence of a dubious, distant relic that few had ever seen.

In Turin the Shroud was still honored, and continued to be exhibited on great occasions, such as a royal marriage or the visit of a pope. Even locally, though, interest in the relic gradually diminished. As the Savoys pursued their dream of ruling a unified Italy, a dream finally realized in 1861, their faithful talisman, which had served the family for so long, went into semi-retirement. In over fifty years it was displayed in public only once. Like an aged cleric living out his days in quiet seclusion, the Shroud belonged, so it must have seemed, to the theological past.

Aged clerics, though, can sometimes surprise. In 1898, during a rare display to celebrate the fiftieth anniversary of the Italian Constitution, the Shroud revealed a hidden aspect of itself that propelled it to worldwide attention—and continues to fascinate us still. The means by which its secret was revealed was that quintessentially modern technology: photography.

Initially, the Shroud's owner, King Umberto I, was reluctant to have the cloth photographed, concerned that it might somehow be inappropriate. Recognizing, though, that it would be useful to have an exact record of the relic's appearance, he eventually agreed to the idea. The photographer chosen for the task was an experienced amateur called Secondo Pia (Figure 14).[15] On May 25, Pia installed his camera and some newfangled electric lights on a specially built platform in front of the high altar, where the Shroud was hung, and attempted to take a couple of exposures. Unfortunately, he was hampered by technical difficulties and time constraints, and he managed only one exposure, which was unsuccessful. On the evening of May 28, he returned to the cathedral and tried again. This time his equipment worked perfectly. Having exposed four photographic plates, he returned to his studio around midnight and began the process of developing them.

What Pia saw that night in his darkroom astounded him. For, as the image on the negative plate took shape before his eyes, he found himself staring not at a confusing array of lights and darks, the usual effect of a photographic negative, but at a coherent likeness of a crucified man. Instead of the flat, enigmatic image seen on the cloth, the negative plate gave the impression of a substantial figure emerging from the background, a figure that looked like a real human body lit from in front (cf. Figure 15).

Instead of the glaring mask of the Shroud, the negative revealed a remarkably convincing, three-dimensional image of man's face, his eyelids closed (cf. Figure 16). It was as if the Shroud itself was a photographic negative that could be developed into a breathtaking, positive image of the crucified Jesus.

"Shut up in my darkroom," Pia later recalled, "all intent on my work, I experienced a very strong emotion when, during the development, I saw for the first time the Holy Face appear on the plate, with such clarity that I was dumbfounded by it."[16]

Pia's photographs ignited the modern debate about the Shroud. As soon as the Italian and international press began publishing them, they caused a sensation. Some hailed the image as a miracle; others denounced it as a fraud. While many marveled, most were wary of putting any faith in photographs of a strange, undocumented relic. Atheists, in particular, were aghast at the thought that modern science might have revealed a miraculous portrait of Christ. Some even accused Pia of deception. Emotions ran high, because the religious significance of the image seemed so profound.

Surprisingly, the chief spokesman for the opposition came from the ranks of the Catholic Church. In the years immediately following Pia's discovery Canon Ulysse Chevalier wrote a series of pamphlets on the Shroud and its medieval history, in which he published and interpreted numerous documents relating to the Shroud's adventures in the fourteenth and fifteenth centuries. On the basis of Clement VII's 1390 judgment, that the Shroud could be exhibited only as a "figure or representation" of Christ's burial cloth, Chevalier concluded that it could not be a genuine relic and that it must have been "cunningly painted," as Bishop Henry of Poitiers had supposedly discovered.[17] This was the conclusion the academic establishment desired, and he was duly rewarded with a gold medal by the Académie des Inscriptions et Belles-lettres.[18]

To this day Chevalier's opinion underpins the presumption that the Shroud is a fake, even though, as we shall see, the idea that it is a painting has long been disproved.

For most the matter was now settled, but one man was not so easily persuaded. Yves Delage was a distinguished scientist at the Sorbonne, a zoologist and biologist with a particular interest in the topic of evolution. He was an avowed agnostic, both before and after his involvement with the Shroud. Viewing the image as an experienced anatomist, he was impressed by its extraordinarily lifelike quality—far more so than by Chevalier's historical arguments. In 1900 he showed Pia's photographs to a young, inquisitive and indefatigable assistant, Paul Vignon, who immediately embarked on a scientific investigation of the image. Delage oversaw Vignon's work and agreed with him that the evidence was in favor of authenticity. In April 1902 the Sorbonne professor presented a paper on the Shroud to the French Academy of Sciences in Paris, in which he argued that its image was medically accurate, that it could not be a painting and that it was probably a "vaporograph" (an image caused by gas). He concluded, on scientific and historical grounds, that the relic was probably authentic, that it was indeed the winding sheet of Jesus.[19]

Although Delage made it clear that he did not regard Jesus as the resurrected Son of God, his paper upset the atheist members of the Academy, including its secretary, Marcellin Berthelot, who prevented its full publication in the Academy's bulletin.[20] This act of scientific censorship marks the beginning of the academic refusal even to discuss the origin of the Shroud, a refusal that continues to this day. Refusing, for his part, to be silenced, Delage published his arguments the next month in a letter to the editor of the *Revue scientifique*, commenting on his paper and the hostile reaction it provoked as follows:

> I willingly recognize that none of the arguments given . . . offer the features of an irrefutable demonstration; but it must be recognized that together they constitute an imposing bundle of probabilities, some of which are very near being proofs . . . If they have not been received by certain people as they should have been, it is only because a religious question has been unduly grafted onto this scientific question, which has stirred up feelings and distorted straight reasoning . . . I consider Christ as a historical personage and I do not see why anyone should be scandalized that there exists a material trace of his existence.[21]

Had other members of the French Academy of Sciences possessed the same equanimity as Delage, his lecture might have initiated a fruitful debate about the nature and significance of the Turin Shroud. The loss of this opportunity is particularly regrettable, since it was just at this time that anthropologists in England were developing new ideas about religion with the potential to unlock the relic's historical significance.[22] And it was just at this time, too, that the debate about the Resurrection, having passed its zenith, was in urgent need of resolution, to prevent Christianity becoming too detached from the relentless juggernaut of modern thought. Had scientists and scholars a century ago followed the example of Delage and viewed the Shroud as an intellectual challenge to be met, rather than as a superstitious threat, the religious life of the twentieth century might have been very different. But prejudice won the day, and the professor's open-minded investigations were consigned to oblivion.

Or so it was hoped. Fortunately, Delage's protégé, Paul Vignon, was not deterred. He published his initial study of the Shroud in the same year, 1902, providing anatomical and archaeological arguments in favor of its authenticity, and over the next forty years became the Shroud's principal champion. Unlike Delage, Vignon was a Christian, but, as a scientist, he was determined to explain the Shroud in purely rational terms, developing the theory that it was a natural phenomenon caused by vaporography. As an exhibited artist, he also brought a painter's eye to the problem and adduced a wide range of art-historical evidence in support of the Shroud's antiquity.

In 1931 the Shroud was put on show to celebrate the marriage of the heir to the Italian throne, Prince Umberto of Piedmont, the first time it had been exhibited since the momentous display of 1898. This time a professional photographer, Giuseppe Enrie, was commissioned to photograph it, and the results were spectacular.

Enrie's photos confirmed the integrity of Pia's originals and permitted the Shroud to be studied in far greater detail than ever before. They soon caught the eye of an eminent Parisian surgeon, Dr. Pierre Barbet, who became fascinated by the relic. During the 1930s Barbet devoted himself to studying the medical aspects of the image, establishing pathology as one of the most important fields of Shroud research—or "sindonology" as it was then becoming known (from the Greek *sindon*, meaning "linen sheet").[23] By 1939 there was enough interest in the Shroud to warrant a conference on the subject in Turin. Nearly four decades after the silencing of Delage, debate about the Shroud was finally underway, albeit in a marginal forum.

The timing was inauspicious, but after the war study of the Shroud resumed. In 1950 it was the subject of a major international conference in Rome, and in 1959 the Centro Internazionale di Sindonologia was formed in Turin. Despite the scoffing of the academic establishment, a number of dedicated researchers began devoting themselves to study of the Shroud, and the trickle of publications steadily increased, soon becoming a lively underground stream of speculative knowledge.

Interest in the Shroud rocketed in the 1970s, the "golden age" of Shroud research. It was in this decade that the cloth was finally made available for scientific testing. A preliminary examination of it had been made in 1969, but it was only in 1973 that scientists were allowed to take samples. Their findings were sufficiently intriguing to encourage further research. And so, in

1978, a group of around thirty American scientists, calling themselves the Shroud of Turin Research Project (STURP), was permitted to subject the cloth to a battery of hi-tech tests in order to try to determine how the image was made (Figure 17). Although unable to reach a definitive conclusion on this score, the STURP scientists gathered a tremendous amount of useful data on the relic and, crucially, they failed to "falsify" the image—failed, that is, to detect any obvious signs of forgery. As far as they could tell, the Shroud was a genuine burial cloth. Their work has attracted plenty of abuse from skeptics, but it was scientifically motivated and their results were published in peer-reviewed journals.[24] Also in 1978, Ian Wilson published his ground-breaking book *The Turin Shroud*, which reconstructed a possible provenance for the cloth, stretching back beyond medieval France to sixth-century Edessa, a city now known as Şanlıurfa in eastern Turkey. By the end of the 1970s sindonologists were in bullish mood and looking forward to what many of them naively saw as the "ultimate" scientific test: carbon dating.

The 1980s were all about the carbon-dating campaign. In 1983 the Holy See inherited the Shroud on the death of the exiled King Umberto II of Italy (putting an end to the Savoys' long ownership of the relic) and soon afterward the increasingly vociferous calls to have the cloth carbon dated received a response. It took several years of wrangling and scientific compromise before the Church was ready to proceed, but the test was finally performed in 1988.

For the Shroud community, the result was dismaying. According to the carbon-dating laboratories, the cloth was manufactured between 1260 and 1390—just as Chevalier had claimed, just as the academic establishment believed. For decades the heirs of Delage and Vignon had been constructing an ever more plausible case for the authenticity of the mysterious relic; now, in one fell swoop, their case was laid low. The skeptics, it seemed, had been right all along.

One might have expected study of the Shroud to take on a new complexion after 1988. Accepting the carbon dating, art historians should have leaped on the Shroud as one of the most fascinating visual creations of the medieval period, a true masterpiece of devotional imagery. Strangely, though, they have remained almost entirely silent.[25] The reason is simple: the negative photo of the cloth is an unmistakable sign that the Shroud's famous image could not have been created by a medieval artist. Technically, conceptually and stylistically the Shroud makes no sense as a medieval artwork. The discipline of art history has had over a century to study the Shroud since it was first photographed, and in all that time no art historian has ever ventured to attribute it to a medieval artist.[26]

Sindonologists, meanwhile, have taken stock, regrouped and continued their discussions, greatly aided in recent years by the rise of the Internet. Inevitably, the carbon-dating result casts a long shadow over their work, and a great deal of effort has been expended in trying to figure out what might have gone wrong. But others simply get on with the task of trying to piece together the obscure history of the cloth, a pursuit that might seem vain to outsiders, but which continues to throw up tantalizing clues.

Overall, the 1988 carbon dating has made little difference to sindonology. It has just made it even more difficult for qualified researchers to dare to involve themselves in studying the world's most intriguing object.

The reaction of the Catholic Church to the 1988 carbon dating is almost as puzzling as the relic itself. To begin with, the archbishop of Turin, Cardinal Ballestrero, accepted the result unhesitatingly, despite the profound importance of the cult and despite knowing that the preponderance of scientific evidence up to that time was in favor of the Shroud being a genuine burial cloth. "We now know the truth!" he proclaimed cheerfully. "The Shroud is not what we thought it was, but at the very least it remains a beautiful icon."[27]

The Church is not usually so precipitate in its acceptance of scientific findings at odds with the feelings of the faithful. It was only in 1996, for instance, a full 137 years after the publication of Darwin's *On the Origin of Species*, that the Pope finally conceded that the theory of evolution was "more than a hypothesis."[28] The Shroud is an exceptionally significant relic, potentially the burial cloth of Jesus, and yet, on the authority of a single, unsupported scientific test, its ecclesiastical guardian pronounced it a product of the Middle Ages.[29]

Just as perplexing is the refusal to permit further testing of the cloth. For over twenty years sindonologists have been clamoring not only for a second carbon-dating test, in the hope of overturning the 1988 result, but also for a chance to test the cloth in other ways that might help solve the mystery of the image. One might have thought the Church would welcome efforts to revive the Shroud's reputation, but the requests for further tests have been resolutely ignored.

Meanwhile, in 2002, the Shroud was subjected to a secret conservation campaign that interfered drastically with its fabric. This involved the removal of all charred material and the vacuuming and stretching of the entire cloth. William Meacham, an experienced archaeologist and acknowledged expert on the Shroud, has called this campaign an act of "vandalism" that has "removed an important part of the relic's historical heritage, destroyed valuable scientific data and altered the cloth and its study forever."[30] The Shroud's custodians in Turin are adamant that the conservation exercise was responsible and necessary, but many dedicated sindonologists fear that the Shroud has now been neutered as an object of scientific research.

Bewilderingly, despite accepting the carbon-dating result, the Catholic Church does not seem to have abandoned its faith in the Shroud. In the quarter of a century since the carbon dating was performed, the Shroud has been exhibited with great pomp and ceremony on no fewer than three occasions (in 1998, 2000 and 2010), a frequency not known since the early nineteenth century. (Another display is scheduled for 2025.) This is hardly compatible with the view that it is a medieval forgery, and it is certainly not presented to the faithful as such.

The words and actions of the two popes who have sanctioned these displays, John Paul II and Benedict XVI, certainly give the impression that the Vatican still believes in the Shroud's authenticity. In 2010, for instance, on the occasion of the latest exhibition, Benedict delivered a homily in front of the relic, in which he meditated, in particular, on the meaning of the blood marks. The Shroud, he said,

> is a burial cloth, which wrapped the body of a man crucified in total conformity with what the Evangelists tell us of Jesus . . . The Shroud is an Icon written with blood, the blood of a man scourged, crowned with thorns, crucified and wounded in the right chest. The image imprinted on the Shroud is that of a dead man, but the blood speaks of his life. Every trace of blood speaks of love and of life. Especially that copious stain near the chest, made of blood and water that flowed from a large wound produced by the thrust of a Roman lance: that blood and that water speak of life.[31]

Ecclesiastical statements on the Shroud are usually models of studied ambiguity, but not this one. Crucially, the cloth is said to be a real, blood-stained burial cloth and the lance that produced the side wound—the source not only of blood, but also, significantly, of water[32]—is said to have been Roman, not medieval. Benedict evidently believes that the Shroud is genuine. So why is he content to let the world at large—and many Catholics—dismiss it as a fake? Why is the result of the 1988 carbon-dating test tacitly upheld and a second test not permitted? If, as John Paul II said in 1998, the Church "entrusts to scientists the task of continuing to investigate, so that satisfactory answers may be found,"[33] why, fourteen years later, are scientists still being denied access to the cloth, even when it is being conserved? These questions become more urgent the longer the

Church equivocates, making spiritual capital out of a relic it has helped to discredit.

If the attitude of the Catholic Church is inscrutable, that of the secular world is entirely understandable. In the eyes of the general public the Shroud is a certified fake, a medieval oddity, nothing more. It might be interesting to find out how it was made, but, if it remains an enigma, so be it. Only crackpots think it might really have anything to do with Jesus. This popular verdict is shared by the vast majority of academics, which is unfortunate, because it means that very few scholars or scientists have spent any time at all thinking about the Shroud. The mystery that surrounds it is largely a product of this consistent lack of thought.

The carbon dating may be the reason most people now dismiss the Shroud as a medieval sham, but for most of the twentieth century, the case against the Shroud rested on Chevalier's interpretation of its fourteenth-century history, an interpretation that is still hugely influential, despite the widespread realization that the image is not a painting. Underlying the continuing skepticism is a fundamental issue that affects everyone's perception of the Shroud, an issue that helped prompt Chevalier's contemporaries to sweep the problem under the carpet and that has blocked academic discussion of the Shroud ever since. This is the issue of *meaning*, specifically the meaning of the Shroud in relation to the Resurrection.

Ever since Pia's discovery of the photographic negative in 1898, the potential meaning of the Shroud has inspired enthusiasm and anxiety in equal measure. The question is inescapable: if authentic, what might the Shroud tell us not only about the death and burial of Jesus, but also about the Resurrection? As soon as Pia's photographs were published, enthusiasts began wondering if, instead of being a miraculous sweat stain as previously thought, the image might actually have been caused by some form of energy generated during the Resurrection. A French journalist, Arthur Loth, suggested that it might have been produced by an electrochemical discharge from Christ's resurgent body.[34] Needless to say, such speculation was regarded with horror by secularists. Concerned that the Shroud might become a banner for belief in the Resurrection, they sought to close down all discussion, refusing even to allow the possibility that it might be genuine.

Caught between the enthusiastic and the anxious, Delage tried to investigate the image as a natural phenomenon, pursuing the hypothesis that it was a regular "vaporograph" without any (conscious) thought for its cultural significance. Such scientific detachment was and remains essential in

the effort to characterize and understand the material properties of the
Shroud, but it is naive to think that the issue of the cloth's *authenticity* is
"purely scientific." In order to explain the Shroud as a cultural object, in
order to decide whether it is authentic or not, one has to go beyond scientific description and integrate it into a complex account of the past based
on the evidence of texts, images and archaeological remains. Delage's
deduction that the Shroud once enfolded the body of a crucified man may
have been "purely scientific," but his claim that that man was probably
Jesus involved interpreting the Gospels. It had implications for the way the
Gospels were read as historical records, how they were perceived and
understood.

That is why Marcellin Berthelot censored Delage. He was afraid, no
doubt, that, judged authentic in a prestigious scientific publication, the
Shroud would be taken by many as material proof of the Resurrection.
The reasoning is spelled out clearly by Ian Wilson:

> If a similar imprint had appeared on the shroud of an Egyptian pharaoh or
> a Chinese emperor, it would be considered just some freak of nature, and
> dismissed with little further thought. But it occurred, from all that one can
> determine, only on the shroud of Jesus of Nazareth, a man reputed to have
> worked miracles and to have risen from the grave.[35]

It is this apparent coincidence that makes the Shroud so exciting for believers, that makes it seem like a potential proof of the Resurrection. And it is
this apparent coincidence—more than any evidence—that has led skeptics
to ignore and defame the Shroud for over a century. Although, theoretically, the Shroud could be authentic and at the same time unrelated to the
mystery of the Resurrection, we instinctively calculate the odds against
such a chance to be vanishingly small. How could two grand enigmas
resulting from the very same burial be unconnected? Surely, an extraordinary imprint on Jesus' burial cloth would imply something extraordinary
having happened to his body. An authentic Shroud, we assume, points to a
real Resurrection.

Ultimately, then, it is worry about what the Shroud might *mean* that
determines its rejection by modern rationalists. But what if we have got the
potential meaning of the Shroud all wrong? What if the fixed assumption
that it might help prove the Resurrection were a giant misconception?
What if, interpreted more carefully in the context of first-century Jewish
culture, it suggests that the founding "miracle" of Christianity was nothing
more than a popular confusion? Would rationalists then be inclined to
look more favorably on the Shroud? Would they then discover unnoticed

virtues in the arguments of the despised sindonologists? Answering these questions, we may come to know ourselves a little better, as well as the Shroud.

It is as if a spell has been cast over the Shroud, a spell consisting of the words: "if the Shroud is real, then so is the Resurrection." This is the unspoken thought that prevents most people from taking the cloth seriously. The way to break the spell is not to find out ever more about the Shroud scientifically and historically; it is to rethink the Resurrection. It is the magic of this word that bedazzles the Shroud's supporters and blinds its detractors.

PART 2

The Historical Riddle

3

Judaism before Easter

"Under Tiberius all was quiet": so wrote Tacitus in the early second century, describing the situation in Palestine at the time Jesus was crucified and Christianity began.[1] From the vantage point of the Roman aristocracy, untroubled by the travails of the Jews themselves, this was, no doubt, an accurate assessment. But on the ground in Judaea all was not quiet. In AD 26 Tiberius appointed a new prefect to Judaea, a governor whose ten-year rule would put a severe strain on the *pax romana* in the east. The name of this prefect was Pontius Pilate.

The Gospels portray Pilate as a spineless ditherer, caught between a worrisome wife who warns him not to have anything to do with the execution of Jesus, and the bloodthirsty Jews who, spurred on by their nefarious leaders, eventually persuade him to deliver up the Son of God to be crucified. This pusillanimous Pilate is a caricature designed to shift the blame for Jesus' death from the Roman prefect of Judaea onto the Jews. The real Pilate was far more sinister, a provocative bully with a reputation for injustice, violence and low cunning.[2] One episode in particular illustrates the febrile state of Judaea under his administration shortly before the crucifixion of Jesus. Recorded by Josephus, a Jewish historian who wrote toward the end of the first century, it apparently took place in AD 26, soon after Pilate's arrival in the province, and it helps set the scene for the sudden emergence of Christianity.[3]

The trouble occurred when the inexperienced Pilate sent a cohort of troops up from the coastal city of Caesarea to Jerusalem, where they were to stay over winter.[4] Each unit of the Roman army marched behind a standard, an emblem of identity mounted on a pole or spear, rather like the colors of a modern army regiment but imbued with religious significance. Some of these standards bore an embossed or sculpted image of the emperor, considered a living embodiment of the (semi-divine) man himself.[5] As even the meanest infantryman knew, these images were deemed

highly offensive by the Jews, who regarded them as abominable idols, forbidden by divine law. So to keep the peace, all Roman troops stationed in
Jerusalem adopted plain, inoffensive standards. Rashly, the new governor
decided to disregard this taboo and ordered the cohort to go up to Jerusalem with standards bearing the emperor's effigy. Warned of the turmoil
that would ensue, he had them smuggled into the city by night, so that,
once the plan was discovered, it would be a fait accompli.

The next day, when the inhabitants of Jerusalem realized what had been
done, they were horrified. As word spread, large numbers of Jews con-
verged on Caesarea, to plead with the governor to respect their law and
have the images removed. Pilate refused, on the grounds that to do so
would dishonor the emperor. The Jews, though, would not disperse; for
five days and nights they remained outside his palace, imploring him to
undo the offense. On the sixth day the prefect's patience wore out. Pre-
tending he would give them a fair hearing, he summoned the protestors to
attend a tribunal in the city's stadium, having first of all concealed a company of soldiers beneath the stands. As soon as the Jews repeated their
petition, Pilate gave a signal, and they found themselves surrounded by a
ring of soldiers, swords at the ready. They were then threatened with death
if they didn't cease their protest. But Pilate misjudged his adversaries.
Instead of withdrawing with their tails between their legs, the Jews "threw
themselves upon the ground, and laid their necks bare, and said they would
take their death very willingly, rather than the wisdom of their laws should
be transgressed."[6] Aware that he couldn't afford to make martyrs of them,
Pilate wisely decided to abandon his threat. The protest was successful,
and the offending standards were returned to Caesarea.

Historical accounts are thin on the ground in this period, and we are
fortunate indeed to have this report of a major incident that took place on
the eve of the Resurrection. It provides us with an invaluable snapshot of
people who breathed the same ideological air as the followers of Jesus, fellow Jews who, like them, experienced a religious crisis during the
governorship of Pontius Pilate. It must be remembered that the first Christians (as we now call them) were Jews and never thought of themselves as
anything else. It is likely, indeed, that some of those who defied Pilate in the
stadium of Caesarea were among the later followers of Jesus, and a few
may even have become eyewitnesses of the Risen Christ. (There were far
more of these witnesses than is usually realized, as we shall see.) Obviously, to get to grips with the astonishing idea of the Resurrection, we need
to understand how the first Christians thought and what they believed
before the events of Easter—before they became Christians. The Caesarea

protestors may serve as their representatives. If we can understand the mindset of these Jewish radicals, we may be able to understand the mentality of those who, shortly afterward, proclaimed the Resurrection.

The ancient Jewish worldview was based on a unique heritage of myth, legend and history, stretching back (as was believed) to the dawn of time. This heritage was embodied in the scriptures of the Hebrew Bible (known to Christians as the Old Testament). Together, these scriptures articulated an extraordinary story about the nation's past: the Story of Israel. It is now thought that only a small percentage of the events narrated in the Hebrew scriptures actually happened; rather than straight history, the Story of Israel is "an epic saga woven together from an astonishingly rich collection of historical writings, memories, legends, folk tales, anecdotes, royal propaganda, prophecy, and ancient poetry" during the eighth to fifth centuries BC.[7] But for first-century Jews the Story of Israel was the only history there was, and it was unassailably true.

The first half of the Story is contained in the first five books of the Bible: Genesis, Exodus, Leviticus, Numbers and Deuteronomy. These books are known in Hebrew as the Torah—the "law" or "teaching"—because, as well as the great narrative of Israel's foundation, they contain the original statutes of the Israelite nation, the Law of God. The Torah was believed to have been dictated to Moses by God on Mount Sinai, and it dominated every aspect of ancient Jewish life. It prescribed various customs and beliefs that distinguished the Jews from other nations, notably monotheism, male circumcision, Sabbath observance, racial purity and dietary laws. It laid down strict ethical rules, ordained festivals and fasts, regulated the consecration of priests, and gave elaborate instructions for sacrificial performances. The finer points of this legal system were undoubtedly lost on the majority of the Jewish populace, but the overall story and the moral/racial code it embodied were digested by all. They were taught it from the cradle (when half of them were circumcised), and they heard passages from the Torah read out in their local synagogue. To be Jewish was to know and observe the Torah.

The Story of Israel begins at the very beginning, with God—called "Yahweh" or "the Lord"—creating the heavens and the earth.[8] Yahweh was not a local sky-god, inhabiting a pre-existent cosmos; nor was he an inferior creator-god, like the Greek demiurge, who formed a largely evil world. He was the Lord of all Creation, and his Creation was essentially good—"And God saw everything that he had made, and behold, it was very good."[9] However, this raised a problem, because it was obvious to everyone that

God's Creation was no longer the best of all possible worlds. Something had gone badly wrong. The whole Story of Israel (and the whole body of law contained in the Torah) was, in essence, a response to the problem of suffering and evil. It explained what had gone wrong, how God had devised a somewhat inscrutable plan to fix his Creation, and why the plan was taking so long to come to fruition.

The problem, needless to say, was caused by humanity. Genesis contains two accounts of the creation of man, and together these determined the Jewish conception of what it was to be human. On the one hand, God created man, male and female, in his own image; on the other, he formed Adam from the dust of the ground and breathed into him the spirit of life.[10] Man may have been blessed with various privileges, such as having dominion "over all the earth,"[11] but it did not take him long to irk his Creator. Beguiled by the serpent, Adam and Eve tasted the fruit of the Tree of Knowledge of Good and Evil, the only tree in the Garden of Eden whose fruit God had forbidden them to eat, and for this they were expelled from Eden. Eve was condemned to endure the pain of childbirth, Adam to labor in the fields, and they were both fated to die—"you are dust, and to dust you shall return."[12] The original sin of Adam and Eve—their disobedience of God's primeval law—was the ultimate source of all human suffering and death. The Resurrection represented the long-awaited lifting of this universal curse.

After Adam and Eve things went from bad to worse. The rot set in with Cain, their first-born son, who murdered his brother, Abel, in a fit of jealousy. Just eight generations later human wickedness was everywhere, and God decided to destroy his creatures in a great cataclysm, warning only the righteous Noah. Even this did not solve the problem. Following the Flood, the repopulated world soon reverted to moral delinquency. But rather than cleansing the earth with a second cataclysm, God decided that this time he would help man redeem himself. He would choose a nation to serve him, a nation whose obedience would atone for all the sins of Adam and his descendants. The father of this nation—the Chosen People—was Abraham, the progenitor of the Jews.

In order to initiate his plan, God made a covenant with Abraham. In return for his exclusive devotion, God would make Abraham "the father of a multitude of nations," and, crucially, he would give to him and his descendants "the land of [his] sojourning, all the land of Canaan, for an everlasting possession."[13] For better or worse, the idea of the Promised Land has always been of central importance to the Jews, feeding their imagination and influencing their fate. For first-century Judaeans, the conviction that Israel had an inalienable, divine right to possess the land made the country's domination by Rome all the more difficult to bear.

Like all good yarns, the Story of Israel takes many twists and turns. After Abraham died, his son, Isaac, became wealthy, living as a nomad in the land of Canaan, but the lives of his grandsons, Esau and Jacob, were rather less prosperous. Esau, the elder, sold his birthright to Jacob (later called Israel) for a bowl of lentil stew. Jacob, though, ended up a refugee in Egypt, along with his twelve sons, the founders of the twelve tribes of Israel. This mythical sojourn in Egypt provided Judaism with its greatest symbol of exile and despair. For 400 years, it was believed, the Children of Israel were enslaved by the pharaohs, used as forced labor on building sites and in the fields.

The covenant, it seemed, had been broken. But God did not abandon his people forever. The great epic of Exodus tells the story of God's deliverance of the Israelites from bondage, a story that stood as the most potent symbol of his power to rescue the Jewish nation from adversity. The hero of the epic was Moses, the foremost Hebrew sage. Having served as God's intermediary with Pharaoh, warning him in advance of each of the ten plagues to be visited upon the Egyptians, Moses then led the Israelites across the Red Sea—when the waters were miraculously parted—and into the Sinai desert.

It was in the desert that God revealed himself most fully to Moses and his followers. The most famous revelation was the issuing of the Ten Commandments on Mount Sinai. These were inscribed "by the finger of God" on two stone tablets, which Moses placed in the Ark of the Covenant, a gilded chest that doubled as the throne of Yahweh. Most of the commandments are simple ethical rules whose validity is universally acknowledged—"You shall not kill," etc.—but three stand out as markers of Israel's distinct religious outlook.[14]

The most fundamental is the first: "You shall have no other gods before me." Monotheism—the worship of a single deity—was the rock on which Judaism was built.[15] This exclusive devotion set the Jews apart from their pagan neighbors, who saw no harm in worshipping a multiplicity of gods. The second commandment, a prohibition against idolatry, the worship of man-made gods, is really an extension of the first:

> You shall not make for yourself a graven image, or any likeness of anything that is in heaven above, or that is in the earth beneath, or that is in the water under the earth; you shall not bow down to them or serve them; for I the Lord your God am a jealous God . . .

In the early days of Judaism, the temptation to supplement the worship of Yahweh with the cults of rival gods seems to have been strong, and the Hebrew scriptures abound with dire warnings of the consequences of such apostasy. Among the direst is the story of the Golden Calf, an idol the Children of Israel fashioned for themselves while Moses was communing with God on Mount Sinai. God demanded that 3,000 of them be slaughtered for this crime, and, just for good measure, he sent a plague on them, too.[16]

Also distinctive was the fourth commandment: "Six days shall you labor, and do all your work; but the seventh day is a Sabbath to the Lord your God." The keeping of the Sabbath was explicitly linked to God's creation of the world: "For in six days the Lord made heaven and earth, the sea, and all that is in them, and rested the seventh day; therefore the Lord blessed the Sabbath day and hallowed it."[17] The Sabbath thus served as a weekly reminder that Yahweh was no mere tribal deity, on a par with other local gods, but the Creator of the Cosmos, the universal God.

The Torah leaves the story of the Israelites' epic journey unfinished. The tale is taken up in the next division of the Hebrew Bible, the so-called Early Prophets, from which the Jews drew their conception of Israel's heroic and troubled past, a time when the promise of the Promised Land was temporarily realized and then forfeited. Thanks to modern scholarship, we now know that the biblical tales of Israel's conquest and rule of the land of Canaan are barely any more historical than the myths of Genesis and Exodus, but their literal truth was unquestioned in first-century Judaea.[18] The first Christians believed wholeheartedly in these stories, and their dream of the Kingdom of God, inspired by the Resurrection, looked back to this time of national achievement.

Under the leadership of Joshua, the conquest of the Promised Land proceeded apace. Once the land was won, it was divided up among the twelve tribes of Israel, to be their perpetual inheritance. After Joshua's death, however, Israelite men began marrying Canaanite women and started worshipping the gods of their foreign wives. God was regularly provoked to wrath, and the Chosen People found themselves caught in a brutal cycle of war and oppression. Fortunately, though, God devised a means of rescuing his people from their self-inflicted woes. What they needed was a king, to galvanize their efforts against their enemies and keep them on the straight and narrow. The first king, Saul, was an abject failure, but his successor, David, was Israel's national hero. So great a warrior was David that, having defeated Israel's internal enemies, he created an Israelite empire stretching out beyond the Jordan and up through Syria, all the way to the Euphrates. Under David the territorial promise made to Abraham was gloriously fulfilled.

David was so favored by God that he received a divine promise that his descendants would rule an everlasting kingdom, centered on Jerusalem:

> When your days are fulfilled and you lie down with your fathers, I will raise up your offspring after you, who shall come forth from your body, and I will establish his kingdom. He shall build a house for my name, and I will establish the throne of his kingdom forever.[19]

David's immediate heir was his son, the wise and fabulously rich Solomon, who, in accordance with the prophecy, built the Lord a "house" in Jerusalem, the fabled Temple of Solomon. When the work was finished, the Ark of the Covenant was taken into the Temple and placed in the inner sanctum, the "most holy place"; "And when the priests came out of the holy place, a cloud filled the house of the Lord . . . for the glory of the Lord filled the house of the Lord."[20] God thus consecrated Solomon's Temple as his dwelling-place on earth. That is how Jerusalem became the Holy City and why, almost a millennium after the time of Solomon, pious Jews could not countenance Roman effigies entering the city.

After Solomon's death Israel's short-lived empire was divided into the northern kingdom of Israel, which spanned the River Jordan, and the smaller, southern kingdom of Judah, the region around Jerusalem. Beginning with Jeroboam, who instituted the worship of a golden calf, every one of the northern kings "did evil in the sight of the Lord." Eventually Yahweh lost patience altogether. He chose as his agent of destruction the king of Assyria, Shalmaneser, who descended on the northern kingdom of Israel, captured its capital, Samaria, exiled the people and replaced them with foreigners. Ten of the twelve tribes of Israel thus vanished from the Promised Land.

The kings of Judah were not much better than their northern counterparts, and Yahweh finally vented his anger by delivering the southern kingdom, too, into the hands of its enemies. In 597 BC Nebuchadnezzar, king of Babylon, conquered Judah, and all but "the poorest people of the land" were taken captive and sent to Babylon.[21] The final blow came ten years later, when, following a rebellion, Nebuchadnezzar returned to Jerusalem and demolished it. Solomon's Temple was stripped of its treasures and destroyed, and the remaining inhabitants were deported. Centuries after the Exodus, the nightmare of exile had returned.

*

The Story of Israel—the grand narrative that structured the way ancient Jews saw the world—came to an unexpected halt with the Babylonian captivity. The Chosen People had been led to the Promised Land, had settled in it, had finally conquered it . . . and had then been ignominiously banished. From then on, the Story itself became the chief object of their religious contemplation.[22] As we move into the period of the exile and beyond, we leave the realm of legend behind and enter the domain of history proper.

After Nebuchadnezzar destroyed Jerusalem, its leading citizens remained captive in Babylon for another forty years, cut off from their land, their Temple and their God. They found solace, it seems, in communal worship, coming together for the first time in synagogues, to pray, sing psalms, read and hear the scriptures, and preach and debate.[23] Another way of responding to exile was prophecy—speaking God's word. Several important prophets appeared in the sixth century BC: Jeremiah, Ezekiel, the so-called "Second Isaiah," and Zechariah.[24] The oracular words of these men had a powerful effect on the Jewish imagination. Most thrilling of all, perhaps, were the vivid visions and allegories of Ezekiel, a former priest, who was among those exiled in 597 BC, before Jerusalem was destroyed.

Ezekiel's prophesying began, so he tells us, with a breathtaking vision of the heavenly chariot and the throne of the Lord, above which was "a likeness as it were of a human form" surrounded by a bright, rainbow-like aura. Following this epiphany, Ezekiel began relaying to his fellow Israelites the vengeful messages of Yahweh. The "rebellious house" of Israel was to "fall by the sword, by famine and by pestilence," and Jerusalem, Yahweh's unfaithful bride, was to be stripped naked and cut to pieces.[25] Once the nation was purged, however, Yahweh would restore his people to the Promised Land.

On this note, Ezekiel introduced two optimistic ideas that would bubble away in Judaism for centuries, finally erupting in early Christianity. The first of these was the notion that after the exile Israel would once again be ruled by a scion of the line of David. Speaking through Ezekiel, God foretold a time when Israel, his flock, would once more live in their own land under a Davidic king: "And I will set up over them one shepherd, my servant David, and he shall feed them . . . and my servant David shall be prince among them . . ."[26] This prophecy was proved wrong; the Davidic monarchy was never reinstated. But it was a dream that would periodically inspire hopes of a national revival until the final destruction of the Jewish state in AD 135, at the hands of the Roman Emperor Hadrian.

Starting with Saul, all the Israelite kings, including David, had been consecrated by being anointed with oil, and they were therefore known as the "anointed" of the Lord. The Hebrew word for "anointed" is *messiah* (which translates into Greek as *christos*—Christ). A messiah, then, was simply a consecrated ruler of Israel. Six centuries after the fall of David's dynasty, a significant number of Judaeans looked forward to the arrival of a new messiah, who would restore their nation to its former glory. This messiah would be a conquering hero, like David himself.[27] By some strange alchemy, this nationalistic idea was transmuted into the Christian concept of an other-worldly, crucified Messiah. That alchemy involved the idea of the Resurrection, which brings us to the second of Ezekiel's optimistic ideas.

Envisioning the time of Israel's return to the Promised Land, Ezekiel conceived one of the most brilliant and influential allegories in the history of literature. In a passage of vital importance for the development of the Jewish concept of resurrection, he envisaged Israel as a mass of dry bones brought back to life by the Spirit of God:

The hand of the Lord was upon me, and he brought me out by the Spirit of the Lord, and set me down in the midst of the valley; it was full of bones. And he led me round among them; and behold, there were very many upon the valley; and lo, they were very dry. And he said to me, "Son of man, can these bones live?" And I answered, "O Lord God, thou knowest." Again he said to me, "Prophesy to these bones, and say to them, O dry bones, hear the word of the Lord. Thus says the Lord God to these bones: Behold, I will cause breath to enter you, and you shall live. And I will lay sinews upon you, and will cause flesh to come upon you, and cover you with skin, and put breath in you, and you shall live; and you shall know that I am the Lord."

So I prophesied as I was commanded; and as I prophesied, there was a noise, and behold, a rattling; and the bones came together, bone to its bone. And as I looked, there were sinews on them, and flesh had come upon them, and skin had covered them; but there was no breath in them. Then he said to me, "Prophesy to the breath, prophesy, son of man, and say to the breath, Thus says the Lord God: Come from the four winds, O breath, and breathe upon these slain, that they may live." So I prophesied as he commanded me, and the breath came into them, and they lived, and stood upon their feet, an exceedingly great host.[28]

So complete was the calamity that had befallen Israel, so complete its debasement, that in Ezekiel's eyes the nation had died, and its restoration would be a symbolic rebirth. It is a wonderfully extreme interpretation of

the misery of exile and the anticipated joy of repatriation. The meaning of
the allegory is made clear by the Spirit of the Lord:

> Then he said to me, "Son of man, these bones are the whole house of Israel.
> Behold, they say, 'Our bones are dried up, and our hope is lost; we are clean
> cut off.' Therefore prophesy, and say to them, Thus says the lord God: Behold,
> I will open your graves, O my people; and I will bring you home into the land
> of Israel."[29]

Ezekiel spoke and wrote these words in the sixth century BC to comfort a
few thousand unhappy Israelites, cut off from their ancestral home and
thus from their God. He could never have anticipated the strange hopes his
imagery would excite in a later generation of Jews, back in their homeland
but still unhappy. How astonished he would have been to learn that his
allegory was eventually taken literally—as a scene he had witnessed and a
miracle that would come to pass!

Ezekiel's hope was not in vain. The skeletal remnant of Israel was given
new life in 538 BC, when the king of Persia, Cyrus the Great, defeated the
Babylonians and issued a decree permitting the captive Israelites to return
to Judah, which was now under his control. The exile was over. But what
sort of nation would the returnees be able to build? And how was the resurrected Israel to relate to its troubled past? Everything that came after the
exile was, in a way, an attempt to restart the Story of Israel, to re-establish
the covenant between Yahweh and his Chosen People, to transform a painful historical struggle into a mythical destiny.

Under Persian rule the people of Judah became truly Jewish, consolidating
their idea of who they were, where they had come from and where they
were going.[30] It was a period of national optimism, but also frustration.
The Chosen People were back in Judah, and the so-called Second Temple,
completed in 516 BC, supplied them with a new focus of national identity.
But, as long as they lacked independence, their exile was, in a sense, ongoing. Freedom and the ultimate fulfillment of God's plan would come
only once Israel had atoned for a multitude of sins. Atonement was to be
achieved by the people's strict observance of divine law, the Torah, including the proper worship of Yahweh in his Temple. It was a simple scheme of
salvation, and, as long as Judah was ruled by Persia, it must have seemed
a realistic hope.

However, in 332 BC the course of Jewish history changed, complicating
the fulfillment of the divine plan. In that year Alexander the Great marched
through Palestine on his way to Egypt, in the course of his titanic struggle

with the Persian emperor, Darius, and Judah was incorporated into his Hellenistic empire. Suddenly the Jews found themselves part of an alien, Greek world. This presented an unexpected and ultimately fatal challenge to the ideology of the Jewish state. For, unlike the Persians, the Greeks went in for cultural imperialism.

During the Hellenistic period Greek cities were planted in territories all around Judaea (the Greek name for Judah), in Samaria and Galilee, in Transjordan, and along the Mediterranean coast. In these cities Jews could encounter all the usual institutions of Greek life—temples, theaters, stadia, gymnasia—as well as Greek literature and philosophy. Many Jews were seduced by this new, sophisticated world, even in Jerusalem, and Greek soon became the language of government, literature and education.

At the same time, the Jews' unique devotion to a single God and their self-isolating practices set them apart from the rest of the Hellenistic world. Inevitably, this led to tension, both between Jews and Gentiles and within Judaism itself. The question was how far Jewish–Hellenistic assimilation should go, especially in Judaea. Over the course of the next four centuries different answers to this question (on the part of Jews themselves and powerful outsiders) would lead to the fragmentation and eventual destruction of Second Temple Judaism.

After Alexander's death in 323 BC, Judaea was incorporated, first of all, into the Egyptian empire of the Ptolemies and then, after 198 BC, into the Syrian-Mesopotamian empire of the Seleucids. The country prospered under the Seleucids until 175 BC, when Antiochus IV Epiphanes came to the throne. The new emperor was an ardent Hellenizer, and his first act was to replace the high priest, Onias, with his brother, Jason, who dreamed of transforming Jerusalem into a Hellenistic city-state. Further machinations, including the murder of Onias, provoked widespread resentment. In 169 BC a rumor began circulating that Antiochus had died on campaign in Egypt, and the inhabitants of Jerusalem rose in revolt.

The report of the emperor's death was exaggerated. Entering Judaea with a formidable army, Antiochus marched on Jerusalem, broke down its walls, butchered and enslaved its citizens and plundered the Temple. Following further unrest the next year, he decided to solve his Jewish problem once and for all by systematically eradicating Judaism in its homeland. A series of decrees was issued, banning circumcision, abolishing the food laws and Jewish festivals, prohibiting observance of the Sabbath and ordering the destruction of all Torah scrolls. Jews were forced to eat pork—an "unclean" animal—on pain of death, and swine were sacrificed on the Altar of Burned Offerings. Finally, on December 14, 167 BC, an idol of Zeus was set up in the Temple, signifying the complete overthrow of Yahweh. The memory of this "desolating sacrilege" haunted Israel as long as the Temple stood.

Soon all Judaea was in revolt. The rebels were led by a priest named Mattathias and then, after his death, by his sons, chief among them Judas Maccabaeus, a master of guerrilla warfare. After a series of victories in the Judaean hinterlands, Judas and his men fell on Jerusalem and seized control of the Temple. The "desolating sacrilege" was torn down and the Altar of Burned Offerings was rebuilt. On December 14, 164 BC, the third anniversary of its desecration, the Temple was rededicated to Yahweh, and, soon afterward, Antiochus was forced to rescind his ban on the practice of Judaism. After another two decades of fighting and diplomacy, full independence was achieved under Judas's brother, Simon.

The Maccabean revolt was a pivotal moment in the history of Israel, and it inspired the writing of a prophetic book that was to be of crucial importance for the creation of Christianity: the Book of Daniel. This pseudonymous text, which purports to contain the prophecies of the prophet Daniel, a legendary figure said to have lived at the time of the Babylonian captivity, offers an apocalyptic commentary on the Jews' struggle against Antiochus. The climax comes with a vision of a snowy-haired man, the Ancient of Days, dishing out victory to "one like a son of man," an angelic figure representative of Israel:

> I saw in the night visions, and behold, with the clouds of heaven there came one like a son of man, and he came to the Ancient of Days and was presented before him. And to him was given dominion and glory and kingdom, that all peoples and nations and languages should serve him; his dominion is an everlasting dominion, which shall not pass away, and his kingdom one that shall not be destroyed.[31]

Like Ezekiel's description of the valley of dry bones, this passage was intended as an allegory of Israel's future, a future still conceived in terms of a return to the glory days of David and Solomon. When the author of Daniel writes of an "everlasting dominion," he is thinking of an independent, righteous, eternal Israel. The first Christians, who identified the "one like a son of man" with Jesus, would have understood this vision literally, as well, as an earthly kingdom ordained by God. It was only in retrospect, once the Romans had annihilated the Jewish state, that the Kingdom of God was reinterpreted as a purely spiritual realm.

The author of Daniel also uttered a vital prophecy about the resurrection of the dead. Speaking of the end-times, when Israel would finally be delivered, he described the fate of the dead on the Day of Judgment as follows:

> And many of those who sleep in the dust of the earth shall awake, some to everlasting life, and some to shame and everlasting contempt. And those who are wise shall shine like the brightness of the firmament; and those who turn many to righteousness, like the stars forever and ever.[32]

Unlike Ezekiel, the author of this passage meant his words to be read literally. He believed that, following a time of unprecedented trouble, there would be a general resurrection of the dead, and God's justice would finally prevail; the wise and righteous would be reborn in glory, while the wicked would suffer damnation. Here we see the first definite expression of the Jewish concept of resurrection.[33]

This ancient Jewish belief must not be confused with the modern belief in a spiritual afterlife. Daniel's resurrected shades are not envisaged as simply going to heaven when they die. Rather, they "sleep in the dust of the earth" for a while and are then reborn—in either physical or celestial bodies—to live new lives (either glorious or shameful, either on earth or in heaven). This is an updating of the old Israelite belief that, after death, all humans were fated to sleep for eternity in a dismal underworld, known as Sheol (the Pit).[34] This bleak idea seemed unacceptable in the wake of Antiochus' persecution, when Sheol began to be populated with large numbers of righteous Jews, who had been killed for the sake of their religion. Many of their fellow Jews, it seems, could not believe that a just God would leave such die-hard devotees to molder in the grave in perpetuity. Surely, they thought, the martyrs would eventually be restored to the life they had so nobly sacrificed. Behind the Christian faith in the Resurrection lies an unshakeable trust in divine justice.

Fundamentally, resurrection is about returning to life (a positive mode of existence) after a period of death (a negative mode of existence). Ancient Jews thought of life in terms of God's Creation, specifically the creation of Adam, and resurrection was conceived, therefore, as a return to embodied, created existence. That a dead person might cease to exist altogether was inconceivable; to die was not to be completely annihilated, but to be *uncreated*. Sheol, into which human shades descended, was a remnant of the dark, formless void that preceded Creation.[35] The resurrected would be rescued from this realm of eternal deathliness by being recreated by God. What form this new Creation would take, though, was a mystery. God might repeat his original design, or he might produce something quite different.

The pre-Christian, Jewish hope for resurrection is expressed most vividly in a book known as 2 Maccabees, written in the late second century
BC.[36] There is a story in this work of seven brothers, representatives of the
so-called "Maccabean martyrs," who defied Antiochus by refusing to eat
pork. The brothers were tortured to death one by one, but, as they died,
they each proclaimed their faith in a future resurrection. Thus, for instance,
one brother "put out his tongue and courageously stretched forth his
hands, and said nobly, 'I got these from Heaven, and because of his laws I
disdain them, and from him I hope to get them back again.'" Meanwhile,
their mother, who was forced to watch her sons being killed, encouraged
them by reflecting on the mystery of Creation:

> Filled with a noble spirit, she . . . said to them, "I do not know how you came
> into being in my womb. It was not I who gave you life and breath, nor I who
> set in order the elements within each of you. Therefore the Creator of the
> world, who shaped the beginning of humankind and devised the origin of all
> things, will in his mercy give life and breath back to you again, since you now
> forget yourselves for the sake of his laws."[37]

The future resurrection of the martyrs is seen here as a form of new Creation, dependent on God's mercy, which he will surely show those who lay
down their lives for his sake. It will involve sleeping with the ancestors for
a while in the earth, before being reconstituted to live again in God's Kingdom.

As the differing imagery in 2 Maccabees and Daniel reveals, the Jewish
idea of resurrection was a vague hope, rather than a well-defined doctrine.
Different attitudes toward the idea prevailed in the three main "parties"
that emerged in the second century: the Sadducees, the Pharisees and the
Essenes. The Sadducees, an aristocratic party, rejected the notion of resurrection outright, presumably because it was associated with the idea of
revolution.[38] The Pharisees, a group who sought to perfect Israel's observance of the Torah, were less satisfied with the status quo than the
Sadducees and looked forward to the future resurrection of the dead.[39]
Their views were influential among the Jewish people at large, but it is
unclear how they envisaged the coming resurrection: they may have taken
Ezekiel's prophecy literally and anticipated a return to physical, fleshly
existence, or they may have believed in something more ethereal, as implied
by Daniel. Probably, different Pharisees imagined the event in different
ways. The Essenes, a monastic sect who awaited the imminent arrival of
God's Kingdom, definitely believed in the immortality of the soul and may
also have believed in some sort of bodily resurrection.[40]

From the second century BC on, then, there was a widespread belief among the Jews in some sort of resurrection of the dead. Somehow, at the start of the new age, God would raise the righteous from Sheol and recreate them in new bodies, just as he had once created Adam and Eve.

In 63 BC, a century after Judas Maccabaeus drove the Syrians from the Temple and rededicated it to Yahweh, the Roman general Pompey marched on Jerusalem and laid siege to the Temple Mount. After three months the walls were breached, and the Romans poured into the Temple, slaughtering the hapless defenders.[41] The priests continued offering up sacrifices as if nothing was happening and were cut down around the altar. Finally, Pompey strode into the Temple Sanctuary and entered the Holy of Holies, God's private chamber, where only the high priest was allowed to tread. Having committed this terrible trespass, he returned to Rome in triumph. Judaea was now a province of the Roman Empire.

Pompey left the nation in the hands of the high priest, Hyrcanus II, but the real power lay with a man named Antipater, governor of the neighboring province of Idumaea.[42] Over the course of the next two decades, Antipater manoeuvred adroitly at home and abroad, gaining favor with successive Roman generals and installing his son, Herod, as governor of Galilee. In 37 BC Herod crushed a revolt and was proclaimed king of Judaea by the Roman senate. It was the start of one of the most notorious reigns in history. Tormented by conspiracies, both real and imagined, Herod ended up executing his beloved wife, Mariamme, and several of his own sons. But, for all his cruelty and paranoia, Herod was an able ruler. He brought peace and order to the realm, and Judaea grew wealthy under his rule. His greatest achievement was the monumental reconstruction of the Temple, begun around 19 BC, one of the most ambitious building projects anywhere in the ancient world. The scheme was so vast that, although the principal structures were completed within eight years, the whole complex was not finished until AD 63—seven years before it was utterly destroyed by the Romans.[43]

On Herod's death in 4 BC, his domains were divided between his surviving sons. Galilee and Peraea went to Herod Antipas, who was still in power during the earliest phase of Christianity. Samaria, Judaea and Idumaea were assigned to Archelaus, who was denounced as a tyrant in AD 6 and exiled to Gaul. Emperor Augustus then placed his territories under direct Roman rule. This necessitated taking a census for taxation purposes, a task undertaken by Quirinius, the imperial legate of Syria. For many Jews this was intolerable: it represented the enslavement of the Chosen People in their own Promised Land. A serious uprising ensued, led by a man named Judas the Galilean, the founder of what Josephus calls "the fourth sect of Jewish philosophy." This zealot movement united the popular doctrines of the Pharisees with a determination to acknowledge none but God as ruler—to achieve, that is, the earthly Kingdom of God.[44] Although Quirinius put down the rebellion swiftly, the "fourth philosophy" never went away and may have fed into the birth of Christianity.

After AD 6 Judaea remained peaceful for twenty years. Four Roman prefects came and went without provoking any trouble. Then Pilate arrived. Within a year this harsh, overbearing civil servant had managed to reawaken the spirit of Judas the Galilean and bring his province to the brink of revolt. Brutal and insensitive as he was, Pilate managed to keep a lid on the civil unrest that his rule provoked, so that Judaea remained, from a Roman perspective, relatively quiet. But after his departure the situation gradually deteriorated until eventually, in AD 66, the country slid into a suicidal war with Rome. The so-called Jewish War culminated in the utter destruction of Jerusalem in AD 70, bringing Second Temple Judaism (and with it the first phase of Christianity) to an end.

We can now understand how the followers of Jesus saw the world before being confronted by the mystery of Easter.

Let us focus on the affair of the standards and on the brave defiance of the protestors in the stadium at Caesarea. What was the point of their lying prostrate in the sand, inviting the circle of drawn swords to carry out the threat of slaughter? What were they expressing by this extraordinary offer of self-sacrifice? What beliefs and hopes drove them to this moment of crisis?

They thought of themselves (and everyone else) as descendants of Adam, whom God had created in his own image from the dust of the ground. Therein lay the root of their suffering, for, ever since Adam's transgression in the Garden of Eden, man had been cursed with toil and death, a return to the primordial dust. They themselves, though, were an elect people, the Children of Israel, chosen by God as instruments of redemption for the whole of mankind. In order to achieve their destiny, God had given them a code of law, the Torah, to which they had to adhere scrupulously. As long as they remained faithful to God's law, they would eventually cancel out Adam's sin and achieve redemption. And in return for their obedience, God had given them the Promised Land as an eternal inheritance.

But things were not going according to plan. Due to past transgressions, their forebears had been exiled from the Promised Land and then, on their return, subjected to Gentile domination. Some time ago they had achieved independence, but now they found themselves subject to a foreign empire once again. No scene could better represent the sorry situation of the Chosen People on the eve of the Resurrection than the mass protest in the stadium at Caesarea. To defend the divine law, to uphold the traditions of their fore-fathers, the protestors had to offer themselves as sacrifices in an arena dedicated to violent, impious sports. Dominated by Roman power and surrounded by a foreign, pagan culture, they had little prospect of realizing their own ideals. No wonder they succumbed to fantasies of future glory.

In the short term, they simply wished to persuade Pilate to remove the imperial standards from Jerusalem, thus preserving the Holy City from idolatry. In the long term, they and many of their compatriots looked forward to the Kingdom of God, when Israel would finally be saved from foreign tyranny and the world would be restored to its prelapsarian perfection. Many harbored a vague hope that God's Kingdom would be achieved through the agency of a messiah, an anointed king, who would lead them to victory and re-establish the glorious kingdom of David. But, as they lay there in the dust of the stadium, Roman soldiers standing over them, the protestors' minds would have been fixed on an even bolder hope: the resurrection of the dead. Having complete faith in God's justice, they anticipated being raised to life again, along with the Maccabean martyrs, once God's Kingdom finally dawned. None could have said how this future resurrection would occur, whether they would take on a celestial form or be recreated in the flesh. All that was certain was that they would be reborn and that their resurrection would involve some sort of re-embodiment, for to be without a body was to be a mere shade in Sheol.

This resolute hope won the day. The prefect backed down, the swords were sheathed, and the petitioners went on their way.

A little while later, these same people must have heard to their amazement that the resurrection of the martyrs had begun ahead of time. A man called Jesus, a descendant of David, had just been raised from the dead, three days after being crucified by the Romans as a would-be king of Israel. It was remarkable news, and, if true, hugely significant. Consulting the scriptures, they could have seen that it was a prophesied event, a signal that the Story of Israel was approaching its inevitable climax. The Christian gospel, as it would come to be known, was a new and exciting chapter in the centuries-old story for which the petitioners in the stadium at Caesarea had been willing to die. A glorious finale was assured.

But it all hung on rather a slender thread: the testimony of those who claimed to have seen Jesus risen from his grave.

4

The Testimony of Paul

Trying to figure out what happened at Easter is like investigating a 2,000-year-old crime. The only clues we have are contained in written sources, which tell us what people of the time said about the episode and what happened in its wake. The challenge is formidable. We are attempting to reach back into the distant past and grasp something that was obscure even to contemporaries. To stand a chance of success, we need to consider the evidence of the written sources very carefully, as if we were detectives interviewing witnesses and identifying significant leads.

Our sources provide three types of evidence.

First, there is the eyewitness testimony of those involved. This is what convinced others at the time—initially Jews, later Gentiles, as well—that Jesus had been raised from the dead. Fortunately, we still possess fragments of this first-hand testimony in the letters of Paul, preserved in the New Testament. One of Paul's letters, his first letter to the Corinthians (or 1 Corinthians), is particularly informative and opens an astonishing window on Easter from the point of view of the apostles. Listening to what Paul has to say about the Resurrection in 1 Corinthians is as close to Easter as we can get.

Second, via a variety of sources (Christian and non-Christian) we can trace the impact the Easter event had on first-century history. That is to say, we can identify specific historical effects—social and cultural developments—that point to something extraordinary having happened soon after the death of Jesus. These effects provide indirect evidence of the nature of the Resurrection phenomenon, and they also help prove that Easter was a real, historical episode.

Third, there are the stories told about Easter by early Christian communities and set down in the Gospels. These stories are relatively familiar and, read superficially, they are easy to understand, so they tend to shape the popular idea of the Resurrection. But they are not nearly as straightforward as they appear. As legendary narratives compiled toward the end of the first century, they are rooted in real history but contain all sorts of biases, contradictions and misunderstandings. In legal terms, they are the equivalent of hearsay.

These three types of evidence—eyewitness testimony, historical effects and Gospel stories—form the subjects of the next three chapters. And just as a detective trying to understand a crime gives priority to eyewitness testimony, generally the most direct and reliable form of evidence, so we should give priority to the testimony of Paul, a man in touch with the founders of the Church and himself a supposed eyewitness of the Risen Jesus.

If anyone can help us understand Easter, Paul can.

We have little or no knowledge of Paul's early life.[1] We do know, however, that as a young man he was a strict Pharisee and that by the early 30s he was a vicious persecutor of the early Church—perhaps the least likely person in Palestine to be converted to its cause.[2] He is introduced in Acts as a bystander at the execution of Stephen, a deacon stoned to death by a Jerusalem mob. This vivid story may owe as much to Luke's imagination as to an actual, remembered martyrdom, but the image of Paul consenting to the killing of a well-known Christian is perfectly plausible. Acts describes him "breathing threats and murder against the disciples of the Lord," and Paul himself says that, in his youth, he "persecuted the church of God violently and tried to destroy it."[3]

Then, suddenly, his whole world was turned upside down.

According to Acts 9, having "laid waste the church" in Jerusalem, Paul set off for Damascus, armed with letters from Caiaphas, the high priest, intending to root out Christians in the city's synagogues and take them back to Jerusalem in chains. Caiaphas must have had every confidence in his energetic inquisitor. But the raid had an unexpected outcome. Somewhere in the vicinity of Damascus, Paul experienced "a revelation of Jesus Christ" (as he would later call it) and went over to the other side. From a rabid opponent of the Church, he became, virtually overnight, one of its boldest champions. In the whole of history, there may never have been a more surprising—or more significant—volte-face. When news of it reached Jerusalem, Caiaphas and his colleagues must have been incredulous. It would have been rather like opening a newspaper one morning to read that Richard Dawkins, scourge of Creationists everywhere, had become a Seventh Day Adventist.

Paul's conversion is as great a mystery as the initial founding of the

Church; in a sense, it is the same mystery. We will consider what actually happened later in this book (where we will discover that the famous scene in Acts of Paul being accosted by a "light from heaven" on the road to Damascus is not an accurate historical account). For the moment, we need only note that Paul definitely had a traumatic, life-changing experience and that, by his own account, it involved seeing the Risen Jesus.

The exact date of Paul's conversion is uncertain, but it must have occurred within a few years of the Crucifixion, probably in AD 33.[4] After his conversion he went away briefly into Arabia (east of Palestine) and then returned to Damascus. It is difficult to say what he was doing during this period. He may have begun working on his own initiative as a preacher, concentrating on the conversion of Gentiles (non-Jews) and reacting strongly against the Jewish codes of law he had once so prized. In or around 36 Paul visited Jerusalem in order to make the acquaintance of Peter. While there, he also met James, one of Jesus' brothers and the head of the Jerusalem Church, a man who will feature prominently in our story. It was probably on this occasion that Paul was appointed an apostle, an official emissary of the Church.

After a fortnight's stay in the Holy City, Paul set out to spread the gospel throughout Syria and Cilicia. He worked as a missionary in these regions for over a decade, being remembered especially as one of the founders of the important church in Antioch. This Syrian metropolis was the scene of a dispute that drove Paul back to Jerusalem fourteen years after his initial visit. The trouble, it seems, was over the issue of circumcision. While Paul was adamant that pagan men who converted to Christianity should remain uncircumcised, some of his colleagues—"false brethren" he calls them—insisted that all Christians were subject to the Jewish law and had to be circumcised. Around 47, therefore, Paul went up to Jerusalem along with Barnabas, a fellow apostle, and Titus, a pagan convert, to lay his case before the "Pillars" of the Jerusalem Church: James, Peter and John.[5] This important meeting, known as the Jerusalem Conference, was a great success from Paul's point of view. As he tells it, the Pillars confirmed his version of the gospel and agreed that he and Barnabas should evangelize the Gentiles, while they themselves concentrated on evangelizing the Jews.

Thus began one of the greatest sagas in the history of early Christianity, Paul's colorful, decade-long quest in pursuit of universal salvation. In the course of three long, arduous journeys he founded churches in major cities across Anatolia and around the Aegean, and it was to these churches that most of his letters were written, letters of greeting and exhortation,

pleading and recrimination, instruction and explanation. They were written in Greek, the original language of every book of the New Testament.

Paul's career effectively ended when he was arrested in Jerusalem in 57.
Following several years of imprisonment in Caesarea, he was sent to
Rome to face trial before Nero. Acts 28.30 informs us that he lived in
Rome for two whole years but says nothing of his eventual fate. It is
unlikely that he survived Nero's purge of Christianity in Rome, following
the Great Fire of 64, for which the Christians were blamed. Tradition has
it that Paul was beheaded just south of Rome at a place that later became
the site of a magnificent abbey called Tre Fontane. His severed head supposedly bounced on the ground three times, and in each of the spots where
it landed, a spring welled up, giving the abbey its name—"Three Foun-
tains."

In contrast to such pious legends, the information contained in Paul's
letters is invaluable. His seven authentic letters (Romans, 1 Corinthians,
2 Corinthians, Galatians, Philippians, 1 Thessalonians, and Philemon)
form a unique archive of apostolic thought and belief.[6] It is of the utmost
significance that Paul was personally acquainted with the original leaders
of the Church. Before any of his letters were written, he got to know Peter
well, not only in Jerusalem but also in Antioch (where they fell out), and
he met James at least twice. On the occasion of the Jerusalem Conference
he laid his gospel before the three Pillars, to make sure he "was not running, or had not run, in vain,"[7] and, since his mission received their blessing,
there can be no doubt that they approved the essence of his teaching. He
was a contentious character, and his views on some issues differed markedly from those of other Jewish Christians, but he was not, as is sometimes
claimed, an ignorant outsider whose doctrines had nothing to do with the
teachings of the Jerusalem Church.

Paul, then, knew everything there was to know about nascent Christianity. In particular, he understood precisely what the apostles meant by the
Resurrection. He himself was understood to have seen the Risen Jesus, and
he must have discussed his "revelation" with the leaders of the Jerusalem
Church, who had seen the Risen Jesus too. This makes his letters exceedingly
valuable as sources for the Resurrection, far more so than the late, anonymous Gospels. Paul was not a would-be biographer of the late first century,
trading in confused Church traditions; he was an eyewitness and emissary of
the Risen Jesus, someone directly involved in the founding of Christianity.

Probably in the spring of 54, when he was staying in Ephesus, the principal city of Asia Minor, Paul wrote an impassioned letter to his former

acolytes in Corinth, prompted by news that they had become factional and dissolute. Paul's first letter to the Corinthians was an attempt to re-evangelize his followers in Corinth at a distance, preserving them in the Lord until he could visit them again in person—or until the Lord himself returned.[8]

One of the key issues the letter addresses is the resurrection of the faithful at the end of the age, a belief which had evidently become a major bone of contention in Corinth. As Paul explains toward the end of his letter, the expectation of a glorious future life is inextricably linked to the Resurrection of Christ, the event upon which the "good news" of Christianity depends. "If there is no resurrection of the dead," he tells his fractious followers, "then Christ has not been raised; if Christ has not been raised, then our preaching is in vain and your faith is in vain."[9]

Determined to clarify this crucial doctrine, Paul tries to spell out, once and for all, what the future resurrection of the dead will involve, in light of his knowledge of the Risen Christ. He begins by reminding his followers of the essential "gospel" he taught them when he first evangelized their city around 49, a gospel he himself was taught by the founders of the Church.[10]

> Now I would remind you, brethren, in what terms I preached to you the gospel, which you received, in which you stand, by which you are saved, if you hold it fast—unless you believed in vain. For I delivered to you as of first importance what I also received, *that Christ died for our sins in accordance with the scriptures, that he was buried, that he was raised on the third day in accordance with the scriptures, and that he appeared to Cephas* [i.e. Peter], *then to the twelve. Then he appeared to more than five hundred brethren at one time,* most of whom are still alive, though some have fallen asleep. *Then he appeared to James, then to all the apostles.*

This is a truly remarkable passage. It apparently preserves the contents of the original Christian gospel (shown in italics) in the very form that Paul taught it to the Corinthians, twenty years or so after the Crucifixion.[11] Long before Mark wrote down his self-proclaimed "gospel," the same title was being applied by Paul to this authoritative creed, which amounts to a historical summary of the birth of the Church.

The precise origin of the First Creed, as it may be called, is disputed, but there can be little doubt that it represents the core beliefs of the men who founded the Church.[12] Paul himself regarded it as having absolute authority, which is why he recites it at the outset of his argument about the Resurrection. He tells the Corinthians that he delivered it to them "as of first importance" and that it is through the gospel preached in these terms that they are saved.[13] It surely featured in the discussion he had with Peter, James and John, concerning the gospel he was preaching to the Gentiles,[14] and the fact that Paul's gospel was sanctioned by the Pillars, two of whom feature in the list of appearances, means that they must have approved its contents. Moreover, Paul states explicitly that it was a creed he shared with the other apostles: "Whether then it was I or they, so we preach and so you believed."[15]

The First Creed, then, is the original Christian proclamation; it is how the apostles themselves reported the Resurrection. But what does it mean?

On one level, it is perfectly straightforward: it simply records that Jesus died, that he was buried, that he rose from the dead and that he was seen subsequently by a large number of witnesses. On another level, though, the Creed seems paradoxical, for it testifies to an apparent impossibility: that a dead man was brought back to life. In due course we will see how we can make historical sense of the series of events the First Creed records. For the moment, though, let us focus on a few aspects of the text that can tell us something about the nature of the Resurrection phenomenon. Eking out these clues is vital if we are to solve the mystery of Easter.

First, the Creed tells us that Jesus was buried. This is significant, because it is sometimes argued that, as a victim of crucifixion, Jesus would not have been buried, but either left as carrion for wild animals or tossed into a common grave.[16] It may be that crucifixion victims in first-century Judaea were generally denied burial, but we know there were exceptions. Philo records instances of the bodies of crucified people being delivered to their kinsfolk so that they could be laid to rest, and Israeli archaeologists have found the remains of a crucifixion victim named Jehohanan in an ossuary (a stone box used for the secondary burial of the bones, once the body laid in the tomb had decomposed).[17] The statement in the First Creed that Jesus was buried shows that he was one of those fortunate souls, like Jehohanan, whose mortal remains were retrieved from the cross and accorded the proper funerary rites.

Note that in this earliest of sources Jesus is already called "Christ" (the Greek for Messiah). The use of this Jewish title as a proper name is peculiar and must have something to do with the Resurrection. Jesus was raised not just as a messiah or the Messiah, but as "Messiah" ("Anointed").

Next, the Creed says that Christ rose "on the third day." This phrase appears to echo Hosea 6.2 ("after two days he will revive us; on the third day he will raise us up, that we may live before him"), but it probably reflects the actual chronology of events as well. The three-day period seems to have been reckoned on the basis of Christ's appearance to Peter (referred to as Cephas, the Aramaic form of his name), since the Creed gives no other indication of how Christ was known to have risen.[18] Significantly, there is no mention of his tomb having been found empty.

The Resurrection is also said to have occurred "according to the scriptures," which indicates that, whatever it was that inspired belief in the Resurrection, it was interpreted from the beginning in terms of scriptural prophecies. The idea of the Resurrection may owe as much to creative reading, therefore, as to witnessing a remarkable phenomenon. It is surely no accident that the cult of the Risen Christ arose in a culture already permeated by the idea of resurrection.

Moving on to the appearances, the same Greek word is used three times to denote the manifestation of the Risen Christ: *ophthe*, meaning "was seen" or "appeared."[19] The construction of the verb phrase is somewhat unusual, which may indicate that the experience was difficult to put into words. Perhaps "he showed himself to" would be the best English translation.[20] It seems clear, at any rate, that some sort of vision was involved, whether natural or supernatural.

The list of witnesses is particularly interesting. First of all, there are a surprising number of them—at least 517 people, probably many more. Conditioned by the Gospel accounts, Christians tend to think of the Risen Jesus appearing only to his twelve disciples and a few other close followers, but the First Creed reveals that he was witnessed much more widely than this. The third appearance—"to more than five hundred brethren at one time"—suggests a great public appearance. Many now find this claim incredible, unable to reconcile it with their idea of the Resurrection, but Paul evidently regarded the testimony of the More-than-500 as vital, stressing that most of them were still around to bear witness in the 50s. The number of the apostles—the fifth group—is uncertain, but we know from Paul's letters that there were quite a number of them, probably dozens (see below, p. 62). Presumably, they all saw the Risen Jesus individually, since it is not said that they saw him "at one time," like the More-than-500. If so, the appearances must have been fairly numerous—almost routine. This hardly chimes with the popular idea of the Resurrection appearances as a few exclusive epiphanies.

Incidentally, the apostles are commonly confused with the Twelve, a confusion Luke was the first (or one of the first) to promote. It is clear from Paul's letters, however, that the title *apostolon* (meaning "emissary") was given to every legitimate Christian missionary, whether or not they were members of the Twelve.[21]

To summarize, the First Creed points to the Risen Christ having emerged from a tomb; having been witnessed by Peter "on the third day" after the Crucifixion; having been seen repeatedly thereafter by individuals, groups and even a large crowd; and having immediately been viewed in relation to—perhaps even identified via—the Hebrew scriptures. This is a fair amount of information, and, however confusing it may appear now, it should eventually help us understand what happened at Easter.

Having recited the First Creed, Paul adds a personal coda, concerning his own encounter with the Risen Christ:

> Last of all, as to one untimely born, he appeared also to me. For I am the least of the apostles, unfit to be called an apostle, because I persecuted the Church of God.[22]

This is virtually all Paul ever tells us about his conversion experience. Quite what he means by saying that Christ appeared to him "as to one untimely born" is, as yet, difficult to say. It certainly doesn't clarify anything, but it does add to the impression, given by the First Creed, of a peculiar phenomenon seen by a wide variety of witnesses.

Paul may never give a full account of his conversion experience, but a little later in 1 Corinthians he does the next best thing. In response to a report that some of his Corinthian followers have started to deny the future resurrection of the dead, he embarks on a lengthy discussion of this crucial doctrine, from which we can extrapolate a detailed description of the Risen Christ.

Paul thought that the resurrection of the dead was imminent, that the Resurrection of Jesus was the "first fruits" of a great resurrection harvest to be reaped at the *parousia*, the arrival of Christ as the cosmic Messiah (popularly known as the Second Coming). The purpose of his discussion is to give the Corinthians a precise understanding of this impending event, to explain to them how the dead would be raised and the kind of body they would inhabit. Since Paul viewed the Resurrection of Jesus as the prototype of these future resurrections, he must have based his description of the risen body on the Risen Christ, the only resurrected person he or anyone else had ever seen.

Indirectly, then, Paul does provide a first-hand account of the Risen Christ. However, despite being beautifully crafted, his account of the risen body is rather complex and hard to follow. In particular, the novel idea of the "spiritual body," which is at its heart, is as elusive as a wriggly fish. It is worth reading the passage through twice, to get a feel for its contents and structure.[23]

But some one will ask, "How are the dead raised? With what kind of body
do they come?" You foolish man! What you sow does not come to life unless
it dies. And what you sow is not the body which is to be, but a bare kernel,
perhaps of wheat or of some other grain. But God gives it a body as he has
chosen, and to each kind of seed its own body. [For not all flesh is alike, but
there is one kind for men, another for animals, another for birds, and another
for fish. There are celestial bodies and there are terrestrial bodies; but the
glory of the celestial is one, and the glory of the terrestrial is another. There
is one glory of the sun, and another glory of the moon, and another glory of
the stars; for star differs from star in glory.]

So it is with the resurrection of the dead. What is sown is perishable, what
is raised is imperishable. It is sown in dishonor, it is raised in glory. It is sown
in weakness, it is raised in power. It is sown a physical body, it is raised a
spiritual body. If there is a physical body, there is also a spiritual body. Thus
it is written, "The first man Adam became a living being"; the last Adam
became a life-giving spirit. But it is not the spiritual which is first but the
physical, and then the spiritual. The first man was from the earth, a man of
dust; the second man is from heaven. As was the man of dust, so are those
who are of the dust; and as is the man of heaven, so are those who are of
heaven. Just as we have borne the image of the man of dust, we shall also
bear the image of the man of heaven.[24]

The opening questions—"How are the dead raised? With what kind of
body do they come?"—represent a hostile challenge.[25] Skeptics were
apparently raising basic objections to the idea of resurrection, such as the
evident impossibility of reconstituting a dead body once it has decomposed.[26] In the face of this challenge, Paul is forced to mount a defense of
his core belief.

His defense is basically this: arguments about reconstituting physical
bodies are irrelevant, because the faithful will be resurrected not in their
flesh-and-blood bodies, but in "spiritual bodies."[27] Resurrection is not
about corrupt flesh being reconstituted and revivified; it is about God giving his people entirely new bodies, of a kind suitable for a new, perfect
Creation. The Risen Christ, to whom the apostles bear witness, is the pre-
cursor and progenitor of the risen, spirit-embodied faithful. The Corinthian
heretics have failed to grasp the crucial idea of the spiritual body and, fools
that they are, have slipped into the trap of conceiving resurrection in terms
of flesh and blood.

Paul premises his argument on the idea that Creation contains various
distinct types of body. Having reminded his audience of the differences

between the flesh of men, animals, birds and fish, he goes on to differentiate terrestrial bodies from celestial ones, such as the sun, moon, and stars.[28] He believed that God had created a range of different bodies, each type having its own particular "glory" (i.e. quality, not shininess).[29] Resurrected bodies, therefore, did not have to be the same as mortal bodies; God could make them fundamentally different.

At the same time, the resurrected body had to preserve the identity of the mortal person. Paul uses the everyday image of a sprout springing from a seed planted in the ground (like a corpse in a tomb) to explain the intimate relationship between the mortal human body and its resurrected counterpart.[30] He makes a clear distinction between the seed (the old, mortal body) and the seedling (the new, resurrected body). The two are not the same. He says explicitly, "you do not sow the body that is to be"—you do not sow a seedling. Immortality is bestowed by God in the form of a new type of body, just as he gives a shoot to the "bare seed" planted in the earth.

Whereas the body that is "sown" (i.e. buried) is perishable, shameful and weak, that which is raised is imperishable, glorious and powerful. By definition, a body that perishes cannot be transformed—to perish is to cease to exist. It is the *spiritual person* that survives and is recreated, not his or her flesh. Paul summarizes the transition from mortality to immortality in this famous line: "It is sown a physical body, it is raised a spiritual body." The physical body and the spiritual body are two different bodies, one of which succeeds the other.[31]

Paul goes on to explain the difference between the physical body and the spiritual body in terms of two archetypal figures: Adam and Christ. The first man, Adam, represents mortal humanity. Three times Paul reminds us that Adam was a "man of dust," emphasizing both the lowliness of his flesh and its inevitable decay—"You are dust and to dust you shall return."[32] Adam is contrasted with Christ, the second man, the pattern and forebear of resurrected humanity. By describing Christ as "from heaven" and opposing him to the man "from the earth," Paul reminds us of his earlier distinction between earthly and heavenly bodies. Clearly, then, the body of the heavenly man, Christ, is of a celestial quality, akin to the sun, moon and stars.[33]

Paul's final statement—that, although we currently bear "the image of the man of dust," in the future we will "bear the image of the man of heaven"— defeats any attempt to reduce the Risen Christ to a heavenly glare, in line with Luke's idea of the vision on the road to Damascus. Christ may have appeared to Paul more like star-stuff than mortal flesh, but there was more to him than pure light—if, indeed, he was luminous at all. He possessed an image, a form analogous to, but distinct from, Adam's. When we are resurrected, Paul thought, our spiritual bodies will share the form of the Risen Christ, who was made in the image of God.

Just in case anyone in Corinth fails to get the point, Paul concludes his discussion with an unequivocal denial of physical resurrection. "I tell you this, brethren," he says, emphasizing the importance of what he is saying:

> flesh and blood cannot inherit the kingdom of God, nor does the perishable inherit the imperishable.[34]

There it is in plain Greek: flesh and blood will not participate in the Kingdom of God, will not be involved in the resurrection of the dead. Resurrection is not about corpses being recomposed and exiting the grave; it is about God's children being reborn in spiritual bodies as part of a new Creation. The usual philosophical objections to the concept of resurrection are thus rendered obsolete.[35]

Taking everything together, we arrive at the following "photo-fit" of the Risen Christ.

The person who appeared to Paul at the moment of his conversion was quite unlike an ordinary human. He seemed like a heavenly being with a body composed not of flesh, but of celestial matter, like the bodies of the sun, moon and stars. This celestial man was "a life-giving spirit," clothed in a spiritual body, which appeared imperishable, glorious and powerful. He appeared so exalted that Paul regarded him as literally God-like, identifying him with the man made in God's image on the sixth day of Creation (to be contrasted with the mortal Adam, made on the second or third day—a new take on a common interpretation of Genesis 1–2).[36]

Yet, mysteriously, Paul also recognized this starry being as Jesus, the would-be Messiah, whose followers he was busy persecuting. And he also somehow recognized that Jesus had been resurrected; he was not merely a ghost, a temporary visitor from the realm of the dead. Here, then, was a fulfillment of the prophecy in the Book of Daniel about the resurrected righteous shining "like the stars." But Jesus had not simply been transformed into a star, like some pagan hero. His celestial, spiritual body had apparently sprung from his dusty flesh as it lay in the tomb, like a seedling emerging from a seed, and was then seen for a period on earth.

This is the portrait Paul paints of the Risen Christ. It is remarkably detailed and covers his nature, form and relation to the mortal Jesus. Paul's failure to describe his conversion experience in detail no longer seems so unfortunate. The problem now is not so much understanding *how* Paul perceived the Risen Christ as understanding *why* he perceived him as he did. Was he delusional? Did he really meet Jesus resurrected in a spiritual body? Or did he experience something else that he interpreted in terms of seeing a resurrected, celestial, God-like Jesus?

Here, we run up against the limits of our historical imaginations. We will discover in due course, though, a means of transcending those limits, enabling us, twenty centuries later, to unlock the workings of Paul's mind and gaze on the same ethereal person as he did.

5
The Impact of Easter

It is generally regarded as a secure historical fact, based on the narratives of the Gospels, that the Church was founded in the wake of Jesus' crucifixion, which took place when Pontius Pilate was governor of Judaea. Fundamental as it is, this idea is surprisingly difficult to corroborate in other ancient sources, which provide scant evidence about the origins of Christianity. Fortunately, though, there is one excellent, non-Christian source that does support the testimony of the four Evangelists: a passage in *The Annals of Imperial Rome* written by Tacitus around 115.

Describing Nero's persecution of the Christians in Rome in 64, Tacitus summarizes the origins of Christianity thus:

> Nero fabricated scapegoats—and punished with every refinement the notoriously depraved Christians (as they were popularly called). Their originator, Christ, had been executed in Tiberius' reign by the governor of Judaea, Pontius Pilatus. But in spite of this temporary setback the deadly superstition had broken out afresh, not only in Judaea (where the mischief had started) but even in Rome. All degraded and shameful practices collect and flourish in the capital.[1]

Tacitus may speak of Christianity "in the tone of voice of one who has come across a dead rat in his water-tank," as Tom Wright puts it, but he knows enough about the "deadly superstition" to say where and when it originated.[2]

The same story is implicit in the First Creed, in which Christ's death and burial are immediately followed by the formation of the Church, reduced to a set of Resurrection appearances. Unlike later creeds, this one does not say explicitly that Jesus suffered under Pontius Pilate, but its references to Peter and James, both well-attested historical characters, makes this timeframe all but certain. There is little or no justification, then, for denying the traditional chronology of Christianity's foundation.[3]

The First Creed introduces us to the founders of the Church: Peter, James, the Twelve, and the apostles. Since all these people were actors in the Resurrection drama we are trying to reconstruct, we need to establish who they were. We should be aware, as we do, that they did not think of themselves as belonging to a new religion and were not initially known as Christians. They were members of a Jewish sect and called themselves Nazarenes, or followers of the Way.[4]

Peter, also called Simon, is a figure almost lost to view beneath layers of Christian legend.[5] From the many stories told about him in the Gospels, we tend to think of him as an impetuous, passionate man, an ardent follower of Jesus, who, despite being full of human weakness, remains ultimately faithful. One moment he is sleeping in the Garden of Gethsemane, when he should be keeping watch; the next he is cutting off the ear of the servant of the high priest in a desperate attempt to prevent his master being captured. Then his courage fails and he denies Jesus three times in the house of the high priest, only to make amends by thrice protesting his love for Jesus a short while later, beside the Sea of Galilee.[6] This fascinating, larger-than-life character—a sort of spiritual Falstaff—is firmly imprinted on the Christian imagination. Little of this Gospel material, though, is likely to be historical. The real Peter was probably a lot less colorful than his legend.

According to Acts, Peter was the initial leader of the Church. It was he who delivered the first sermons in Jerusalem and performed the first signs through the power of the Holy Spirit. After the death of Stephen, he became the principal Christian missionary "throughout all Judaea and Galilee and Samaria."[7] Peripatetic though he was, Peter spent a good deal of time in Jerusalem, as his meetings with Paul confirm. The final period of his life is hopelessly obscure. According to a dubious Church tradition, he ended up in Rome and was crucified there under Nero.[8] He is supposed to have chosen to be crucified upside-down, feeling unworthy to imitate the manner of Christ's death. If he did suffer an upside-down crucifixion, his own wishes can have had nothing to do with it. Roman soldiers enjoyed experimenting with torture and regularly crucified people in odd positions.[9]

Although Peter is remembered as the principal hero of the early Church, he soon ceded authority to James, the brother of Jesus.

Almost forgotten today, James was the dominant figure in Christianity until his judicial murder in 62.[10] His authority stemmed from his relationship to Jesus. They were definitely full brothers, not cousins or half-brothers, as theologians have often claimed. This fraternal relationship is attested by both Paul and Josephus, and their testimony is supported by early Church traditions.[11] No one thought to deny that Jesus had brothers until the fourth century, when the doctrine of the perpetual virginity of Mary gained influence, and theologians saw a need to reinterpret them as half-brothers or cousins in order to preserve Mary's womb intact. In reality, it seems, Mary and Joseph parented five boys and at least two girls. James was probably the eldest brother after Jesus, making him his natural heir.[12]

We have already seen how, on the occasion of the Jerusalem Conference, Paul and Barnabas met in private with the three Pillars, James, Peter and John, and persuaded them to sanction their mission to the Gentiles. Evidently, the Pillars formed the supreme council of the early Church.[13] The more famous council of the Twelve is practically invisible from a historical point of view. Everyone is familiar, of course, with the twelve disciples of Jesus portrayed in the Gospels, his loyal, if erratic, followers who often struggle to understand his divine mission. It is debatable, though, how much credence should be given to this group portrait. The fact that the Twelve are listed in the First Creed as the recipients of the second Resurrection appearance strongly suggests that such a body did exist before the Crucifixion, but it is unclear how long it remained an important institution, or even if it survived into the era of the Church.[14] Their number, an allusion to the twelve tribes of Israel, had religio-political implications, since the reassembly of the twelve tribes was associated with the Messianic age to come. This ties in with the fact that Jesus was executed by the Romans as a Messianic pretender—a would-be king of the Jews.[15]

Then there were the "apostles," an order of which Paul was a prominent member.[16] These official envoys of the faith were the means by which Christianity spread. They preached the gospel and set up churches at home and abroad, Peter being regarded as the principal apostle to the Jews, Paul as his counterpart among the Gentiles.

Unfamiliar apostles pop up occasionally in Paul's letters, giving the impression that there were quite a number of them. Silvanus and Timothy, co-senders of Paul's first letter to the Thessalonians, are called apostles, as are two other of Paul's companions, Apollos and Barnabas, and two unnamed brethren sent to preach the word in Corinth.[17] Particularly interesting is a reference to two people in Rome named Andronicus and Junia (probably husband and wife), whom Paul describes as "prominent among the apostles."[18] In the Middle Ages careless (or prejudiced) copyists transformed Junia into "Junias," a man, but it is clear that she was, in fact, a woman. So, at least one of the apostles—and a prominent one, at that—was female.[19]

According to the First Creed, all the apostles saw the Risen Jesus. Those who were not among the first witnesses (i.e. Peter, the Twelve, the More-than-500 and James) must have seen him later, as did Paul. This may come as something of a surprise, for there is nothing in the Gospels about obscure Christian missionaries seeing the Risen Jesus. The Gospels, though, provide a very incomplete record of the Resurrection appearances. Strange as it may seem, the Mediterranean world of the mid first century was buzzing with supposed eyewitnesses of the Risen Christ.

These, then, were the acknowledged leaders of the early Church, all of whom derived their authority, at least in part, from having seen the Risen Jesus. Beneath the apostles, according to Paul, there was a hierarchy stretching down through prophets and teachers to miracle-workers, healers, helpers, administrators and "speakers in various kinds of tongues."[20] It was a busy organization, and within a few decades of its foundation it was making a lot of noise, both literally and figuratively, right round the Mediterranean.

The spread of the gospel was highly controversial. Wherever he went, Paul tended to receive a hostile reception, and on at least two occasions, it seems, his teaching provoked a riot.[21] Other apostles, who went to preach the word in Rome, were equally controversial. Suetonius records that the Jews were expelled from Rome by Emperor Claudius, because they "caused continuous disturbances at the instigation of Chrestus" (i.e. Christ).[22] This episode probably took place around 49 and suggests that by as early as the mid first century the Nazarenes were deemed something of a menace.

More than anything, though, this new Jewish sect was a puzzle. A knowledgeable outsider could have identified at least five aspects of the Christ cult that were difficult to comprehend, features that differentiated it from regular Judaism and pointed to something very mysterious at the heart of the movement.

The first and most obvious puzzle associated with Christianity is that its founders, the former followers of Jesus, were inspired by his crucifixion. Nowhere in early Christian literature is there even a hint that the Crucifixion was considered a setback (as Tacitus mistakenly called it). On the contrary, it was regarded almost immediately as a great sacrificial act by which God had redeemed mankind.

This is as extraordinary a response to an execution as it is possible to imagine. Revolutionaries frequently cherish the memory of a martyr, but they never usually hail a martyrdom as the means of their salvation. When Martin Luther King was killed, for instance, his congregation did not

rejoice in the shooting and found a new denomination focusing on its significance. Yet, somehow, the first Christians did just that. Had Tacitus been
informed that Christianity did not merely survive the Crucifixion but actually sprang from it, he would have been flummoxed. Revolutionary
movements are supposed to die when they are decapitated, not start cele-
brating their severed head.

The Gospels try to explain how the disciples arrived at their positive
view of the Crucifixion as follows. Three days after being laid in the tomb,
Jesus reappears in a resurrected form and explains to them that it was
necessary "that the Christ should suffer and on the third day rise from the
dead."[23] And he then appoints them his "witnesses in Jerusalem and in all
Judaea and Samaria and to the end of the earth."[24] In the Gospels, Jesus is
always being let down by his disciples, most notably when they flee at the
moment of his arrest, but this time, stirringly, they step up to the mark.
More than an unexpected cause for joy, Jesus' death is a moral turning-
point in the lives of these lily-livered Galileans. After the Crucifixion they
are transformed from a bunch of obtuse, undependable hangers-on into a
band of sagacious heroes—a transformation symbolized, above all, by the
figure of Peter.

We may find this scenario incredible, but, if so, we have to come up with
a more plausible, alternative explanation. As the biblical scholar Reginald
Fuller puts it, "even the most skeptical historian has to . . . account for the
complete change in the behavior of the disciples."[25]

A second puzzle is that, following his death, the Nazarenes hailed Jesus as
the Messiah, the anointed leader of the Jewish nation. Jesus is called Christ
in the earliest Christian traditions that scholars have been able to identify.[26] Moreover, the belief that Jesus' death achieved the forgiveness of sins
(a belief attested in the First Creed) had Messianic connotations: it signified forgiveness not merely for individuals but for Israel as a whole, a
collective absolution associated with the dawning of the Messianic age.[27]

Christians are now so used to thinking of Jesus as their "Messiah," by
which they mean their spiritual savior, that it can be difficult for them to
understand how strange—indeed, how wrong—this title would have
seemed to most first-century Jews. As we have seen, the Messiah was traditionally conceived as a conquering hero, a new David who would liberate
the Jews from foreign rule, and he would be recognized as such only after
he had driven the Gentiles from the Promised Land and established his
righteous rule. So, if, before his death, people had hoped that Jesus might
be the Messiah, they would have been more than disheartened by his arrest

and crucifixion: they would have had their faith in him destroyed, because his execution would have been perceived as proof positive that he was not God's "Anointed." Hailing Jesus as the Messiah in mid-first-century Palestine would have been as paradoxical as declaring Che Guevara president in late-twentieth-century Cuba.

The idea of a crucified Messiah, moreover, would have been seen by many Jews as an insult to the Jewish nation.[28] Death by crucifixion came under the rubric of hanging, and, according to the Torah, "anyone hung on a tree is under God's curse."[29] To exalt a crucified man as Israel's divinely ordained king would have been seen as morally reprehensible, a betrayal of the nation and an affront to God. Gentiles would have been inclined to view the idea with similar disdain, crucifixion being considered shameful throughout the ancient world. Dead, shamed and accursed, Jesus was the most unlikely Messiah imaginable.

What could possibly have prompted the first Nazarenes to hijack the nationalistic idea of the Messiah and apply it to the pitiable figure of Jesus? They must have witnessed or experienced something very powerful after his death, something that made them think he had been vindicated by God. Otherwise, his claim to be the Messiah would have died with him on the cross.

A third peculiar aspect of Christianity was its obsession with, and development of, the Jewish notion of resurrection. As we have seen, the idea that God would resurrect the dead had been prevalent in Judaism since the second century BC, but most first-century Jews would have been astonished by the Nazarenes' views on the subject.[30]

Whereas their Jewish contemporaries regarded resurrection as a peripheral issue, the Nazarenes considered it absolutely central. Paul drives home the fundamental significance of the belief in his first letter to the Corinthians: "For if the dead are not raised, then Christ has not been raised. If Christ has not been raised, your faith is futile and you are still in your sins."[31] Ordinary Jews accepted that they were still "in their sins" and looked forward to God's eventual forgiveness of Israel, which might or might not involve the resurrection of the dead. For many, this communal resurrection was an event to be expected, but it was not a symbol like the Promised Land, the Temple or the Torah, which defined Jewish belief.[32] For the Nazarenes, though, it was all-important. The apostles were primarily witnesses of the Risen Christ, and their mission was to ensure the future resurrection of as many people as possible.

Also revolutionary was the idea that the general resurrection at the end of the age had already started happening. It was not merely a hope for the future, but a two-stage process that had begun with the Resurrection and would conclude with the (re)appearance of Christ on earth—the *parousia*— when he would be joined by his followers.[33] The Risen Jesus was the "first fruits" of the resurrection harvest to come.

Because the resurrection of the dead was strongly associated with the inauguration of the revolutionary Kingdom of God, this implied that the Kingdom of God was already somehow present or starting, even though the Romans were still in charge. For a zealous Jew outside the Nazarene fold, such talk would have been incomprehensible: the fact that Rome still ruled the country would have been ample proof that the resurrection had *not* begun to happen. How could the Nazarenes have abandoned Ezekiel's idea of the resurrection as the resurgence of Israel? How could they have hived off the resurrection of one martyr from those of all the rest? For contemporary Jews, these questions would have been urgent. The Nazarenes had hijacked the regular conception of resurrection, just as they had hijacked the idea of the Messiah.

The Nazarenes also spoke about themselves as if they had already been resurrected, in some sense, in this life—or were in the process of being resurrected. Paul articulates this belief most clearly in his letter to the Romans:

> If Christ is in you, although your bodies are dead because of sin, your spirits are alive because of righteousness. If the Spirit of him who raised Jesus from the dead dwells in you, he who raised Christ Jesus from the dead will give life to your mortal bodies also through his Spirit which dwells in you.[34]

The outward sign of this metaphysical rebirth was baptism, a mystical union with Christ that incorporated the believer into the unfolding Kingdom of God.[35]

The novelty of this doctrine is best illustrated by John's story of Nicodemus, a Pharisee who struggles to understand the concept of spiritual rebirth. When Jesus tells him that he must be "born anew" to see the Kingdom of God, Nicodemus asks, "How can a man be born when he is old? Can he enter a second time into his mother's womb and be born?"[36] Jesus then explains that he must be "born of water and the Spirit," but the Pharisee is still confused—"How can this be?" Many conversations like this must have occurred between Nazarene preachers and their would-be converts, for whom the idea of being "born anew" while still alive would have been extremely puzzling.

Tom Wright calls the Christian "mutation" of the Jewish resurrection hope "a phenomenon so striking and remarkable that it demands a serious and well-grounded historical explanation."[37] No such explanation has yet been proposed.

Fourthly, there is the remarkable fact that the Nazarenes adopted Sunday, the first day of the week, as a new day of worship, compromising the unique importance of the Sabbath. Indeed, Sunday was evidently accorded greater significance than the Sabbath, since the celebration of "the Lord's Day" was imposed on Gentile converts, while Sabbath observance was not.

The evidence for Sunday worship in the primitive Church is sparse but compelling. In Acts 20.7, for example, it is recorded that Paul and his companions "gathered together to break bread" on the first day of the week. The "breaking of bread" was a way of referring to the weekly symbolic meal, the Lord's Supper, which developed into the Eucharist (or Holy Communion).[38] Conversely, there is no evidence of any Christian group ever meeting for worship on any other day—on Friday, for instance, the day of the Crucifixion, or on Thursday, the day of the Last Supper. To have been observed universally, Sunday worship must have been established at a very early date indeed, probably before the first Jerusalem community was dispersed by persecution. This must have been within a few years of the Crucifixion, since Paul was pursuing Nazarenes in Damascus by around 33.[39]

By good fortune, a brief account of the weekly meetings held by a community of early second-century Christians has come down to us in a letter written by Pliny the Younger. As governor of the province of Bithynia in northwestern Anatolia, Pliny was involved in prosecuting Christians as enemies of the state. In the course of interrogating them, he found out a little about their religious practices:

> [They] met regularly before dawn on a fixed day to chant verses alternately among themselves in honor of Christ as if to a god, and also to bind themselves by an oath, not for any criminal purpose, but to abstain from theft, robbery and adultery, to commit no breach of trust and not to deny a deposit when called upon to restore it. After this ceremony it had been their custom to disperse and reassemble later to take food of an ordinary, harmless kind . . .[40]

Pliny doesn't specify the day on which they met, but we may be sure that (as elsewhere) it was Sunday, the first day of the week. For some reason they met twice, first before dawn, to sing antiphons and to swear an oath, and then again, after the day's work was done, to share a communal meal—the Lord's Supper.

Why did the Nazarenes create a new "holy day" to rival the age-old institution of the Sabbath? Such a major shift in religious practice has to have had a profound impetus. It is hard to avoid the conclusion that Jesus' followers were convinced that something supremely significant had happened on a Sunday, something that had to be memorialized week after week on the day that it actually happened.[41]

"Our curiosity is naturally prompted," wrote Edward Gibbon in *The Decline and Fall of the Roman Empire*, "to inquire by what means the Christian faith obtained so remarkable a victory over the established religions of the earth."[42] Until the eighteenth century, when Gibbon was writing, there would have been nothing natural at all about this question: Christianity had prevailed, so it was thought, because it was true, because it was founded by the Son of God and because it was guided by Divine Providence. For Gibbon such glib explanations were no longer adequate. He was interested in identifying the social and psychological factors that helped Christianity flourish throughout the Roman Empire.[43] This new approach made the rise of Christianity subject to rational inquiry, but it also masked a deeper problem that the notion of Divine Providence did at least address, however unsatisfactorily. This—the fifth and greatest puzzle concerning the Nazarenes—is the relatively short-term question: how did the apostles manage to create a church in the first place, an assembly that had the capacity to grow? In other words, why didn't Christianity disappear almost as soon as it was born, like many a flying-saucer cult today?[44]

Once the Church was established, and once Nazarene communities were up and running in Palestine and abroad, social forces came into play that would have made the sect self-sustaining and aided its continual growth. But in order for this to happen, the Church needed to achieve a certain critical mass, so that following Christ became a socially viable option. Somehow, instead of stagnating and appealing only to a few gullible eccentrics, Christianity achieved that critical mass. In a way, the initial establishment of the Church is a large-scale, social equivalent of the unlikely conversion of Paul. There is a major difference, though: Paul saw something that persuaded him of the reality of the Resurrection; thousands of others saw nothing but put their faith in the Risen Jesus none the less. The "miracle" of mass conversion was achieved purely by preaching.

The success of that preaching was remarkable, given the immense obstacles facing the apostles. As we have seen, the gospel would have struck most Jews as implausible, unpatriotic and immoral. They would have balked at the idea that the Messiah, their national hero, was a man who had just been crucified by the Romans, and, even if they believed in the future raising of the dead, they would have scoffed at the idea that a lone martyr had been resurrected while the Promised Land was still overrun by Caesar's troops. The apostles had to convince their fellow Jews to rethink the two great symbols of Israel's redemption, based on nothing other than their own say-so. At the same time, they had to contend with a hostile Jewish establishment. Caiaphas and his allies must have attempted to silence the Nazarenes from the outset.[45] Certainly, the persecution in which Paul played a leading part was underway within a few years of the Crucifixion.

Despite this formidable opposition, the Church in Palestine seems to have grown remarkably fast. Paul makes reference to the "churches of Christ in Judaea" rejoicing at the news of his conversion, indicating that there was more than one Christian community in the region by 33. According to Acts 9.31, the Church then existed "throughout all Judaea and Galilee and Samaria," which tallies with the fact that Paul was chasing Nazarenes as far north as Damascus. During the 30s the followers of the Way seem to have established themselves in such centers as Antioch, Lydda, Joppa, Caesarea, Ptolemais and Tyre.[46] The people of Israel were surprisingly receptive to the gospel of the crucified Christ.

Just as surprising was the spread of the gospel among the Gentiles. The first Gentile converts were probably God-fearers, i.e. Gentiles who were sympathetic to Judaism and attended meetings in the local synagogue. These people would have been familiar with the Nazarenes' Jewish heritage, and they probably welcomed Paul's rejection of the Jewish law—in particular, the food laws and circumcision. But how were regular, idol-worshipping pagans, such as Paul's Galatian and Corinthian followers, won over to the "folly" of Christ crucified? As Charles Freeman emphasizes, Christianity was "in conflict with Greco-Roman society and traditions, over sexuality, art and philosophy" and required Gentiles "to turn their backs on significant aspects of their traditional culture."[47] Yet many were persuaded to lay aside their ancestral traditions and join the paradoxical cult of a Jewish martyr.

They were certainly not opting for an easy life. Paul and his companions were regularly abused by mobs, and any who followed them risked similar treatment.[48] It was not just the locals they had to worry about. The Roman state was an even greater threat. Worshipping a divine king, other than the Roman emperor, and working to bring about the Kingdom of God, as opposed to the kingdom of Caesar, could be considered highly subversive. There is no evidence of concerted persecution of Christians until 64, when Nero had those in Rome crucified, burned and thrown to the dogs, but it is likely that harsh punishments had previously been meted out to members of provincial churches. As Tom Wright says:

> For a pagan of whatever background, Christianity demanded, and was known
> from quite early on to demand, an allegiance that might very well involve not
> only a previously unimagined self-denial, but also social ostracism, imprison-
> ment, torture and death. Early Christianity certainly does not look as if it spread
> because demands were being trimmed to the hearers' expectations or wishes.[49]

The first adherents of the Way were not making a lifestyle choice. They were not like New Age seekers, adopting an exotic Eastern religion that appealed to their spiritual sensibility, or like some modern Christians, participating in a socially acceptable religious club. They followed the Way, hard as it was, because the preaching of Paul and his colleagues was compelling. Somehow, they were persuaded it was true.

More than two centuries after Gibbon wrote, we still cannot account for the wildfire spread of the Christian gospel. Why weren't the apostles just dismissed as charlatans? How come so many listened to their outlandish claims? Luke attributes the power of their preaching to the influence of the Holy Spirit; modern historians have ditched this metaphysical explanation, but they have yet to come up with a physical one to replace it. Once again, something seems to be missing from our picture of Christian origins.

Five remarkable aspects of the early Church: five enigmatic pointers to its origin. Together, these developments reveal the historical impact of Easter, seen against the background of Second Temple Judaism and the wider Roman Empire. These were all facts about the Nazarenes that well-informed contemporaries would have known, even if they had no idea why the sect was so unorthodox or what gave it such power to convince.

The Nazarenes themselves traced everything back to the supposed miracle of Easter. At the root of the cult was a single, incredible idea: that, soon after his death and burial, Jesus had been raised from the dead and had been seen alive again by numerous witnesses. Unable to comprehend this madness, outsiders would have been at a loss to explain the social revolution occurring in their midst. We are in much the same position today. It is not so much that we lack information, but that we cannot make sense of the information we have. Maybe, then, we should stop trying to make sense of it and simply accept the apostolic claim—just trust in the literal truth of the Resurrection. That would be premature, however. A rational explanation may be just round the corner. And we have yet to consider the important evidence of the Gospels.

6

The Gospel Stories

Fascinating, disconcerting and, above all, tantalizing, the four Gospels are the oracles of an entire generation of Christians trying to come to terms with their confused religious heritage. To be properly understood they have to be viewed in context, as the products of an ecclesiastical age both close to and distinct from the age of Paul and the apostles.

By the end of the first century, Christianity was no longer just a sect of Judaism. It was now an independent faith, recognized as such by insiders and outsiders alike. The split from Judaism was precipitated, above all, by the Jewish War of 66–70, during which the Jerusalem Church was effectively destroyed, along with Jerusalem itself.[1] Jewish antagonism toward the Church probably increased in the wake of the war, since Messianic expectations were seen as having contributed to the national disaster. Moreover, many Christians outside Judaea held an ambivalent—even hostile—attitude to the Jewish law, often being uncircumcised Gentiles. Without its Judaean core, politically and theologically suspect and increasingly Gentile in composition, the Church was rapidly disowned by mainstream Judaism. Sometime in the late first century the Jews incorporated a curse against heretics into the Eighteen Benedictions (their regular prayers), and the Christians were formally expelled from the synagogue. Thereafter, Jews and Christians were to be seen as distinct tribes.[2]

Formerly part of a recognized, tolerated religion, a Jewish sect with its headquarters in Jerusalem, the Church was now a loose association of vulnerable, unaffiliated assemblies. Adrift in the world, like a flotilla of small boats battling to reach harbor through a stormy sea, Christian communities across the empire were forced to regroup. Right from the start, it seems, provincial churches contained a number of bishops, who oversaw the community, and deacons, who performed liturgical and pastoral duties. Now spiritually orphaned, these local bishops and deacons took over the leadership of the Church.[3]

Issues of religious authority and church governance were of crucial importance at the time the Gospels were composed. Of particular concern was the issue of female authority. Tension between entrenched patriarchal attitudes and the aspirations of women probably goes back to the very dawn of Christianity. There is scattered, but persistent, evidence that Mary Magdalene was an important figure in the early Church and that her prominence and assertiveness brought her into conflict with certain male apostles, particularly Peter.[4] Women definitely served as ministers of the gospel in the very early Church,[5] and the equality of men and women was enshrined in the saying, quoted by Paul, that "there is no longer male and female; for you are all one in Jesus Christ."[6] But, despite this principle, treating women as church leaders was highly contentious in the patriarchal world of antiquity, and women were gradually excluded from the Christian hierarchy.

The battle of the sexes is plainly visible in 1 Timothy, one of the so-called Pastoral Letters, whose unknown author acknowledges the existence of female deacons and presbyters (the order of "elders" that evolved into priests) but states categorically, "I permit no woman to teach or to have authority over a man; she is to keep silent."[7] As the New Testament scholar Bruce Chilton comments, this is "the party line of the up-and-coming Christian hierarchy that wanted to make sure that, as in a well-run Roman household, men were firmly in positions of leadership throughout the Church and that women did not abandon the roles of wives and mothers."[8] By the end of the second century, female priests were deemed heretical, and women had been completely subordinated to men in the mainstream churches.[9] A century before, however, when the Gospels were written, the struggle was still ongoing. We will find it reflected in the tales told about the Resurrection.

Despite such controversies, and despite the continuing, disturbing delay of the *parousia*, the men and women of the post-apostolic Church managed to keep Christianity afloat. Indeed, the new religion positively thrived. As it spread, it gave rise to a wide range of literature, including texts which came to define the beliefs of later generations of Christians. Tales and traditions about Jesus were already circulating before the Jewish War, but after AD 70 scribes around the Mediterranean took up this material and molded it in accordance with the ideas and requirements of their own communities. Thus came into being the texts we know as the Gospels. Numerous different gospels were produced, each bearing the ideological imprint of the church for which it was written. At least twenty are recorded, though fewer have survived. Over time, four of them—Matthew, Mark,

Luke and John—assumed special status and were included in the canon of the New Testament. The rest were consigned to oblivion. Fortunately, fragmentary remains of these forgotten gospels have survived here and there in ancient libraries and in the dry sands of Egypt, giving us an inkling of the early Christian stories that were suppressed.[10]

The four canonical Gospels, whose Easter stories dominate the traditional idea of the Resurrection, are all anonymous. They are first attributed to their traditional authors by Irenaeus, bishop of Lyons, in around 185, but there is little or no reason to regard these attributions as authentic.[11] It is nevertheless customary to refer to them by the names of their traditional authors. Mark is usually considered the earliest and is dated to around 70; Matthew and Luke are placed a decade or two later; and John is generally considered the latest, composed around 100.[12] This broad consensus is relatively stable, but it is based on little more than supposition.

Mark is the shortest of the Gospels. Matthew and Luke, which are rather more elaborate, contain a large amount of material in common with Mark, much of it corresponding verbatim. Because their texts can be laid alongside one another and compared word for word, the first three Gospels are known as the Synoptics (from the Greek *synopsis*, meaning "with the same eye"). The fourth Gospel is distinct, although it bears similarities to the Synoptics. It is sometimes supposed that John was aware of the Synoptic tradition, but there are barely any verbal correspondences between his Gospel and the others, and such as there are may well be accidental. John may reasonably be regarded, therefore, as an independent source.[13]

The Resurrection narratives in the Gospels can be divided into two categories: the "tomb-stories," which tell of people going to Jesus' tomb early on Easter morning, and the "appearance-stories," which describe the subsequent appearances of the Risen Jesus to his close followers.

In John, the only woman to visit the tomb on Easter morning is Mary Magdalene.[14] Arriving while it is still dark, she sees that the stone has been taken away from the tomb's entrance and immediately runs off to tell Peter and the anonymous "disciple whom Jesus loved" that Jesus' body is missing.[15] These male disciples come and check the tomb for themselves, while Mary hangs around outside, weeping. Once the men have gone, she looks into the tomb and sees "two angels in white, sitting where the body of Jesus had lain, one at the head and one at the feet." They ask her why she is weeping, and she replies, "Because they have taken away my Lord, and I do not know where they have laid him." The moment she says this, she turns round and sees the Risen Jesus, though she initially thinks he is

the gardener. He repeats the angels' question and then, once she has recognized him, tells her not to touch him. Finally, he commissions her to tell
his disciples that he is ascending to heaven. This she does.

John's narrative differs considerably from the Synoptics' tomb-stories.

In Mark, Mary Magdalene is accompanied by two other women, named
as Salome and Mary, the mother of James.[16] The three women make their
way to the sepulchre not while it is still dark, but after the sun has risen.
When they see that the stone has been rolled away from the entrance, they
decide to investigate and enter the tomb themselves, rather than hurry off
to tell Peter. Inside, they see a "young man" (not two angels) sitting on the
right-hand side, wearing a white robe. He tells them that Jesus has been
raised, points out the empty slab where the body lay and instructs them to
tell Peter and the other disciples that Jesus will appear to them in Galilee.
The women flee in terror and say nothing to anyone. None of this tallies
with John's description of Mary Magdalene encountering both the angels
and the Risen Christ.

The tales told by Matthew and Luke are reminiscent of Mark's story in
some respects, but, once again, discrepancies abound.

Matthew has only two women, Mary Magdalene and "the other Mary,"
going to the tomb just before dawn.[17] The moment they arrive, there is a
great earthquake and "an angel of the Lord" descends from heaven, rolls
away the stone from the entrance of the tomb and sits on it. This terrifies
the Roman soldiers guarding the tomb, a group of men mentioned in none
of the other Gospels.[18] The angel then delivers virtually the same speech to
the women as the "young man" in Mark, and the two Marys set off quickly
to tell the disciples. There is no suggestion here of disobedient silence. As
they hurry along, they are met by the Risen Jesus, recalling his appearance
to Mary Magdalene in John. In this version, however, the women are
allowed to take hold of his feet. And instead of asking them why they are
weeping and telling them of his imminent Ascension into heaven, he simply repeats the angel's message that the disciples will see him in Galilee.

Luke's account of the women's visit to the tomb is more straightforward,[19] but he is worryingly vague about the witnesses involved: he names
them as Mary Magdalene, Joanna, Mary the mother of James, and "the
other women with them"—so, five or more in total. This female posse goes
to the tomb at early dawn, intending to complete the burial rites. They find
the stone rolled away from the entrance, venture inside and discover that
the body is no longer there. Suddenly, two men in shining clothes are
standing beside them. The women are frightened and bow their heads to
the ground. "Why do you look for the living among the dead?" the men ask,

and then remind them that Jesus had prophesied he would be resurrected "on the third day." As in Matthew, the women return home and tell the disciples what they have witnessed. But they do not meet the Risen Christ along the way.

Clearly, the four Evangelists are building on the same tradition, but as a collection of witness statements their stories are horribly unsatisfactory. They disagree about who went to the tomb, why they went there, whether the tomb was guarded, whether it was open when they arrived, who they saw there, what the messenger(s) said, and how they reacted. The Evangelists even disagree as to whether the women saw the Risen Christ or not. Some of the discrepancies could simply be the result of errors or variations in oral transmission, while others, such as the descent of the Angel of the Lord in Matthew, look like creative editing on the part of the Gospel writers themselves. Either way, the female tomb-stories are hopelessly inconsistent. Even an evangelical scholar like Tom Wright admits that, with regard to the tales of the women's visit to the tomb, "one could be forgiven for thinking that the evangelists had set out to see how different from one another they could possibly be."[20]

There is one clear sign, nevertheless, that these tomb-stories go back to a real event: the fact that they concern women. In the ancient world women were generally regarded as inferior witnesses, and they did not usually speak or testify in public.[21] Given this prejudice, it is remarkable that women are presented in these stories as the sole or primary witnesses of the Resurrection. Predictably, Celsus, the second-century satirist of Christianity, stressed that "a hysterical female" was the first to see the Risen Jesus.[22] As proofs of the Resurrection, then, these tomb-stories were far from ideal. This suggests that they go back to a well-known historical episode, whose protagonists were indeed women.

As yet, though, there is no evidence to support any other aspect of the tomb-stories. This includes the idea that the body of Jesus was found to be missing. The tomb-stories are clearly a blend of fact and fiction, and no particular detail can be considered historical unless it is supported by external evidence.

To the "female tomb-stories" John and Luke add briefer "male tomb-stories."

According to John, as soon as Mary Magdalene sees the stone rolled away from the entrance to the tomb, she goes to tell Peter and the Beloved Disciple that Jesus' body has been taken away.[23] The two men run to see for themselves, but the Beloved Disciple runs faster and arrives at the tomb first. Stooping to look in, he sees the burial cloths lying there, but does not enter. Although Peter reaches the tomb second, he is the first to go in and inspect its contents, consisting of the linen cloths in which Jesus was buried and another cloth, arranged tidily "in a place by itself."[24] The Beloved Disciple then follows Peter in and sees something that makes him believe that Jesus has risen from the dead—a cryptic epiphany left unexplained. The disciples then return to their homes.

A much briefer version of this tale appears in Luke 24.12, which many scholars think was added to the Gospel after its initial composition. No mention is made here of the Beloved Disciple, a character found only in John. Instead, once the women have returned from the tomb and told the disciples of their strange experience, Peter alone runs off to check their story. Stooping and looking in, he sees "the linen cloths by themselves," but he does not enter the tomb, and, unlike John's Beloved Disciple, he does not realize about the Resurrection, merely "wondering at what had happened" on his way home.

Further on in Luke 24 the two disciples who encounter the Risen Jesus on the road to Emmaus refer to the same episode, saying, "Some of those who were with us went to the tomb, and found it just as the women had said."[25] Unlike verse 12, this brief reference is definitely an authentic part of the Gospel, and it may well represent an independent attestation of the episode. If so, the likelihood that Peter did visit the tomb (accompanied or not) is increased, though, given the scarcity of the tradition, it is difficult to decide which elements of the male tomb-story to believe.

The tomb-stories do at least agree on a few basic facts, such as the location, the day and (roughly) the hour. No such unities of time and place connect the appearance-stories, which are a ragbag of different tales.

The first surprise is that Mark does not narrate a single appearance of the Risen Jesus. The Gospel breaks off unexpectedly with the flight of the women from the tomb. Some early manuscripts of Mark add verses 16.9–20, which narrate three appearances—to Mary Magdalene, to two unnamed disciples "walking into the country," and to the Eleven at table (the Twelve having been reduced to the Eleven by the betrayal of Judas Iscariot)—but there is general agreement among scholars that this material, dubbed "Pseudo-Mark," was added to the Gospel in the early second century.[26]

John narrates three appearances of the Risen Christ, besides that to Mary Magdalene. The first of these occurs on the evening of Easter Sunday.[27] The disciples, afraid to be seen by their fellow Jews, are gathered together behind closed doors, when Jesus suddenly appears standing in their midst. The disciples are glad, and he blesses them and shows them his hands and side, implying that, despite his ability to materialize from nowhere, his body is still marked with the wounds of the Crucifixion. He then commissions them to go out and preach the gospel and breathes on them the Holy Spirit, telling them that they now have the power to forgive sins.

John does not say how many disciples were present on this occasion, but the next story, the famous episode of Doubting Thomas,[28] suggests that there were ten, since Thomas is said to have been absent. When told of the Easter Day appearance, Thomas refuses to believe unless he himself sees and touches the nail marks in Jesus' hands and the wound in his side. Eight days later, the disciples have locked themselves away in their safe house once again, and this time Thomas is with them. Suddenly, the Risen Jesus appears, just as before, and tells Thomas to touch his wounds. Thomas responds with his famous confession, "My Lord and my God!" But Jesus belittles his faith, saying, "Blessed are those who have not seen and yet believe."

In John 21 the scene switches to the coast of the Sea of Galilee. Seven disciples (Peter, Thomas, Nathanael, the sons of Zebedee and two others, unidentified) have apparently ignored Jesus' command to preach the gospel and have gone fishing instead. During the night they catch nothing. At daybreak they see a figure standing on the beach, who asks if they have caught any fish. When they reply that they haven't, he tells them to cast the net out on the right-hand side of the boat, where they will find plenty. Needless to say, the catch is spectacular, causing the Beloved Disciple (one of the unnamed members of the crew) to recognize the mysterious figure on the beach as Jesus. Peter then leaps into the sea and swims ashore, while the others drag in their net bursting with fish. On the beach there is a charcoal fire and a meal of fish and bread. Jesus tells the disciples to bring some of the fish they have just caught, which Peter does, and then, having invited them to have breakfast, he hands out the food. Strangely, the Gospel writer tells us that none of the disciples dared ask Jesus who he was, even though they knew it was him.

Matthew knows of only one appearance to the disciples,[29] and it bears no relation to anything in John. According to Matthew, the Eleven went to a mountain in Galilee, where Jesus had said he would meet them. When he appears, they worship him, but we are also told, rather surprisingly, that "some doubted." Jesus then gives the disciples the so-called Great Commission, telling them that they should go to "all nations," baptize in the name of the Father, Son and Holy Spirit, and pass on his teachings.

Finally, he assures them that he is always with them, "to the close of the age."

This tale cannot be squared with John's story of the Risen Jesus sending out the disciples. The numbers are different (not ten, but eleven, meaning that Thomas was present); the location is different (not Jerusalem, but Galilee); the setting is different (not a room, but a mountain); the disciples' reactions are different (not gladness, but worship and doubt); and the commission is different (not the grace to forgive sins, having received the Holy Spirit, but the command to baptize and teach). Nor can it be matched with the appearance by the Sea of Galilee in John 21. Put plainly, John and Matthew give completely irreconcilable accounts of the disciples' encounter with the Risen Jesus.

Luke complicates matters further by introducing the celebrated story of the Emmaus disciples.[30] On the evening of Easter Day two disconsolate disciples (one named Cleopas) are walking to a village called Emmaus, several miles from Jerusalem, and talking about recent events. They are joined by the Risen Jesus, whom they fail to recognize, and he asks them about their topic of conversation. Surprised by his apparent ignorance, they tell him about his own arrest and crucifixion and the discovery of the empty tomb. When they have finished, Jesus upbraids them for their failure to believe the Messianic prophecies and interprets for them "the things about himself in all the scriptures."[31] They are fascinated by his discourse and invite him to stay with them in Emmaus—still unaware of his identity. At supper, Jesus takes the bread, blesses it and gives it to them, and, as he does so, the two disciples suddenly recognize him. In that moment he vanishes. Reflecting on the emotion his words kindled in their hearts, they return to Jerusalem immediately, despite the late hour, to tell the Eleven what they have witnessed.

There is not a word about this Emmaus encounter in John or Matthew. And, as the story reaches its conclusion, Luke springs another surprise. Before the two disciples can report what they have witnessed, the Eleven inform them, "The Lord is risen indeed, and has appeared to Simon!"[32] Nowhere in any of the Gospels is this appearance to Simon (i.e. Peter) narrated.

Luke finishes his Gospel with the story of an appearance to all the disciples.[33] This takes place in Jerusalem, and those present include the Emmaus pair, the Eleven, and an unspecified number of others with them—so, fifteen people or more. As they are talking, Jesus suddenly appears in their midst. Startled and frightened, the disciples think he is a spirit. But Jesus reassures them and shows them his hands and feet, demonstrating that, unlike a spirit, he is made of "flesh and bones." Their doubt is only finally overcome, however, when he eats a piece of broiled fish. Having convinced them of his resurrection, Jesus then reminds them of the prophecies concerning him in the books of Moses and the prophets and interprets the scriptures—just as he did on the road to Emmaus. He concludes by affirming that he has died and risen from the dead, according to the scriptures, and by announcing that the forgiveness of sins will be preached to all nations. The disciples, he says, are witnesses to these things, and they must stay in Jerusalem until they are "clothed with power from on high." He then leads them out to the nearby village of Bethany, where he lifts up his hands, blesses them and disappears.

This story corresponds to the first appearance in John. The action takes place in Jerusalem on the evening of Easter Day, Jesus comes and stands among the disciples, he shows them his hands and feet, and mention is made of the forgiveness of sins. This hints at a common source underlying the two texts. But there are discrepancies. Whereas John has ten witnesses, Luke has fifteen or more. John describes the appearance taking place in a house, but Luke fails to specify the location and finishes with a walk to Bethany. In John the disciples recognize Jesus as soon as they see his hands and feet; in Luke they persist in their disbelief until he eats some fish. John's Jesus bestows the Holy Spirit on the disciples there and then; Luke's Jesus promises them "power" in the near future. Even when they agree on a basic story, the Evangelists disagree about the details.

The appearance-stories told by the Evangelists may seem, at first glance, to flesh out the skeletal history of the Resurrection provided by the First Creed. Unfortunately, though, they contain obvious elements of fiction and, on the whole, agree neither with each other nor with the testimony of Paul. The theologian Hans Zahrnt sums up the situation thus: "the New Testament narratives of Easter contain many legendary features, contradictions, absurdities and discrepancies ... To harmonize the different independent traditions which are collected together in them ... is an extremely delicate, if not a hopeless, task."[34] It is a rash historian indeed who bases his or her understanding of Easter on the Resurrection narratives in the Gospels.

The discordances with the First Creed (illustrated in Table 1 overleaf) are particularly unsettling. Four appearance-stories—concerning Mary Magdalene (alone or accompanied), the Emmaus disciples, Doubting Thomas, and the seven disciples by the Sea of Galilee—are conspicuously absent from the First Creed. What are we to make of these omissions?

Table 1: Reported Appearances of the Risen Christ in the Gospels and the First Creed

First Creed	Matthew	Luke	John	Mark
—	Mary Magdalene & Mary	—	Mary Magdalene	—
—	—	Road to Emmaus	—	—
Cephas	—	(Simon)	—	—
The Twelve	The Eleven	The Eleven & others	The Eleven (minus Thomas)	—
—	—	—	Thomas (& the other ten)	—
More than 500 Brethren	—	—	—	—
James	—	—	—	—
All the Apostles	—	—	—	—
—	—	—	The Seven by the Sea of Galilee	—

The First Creed's failure to mention an appearance to Mary Magdalene is undoubtedly significant, but it need not be a sign that the story is fabricated. The Creed was devised by the male hierarchy of the Jerusalem Church, and these men would have had two powerful motives to exclude Mary Magdalene (and any other women) from the list of witnesses: to increase the collective authority of the testimony by making it all-male (especially important if she was the initial witness), and to enhance their own authority by removing a female rival (especially important if she preceded them). So the story of the appearance to Mary Magdalene, told independently by John and Matthew, may well have a historical basis, representing a claim the author(s) of the First Creed wished to deny.

No such argument can be used in support of the appearance to the two Emmaus disciples. If Cleopas and his companion really did encounter the Risen Jesus on the evening of Easter Day, why was it not recorded in the First Creed (or in Matthew, Mark and John)? Apologists are keen to save the Emmaus story for history, but, for all its emotional appeal, it appears to be nothing more than a sophisticated fiction.[35] The famous tale of Doubting Thomas is equally dubious. It, too, is missing from the First Creed and from three of the four Gospels, which completely undermines its historical credibility. And the same goes for John's tale of the appearance by the Sea of Galilee.[36] It must be emphasized, however, that, even if these stories depict events that never happened, they are not necessarily devoid of historical content. Like all legends, they may incorporate elements of tradition based on authentic memories.

As well as creating fictional appearances, the Gospel writers omit ones listed in the First Creed. With the exception of Luke, they are entirely ignorant of the appearance to Peter, and none of them shows any awareness of the appearances to the More-than-500, to James, or to all the apostles. These forgotten appearances combine to create an impression of the Easter event which differs considerably from that created by the Gospels. Together, they make the witnesses' experience of the Risen Christ seem far more public and frequent than the few private revelations described by the Evangelists.

The only appearance listed in the First Creed that corresponds, more or less, to stories told in the Gospels is that to the Twelve. This must be the event remembered in John and Luke as the appearance to the (ten or eleven) disciples in a safe house in Jerusalem and in Matthew as the appearance to the (eleven) disciples on a mountain in Galilee.[37] Nothing could better illustrate the corrupt nature of the Gospels as historical sources.

The evidence of the Gospels, then, is too flimsy on its own to prove anything, let alone that Jesus rose from the grave. Nevertheless, buried deep within these odd, confused narratives there may well be clues to the events and experiences of Easter. It is worth reflecting on the words of Strabo, a Greek geographer who wrote in the first century AD:

> the ancients expressed enigmatically their physical notions concerning the nature of things, and always intermixed fable with their discoveries. It is not easy therefore to solve these enigmas exactly, but if we lay before the reader

a multitude of fabulous tales, some consistent with each other, others which
are contradictory, we may thus with less difficulty form conjectures about the
truth.[38]

This is sage advice from someone familiar with the thought-processes and
story-telling practices of the ancient world. In order to form "conjectures
about the truth" of the fabulous Gospel tales, however, we need to compare them not only with one another, but also with the apostolic testimony
and historical evidence looked at previously.

Was there, at the heart of Christianity, a real discovery, one that has
been obscured for nearly 2,000 years by ancient "notions concerning the
nature of things?"

7

The Way Ahead

According to Acts, when the Roman procurator, Festus, listened to Paul trying to explain himself, he simply declared him insane: "'Paul, you are mad; your great learning is turning you mad.'"[1] There is a strong temptation for modern rationalists to agree with him, to dismiss the whole idea of Easter as an extravagant fantasy. But the charge doesn't bear scrutiny. Paul and his fellow apostles were not crazy fantasists: they were struggling to comprehend and express something outside the realm of ordinary, everyday experience.

We will endeavor to explain their behavior in due course. But first, we need to review the historical evidence, so as to determine, as precisely as possible, what has to be explained. And we also need to think carefully, at the outset, about the sort of explanation that might work.

Easter was a moment in first-century Jewish history that saw a mysterious shattering of the religious landscape. To start with, there was the lively, established world of traditional Judaism, a world in which hopes for a glorious future, modelled on a mythical past, were continually being frustrated by the imperial realities of the time. There then erupted into this world the heretical sect of the Nazarenes, the early Christians, who believed that, whatever the facts on the ground, the Kingdom of God was finally being inaugurated. Between these two worlds resounded the spiritual explosion known as Easter.

As we have seen, Easter had discernible historical effects. It inspired Jesus' followers to view his death as a means of salvation, to hail him as the Messiah, to reinvent the Jewish idea of resurrection, and to meet together every Sunday for a ritual meal. It also led, within a short space of time, to the conversion of many Jews and Gentiles throughout the Mediterranean world (including, most remarkably, the Damascene conversion of Paul). To be convincing, a solution to the Resurrection problem must be able to account for each and every one of these mysterious historical developments.

A satisfactory explanation must also be able to explain the reports that the crucified Jesus was seen alive again, soon after his death, by numerous eyewitnesses. We have an authoritative summary of this teaching in the First Creed, which states that Christ died "for our sins in accordance with the scriptures," that he was buried, and that he was raised from the dead three days later, again "in accordance with the scriptures." Thereafter, he was seen by Peter, the Twelve, by more than 500 brethren at one time, by James, and by all the apostles, including Paul. This list appears to be a straightforward chronological sequence. It reveals that the Risen Christ was perceived visually; that he appeared to a large crowd, as well as to individuals and a group of twelve; and that he was seen frequently— probably dozens of times, if all the apostles witnessed him individually.

This first-hand testimony, implicitly agreed by a large number of witnesses, is undoubtedly impressive, but, from a historical point of view, it is weakened by the claim that Christ died and rose "in accordance with the scriptures." This raises the possibility that the witnesses' interpretation of what they saw was influenced, perhaps decisively, by knowledge of the Hebrew scriptures.

It is also historically significant that the First Creed makes no mention of an empty tomb.[2] This implies that the fate of Jesus' corpse was irrelevant to the original belief in the Resurrection. If the emptiness of the tomb was an essential component of the belief, why was it not proclaimed in the apostolic gospel?

This fits in with Paul's account of the risen body, based on his knowledge of the Risen Christ. He describes the risen body as quite unlike, and quite distinct from, the physical body of flesh and blood. He conceives it as derived from a separate act of Creation. The mortal body, descended from the "first man" (Adam), is formed from the dust of the earth and is perishable; the risen body, descended from the "second man" (Christ), is a celestial, spiritual body and will last forever. Flesh is shameful and weak, while the spiritual body is glorious and powerful. As well as describing the quality of the spiritual body, Paul hints at its relation to the physical body. His analogy of the seedling growing from the seed suggests that the spiritual body sprang directly from the physical body, as it lay underground. It is significant, too, that the Risen Jesus was not only visible (or visualizable) but also recognizable as one and the same as the crucified Jesus. Christ's mortal and risen bodies were like identical twins made from fundamentally different stuff.

Paul's personal testimony, combined with the First Creed, speaks of just the sort of extraordinary phenomenon that could have generated Christianity. There is just one problem: as a historical scenario, it looks like nonsense. Taken at face value, the idea of a heavenly, resurrected man appearing to a series of eyewitnesses seems utterly incredible. But do we have to take it at face value? Perhaps there is a way of understanding the appearances non-literally—and thereby interpreting them rationally. Maybe the apostles really did see something unusual, something outside their normal, everyday experience, something they *interpreted* as Jesus raised from the dead. If so, we may still be able, even now, to identify the astral body that crashed so spectacularly into first-century history.

Can the Gospels help us understand the situation?

The Evangelists may be ill-informed and worryingly creative, but, as we have seen, one or two of their Resurrection stories do appear to reflect historical events, and even those that don't may reflect aspects of the apostolic experience of the Risen Christ.

One general characteristic of the narratives helps confirm that, however fanciful they may be in some respects, they are rooted in history. This is the fact that they contain barely any allusions to the Hebrew scriptures, which is odd, because the Resurrection was supposed to have occurred "in accordance with the scriptures" and because the Gospels generally abound with scriptural references.[3] So the Easter stories were not conceived as fulfillments of Hebrew prophecies, which is what we would expect if they were purely fictitious. This makes it more likely (though it does not prove) that they derive from real experiences.

Also, a couple of recurrent themes in the Gospel narratives accord with, or are compatible with, the "photo-fit" of the Risen Christ provided by Paul.

First, the Gospel stories repeatedly represent Jesus' friends and companions having difficulty recognizing him. The most famous example occurs in John, when Mary Magdalene mistakes the Risen Jesus for the gardener. Then there is the reported experience of the two disciples on the way to Emmaus, who meet the Risen Jesus and talk with him all evening before finally recognizing him "in the breaking of the bread." This is echoed in Pseudo-Mark's brief parallel to the Emmaus tale, in which it is said that Jesus appeared to two disciples "in another form."[4] Finally, the seven disciples who see Jesus by the Sea of Galilee in John 21 fail to recognize him at first, doing so only when he helps them catch a vast quantity of fish. The consistent idea that his followers did not initially recognize the resurrected

Jesus accords with Paul's emphasis on the difference between the mortal, physical body and the immortal, spiritual body. If the man who was crucified had simply come back to life "in the flesh," it is hard to imagine his friends and companions not knowing him immediately. But if he came back "in another form"—a celestial spirit-form—their confusion would be quite understandable.

Even more startling, perhaps, is the repeated notion that the disciples doubted the identity of the Risen Jesus *even after they recognized him*. In Matthew some of the disciples doubt the appearance of the Risen Jesus on the mountain in Galilee, even though he had directed them there.[5] Luke describes the disciples struggling between doubt and belief when the Risen Jesus appears to them in Jerusalem: although they recognize him from his appearance, they initially think he is a ghost, and he has to convince them otherwise by eating some fish. Most explicit of all is John's account of the puzzlement of the disciples when the Risen Jesus appears to them beside the Sea of Galilee. First of all, they fail to recognize him, and then, once they do, they dare not ask him who he is. Somehow, they consider his identity to be distinct from his semblance. This may seem strange, but it is what we should expect, if, after the Resurrection, Jesus inhabited a new type of body, one sprung from the seed of his mortal flesh, but of a different quality.

Despite these signs of authenticity, the Gospel stories conflict with the testimony of Paul in one major respect: they preach a physical, fleshly Resurrection. This is an idea that, from a purely historical point of view, is looking untenable. Paul's detailed account of the celestial, resurrected body and his flat denial of flesh-and-blood resurrection count decisively against the notion of Jesus exiting the tomb "in the flesh." As 1 Corinthians makes clear, the idea that Jesus' corpse was revivified is a crude misunderstanding of the original idea, a confusion that gained currency a generation or so after Easter, as the influence of the apostles started to wane. That is why the empty tomb is not mentioned in the First Creed.

Intriguingly, however, Paul's description of the spiritual body as a seedling emerging from its seed does suggest a physical connection between the Risen Christ and the mortal body of Jesus. Furthermore, the First Creed testifies that Christ was buried, meaning that the Resurrection must have been thought to have occurred in a tomb, and, as we have seen, the female tomb-stories probably have a historical basis, indicating that the earliest Easter experience took place at a tomb. The Resurrection may not have been a physical, flesh-and-blood affair, but it seems to have been connected with Jesus' burial, none the less.

One final aspect of the Gospel stories should be highlighted: they contain no direct account of the Resurrection itself. Luke confidently narrates Christ's Ascension into heaven (twice), but none of the Gospel writers describes his emergence from the tomb.[6] Instead, they recount stories about what happened after the Resurrection, stories about his followers going to his tomb on Easter morning and about the Risen Jesus appearing to them later on. The Gospels do not pretend to bear witness to the miracle directly; they supply indirect, circumstantial evidence, accounts of experiences which are *interpreted* as pointing to the Resurrection. As in all the best conjuring tricks, the miracle itself is veiled from view.

The same is true of the First Creed. None of the witnesses listed in the First Creed is said to have seen the supposed miracle happen: they all just inferred it from seeing (what they took to be) the Risen Christ. Inferences, which depend on background theories and assumptions, as well as observations, are always uncertain.

The situation recalls a famous incident that occurred about three-quarters of a century earlier in ancient Rome. Soon after the assassination of Julius Caesar in 44 BC a comet appeared, which "the common people believed . . . signified the soul of Caesar received among the spirits of the immortal gods."[7] There is no suggestion the apostles saw a comet, of course, but the story stands as a warning against putting too much faith in the inferences of ancient witnesses. In the absence of a scientific worldview, unusual phenomena could easily be misunderstood.

Approached as a regular historical problem, Easter is frankly imponderable—hence the last 200 years of fruitless theorizing. To view it as a divine mystery, on the other hand, is naive and hasty—hence the last 2,000 years of Christian disappointment. What we need is a new approach, one that can explain Easter in rational terms, while simultaneously embracing the sheer mysteriousness of the episode. The way ahead, I think, is to presume that the apostles saw something real but out of the ordinary, a phenomenon they interpreted naively in terms of a resurrection. This enables us to take the apostolic testimony as seriously as it deserves, while at the same time attributing it to an earthly, if wondrous, cause.

This approach is not entirely new. Scholars have occasionally speculated that the Resurrection was a belief inspired by a rare natural phenomenon, citing such "paranormal" manifestations as UFOs and Bigfoot.[8] Gary Habermas dubs these suggestions "illusion theories," since they involve the "misperception or misinterpretation of real external sensory stimuli."[9] As yet, though, no one has come up with an illusion theory that is plausible and can account adequately for the historical evidence.[10] But, since natural phenomena were widely misinterpreted in the first century (as the example of Caesar's comet reveals), it is surely worth asking whether, instead of witnessing a miracle, the apostles simply mistook a marvel.

It so happens that a long-forgotten resurrection myth from the ancient world—a close analogue to the Resurrection of Jesus—has recently been explained in precisely these terms. It is worth considering the solution to this parallel mystery, because it proves that in antiquity belief in a resurrection could indeed be prompted by witnessing something natural but unusual. The Christian belief in the Resurrection of Jesus was not entirely unique, and understanding this pagan parallel may help us finally demystify Easter.[11]

Of the myriad cults that flourished in ancient Greece one, in particular, resembled Christianity, in that it concerned a mortal who was thought to have been resurrected by divine agency. This distinction was accorded Pelops, king of Pisa in the western Peloponnese. According to a rather gruesome myth, the youthful Pelops was killed by his father, Tantalus, who chopped up his body and cooked it in a stew, which he then served up surreptitiously at a banquet attended by the gods. Oblivious to the outrage, Demeter, the goddess of fertility, began eating the stew, but the other Olympians were suspicious. Once they realized what Tantalus had done, they decided to reassemble his son's body and restore him to life. Unfortunately, Demeter had already eaten one of his shoulders, so Hephaestus had to fashion him a new shoulder out of ivory. Pelops was thus resurrected in a reconstituted body—not quite the same as his original one—and went on to become the legendary founder of the Olympic Games, the great pan-Hellenic festival held every four years at Olympia.[12]

This myth of Pelops—a spiritual protector who was unjustly killed and miraculously restored to life in a partially new body—provides a close analogy to the Resurrection. It is certain, moreover, that the Greeks believed in the resurrection of Pelops, just as Christians believe in the Resurrection of Christ. For they possessed, so they thought, the ultimate relic of the event: the ivory shoulder blade of the Hero—physical proof of the miracle![13] As well as being made (supposedly) of ivory, the shoulder blade was of gigantic size, befitting the idea that Pelops, like all the Heroes, was a man of superhuman strength and stature. This notable relic, whose fame was widespread in antiquity, was kept for centuries in a dedicated shrine at Olympia, known as the Pelopion.

This shoulder blade is the key to understanding the imagined resurrection of Pelops. That such a relic existed might seem implausible, but, in fact, there is good reason to believe that it did. In 2000 Adrienne Mayor published a well-received book, *The First Fossil Hunters*, in which she drew attention to numerous reports of discoveries of giant bones in ancient Greece and explained them in terms of paleontology: the Greeks were finding semi-fossilized bones belonging to huge, extinct mammals, such as mastodons, elephants and mammoths.[14] Until now, as she says, classicists have tended "to read the ancient allusions to the bones of giants or monsters as mere poetic fantasies or as evidence of popular superstition."[15] By painstakingly matching the ancient reports with modern paleontological data, Mayor shows that they were actually based on finds of spectacular fossils.

The nature of the Pelops relic is now clear. Mayor reckons that it was probably the semi-fossilized scapula of a mammoth.[16] Installed in the Pelopion, this great shoulder blade inevitably provoked questions, and the answers to those questions inevitably took the form of myths.[17] Particularly puzzling, it seems, was the odd appearance of the bone. It was thought to be made of ivory—an understandable confusion, since semi-fossilized bone has the appearance of old ivory, especially when burnished.[18] But how on earth did Pelops come to have an ivory shoulder blade?

The elaborate story of his resurrection was designed to answer this question. Reckoning that Pelops must have been given the fabulous shoulder blade by the gods, in order to replace one he had lost, some ingenious myth-maker came up with the story of Tantalus's stew. The myth of the young Hero's resurrection was a way of making sense of the mammoth bone enshrined in the Pelopion, an object that the ancients could not explain scientifically. As Gary Habermas might say, it was an illusion due to the misinterpretation of an external sensory stimulus.

Could some equivalent prodigy, hitherto neglected by scholars, have inspired the birth of Christianity? Could the first Christians, emulating the ancient myth-maker of Olympia, have inferred the Resurrection on the basis of a similarly bizarre relic? Just as generations of classicists have missed the mythic significance of giant fossils, generations of New Testament scholars may have been overlooking a relevant marvel of their own.

But Jesus was no Hero of the legendary past. What sort of marvel could possibly have generated the idea that a first-century Jew had been raised from the dead?

It is time to turn our attention, once more, to the Shroud of Turin.

PART 3

The Unthinkable Shroud

8

A Unique Spectacle

May, 2010. Our taxi patters over the tramlines and paving stones in the Piazza San Giovanni and draws to a halt in the center of the square. Getting out, we are presented with our first view of Turin Cathedral, a Renaissance basilica whose plain, elegant design strikes a reassuring note of religious sobriety. It is not the Baroque extravagance I had imagined. The atmosphere in the square seems remarkably calm and relaxed, given the religious importance of the occasion—the first public display of the Turin Shroud since the turn of the millennium. It is busy enough, with people dawdling at the foot of the cathedral steps, dodging the cars and occasional trams, heading off in search of cappuccinos and gianduja ice-creams, but it hardly feels like the forecourt of the most extraordinary shrine in Christendom. I was expecting a great press of pilgrims, currents of people swirling around in the wake of gabbling tour guides, all interspersed with pushy souvenir sellers, along the lines of Lourdes. The Turin pilgrimage, though, is a much more quiet, urbane affair. Most of the pilgrims are queuing patiently behind the cathedral to see the Shroud. The only hawkers in evidence are touting umbrellas, praying that the promised showers will soon materialize.

We make our way to the cathedral steps, bedecked with garlands of white-and-yellow chrysanthemums, and await the arrival of a couple of friends who have seen the Shroud already. I assume at this stage that the relic is closeted in its chapel at the back of the cathedral, visible only to those who have booked to see it. It doesn't occur to me that, if I just tripped up the steps and peered through the doorway, I would be able to set eyes, at long last, on the object that has occupied my thoughts for the past six years.

Our friends arrive, and, instead of going into the cathedral, we amble off in the direction of Turin's grand central square, the Piazza Castello. Along the way we pass a couple of stalls selling Shroud tea towels and

Shroud playing cards, small cloth replicas of the relic, framed portraits of Christ and so on—none of it too kitsch. The usual pilgrimage tat is conspicuous by its absence. The official exhibition shop, selling nothing but books on the Shroud and theology, is so packed we are denied entrance. It begins to dawn on me that Turin 2010 is a pilgrimage of the head, rather than of the heart.

Several hours later, well fed and briefed about the Shroud's display in the cathedral, we return to Piazza San Giovanni. It is with a rare sense of anticipation that I climb the steps up to the gleaming cathedral façade, past the swathes of flowers, and approach the dark doorway. Passing through the interior porch, we enter a different world—darkness replaces light, murmur replaces chatter. Glancing ahead, my eyes still attuned to the sunlit marble outside, rather than the cavernous interior of the church, I catch sight of a small white rectangle of light hovering in the blackness—the Shroud. Lit up and suspended behind glass above the high altar, it is displayed, as always, horizontally, drawing the gaze like a motionless movie screen.

For a moment, it is all I can see. Then I begin to perceive the arcaded space of the nave and the people milling around. Some sit quietly in the pews, meditating and taking in the spectacle; others kneel and pray; a few study the cloth intently through binoculars. Bizarrely, the nave is dotted with a series of TV screens giving a bird's eye (or God's eye) view of the scene.

We join the crowd going forward to the barrier that closes off the altar area, where we can peer at the cloth from a distance of twenty-five yards or so. Even at that distance the two Shroud figures, frontal and dorsal, are readily apparent, although my companions, less familiar with the image, have difficulty discerning which is which. Ahead, those who have booked to view the relic up close shuffle into position and stand motionless before it, their heads silhouetted against the cream-colored cloth (Figure 18). Every three or four minutes, one group moves aside to let another take its place, a slow ebb and flow of rapt contemplation. It reminds me of the old allegory of Plato's cave. The mysterious silhouettes on the cloth really do seem like shadows cast by the light of a higher reality, shadows almost bound to seduce any Platonist standing before them.

After a while, unable to make out the Shroud's image in any detail, I transfer my attention to my fellow pilgrims. Here and there are signs of undoubted emotion—an elderly lady falling to her knees, a young man wiping away a tear to look through his camera—but, on the whole, people's faces and attitudes speak of simple, earnest curiosity. Despite the setting, there is nothing particularly religious about the atmosphere in the nave. We might almost be a crowd of scientists witnessing something unprecedented, like the first pictures from the surface of an unexplored moon or the spiral track of a new subatomic particle, something touching our existing knowledge, but still unfathomable and strange. The Shroud, though, is a very human mystery. It concerns us directly and so prompts a far more ancient, essential response than is experienced in front of any scientific marvel—or, for that matter, any other relic. It belongs to the lost world of religious awe and stupefaction. The congregation seems moved not so much by pious enthusiasm as by an atavistic sense of wonder.

I find my thoughts wandering back to ancient Olympia, which every four years hosted its own religious festival. I imagine a Greek athlete of the fifth century BC, about to compete in the Games, making his way to the shrine of Pelops to ask for protection and to gain strength from the marvelous shoulder blade of the Hero. As he entered the Pelopion, would his expression have differed greatly from the faces of those now gazing at the Shroud? If he doubted the literal truth of the myth of Pelops (as Pindar did), would the sight of the relic not have caused him to think again, just as the sight of the Shroud is forcing Christians, here and now, to reflect on the true nature of the Resurrection? Would his perplexity have been far removed from that of these present-day pilgrims, peering, in a sense, at the earthly remains of their immortal hero? I cannot escape the feeling that I am taking part in a communal rite whose origins go back much further than the first century AD.

Everyone in the cathedral must be aware that the Shroud's authenticity is a matter of dispute and that it is regarded by the world at large as a medieval fake, but this does not seem to detract from its fascination. If the image is man-made, is it any less astonishing? Just across from the Pelopion at Olympia was the great Temple of Zeus, home to a 40-foot-high statue of the god, one of the Seven Wonders of the World. Anyone who stood in the half-light before this extraordinary work of art, a giant figure fashioned out of ivory and gold, would have been quite as awe-struck as a visitor to the shrine of Pelops. In the twenty-first century there is perhaps only one place we can stand and experience the religious thrill of the ancient pagan: in Turin Cathedral, before the Shroud.

Whatever the Shroud may be, it connects us with our distant past, with instincts we have now so thoroughly repressed we barely know they are there.

Early the next morning I join the queue to view the Shroud up close. After an hour or so I make it into the cathedral and walk up the aisle to await my turn. From where I am standing the Shroud is hidden behind a column, so I spend a few minutes contemplating the altarpiece in the side chapel next to me, a colorful scene of the Resurrection. A helpful notice explains that it was painted in 1575 by Giacomo Rossignolo, court artist to the Savoys. It shows Christ, naked but for a swathe of white drapery tied around his hips, flying up out of a sarcophagus in a blaze of heavenly glory, while the soldiers guarding the tomb look on in startled amazement.

I reflect that, three years after he painted this drapery fluttering around the Risen Savior, Rossignolo would have had a chance to see the Shroud, on the occasion of its transferral to Turin. As a court artist he may even have been admitted to a private viewing. If so, he would have found it a daunting experience. Naturally, he would have wanted to understand the process via which the image was formed, but he would surely have been mystified, like competent investigators ever since. He would have realized, no doubt, that, however well he could paint the Resurrection, he could never hope to emulate this image of Christ's death. Numerous attempts throughout the sixteenth and seventeenth centuries to reproduce the Shroud, all hopelessly inadequate, prove the point (cf. Figure 11). It is no mere piece of handiwork.

My own chance to inspect the relic finally arrives, and, along with a score of other pilgrims, I am ushered into its presence. At last, I can see it properly with my own eyes. I already have a detailed knowledge of the image from the many photographs I have pored over in the past, but I am still not prepared for the sight of the real thing. It is infinitely more impressive than any photograph can convey.

Mentally, I erase the burn marks and concentrate on the head-to-head figures, spreadeagled across the cloth like a macaber heraldic emblem. They appear almost the same color as the linen, but just a tone or half a tone darker, virtually the color of pale white skin. It looks almost as if they have been dabbed on with pure water, or as if the cloth has been gently inflated with their presence.

The image is subtler than it appears in photographs, yet the figures also seem more coherent, perhaps because of their human scale, perhaps because their extreme faintness encourages the mind to supply the missing definition. Visually, it is difficult to locate them with respect to the cloth—they could be resting on it, or just behind it, or within it. Lose focus, and the whole thing can seem like an illusion, like a giant Rorschach test, but look again, and the figures remain stubbornly there, as if a mental image had somehow projected itself out into the world and settled on the cloth.

Fortunately, I am standing near the center, so I can twist my head and regard the figure face-to-face. The effect is mesmeric. Seen horizontally, the figure is eerie and evocative; seen vertically, it is faintly terrifying. The vacant, glaring eyes—two white discs amid a face that is barely there— hold me spellbound. No other image I have ever seen comes close to it—not the frowning visage of Michelangelo's Moses, not the frightful stare of Goya's Saturn. The sense of a veiled presence is inescapable. With my head cocked awkwardly on one side, I find it easy to imagine there is someone there behind the image, returning my gaze. But, like all illusions, he gives nothing away; he just stares back, silent and unblinking.

As I stand there, I notice myself willing the face to become clearer, even though I know it is, in essence, indistinct. When we are asked to move on, I linger for a few moments, still hoping to catch something more. The desired communion, though, remains elusive. Slowly, I pass along to the exit, my eyes traversing the full length of the dorsal figure as I go. The man in the Shroud has turned his back on me; the encounter, sadly, is over.

According to the philosopher Richard Wollheim, it takes a couple of hours for a great painting to disclose itself to the viewer. I have been able to scrutinize the Shroud for only a few minutes, but in that time, I feel, it has revealed as much of itself as it ever will. My expectations have been fulfilled; a theory six years in the making has received its imprimatur. Feeling rather light-headed, I make my way out of the cathedral and wander along to the Piazza Castello, ruminating on the experience I have just had, trying to fix it in my memory.

Eventually, walking aimlessly down a side street, I stop before a shop window displaying various prints and posters of the Shroud. Instantly, the vision in my head is reduced to a set of glossy photographs. The spell is broken. I flip open my mobile and arrange to rejoin my family.

Until the end of the nineteenth century, everyone who saw the Shroud experienced it as I have just described, as a unique spectacle. It might have been seen once, fleetingly, and then never again. There was no way to accurately record its appearance. Each viewing was an occasion—an encounter—that had to be stored and worked over in the memory. The image had a powerful impact, but it was known only in this limited way.

Today, most people know the Shroud via photography. This, too, is limited. Although photographic techniques are becoming ever more sophisticated, they will never be able to capture the visual effect of the cloth itself, let alone its emotional resonance. The small photos reproduced in books, including this one, omit a great amount of detail visible on the cloth itself, and the change in scale drastically reduces the psychological impact of the figure. Photographs also tend to exaggerate the contrast between the image and the background. Most seriously of all, perhaps, photos of the Shroud fix an image that is inherently vague and elusive.

So saying, I am speaking only of the body-image (the anthropomorphic stains), not the blood-image (the apparent traces of the wounds), which is relatively clear and substantial. All those who have seen the Shroud at close quarters agree that, within a few feet, the body-image fades entirely from view. I was unable to observe this effect myself, as the public were not allowed that close at the 2010 exhibition, but the effect is vividly described by Ian Wilson, who was admitted to a private viewing of the cloth in 1973: "the image color was the subtlest yellow sepia, and as you moved in closer to anything like touching distance . . . it seemed virtually to disappear like mist. Because of the lack of outline and the minimum contrast to the ivory-colored background, it became well-nigh impossible to 'see' whatever detail you were trying to look at without stepping some distance back again."[1]

The importance of this observation cannot be overemphasized. Wilson cites it as evidence against the idea that the image was painted, pointing out that it would have been difficult for an artist to paint a picture that he could only see from a distance of 6 feet or so (necessitating the use of a 6-foot paintbrush).[2] This is true, but, besides reducing the likelihood that the image is a painting, the ethereal quality of the figure may also have affected the way it was once perceived. Wilson describes a dynamic image, like a hologram, one that alters its appearance as the viewer changes position. How might this have been interpreted in the past? This is a question we should keep at the forefront of our minds. The effect may originally have been less pronounced, when the cloth was whiter and the contrast between figure and ground slightly clearer, but the image must always have been fugitive.

Just as compelling as the elusive form of the image is its paradoxical content, its uncompromising display of etherealized torture. The body-image may fade away into the cloth, but the blood-image is emphatically corporeal. However they were produced, the gory stains that disfigure the Shroud evoke the presence of a real, crucified body. The fact that the image is life-size makes it seem almost like the flayed skin of the victim it represents. At the same time, the figure appears other-worldly, and the face, in particular, is quite surreal. The eyes appear huge, like the eye sockets of a skull, and gleaming with inner light. This is not an ordinary human visage; it is more like a theatrical mask. As well as being entrancing, the Shroud is also deeply disturbing.

All this adds to the power and fascination of the image, but, ultimately, it is its sheer inexplicability that captures the imagination. The sense of the uncanny that emanates from the cloth is due, above all, to its singularity, its radical dissimilarity from anything else known. The sensation of being in the presence of a bona fide mystery, something so anomalous that it defies, to some extent, the human capacity to understand, is one that no mechanical reproduction can possibly convey. The Shroud makes present the daunting power of the unknown.

In the past this power was labelled miraculous and ascribed to God; today it is attributed to nature and understood as a scientific challenge. If we are ever to come to terms with the Shroud, we must learn to see it simultaneously from these two different points of view. We must see it both as an object of modern, scientific analysis and, just as importantly, as an object of premodern, unscientific wonder. Maintaining this double vision is the key to unlocking the mystery of its origin.

9

The Cloth Examined

When Secondo Pia first photographed the Shroud in 1898 he was not so much producing an exact copy of the relic as conducting the first scientific investigation of it. Besides making people across the globe aware of the mysterious image, Pia's work enabled scientists to begin researching the Shroud's nature and origin, even with the cloth itself locked away in its shrine. And the photos revealed a remarkable property of the image that could never have been discovered with the naked eye: its extraordinary realism when viewed "in negative" (Figures 15 and 16).

The negative photo of the Shroud is Exhibit A in the case for the cloth's authenticity. It demonstrates that the image possesses a hidden structure, which could hardly have been conceived in the fourteenth century, when the relic is first documented in Europe. Simply glancing at the automatic inversion of the image is enough to dispel the idea that it is a regular work of art.

If it is a fake, it would have to be the most ingenious and improbable fake in history, a work of supreme skill and cunning. If it is not a fake, then the chances are that it is connected, as traditionally supposed, with the death and burial of Jesus.

It was Pia's photonegative that inspired a small group of scientists at the Sorbonne to start studying the relic at the turn of the twentieth century, culminating in the 1902 publication of *The Shroud of Christ* by Paul Vignon. Dated though it is, Vignon's work remains, even today, one of the most perceptive and instructive studies of the Shroud, demonstrating the image's dissimilarity to medieval works of art and explaining its form in terms of regular physical processes (see below, pp. 153–4). Most importantly, working from Pia's relatively crude photographs, Vignon managed to deduce a remarkable fact about the body-image, one that sindonologists stress even today as evidence of the relic's authenticity.

Examining the image minutely, Vignon observed that it appears to involve some sort of projection, or action at a distance, implying that the cloth was discolored by an emanation from a human body. He then proceeded to demonstrate with careful geometrical arguments "that the action diminished in proportion as the distance of the body from the Shroud increased."[1] That is to say, *the intensity of every part of the body-image is determined by a distance ratio (actual or imagined)*. This is extremely important. The same is *not* true of a photograph, in which the intensity of the image is determined by the amount of light received by the photosensitive film or plate, not its distance from the object. It is not true of paintings either, which mimic the fall of light on an object. The Shroud is more like a technical blueprint for a sculpture.

Seventy-four years later, Vignon's insight received dramatic confirmation. In 1976 John Jackson, the leading light of the Shroud of Turin Research Project (STURP), was trying with some colleagues at the U.S. Air Force Academy in Colorado Springs to demonstrate the relationship between the Shroud and an underlying body by obtaining measurements from a draped volunteer and correlating them with the Shroud's body-image. Although suggestive, their results were far from conclusive.[2] Then Jackson met up with Bill Mottern, a physicist at the Sandia Laboratory in Albuquerque. Hearing about the problem the Air Force group was working on, Mottern suggested feeding a photo of the Shroud into a state-of-the-art machine called a VP-8 Image Analyzer, a device developed by NASA "which plots shades of image intensity as adjustable levels of vertical relief."[3] In other words, it can translate the tonal gradations of an image into a 3-D graphic, representing a contour map.

The result was impressive. The VP-8 spewed out a relatively coherent, three-dimensional portrait of the Shroud-man (Figure 19), proving that the image accurately represents the contours of a human body.[4] Vignon was vindicated. Far too much has been read into the VP-8 analysis of the Shroud in recent years, but it does neatly demonstrate the distance-dependency of the body-image and thus helps prove that it was formed in close proximity to a real or sculpted body. Any viable theory of the Shroud's origin must take this into account. Because photos and paintings represent light levels rather than distance levels, they yield distorted, incoherent results in the VP-8.

In 1978 Jackson and the rest of the STURP team rolled up in Turin and began looking at the Shroud in entirely new ways.[5] The earlier scientific investigations of 1969 and 1973 had been extremely limited; the STURP one, though far from exhaustive, was wide ranging and thorough. Working round the clock over five days, the team subjected the

Shroud to one type of non-invasive test after another. Using custom-built reflectance spectrometers, Roger and Marion Gilbert and Sam Pellicori measured the light spectra reflected from various areas of the cloth, yielding detailed information about the surface of the material.[6] Roger Morris, Larry Schwalbe and Ron London scanned it with an X-ray fluorescence spectrometer, which could detect the presence in the cloth of all but the lightest chemical elements.[7] Joe Accetta and Stephen Baumgart surveyed it using infrared spectrometry and thermography, in an effort to detect different compounds and materials that might have been applied to it.[8] The photographic team, meanwhile, not only documented the Shroud's appearance under normal lighting conditions, but also under raking light, to show up the creases, and via transmitted light (i.e. lit from behind). The cloth was studied under the microscope, and photomicrographs were taken, showing the minute structure of the blood-image and body-image. Finally, Ray Rogers lifted material from the surface of the cloth in a number of locations using a specially designed sticky tape, so that fragments of fibers from different areas could be analyzed back in the lab.

All this effort was directed toward one primary goal: to see whether any sign of forgery could be detected. In particular, the STURP scientists were on the lookout for evidence that the image might have been painted, this being the default assumption of skeptics at the time. Otherwise, they were just keen to record as much data as possible regarding the physics and chemistry of the cloth, hoping it might help answer any questions asked subsequently. Given the constraints they had to work with, they achieved a remarkable amount, and it is to STURP that we owe practically all our scientific knowledge of the Shroud. Astonishingly, in the thirty-four years since they ran their tests, no further, proper scientific work has been permitted. A few useful observations were made during the secret conservation in 2002, but that is all. We should be grateful, then, that STURP managed to gather as much information as they did, before the Catholic Church called a halt to the scientific examination of the Shroud (with the exception of the carbon-dating test).

The material evidence gathered by STURP and others can be divided into four main categories: the composition of the blood-image; the composition of the body-image; the textile itself; and debris found on the cloth.

Is the blood-image made of blood or of paint? This is a crucial question—perhaps *the* crucial question—in the scientific study of the Shroud. If it is paint, then the Shroud is definitely a forgery; conversely, if it is real blood, then the case for the Shroud being a genuine grave-cloth is considerably enhanced. "Blood or paint?" is the sort of black-and-white question scientists love, and the STURP team had the equipment and expertise to answer it. Tests for blood had been carried out previously in 1973, but the results were inconclusive.[9] This time they were far more illuminating.

The simplest imaging technique performed by the STURP team in Turin was taking ordinary color photographs of the cloth lit from behind. While the body-image disappears in these photos, the blood-image remains clearly visible, demonstrating that it is composed of material that is relatively substantial and opaque.[10] Photomicrographs of blood-image areas of the cloth show that the substance is a form of particulate matter, deep red in color, which lies on the surface of the threads and collects in the interstices (Figure 20). In places it has soaked through to the other side.[11] X-ray fluorescence spectrometry revealed significantly high levels of iron in the blood-image areas, consistent with the stains containing hemoglobin, an iron-containing constituent of blood, and this was supported by the reflectance spectrometry.[12] To be sure that the substance was blood, however, rather than an iron-based pigment such as red ochre, STURP needed to do some chemistry.

Back in the U.S. two respected chemists, John Heller and Alan Adler, set about analyzing the red particulate matter found on samples taken from the blood-image. Testing it in various ways, they were able to conclude unequivocally that it was blood and soon published their findings in respected, peer-reviewed journals. Here, for the scientifically minded, are the array of proofs they cited for their conclusion (including the results of the X-ray fluorescence spectrometry and the reflectance spectrometry conducted in Turin):

1. High iron in blood areas by X-ray fluorescence
2. Indicative reflection spectra
3. Indicative microspectrophotometric transmission spectra
4. Chemical generation of characteristic porphyrin fluorescence
5. Positive hemochromogen tests
6. Positive cyanomethemoglobin tests
7. Positive detection of bile pigments
8. Positive demonstration of protein
9. Positive indication of albumin
10. Protease tests, leaving no residue
11. Microscopic appearance as compared with appropriate controls.[13]

Regarding points 2 to 7, Heller observes that any one of them "is proof of the presence of blood, and each is acceptable in a court of law."[14] Moreover, although they were unable to state categorically that the blood tested was human, Heller and Adler did determine that it was definitely primate. So far, no skeptic has argued that it comes from an ape or monkey.[15]

Returning to the image on the Shroud, one of the clearest signs that the reddish stains are composed of blood is that they are surrounded by traces of a much clearer substance, identifiable as blood serum, which has separated from the clots and seeped out across the cloth. A good example of such serum separation is seen around the wound in the wrist. As Dr. Gilbert Lavoie observes, "Paint does not separate and create the serum lines that are seen here. Only blood does this."[16] Doctors noticed these characteristic traces of bloodstains long before 1978,[17] and the judgment of the medical men has been usefully corroborated by STURP. The serum deposits are barely perceptible to the naked eye, but photographed under ultraviolet light, they fluoresce like "haloes" around every bloodstain.[18] Indeed, some of the scourge marks are only detectable by this method, implying that they are either exudations of serum from genuine wounds or the work of a medieval artist who knew how to paint in ultraviolet. Fibers sampled from these areas have also tested positive for serum albumen.[19]

Leaving the serum aside, could a medieval artist have used human blood to paint the obvious wounds on the Shroud? It is perhaps conceivable, but he would have had to have worked astonishingly fast with a constant supply of fresh blood, given that blood starts clotting within a minute or two of exposure to air. There is no art-historical evidence for medieval craftsmen producing images with blood. And there would have been no point in doing so, since no one in the Middle Ages could have tested the relic to check whether the blood was real or not.

Another observation indicates that the blood-image could not possibly have been painted. When Adler removed the blood from fibers sampled within the region of the body-image, he discovered that, underneath, they are white, the color of the background linen. This proves that the blood-image was on the cloth before the body-image was created.[20] An artist, of course, would have proceeded in the opposite way: needing to know where to place the wounds before painting them, he would have established the overall form of the figure first. The fact that the blood-image precedes the body-image is excellent evidence that the wounds were not painted, but imprinted directly from an injured figure.

Experiments undertaken by Lavoie have shown that a bloodstain with characteristics similar to those seen on the Shroud can be produced when linen is placed on a blood clot within 1½ to 2 hours of the initial bleeding. The transfer depends on the moist serum that collects on the surface of the clot, and it exhibits the same fluorescent halo under ultraviolet light as the bloodstains on the Shroud.[21] This indicates that the blood-image, at least, could have formed naturally around the body of a crucified man.

The only caveat is that Lavoie used blood from a live, healthy volunteer, whereas the blood on the Shroud is likely to be post-mortem. In cases of violent death, according to Dr. Frederick Zugibe, the foremost authority on the pathology of the Shroud, post-mortem blood may coagulate, but it may also remain fluid (owing to the presence of enzymes known as fibrinolysins), or it may simply dry, in which case it reliquefies if dampened.[22] So the bloodstains on the Shroud might have been caused by either clotted or fluid blood.

There may be evidence that the blood on the Shroud came from an individual who was badly injured. Adler discovered that the bloodstains contain high levels of bilirubin, a bile pigment produced when hemoglobin is broken down in the liver. This occurs when someone is beaten or subjected to severe traumatic shock. The bilirubin may also help account for the color of the blood, which is surprisingly reddish, given that blood tends to become dark brown with age. Bilirubin is yellow-orange in color, and, in combination with other orangey-brown residues, it could increase the blood's reddishness.[23]

Based on the scientific analysis of the bloodstains, then, there must be a very strong presumption that the Shroud was used to enfold the corpse of a badly wounded man. This presumption is supported by the positive evaluation of the blood-image by medical experts (and also, one might add, by the deafening silence of art historians). As the Jewish-born Adler comments:

> The chemistry is saying the same as the forensics. There is only one way that this kind of chemistry could appear on the cloth. This cloth had to be in contact with the body of a severely beaten human male.[24]

Although this does not prove that the Shroud is the authentic burial cloth of Jesus, it certainly allows that possibility. It also casts doubt on every alternative explanation that involves the wounds having been painted (in effect, every hypothesis involving deliberate forgery). Round 1 to the sindonologists.

The body-image was always going to present more of a challenge than the blood-image. STURP's primary aim was to look for traces of paint, which

would be an obvious sign of forgery, but, failing that, they had no idea
how the image might have been made. The 1973 commission had said
nothing about the body-image, besides noting its extreme faintness. So, the
STURP team found themselves approaching a virtually invisible phenomenon more-or-less blind.

The mystery deepened as soon as they trained their microscopes on the
cloth. Close up, the body-image areas look much like ordinary linen, as
photomicrographs show (Figure 21). All that can be seen are the squares
and rectangles of the interweaving threads, each composed of thousands of
tiny plant fibers. There is no sign of anything else. Instead of being white,
however, some of the fibers appear golden brown or straw-yellow (depending on the lighting conditions). The sepia-colored image evidently consists
of these colored fibers, not of any substance applied to the cloth. Teasing
the threads apart, the STURP scientists discovered that the yellowed fibers
reside only on the crests of the threads; the image is just a single fiber deep,
and, where the surface of a thread dips down, the color disappears.[25] This
is true of the dorsal image as well as the frontal image, indicating that
the process of image formation was unaffected by the pressure of a
body.[26] The yellowed fibers are not cemented together in any way, which
would be the case if they were covered by a liquid paint medium.[27] The
scientists also observed that the tone of the colored fibers is uniform. The
intensity of the image in any given area is determined by the number of
colored fibers present, not the varying strength of the color itself.[28]

The extraordinary insubstantiality of the image was further demonstrated by a couple of STURP's tests. Backlit, the body-image is completely
invisible (unlike the blood-image), so it cannot consist of opaque material.[29] It is also indistinguishable from the background cloth via X-rays,
proving that it is not composed of a heavy metal pigment, such as iron
oxide.[30] The body-image could be seen, however, via reflectance spectrometry, because it does not fluoresce at all under ultraviolet light, whereas the
background cloth does. Whatever the golden coloration of the image fibers
may be, it cancels out whatever it is that makes the rest of the cloth fluoresce.[31]

As if all this were not perplexing enough, Italian scientists recently
announced the discovery during the secret conservation campaign of 2002
of an even fainter image on the reverse side of the cloth. According to the
official report by Monsignor Giuseppe Ghiberti, this reverse image is of
nothing more than the hair of the frontal figure, although image processing
of the photo published in the report indicates that other features may be
discernible, as well, such as the moustache, beard, eyes, nose, and hands.[32]

There is apparently no hint of a reverse dorsal figure. Unfortunately, the Turin authorities have refused to make original photographs of the reverse side of the cloth available to qualified researchers, so the precise scope of the reverse image is uncertain.[33] Because the reverse image appears to be as superficial as the familiar obverse image, sindonologists have taken to referring to the "double superficiality" of the body-image, meaning that it exists (in places) on both surfaces of the cloth, but not in between. Ray Rogers, a senior STURP scientist, considers "the slight penetration of the color in all areas but the hair to be one of the most important observations with regard to developing image-formation hypotheses."[34]

To try to understand what the straw-yellow color might be, it was nec-essary to look at body-image fibers under much higher magnifications and analyze them chemically in the lab. The initial work was done, once again, by Heller and Adler, using the samples obtained by Ray Rogers. They found, to begin with, that the body-image fibers are not colored right the way through; they are golden yellow only on the surface, their medullas (interiors) remaining quite clear (Figure 22).[35] They differ in this respect from scorched fibers, which are colored throughout, due to the penetrat-ing effect of the heat.[36] On the other hand, the pattern of discoloration does resemble the natural yellowing of linen fibers with age, due to oxidi-zation and dehydration of the cellulose. (It is this aging process that has turned the whole cloth, originally white, the color of old ivory, reducing the contrast between the image and the background.) Heller and Adler then found that they could get rid of the yellow color from body-image fibers by applying a strong reducing agent (diimide), indicating that it was indeed a product of oxidization.[37] They assumed that the cellulose itself was involved, and, when they managed to mimic the appearance and chemistry of the body-image fibers by soaking linen in concentrated sul-furic acid, they took this as confirmation.[38] But they were at a loss to understand how the fibers of the body-image could have been prema-turely "aged."

This analysis of the body-image fibers represented STURP's official con-clusion, and so most sindonologists believe to this day that the body-image is the result of a chemical alteration of the linen fibers themselves. Recently, however, the evidence has been reviewed by Ray Rogers, who has come to a very different conclusion, one with tremendous significance for the scien-tific understanding of the image.

According to Rogers, the fact that, using a reducing agent, the golden color can be removed from body-image fibers, leaving them undamaged, is a clear sign "that the cellulose was not involved in image formation."[39] He then draws attention to some surprising observations he and Adler made in 1981, though they didn't understand their significance at the time. Having shared his initial findings with the STURP team,

> Adler went back to his laboratory to make more detailed observations on the tape samples. He immediately reported that he had seen "ghosts" in the adhesive tape. It appeared that some image fibers had been pulled out of the adhesive, *and their colored coating had been stripped off of the fiber and remained in the adhesive*. He found that the colored "ghosts" showed the same chemical properties as the authentic image fibers from the Shroud.[40]

Rather than being composed of degraded cellulose, then, the golden color of the body-image is due to some sort of "coating" on the fibers. According to Rogers, this coating consists of dehydrated carbohydrates, containing complex conjugated double bonds, like degraded cellulose, which accounts for its earlier misidentification.[41]

The body-image, then, is far more difficult to understand than the blood-image and is evidently the result of complicated physical and chemical processes. Valuable as their investigations were, Heller and Adler were ultimately unable to solve the problem, and it was left in abeyance until Rogers resumed study of the Shroud in 2000.[42] We are fortunate that he did. Tackling the problem afresh, Rogers succeeded in developing a hypothesis that promises, at long last, to provide a coherent, naturalistic explanation for the formation of the body-image, one dependent on the presence of a dead body. We shall return to this issue in Chapter 12.

What about the evidence of the cloth itself?

STURP focused their effort on analyzing the images, making only incidental observations regarding the rest of the Shroud, so the 1988 carbon dating took place in a virtual vacuum of knowledge about the cloth, which was extremely unfortunate. Most of the evidence has been uncovered since then—indeed, since the turn of the millennium—and has not yet attracted the attention it deserves.

The first serious study of the Shroud as a textile was undertaken in 1973 by Professor Gilbert Raes of Ghent University, who was permitted to take some samples, including a small swatch, the size of a postage stamp, from one of the corners (adjacent to the area subsequently sampled for the carbon dating).[43] Raes confirmed that the cloth was made of linen and that its weave is a rare type known as a three-to-one twill, created by passing each weft thread under three warp threads and then over one, building up a herringbone pattern (Figure 44). Not much can be gleaned from this, except that the cloth was more expensive than average. Three-to-one twill weaving was practiced both in antiquity and in the late Middle Ages, although more examples exist from the earlier period, including ones found in Syria and Egypt, countries bordering Palestine. These are all of silk or wool, but the same technique could well have been used for linen.[44]

Raes reached no conclusion regarding the age of the Shroud, but he was unable to examine the whole cloth at leisure and had to make do with tiny samples. Another textile specialist, Dr. Mechthild Flury-Lemberg, enjoyed much more favorable conditions in 2002, as the leader of the secret conservation exercise. Besides having access to the Shroud over a period of weeks, Flury-Lemberg was able to examine its underside for the first time, when she removed the old backing cloth that was attached by the nuns in 1532. This revealed something that no one had seen before, something that links the cloth specifically to first-century Judaea.

Right the way along the left-hand side of the Shroud (looking at the frontal figure upright) is a thin strip of linen, of the same herringbone weave, which has been stitched very skillfully to the main body of the cloth. The joining seam has always been apparent, but until 2002 it had never been properly examined, since the underside was inaccessible. When Flury-Lemberg finally had the opportunity to study it, she saw that the stitching was extremely unusual. In fact, only one other example of such a seam has ever been found on a historical textile, and that was a scrap of clothing from Masada, the fortress in southern Israel where Jewish rebels made their last stand against the forces of Rome at the end of the Jewish War. The clothing belonged to one of the rebels and can therefore be dated securely to AD 73, when the fortress fell. According to Flury-Lemberg, the seam found on this first-century Jewish cloth is identical to that found on the Shroud and nowhere else. Moreover, other fragments of clothing found at Masada exhibit the same unusual selvedge as the Shroud, i.e. the same way of binding and finishing the edges of the cloth.[45] These technical parallels are extremely impressive, linking the Shroud, as they do, to the very region and period in which Jesus died.

The side strip may have more to tell us. An obvious question is: why would a piece of cloth 3½ feet wide have had an extra 3½-inch-wide strip added to one side? This was a puzzle, until Flury-Lemberg explained that it has to do with the manufacturing of the cloth on a much wider loom.[46] The selvedges, which run down either side of the Shroud, indicate that the side strip and the main body of the cloth were manufactured at either end of the loom; between them there would have been an expanse of cloth that was cut out and used separately. The missing section, which was seamless, is unlikely to have been any narrower than the Shroud, making the entire loom at least 7½ feet wide. During the Middle Ages, it seems, looms were never this large, since there was no demand for especially wide pieces of cloth, but in antiquity, when broad, seamless robes were in fashion, large looms were relatively common. Ancient Egyptian looms could be up to 11½ feet in width, being needed "particularly for the production of the 'tunica inconsutilis,' the seamless tunica."[47]

Like their Hellenistic contemporaries, ancient Jews wore tunics and mantles and would have been in the market for relatively large linen cloths. Interestingly, Josephus tells us that, by tradition, the Jewish high priest wore a blue tunic made without any seam.[48] This may relate to the coats "woven of fine linen" made for Aaron and his sons, the priestly line, in Exodus 39.27. The Shroud's herringbone weave is exceptionally fine, and, given the link with the Masada textiles, it could well represent the sort of linen produced in first-century Jerusalem for the Temple priests.[49]

That the Shroud was manufactured in antiquity rather than the Middle Ages is further indicated by a couple of observations made by STURP scientists. First, Ray Rogers has drawn attention to the "banding" of the Shroud's linen, due to slight color variations in the hanks of yarn. He explains this effect in terms of the way linen was produced in Roman times, a process described by Pliny the Elder in his famous encyclopedia, *Natural History*, composed around AD 77–9.[50] According to Pliny, harvested flax was divided into small sheafs, which were soaked in water, dried in the sun and pounded with hammers, before being carded and spun into threads. The linen threads were then soaked, dried and pounded in turn, to increase their pliability. The sunlight would have had a mild bleaching effect, and, because each hank of yarn would have been treated slightly differently, they would have been slightly variegated in color. Impurities picked up in the wash may also have affected their color. So, ancient linen appears faintly striped, due to the way the thread was processed in separate batches. Medieval linen, apparently, is more homogenous, since the material was bleached after being woven, not before.[51]

Once linen textiles were woven, they were often washed with an extract of soapwort (*Saponaria officinalis*). The purpose of this was to further bleach and soften the cloth. Pliny says that soapwort was used extensively for washing wool, and that it contributed greatly to its whiteness and softness, but he should have said linen, not wool, because his source, Theophrastus, tells us that soapwort was used to bleach linen.[52] Textile conservators have also found that ancient cloths which were washed in soapwort tend to be relatively well preserved, which is suggestive in relation to the Shroud, given its excellent condition.[53] Suspecting that the Shroud might have been washed with soapwort, Rogers tried to detect tell-tale pentose sugars on some of its fibers, but without success. He did observe, however, that the reflectance spectrometry supported the idea, since the cloth fluoresced at a particular wavelength, indicating the presence of chemicals derived from soapwort.[54] The significance of this will become apparent later on, when we look into the possible cause of the body-image.

It is worth noting that, if the cloth was washed using soapwort, it might also help explain the reddish color of the bloodstains, since *Saponaria* solutions are hemolytic, i.e. they break down red blood cells and release the hemoglobin. Apparently, this was tested before the STURP team went to Turin by applying blood to linen washed with soapwort, and twenty-five years later this blood was still red, whereas control samples on ordinary linen had turned black.[55] This is an alternative explanation to that proposed by Adler, but it does not necessarily invalidate his conclusion that the blood belonged to a badly injured person.

Over the course of three or four decades, then, scientists and textile conservators have discovered enough about the cloth to make a strong case that it dates from antiquity, rather than the Middle Ages, and that its place of manufacture was Palestine. Unfortunately, this detailed evidence has been overshadowed by the contradictory carbon dating, which is all most people know—or want to know—about the Shroud.

We shall look into the dubious science and politics behind the carbon-dating headlines soon, but we may note here that the carbon-dating result has been challenged on its own terms by the indefatigable Ray Rogers, who discovered an alternative way to estimate the age of the flax. While relatively imprecise, his method indicates that the cloth is probably pre-medieval.

The method depends on a straightforward chemical test for lignin, the substance that gives the cell walls of plants their rigidity. Lignin produces vanillin, and it is this substance that the test detects. Rogers noticed that, although he could see dark patches of lignin in Shroud fibers under the microscope, they did not give a positive test, meaning that the Shroud's lignin must have lost all or nearly all its vanillin. It turns out that the rate at which lignin loses its vanillin is very low. Along with a colleague at Los Alamos National Laboratory, Stanley Kosiewicz, Rogers calculated that, in order to lose 95 percent of its vanillin, a piece of linen would have to be 1,319 years old, if stored at up to 25°C, and 3,095 years old, if stored at up to 20°C. At a conservative estimate, then, a linen cloth without detectable vanillin is unlikely to date from after 700. Confirming this, he found that medieval linens in which lignin was visibly present all tested positive, whereas samples of linen found with the Dead Sea Scrolls, roughly contemporary with Jesus, did not.

The Shroud, then, is probably much older than is indicated by the carbon dating. If it had been made as late as 1260, the lower limit implied by the carbon dating, it should have retained about 37 percent of its vanillin, which would be easily detectable. The fact that it is vanillin-free is a clear sign that the Shroud is more than 1,300 years old. It could well have been produced in first-century Judaea, like the cloth found with the Dead Sea Scrolls.[56]

This argument was published in a peer-reviewed article in *Thermochimica Acta* in 2005, an article in which Rogers further undermined the validity of the carbon-dating result by casting doubt on the representativeness of the carbon-dating sample. This article has been ignored by the academic establishment, which is not interested in re-opening the debate, but, as a contribution to understanding the origin of the Shroud, it is far more significant than the 1989 *Nature* report concerning the carbon dating. Instead of orphaning the cloth in the Middle Ages, it helps locate it in the world of Pliny and Masada, a far more suitable context in terms of the history of textile production.

The final category of evidence consists of minute particles of debris found on and within the cloth. Wherever and whenever it has been exhibited, the Shroud has acted like a fine net trawling the atmosphere, catching tiny particles of dust floating in the air, and it has also picked up traces of the various materials with which it has come into contact. By thus sampling its environment, the cloth has built up a large reservoir of information over the years relating to its conditions of storage and even its various geographical locations. That is why the decision to vacuum the Shroud during the 2002 conservation was so contentious.

Study of the detritus on the Shroud began in 1973, when Max Frei, a Swiss botanist and criminologist, was permitted to take some samples by pressing adhesive tape onto the cloth, a method he had devised to sample the clothing of suspects in criminal cases. Frei was looking for a very specific type of evidence: pollen. As forensic scientists know well, pollen grains trapped in a fabric can help indicate its past whereabouts, and Frei, who pioneered this technique, reckoned that it might help establish the historical locations of the Shroud.

The scientific study of pollen, palynology, is based on the fact that the pollens of different plants are distinguishable under the microscope by their shapes and microstructures. In theory it is possible to ascribe an individual pollen grain to a particular species of plant on the basis of its appearance, though, in practice, palynologists are rarely confident identifying more than the genus of the plant (the category above species). Pollen is borne either by the wind or by insects; in either case, it rarely travels far from the parent plant.[57] This means that, if the pollen of a plant becomes entrapped in the weave of a cloth, the cloth was almost certainly in the vicinity of that plant, not miles away. Since different plants are native to different parts of the world, the geographical distribution of plants whose pollen can be found on the Shroud should "map" the places where the Shroud has been. Fortunately, pollen grains are extremely durable and can exist for thousands of years without deteriorating—especially if tucked up in a piece of linen.

Frei, it seems, was initially skeptical of the Shroud's authenticity, as would be expected of a Zwinglian Protestant.[58] What he saw under the microscope, though, changed his mind.

As he analyzed the plentiful pollen picked up by his sticky tapes, he began to realize that the Shroud could not have spent all its time in France and Italy. For, besides pollen grains from central European and Mediterranean lands, which could easily have blown onto the Shroud in the previous 600 years, he found large numbers of grains from much further afield. A significant proportion of these indicate, Frei says, that the Shroud was once kept in Turkey: "According to the palynology, the Shroud must have been exposed to the open air also in Turkey, since twenty of the verified species are abundant in Anatolia . . . and four are abundant in the environs of Constantinople; these are completely absent from central and western Europe."[59] This is extremely interesting in relation to certain historical evidence, which suggests that, long before it was brought to Europe, the Shroud was kept in Constantinople and Edessa, a town in eastern Turkey.

Furthermore, on the basis of finding pollen from thirteen species of halophytes—a genus specially adapted to living in salty environments, many of them exclusive to the Negev desert and Dead Sea area—Frei affirms that "in the course of its history (including its manufacture) the Shroud has been in Palestine."[60] Just as significant, in Frei's view, as the identification of individual species or genera is the overall proportion of Middle Eastern to European pollen grains: "the Shroud must have stayed in Palestine or in Turkey, since plants that grow in these areas . . . are dominant in the pollen spectrum."[61]

It is important to emphasize that Frei does *not* claim to be able to date the Shroud on the basis of the pollen evidence. But it is clear, nevertheless, that his data have chronological implications, since the Shroud's whereabouts since its fourteenth-century appearance in Lirey are well known, and thus, if it was ever in Palestine and Turkey, it must have been before then.

Since Frei's death in 1983 his work on the Shroud has been reviewed by a number of other palynologists. One or two have expressed doubts about his methodology and conclusions; others have broadly endorsed his work.[62] There seems to be general agreement that, although he is likely to have been able to identify the genus of each pollen grain correctly, his species identifications are suspect. Perhaps the most balanced view is that of Silvano Scannerini, a Turinese botany professor, who, while critical of Frei's publications, concludes nevertheless that "the pollens of plants from the Near East are an indirect confirmation of the plausibility of the voyage of the Shroud from Asia to Europe."[63] However, he says, "to transform this evidence into an irrefutable proof of the presence of the Shroud in the Middle East and in Palestine requires a more thorough palynological analysis than has hitherto been conducted."[64] Regrettably, those now in possession of Frei's sticky-tape samples, an American Shroud group called ASSIST, have not managed to arrange a more thorough analysis in over two decades. They did have them checked by an Israeli palynologist, Uri Baruch, who concurred with Frei's findings, but Baruch's work has since been shown to be inadequate.[65] The world still awaits a definitive investigation of the Shroud's pollen.

Perhaps the most impressive corroboration of Frei's work comes from an analysis of particles of limestone (mainly calcium carbonate) lifted from the surface of the Shroud.[66] Around the time of Frei's death, optical crystallographer Joseph Kohlbeck was given access to STURP's sticky-tape samples and began investigating this limestone dust in the hope that, like the pollen, it might shed light on the past whereabouts of the cloth. The crystalline structure of limestone varies depending on the conditions under which it is deposited, and the rock also bears a "chemical signature," a particular spectrum of trace elements. Obtaining a sample of limestone from a tomb near Jerusalem, Kohlbeck found that it was of the rare aragonite variety and "also contained small quantities of iron and strontium but no lead."[67] When he analyzed a speck of calcium carbonate from the Shroud, he found that its composition was similar.

Not content with this, Kohlbeck took his samples to the Enrico Fermi Institute at the University of Chicago, where Dr. Riccardo Levi-Setti put them through a high-resolution scanning ion microprobe, so that their chemical signatures could be compared in detail. The match was extremely close, indicating that the traces of limestone on the Shroud could have been picked up in the Jerusalem area. Samples of limestone taken from nine other sites in Israel failed to provide a good match. While Kohlbeck points out that limestone similar to the Jerusalem type may exist elsewhere in the world, the onus is on skeptics to show where and to explain how it might have ended up on the Shroud. Even more than Frei's halophytes, those salt-loving plants native to the Dead Sea region, Kohlbeck's aragonite limestone points to the relic having once been in the vicinity of Jerusalem.

Besides the pollen and calcium carbonate, many other bits of debris were found on STURP's sticky tapes: particles of iron, bronze, silver and gold, deriving presumably from the various containers in which the Shroud has been kept and liturgical objects with which it has come into contact; droplets of candle-wax; fly ash from the power stations of Turin; animal hairs, feather fragments and insect parts; red silk, blue linen and white cotton from cloths with which the Shroud has been stored; and wool, nylon and polyester from the clothes of those who have handled it.[68] None of this has any significance for the early history of the cloth.

Also found on the tapes were a few particles of paint. These were seized upon by an associate of the STURP team, a microscopist called Walter McCrone, who took them as evidence that the cloth had once been in an artist's studio and was therefore a painted fake.[69] This argument is baseless. Artists have been making copies of the Shroud since the sixteenth century, at least, and several of these are known to have been laid directly on the original in order to be sanctified.[70] Tiny fragments of paint would undoubtedly have been transferred in the process. Other particles could easily have come from nearby paintings. For instance, when STURP examined the Shroud in the Royal Palace of Turin, they did so in a room whose ceiling was covered in frescoes, "from which tiny paint fragments would fall like confetti as the team members worked below."[71] McCrone's paint particles could have fetched up on the Shroud just as easily as any of the other debris.

It was the opinion of the Sorbonne scientists who initiated study of the Shroud in the early twentieth century that arguments proceeding solely from Pia's photographs constituted "an imposing bundle of probabilities" in favor of the relic's authenticity. The much broader evidence presented in this chapter does not indicate a specific connection with Jesus, but it does point to the Shroud being an oddly stained, first-century, Jewish burial cloth.

The case for authenticity looks promising, but it is still far from proven. To determine whether the Shroud is authentic or not, we have to understand it not only scientifically, but also historically, as the representation of a past event. It is as an image that the Shroud will reveal its cultural origin most clearly. The next two chapters concern the blood-image and the body-image, respectively. Now that we have a basic understanding of their material properties, we can step back and view these images as twin representations of a crucified man.

This is where the interpretation of the Shroud starts to impinge upon (sacred) history and the (sacred) texts that represent that history. This is where things start to get meaningful.

10

The Blood-Image

Why start with the blood rather than the body? Because the identity of the Shroud-man, the real or imagined person wrapped in the cloth, is written in his blood. The blood-image is the Shroud-man's birthmark—or death-mark.

Clearly defined and relatively easy to analyze medically and historically, the blood-image conveys a great deal of information about the hypothetical treatment of the Shroud-man, how he was tortured, killed and laid to rest. Since people are executed and buried in different ways at different times, this treatment enables us to work out roughly where and when the image came into being.

What is more, the wounds represented on the Shroud recall the execution of a particular historical individual—Jesus. Might the Shroud genuinely have wrapped the crucified body of Jesus? Or does it merely represent his body as imagined by a cunning medieval forger? The blood-image, above all else, can help us decide.

Scientific investigators of the Shroud have been impressed by the apparent blood flows on the cloth from the beginning. When the agnostic professor of anatomy, Yves Delage, presented his paper to the French Académie des Sciences in 1902, he drew attention to the complexity and naturalistic quality of the bloodstains, maintaining that they were medically convincing in every detail.[1] His paper was enthusiastically reported in the *Lancet*, the leading British medical journal, which spoke of "an exact image, even to minute details such as wounds produced by the thorns and the marks of the blood drops."[2] Delage's arguments—underpinned by the careful research of his protégé Paul Vignon, who published his findings later in the same year—were never challenged on their own terms; they were just shelved and forgotten.

However, following the 1931 exhibition of the Shroud, when excellent new photos were taken, Pierre Barbet and a handful of other doctors took up the baton and began to confirm the observations of Delage and Vignon. Since then numerous medics have devoted time and effort to investigating the Shroud, and their collective opinion is unanimous: the image displays convincing signs of injury and death, and the cloth is therefore likely to have enveloped a man tortured and crucified in the manner of Jesus, as narrated in the Gospels.

In his book *The Resurrection of the Shroud* Mark Antonacci lists twenty-four of the most notable of these experts, among them surgeons, pathologists and professors.[3] We are not talking about a couple of mavericks, but a large number of eminent doctors who discuss the problem in scientific terms and present detailed arguments in support of their conclusions. Art historians, meanwhile, who should be able to spot wounds painted by a medieval artist a mile off, have remained tellingly silent. Everyone agrees that, if the Shroud is a deliberate fake, the blood, at least, must have been applied with a paintbrush, so it is notable that experts in medieval art have declined to discuss the image. Have they been ignoring a remarkable medieval blood painting, or are the Shroud's bloodstains really a subject for medical research?

To decide whether or not the blood marks visible on the Shroud could possibly be the work of a painter, we need to compare the Shroud with images of the dead Christ produced by artists of the fourteenth century, when the relic is supposed to have been forged. Perhaps the most useful comparison is with the figure of the entombed Christ in the famous *Parement de Narbonne* (Figure 23), created for Charles V of France sometime between 1364 and 1380 (just after the alleged forging of the Shroud).[4] This ink-wash image on silk, painted by an artist of exceptional ability, provides the closest approximation to the Shroud in all fourteenth-century art.

For good measure, we may also compare the Shroud with an exquisite "Man of Sorrows" by Naddo Ceccarelli (Figure 24). Naddo was a follower of the renowned Sienese artist Simone Martini, who worked in Avignon from 1336 until his death in 1344 and who had a profound influence on French painting of the fourteenth century. Although the "Man of Sorrows" was probably painted in Italy around 1347, Naddo worked with his master in Avignon, and it is representative of the best work produced by Simone's pupils.[5] Fourteenth-century painting did not get any more lifelike than this—in Italy, France or anywhere else.

If the medics who have studied it are wrong, and the Shroud really is an artistic forgery of the Middle Ages, we should expect the blood-image to relate to the wounds depicted in these contemporary pictures of the dead Christ.

The most clearly defined wound on the Shroud is that located in the area of the figure's left wrist. The existence of a corresponding wound to the right wrist, obscured beneath the left hand, can be inferred from the trickles of blood running down the right forearm, similar to those on the left. Together, these wounds indicate that the man represented via the Shroud—real or imagined—was subjected to crucifixion.

The bloodstain visible in the left wrist is an exit wound, the nail having been driven in from the other side. A small stream of blood appears to have issued from a circular patch, which represents the wound itself (Figure 25). Because of the vagueness of the body-image, it is impossible to be sure exactly where this wound is located, but it is clearly in the region of the wrist, rather than the center of the hand.[6] This casts doubt on the idea that it was painted by a medieval artist, for in the art of that period the wounds are conventionally depicted in the center of Christ's hands, never in the wrists (cf. Figures 23 and 24). This convention mattered. Today, it might seem unimportant whether the hands or the wrists were pierced, but in those days there was intense devotional interest in Christ's wounds, and they had to be depicted correctly, i.e. according to the traditional understanding.[7] If the blood-image was the work of a medieval painter, then, the wound would almost certainly have been located in the back of the hand.

This traditional imagery is now known to be mistaken. Medics who have studied crucifixion and the Shroud all agree that, in order to have supported the weight of the body, the nail must have been driven into the relatively strong region of the wrist. Had it been driven through the center of the palm, as depicted by medieval artists, it would have torn through the ligaments of the hand, and the victim would have fallen off the cross. So the exit wound appears in the right place anatomically, the wrong place artistically.

Concerning the invisible entrance wound, the medical arguments are more problematic. After experimenting with an amputated arm, Dr. Barbet concluded that the nail must have been driven through a hole found in among the complicated array of carpal bones (wrist bones) known as Destot's space. This idea has been enthusiastically endorsed by sindonologists, partly because it is thought to fulfil a scriptural prophecy ("He keeps all his bones; not one of them is broken"), a consideration advanced by Barbet himself.[8] The use of scripture to support this interpretation is worryingly unscientific, and it has been challenged on medical grounds by Dr. Frederick Zugibe. Confident that the exit wound is on the thumb side of the wrist, Zugibe explains that Destot's space is on the little-finger side and so could not have been the region pierced.[9] His preferred interpretation is that the nail was driven at an angle through the "thenar furrow" in the upper part of the palm (popularly called the "life-line"). This is plausible, since Zugibe goes to great lengths to demonstrate that the bones and tissues of the upper palm would have been strong enough to support the weight of the body.[10] Unfortunately, the reasoning is infected, once again, by a credulous attitude toward Christian tradition, including the belief that the upper palm pathway is in accord with the "prophecy" of Psalm 22.16 ("they have pierced my hands and feet").[11]

It is worth focusing on this debate about the precise method of fixing the nails through the wrists, because it highlights two aspects of medical discussion about the Shroud that need to be borne in mind. On the positive side, it is significant that learned physicians can engage in meaningful discussion about the process of crucifixion on the basis of a wound mark represented on the Shroud. That in itself demonstrates the extraordinarily realistic quality of the bloodstain. On the negative side, it warns us to be on our guard when assessing the medical arguments, since doctors who are devout Christians may be influenced by an unscientific regard for the evidence of scripture.[12] Barbet, Zugibe and other medics have contributed enormously to our understanding of the Shroud, but, at the same time, they have often been too ready to view it as a mere reflection of biblical texts.

In my view, it is impossible to say whether the nail that pierced the left wrist was driven through the carpal bones or at an angle through the upper palm. Either way, the Shroud shows a plausible location for the exit wound, unlike medieval representations of Christ's stigmata, which invariably show the wounds in the center of the hands. Did some artistic genius of the fourteenth century have a unique insight into the practice of crucifixion? Or does the Shroud genuinely document this ancient torture?

The bloodstains that cover the forearms of the Shroud figure are evidently connected to the wrist wounds. A great deal has been read into these bloody meanders in the past, far more than is warranted. It has been argued, for instance, that they provide evidence of the man having raised himself up and down on the cross, in order to breathe.[13] Zugibe regards this idea as completely untenable. "It is obvious," in his view, "that the blood flows on the arms occurred right after the removal of the nails (which had sealed the wounds during suspension) from the hand area, causing the blood . . . to flow down the back of the arms from the nail exit wound . . ."[14] The small quantity of blood speaks in favor of a post-mortem interpretation, as Zugibe explains: "The blood seen on the Shroud is a very small amount although it may seem like a lot to the uninitiated . . . Forensically speaking, the reason for the small amount of blood on the arms is due to the fact that the heart was not beating when the nails were removed and the arms were in a suspended position."[15]

Zugibe seems to think that the nails were removed while the man was still upright on the cross, but it is much more likely, for practical reasons, that he was detached from the cross-beam while laid out supine on the ground. (As I explain later, the cross-beam would have been easily removable from on top of the vertical shaft.) Lying in this position, the blood still in his hands and wrists would have drained from the holes left by the nails and trickled down the undersides of his arms, exactly as we see on the forearms of the Shroud figure (cf. Figure 26).

As far as I am aware, medieval artists never depicted such blood flows on the body of the dead Christ. They imagined blood dribbling from the hand wounds, but left the forearms clean (cf. Figures 23 and 24). Moreover, the irregular, asymmetrical character of the blood flows is unlike anything a medieval artist might have imagined, and their fragmented appearance would have seemed quite illogical to medieval minds. (Compare the continuous trickles of blood depicted on Christ's side in the *Parement de Narbonne*.) The likelihood that the forearm stains are the work of a medieval painter is virtually nil.

Turning to the feet, we are presented not with clear clots, but with bloody smears (Figure 27). Usually, medics identify the exit wound in the right foot—the foot whose sole is represented in its entirety on the dorsal image—with what appears to be "a square image surrounded by a pale halo" in the middle of the instep,[16] but others locate it in the heel, from which a conspicuous bloodstain trails out laterally across the cloth.[17] Although a wound in the center of the foot would make more sense, it is impossible to be sure from the blood on the Shroud where exactly it was pierced. Even less can be said about the wounding of the left foot, since the bloodstains on this side are quite formless.

The lack of clarity regarding the stigmata in the feet is itself significant. If the Shroud were a medieval forgery, the wounds in the feet (along with every other wound) would surely have been clearly marked (cf. Figure 23). Christ's wounds were not just incidental traces of torture in the Middle Ages. As the source of the blood that bought salvation, they were considered profoundly meaningful and were a focus of devotion. Accordingly, when medieval artists depicted Christ's wounded feet, they were always careful to indicate the marks of the nails. Paul Vignon had it right over a century ago: "Had a forger at that date desired to simulate the wounds made by the nails, he would, we think, have drawn them carefully, showing them in circular form; the essential thing in his eyes would have been that the wounds should have been easily recognized in the traditional positions."[18]

The sort of impressionistic effect of the Shroud might seem "convincing" to us today, but it would have been nonsensical and shocking—even unthinkable—in the Middle Ages, when artists were bound by theological and devotional requirements.

The blood-image in the areas of the hands and feet, then, is incompatible with the notion that the Shroud was forged in the late Middle Ages and supports the idea that it was used to enfold the body of a crucified man. Crucifixion was outlawed in the Roman Empire in the fourth century by Emperor Constantine and his successors, which would indicate that the image was created before that time.

Further evidence that the man was executed by the Romans is supplied by the distinctive marks of flagellation. Scourge marks are present all over the Shroud figure, except in the regions of the head, arms and feet. They can be seen on both the frontal and dorsal figures, but are best seen on the man's back (Figure 28). As Dr. Bucklin, a medical examiner, observes, the injuries "appear to have been made by some type of object applied as a whip, leaving dumbbell-shaped imprints in the skin from which blood has issued."[19]

It so happens that these distinctive injuries correspond with what we know of the Roman *flagrum*, a type of scourge whose thongs were tipped either with knuckle bones or with lead buttons known as *plumbatae*. It was routine for victims of crucifixion to be scourged with such an instrument before being put on the cross. A relatively intact *flagrum* was apparently discovered in the ruins of Herculaneum, with *plumbatae* not dissimilar to those that afflicted the Shroud-man (cf. Figure 29).[20] This is good evidence that the Shroud is of the same period as Herculaneum, a town buried, like its neighbor Pompeii, by the volcanic eruption of Vesuvius in AD 79.

About a hundred scourge marks can be detected on the two Shroud figures. The *flagrum* had either two or three thongs, so the Shroud-man would have received at least thirty lashes—quite possibly many more. According to Jewish law, a prisoner could receive up to forty lashes, but Roman executioners were not bound by this law and were limited only by

the need to keep the victim alive and able to stagger to the place of crucifixion.[21] Since the scourge marks on the back are in a criss-cross pattern, it
is evident that the blows were delivered from two different directions,
either by two flagellators or a single flagellator who changed position.
Apart from the head and feet, only the arms were spared, which implies
that the man's hands were tied above his head when the scourging took
place. It was apparently the regular Roman practice for those scourged to
be tied to a column.[22]

Observing all this, doctors are agreed that the scourge marks on the
Shroud are convincing, both medically and historically, as the sort of injuries that would have been sustained by a victim of Roman flogging prior
to crucifixion.

Once again, though, it differs dramatically from anything envisaged in
the Middle Ages. The vast majority of medieval images of the dead or
dying Christ fail to depict any scourge marks at all (cf. Figures 23 and 24).
This may be because it was generally assumed that the flogging affected
only Christ's back, or it may be to avoid distracting from the more significant wounds in the hands, feet and side. Christ is sometimes shown
bleeding in depictions of the flagellation, but the effect is always rather
crude. In Duccio's rendering of the scene, for example, the scourge marks
are represented as red dribbles all over the body, including the arms but
not the legs (Figure 30). The artist displays no knowledge of the Roman
flagrum, nor any conception of how it was wielded.[23] Even a fifteenth-
century artist as accomplished as Jean Colombe, who definitely knew the
Shroud, was unable to reproduce its convincing pattern of scourge marks
(Figure 10). To attribute the marks on the Shroud to a provincial unknown
working in the mid fourteenth century is therefore ridiculous.

In one area, according to medics who have studied the Shroud closely,
the scourge marks are slightly less well defined than elsewhere: at the top
of the back, where the shoulder blades appear.[24] The flesh here seems to
have been rubbed and bruised, making the scourge marks less distinct. The
effect is described by Bucklin thus: "Two large discolored areas over the
shoulder blades are consistent with bleeding from surface abrasions as if a
heavy, rough object had been in contact with the skin at these points."[25]
The object in question is likely to have been the horizontal beam of the
cross. Roman crosses consisted of a vertical shaft, called the *stipes*, which
remained permanently fixed in the ground, and a cross-beam, called the
patibulum, which was carried to the site of execution by the condemned
man himself. (The idea that the entire cross was carried is a medieval fiction.) It has been estimated that a *patibulum* could weigh in the region of

100 pounds.[26] Scholars debate how the beam would have been carried, some imagining it balanced on one shoulder, others reckoning that it was tied to the outstretched arms across the back. For practical reasons, the latter is much more likely. A scourged prisoner would have been weak and would have had great difficulty balancing a heavy beam on his shoulder. Tied to his outstretched arms, the burden would have been secure, eradicating any risk to the accompanying guard. This arrangement would also have made the subsequent business of nailing the wrists relatively straightforward. Laid across the Shroud-man's back, the *patibulum* would have chafed precisely in the area of the shoulder blades.[27]

In the Middle Ages, Christ was invariably depicted bearing the whole cross—shaft and cross-beam together—over one shoulder. An artist attempting to portray the effect of this labor on Jesus would probably have represented it as a bruise at the top of a shoulder, either on his front or back, or both. He is unlikely to have thought of a pair of damaged shoulder blades. This is yet another sign that the Shroud is not a medieval invention.

Convincing as they are, there is something very odd about the marks of flagellation seen on the Shroud: the lack of blood. A body subjected to this severe laceration would have been smothered in streams of clotted blood.[28] What can account for the relatively clean appearance of the body and the clarity of the scourge marks?

The answer is simple: the body was washed before being buried. Washing would have removed the messy blood clots, exposed the wounds and induced a limited amount of post-mortem seepage of blood and serum. As Zugibe explains, "if the body was washed, the dried blood around the wounds would be removed, causing an oozing of bloody material within the wounds. This should result in the production of relatively good impressions of the wounds."[29] Anyone who has removed a scab from a cut or graze and then dabbed it with a cloth will be familiar with this phenomenon.

In order to test the idea, Zugibe experimented on the bodies of accident victims. He found that, if he washed the blood clot from a small wound and then touched the flesh gently with a linen cloth, he could obtain a fairly accurate impression of the wound (a claim he supports with photographic evidence).[30] This demonstrates beyond doubt that the neat scourge marks on the Shroud could have been imprinted by the washed corpse of a crucified man. Apparently, every other forensic pathologist Zugibe consulted "agreed that the wounds would have caused a large amount of bleeding and that the body had to be washed, to account for the preciseness of the wounds on the Shroud."[31]

The realization that the body was washed is profoundly significant. Washing the deceased all over was (and is) an important Jewish funerary rite. Known as *taharah*, the practice is recorded in the Mishnah, a book of traditional Jewish regulations compiled toward the end of the second century AD, and was almost certainly customary in the first century.[32] It is a clear sign that the man whose scourged body produced the image was Jewish.

Unfortunately, sindonologists have been confused in the past by the fact that there is still plenty of blood on the figure. This has been thought to indicate that the body was not washed and has been linked to a special provision in the sixteenth-century Code of Jewish Law that prohibits the washing of anyone who dies violently:

> If a person falls and dies instantly, if his body was bruised and blood flowed from the wound, and there is apprehension that his lifeblood was absorbed in his clothes, he should not be ritually cleansed, but interred in his garments and shoes. He should be wrapped in a sheet, above his garments. That sheet is called *sobeb*.[33]

Despite its late composition, the Code is thought to preserve very ancient traditions, so it may well have a bearing on the ritual treatment of the Shroud-man.[34] The trouble is that the scenario it describes is not applicable to him in crucial ways: he did not die instantly from his wounds, and he was not wearing any clothes. Once we understand the underlying rationale of the provision, we will see that it is perfectly compatible with the conclusion that the body of the Shroud-man was washed.

Everything turns on the issue of "lifeblood." The prohibition against ritual cleansing in the special case of violent death is designed to ensure that the person is buried with his or her lifeblood (which, under normal circumstances, remained within the body). Lifeblood, in Jewish thought, is blood that issues from someone while they are dying (or just after they have died); it does *not* include blood lost while the person is still alive.[35] It is important to preserve it, because, having been essential to the life of the body at the moment of death, it will be again at the moment of resurrection. Blood that leaves the body while the person is still alive does not need to be preserved, even if it has issued from wounds that ultimately cause death, because it is inessential to the person's life. The next provision in the Code of Jewish Law makes this clear, in a way that sheds considerable light on the treatment of the Shroud-man:

If blood has flown from the injured body, but it stopped and his clothes were removed, after which he recovered and lived for a few days and then died, he must be cleansed and dressed in shrouds. Even if his body is stained with the blood which issued forth from him, he must be cleansed, for the blood lost while being alive is not to be regarded as lifeblood; we are only concerned with the blood which one loses while dying, for it is likely that this was his lifeblood, or it is possible that lifeblood was mixed with it.[36]

The situation of someone who was flogged and died on the cross would have been midway between this scenario and the first. He would have had to have been "cleansed" of the blood he lost while he remained alive, as per the second provision; but his "lifeblood" would have had to have been buried with him, as per the first.

This is exactly the pattern of washing seen on the Shroud. All the blood on the Shroud is post-mortem, i.e. lifeblood, required for the man's anticipated resurrection. Only the superfluous blood that fell from him prior to death has been washed away. Since he was naked, this presented little difficulty.

The circumstances also required the use of a *sobeb* (or *sovev*)—a winding sheet. As Ian Wilson observes, the Code of Jewish Law further stipulates that "whatever garments the deceased may have worn when he died were all that he should be buried in, clearly implying that if he had died naked, then he should be left that way, except for the *sovev*."[37] Interestingly, according to Victor Tunkel, a Jewish law professor, a *sovev* is a single sheet wrapped carefully right round the body, in order to avoid disturbing the bloodstains as much as possible. The word *sovev* actually derives from a Hebrew verb meaning "surround" or "envelop."[38] This accords with the form and use of the Shroud.

The overall pattern of the blood-image and the use of a *sovev*-like winding sheet tell us that the Shroud-man was buried by pious Jews, who believed in the future resurrection of the dead. Once again, this militates against the idea of forgery, for, on top of all his other accomplishments, the hypothetical forger would have had to have researched Jewish burial practices and worked out precisely how the body of Jesus would have been prepared for burial, ignoring the fact that the Gospels fail to say anything about a ritual washing. This sort of historical reconstruction would have been utterly beyond any medieval craftsman.

Presuming, therefore, that the blood-image was imprinted by a real, Jewish body, we can say confidently that it must have been created before the abolition of Roman crucifixion in the fourth century. As far as we know, Jews were never crucified after that time (let alone in imitation of Jesus).

The treatment of the Shroud-man proves he was considered dead by those who buried him. Further evidence of his death is provided by the large bloodstain on the right side of his chest (Figure 31). The wound itself is identifiable with a solid, oval area at the top of the stain, roughly an inch and three-quarters by half an inch, from which the rest of the blood appears to have oozed.[39] A wound of this sort could easily have been inflicted by a Roman lance, whose long, leaf-like blade was of approximately the same breadth.[40] It appears that, whenever the body of a crucified man was handed over for burial, it was pierced in this way by a spear. Rather than a *coup de grâce*, it was a reliable means of checking that the prisoner was dead. Origen, a third-century author, tells us that the lance-thrust was made *sub alas* ("under the armpit"), and this agrees with the evidence of the Shroud.[41]

Beneath the wound area, the blood has trickled down 6 inches or so in a strangely irregular manner. It must have dried and clotted while the body was still in a vertical position. It might be thought surprising that a major hemorrhage in the side should result in such a small amount of blood.[42] Medics are quite clear, however, that the small quantity of blood is consistent with a post-mortem injury. As Dr. Bucklin observes, the blood appears to have flowed "without spatter or other evidence of the projectile activity which would be expected from blood issuing from a functional arterial source."[43]

The outline of the stain is oddly angular. One theory is that the undulations on the inner edge of the clot correspond to the positions of the muscles over the ribs, which would have protruded when the body was on the cross. As the blood dribbled down, it would have pooled a little in the indents between these muscles.[44] This is possible, but the main indent may have more to do with the adjacent waterstain.[45] What is absolutely clear is that no artist would have come up with the virtually rectangular form of the lower part of the clot. Look at the glistening streamlets running from the side wound in the *Parement de Narbonne*, as delicate and rhythmical as the tresses of hair falling over Mary's shoulder above (Figure 23). Less stylized, but no more lifelike, is the single drip that issues from the side wound in Ceccarelli's painting (Figure 24). Though they depicted the muscles of the ribcage, neither of these artists imagined the effect they would have on a flow of viscous blood.

Doctors have determined that the wound was inflicted between the fifth

and sixth ribs (the fifth intercostal space),[46] but, beyond that, their interpretations of this bloodstain are somewhat dubious. There has been much
speculation about the damage to internal organs, even though the angle of
the blade's entry is unknown.[47] And, once again, medical opinion has been
unduly influenced by a reading of scripture, in this case by John's statement that, when Jesus' side was pierced by a spear, there came out not only
blood, but also "water."[48] Thus, Bucklin claims that "close examination
shows a variance in intensity of the stain consistent with the presence of
two types of fluid, one comprised of blood, and the other resembling
water."[49] This is wishful thinking. Other bloodstains on the Shroud vary in
intensity as well, due not to the presence of watery fluid, but to differing
levels of hematic material on the cloth (cf. Figure 25). The only reason
some observers think "water" can be detected in this bloodstain is because
they are keen to validate the biblical text. In reality, it provides no evidence
of anything other than blood having issued from the wound.

Water *can* be detected, though, in another region of the blood-image:
the two pools of watery blood that flank the Shroud's dorsal figure (Figure
5). Compared with the wounds these stains may seem incidental and unin-
teresting, but they are in fact among the most illuminating marks on the
cloth.

Unfortunately, the dorsal pools were partially obliterated by the fire of
1532, and we have to be careful not to confuse them with the staining connected with that event. The pilgrim's badge of around 1355 indicates that,
before the fire, the pools extended outward either side of the body, but not
up alongside it (Figure 9). The main area of either stain measures approximately 12 inches across and roughly 8 inches high, and it is evident from
their blotchy appearance that they were caused by two pools of intermin-
gling fluid, two bloody, watery puddles. The pools are connected by one or
two trickles of blood that traverse the small of the back.

These stains have always been misinterpreted. Louise de Vargin, the
sixteenth-century mother superior in charge of mending the cloth after the
devastating fire, thought that they were the bloody traces of a chain used
to bind Christ to the column of flagellation.[50] A similar interpretation may
have prevailed earlier, since the stains are apparently depicted in the
fourteenth-century pilgrim's badge as a length of rope. Such ideas may
now seem naive, but modern interpretations of the stains are no more
logical. Most sindonologists connect them with a second, hypothetical flow
of blood from the lance wound, thought somehow to have poured out and
pooled across the back. Barbet and Bucklin both imagine a hemorrhage

occurring as the body was carried to the tomb.[51] The most obvious problem with this idea is that it is incompatible with the way the stains extend outward from the body-image onto the cloth. Others assume that an outflow took place when the body was laid in the Shroud and perhaps tilted back and forth.[52] These suggestions proceed from the same basic misconception: that the dorsal pools of "blood and water" are connected with the side wound. This is demonstrably incorrect; these stains have no more to do with the side wound than they do with a rope or chain.

To begin with, they are in the wrong place. The top of the left-hand pool is 8 inches or so below the side wound, from which the "blood and water" is supposed to have issued. Any "blood and water" from the side wound that fell down the side of the body would have traversed the back much higher up. Secondly, blood and serum are not like oil and water—they mix—so it is hard to see how they could have remained separate. Thirdly, the clot visible beneath the side wound shows that only a very small amount of blood oozed from it when the body was on the cross. Why would a great stream of blood and serum have poured forth from the wound subsequently, when the body was horizontal? Fourthly, the image of the side wound disproves the idea that there was a second, major flow down the right flank of the body: not only does the clot appear intact, but also, had there been such a flow, blood would have covered the area to the right of the wound. Fifthly, if the body had been tipped to the left, causing the spillage to traverse the back, fluid from the wound would also have traversed the front of the figure. Finally, the pool on the right cannot have had its source in the pool on the left: the trickles that connect them cannot have conveyed more than a fraction of the liquid required, and they cannot have separated out again into distinct areas of blood and serum. What we have are two separate pools that formed on the cloth either side of the body, one of which dribbled across and met the other.

So, if the stains cannot logically be linked to the side wound, how are they to be explained? The answer, I think, is that they were created during the ritual washing. The reason they look like pools of intermingled blood and water is because they were caused by . . . intermingled blood and water. There is no need to invoke vast amounts of separated blood serum. And, if we think carefully about the washing of the corpse, we will see that the position of the pools relative to the body makes perfect sense.

In most places on the body water did not come into contact with fresh, uncongealed blood. As we have seen, the scourged legs and torso of the Shroud-man would have been covered in clots, which were washed off the body and discarded. These clots did not mix with the water and left no trace on the Shroud. The major post-mortem blood flows, which were probably still moist when the body was laid on the Shroud, were those connected with the side wound, the feet and the wrists and forearms. This lifeblood had to be preserved, while the corpse had to be washed all over. It would have been relatively easy to avoid the side wound while washing the torso; it would have been more difficult to avoid the blood on the feet, but it seems the feet were not washed very thoroughly.[53] The trickiest area, undoubtedly, would have been the wrists and forearms. And it was just beneath the forearms that the symmetrical pools of blood and water formed.

Imagine someone kneeling down beside the body and washing one of these limbs. The water would have flowed down the forearm and dripped onto the cloth in the vicinity of the elbow, just where the dorsal pools are located. Elsewhere, the water falling on the cloth would have been clear, but here it became mixed with the fresh blood on the forearm, which had oozed out when the nail was removed from the wrist. As dirt and old, clotted blood were removed, some of the lifeblood would have reliquefied and washed down onto the cloth.[54] Splashes of pure water would have followed, creating the marbled effect that we see. It would not have mattered to the buriers that the lifeblood did not remain in situ, as long as it remained with the body.[55] Just off the right elbow we can witness the last dribble to descend: a large drop of viscous blood seems to have trickled down the underside of the cloth (once it was laid over the arm) and pooled on the surface below.[56]

The ritual washing of the arms also helps explain the fragmentary state of the forearm bloodstains. But for a gentle wiping with wet cloths, they would appear intact. The most vivid sign of the washing, other than the dorsal pools themselves, is the blood on the left wrist. This stands out on its own, implying that it seeped from the wound after the surrounding area was washed clean. Zugibe has argued that this pattern was created when "a clot or pseudo-clot of dried blood was disturbed, causing an oozing of the blood."[57] He suggests that this occurred when the nail was drawn from the wrist, but it is more likely, in my opinion, that it resulted from the ritual washing. The hand was in the same position we see now, and the blood dribbled down naturally across a clean wrist.

The watery bloodstains beside the dorsal figure are explicable, then, as residues of the ritual cleansing. Misunderstood by modern sindonologists and Renaissance observers alike, they provide unexpected confirmation that the Shroud once wrapped the body of a crucified Jew.

The only skeptic to have ventured an interpretation of the dorsal pools, as far as I am aware, is Joe Nickell, who claims that they resemble rivulets of blood in medieval paintings and dismisses them as "a clever touch by a shrewd artist anxious to impart 'realism.'"[58] This does not make sense. No medieval artist ever painted anything resembling the dorsal pools on the Shroud. Suppose some out-of-time genius had come up with this "clever touch": it would have been utterly lost on his contemporaries, who had no idea that the body of Jesus had been washed and would hardly have been able to reconstruct the hypothetical process that resulted in the stains. Moreover, the concept of "realism" that Nickell invokes did not exist in the fourteenth century. In the Middle Ages, the "real" was the realm of abstract ideas thought to be behind and above the transient, perceptible world, and paintings seemed more "real," therefore, the better they expressed that ideal realm. Christ was a manifestation of the divine on earth, and no one would ever have represented his Holy Blood as a messy puddle, unconnected with his wounds, in order to indicate an incidental fact about his burial. More than any other mark on the cloth, the blood and water across the back are inconceivable as part of a medieval forgery.

Perhaps the most surprising feature of the blood-image is the pattern of bloodstains on the head. There are a number of prominent blobs and dribbles on the facial image above the level of the eyebrows, some of them ill-defined, others quite distinct. More bloodstains are found on the back of the head (Figure 32). Here, despite a marked asymmetry, there is a rather more ordered arrangement. A few smudges of blood are visible on top of the scalp, but the majority of the marks form a loose ring around the base of the skull. The Shroud-man's head evidently suffered numerous small puncture wounds. Given this evidence, "it is virtually impossible," as Wilson says, "not to envisage an object very like a crown of thorns."[59] It does not suggest a spiky circlet, though, of the sort invariably depicted by medieval artists (cf. Figures 23 and 24). The bloodstains near the top of the head, especially those on the dorsal view, imply a sort of cap that covered the whole head. It is unlikely that a medieval artist, trying to imagine the effects of the crown of thorns, would have so departed from convention.[60]

Indeed, the bloodstains on both the frontal and dorsal images of the head look like no artistic representation of blood that I know—medieval or otherwise. It is extraordinarily difficult to disguise habitual methods of depiction, and when artists try to simulate blood flows the results are always more-or-less formulaic. It stretches credulity to think that in the Middle Ages, an era of rigid stylization, anyone could have designed such a convincing spattering—or would have wanted to. The blood we see on the Shroud is not crafted as a sign, as it would have been in the fourteenth century; it is not controlled by convention or technique. To regard these haphazard dabs and runnels of blood as fourteenth-century brushwork is to ignore the limits of medieval art and to misunderstand the whole tenor of medieval thought.

So, how were these marks produced? Exactly as it appears: by the removal of a crown of thorns. This operation appears to have occurred when the body was laid out horizontally. With the head tilted forward in rigor mortis (a condition discussed in the next chapter), the blood would have flowed down naturally, as if on a semi-upright figure (cf. Figure 26). The head must have been washed first, so that, when the crown was removed, any lifeblood that seeped out could be left undisturbed. This may account for the rather wishy-washy appearance of some of the bleeding, particularly on the back of the head. Rather than stemming directly from wounds, some of the stains, such as the prominent inverted-3-shaped one on the forehead, may represent drops that fell from the thorns as they were removed.[61]

The bloodstains on the head, then, are traces of a crown of thorns, removed from the head of a man who was crucified in the Roman manner and buried according to the custom of the Jews. Historically, we know of only one Roman Jew who was crucified wearing a crown of thorns: Jesus. The implication is that the Shroud is the very cloth in which Jesus was wrapped for burial.

"Too good to be true"—that is a regular response to the Shroud of Turin. Without even looking at it, most people make a rough calculation (based on all sorts of hidden assumptions) that it is plainly incredible, not even worth considering. The doubts creep in only when and if—a rare event— they start studying the cloth. Surprisingly, perhaps, the overwhelming majority of those who consider the matter carefully (including atheists, agnostics and non-Catholic Christians with a healthy disregard for religious relics) conclude that the Shroud might very well be what it purports to be: the winding sheet of Jesus. And the primary evidence that leads to this conclusion is the pattern of injuries apparent on the cloth. Far from being too good to be true, the Shroud's blood-image seems too good to be false.

Medically attested as a convincing representation of severe injuries and chemically proven to consist of blood, there is no rational reason to deny that the bloodstains are natural traces of a man crucified in accordance with Roman practice, crowned with thorns and buried as a Jew. The notion that such a physiologically and archeologically accurate image could or would have been painted (in blood) by a medieval artist is patently absurd. As the great Jewish art historian Ernst Kitzinger is reported to have said, "there are no paintings that have blood marks like those of the shroud. You are free to look as you please but you won't find any."[62] If the blood-image is not painted, it must derive from a genuine death and burial. Comparing it with the texts of the Gospels, the historical origin of the Shroud seems clear. As Yves Delage concluded over a century ago, it shows every sign of being the burial cloth of Jesus, a "historical personage" whose body could have left "a material trace of his existence" as well as any other.

Perhaps, if the Shroud had borne only blood marks, its authenticity would have been accepted long ago. After all, there is nothing particularly marvelous, to most people's minds, about a bloodstained linen cloth. But the blood-image is not alone; it is ghosted by the body-image, wherein lies the enduring mystery of the Turin Shroud. It is this that causes such anxiety among skeptics—and such enthusiasm among devotees.

11

The Body-Image

Given the evidence of the blood-image, backed up by the scientific findings described in Chapter 9, we might be forgiven for presuming that the body-image must be the genuine imprint of a crucified man (of whatever date). In a case as controversial as the Shroud, however, we cannot afford to make any such presumption. The bloodstains may be real, but perhaps the body-image was superimposed on them by an artistic mastermind of the Middle Ages (explaining why the yellow body-image fibers are not found beneath the blood). To be sure that the body-image is a genuine human imprint, we need to analyze it on its own terms, piecing together the evidence just as we did for the blood-image.

This means that we have to confront head-on the idea that the Shroud is a forgery. Every now and then, an intrepid investigator claims to have rediscovered the method by which a medieval artisan managed to endow the Shroud with a faint, life-sized, front-and-back portrait of a naked man. First we are told that it is a scorch produced by a hot metal statue; then we are asked to believe that it is a unique example of medieval photography; next it is claimed to be nothing but the "shadow" of a figure painted on glass. Recently, an Italian professor "recreated" the Shroud's body-image by draping a cloth over a volunteer and dabbing it with dilute sulfuric acid.[1] There appears to be no end to the ingenuity of modern Shroud-sleuths, hot on the trail of a dastardly medieval hoaxer. And then there is the old claim that it is just a clever painting, the default assumption of skeptics until the 1970s and an idea doggedly maintained by the Shroud's would-be debunker, Walter McCrone.

Art historians, who are familiar with the forms, ideas and techniques of medieval art, have studiously ignored all these suggestions, as if tacitly denying that the Shroud can be understood as a medieval artifact. So how should we judge the various forgery theories? Are they serious contributions to an art-historical debate that qualified academics have been too timid and unimaginative to join? Or are they just half-baked ideas, contradicted by the opinion of numerous medics that the body-image, like the blood-image, reflects a real, crucified body? Only careful scrutiny of the cloth can help us decide.

Rather than consider every forgery theory, we shall look at three prominent ones that illustrate the main issues: McCrone's painting theory; Joe Nickell's rubbing theory; and Nicholas Allen's proto-photography theory. We will then consider the obvious alternative, that the Shroud's body-image is a stain produced by a human body enveloped in the cloth. This will enable us to determine whether or not it is consistent with the evidence of the blood-image and prepare the way for a full explanation of the Shroud's origin.

From an art-historical point of view, the idea that the Shroud's body-image was painted shortly before 1356, the approximate date of its first display in Lirey, is untenable. The Shroud's image is quite unlike any painting of the period—or, indeed, of any period. In the words of Ernst Kitzinger, "The Shroud of Turin is unique in art. It doesn't fall into any artistic category."[2] You only have to compare the frontal figure (Figure 2) with Duccio's delicate, awkward image of the flagellated Christ (Figure 30) to see that it could hardly be the work of even the most skilled fourteenth-century painter.

Walter McCrone was of a different opinion. Based on nothing other than an examination of some fibers lifted from the cloth (his motto was "think small"), McCrone came to the conclusion that the Shroud was merely an "inspired" painting, produced using red ochre and vermilion pigments bound in a very dilute watercolor medium. In an effort to bolster his argument, he drew attention to a couple of *sinopie* paintings by Simone Martini—in his words "two excellent monochrome examples of paintings in the style of the Turin 'Shroud' "—which he happened across on a trip to Avignon. He even toyed with the idea that Simone could have painted the Shroud.[3]

To appreciate the emptiness of this claim, compare the Shroud-face with Simone's *sinopia* portrait of Christ (Figure 33). (*Sinopie* are underpaintings executed in red ochre that exist beneath all fourteenth-century frescoes; they are not a particular "style" of painting, but part of a regular wall-painting technique.) Sketchy though it is, Simone's painting is confident and bold. It represents an elegant, sinuous ideal, characteristic of Gothic art, compared with which the Shroud-face is lumpen and rough. Christ's countenance was conceived in the Middle Ages as an image of perfection—beautiful, symmetrical and unblemished. Yet the Shroud-face is thoroughly awkward and asymmetrical—by the standards of Simone's time, ugly. As a representation of the human face of God it would have been regarded as hopelessly inadequate.

Having established the oval form of Christ's face, Simone delineates his features, including a delicate mouth and some beautiful, almond-shaped eyes, then brushes in the hair and a few shadows, always following the imagined contours of the form. This is how all fourteenth-century painters operated, and it is hard to believe that an anonymous genius could have abandoned this practice and painted an image as impressionistic as the Shroud. The difference is most strikingly apparent in the eyes: in place of Simone's finely drawn eyelids and irises, the Shroud-face has two vague hollows, which seem lit from within. No fourteenth-century painter could possibly have imagined Christ's gaze as bright and vacant as this.

Of course, we now know why this face looks the way it does. Seen "in negative," the odd blotches are transformed into a stunningly realistic representation of a bearded man, his eyes firmly closed (Figure 16). It is important to remember, though, that, until the end of the nineteenth century, only the actual image on the cloth was known (Figure 3), and it was this image with which any medieval artist would have been concerned. It is not the sort of image that a medieval artist would have produced, and the fact that it has an invisible structure, which could not have been appreciated then by anyone, is utterly damning for the painting hypothesis. What artist is going to work from a vision as coherent as that of the photographic negative and deliberately transform it into the peculiar image on the Shroud? How could a fourteenth-century artist have achieved such a transformation, even if he had wanted to?

Then there are the scientific objections. For a start, there is no sign of any pigment or binding medium.[4] No artist could or would have colored just the topmost fibers of the cloth with an undetectable, non-liquid substance and then turned it over and done the same in the region of the hair. STURP also observed that the colored fibers remained the same next to the 1532 scorches, indicating they had nothing to do with an organic pigment, which would have been discolored by the heat. The body-image was equally unaffected by the water damage represented by the diamond-shaped water stains, meaning the color is insoluble, ruling out the use of a water-based paint medium.[5] Finally, Don Lynn and Jean Lorre used a microdensitometer to show that the coloring of the body-image is entirely directionless, i.e. there is no sign of any brushwork.[6]

McCrone based his interpretation of the Shroud as a painting on his observation of certain "pigment particles" on the fibers of the cloth, but these are best interpreted in other ways. Particles of iron oxide (the constituent of "red ochre") can indeed be observed on and in the fibers of the cloth, but they are not the cause of the image.[7] Unlike pigment particles, they are tiny and very pure and must have formed during the process of manufacture, when the cloth was retted (i.e. soaked) in iron-containing water.[8] The odd particle of vermilion, on the other hand, which McCrone linked to the blood-image, should be understood as contamination, probably derived from the painted copies laid on the Shroud in centuries past.[9]

For a number of reasons, then, it is inconceivable that the Shroud is a medieval watercolor. Keen to be the one to solve the mystery and unwilling to look up from his microscope, McCrone interpreted his observations hastily and unrealistically, ignoring a great deal of evidence to the contrary. Tellingly, he failed even to convince his fellow skeptics, which is why, decades later, they continue to explore more exotic solutions.[10]

The photographic negative of the Shroud-face proves that the image involves some sort of automatic transformation. However it was produced, it evidently derived from a model that resembled the photographic negative, not just from an idea in an artist's head. Any plausible theory of its creation, then, must be able to account for this transformation. Recognizing this, skeptics more visually astute than McCrone have tried to come up with a technique that might achieve the requisite transformation and also satisfy STURP's observations regarding the appearance and chemistry of the body-image. A relatively well-known "solution" is that proposed by Joe Nickell, one of the Shroud's most determined opponents.

Essentially, Nickell thinks that the body-image is a type of rubbing.[11] He presumes, first of all, that an unknown fourteenth-century artist made a life-size, front-and-back, bas-relief (low-relief) sculpture of the dead Christ—a monumental task he takes for granted. He then supposes that, having loosely molded a wet cloth over the sculpture and allowed it to dry, the artist dabbed the whole figure with powdered iron-oxide pigment (red ochre), producing an impression. This could have achieved a sort of "negative" effect, if the artist avoided dabbing the hollows.

When Nickell first expounded his theory in February 1978, he thought this was all there was to it.[12] STURP's investigations forced him to concede, however, that the body-image is not due to iron oxide (only trace amounts of which can be detected on the cloth) but to the straw-yellow color of some of the linen fibers. To accommodate this awkward finding, he now says that all the pigment must have fallen off the cloth and that the present image is an unintended "ghost," the result of the vanished iron oxide having degraded (dehydrated and oxidized) the underlying cellulose.[13] (Regarding the blood marks, he simply denies STURP's findings and assumes they were brushed on by a painter.)

Nickell's theory is no more plausible than McCrone's. If the body-image was made by dusting red ochre on the cloth, significant residues of the pigment should remain, which is not the case. And the idea that powdered pigment would have affected only the topmost fibers is untenable. Rather than sit on top of the cloth, the pigment particles would have become lodged between the threads, discoloring fibers throughout the weave.[14]

Perhaps the clearest refutation of Nickell's hypothesis is his own attempt to produce a copy of the Shroud (Figure 34). Like most such attempts, it is limited to the area of the face. If a modern debunker cannot be bothered to reproduce the whole figure, front and back, it is difficult to see why a medieval hoaxer would have been any more industrious. A "Holy Face" would have been much easier to make than a full-body image, and it would have been much more saleable, too. The main problem, though, is the quality of the image. Can Nickell really believe that his crude daub is equivalent to the astonishingly lifelike and subtle Shroud-face?

This returns us to the essential problem with most forgery hypotheses: the fundamentally *inartistic* quality of the Shroud. Medieval artists were not merely incapable of representing Christ as realistically as he appears in the Shroud; they had no wish to represent him that way. In medieval art Christ's face, an unalterable sign of his divinity, remained perfect even after the Passion (cf. Figures 23 and 24). The rugged Shroud-face is completely different, displaying clear signs of injury (Figure 16). The nose is disjointed, and medics are agreed that this represents "a clear separation of the cartilage from the nasal bone."[15] There is also a severe swelling just below the right eye. It seems as if the face was struck a heavy blow, breaking the nose and wounding the area of the right cheekbone.[16] This is consistent with its being the imprint of a bruised and battered face; it is not consistent with its being based on an artistic model of the Middle Ages.

Besides the stylistic difficulties, the proposed technique is inherently unlikely. Nickell supposes that instead of simply painting a cloth—a method that satisfied plenty of other relic-mongers and relic-consumers in the Middle Ages—some eccentric genius invented an expensive and laborious image-making process that lessened his control of the final image and involved the production of a disposable, 14-foot-long bas-relief. The imagined sculpture would have been extraordinary: it would have been vast compared with any other bas-relief of the time; it would have portrayed

Christ naked, which was virtually never done; it would have shown his face disfigured; and it would have been without any discernible trace of medieval style. This unlikely object was then allegedly used as the basis for an unprecedented, undocumented rubbing technique, which has not been adequately demonstrated and is itself artistic, rather than automatic.[17] Supposing, for a moment, that all this could have been accomplished, why would the artist have left the frontal figure incomplete, omitting the feet? Why would he have produced just a single fake relic when, using the same bas-relief, he could have produced dozens? And why go to such trouble to produce an item so extraordinary that it was bound to be considered suspect?

Nickell implies an art-historical episode so bizarre, speculative, impractical and anachronistic that it is quite unbelievable. The Shroud is not the rubbing of a fourteenth-century sculpture, any more than it is a painted icon. In fact, as many skeptics have now realized, given its astonishing lifelikeness and dissimilarity to any medieval work of art, the image can only be the automatic likeness of a real human body.

Working on the assumption that the cloth is medieval, skeptics have come up with several suggestions as to how the likeness of a naked man might have been imprinted on the Shroud. The most popular idea, publicized via recent TV documentaries, is that the Shroud is the world's first photograph, a technological feat centuries ahead of its time. The notion is instantly intriguing, and, at first glance, the negative photo of the Shroud does look quite like a photograph. But is it genuinely photographic? And could photography really have been invented—and then forgotten again—500 years before its development in the nineteenth century?

The "proto-photo hypothesis," as it may be called, was developed during the 1990s by two British researchers, Lynn Picknett and Clive Prince, and also, independently, by a South African art historian, Nicholas Allen. Prompted by a shadowy informant named "Giovanni," a self-proclaimed member of the Priory of Sion, Picknett and Prince swallowed the idea that the Shroud was created in 1492 by Leonardo da Vinci, the only person capable, in their view, of such a brilliant, audacious fraud. He did it by photographing one of the corpses he used for dissection (except for the head, which is apparently a self-portrait) and then painting on the bloodstains.[18] Fun as it is, this scenario is wholly implausible and is contradicted by mountains of evidence, not least the fact that the Shroud was being displayed in France a hundred years before Leonardo was born. Allen's theory, that the Shroud was created by an unknown alchemist working in the late thirteenth or early fourteenth century, is slightly more satisfactory from a historical point of view, and his experimental results are rather better. It represents the best case that can be made for the proto-photo hypothesis.[19]

Unlike the majority of Shroud theorists, Allen has gone to the trouble of producing a full-size, front-and-back replica of the Shroud (minus the bloodstains), using his proposed technique. Best appreciated via a negative photograph, his pseudo-Shroud certainly bears a superficial resemblance to the original (Figure 35). It was created as follows. First of all, Allen set up a large camera obscura, a device known since antiquity, consisting of a darkened chamber into which light is admitted via a small aperture. Light entering the chamber is projected onto a surface, where it casts an upside-down image of the view outside the chamber. Allen's camera obscura was a blacked-out shed with an aperture in one of the windows. Finding that a pinhole could not produce a sufficiently bright image, Allen fitted the aperture with a large, optical-quality, biconvex lens made of quartz crystal. (A glass lens, he found, would not let in enough ultraviolet light to achieve his purpose.) He then placed a long linen cloth on a vertical screen within the room and positioned it to receive the focused light entering through the lens. The cloth had previously been soaked in a silver sulphate (or silver nitrate) solution and dried in the dark, rendering it mildly sensitive to ultraviolet light. Next, Allen hung a plaster cast of a human body (in place of a real, dead body) outside the room in front of the aperture, so that its image was projected onto the linen cloth (Figure 36). He then left the apparatus in place for four days, over which time a faint image formed. The plaster cast was then rotated, so that its back faced the camera, and the other half of the cloth was exposed for a similar period of time. Finally, the cloth was washed in an ammonia solution (or urine), removing the silver sulphate and fixing a straw-yellow image, something like the body-image of the Shroud.

Before analyzing this experiment, let us consider the basic historical proposition: that some lone genius invented a form of photography around 1300 and used it—just once—to produce an extraordinary fake relic. Is this credible?

It is true that educated individuals knew about the camera obscura in the Middle Ages, and Allen was careful to use only materials and compounds that were available at the time, but putting everything together to produce his photographic apparatus would have been a feat of unparalleled scientific genius. It could only have been the result of prolonged research and development. The nineteenth-century pioneers of photography, men such as William Henry Fox Talbot, worked on the problem for decades, experimenting with various procedures and taking account of each other's experiments. It took a great deal of trial and error, in other words, in an age far more technologically advanced than the fourteenth century, to produce the modest results hailed as revolutionary by Fox Talbot's contemporaries. Inevitably, the process left a trail of documentary evidence. Allen's medieval alchemist, though, is presumed to have worked in utter secrecy, perfecting his technique in isolation, leaving no trace of his ideas and experiments other than the Shroud itself. This is implausible. Over the course of the succeeding five centuries many clever people were intensely interested in optics and alchemy without ever coming close to inventing photography. When the idea did arise in the nineteenth century it did so in a culture that was visually experimental and alive with the spirit of scientific collaboration.[20]

The idea of a medieval proto-photo, then, is extremely dubious. And the practical problems inherent in producing the particular image on the Shroud—a life-size image of a dead man—make the scenario even less likely. To get enough focused light entering the room, Allen's hypothetical forger would have needed to have fitted the aperture with a very special lens, long before the earliest recorded use of a lens in a camera obscura.[21] Moreover, as Antonacci comments, "Since optical-quality quartz lenses do not appear historically until the nineteenth century, Allen has the burden of demonstrating how a 7-inch, optical-quality, biconvex quartz-crystal lens without any imperfections" could have been made in the Middle Ages.[22] Once the equipment had been assembled, including this unlikely optical tool, the forger would have had to have procured a dead body and prevented it decomposing over the course of an eight-day exposure. If he knew how to do this, he knew more than modern doctors.[23]

Allen's theory is also in conflict with several important observations. If the cloth was soaked in silver nitrate or silver sulphate, traces of it would remain, yet the X-ray fluorescence spectrometry conducted by STURP found no trace of silver on the Shroud.[24] Even more damning is the recent detection of an image on the reverse side of the cloth. There is no way light could have penetrated the threads (mainly in the region of the hair) and reacted with silver nitrate/sulphate on the other side. Finally, although Allen acknowledges that blood is present on the Shroud, he believes the bloodstains were applied by an artist and ignores STURP's finding that they were present on the cloth before the body-image.[25] Tellingly, he does not even attempt to replicate them.

What about Allen's replica of the Shroud? Might this stand as evidence that some sort of photographic technique produced the image, even if the precise details have yet to be worked out? Quite the reverse. As one of STURP's professional photographers, Barrie Schwortz, has argued, Allen's experiment serves as a very useful demonstration that the Shroud-image is *not* photographic.[26]

The first and most important way in which the proto-photo differs from the Shroud is in its lighting. Allen's figure is noticeably top-lit, due to the sun passing daily overhead. The tops of the head, shoulders, chest, forearms, knees and feet all register as particularly bright, these being the areas on which sunlight fell most consistently and intensely. The Shroud figure, by contrast, looks as if it were lit from directly in front, since only the most forward parts of the body are visible.

We can also tell that Allen's plaster cast was lit, during the course of the day, from either side. For example, the left calf is most strongly illuminated on the left, the right calf on the right, an effect that registers the shifting position of the sun. The Shroud figure, though, is not side-lit at all; it actually fades out completely at the edges.

This highlights—literally—another major difference between the two images: the Shroud is much less sharp and focused than Allen's proto-photo. The outlines of the latter are relatively distinct, and it registers more accurately the form of small features such as the kneecaps and ribs. Compared with the clearly defined proto-photo, the Shroud figure looks like an anthropomorphic cloud. It was evidently the result of a much vaguer image-forming process than photography.[27]

The starkest difference between the two images is in the area of the feet. In Allen's proto-photo the feet are so strongly illuminated that it looks almost as if the figure was wearing white socks; on the corresponding section of the Shroud, there is no sign of the feet at all. On the one hand, this is conclusive evidence that the Shroud was not produced by light reflected from a suspended body. On the other hand, it is a very strong indication that the image is some sort of stain produced by a body draped in the cloth. To understand why, we need to move on from the fantasy of medieval photography and think about the Shroud as a potential burial cloth.

Supposing a body could leave an impression of itself on a cloth, might it have left one resembling the image we see on the Shroud?

Let us look, first of all, at the feet. As just noted, the feet are not represented on the frontal figure. They are clearly discernible, however, on the dorsal figure (Figure 27). The sole of the right foot can be seen in its entirety, while the left presents an image of only the heel. The toes point inward, as if the feet were overlapping slightly, left over right.

These imprints have caused a good deal of confusion in the past, it being commonly supposed that the feet must have lain on the cloth more or less horizontally. This is the opinion of Isabel Piczek, a professional artist, whose reconstruction of the Shroud-man's pose has been particularly influential. Piczek surmises from the position of the hands that the legs must have been bent considerably at the knees, allowing the feet to rest almost flat on the ground.[28] (Anatomically, it is impossible to plant your foot flat on the ground while lying down, unless your legs are bent almost at a right angle.) With all due respect to Piczek, the idea that the Shroud-man's knees were bent is entirely unfounded. The position of the hands can be explained otherwise (see below), and, given their length, there can be no appreciable foreshortening of the legs. Instead, the backs of the knees must have rested close to the cloth, which means that the feet must have been pointing upward. How, then, did the man's soles leave an imprint on the cloth? Very easily, because, however inflexible the human body may be, linen is extremely flexible. All that was needed was a simple fold.

Imagine a body lying supine on a linen cloth with its legs almost straight and its feet pointing upward, slightly overlapping. The cloth extends 18 inches or so beyond the heel. Then suppose that the end of the cloth is wrapped up over the toes, and that, while it is in that position, the legs and feet leave a mark on the linen. (This arrangement is illustrated in Figure 37.) When straightened out again, the cloth would exhibit an image exactly like that seen on the dorsal section of the Shroud.

The same pose can account for the absence of any image of the feet on the frontal view. If the legs were more-or-less straight and the feet were pointing upward, the upper half of the cloth could have been stretched from beneath the knees up and over the toes, losing contact with the shins and hanging clear of the feet. The wrapping and draping of the cloth over the feet is the only rational explanation for the way the feet are both represented and not represented on the Shroud.[29]

This begins to reveal the character of the image-forming process. Clearly, the image appears wherever the cloth was in contact with the body, but it is not dependent on contact, because, instead of stopping abruptly at the edges, it fades away gradually. This fits in with what we have already learned about the 3-D character of the image: the intensity of the image is proportional to the cloth's distance from the body, soon fading away to nothing. The image of the feet also indicates that the cloth was draped over the body rather loosely, not tied in place, as a shroud would usually have been. This is interesting, because it indicates that the burial was left unfinished, a circumstance suggested also by the absence of any traces of aloes or myrrh on the cloth.[30] Whoever laid the man to rest must have envisaged the burial being completed later. Moreover, the fact that the Shroud appears unaffected by any signs of liquid decomposition implies that the cloth was separated from the body within a few days, perhaps by those who came to complete the burial, perhaps through some agency unknown.[31] Anyhow, people must have visited the tomb for the cloth to have been retrieved.

The loose draping of the cloth helps explain the relatively undistorted appearance of the frontal figure. Had the cloth been wrapped around the man tightly, his sides would have stained the cloth, too, and the image would appear much "fatter." Laid over him loosely, however, the cloth would have fallen away from the body at the sides, and only his frontal aspect would have been imprinted.[32]

Nevertheless, we should expect to be able to detect some lateral distortion of the figure, and, in fact, we can.[33] Careful examination of the legs reveals some telling signs. The image is thinnest at the knees. Just above this level, the base of the right thigh bulges out quite markedly—much more so than its counterpart on the left. The image of the right shin also extends out from the knee further than the left. These effects are subtle but discernible in all photos of the Shroud. To account for the apparent discrepancy between the widths of the two legs and the slight "indent" in the image beside the right knee, we need only presume that the cloth was slightly less taut on this side, remaining closer to the thigh and shin for longer as it descended to meet the other half of the cloth below. This would have exaggerated the width of the muscles with respect to the knee. The side of the kneecap is fairly vertical, so the cloth would have lost contact with the flesh here relatively swiftly, halting the formation of the image.

Also worth pointing out is the way the thighs widen out on either side toward the top, making it seem almost as if the man had child-bearing hips.[34] This looks very unnatural (a useful comparison is provided by Allen's proto-photo, Figure 35), but it can be explained by the gradual descent of the cloth from the kneecaps to the outer edges of the hips. It is effects such as this that give the lie to all forgery theories.

The dorsal view of the legs provides crucial evidence of the state of the body and its position in death. As we have seen, the left foot appears half-hidden, as if it slightly overlapped the right, and this ties in with the fact that the right calf is much more strongly marked than the left, implying that the left leg was raised a little off the cloth. This arrangement, which is not how the lower legs and feet rest naturally, is best understood in terms of rigor mortis. When someone dies, their body initially goes limp, but within three hours (sooner if the body is hot) a complex chemical reaction in the muscles causes them to become rock hard, and the body remains fixed in position.[35] This is the condition known as rigor mortis. The man wrapped in the Shroud would seem to have died with one foot crossed over the other, his left leg fractionally bent, a position maintained after death.

It might be argued, alternatively, that the Shroud-man was alive and deliberately held his feet in this position for some reason, but, besides being inherently unlikely, this is disproved by the imprint of the buttocks. As pointed out by Keith Laidler, "the gluteus maximus of the buttocks is one of the largest muscles in the human body and would have shown a much greater degree of compression,"[36] assuming it was still supple when laid on the cloth. Laidler takes this as proof that the body was hanging vertically when the image was made, but it is consistent with the man having died in a vertical position and then having been laid on the cloth after the onset of rigor mortis. Doctors who have studied the Shroud are in agreement that rigor mortis is implied by the imprints of the legs and that the pose implies crucifixion.[37]

With regard to crucifixion, the crossing of the feet implies strongly that they were fixed in place by a single nail, driven first through the left foot, then the right. The only practical way for the executioners to achieve this would have been to lash the legs of the victim to the vertical shaft of the cross—otherwise it would have been difficult to hold them still. Since the feet would then have pointed out from the cross, there must have been a footrest beneath the right heel, into which the nail was driven. We know that Roman crucifixions sometimes involved the use of such a footrest, called a *suppedaneum*, because one is illustrated in a third-century graffito of a crucifixion found on the Palatine Hill in Rome.[38] The crossed feet position definitely implies the use of a *suppedaneum*. This is significant, because the use of a single nail and a *suppedaneum* implies expertise on the part of the executioners, expertise that died out following the abolition of crucifixion in the fourth century.

Moving up the frontal figure we come to the hands and forearms. The blank areas around these limbs are very telling: they are where the cloth fell away from the hands and arms and thus avoided being discolored, until it reached the thighs and stomach. This is one of the clearest signs that the image was produced by proximity to the Shroud-man's flesh, not by reflected light (i.e. photography).[39]

The position of the hands is also revealing. They are crossed over the genitals, which is lower on the body than we might expect. If you lie down on a flat surface and attempt to recreate the pose, you will find that your upper arms naturally rest on the ground and your hands cross nearer your navel, about 6 inches higher up the body than on the Shroud.[40] To imitate the Shroud's image, you have to lift your arms and hold them almost straight—an unnatural resting position. What can account for this posture? The answer, I think, is that the man's arms were fixed in rigor mortis and maintained the stiff position they had on the cross, except that they would originally have been splayed out either side of his head. The rigor in the shoulders must have been broken—an operation requiring quite a bit of force—so that the arms could be contained within the narrow sheet (and help preserve the man's modesty).[41]

A point of particular controversy in recent years has been the location of the head on the frontal figure relative to the torso. Comparisons with normal figures (such as Allen's proto-photo) seem to show that the head is situated far too low. It looks, in effect, as if the Shroud-man had no neck. This has encouraged sensationalist claims that the head and body belonged to different people, the image having been cobbled together by whoever faked the Shroud.[42]

The real reason the head appears to rest almost directly on the shoulders has to do, once again, with rigor mortis. From studying the legs of the figure we have deduced that when the Shroud-man died he was suspended vertically. The indications are that he was crucified. At death, therefore, his head would have dropped forward at an angle of about forty degrees to the vertical, bringing his chin down close to the base of his throat. The head remained bowed as the neck muscles developed rigor and was then fixed in that position even after the body was taken down from the cross and laid horizontally. When the cloth was laid over the body, it would have passed almost directly from the top of the chest to the beard (cf. Figure 37), making it seem, when stretched out later, as if the neck was missing.[43]

Of course, this affects the apparent height of the figure. A lot of nonsense has been written about the man's height, based on faulty reconstructions of his pose and failure to distinguish between the Shroud-image and the body itself.[44] Any calculation should take account of the folds and undulations of the cloth, as illustrated in Figure 37. Zugibe is probably right to estimate the man's height at approximately 6 feet.[45] Given the vagueness of the image, the flexibility of the cloth and complications in the areas of the feet and head, no precise measurement can be made.

The other major query concerns the undistorted appearance of the face. It is obvious that, had the cloth been wrapped tightly around a head, the facial image would have been grossly distorted, somewhat resembling a Halloween pumpkin. Books on the Shroud sometimes contain a photo of a cloth imprinted with such an image, in order to demonstrate the problem,[46] and skeptics often argue that the undistorted face is proof that the Shroud was created artificially. The trouble with this argument is that it ignores the particular qualities of the facial image and the likely circumstances of its formation.

To begin with, the angle of the head was a significant factor. It is usually assumed that the head would have been horizontal, maximizing the weight of the cloth on the face and hence maximizing the potential distortion. But this is incorrect. As we have seen, the head was bent forward at an angle of roughly forty degrees. This would have significantly reduced the weight of the cloth on the face, making the undulations less pronounced.

Even so, slight traces of distortion should be apparent, and, in fact, they are, at least on the left-hand side of the face.[47] This is best seen in high-contrast photographs, which show the left eye socket extending further out than it would in a straightforward, frontal view (such as a photo). As luck would have it, the effect of this distortion is minimized, because the image is "cut" at just this point by a batch of warp threads that, for some reason, barely discolored. No such "artifact" appears on the right-hand side, but here the situation is affected by the large swelling discernible just below the right eye, which would have raised the level of the cloth and made it appreciably flatter. We must also bear in mind the condition of the man's nose. Unlike the healthy proboscises that contribute to the pumpkin-face comparisons, the Shroud-man's nose was apparently badly beaten, and it would therefore have been less prominent. Stretched over a swollen cheekbone and a flattened nose (and a moustache and beard), the cloth would have been relatively flat, virtually eliminating any distortion of the face.

But why are the sides of the head not marked at all? And why, instead, is the face framed neatly by the hair? The answer is provided, once again, by Jewish burial practice. It is customary in many cultures to tie a band around the head of a corpse, underneath the chin and over the crown, to prevent the lower jaw dropping and the mouth gaping open. Among ancient Jews, this was considered such an essential duty that it was even permitted to bind up the chin of a corpse on the Sabbath, when no work was allowed.[48] If the Shroud is that of a first-century Jew, we can be virtually certain that, as well as being enshrouded, he would have had his head tied round with a bandage (most likely a rolled-up linen cloth).

There is, in fact, clear evidence that such a band covered the crown of the head: the gap between the frontal and dorsal images. If the Shroud had lain directly on the man's crown, the body-image would have formed here as elsewhere, joining the two figures via a long, sausage-shaped head. The length of the gap, roughly 6½ inches, is too short to allow the cloth to have been raised beyond the range of the image-forming process (somewhere in the order of 2 inches).[49] Therefore, something fairly thin must have lain across the crown of the head, preventing the imprint forming on the Shroud. Given its apparent shape and the ritual requirement to bind up the jaw, this can hardly have been anything other than a bandage.

How can this help explain the undistorted appearance of the face and the locks of hair? Tucked behind the beard, the cloth band would have passed up the sides of the face just in front of the ears, before arching over the top of the head. Its effect would have been to push forward the hair at the sides, and perhaps also above the forehead. Remember that the hair would have been matted with blood and sweat, and that it would have dried while hanging down either side of the bowed head on the cross. Remember, too, that the head did not lie flat in the tomb, but was bent forward. These circumstances would have caused the hair to rest relatively far forward, propped up by the headband, so that it created, in effect, a facial frame.[50] The result was a fortuitous impression of the hair falling down either side of the face like regular locks.

Every part of the body-image, then, even the remarkable image of the head, can be explained in terms of a stain produced by a real human body. Indeed, certain distortions and gaps in the image demand to be explained in these terms. The missing feet and neck of the frontal figure, the blank areas around the hands and forearms, the soles of the feet in the dorsal figure: these speak of the cloth having been draped loosely over the body of a man, not tinted by a medieval artist or subjected to a primitive form of photography.

Moreover, we can tell that the body was fixed in rigor mortis and that, when the man died, he was suspended vertically, his feet crossed one over the other, his head bowed. There can be little doubt that he died of crucifixion. It may be regarded as certain, therefore, that the body-image was imprinted on the Shroud by the same corpse as was responsible for the blood-image. The two superimposed images are in perfect accord; they reinforce each other, proving beyond doubt that the Shroud really did enfold the dead body of a crucified man.

The question is: who was the man, and how did his body leave an eerie stain on its winding sheet?

12

A Natural Image of Jesus?

The signs are that the Shroud once wrapped the dead body of a man crowned with thorns, crucified in accordance with Roman custom and buried as a Jew. There is also strong evidence that the cloth originated in first-century Judaea. We now face the question: who was the man?

The obvious answer—the answer that fits the historical and archaeological evidence—is that he was Jesus, a first-century Jew executed by the Romans as a mock "king." This is what a rational analysis of the Shroud indicates, however astonishing it may seem. The only other conceivable options, taking account of the evidence surveyed so far, are that the Shroud was used to wrap the body of some other ancient Jew crucified as a would-be Messiah, or that it was used to wrap the body of some later unfortunate crucified and buried in deliberate imitation of Jesus. Neither of these options is remotely plausible.

Regarding the first, plenty of Jews were crucified by the Romans, but none other than Jesus, as far as we know, was executed as a Messianic pretender.[1] There is certainly no record of anyone else being crowned with thorns. Moreover, we know that the Shroud-man's burial was left incomplete and that his body was separated from its winding sheet within days of being buried, two unusual circumstances that are compatible with the Gospel accounts of Good Friday and Easter. It would be absurd to suppose that the same circumstances occurred in the wake of the crucifixion of a second would-be Messiah. There is no need to invent a hypothetical Jesus-double when the evidence points to Jesus himself.

Skeptics have concentrated, for obvious reasons, on the second option. Realizing that neither art nor photography can explain the extraordinary body-image, several have speculated that it might be the imprint of a man crucified in imitation of Jesus in the Middle Ages. Thus, for instance, two investigators of Masonic mysteries, Christopher Knight and Robert Lomas, have put forward a scenario in which the Shroud enfolded the still-living body of Jacques de Molay, last Grand Master of the Knights Templar.[2] There is not a shred of evidence, though, that this Templar leader was tortured by crucifixion, and the Shroud-man was definitely dead when he lay in the cloth, which would rule out de Molay, who was burned at the stake. Slightly more sensible is the suggestion of another doubter, Dr. Michael Straiton, that the body was that of an unfortunate Crusader, captured and crucified by Mamluk Turks in the last years of the thirteenth century.[3] This is probably the least implausible idea regarding the Shroud's origin that a skeptic has ever offered, though that is not saying very much.

The Turks may have practiced crucifixion occasionally at the time of the Crusades, but it is a massive leap of faith to imagine that they ever crucified anyone in exact imitation of Jesus. Even if they had wanted to, they could hardly have recreated the complex torture, execution and burial of a first-century Jew without introducing a single anachronism. Just consider what would have been involved.

First, our archeologically minded Muslims would have scourged their prisoner with a Roman-style *flagrum*, before making him carry a crossbeam on his shoulders, in imitation of the Roman custom. Then, rather than bang a nail into the upright through either foot, they would have expertly driven a single nail through both feet, having furnished the cross with a Roman-style *suppedaneum*. Once he was dead, they would have pierced him in the Roman manner beneath the armpit, using a spear like a Roman *lancea*. The reconstruction would have continued after the man was taken down from the cross. Rather than toss him into a simple grave, they would have given him an appropriate Jewish burial, washing away all the blood clots, carefully avoiding the post-mortem "lifeblood," binding up the jaw, and wrapping him in a *sovev*. This linen sheet, of very fine material and manufactured in conformity with ancient Jewish textile-making techniques, would have been sourced from the Jerusalem area, as indicated by the pollen and limestone dust embedded in its weave. Finally, they would have left the burial unfinished, draping the body rather than tying it up, and then they or someone else would have removed the cloth from the body within a few days. All this would have been done, moreover, to a man bearing an uncanny resemblance to the traditional portrait of Jesus (e.g. Figure 33).

The odds against the Mamluk Turks (or anyone else) having performed such a bizarre "action-replay" of the events of Good Friday must be astronomical. As a historical scenario, it is speculative, nonsensical and implausible.[4]

Proponents of this type of coincidence scenario also have to account for the formation of the Shroud. Was it produced intentionally, in order to create a fake relic? Then how was it done? How did the medieval perpetrators devise an automatic image-making technique that has bamboozled generations of modern scientists and has left no other trace in the annals of art and science? Pursuit of this question leads directly into pseudo-historical speculation about proto-photography and the like. Alternatively, was the image just a natural accident, discovered by chance when someone looked inside the burial cloth? But then why not accept that it could have been produced equally well by the dead body of Jesus? If we are prepared to regard the Shroud as the natural result of an execution and burial precisely similar to his, it would be illogical to deny that it could have resulted from the execution and burial of Jesus.[5]

To admit that the Shroud once covered the body of a crucified man, but then to try to pass it off as an accident or forgery from the Middle Ages, introduces all sorts of unnecessary and unlikely complications into the story of the Shroud's origin. There are essentially two reasons to entertain such ideas. The first is an absolute refusal to contemplate the possibility that the Shroud is authentic, that it really is the sheet in which Jesus was (initially) buried. This refusal stems primarily from rationalist fears about the Shroud's meaning. If we think about the potential connection between Jesus and the Shroud a little more deeply, this anxiety should vanish. The second reason is excessive faith in the result of the 1988 carbon-dating test. We shall see just how unsafe this result is in the next chapter.

Fears and faith aside, the empirical evidence we have examined so far is sufficient, in my view, to conclude that the Shroud is indeed the burial cloth of Jesus. This is the only viable explanation for the appearance of these particular marks on this particular piece of linen cloth. The explanation is not yet complete, however: we still have to consider the process by which the body-image was formed.

The great pioneers of sindonology regarded the Shroud as a purely natural phenomenon, the product of an ordinary chemical reaction, whose secret would ultimately be discovered by science.[6] This naturalistic view of the problem has recently borne fruit, as we shall see, in the form of an excellent new hypothesis concerning the image-forming process, based on rigorous scientific research. Since the 1970s, however, many sindonologists have become enthused by the idea that the image is the trace of a miracle, and some have even tried to give this idea a veneer of scientific intelligibility. Traditionally, the Shroud was seen as a miraculous imprint of Christ's sweat-soaked body—a memorial of his death; the new idea is that it was caused by a brief flash of radiation emanating from Jesus' body at the moment of the Resurrection. The Shroud is now frequently thought to provide evidence for the "physics of miracles."

The radiation theory comes in a variety of forms, including the idea that the body suddenly dematerialized, giving off radioactive particles, and the milder suggestion that it emitted X-rays.[7] Some variants, such as the idea that a corona discharge (a type of plasma) was generated between the body and the cloth, do not necessarily involve a miracle, although the sense of the supernatural is never far away.[8] What they all have in common is the assumption that the body became extraordinarily hot and that the image on the Shroud is due to a slight scorching of the cellulose. This basic assumption is at odds with the microscopic analysis of the body-image fibers. As explained previously, it has now been shown that the straw-yellow substance that constitutes the body-image lies on the surface of the fibers and is not part of the cellulose itself. Contrary to STURP's initial conclusion, the cellulose was not scorched or damaged during the image-making process. As Ray Rogers, a pyrolysis expert, has shown, any heat strong enough to discolor the outside of a fiber would have scorched it right through, yet the interiors of the fibers are clear.[9] Having studied the evidence thoroughly, Rogers is adamant: "High-energy radiation can not have been responsible for the color of the image."[10]

The problems with the idea go beyond microscopic contradictions. Even if we accept, for the sake of argument, that a corpse might suddenly emit a burst of radiation, the event would hardly have produced an image like that seen on the Shroud. Take the theory propounded by Mark Antonacci that the body instantaneously dematerialized, letting loose protons and alpha particles (among other things) whose energy was absorbed into the topmost fibers of the cloth, causing them to discolor.[11] Rogers calls this "an outstanding example of goal-directed pseudoscience" and observes drily that "one bothersome problem with Antonacci's 'theory' is that complete conversion of the mass of a normal human body into energy would have the effect of a huge H bomb, on the order of 200–300 megatons of TNT."[12] The Shroud would not have been lightly scorched: it would have disappeared, along with Jerusalem.

Like the French journalist Arthur Loth's suggestion in 1900 that the image was a kind of "electrical impression," a notion obviously indebted to the story of Frankenstein, these recent attempts to interpret the Shroud in terms of the "physics of miracles" owe more to science fiction than scientific fact. They are where sindonology meets *Star Trek*.[13]

When faced with a mysterious phenomenon, it is generally wise to presume that it has a natural cause. Although the Shroud appears to be the result of an otherwise unknown image-forming process, there is no reason to doubt that this process operated in accordance with the known laws of physics. After all, other strange, automatic images are known, and no one invokes miracles to explain them. In 1942 Jean Volckringer, a French pharmacist, drew attention to the beautiful imprints sometimes made by pressed plants on the papers in which they are kept (e.g. Figure 38). These imprints are even more detailed and accurate than the Shroud, and, seventy years later, they have still not been definitively explained.[14] Similarly, in 1981 a remarkable imprint was found on a mattress in a Lancashire hospice, which preserved an outline image of the man who had just died in the bed (Figure 39). He had been suffering from incontinence and pancreatic cancer, and it has been argued that the image was caused by enzymes in his urine reacting with the mattress material.[15] As far as we know, there has never been another image like it, but it is hardly miraculous, and we know that it was not the result of a resurrection. Human bodies, like plants, can sometimes create odd, accidental stains.

The first scientists to ask themselves how the Shroud's image might have formed naturally were Yves Delage and Paul Vignon, over a century ago. Vignon soon realized that two properties of the image—its diffuse character and the apparent correlation between its intensity and the relief of the underlying form—suggested that it had been produced by vapors emanating from a human body. Taking his lead from contemporaries interested in the way photographic plates could be affected by gases (as well as light and other forms of radiation), he conducted an experiment to show how an image similar in quality to the Shroud's body-image could be created by "vaporography." Exposing a suitably sensitized plate to a silver medal coated in zinc powder, which slowly vaporizes, he proved that it was possible to obtain a reasonably clear vaporograph (Figure 40).[16] Moreover, Vignon observed that, like the Shroud's body-image (and unlike a photograph), his "chemical projection" conveyed accurate 3-D information about the medal—it was a contour map.[17] A vaporograph even more three-dimensional in effect was produced by one of Vignon's collaborators, the physicist René Colson, from a small zinc-coated plaster cast (Figure 40).

In recent years sindonologists have completely ignored these experiments and are mostly under the illusion that vapors cannot create a coherent image at all, let alone one containing 3-D information.[18] Had the Frenchmen been able to plug their vaporographs into a VP-8 Image

Analyzer, the enduring significance of their work might have been more widely appreciated.

Unfortunately, having demonstrated a viable physical process, Vignon took a wrong turn regarding the chemistry. Reckoning that the cloth had been anointed with a mixture of myrrh and aloes,[19] he hypothesized that the image was due to a reaction between chemical constituents of the aloes and ammonia vapors rising from sweat on the body (which he thought was unwashed).[20] There were theoretical problems with this idea, and it did not work well experimentally. It was finally put to bed by STURP, whose investigations failed to find any trace of aloes (or myrrh) and revealed that the image resided solely on the surface of the cloth, whereas the ointment hypothesized by Vignon would have penetrated right through.[21] This meant that the particular vaporographic theory developed by Vignon was wrong, but it did not mean that the general concept of vaporography had to be abandoned. STURP, however, threw the baby out with the bathwater. Instead of rethinking Vignon's theory, they ruled out vaporography altogether and began exploring much less promising avenues of research, including direct-contact theories, which Vignon had effectively disproved, and radiation theories, which he had (very sensibly) dismissed out of hand.[22]

Eventually, one of the STURP scientists, Ray Rogers, worked his way back to the idea of vaporography via a meticulous review of all the chemical and microscopic observations of the body-image fibers. In 2003 he co-authored a peer-reviewed paper with another chemist, Anna Arnoldi, which provided, at long last, a convincing chemical explanation for the formation of the body-image, one dependent on the idea of vapors rising from a dead body.[23] A full century after Vignon wrote, scientists may be on the verge of proving that the Shroud is the world's most spectacular vaporograph.

Rogers started by listing everything that was known about the body-image from a scientific point of view: the color and distribution of the body-image fibers, their location on the topmost surfaces of the threads, the lack of any foreign materials on the cloth, and so on. He knew there was no point pursuing a hypothesis unless it could account for all these characteristics of the image. He then concentrated on the structure and appearance of the body-image fibers. The fact that there was no clear sign of any cellulose degradation indicated that, whatever reaction caused the discoloration of the fibers, it must have occurred at a relatively low temperature (under 200°C). Spectral analyzes suggested that the colored layer of each fiber consisted of dehydrated carbohydrates.[24] At first it had been assumed that this layer was part of the cellulose itself, but, as he and Adler had discovered, it could easily be stripped off the fibers, implying that it was composed of impurities on the surface of the cloth. Identifying these impurities was key.

To discover what substances might have been present on the cloth when it was new, Rogers researched the ancient manufacture of linen. During weaving, he discovered, the warp threads would have been protected and stiffened by being coated in starch, a carbohydrate. Then, once the cloth was woven, it would have been washed using soapwort to further whiten it and restore its suppleness. This would have removed most but not all of the starch, and sugars derived from the soapwort would have added to the carbohydrates present in the cloth. Significantly, traces of starch have been found on the Shroud, and there is also evidence that it was washed in soapwort.[25] Finally, the cloth would have been laid over bushes to dry.[26] And it was thinking about this process that gave Rogers the first clue that he was on the right track. He realized that, as the water evaporated, materials dissolved and suspended in it would have been drawn to the surface of the cloth and would have precipitated there, forming a concentrated layer. If these materials were involved in the image-forming process, it would explain why only the topmost fibers bore the image color.

He could now confidently conjecture that the carbohydrates involved in the formation of the image were residues of the manufacturing process. But how had they become dehydrated? Eventually, he hit on an answer, one with major implications for the origin of the Shroud.

Rogers realized that he could be looking at the result of a Maillard reaction: a reaction between carbohydrates and amines (or amino acids). Maillard reactions are very well known, because they are important in food chemistry. They take place at relatively low temperatures, are rapid and produce browning—the golden brown crust on bread, for instance, is due to a Maillard reaction. The reason this idea is so significant is that the amino acids needed to react with the carbohydrates on the cloth *could have emanated from a dead body*. The rank smell of a corpse actually derives from ammonia and amines, such as putrescine and cadaverine, which begin to be produced fairly quickly after death. As Rogers says, "The potential source of amines, a decomposing body, involves support for the hypothesis that the Shroud is a real shroud."[27]

Furthermore, given the right funerary conditions, such a reaction would be inevitable. "When amines and reducing sugars come together, *they will react. They will produce a color*. This is not a hypothesis: this is a fact. A cloth with crude starch on it *will* ultimately produce a color, if it is left in close proximity to a decomposing body."[28] It is worth noting in this regard that cloths enveloping Egyptian mummies are sometimes stained brown, although none is known to bear an imprint like that of the Shroud.[29]

In order to test this, Rogers teamed up with a food chemist, Anna Arnoldi, and ran some experiments. Having obtained a sample of linen made according to ancient methods, they treated it with solutions of soapwort and a starch substitute (dextrin) and then exposed it to ammonia vapors for ten minutes (Figure 41). "A very light color could be observed on the top surface after standing twenty-four hours at room temperature."[30] Looked at under the microscope, the colored fibers had all the characteristics of fibers from the Shroud's body-image: they were golden brown on the outside, clear on the inside, and there was no scorching of the cellulose. The color barely penetrated the cloth, and it was insoluble, as on the Shroud. Rogers and Arnoldi seem to have effectively mimicked the composition and distribution of the color on the Shroud's body-image fibers. This is good empirical evidence that the body-image was caused by a Maillard reaction involving a dead body.

The hypothesis makes sense in various other ways, as well, and may be able to account for some puzzling features of the image. The vapors would not have been able to penetrate the blood on the Shroud, explaining why there is no body-image beneath the blood. Since the intensity of the image is limited by the amount of impurities on the surface of the cloth and has nothing to do with pressure, this would explain why the dorsal image is no more intense than the frontal image.[31] Rogers also argues that the release of ammonia from the mouth and nose of the dead man may help explain the relative darkness of the moustache and beard (and the tip of the nose). Some of the highly volatile ammonia would have diffused across the underside of the cloth, becoming concentrated in the porous mats of hair, which would have inhibited its diffusion. The concentration of ammonia in these areas would have yielded a darker image.[32]

Even more significantly, the Maillard reaction hypothesis can account for the so-called "double superficiality" of the image, the observation that parts of the frontal image (in particular, the hair) show up very faintly on the reverse side of the cloth. Carbohydrate impurities would exist on both surfaces of the Shroud, and, as the amines diffused through the cloth, they would occasionally have come into contact with the impurities on the far side. Generally, the reactions would have been too few to create a visible stain, but where hair acted as a porous barrier to diffusion, more ammonia would have collected and penetrated the cloth, resulting in a very faint reverse image.

The cogency of the Maillard reaction hypothesis is recognized by Zugibe, who concludes that it holds "the most promise" out of any mechanism so far proposed. The only query he has concerns the potential resolution of the image.[33] Rogers and Arnoldi address this issue briefly in their article, citing various factors (such as the rapid diffusion of the amines through the cloth and steep temperature gradients across the cloth's surface) that "would cause a rapid reduction in amine concentrations away from contact points" and hence a relatively focused image.[34] This argument was purely theoretical, but, before his death in 2005, Rogers conducted a couple of experiments to test the theory. These experiments show that, as predicted, reasonably precise images can be created by amine vapors acting on a suitably prepared cloth. To obtain good resolution, the body temperature must be low (to minimize convection), the amines must be released slowly (to avoid "flooding"), and the environment must stay cool and still. These conditions would be met in the case of a corpse laid in a tomb soon after death.[35]

Clearly, then, there is every chance that a dead body could have stained the Shroud via a Maillard reaction, as outlined by Rogers and Arnoldi. Their work has been endorsed in a recent review by Denis Mannix, a retired chemist and former fellow of the Royal Society of Chemistry. Mannix concludes by saying, "Rogers and Arnoldi have been able to show that the image could have been formed through a sequence of well known scientific steps and without any mystery or unproven scientific theory. Their hypothesis provides an explanation for every aspect of the image that has been noted."[36]

Can the Maillard reaction be said to be scientifically proven? Not yet, as Ray Rogers himself was careful to insist. While others have been all-too-ready to say that they have solved the riddle of the Shroud's body-image on the basis of flimsy evidence, Rogers, ever the cautious scientist, knew that further tests were required before his hypothesis could be accepted as fact. What is needed now is for scientists to take his work forward and test whether a Shroud-like image can be formed on appropriately prepared linen using body parts or a whole corpse—a rather gruesome task, but one potentially of huge cultural significance. Only if the Maillard reaction hypothesis can pass this test will we be able to say that a complete explanation of the body-image has been achieved.

Such testing would also shed light on a key question regarding the potential relation of the Shroud to the Gospel accounts of Easter. Sindonologists often assume that the body-image cannot have appeared on the Shroud until after Easter, since there is no apparent mention of it in any of the Gospels.[37] However, Rogers reports that the color was visible after only twenty-four hours in the experiment he ran with Arnoldi, and he also says that Maillard reactions "are rapid at room temperature, or even lower."[38] This issue needs to be studied urgently, for, as we will see, the rate at which the image might have appeared is no side issue: it is of central importance to the interpretation of the Resurrection narratives in the New Testament.

Strangely, despite its tremendous promise, Rogers's hypothesis has been generally ignored. It is now nearly a decade since the publication of the article he co-authored with Arnoldi, yet few sindonologists seem to have recognized its significance, and, as far as I am aware, no further testing is being done. Ian Wilson, the most influential writer on the Shroud, makes no mention of it in his latest book, *The Shroud: The 2000-year-old Mystery Solved*, nor is it mentioned in David Rolfe's film *The Shroud*, produced to accompany the 2010 exhibition. This is curious. One of the most respected and knowledgeable of the STURP scientists finally comes up with a rigorously researched hypothesis that promises to solve the mystery of the image, one that provides strong support for the contention that the cloth once wrapped a dead body, yet sindonologists don't want to know.

One of the reasons, it would seem, is that, although they pay lip-service to the scientific method, many of those involved in studying the Shroud have come to believe, ahead of any scientific evidence, that it is the material trace of a miracle, that its image represents the bright flash of the Resurrection. They do not want to believe that it is a purely natural phenomenon; they prefer to think of it as the result of some sort of divinely induced radiation. Another reason is the widespread misconception that vapors cannot produce a well-resolved image. The fact that the founding text of sindonology, Vignon's *The Shroud of Christ*, proves not only that vaporography is possible, but also that it can record 3-D information in a way that photography cannot, has apparently been forgotten.[39]

Perhaps the main reason for the unpopularity of the Rogers–Arnoldi explanation is its disturbing implication that the body of Jesus began to decompose. This contradicts the "prophecy" quoted by Peter in Acts 2.27—"For thou wilt not abandon my soul to Hades, nor let thy Holy One see corruption"[40]—and it makes the idea of the resurrection of Jesus' body just that little bit harder to believe. Did God have to reverse the rotting of his corpse, as well as restore its vital energy? And what of the molecules that were lost, those tiny parts of Jesus that floated off into the air of the surrounding tomb, those atoms that may inhere, even now, in the Shroud? An image dependent on the decomposing flesh of Jesus might not be as damning for the traditional doctrine of the Resurrection as the discovery of his bones or ossuary would be, but the idea still sits uneasily with Christian sensibilities. Rogers's hypothesis might help prove that the Shroud is a genuine grave-cloth, but at what religious cost?

For those less enamored of the idea of the Resurrection, the virtues of the hypothesis should be clear. As well as being cogent in itself, it fits in with the combined evidence of the bloodstains and the body-image, to the effect that the Shroud once enveloped a dead body. We now have a theory of the formation of the Shroud's image that is unified and virtually complete. And it points unequivocally to the Shroud being the very linen sheet in which the crucified corpse of Jesus was buried on Good Friday. As Yves Delage argued so valiantly at the beginning of the twentieth century, there is no reason to doubt the possible existence of such a relic, however unique it might seem. We possess the burial cloths of Charlemagne and Ramesses the Great—why not the burial cloth of Jesus?

There is just one snag: the carbon dating. It is all very well deducing that the Shroud is authentic on the basis of its image and material characteristics, but what about the physicists' claim that the cloth itself is medieval? Does this not instantly invalidate our conclusion and throw us back, perhaps, on Straiton's dubious idea of a Crusader crucifixion? Well, it would, if nuclear physicists pronouncing *ex cathedra* were infallible, like the Pope. But this is very far from being the case. Carbon-dating scientists, like all human beings, make mistakes. And the medieval dating of the Shroud may be the biggest mistake they have ever made.

13

The Carbon-Dating Fiasco

As far as most people are concerned, the 1988 carbon dating of the Shroud was a definitive test that proved the cloth to be a product of the Middle Ages. The results were presented in a multi-authored article in *Nature*, which claimed that they provided "conclusive evidence that the linen of the Shroud of Turin is medieval."[1] To be precise, the authors found (at a 95 percent confidence level) that the flax of the samples they tested was harvested between 1260 and 1390. The Shroud could not be the burial cloth of Jesus.

Doubting *Nature*, the voice of Science, is quite a proposition. It is tempting, therefore, to bow to the authority of this scientific pronouncement and to give up the complex and difficult struggle to understand the Shroud. But, on reflection, we know that all scientists can err, and even the most polished scientific article can mask errors and false assumptions. So anyone who is serious about comprehending the Shroud will want to subject the carbon-dating result to rigorous scrutiny—the sort of scrutiny used to evaluate all scientific evidence.

As soon as we begin to investigate the carbon dating of the Shroud, its authority starts to fray. Carbon dating is not an "ultimate" test, as is often assumed. Though undeniably useful, its results are often doubtful, and scholars, scientists and conservators are less than sanguine about its reliability. Furthermore, the conduct of the actual test on the Shroud was as messy and unsatisfactory as the conduct of a major scientific project could be. The popular perception that the carbon dating of the Shroud was definitive is simply mistaken.

It should be realized, first of all, that, like any highly complex operation, carbon dating can easily go wrong.

Carbon dating involves measuring the ratio in any carbon-containing material of different carbon isotopes (that is, two different forms of carbon atoms whose nuclei have a different mass). The vast majority of natural carbon is carbon-12 (C-12), a stable isotope, but one in a trillion carbon atoms are carbon-14 (C-14), a radioactive isotope that decays at a known rate. C-14 is constantly being produced in the atmosphere, replenishing the overall stock of C-14 at the same rate that it decays. Along with the much more common C-12, this C-14 then combines with oxygen to form carbon dioxide (CO_2). Photosynthesizing plants, including the flax used to make linen, constantly absorb this CO_2, which then travels on through the food chain. In this way all organisms incorporate throughout their lives a stream of C-14 and C-12 atoms in the same ratio as is found in the atmosphere. Once an organism dies, however, it ceases to absorb carbon, and the ratio of the two isotopes in its remains begins to alter, because the radioactive C-14 decays, while the stable C-12 stays put. It is this difference that allows scientists to measure the amount of time elapsed since the organism's death. They can do so because the precise rate at which C-14 decays is known. Its half-life is 5,730 years; in other words, every 5,730 years its quantity will decrease by half. So by measuring the amount of C-14 in relation to the amount of C-12, it is possible to work out the number of years since the organism died.

The theory of carbon dating, then, is fairly straightforward. The practice, however, is fraught with difficulties. Calculating the ratio of C-14 to C-12 in an organic material is not like counting beads on an abacus; it is a technological feat near the limits of scientific capabilities. A major problem is how to detect the infinitesimal amount of C-14 radiation against the background radiation from other sources. Solving this problem was one of the achievements of Willard Libby, who invented carbon dating in the 1940s. Subsequently, it was discovered via dendrochronology (the study of tree rings) that, due to variations in solar activity, the rate of C-14 production in the atmosphere is subject to minor fluctuations, disturbing the neat ratio of C-14 to C-12. A calibration curve has been derived from the tree-ring data so that this natural variation in C-14 can be accounted for, but the issue highlights the complexity of the problem of age determination, even once the relevant pulses of radiation have been detected.[2]

Other factors can introduce a significant degree of uncertainty into the interpretation of the data as well. Contamination is a major problem. Although various potential sources of contamination are known, including volcanic activity and carbon exchange with the surrounding environment (air, smoke, groundwater, etc.), it is not always possible to explain the cause of an erroneous reading. Due to the ever-present possibility of contamination, no radiocarbon date is absolutely certain. A recent review of the history of carbon dating concludes, with direct reference to the Shroud, that "the issue of organic reactions and non-contemporaneous contamination of ancient materials can be a very serious and complex matter, deserving quantitative investigation of the possible impacts on measurement accuracy."[3] In other words, the problem of contamination is severe and difficult to quantify.

The rejection of carbon-dating results that are incompatible with other evidence is routine in archeology.[4] Since carbon dating sometimes yields such conundrums as an ice-age mammoth dating to around 3600 BC, one can understand why.[5] According to William Meacham, a professional archaeologist, "No responsible field archaeologist would trust a single date, or a series of dates on a single feature, to settle a major historical issue."[6] Unfortunately, the interpretation of the 1988 carbon-dating results was left to the physicists who performed the tests, men who knew little about the Shroud and had no experience in interpreting such a complex artifact.

The problems with carbon dating are most starkly revealed when the results produced by different labs differ among themselves. In 1989, for instance, a year after the Shroud test, the Greek archaeologist Spyros Iakovidis was confronted by a totally incoherent result: "I sent to two different laboratories in two different parts of the world a certain amount of the same burned grain. I got two readings differing by 2,000 years, the archaeological dates being right in the middle. I feel that this method is not exactly to be trusted."[7]

That there are general problems with the technique is acknowledged by carbon-dating scientists themselves. Consider, for instance, the following caution in a 1985 conference paper, one of whose joint authors was Willy Wölfli, one of the professors responsible, three years later, for the carbon dating of the Shroud:

> The existence of significant indeterminate errors can never be excluded from any age determination. No method is immune from giving grossly incorrect datings when there are non-apparent problems with the samples originating in the field. The results illustrated [in this paper] show that this situation occurs frequently.[8]

This is a startling admission. According to Wölfli and his colleagues, in the field of carbon dating gross errors occur frequently. But, while the scientists discuss these problems among themselves, they are less ready to dent the prestige of their discipline in public.

An insight into the potential pitfalls of carbon dating is provided by the record of an inter-laboratory comparison exercise conducted in 1983, in order to prepare the way for the Shroud project.[9] The coordinator of this exercise, as of the 1988 test, was Dr. Michael Tite, head of the British Museum's Research Laboratory. Tite sent three samples of cloth to each of the six participating laboratories (including Arizona, Oxford and Zurich, who would later date the Shroud) and asked them to determine their age. Wölfli's Zurich lab managed to date Sample no. 1 1,000 years too young and Sample no. 3 1,000 years too old. The errors were blamed on mistakes made in cleaning the samples, but, whatever the cause, they hardly re-inforce confidence in the carbon-dating technique.[10] The Zurich "outliers" were a major cause for concern among those who subsequently developed a protocol for carbon dating the Shroud.

The inter-laboratory comparison exercise shows how unreliable the car-bon dating of cloth was prior to the 1988 Shroud test. It was still unreliable immediately afterward. In 1989 Britain's Science and Engineering Research Council (SERC) decided to conduct a trial in which the carbon-dating technique itself would be tested. Thirty-eight laboratories were involved in the trial, each being asked to date artifacts whose age was already known. (For some reason the Oxford lab, one of those that had dated the Shroud the previous year, declined to participate.) The findings, reported in *New Scientist* under the headline "Unexpected errors affect dating techniques," were salutary. It was found that "The margin of error with radiocarbon dating . . . may be two to three times as great as practitioners of the tech-nique have claimed . . . Of the thirty-eight [laboratories], only seven produced results that the organizers of the trial considered to be satisfac-tory."[11] In other words, about 80 percent of the labs failed the test. The three laboratories that dated the Shroud the previous year employed a technique known as Accelerator Mass Spectrometry (AMS), which "came out of the survey badly." According to one of the organizers of the trial, "some of the accelerator laboratories were way out when dating samples as little as 200 years old."[12] So, just a year after the Shroud was damned by AMS, the authority of this carbon-dating technique itself took a severe blow.

There is a vast discrepancy, then, between the popular perception of carbon dating as infallible and its true scientific status. The fact is that carbon-dating results are often wrong, that the claims made on behalf of carbon dating are often inflated, and that the AMS technique used in 1988 to date the Shroud is (or was) particularly error prone. The purvey-ors of any technology, carbon dating included, are inclined to exaggerate its power and usefulness. Also, being physicists, so not embroiled in the business of making historical sense of their findings, they probably have a tendency to underestimate the method's rate of failure. Those responsible for the historical interpretation of ancient artifacts, usually archaeologists, are the ones who decide whether or not to reject carbon-dating results. But, because archaeologists were excluded from the 1988 testing of the Shroud, scientific caution was thrown to the winds when the results of this high-profile test were announced.[13]

How was this situation allowed to occur? The answer lies in the sorry history of the project. People tend to envisage the carbon-dating result as a nice, neat number churned out by a machine, an impersonal, objective answer to a human query. If only the contents of science journals were so straightforward. All scientific work is conditioned by human concerns, and the Shroud carbon dating, in particular, was the product of a lengthy, messy process of politicking that resulted in a deeply flawed procedure, dictated by the Vatican. The public is for the most part ignorant of the quagmire of self-interest and scientific compromise on which the "fact" of the Shroud's carbon dating rests.

Concerted efforts to persuade the Catholic Church to have the Shroud carbon dated began in the late 1970s. Previously, the idea had been discounted, because it would have required a sizeable piece of cloth, which would have been destroyed in the process. In 1977, however, the AMS technique was developed, which could work with samples no bigger than a postage stamp. Professor Gilbert Raes had already been allowed to cut a sample this size in 1973, and it seemed reasonable to expect that the Church might allow a similar piece to be taken for carbon dating. STURP, though, was only allowed to carry out non-destructive tests, and the issue of carbon dating was put on the back-burner for several years.

Keen to be involved in the carbon dating of the Shroud, should it be permitted, was Harry Gove, one of the inventors of AMS. A rather egotistical character, Gove was interested in the project not because he wanted to find out about the Shroud, but because he reckoned it would provide "a highly public demonstration of the power of carbon dating by AMS."[14] In the 1980s he assumed leadership of a group of carbon-dating scientists which began lobbying the Catholic Church for the opportunity to date the Shroud. All were conscious of the potential publicity value of such a test. Prominent among them was Teddy Hall, a professor at Oxford, who was trying to raise funds to endow a chair at the university, a cause he knew would be well served by the high-profile Shroud project. Gove, meanwhile, saw STURP as a biased, Christian organization and a rival to his own group, and agitated to have them excluded from the carbon-dating exercise, despite their detailed knowledge of the cloth.

A "workshop" with the Church authorities in Turin was eventually held in 1986, at which a protocol was agreed to ensure the scientific validity of the test.[15] In retrospect, the most important stipulations were those concerning the sampling procedure, which, as we shall see, lies at the heart of the controversy. It was agreed that "the samples should be taken from an unobtrusive part of the Shroud" and that the "selection of this material to be removed and the actual removal will be the responsibility of Madame Flury-Lemberg." (Two delegates at the workshop—Meacham and Adler—argued in favor of the samples being taken from several different areas of the cloth, but this sound advice was ignored.)[16] The "certifying institutions" responsible for the distribution of the samples to the scientists were to be the British Museum, the archbishop of Turin, and the Pontifical Academy of Sciences (whose president, Professor Carlos Chagas, chaired the workshop). It was also agreed that the carbon-dating samples would be removed "immediately prior to a series of experiments planned by other groups." That is to say, STURP and other interested scientists would be given the opportunity to carry out further tests on the cloth. The number of laboratories to be involved in the carbon-dating test was set at seven, ensuring that, when the results were analyzed, any "outliers" could be statistically identified. And it was explicitly stated that the "taking of samples will be done so that the representatives from the seven laboratories will have complete knowledge of the process." This was because the scientists were concerned to be sure that the samples they received were indeed part of the Shroud.

Remarkably, however, the Turin Protocol contained another clause that compromised the stated need for the lab representatives to have "complete knowledge" of the sampling process. To enhance the credibility of the test with the general public, the lab representatives undertook to receive the Shroud samples and control samples blind: "These shroud samples will be distributed to the seven laboratories in such a way as to ensure that the seven laboratories are not aware of the identification of their individual sample."[17] Obviously, this meant that they could not witness the entire process of which they were supposed to have "complete knowledge."

There was no scientific justification for this decision. In fact, it was a sham. Everyone at the Turin workshop understood that it was impossible for the tests to be conducted blind, for the simple reason that no control cloth could be found matching the distinctive weave of the Shroud. They knew that the Shroud samples would be recognized the moment they were unpacked.[18] However, the majority of the delegates at the workshop—all except Gove and Meacham—were concerned that the carbon-dating test should be *seen* to be done blind.[19] And so they settled on a faux-blind sampling procedure, designed to reassure people that the test was "objective," even though it meant that they themselves would not be able to keep track of the samples, jettisoning a crucial bulwark against any imputation of fraud. Frankly, it beggars belief that a group of eminent scientists should agree to compromise and misrepresent a scientific test for the purposes of propaganda.

Having settled everything with the authorities in Turin, the carbon-dating scientists expected to be invited to carry out the tests forthwith. Instead, everything went quiet. Then, in October 1987, they received a letter from Cardinal Ballestrero, archbishop of Turin, in which they were informed that the number of labs was to be reduced to three and that important provisions agreed in Turin were to be discarded. The Vatican had stepped in and decreed a new protocol. Gove, whose lab was one of those excluded, lobbied furiously against the changes, even writing a letter to the editor of *Nature*, in which he said that the changes "will produce an age for the Turin Shroud which will be vastly less credible than that which could have been obtained if the original Turin Workshop Protocol had been followed."[20] But it was to no avail. The three chosen labs, Oxford, Arizona and Zurich, could not resist the opportunity to make headlines, so they agreed to the terms laid down by the Vatican.[21] Gove consoled himself with the thought that at least STURP had been excluded from the process, as well.[22]

The test went ahead the next year. The most critical procedure, the sampling, was utterly shambolic. It took place in the Sacristy of Turin Cathedral, with the carbon-dating scientists in attendance. The two men deputed to cut the sample, Professors Giovanni Riggi and Luigi Gonella, argued for an hour or more over which site on the cloth to choose, a vital issue that should have been decided well in advance.[23] Eventually, they snipped it from the corner next to the Raes sample, an area members of the (absent) STURP team suspected was unrepresentative of the rest of the cloth.[24] This single sample was cut into three pieces, one for each of the labs.

Then, instead of being handed over directly, the pieces of cloth were taken into the Sala Capitolare, the room adjoining the Sacristy, by Cardinal Ballestrero and the representative of the British Museum, Michael Tite. There, in complete secrecy, the samples were wrapped in foil and placed in sealed canisters, along with control samples from other cloths. Finally, the canisters were brought out and handed over to the carbon-dating specialists.

It took six months for the labs to perform their tests and send their results to Tite at the British Museum, who served as the coordinator. They were relieved to find that the results were fairly consistent with each other, which was a necessary condition for the test to be considered reliable. At two simultaneous press conferences held on October 13, 1988, one in Turin, the other in London, the world was solemnly informed that the Shroud was manufactured sometime between 1260 and 1390 (Figure 42). The Church, in the person of Cardinal Ballestrero, accepted the result unreservedly.

The Shroud, it seemed, was a certified fake, nothing but a piece of religious tomfoolery from the Middle Ages.

How much faith should we have in the 1988 carbon-dating result? Not as much as is generally assumed. Given the patchy record of the scientific technique and the shenanigans of the Shroud carbon-dating project itself, it would hardly be surprising if an error was made. On what grounds can this badly organized test be considered immune to the many problems that afflicted the science of carbon dating in the 1980s? Recognizing the potential for error is one thing, though; deciding that something actually did go wrong is another. What reasons are there in this particular case for disbelieving the carbon-dating result?

First of all, dating the Shroud to the Middle Ages makes it literally incomprehensible. For over a century mainstream scholars have viewed the Shroud, a priori, as a medieval artifact, and for over a century they have completely failed to make sense of it. This is unsurprising, for, as we have seen, the Shroud is inconceivable as a medieval work of art and can be understood neither as a deliberate "recreation" of Christ's burial cloth nor as a bizarre accident. The onus is on those who uphold the carbon-dating result to integrate it into a full and adequate description of the Shroud's origin—just as archaeologists would do with any other carbon-dating result. This they have been conspicuously unable to do. The poverty of the carbon-daters' own understanding of the problem is illustrated by Teddy Hall's comment at the London press conference that someone in the fourteenth century "just got a bit of linen, faked it up and flogged it."[25]

Given credence, the carbon-dating result effectively raises the Shroud to the status of a miracle, an object that defies, if not a law of nature, a law of culture. All artifacts are linked to the art and technology of the society in which they originate. Something that cannot be explained in terms of its (presumed) cultural context invites a supernatural explanation. As far as I am aware, no one has yet argued that the Shroud was deposited in medieval France by aliens, but after the carbon dating Cardinal Ballestrero did suggest attributing it to "the supernatural intervention of God," likening it to the famous Madonna of Guadalupe, a painting that, according to Catholic belief, appeared miraculously on the cloak of a Mexican peasant in 1531.[26] Those of a more critical frame of mind may find this idea difficult to accept. There is no better explanation, though, for a fourteenth-century Shroud.

The other reason to reject the 1988 result—really a raft of reasons—is that it conflicts with all the evidence that points to the Shroud having been in existence long before 1260: the fact that the lignin in the fibers of the cloth has lost its vanillin, indicating that it is over 1,300 years old; the fact that the image derives from an actual victim of crucifixion, a practice outlawed in Christendom in the fourth century; the fact that the scourge marks testify to the use of a Roman *flagrum*; and the fact that the technical features of the weaving and stitching conform to practices known in antiquity, not the Middle Ages. And this is only the evidence we have adduced so far. In the next chapter we will consider various historical and art-historical arguments that enable us to say where the Shroud was long before 1260—as far back, indeed, as the sixth century. To stick dogmatically to a fourteenth-century date for the Shroud in the face of all this counter-evidence would be quite irrational, especially when the carbon-dating project was so manifestly flawed.

So, what could have gone wrong? This is a much more difficult question, and nearly a quarter of a century after the event sindonologists are still scratching their heads over it. The strange refusal of the Catholic Church to permit further examination of the cloth has been a major impediment to understanding. Essentially, though, there are three possibilities.

The first is that the Shroud sample given to the laboratories was contaminated in some way or chemically altered, so that the C-14 levels they detected were greater than they should have been. In the vast majority of cases, when carbon-dating tests yield suspect results, it is because some natural process has interfered with the regular ticking of the radiocarbon clock. The most obvious explanation for the dubious carbon-dating result is that some form of contamination was present or that the level of C-14 in the material was otherwise enhanced. As noted above, the measurement errors caused by such processes can be spectacular—in the range of thousands of years.

There is evidence that tests on linen are particularly prone to distortion. In the late 1970s Dr. Rosalie David of the Manchester Museum had samples from an Egyptian mummy carbon-dated at the British Museum, only to find that the bandages were dated 800 to 1,000 years younger than the body.[27] She didn't believe the mummy could have been re-wrapped, and she had received other anomalous results as well. In 1997 David co-authored an article (along with Harry Gove and others) in which new experiments conducted on ancient Egyptian ibis mummies were reported. It was found that "there was a very significant discrepancy, an average of 550 years, between the dating of the mummy's linen wrappings and the mummy itself."[28] Two reasons have been suggested for the anomalous linen results: either that the porosity of the fibers makes them particularly susceptible to contamination, or that, because crop plants have a short life span, they reflect short-term fluctuations in the C-14 levels.

The samples used in the 1988 test were cleaned using standard methods, but, as Gove remarks, "One of the problems with small samples is that one never knew when the cleaning procedure was sufficient." And he also makes the following point: "All of the labs used the same cleaning technique, and if there's some kind of contaminant that was not taken care of, it would give the same answer to all three labs, and all three would be wrong."[29]

Various suggestions have been made regarding potential sources of contamination. An early suggestion was that some form of C-14 enrichment took place in 1532, when the Shroud was scorched and burned.[30] An alternative argument, popular in some quarters, is that the Resurrection was a radioactive event which converted some of the C-12 in the cloth into C-14.[31] Another theory is that developed by Dr. Leoncio Garza-Valdes, a Texan microbiologist, who believes that the Shroud sample was covered with a "bioplastic coating," i.e. a transparent, natural varnish produced by bacteria and fungi.[32] Some of these theories are more plausible than others, but none has gained widespread acceptance, let alone been proven. Without access to the Shroud, it is difficult to see how any further progress can be made in this type of investigation.

The second possibility is that the cloth cut from the Shroud was not actually part of its original fabric but was a careful repair made during the late Middle Ages or Renaissance. This idea has been vigorously promoted by two amateur researchers, Sue Benford and Joe Marino.[33] The basic claim is that the relevant corner of the Shroud was repaired "invisibly" using a technique known as "French weaving," which even textile experts cannot necessarily detect by eye. Opinion seems to be split regarding the plausibility of this claim. Benford and Marino quote experts willing to entertain their suggestion, but it is strongly opposed by Flury-Lemberg, who says, "even the most successful execution can ultimately not conceal

the operation completely to the trained eye, and it will always be unequivocally visible on the reverse of the fabric."[34] She has inspected the back of
the Shroud and denies there is any sign of reweaving.

Nevertheless, the repair hypothesis has recently received a shot in the arm
from Ray Rogers, whose meticulous investigation of various Shroud samples,
published in *Thermochimica Acta* shortly before he died in 2005, lends it a
measure of support. Studying threads obtained from both the Raes sample
and the adjacent carbon-dating sample, Rogers found that they were coated
in a gum containing alizarin and red lakes—in other words, a dye. None of
the threads he examined from the main body of the Shroud shared this dye.
"The presence of alizarin dye and red lakes in the Raes and radiocarbon
samples indicates that the color has been manipulated," he wrote. "Specifically, the color and distribution of the coating implies that repairs were made
at an unknown time with foreign linen dyed to match the older original material."[35] At the very least, Rogers's observations constitute evidence that the
carbon-dating sample was taken from a suspect corner of the Shroud. Once
again, though, it is impossible to say anything more until the Church fulfils
John Paul II's promise and gives scientists further access to the cloth.

The third possibility is that a fraud was perpetrated, that genuine
Shroud samples were deliberately swapped with cloth of a later date. Arguments to this effect have come from quarters as diverse as members of an
ultra-conservative Catholic Counter-Reformation group, who think there
was a Masonic plot to discredit the Shroud, and the "heretical" German
writers Holger Kersten and Elmar Gruber, who believe that the Catholic
Church rigged the result, fearful that the Shroud might prove Jesus did not
die on the cross.[36] Most sindonologists regard these fraud theories as
plainly incredible. Some, like Ian Wilson, refuse to contemplate such
"unworthy" accusations. However, scientific fraud is by no means
unknown, as the editors of science journals are well aware. One only has
to recall the infamous Piltdown Man hoax (which, incidentally, Teddy Hall
was instrumental in unmasking) or the more recent case of Professor
Hwang Woo-suk, whose fabricated research into human stem-cells was
published in *Science* in 2004 and 2005.[37]

One important consideration weighs in favor of the possibility of deception. If the carbon-dating error was accidental, then it is a remarkable
coincidence that the result tallies so well with the date always claimed by
skeptics as the Shroud's historical debut. But if fraud was involved, then it
wouldn't be a coincidence at all. Had anyone wished to discredit the
Shroud, "1325 ± 65 years" is precisely the sort of date they would have
looked to achieve.

The argument draws attention to the most absurd aspect of the whole affair: the unnecessary secrecy surrounding the packaging of the samples. Although they were present at the sampling, the carbon-dating scientists themselves could not be 100 percent certain that the samples they received were from the Shroud. The "complete knowledge" they wanted of the sampling process was broken the moment Tite and Ballestrero took the samples into the Sala Capitolare. From then on, the entire validity of the test rested on the competence and integrity of the cardinal and the representative of the British Museum. No one else knows what went on in that room. The conclusion that the linen of the Shroud is medieval rests ultimately, then, on the unseen behavior of two men over the course of about half an hour— on trust, therefore, not on science. Given the magnitude of the issue, especially for the Church, the possibility of tampering cannot be discounted. As Meacham says, "chain of evidence is important, to insure and be seen to insure that no tampering could have taken place."[38]

Contamination, reweaving or fraud: three potential sources of error, any one of which could have caused the incorrect carbon dating of the Shroud. But can we legitimately reject the carbon-dating result without determining exactly what went wrong? Of course we can. Archaeologists routinely dismiss "rogue" radiocarbon dates out of hand. The success of a carbon-dating result should never be declared unilaterally; it is always measured against other evidence. The 1988 test may therefore be declared null and void, even though, without further direct study of the Shroud, it is unlikely we will ever be able to say definitively what went wrong.

It is not just sindonologists who consider the carbon dating of the Shroud questionable. The thoroughly inconclusive nature of the "conclusive evidence" trumpeted in the 1989 Nature article is acknowledged by the current head of the Oxford Radiocarbon Accelerator Unit (ORAU), Professor Christopher Ramsey:

> Anything is always provisional . . . most scientific experiments are only verified by being repeated many times . . . With the Shroud you're in a slightly difficult position, because obviously you can't go on dating it lots and lots of times. As a scientist I'm much more interested in getting the right answer than in sticking to an answer which we came to before.[39]

Ramsey speaks here as a prudent scientist. The 1988 carbon-dating result has not been verified by subsequent experiments, so we cannot be sure that the right answer has yet been obtained.

In 2008 Ramsey and his team worked with John Jackson in testing a new hypothesis regarding a possible source of carbon contamination that might have affected the linen of the Shroud. On the ORAU website, Ramsey justifies his lab's continuing interest in the Shroud as follows:

> There is a lot of other evidence that suggests to many that the Shroud is older than the radiocarbon dates allow and so further research is certainly needed. It is important that we continue to test the accuracy of the original radiocarbon tests as we are already doing. It is equally important that experts assess and reinterpret some of the other evidence. Only by doing this will people be able to arrive at a coherent history of the Shroud which takes into account and explains all of the available scientific and historical information.[40]

This is an eminently sensible statement. Oxford's participation in this ongoing research underlines the dubious status of the 1988 result.

The carbon dating of the Shroud will probably go down in history as one of the greatest fiascos in the history of science. It would make an excellent case study for any sociologist interested in exploring the ways in which science is affected by professional biases, prejudices and ambitions, not to mention religious (and irreligious) beliefs. And it should certainly serve as a warning to practitioners of any discipline tempted to see their work as more important and "fundamental" than any other. Research on the Shroud is like a microcosm of all human knowledge, a great multidisciplinary effort to describe a perplexing phenomenon as elegantly and comprehensively as possible. It so happens that, in the case of the Shroud, carbon dating has so far turned out to be less useful than a study of needlework. (Stitches are easier to observe and interpret than atom ratios, which makes them a relatively reliable source of information about old textiles.) Carbon dating may still make a valuable contribution to sindonology, if the Catholic Church ever allows further tests, and if those tests are integrated into a full, interdisciplinary research program, as Professor Ramsey recommends. In the meantime, we can safely ignore it and concentrate on more productive avenues of research.

Long before the Shroud was even a twinkle in the eye of Gove and his carbon-dating crew, sindonologists were aware of historical evidence—scattered references to a relic of Christ's burial cloth in Byzantium—that hinted at the Shroud's existence centuries before its appearance in the French village of Lirey. In 1978, as the campaign to carbon-date the Shroud cranked into gear, Ian Wilson published a remarkable new theory that offered to explain precisely where the Shroud had been—and why it was virtually unknown—for most of the first millennium AD. In the decades since, sindonologists have been patiently adding to this theory, so that the ancient provenance of the Shroud can now be reconstructed with a fair degree of confidence. This historical and art-historical research complements the scientific clues regarding the cloth's age discussed in earlier chapters and fulfils the demand that the Shroud's whereabouts be traced back to antiquity, perhaps even to the first century.

14

The Shroud in the East

On June 24, 1203 a brutal, ill-disciplined fighting force sailed into view of Constantinople, the self-styled Queen of Cities, and prepared to lay siege. The Fourth Crusade, conceived as yet another attempt to liberate the Holy Land from the Saracens, was about to shift focus and become nothing more than an infamous act of pillage. En route to the Levant, the Crusader leaders had picked up the exiled heir to the Byzantine throne, Alexios Angelos, and decided to escort him back to his native city. It seems to have been their intention to restore his dynasty to power and then move on to the Holy Land, having been handsomely rewarded. But, if that was the plan, it was soon undermined by the deep-rooted hostility between the ancient capital of the Eastern Roman Empire and the feudal West.[1]

Three weeks after its arrival, the expedition achieved its first aim. The walls of the city were breached, the imperial usurper, Alexios III, fled, and the citizens, acquiescing to the Crusaders' demands, swiftly reinstated the blind Isaac Angelos II as their emperor, with his son Alexios as co-emperor and de facto ruler. By this means, the city was initially spared any further violence, but the threat did not go away. Camped outside the city walls, the Crusaders awaited payment for their services, but this failed to materialize, owing to the bitter resentments of the Byzantine populace. Meanwhile, the soldiers were free to come and go in the city as they liked, and tension mounted between the relatively refined local citizens and the uncouth Franks and Flemings in their midst.

In February 1204 the Byzantine populace defied a Crusader delegation and rose up against their puppet rulers. The die was cast. In early April the Crusaders attacked the city once again, and this time they spared no one and nothing. Fuelled by drink, greed, hatred and envy, they tore the heart out of one of the most venerable civilizations of the age. Women were raped and murdered, children butchered, palaces and churches looted, altars desecrated. A prostitute was placed on the throne of the Patriarch and made to sing and dance, in mockery of the unfamiliar Eastern liturgy. The embalmed body of the revered Emperor Justinian, which reposed in the city's cathedral, Hagia Sophia, was stripped of its finery.[2] Four great bronze horses were taken down from the Hippodrome and carted off, later to be proudly installed on the façade of St. Mark's in Venice. But the bronze horses were not the most valuable treasure seized by the Crusaders. In the midst of all the chaos a priceless cloth was stolen from the Church of St. Mary of Blachernae, a cloth that seems to have been very similar, if not identical, to the present-day Shroud of Turin.

We know about this cloth thanks to Robert de Clari, a minor Frankish knight who was a member of the Fourth Crusade and who later wrote (or dictated) *The Conquest of Constantinople*. Robert, like his fellow knights, wandered freely in the city during the latter half of 1203 and took in the sights. It is difficult for us to understand, perhaps, the impact of this great metropolis on the minds of such men. It was unlike anything they had ever seen, a city of such breathtaking magnificence that it put Paris and Ghent, the greatest cities of the West, to shame. Besides its visual splendor, Constantinople was also a vast urban reliquary, a container of innumerable objects of spiritual power. Relics were the most precious objects in the medieval world, and Robert, a diligent observer, was careful to describe as many as he could.

His attention was caught, in particular, by the Shroud-like cloth at the Blachernae church, a cloth which was the subject of a ritual performance every Friday:

> there was another church which was called My Lady Saint Mary of Blacher-nae, where was kept the sheet [*sydoines*] in which Our Lord had been wrapped, which every Friday rose up straight, so that one could clearly see the figure [*figure*] of Our Lord on it; and no one, neither Greek nor French, knew what became of this sheet after the city was taken.[3]

Sindonologists have long regarded this as a likely reference to the Shroud. The word Robert uses to denote the cloth, *sydoines*, is simply an Old French spelling of the Greek word *sindon*, meaning a "linen sheet," the word used in the Synoptic Gospels for the cloth in which Jesus' body was wrapped.[4] This *sindon* is identified as the actual burial cloth of Christ, and, crucially, it is said to have manifested the *figure*, i.e. the bodily form, of Christ.[5] The description matches the Shroud. And Robert says that the *sindon* disappeared after the sack of the city, presumably looted by a Crusader, which may help to explain how the Shroud ended up in France.[6]

Writing in 1981, before the carbon dating of the Shroud, the eminent art historian Hans Belting was happy to assert that Robert's *sindon* was "probably identical with the 'Shroud of Turin.' "[7] Ernst Kitzinger, a fellow art historian, was of the same opinion. Interviewed by Gilbert Lavoie in 1979, he remarked, "For us, a very small group of experts around the world, we believe that the Shroud of Turin is really the Shroud of Constantinople. You know that the crusaders took many treasures back to Europe during the thirteenth century, and we believe that the shroud was one of them."[8] In other words, taking the historical evidence on its own, it is perfectly reasonable to connect the cloth seen by Robert de Clari with the Shroud.

If Robert's *sindon* was the Shroud, it would predate 1260—the earliest date indicated by the carbon dating—by over half a century.

A couple of years before Robert de Clari and his companions-in-arms arrived in Constantinople, the Sindon was kept in the spiritual epicenter of the city, the Pharos Chapel, which housed the magnificent collection of relics owned by the Byzantine emperors. In 1201 the Overseer of the collection, Nicholas Mesarites, delivered a speech in which he described the Sindon in some detail:

> The funerary sheets [*sindones*] of Christ: they are of cheap and easy-to-find material, still smell of myrrh, and defy destruction, because they wrapped the unoutlined [*aperilepton*], dead, naked and embalmed [body] after the Passion.[9]

There can be no doubt that Nicholas is referring to the same relic as that seen by Robert de Clari. He calls it the *sindones*, just as Robert refers to it as the *sydoines*—the same word in Old French. Both witnesses identify it as the linen in which Jesus was wrapped, and there cannot have been more than one cloth claiming this distinction at the same time in the same city.[10]

If the cloth relic described by Nicholas Mesarites was one and the same as that seen by Robert de Clari, then it would follow that it also manifested "the figure of Our Lord." Although Nicholas omits to mention this crucial point, his words do evoke the Shroud in several specific and surprising ways.

First, Christ's body is referred to as naked. This is significant, as in this period the dead Christ was almost invariably conceived as wearing a loin-cloth (cf. Figures 23 and 24).[11] The novel idea that Christ was naked when wrapped in his winding sheet could have been inferred from the Shroud. Secondly, the adjective *aperilepton*, meaning literally "unoutlined," is a word that is obviously applicable to the blurry, un-outlined Shroud-image.

What better way of describing the figure seen in the Shroud?[12] Thirdly, the odd remark about the cloth defying destruction might hint that it was conspicuously damaged. This would fit in with evidence to be adduced below that the so-called "poker-holes" were burned into the Shroud before the thirteenth century.

On its own, Nicholas's account of the Sindon would mean little, but in combination with Robert de Clari's account it is highly significant. Together, these two reports indicate that, at the beginning of the thirteenth century, a (possibly damaged) linen sheet was kept in Constantinople that bore a blurry image of the naked, crucified Jesus. This sounds like a description not just of a burial cloth relic similar to the Shroud, but of the Shroud itself.

But why would the Overseer have failed to mention the all-important image? The answer may have to do, at least in part, with the problematic discovery of the relic. Originally, as we shall see, the cloth was probably framed and interpreted as something else entirely, a miraculous portrait of Jesus, an image whose cult was too important to be discredited or compromised. There was also a more general reason: religious mystique. That the Pharos Chapel housed the burial cloth of Christ seems to have been common knowledge, but awareness of the "miraculous" image on the cloth appears to have been reserved to a privileged few. Byzantine society was extremely hierarchical, and the awe-inspiring image was probably deemed too sacred a sign to be shared with hoi polloi. Before the Crusaders arrived on the scene in 1203 there would have been no question of advertising the existence of the image, let alone displaying it in public. Had Nicholas Mesarites mentioned it in 1201, he would have betrayed a royal and aristocratic secret.

How far back can we trace the Byzantine relic of the Sindon? The references are few and far between. The chronicler William of Tyre records the Sindon among various relics shown to King Amaury of Jerusalem and his entourage in 1171.[13] Going further back, a letter of 1092 purporting to be from the Byzantine emperor to various Western princes tells us that "the linen cloths [*linteamina*] found in the sepulchre after his Resurrection" were then in Constantinople. Although the source is somewhat problematic, this is presumably a reference to the same relic.[14] The Sindon is first mentioned more than a century earlier, in a letter of encouragement sent by Emperor Constantine VII Porphyrogenitus to his troops in 958. The emperor says that he is sending them some holy water consecrated by contact with various relics of the Passion in the Pharos Chapel, including the *theophoron sindonos*—the "God-worn linen sheet."[15] Whatever the precise meaning of the word *theophoron*, this is a clear sign that the Sindon seen by Robert de Clari was in the imperial relic collection by the mid tenth century—a full 300 years before the earliest date indicated by the carbon dating of the Shroud.

The million-dollar question remains: can we be sure that the Sindon of Constantinople was one and the same as the Shroud of Turin? The Byzantine cloth certainly seems to have been a close match for the present-day Shroud, but is there any evidence that proves they were identical? Indeed, there is. But it is not a written description: it is a rather crude drawing in a medieval manuscript.

One of the greatest treasures in the National Library of Budapest is the Pray Codex, a manuscript which contains, among other things, the earliest Hungarian annals and the earliest work of Hungarian literature. The main part of the codex, including the part that interests us here, was produced around 1192–5 in one of the country's Benedictine monasteries. Hungary was ruled at the time by King Béla III, a staunch ally of the Byzantine Empire, who had spent eight years as a young man in the imperial court at Constantinople. During his reign, therefore, cultural links between Hungary and the Byzantine capital were strong.

On folio 28r of the Pray Codex, in the midst of a liturgical text relating to the celebration of Holy Week, are a couple of drawings that together document the existence of the Shroud in the late twelfth century (Figure 43). The artist's idiom is rather crude, making interpretation of the pictures slightly tricky, but his intentions are none the less reasonably clear.[16]

There are two scenes, one above the other.

The upper scene is a rare depiction of the Anointing of Christ, in which Jesus' corpse is prepared for burial on Good Friday.[17] In the center we see Nicodemus pouring a flask of ointment over the dead body, which is laid out on a rectangular tomb-slab and a large sheet characterized by conspicuous folds. To the left and right stand Joseph of Arimathea and St. John the Evangelist, respectively, holding the other half of the winding sheet between them.

The bottom half of the page represents the much more common scene of the Three Marys at the Sepulchre. The women are on the right, while on the left appears the angel they encounter at the tomb, who informs them of the Resurrection.[18] At the base of the composition are a couple of highly patterned rectangles, one predominantly zigzagged, the other cross-covered, whose significance we will investigate in a moment.

It was Ian Wilson who first drew attention to the potential relevance of this page of the Pray Codex to the subject of the Shroud.[19] He noticed two unusual aspects of the depiction of Christ in the Anointing that reminded him of the Shroud. First, the wrists are crossed, right over left, at the level of the groin. This pose, which is uncommon in the art of the period, corresponds to the pose of the Shroud figure. Secondly, the figure of Christ is represented naked. As noted earlier, in medieval art Christ's modesty was almost always preserved by a loincloth or by his burial cloth, yet he also appears naked in the Shroud.

Researchers have since noticed several other features of the same drawing that recall the Shroud. Heinrich Pfeiffer has suggested that the red mark above Christ's right eyebrow is intended to represent the noticeable bloodstain in the same place on the forehead of the Shroud figure.[20] It could perhaps be an accidental smudge, but the placing is perfect, and a chance coincidence seems unlikely. More significant is the fact that the hands of Christ lack thumbs, as they do on the Shroud. This is notable especially in the case of the left hand, whose thumb should definitely be visible (cf. Figure 23). Also significant is the artist's conception of the winding sheet, which corresponds to the bi-fold form of the Shroud:[21] the upper half of the sheet is held by Joseph and John, and, when Nicodemus finishes the anointing, they will wrap it around the head and lay it over the rest of the body.

The scene of the Anointing corresponds to the Shroud, then, in five telling respects: it represents Jesus naked, his wrists crossed over his groin, his hands lacking thumbs, a prominent red stain above his right eye, about to be enfolded in a long sheet drawn up and over his head. Does this not look like an attempt to imagine the burial of Christ on the basis of the Shroud? What are the odds in favor of all these rare correspondences with the Shroud occurring in the same image just by chance?

We have yet to consider the most impressive evidence, which is found in the scene of the Three Marys below. The most conspicuous and peculiar features of this composition are the large, ornate rectangles beneath the figures. At first glance, these shapes seem quite incomprehensible. Anyone well versed in medieval iconography would expect this part of the picture to be occupied by an empty sarcophagus, but no sarcophagus was ever painted with crosses and zigzags like this. It is the zigzags that give the game away. As André Dubarle observes, they look like an attempt to imitate the herringbone weave of the Shroud.[22] The artist has struggled to work out the design, but the stepped-pyramid pattern that fills the upper rectangle clearly evokes the visual effect of the Shroud's three-to-one twill weave (see Figures 44 and 45).

If we follow the sloping, zigzagged rectangle downward, we find that it meets the horizontal, cross-covered rectangle at an acute angle in the bottom left-hand corner of the page. This implies that the two rectangles are two halves of the same cloth, folded over on the left, in accordance with the depiction of the winding sheet in the scene above—and with the Shroud.[23]

This interpretation is confirmed by the most important details in the whole drawing: two tiny sets of circles, one on either half of the cloth. In the midst of the herringbone pattern is a group of four circles disposed like a knight's move in chess (Figure 45), while to the right, in among the crosses of the lower rectangle, is a similar group of five circles. These circles make no sense whatsoever as decorative motifs. They are plainly meant to signify something, and their meaning becomes clear the moment we recall the "poker-holes" that disfigure the Shroud (Figure 6). There are four sets of poker-holes, each set resembling a knight's move in chess, perfectly matching the configuration of the circles in the drawing.[24] The artist has depicted the circles on either rectangle to show how the holes went through the cloth. Given that he was working from memory and was not particularly skillful, his rendering of the poker-holes is astonishingly accurate. They are an unmistakable mark of identity.

We have now identified eight telling correspondences between the Shroud and the drawings on a single page of the Pray Codex. The first five, found in the scene of the Anointing, are sufficient on their own to indicate that the artist of the Pray Codex knew the Shroud. Conclusive proof is provided by the three correspondences in the lower scene: the stepped-pyramid pattern in the upper rectangle, evoking the distinctive herringbone weave of the Shroud; the folding of the object in two halves; and the small circle formations, which match the pattern of the poker-holes. It is inconceivable that all these detailed links with the Shroud, several of which are found nowhere else, could have occurred on a single manuscript page by chance. The only reasonable conclusion is that the artist of the Pray Codex was aware of the Shroud.

The Shroud existed and was already damaged, then, by 1192–5, when the illustrations in the Pray Codex were drawn. Given the close links at the time between Hungary and Byzantium, it can hardly be doubted that the artist saw the relic in Constantinople. The Shroud was the Byzantine Sindon.

The realization that the Pray Codex contains a depiction of the Shroud begs an obvious question: why did the artist not depict the cloth's figure? There are several likely reasons. As someone privileged to view the relic, the artist may have been bound by the same code of secrecy as Nicholas Mesarites. He may have wanted to provide himself with a vivid portrayal of the events of Good Friday and Easter morning, focusing on the Shroud, but without revealing the secret to others. Knowledge of the "miraculous" image was not to be divulged to all and sundry. Moreover, he would have found the Shroud figure virtually impossible to draw. It could be defined, as we have seen, by its lack of outline (aperilepton), but, like every other draftsman of the age, the Pray Codex artist depended on outline. If he had simply ignored this problem and drawn the figure in anyway, it would have looked as if the body of Christ was still lying in the tomb—a heretical idea.

Fortunately, he had a much better solution. Instead of representing the Shroud figuratively, he could represent it symbolically. That is why the lower rectangle, representing the interior surface of the Shroud, is covered in red crosses: they symbolize the sacred, bloodstained image.[25] This opens up a broad avenue of art-historical research, since cross-covered cloths of one sort or another were relatively common in the Middle Ages. Only the most important analogy can be mentioned here. From the mid eleventh century onward the patriarchs of the Byzantine Church took to wearing a new type of liturgical garment, a robe covered with a field of black or red crosses, known as a polystaurion ("many-crossed").[26] The design of this garment matched the pattern drawn on the interior surface of the Shroud in the Pray Codex, and the liturgical context in which it was worn suggests that the symbolism was exactly the same. Dressed in his liturgical robes, the priest stood in for the figure of Christ, a function emphasized by the multiple crosses.[27] The Hungarian artist has simply appropriated this sign, using a "many-crossed" cloth to stand in for the absent Shroud figure. In doing so, he revealed, I suspect, the origin and meaning of the polystaurion itself, and he also confirmed the Byzantine provenance of the Shroud.

The Shroud of Turin, then, was once the Sindon of Constantinople. Seen in public by Robert de Clari and his fellow Crusaders in 1203–4, it was kept before then in a state of religious purdah, witnessed only by members of the Byzantine court and esteemed visitors, who, once initiated, could be trusted to keep the secret of its astonishing image. Historical records show that the Sindon was kept in the Pharos Chapel as part of the imperial relic collection, being first documented there in 958, 400 years before it was put on show in the small French village of Lirey.

The case against the Shroud rests largely on a dubious reading of the documents concerning its emergence in the mid fourteenth century. To begin with, skeptics have leaped on the claim of Pierre d'Arcis, bishop of Troyes, that "thirty-four years or thereabouts" before he wrote, i.e. in about 1355, one of his predecessors, Henry of Poitiers, had investigated the Shroud and found it to be "a work of human skill."[28] In the late nineteenth century, when scholars first became aware of this claim, they were understandably inclined to take it seriously, since little or nothing was then known about the Shroud and its image.[29] In the early twenty-first century, however, there is no longer any excuse for believing the Shroud to be a fourteenth-century work of art. Enough is now known about it (and about fourteenth-century art) to render the idea risible. We might as well dismiss the fossils of archaeopteryx found in Germany from the 1860s on as fakes on the basis that they were denounced as such by a few contemporary scientists.[30] Rather than swallow Bishop d'Arcis's claim, we should recognize it as hearsay evidence that tells us something about fourteenth-century events at Lirey, but nothing about the origin of the Shroud.

Suspicion has also been aroused by the failure of the cloth's owners, the de Charnys, to explain how they came by their extraordinary treasure. They did no more than offer conflicting hints, Geoffrey II de Charny saying that his father had been given it, Geoffrey II's daughter, Margaret, saying that Geoffrey I had won it as a spoil of war.[31] This shiftiness has been taken as a sign that the de Charnys knew the relic was a fake, but it might just as well indicate that their ownership of the cloth was somehow illegitimate.[32] Having identified the Shroud as the Sindon of Constantinople and remembering the Fourth Crusade, we can now see that this was the case. The de Charnys could not divulge the provenance of the Shroud or openly declare it to be the true Shroud of Christ, because it was not rightfully theirs—or any other Westerner's. They would have risked having it confiscated. It was preferable to pay lip-service to the idea that it was a copy, maintain possession of the cloth and look for a future opportunity to promote its cause.

The Shroud's problematic provenance also explains why Pope Clement VII permitted displays of the cloth to continue (to the dismay of Pierre d'Arcis), but only if it was publicly proclaimed to be "a figure or representation of the Shroud of Our Lord," not the real thing.[33] As a relative of the de Charnys, Clement almost certainly knew the cloth's provenance, but he could not allow it to be recognized as the true Shroud of Christ, for fear of causing a diplomatic incident. The Shroud was a cultural treasure that meant as much to the Greek emperors of Byzantium as the Elgin Marbles do to Greeks today, and it had been stolen from them in a looting campaign as brazen as any perpetrated by Napoleon or the Nazis. Nearly two centuries after the Fourth Crusade, the Sack of Constantinople was still an extremely sore point in Byzantium, and, if John V Palaiologos, the Byzantine emperor at the time, had heard that the priceless Sindon was being displayed in France, he would have made moves to recover it.[34] Pope Clement would have been put on the spot, and the anticipated reunion of the Roman and Byzantine Churches, which was being actively discussed at the time, would have been put in jeopardy. Clement, then, had good reason not to acknowledge the real identity of the Shroud and to enjoin perpetual silence on Bishop d'Arcis as well.

There is no substance to Chevalier's claim that the fourteenth-century documents concerning the Shroud at Lirey prove that it was a recently executed painting—or any other sort of artwork.[35] This was a conclusion reached in ignorance of the Shroud's exceptional qualities as an image and its early, eastern history, proved by the Pray Codex. The poker-hole patterns represented in the Pray Codex drawing, first noticed in 1998, are also the final nail in the coffin of the carbon-dating result. The cloth now in Turin must be at least three centuries older than the earliest date indicated by the radiocarbon age of the sample tested—a sizeable error. The 95 percent confidence level the laboratories cited is meaningless, except, perhaps, as a measure of scientific hubris. Physics is not the only way to date the Shroud; historical and art-historical records have their part to play, as do the various indications gleaned from medical, chemical and archaeological investigations. This broad spectrum of research indicates that the Shroud dates not from the Middle Ages, but from antiquity.

The evidence regarding the Shroud's earlier incarnation as the Sindon of Constantinople is consistent with this. Indeed, beyond proving that the Shroud existed over a millennium ago, it helps confirm the conclusion that the cloth is nearer 2,000 years old, that it is, in fact, what it purports to be. Everything we have learned from a study of the cloth itself supports its authenticity, and, in the absence of any credible evidence to the contrary, it is reasonable to conclude that the Shroud was used to wrap the dead body of Jesus.

This conclusion holds whether or not the Shroud's history can be retraced in its entirety. Skeptics like to assert that the Shroud cannot be ancient, since nothing is known of it before the fourteenth century, but, even if this were true, it would prove nothing.[36] We could remain entirely ignorant of the cloth's whereabouts before 1355—or 958—and still logically conclude that it must have been used for the burial of Jesus. As Meacham, writing in the journal *Current Anthropology*, explains:

Being confronted with genuinely ancient objects of unknown provenance is a common experience for the museum curator . . . The "lost" 1300 years and the image origin may always remain unexplained . . . but data sufficient for authentication have been obtained from other aspects of the Shroud. The dating, geographical origin, and association with Christ are indicated not by an isolated feature or datum, but by a web of intricate, corroborating detail as specific as that used in the authentication of a manuscript or painting and certainly as reliable as many other archaeological/historical identifications which are generally accepted.[37]

Consider, for example, the case of one of the most celebrated artifacts in the British Museum, the Portland Vase. This remarkable piece of glasswork, exhibiting a refined cameo technique invented by the Romans in the first century BC, is first documented in 1600–1, when it was in the collection of an Italian cardinal. No one knows where the vase came from, but scholars are sure, none the less, that it is a genuine Roman treasure, based purely on their study of the object. The 1,600-year gap in its history does not make it a Renaissance forgery.[38] Similarly, the Egyptian shroud in the Metropolitan Museum of Art illustrated in Figure 7 turned up out of the blue in the hands of a Cairo antiquities dealer in the early twentieth century, but no one doubts that it is an authentic, second-century artifact. If the object is convincing in itself, lack of provenance means nothing.

The Shroud of Turin can be traced back 1,000 years, at least. That earns it the right to be judged by the same sort of criteria as are used to authenticate the Portland Vase and the Metropolitan Museum shroud. Like them, it stands as "testimony to its own authenticity."[39] Its early history is a separate matter entirely.

It was 1978 before anyone came up with a theory that might explain where the Shroud was—and why it was virtually unknown—throughout most of the first millennium of its existence. In that year Ian Wilson proposed that the Shroud was one and the same as a famous Byzantine relic known as the Mandylion (or Image of Edessa), which was kept for centuries in the Pharos Chapel and seems to have disappeared in 1204, during the Sack of Constantinople. The form and display of the Mandylion is controversial, and we cannot hope to iron out all the difficulties here, but even a brief review of the evidence demonstrates that Wilson's theory has much to commend it.[40]

The Mandylion was the most famous relic in Christendom, valued as a *palladium*—a spiritual protector—and as a prototype for all icons of

Christ. It was reputed to consist of a miraculous imprint of Christ's face on a cloth. Known as an *acheiropoietos*—an image "not made by hand"—it was said to have been produced by Christ as a gift for King Abgar of Edessa, a small city-state just east of the Upper Euphrates. Edessa had been the cloth's home since at least the mid sixth century, but in 944 it was extorted by an imperial army and taken to Constantinople—just fourteen years before we first hear of the Sindon.

What sort of image did the relic bear? The traditional claim that it was "not made by hand" does not tell us much, since there were then (and still are) quite a few man-made images reputed to be *acheiropoietoi*.[41] Conventional wisdom holds that the Mandylion was simply "an old icon" of Christ's face that was discovered in Edessa in the mid sixth century and was thought to be of miraculous origin, becoming the focus of a local legend.[42] This theory can only be maintained by ignoring a great deal of evidence to the contrary. If we pay attention to eyewitness accounts of the cloth, descriptions of it in contemporary sources and striking aspects of its legend, a very different picture emerges.

When the Mandylion was brought to Constantinople from Edessa in 944 it was briefly the object of intense scrutiny, before being plunged into the relative obscurity of the Pharos Chapel. Accounts written by several of those who saw the cloth on this occasion survive, and they suggest that the image was no ordinary icon. One of these authors was the future emperor, Constantine Porphyrogenitus, who penned—or supervised—the official history of the relic, a work known as the *Narratio imagine edessena* ("The Story of the Image of Edessa").[43] Like every other source from the sixth century onward, the *Narratio* tells how the image was imprinted on the cloth by direct contact with Christ's face. In the introduction to the *Narratio*, however, Constantine is rather more specific, saying that "the form of the face" was "imparted onto the linen cloth from a moist secretion with no paint or artistic craft."[44] Plenty of other sources corroborate this description, denying that the image was made with paint and interpreting it as a sweat stain.[45]

Astonishingly, some writers told how the Mandylion was produced on the occasion of the Agony in the Garden, when Christ prayed to be released from his impending ordeal and "his sweat became like great drops of blood falling down upon the ground."[46] This fantastic scenario was entertained by Constantine Porphyrogenitus, and it was believed wholeheartedly by another eyewitness, Gregory Referendarius, who delivered a sermon on the subject of the Mandylion in 944.[47] For Constantine, Gregory and others to have associated the Mandylion with the Agony in the Garden, the image must have exhibited signs of dripping blood—hardly usual in an icon of Christ.[48] Another person present on the occasion of the cloth's arrival in Constantinople, Symeon Metaphrastes, describes the emperor's sons being unable to see the eyes and ears of the face, implying that it was faint and indistinct.[49]

These remarks indicate that the Mandylion was similar to a relic known as the Veronica, which was kept in the church of St. Peter's in Rome. The Veronica was a napkin-sized cloth that also bore a supposedly miraculous portrait of Christ, said to have been created on Good Friday, when Christ, being led along the Road to Calvary, stopped to wipe his bruised and battered face on the cloth.[50] But, however similar the two images may have appeared, there are signs that the Mandylion was quite unlike the Veronica in its overall format.

The Mandylion's appearance is preserved in numerous copies of it made to adorn the churches of the Byzantine Empire (e.g. Figure 46). None of these extant copies is likely to be based on direct observation of the relic, but the iconographic tradition they represent must depend on the work of an artist (or artists) who had the rare privilege of seeing the image. They are distinct from copies of the Veronica in that they all show the haloed, disembodied head of Christ floating in the midst of a *horizontal* rectangle. The use of this "landscape" format, instead of a vertical "portrait" format, is extremely odd, resulting in an empty expanse either side of the face. If the Mandylion was just "an old icon," why would the artist have violated one of the most basic norms of portrait painting?

Moreover, there are consistent indications that the Mandylion was not simply a face-cloth, but something much larger. Four early sources, dating from the seventh to the tenth century, refer to the cloth as a *sindon*, a large linen sheet (like the Shroud).[51] The Mandylion is also termed a *sindon* in versions of a liturgical text called the *Synaxarion*, composed after its arrival in Constantinople and based on the work of Symeon Metaphrastes, who saw the cloth in 944.[52] And writing around 730, John Damascene calls the Mandylion a *himation*, meaning a "cloak" or "mantle," the word used in the Gospels for the clothing stripped from Jesus at the Crucifixion.[53]

If the Mandylion was just a face-cloth, like the Veronica, why would it have been called a sheet or mantle? It seems as if the cloth possessed a hidden dimension. Could it, perhaps, have been a large cloth *folded* to look like a small face-cloth? This idea is dramatically confirmed in two texts, the aforementioned *Synaxarion* and the seventh-century *Acts of Thaddeus*, both of which refer to the relic as the *tetradiplon* ("four-doubled"), a word that can only mean that the cloth was folded over into eight layers (4 x 2).[54] This, Wilson suggests, is the key to the mystery. For if one takes the Shroud and folds it over on itself three times, so that the facial image is still visible, one is left with an eight-layered, four-doubled arrangement that corresponds to the traditional image of the Mandylion—Christ's face set within a horizontal rectangle of cloth (cf. Figures 46 and 47). Framed like this, the Shroud would have been perceived as a miraculous image of Christ's face imprinted on a towel, not the winding sheet it really was.

Everything now falls into place. The peculiar "landscape" format of the Mandylion was not an artistic aberration but was determined by the folded form of the Shroud. The cloth was mounted on a wooden board and embellished with a golden frame that covered the area surrounding the facial image but left the sides of the cloth visible—hence the occasional use of the term *tetradiplon*.[55] Anyone who inspected the cloth could have deduced that it was a large, folded sheet, but it was kept well away from prying eyes most of the time, so its true size would not have been commonly known.[56] Wilson's theory accounts for the Mandylion's reputation as an *acheiropoietos* (an image "not made by hand") and for the testimony of the tenth-century eyewitnesses, who perceived the image as "a moist secretion with no paint or artistic craft." And it also explains why some thought it had been made during the Agony in the Garden, when Christ's face was covered in sweat "like great drops of blood."[57] On top of the exact description of the cloth as the *tetradiplon*—"four-doubled"—this catalogue of connections with the Shroud is extremely impressive.

What is more, various Western sources testify that the Mandylion comprised an image not just of Christ's face but of his entire body. A work known as the Oldest Latin Abgar Text, for example, whose earliest manuscript dates from the tenth or eleventh century, narrates how Christ sent a letter to King Abgar, saying, "I am sending you this linen cloth, on which you will be able to see not only the form of my face but the divinely transformed state of my whole body."[58] Texts such as this provide clear evidence that the Mandylion shared the form of the Shroud, rather than the face-only Veronica.

So far, historians and art historians have conspired to ignore all this evidence, dismissing it as so much legendary whimsy. Wilson's theory is traduced, and it is simply assumed that the inherited idea of the relic as a small face-cloth was correct. The references to it as a *sindon*, *himation*, and, most significantly of all, *tetradiplon* are left unexplained, as are its landscape format, its perceived connection with the Agony in the Garden, the eyewitness denials that it was painted, and the descriptions of it as a full-body image. Able to account for all these aspects of the historical record, Wilson's theory is patently better than the current orthodoxy. Although much remains to be clarified, I conclude, therefore, that the Mandylion was indeed the Shroud.[59]

If the Shroud was the Mandylion, then its known history would go back to the mid sixth century, when the relic was rediscovered in Edessa. According to a legend preserved in the *Narratio*, it was found walled up in a niche above one of the city's gateways, a tale which is by no means implausible and may explain why all knowledge of it had been lost.[60] The problem of the Mandylion's early history, before the 550s, cannot be discussed here, but it may be noted that, if the Shroud turned up unexpectedly in sixth-century Edessa, it was probably lost there centuries earlier—perhaps as far back as the first century. This in turn suggests that the legend of King Abgar, a historical character known to have ruled Edessa from AD 13–50, may have a kernel of truth, in that the Shroud may have been taken to Edessa during his reign.

It is clear, in any case, that the Shroud's history does go back, one way or another, to the first century—and to the tomb of Jesus. Enough was known about the Shroud in 1902, when Delage stood up and gave his pioneering paper at the Académie des Sciences in Paris, to make this a valid conclusion. A hundred and ten years later a huge amount more is known about the Shroud's physical make-up, image and history, and the conclusion is now far more secure: the only coherent way to understand it is as the burial cloth of Jesus.

Between 1902 and 2012 virtually the only aspect of the Shroud that has not been subjected to rigorous scrutiny is its meaning. Its supporters and detractors alike have simply assumed that, if real, the Shroud would confirm the message of the Gospels, an assumption vaguely shared by the world at large. The understanding of Christian origins has traditionally been shaped by the Gospels, and, as a wordless object, the Shroud has generally been considered no more than a supplement to these scriptures, albeit one that could potentially prove the central miracle of the faith. Supplements, though, can be dangerous. Meaning is not something inherent in texts or images, however sacred, but a voice we lend them. And, if we start to think more carefully about the Shroud's meaning, we may hear it speaking with a new voice and telling an altogether unexpected tale.

PART 4

Seeing through the Shroud

15

The Animated Shroud

One hot, bright morning in the early summer of 2004 I ambled out into the orchard beside my house in Cambridge, lay down on the grass and immersed myself in *The Turin Shroud* by Ian Wilson. Overhead, white blossoms clustered along the sparse branches of the apple tree in whose shade I settled; beside me, blackbirds bounced around on the grass, looking for worms; a lawnmower droned back and forth on the neighboring cricket pitch. I wanted a place to think and reflect, somewhere well away from the dingy factories of academic research. The suburban idyll on my doorstep was the perfect spot.

I had spent the previous few days reading up on the Shroud, my interest having been kindled by a TV documentary screened that Easter, which cast serious doubt on the reliability of the carbon-dating test.[1] I was now thoroughly hooked on the subject. Since no one else seemed able to unravel the history and significance of the relic, I was determined to think it through for myself. But to do so, I needed to get some purchase on the problem, to come up with an idea or observation that would give me a new angle on it, a point of departure for my own investigation. I hoped Wilson's book, brought out into the fresh air, might act as a catalyst. It did. Leafing through its arguments and illustrations, I became caught up in the Shroud's mystery as never before, exploring its apparent paradoxes with a refreshing sense of intellectual abandon. After a while *The Turin Shroud* slipped from my lap, and I entered a state of rare contemplation—part reverie, part pure concentration.

Though skeptical of the relic's authenticity, for all the usual reasons, I was nevertheless fascinated by some of the historical evidence Wilson presented. Various texts he cited—such as Robert de Clari's account of the Byzantine cloth on which "the figure of Our Lord could be plainly seen"— did seem to point to a Shroud-like relic existing long before the fourteenth century, the date indicated by the problematic carbon-14 test. Moreover, I was aware by then of the major clue first recognized by André Dubarle: the distinctive pattern of the "poker-holes" found on the representation of Christ's burial cloth in the Pray Codex. Unable to dismiss this as a coincidence, I found myself forced to reckon with the heretical idea that the Shroud was already known in the twelfth century. I also had to admit that Wilson's identification of the Shroud with the Mandylion was plausible and accounted for a good deal of evidence that, as far as I could see, orthodox opinion either ignored or dismissed without proper justification.

For a while I lay there in the shade of the apple tree, turning these issues over in my mind. If Wilson's theory was correct, the Shroud's provenance could be traced back to the sixth century. And if it was that old, the chances of its being a fake were drastically reduced. As an agnostic, used to thinking about Jesus in conventional Christian terms, I was extremely uncomfortable with the idea that the Shroud might be an authentic marvel; and, as an art historian familiar with the merry-go-round of medieval relics, I was extremely skeptical that this one—the most astonishing of all—might be genuine. Nevertheless, having considered every alternative explanation and found it wanting, I felt pinned down and forced to think the unthinkable. The execution and burial of Jesus, I told myself, is the only recorded event that could have resulted in a length of linen becoming stained by the body of a man flogged, crucified, crowned with thorns and speared in the side, and it is an event that is unlikely ever to have been exactly repeated. I couldn't avoid the conclusion: from a purely historical point of view, the death and burial of Jesus seemed to be the best explanation for the Shroud.

For a skeptical agnostic, this was a suffocating thought. The idea that the Shroud might be authentic hinted at something uncanny happening to Jesus' body in the tomb. Preconditioned as I was, my thoughts inevitably turned to the supposed miracle that lies at the heart of Christianity, the Resurrection, an idea that challenged some of my deepest convictions. It was as if the Shroud, backed by the vast weight of Christian tradition, was pressing down on me, threatening to stifle my secular worldview. Instead of enjoying a quiet loll in the summer sun, I found myself battling with a fierce metaphysical adversary, like Jacob wrestling with the angel.

It was then that I glimpsed, for the first time, the potential significance of the relic. Grappling with the idea that it might have been found in the tomb of Jesus, I asked myself a question that has baffled generations of Shroud-enthusiasts: if the relic is authentic, why do none of the Gospels mention its discovery in the empty tomb? And then it struck me: maybe they do. Maybe the Gospels contain descriptions of the Shroud that no one has recognized as such since the days of the apostles, because it appears in their legendary narratives not as an image but as a supernatural person.

Seized by this stunning thought, I leaped up from the grass and bounded indoors to check the biblical stories of the empty tomb.

Confusing the Shroud figure with a person might be taken for a sign of madness, but I had not been struck by a fit of insanity. Rather, I had engaged a form of historical consciousness that becomes second nature to all historians of medieval art. For a split second I saw the Shroud as it would have been seen before the Enlightenment, the eighteenth-century Age of Reason that cuts us off from our more suggestible forebears.

All too often history is conceived as a series of recorded events driven by dry, rational motives. It is forgotten that events are frequently determined by weird and wonderful beliefs and that to understand the past we have to take seriously the strange imaginings of its participants. We cannot make sense of the terrible witch-hunts of early modern Europe, for instance, without understanding that, among pre-Enlightenment peasantry and intelligentsia alike, many of the folkloric horrors with which we amuse ourselves at Halloween were thought to be real. Martin Luther, for one, was a firm believer in witchcraft. History is not just about facts; it is also about beliefs. To understand the past we have to enter into other people's minds—minds generally very different from our own.

So far, I have described the Shroud and its history in terms of (often controversial) facts: what it is, where it was when, how it was displayed, what it was called and so on. It is now time to start investigating the thoughts it would have inspired in those first-century Jews who (if I am right) were its first interpreters. What would they have made of an elusive image of Jesus manifested on his burial cloth? What might they have imagined the Shroud figure signified? One thing is certain: they would not have thought about it the same way as us. They were premodern, unscientific people, whose beliefs about the world were conditioned by ancient folklore and religious tradition. More fundamentally still, they were susceptible to ways of thinking about images, both natural and artificial, that would seem highly irrational to us, just as people in the seventeenth century were apt to think bizarrely about old crones.

Today we tend to think of images as mere representations of mundane reality. We regard them aesthetically—that is, we perceive them as more or less beautiful artifacts, as the passive objects of our gaze. Occasionally, we are surprised by the intensity of our reactions to them, as when we shout at a politician on TV or stroke the image of a loved one, but we interpret such behavior as a stray, irrational impulse or as a symbolic gesture. It would never occur to us to hold the image itself, or even the person represented, responsible for our actions. Living in a rationalistic age, we think of images as nothing but inert visual stimuli.

Before the eighteenth century, however, images were not generally viewed with such rational detachment.[2] Surveying a broad spectrum of human societies, including the ancient Near East, it is clear that people have traditionally treated images in ways that we would regard as plainly superstitious. Throughout most of history images have been viewed as mysterious, metaphysical beings. Like the inaccessible world of the looking-glass, the realm of images is generally conceived as a separate plane of reality. Moreover, before the Enlightenment, images of gods, saints, spirits and ancestors were routinely credited with power, not only affecting the emotions of those who looked at them, but also influencing the course of events. In the premodern world images were perceived to be, in some sense, alive.

To perceive images as alive is to succumb to a form of "animism," the attribution of life to inanimate things. And whenever images of people are considered animate, they are also anthropomorphized, i.e. credited with human-like thoughts and emotions.[3] However odd such ways of thinking might seem to those of us brought up to think rationally and scientifically, both animism and anthropomorphism are deep-seated impulses, found the world over.[4] Images, we might say, naturally come alive in human minds. But they are obviously not alive like us. Animated images belong, therefore, to the domains of the magical, the uncanny, the supernatural and the divine.[5] Some examples will indicate how powerfully the life of images is experienced in traditional societies and the wide variety of beliefs and practices it informs.

Among the most important of all Hindu shrines is the temple of Jagannath in Puri, which contains the idols of Jagannath and his divine relatives.[6] These statues are renewed every twelve to nineteen years. Every part of the process is attended by ceremonies and rituals. The tree trunks from which the idols are carved have to have come from a *daru* tree, that is, a tree identified on the basis of its form and location as a source of sacred wood. The images are carved by low-caste Daitas, who employ secret, prescribed methods to create the images, and it is their duty to transfer the life-force from the old idols to the new. This is done very literally. Taking off the cloth wrappings from an old statue, the man entrusted with the task gains access to a hollow compartment inside the idol, in which a casket containing the *brahmapadartha*—the "life-substance"—of the god is located. The *brahmapadartha* must not be seen or touched, and so the Daita wears a blindfold and wraps his hands in cloth. Once recovered, the "life" of the old statue is transferred to the new, the *brahmapadartha* casket being placed in its cavity and sealed with a lid. The "dead" statue is then mourned, given an elaborate funeral and buried, while the new statue, pulsing with life, is invested with the remaining parts of its body. Long red threads are wound around the wood to serve as blood vessels, and strips of red cloth soaked in resin and bodily substances are applied to serve as the god's skin. Finally, the idol is painted, a task which culminates in forming the pupils of the enormous eyes. It is this that makes the image not merely alive but sentient.[7]

There can be no doubt that the devotees of Jagannath view the statue as a living presence, the actual god who watches, considers and intervenes. The idol may seem inactive to a skeptical observer, but the worshippers attribute to it desires and motivations and perceive its power in the world around them. The image, to them, is no mere representation; it is an agent formed from a sacred substance, a supernatural person, the strange body of a god.

Such idols abounded in the pagan world of the ancient Mediterranean, a prime example being the statue of Artemis at Ephesus, one of the most famous images of antiquity (cf. Figure 48). The strength of devotion to this statue is vividly conveyed by the account in Acts of an uproar in Ephesus caused by the preaching of Paul.[8] Afraid that the success of the Christian gospel would diminish worship of the goddess, on which their livelihood depended, the local silversmiths apparently stirred up the people of the city against Paul and his followers, a couple of whom were seized and dragged into the theater, amid cries of "Great is Artemis of the Ephesians!" They might well have been lynched, had it not been for the timely intervention of the town clerk.

The opening words of the clerk's speech shed light on the perceived nature of the city's divine patroness: "Men of Ephesus, what man is there who does not know that the city of the Ephesians is temple keeper of the great Artemis, and of the sacred stone that fell from the sky [*diopetous*]?"[9] The Greek word *diopetous* literally means "Zeus fallen" and was used of a number of cult images thought to have dropped from heaven. Some of these statues appear to have incorporated, or been associated with, meteorites. The crucial thing from our point of view is that they were considered of divine origin; like the Shroud, they were supposedly "not made by hand."[10]

Besides meteorites, other *objets trouvés* could also be associated with divine beings. Consider the story told by Pausanias of a face made of olive-wood, which some fishermen of Lesbos caught in their nets and afterward worshipped as an idol.[11] This is an episode that resonates strongly with the discovery of the Shroud. What would the fishermen of Lesbos have thought of the strange figure discovered on Jesus' burial cloth?

Cult statues were by no means the only images in the ancient world imbued with life. Even the simplest, crudest images could serve animistic purposes. In the Louvre there is a small figurine, made in Egypt during the third or fourth century AD, which represents a naked woman pierced with eleven needles (Figure 49).[12] As we know from an accompanying inscription, it was intended as a love charm, designed to help a young man named Sarapammon win the heart of a girl called Ptolemais. For the purposes of the spell, the pierced figurine was understood to be one with the person it represented; its ersatz life was mingled inextricably with that of Sarapammon's beloved. This intimate act of sympathetic magic reveals the depth of the popular animism that pervaded ancient Mediterranean societies.

In the world of antiquity, then, as in many places today, images were not perceived simply as objects, as mere representations of something or someone else. Images of people, in particular, were seen as persons—often supernatural persons—who acted within the social world of their viewers. The anthropomorphic instinct was experienced in that period as a perception of reality, rather than as a delusion to be repressed.

All this was in the back of my mind as I lay beneath the apple tree ruminating on the Shroud. I had recently attended a seminar on Alfred Gell's *Art and Agency*, a book which emphasizes the perception of images as active participants in human affairs, and my own work on certain frescoes in the medieval town hall of Siena—including portraits which were occasionally attacked as if they were real people—served as a continual reminder of the magical "life" of images. I was predisposed, then, to think about the Shroud in premodern terms, as a living person. And encountering it that day as more than just an intellectual puzzle, as a disturbing moral challenge, I felt something of the peculiar power it would have had over its original audience.

Thus, my initial hypothesis is very simple: if the Shroud was discovered in first-century Judaea, its figure would have been perceived in animistic, anthropomorphic terms. Before seeking to confirm this idea by re-examining the Gospel tomb-stories, we need to ensure that it is historically sound. Is it appropriate to see animism at work in first-century Judaea? After all, Judaism is founded on the principle of monotheism and prohibits the worship of images. Could first-century Jews have even countenanced the Shroud figure, let alone regarded it as a living person? Wouldn't they have been as immune to the power of images as we moderns?

It should be emphasized, first of all, that animism is a universal human propensity. Across the globe, people interact with figural images in ways that correspond to their treatment of living, breathing persons: they talk to them, beg them, clothe them, offer them food, stroke them, kiss them, become angry with them, attack them, mutilate them, bury them, and so on. No indigenous culture has ever been found that does not engage in some form of animistic behavior. Moreover, a little self-examination will show that we ourselves still lapse into this type of thinking.[13] Why do so many of us enjoy the vague thrill of meeting famous people at Madame Tussaud's? How upset would you be, even now, if someone mutilated your old teddy-bear? Modern adults generally learn to repress their animistic instinct, reducing it to a temporary sensation in front of certain films and works of art, but it is still there beneath the surface.

Listen to the art historian Richard Brilliant describe his fascination with portraits:

> I, too, am drawn to the avid contemplation of Roman and all other portraits because they give life to historical persons, freed from the bonds of mortality . . . It is as if the art works do not exist in their own material substance but, in their place, real persons face me from the other side or deliberately avoid my glance. Quickly enough, the illusion dissipates; I am once more facing not a person but that person's image.[14]

The illusion lasts longer in the cinema, where even determined rationalists can find themselves caught up emotionally in the "life" of an artificial being. How many have had a lump in the throat while witnessing the plight of the friendly latex alien E.T.? We may not believe in E.T., once the credits roll, but we are still capable of endowing a mere image with a soul. We can't help it: we are predisposed to treat images of living things—especially images of people—as animate, sentient beings.[15]

Since the survival of any organism depends on being prepared for encounters with other living things, animism makes good evolutionary sense. We err on the side of caution, betting, for instance, that the large object ahead on the woodland path is a bear not a boulder, since betting the other way might prove fatal. Instead of being a sign of irrationality or childishness, then, animism should be understood "as an inevitable result of normal perceptual uncertainty and of good perceptual strategy."[16] Moreover, as humans, we are attuned, in particular, to the presence and activity of other humans, the most important living things in our environment, and so we have an inbuilt tendency to interpret the world anthropomorphically.[17] Although it may foster a profound sense of mystery, the universal human tendency to interpret images of people as real (or surreal) is not in itself mysterious.

First-century Jews cannot have been exempt from this tendency. They tried to repress their animistic instincts, as we do, but this does not mean that they viewed images any more rationally than their Gentile neighbors. Indeed, the biblical battle against idolatry is testament to the strong appeal of the "graven image" among the ancient Israelites. While Moses was up on Mount Sinai receiving the Ten Commandments, the Children of Israel were down in the valley dancing round the Golden Calf. Later, the famous Brazen Serpent Moses erected at God's behest to protect the Israelites against snake bites had to be destroyed by King Hezekiah because the people had begun offering sacrifices to it.[18] The fear of lapsing into this sort of behavior haunted Second Temple Jews precisely because they recognized their own susceptibility to man-made gods. And we know of some who, like their ancestors, succumbed to the temptation of idolatry. During the Maccabean revolt, it was discovered that certain followers of Judas Maccabaeus who had fallen in battle had worn under their tunics "sacred tokens of the idols of Jamnia, which the law forbids the Jews to wear."[19] These Jewish warriors evidently believed in the protective power of images as sincerely as did their pagan enemies. It is a myth that monotheism somehow made the ancient Jews immune to superstition, a myth that recent work on Jewish magic, in particular, has begun to explode.[20]

But still, it might be argued, the majority of Jews undoubtedly respected the second commandment, the divine injunction against making and worshipping "graven images." Wouldn't this have prevented the followers of Jesus from taking an interest in the Shroud? No, because they would have regarded the second commandment as quite irrelevant to their situation. The original Jewish opponents of Christianity might well have considered the Shroud an idol, but as far as the Christians themselves were concerned, its veneration would have been perfectly innocent.[21] On the one hand, they knew that the Shroud figure was not "graven"—it had been found, not manufactured. On the other hand, as long as they did not bow down to it as an alternative god, there was no danger of committing idolatry. There were plenty of ways they could have interpreted it as a spiritual presence without treating it as a rival divinity.[22]

In any case, the Jewish aversion to imagery is often exaggerated. Although there was a ban on any visual representation of Yahweh (or other gods), figurative art was not entirely eschewed.[23] The famous third-century synagogue at Dura Europos contains one of the most extensive cycles of mural painting to have survived from antiquity. In Jerusalem itself wall paintings, representing among other things fish and birds, have been found in first-century houses and tombs, while Josephus describes figurative sculptures that adorned Herod's Palace and Temple.[24] The Hebrew scriptures themselves relate how, at the command of the Lord, Moses not only erected the Brazen Serpent but also had made the two cherubim whose wings spanned the Ark of the Covenant, a task later emulated by Solomon in the Holy of Holies.[25] As long as the prohibition against idols was not violated, images were evidently tolerated in ancient Jewish society and even had an important religious role.

The Jewish discoverers of the Shroud, then, would have been more at ease with visual imagery than is often supposed, and they would have had no difficulty reconciling an animistic perception of the Shroud with their monotheistic faith. (Throughout the last 2,000 years, most Christians have managed to combine monotheism with an instinctively animistic perception of church icons.) There is thus no reason to doubt that, if the Shroud figure was known in first-century Judaea, it would have been viewed as a living presence.

But as what kind of being would the Shroud figure have been perceived? How would it have been categorized? Once again, my tussle with the Shroud out in the orchard suggests an answer. It felt almost as if the figure was whispering to me news of a distant, metaphysical reality, as if I was hearing the echo of a once vibrant voice—the voice of a divine emissary. The experience was unsettling, and to a first-century Jew it would have spoken of divine revelation. That is to say, the Shroud would have been perceived by its discoverers as a celestial messenger—as an angel.

The Hebrew scriptures speak occasionally of angels, appearing in various forms. First, there is the Angel of the Lord, identifiable with God himself, who appears to Hagar by a spring on the way to Shur and to Moses on Mount Horeb. During the Exodus, God's angel leads the Israelites through the desert to the Promised Land, appearing in the form of a pillar of cloud by day and a pillar of fire by night. Then there are the generic angels, the heavenly host, such as those that Jacob sees ascending and descending on a ladder set between earth and heaven. Lastly, on several occasions the Lord appears to the patriarchs as a man or as men, such as the three divine men who visit Abraham by the oaks of Mamre and foretell the birth of Isaac.[26] It is now generally agreed that all this talk of angels and divine men was originally meant to express God's interaction with his people; it was a way of speaking about his immanent presence on earth and his occasional manifestation in visible form. The authors of the Hebrew scriptures did not believe in heavenly beings separate from God himself.[27] However, the texts are easily read as descriptions of independent beings, and that is how they were often read during the Second Temple period, when there was a tremendous growth of interest in angels.[28]

Probably the best-known pre-Christian text that deals extensively with angels is the *Book of Enoch*, which narrates the fall of the rebel angels, known as the "watchers," and the apocalyptic journey of the patriarch Enoch through the seven heavens.[29] Just as popular was the *Book of Jubilees*, a retelling of the stories of Genesis and Exodus composed in the second century BC, which vividly conveys the new interest in angelology in its account of the first day of Creation:

> For on the first day he created the heavens that are above, the earth, the waters and all the spirits who serve before him, namely: the angels of the presence; the angels of holiness; the angels of the spirits of fire; the angels of the spirits of the winds; the angels of the spirits of the clouds, of darkness, snow, hail and frost; the angels of the sounds, the thunders, and the lightnings; and the angels of the spirits of cold and heat, of winter, spring, autumn, and summer, and of all the spirits of his creatures which are in the heavens, on earth, and in every [place].[30]

These abstract heavenly beings soon came to include angels specifically concerned with the welfare of people. In the *Testament of Levi*, for instance, we find reference to "the angel who intercedeth for the nation of Israel."[31] On a more personal level, the archangel Raphael is introduced in the Book of Tobit as the companion and protector of Tobit's son, Tobias—as his "guardian angel." He masquerades as a mortal throughout their adventures, but eventually reveals himself to be "one of the seven angels who stand ready and enter before the glory of the Lord."[32]

At the time the Shroud was discovered, then, there was a widespread interest in angels among the Jews, and these semi-divine figures were conceived in various ways. They were ranged in hierarchies of holiness, performed different roles, possessed varying degrees of glory, were called by various names and were identified in numerous passages of the Hebrew scriptures.

Might the Shroud have been seen as one of the "watchers" or fallen angels described in the *Book of Enoch*? It is certainly possible that it was seen negatively by some, at least initially, but any fear it prompted would have been dispelled as soon as it was identified via the scriptures (see below, pp. 287–95). Those who saw it would also have been reassured by the whiteness of the cloth, a color associated with purity and holiness,[33] and by the effect of inner light produced by the "photo-negative" tones of the image. The implied luminosity of the figure would have marked it out as a true denizen of heaven. It was of a kind with the Prince of Light who features in the Dead Sea Scrolls, otherwise known as the Angel of Truth and the Great Angel, the triumphant adversary of the Angel of Darkness.[34]

One aspect of the Shroud would undoubtedly have caused consternation: the ritual impurity of the grave-cloth. In Jewish law anything that comes into contact with a corpse is regarded as unclean.[35] However, this need not have affected the evaluation of the Shroud figures. Nowadays, we think of the image as one with the cloth, as a discoloration of the linen fibers, but a first-century Jew or Christian would no more have equated the cloth with the living presence it revealed than a good Catholic would regard a wooden icon of St. Peter as the saint himself. The unclean Shroud could thus have been preserved for the sake of its associated figures, interpreted as separate, living entities. Indeed, the cloth's contagious impurity might well have added to the frisson of excitement that its figures produced.

So, we can say with confidence that any Jew narrating an account of the Shroud's discovery in the first century would have told a story about an encounter with a beneficent angel (or pair of angels) in the tomb of a recent victim of crucifixion. This much can be inferred purely on the basis of the Shroud itself.

Even as I ran into the house and dashed for the bookcase, I knew that the idea of the animated Shroud had remarkable potential. But my sense of epiphany was checked by the thought that I might have misremembered the Gospel accounts of the empty tomb. My hands were shaking as I reached for my battered copy of the Bible. I flicked, first of all, to the final chapter of Matthew:

> Now after the Sabbath, toward the dawn of the first day of the week, Mary Magdalene and the other Mary went to see the sepulchre. And behold, there was a great earthquake; for an angel of the Lord descended from heaven and came and rolled back the stone, and sat upon it. His appearance was like lightning, and his raiment white as snow. And for fear of him the guards trembled and became like dead men . . .[36]

A frightening angel with a face like lightning, clothed in white, appearing at the tomb of Jesus: I thought I recognized the figure instantly. Quickly, I scanned the tomb-stories in the other Gospels—it can't have taken more than a minute, but the suspense made it feel like an hour—and found apparent references to the Shroud in each of them. Propping myself against the bookcase, I went through the texts again several times, making sure they said what I thought they said. Gradually, excitement turned into elation. One simple act of reinterpretation had transformed the familiar Easter legends into gripping historical reports. I was reading about the discovery of the Shroud.

16

The Risen Jesus

It was a few days later, as I lay in bed and reflected on the implications of my discovery, that I tumbled to the astonishing meaning of the Shroud.

I had realized that the Shroud, like other images, could come alive in the imagination, and I had quickly found references to it in the Gospels. But, initially, I was so focused on identifying the animated Shroud figure in the tomb-stories that I gave no thought to its further significance. Fortunately, having convinced myself that the Shroud really might be genuine, I couldn't leave the subject alone. And so, a little while later, lying awake in the small hours, I began to reflect on the original meaning of the cloth—that is, how it would have been interpreted by its original audience.

What would the Shroud have meant to the women at the tomb? How would they have viewed the figure? As an angel, yes, but also, perhaps, as something more. Drowsily, I tried to put myself in the position of those who found it, to see the Shroud though their teary eyes. Ironically, it was modern photography that gave me the necessary perspective. Instead of the eerie, other-worldly mask on the cloth (Figure 3), I saw in my mind's eye the realistic face revealed by the photographic negative (Figure 16), a face that must have been dear and familiar to the female mourners at the tomb. Suddenly I realized that, for his friends and family, the figure would not have been an anonymous specter. They would have recognized it—with difficulty—as a blurry likeness of the man they loved, of the man they yearned to have restored to them. They, too, could have looked through the image and seen the face of Jesus.[1]

This was a remarkable thought. For, as art historians and anthropologists are well aware, in premodern societies likenesses tend to be identified or equated with their models, to be regarded *as* their models.[2] Recall the little figurine of Ptolemais, seen by Sarapammon as a living double of his beloved (Figure 49). The first Christians would have seen the Shroud figure, therefore, as a form of Jesus himself; it would have shared his identity, and he would have partaken in its supposed liveliness. The Shroud would have been understood not to represent the dead-and-buried Jesus, but to make present a sort of living Jesus—a *reliving* Jesus. In other words, if the Shroud originated in first-century Judaea, it would have been interpreted as a kind of resurrection.[3]

Even as I framed this thought I saw that it would lead into a whole new realm of inquiry—and religious controversy. But, despite its profound implications, it appeared to me quite straightforward, almost like a routine research finding. This time I didn't bother to leap up and consult the Gospels; I knew instinctively that the idea was sound. I was already thoroughly familiar with the tendency of devout Christians to see Jesus as alive and present in his image. Just as a pierced figurine can be confused with a desirable girl, icons of Jesus are apt to be identified with the living Christ.

There floated into my mind, I remember, the famous story of the San Damiano Crucifix (Figure 50), a painted medieval cross which allegedly spoke to St. Francis of Assisi one day in 1206. According to the legend, St. Francis ventured into the half-derelict church of San Damiano, near Assisi, and prostrated himself before this austere icon. The miracle that followed was recounted by Brother Thomas of Celano, the saint's first biographer:

> Even though its lips were only painted, the image of Christ crucified spoke to this man . . . and called him by name. "Francis," it said to him, "go and repair my house which, as you can easily see, is in ruins." . . . [T]hrough a new miracle, from the wood of the cross Christ spoke to Francis . . ."[4]

For the duration of the miracle the San Damiano Crucifix effectively became the living Jesus. It was the image that spoke, but it spoke self-reflexively, as if it were Christ; his person was located within the Crucifix, transforming it into a kind of surrogate body. I knew the story of this miracle well, and I could see how it might illuminate the founding miracle of the Church—now an animated Crucifix, then an animated Shroud. If a medieval saint could see Jesus alive in an unremarkable crucifix, the apostles could surely have seen him alive in the amazing Shroud.

But there was one important distinction between the two cases. Francis's vision took place within an established framework of Christian belief, in which images of Christ were already associated with his living presence, whereas the followers of Jesus were first-century Jews, who had no prior conception of their leader as anything other than a mortal human being. If I was right, the Shroud must itself have generated the idea of the posthumously living Jesus. On one level, this notion would have been an inevitable consequence of the animistic perception of the Shroud: when images "come alive" they are identified with whomever they represent. But on another level, the Shroud's re-embodiment of Jesus would have had to have been understood intellectually, as a miraculous, metaphysical process. This process, I suspected, was what was meant by the Resurrection. But what did it involve? How would it have been conceived?

Lying there in the dark, mulling over these new questions, I realized that the meaning of the Shroud was potentially far more complex and surprising than that of any mere work of art. The idea that the Resurrection was a belief inspired by the Shroud opened up vast vistas of interpretation that, as yet, I could barely glimpse. The first task, though, was to try to understand how a group of first-century Jews might have understood and rationalized their animistic perception of the Shroud. Only then would I be able to develop this radical new idea on a secure theoretical footing.

To see the Shroud as it would have been seen by the first Christians, we need to acquaint ourselves with contemporary ideas about persons, bodies and images, especially natural images.

Saying what constitutes a person is tricky, but generally we tend to think of persons as other people like us—as live human beings. Sometimes we identify people with their physical bodies, as when we speak of injuring someone's person, but this is more often combined with a belief in the independent reality of mind or soul.[5] Our ideas of what it is to be a person are brought most sharply into focus when we contemplate death. The materialist view is that death means extinction, but even today many people find it impossible to believe that, when the body dies, the person ceases to exist. Instead, they envisage the soul—the essence of the person—surviving in some immaterial form, perhaps in heaven.[6] They see the person as separable from the body, as a metaphysical entity that can exist independently of flesh and blood.

This view was standard in the ancient world. Although the immaterial aspect of a person was conceived in various ways (often, it seems, as a combination of "life-force" and "mind"),[7] there was widespread agreement that the physical body was only part of a person and that some non-physical part could continue to exist after death. In Homeric Greece, for example, the dead were thought of as insubstantial shadows— "after-images of used-up men"—milling around in a joyless underworld, the kingdom of Hades.[8] Ancient Jews, as we have seen, shared a similar conception: once people died, they were thought to descend as shades to Sheol, the Pit in the depths of the earth, where they would fall into a dreamless sleep. The dead entered "a different, diminished, inferior state of existence," reduced to mere shadows of their former selves.[9]

A vivid description of such a shade is found in the First Book of Samuel, when the ghost of Samuel is summoned from Sheol at the behest of his protégé, Saul. Fearful of the outcome of a battle against the Philistines and unable to learn the future by any lawful means (dreams, divination and prophecy), Saul seeks out a woman reputed to be a medium, so that, via her, he can consult his recently deceased mentor. As the séance begins, Saul asks her what she sees, and she describes "a god ['elohim] coming up out of the earth . . . an old man . . . wrapped in a robe."[10] The word 'elohim denotes an incorporeal being (either a god or an ancestral spirit), and the robe in which he is wrapped evokes a shroud—the clothing of the dead. This famous incident would surely have echoed in the mind of any first-century Jew who witnessed the shadowy figure.

The person might survive death, after a fashion, as a shade, but the physical body was doomed to decay. In Jewish belief, Adam was formed "of dust from the ground," and, following his misdemeanor in the Garden of Eden, he was condemned to become dust once again: "you are dust, and to dust you shall return."[11] Flesh, therefore, could be conceived as a sort of animated clay vessel in which the person temporarily resided, before being consigned to the underworld. This is precisely how Paul saw human bodies, referring to them as "earthenware vessels."[12] But, as well as being earthy containers, bodies were also images—images of God. This second aspect of the Jewish conception of man was based on Genesis 1.27: "So God created man in his own image, in the image of God he created him . . ." Meanwhile, the wider Hellenistic culture that surrounded (and infiltrated) first-century Judaism was strongly influenced by Plato's belief that material things, including human bodies, were inferior copies—images—of divine forms. So Jews and Gentiles alike thought of man's flesh as a living image that was briefly home to his immaterial "soul." This is how Jesus' relatives would have regarded his mortal remains in the rock-cut tomb: as a sort of clay image from which his shade had recently departed, or was in the process of departing.

The next point is crucial. If the physical body is just a temporary location for the immaterial person, it raises the possibility that, under special circumstances, the person might migrate to another suitable location—to another "image." If this relocation occurs after death, it is generally known as reincarnation (or metempsychosis), a fairly common belief in the ancient world. In Plato's *Myth of Er*, for instance, various men of legend are said to have been reincarnated as animals—Agamemnon as an eagle, Ajax as a lion, Orpheus as a swan.[13] But reincarnation is by no means the only way in which people can be envisaged transferring from one body/image to another. For instance, we might imagine the spirit of a young man entering mysteriously into his painted portrait while he is still alive—the premise of Oscar Wilde's famous novel *The Picture of Dorian Gray*. The story of Dorian Gray may be fantastical, but it plays on the incessant superstition that portraits capture something of our inner lives.

For the majority of human history, Wilde's scenario would have been deemed perfectly plausible. It is well known, for instance, that European explorers caused consternation among native peoples when they first began recording their appearance, particularly via photography.[14] Across the world, indigenous people drew the same conclusion: the portrait image was nothing less than the physical embodiment of a person's vitality or soul. This belief is an inevitable product of the ways in which we conceive persons and interpret images, especially natural or "automatic" likenesses.[15] Tellingly, the Shroud is now routinely (if wrongly) described in photographic terms, and its first-century discoverers would surely have viewed it in much the same way that nineteenth-century natives viewed photographs.

There is little evidence that Second Temple Jews believed in reincarnation or that they worried about their souls fleeing into portraits.[16] But they would certainly have regarded these types of belief as intelligible and logical, and many of them did believe in the closely related notion of resurrection, the re-embodiment of a person in a recreated human body—a recreated image of God. Though distinct in theory, it would have been difficult or impossible in practice to distinguish a resurrection from a reincarnation, since no one would have known in advance what a resurrected body would look like or how to distinguish it from a natural body.[17] What an ancient Greek might have interpreted as a psychic transference from one body to another an ancient Jew might have seen as a resurrection.

Moreover, given the animistic assumptions of the time, the second body might have been something we would now categorize as an inert image. So, for the followers of Jesus, a dead person, having left their perishable, physical body, could theoretically have taken up residence in a new, anthropomorphic image created by God, and that image could have been constituted or signified by a posthumous, automatic likeness of their original body. This process would have made sense to them as a form of resurrection, even if it was not the sort of resurrection any of them expected.

Faced with the Shroud, though, they would have been forced to revise their expectations. Why? Because this unique phenomenon could only have been understood at that time as the result of such a process.

*

Modern scientists, using microscopes, imaging techniques and chemical testing, have determined that the Shroud figure is essentially a stain caused by the chemical alteration of something on the surface of the cloth. The stain may not yet have been definitively explained, but it is agreed to be a physical phenomenon none the less. Even the most zealous Shroud-enthusiast accepts the scientific view of the image as a remarkable optical effect produced by the discoloration of the linen. Two thousand years ago microscopes, cameras and chemistry did not exist; scientific inquiry did not exist. First-century people, trying to determine the nature of the Shroud-image, would have asked not what it was made of, but what it resembled, what it was like. For them, as for all pre-scientific people, it was via resemblance that the meaning, order and structure of the world were discerned.[18]

What, then, is the Shroud most like? As the modern photographic analogy indicates, it is akin to automatic or natural images, such as imprints, shadows and reflections. The ancients were fascinated by such natural images and saw them as vitally connected to their parent persons. Philosophers may have speculated about the optical causes of such phenomena, but most people simply viewed them as metaphysical doubles, related to the living in mysterious ways. The Shroud would have been viewed as a type of natural image, and its interpretation would have been strongly influenced by—even determined by—beliefs about these related likenesses.[19]

It is still relatively easy to understand and to feel the psychological power of a human imprint, a power that has always been associated with the lingering presence of the vanished person. Can anything bring us closer to our prehistoric ancestors, for example, than seeing their busy footprints preserved in a patch of hardened mud, as at the cave of Pech Merle in southern France? Can we evade the feeling, however momentary, that the people remain somehow there with us, somehow present in the physical traces of their lives? We ourselves may regard such sensations as fanciful, but in the ancient world they were considered deeply meaningful. Imprints were regarded as detached members of a person's body. Followers of Pythagoras, for instance, were careful, when rising from their beds, to smooth away the impressions left by their bodies on the sheets, lest they be used to gain power over them, and they also forbade anyone to pierce a footprint with a nail or knife, a magical way of making someone lame.[20] In a world where such beliefs were typical, it is easy to see how the Shroud— the impression of a body left on a sheet, its feet pierced and bleeding—could have been seen as a live counterpart of the person it represented.[21]

Even more suggestive, perhaps, was the figure's resemblance to a shadow. The belief that a person's shadow embodies their soul or vitality was ubiquitous in premodern societies, and it was a belief apparently shared by ancient Jews.[22] As implied by the idea of a person's shade inhabiting Sheol, they understood their shadows to be essential elements—the only inextinguishable elements—of their being. Just as we might regard ourselves as partly composed of our thoughts, words or deeds, which live on after we die, they regarded themselves as partly composed of their eternal shadow. We encounter a related belief in the vital power of the shadow in the description in Acts of the sick being laid out in the streets of Jerusalem, "in order that Peter's shadow might fall on some of them as he came by."[23] To be touched by his shadow was to be touched by Peter himself.

It is worth comparing the Shroud with a more recent image that suggests the same sort of shadowy metaphysic. When an anonymous engraver of the seventeenth century wished to depict the human soul, he could think of no better sign than a dappled silhouette resting on—or veiled by—a white sheet (Figure 51). The sign is as intelligible today as it would have been two millennia ago. It is particularly reminiscent of a passage in the sixth-century *Book of the Resurrection of Christ by Bartholomew the Apostle*, in which Siophanes, the resurrected son of the apostle Thomas, tells of "the taking of his soul by Michael [the archangel]: how it sprang from his body and lighted on the hand of Michael, who wrapped it in a fine linen cloth"—a passage possibly inspired by knowledge of the Shroud.[24]

Confronted by the Shroud, the apostles would have been struck by its shadowy appearance: flat, dark, colorless and indistinct. It would have seemed to them as if something resembling Jesus' shade had settled on or in the cloth—a sort of wispy avatar. At the same time, the Shroud figure was obviously not a shadow: it was stable, revealed features and bloodstains, disappeared at close range, showed front and back, and seemed strangely luminescent. It was something they had never seen before, something rather like a shadow, but far more complex.

In some ways it would have seemed more like a reflection. Like a mirror-image, the Shroud-image is left-right reversed and shows detail within its fuzzy outlines. As well as echoing the obscure reflections seen in the imperfect mirrors of the time, mirrors made of materials such as silver, bronze and obsidian,[25] the dim figure would have recalled the fleeting likenesses caught here and there in polished surfaces and pools of water. In antiquity people believed that these reflected images possessed a spiritual reality. The ancient Egyptians buried mirrors with the dead, presumably so that their reflections could accompany them into the underworld.[26] The Shroud could have been understood similarly, as a mirror-image that accompanied Jesus through death.

The lore surrounding mirror images goes back to the Greek myth of Narcissus, the youth who fell in love with his own watery reflection. "At its origin," explains Sabine Melchior-Bonnet, "this myth can be read as an archaic belief in the existence of the double, or of a soul taking on substance ... Homer attributed a double existence to man, one in his perceptible physical being, the other in an invisible semblance unleashed only at his death."[27] The belief that this second self, leaving the body at death, can be captured in a reflection lies behind certain perennial superstitions to do with mirrors, such as the common practice of covering mirrors in rooms where someone lies dead.[28] It is vividly portrayed in a famous mosaic from Pompeii, representing Alexander's defeat of the Persian emperor, Darius. Lying wounded on the ground, one of Darius's bodyguards glances up and sees his departing double reflected in his shield—a chilling signal of his imminent demise (Figure 52).[29] What would the original viewers of this mosaic have made of the Shroud figure, a similar alter ego fixed forever on a cloth?

Mirrors also featured in the initiation rites of the Dionysiac mysteries, especially dark mirrors, which, as the psychologist Richard Gregory says, "stimulated the imagination more than the eye."[30] This is particularly interesting in connection with Paul's famous remark concerning spiritual knowledge: "For now we see in a mirror dimly, but then face to face."[31] It has been convincingly argued that this statement alludes to the use of mirrors in contemporary pagan mystery rites, where they were used to stimulate the imagination of the initiate prior to the climactic revelation.[32] Paul's remark would make perfect sense as an allusion to the Shroud. He could have seen the face of the Shroud figure as a dim reflection of the true face of Christ, analogous to the enigmatic perception of deities in contemporary mystery rites.[33]

As a unique, shadow-like, mirror-like double of Jesus, the Shroud spoke of Jesus' presence in multiple ways. Since natural images were interpreted in antiquity as integral components of a person, the Shroud could hardly have been viewed with rational detachment as an inert, discolored cloth. Decoupling a man and his double would not have seemed at all rational in the first century. Today, if we see someone's shadow or reflection, we rightly deduce that they must be present, even if we cannot see them directly. By the same token, first-century witnesses of the Shroud would have deduced from the figure that Jesus was present, even though he was otherwise unseen.

For the first Christians, the Shroud showed Jesus alive in a sort of looking-glass world. Their hope was that the surface of the mirror would soon dissolve—that the mask would be removed—and they would meet him face to face.

The appearance of the figure would not have been the only factor determining its interpretation. The circumstances in which it formed would have conditioned its interpretation as well. Had the image been created during Jesus' lifetime (as the Abgar legends tell), it might have been seen as his spiritual double, but it would hardly have inspired talk of his resurrection. It is significant that the Shroud was an imprint/shadow/reflection sprung, as it were, from his dead body. That made it an image of rebirth.

The Shroud's envelopment of Jesus' body would have fostered the idea of the transference of his soul from flesh to cloth. Not only was physical contact considered a conduit of spiritual power, but ancient Jews, like premodern people everywhere, also believed that a person's presence inhered in their clothing. This belief is found, for instance, in the Gospel story of the woman with an issue of blood, who reached out to touch the hem of Christ's garment. The moment she did so, Jesus sensed "that power had gone forth from him," and the woman "felt in her body that she was healed of her disease."[34] Christ's clothing (like Peter's shadow) contained or conveyed something of his spiritual presence. The Shroud, which clothed Jesus in the tomb, would surely have been infused with similar power—a power focused and increased by its "miraculous" image.[35]

Given these circumstances and beliefs, we can say with confidence that, if the Shroud is authentic, its original spectators would have viewed its image as the manifestation of a new type of body into which Jesus had posthumously passed. It would have signaled a rebirth, albeit in an unexpected fashion. For first-century Jews the concept of resurrection would have provided the only plausible, satisfying explanation for the appearance of the Shroud figure. And the Shroud would have been quite sufficient on its own to generate and sustain the notion that Jesus was resurrected. No visions of the Risen Christ would have been necessary: the Shroud provided its own "objective vision." No empty tomb would have been necessary, either: the Shroud revealed a new body into which Jesus had passed, making the fate of his old, fleshly body irrelevant. Nor need the Shroud's interpreters have been aware of contemporary myths and rituals in other cultures pertaining to the idea of resurrection (though they probably were). A cool appraisal of the Shroud, employing ancient Jewish common sense, would have been enough to lead to the conclusion that Yahweh had raised Jesus from the dead.

That said, it is worth drawing attention to a venerable religious custom in a neighboring culture that illustrates a type of resurrection process very similar—if not identical—to that which I am describing here. In Egypt the dead had long been envisaged as returning to life in images enveloping their physical body. The *ka* (spiritual double) of a person was thought to require a body to survive, and so deceased Egyptians were provided with effigies to serve as substitute bodies, in case something happened to their embalmed corpse. Originally, these effigies were separate statues, but by about 2000 BC they had evolved into anthropoid coffins.[36] When we look at the magnificent coffin of Tutankhamun, for example, we are witnessing a "spiritual body" of the boy-king, a post-mortem abode for his *ka* (Figure 53). In fact, we are witnessing the body of his *resurrection*, because the elaborate funerary rites performed on the dead pharaoh were designed to achieve his rebirth as Osiris, the resurrected god of the underworld. In time, all those who could afford the necessary funerary arrangements aspired to be reborn as Osiris (or, later, another god). According to ancient Egyptian belief, whenever we meet a sculpted coffin in a museum we are coming face-to-face with a resurrected person.

In the Roman era, the great tradition of Egyptian funerary art took on a new, demotic form. During the fourth decade of the first century (contemporaneously with the emergence of Christianity) Egyptian mummies began to be adorned with painted portraits (called "Fayum portraits" after the region where many of them were found).[37] Two different types of painting were made. Usually, the face of the dead person was painted on a small panel of wood and inserted into the linen wrappings (e.g. Figure 54). Sometimes, though, a half-length or full-length portrait was painted directly onto a linen shroud wrapped around the mummy (e.g. Figure 8). Relatively modest though they were, such images performed the same magical task as the anthropoid coffin of Tutankhamun: "they were deputies which could provide the spirit with the physical form necessary for survival, in case the actual body should perish."[38] The painted shrouds, especially, invite comparison with the mysteriously figured Shroud found wrapped around the body of Jesus. A closer parallel could hardly be imagined.

So, rebirth in an image surrounding the corpse was not just conceivable in the ancient Mediterranean world; it was already an article of faith across Judaea's southern border. Most Judaeans probably knew of the elaborate funerary customs of their Egyptian neighbors.[39] But my point is not that Jesus' followers knew about the Egyptian *ka* relocating to the mummy-portrait and used this foreign doctrine to interpret the Shroud. Rather, it is that, given certain beliefs about the immaterial person, the possibility of rebirth and the nature of images—beliefs that ancient Jews and Egyptians more or less shared—interpreting an image enveloping the corpse as a resurrected body would have been fairly straightforward. Egyptians were used to doing it; Jews could have done it. And the eerie Shroud—a figure that evoked and surpassed the other double selves seen in nature—was far more suggestive than any man-made effigy.

We can now make sense of the Shroud in first-century Jewish terms (see Figure 55).

As soon as Jesus died, his person began detaching itself from his physical body to become a shade, a potential sleeper in Sheol. His flesh and bones still needed to be honored with a proper burial, but the bond between his person and his physical body was loosed. His friends and family might have hoped that he would be resurrected at the end of the age (in whatever form Yahweh saw fit), but they knew that until then he was destined to be nothing but a dormant wraith.

This picture would have changed the moment the Shroud was discovered. It would have been seen immediately as a miraculous sign and as some sort of metaphysical being connected with the dead man. Once its likeness to Jesus was recognized, it would almost certainly have been seen and interpreted as signifying a newly created vessel into which his person had been transferred, a successor to his earthy, physical body, which was returning to dust. It would have been seen as a body formed in the image of God, a body like Adam's but spun from much finer, celestial stuff.[40]

The figure's resemblance to shadows and reflections, its luminous effect, its staring eyes, and, last but not least, its overwhelming presence: all these qualities of the Shroud would have assured Jesus' followers that it revealed him to be once again *alive*. The Shroud figure was not a ghost, like the awoken shade of Samuel, but a glorious, transfigured, re-embodied person. God had performed a miracle of rebirth, a divine version of the human magic practiced by the Egyptian priests.

17

The Ascended Jesus

We have seen how the Shroud could have inspired the idea that Yahweh had raised Jesus from the dead, but we are still only halfway to understanding the early Christian concept of the Resurrection. For God was thought not only to have restored Jesus to some kind of earthly existence, but also to have raised him above the world, to have made him a power in heaven. The resurrected Jesus was a heavenly being, not just a fortunate human.

This extra dimension of the Resurrection—its celestial dimension—is most vividly expressed in the tale of Paul's conversion on the Damascus road. Paul was an undoubted eyewitness of the Risen Christ: Jesus appeared to him just as he did to Peter, James, the Twelve, and all the rest. Yet Paul's experience is represented in Acts not as a terrestrial encounter, but as a celestial call: "a light from heaven" suddenly bursts upon him, and he hears a voice addressing him from heaven.[1] In this story, the resurrected Jesus is not a visible person displaying his body and wounds on earth; he is an invisible, spiritual power.

The Resurrection of Jesus, then, was no "ordinary" resurrection, like those of Lazarus and Tabitha.[2] These miracles were impressive, for those who believed in them, but they were not world-changing, because the people concerned remained humble mortals, destined to die once more. Such tales did not affect how the resurrected person was perceived. The Resurrection of Jesus was different. Jesus was thought not merely to have been restored to life, but to have been restored to *eternal* life and installed alongside Yahweh as co-regent of the universe. It was this that made Christianity not merely the proclamation of a miracle, but a radical reinvention of Jesus and Judaism.

But am I not confusing two separate phases in Jesus' post-mortem career? Traditionally, Christians have understood the Resurrection and the Ascension as two successive events, separated by a period of forty days:

first of all, Jesus was raised from the dead and appeared to his disciples on earth (the Resurrection); then he was taken up into heaven (the Ascension). This neat scheme, which depends upon belief in the physical, flesh-and-blood Resurrection, is laid out in Acts 1.1–11, and it helps explain the distinction Luke makes between Paul's late conversion experience, which takes place after the Ascension, and the Resurrection appearances proper, which take place beforehand. The trouble with Luke's scheme is that no other early-Christian source supports it, and quite a few contradict it.

Throughout the New Testament (and the Christian apocrypha) the Resurrection is spoken of in terms of "exaltation," that is, celestial ascent and enthronement. The pattern is set by one of the earliest Christian texts we have, a hymn quoted in Paul's letter to the Philippians, which describes Jesus' death and afterlife as follows:

> he humbled himself and became obedient unto death, even death on a cross. Therefore God has highly exalted him and bestowed on him the name which is above every name, that at the name of Jesus every knee should bow, in heaven and on earth and under the earth . . .[3]

This simple scheme of death followed by heavenly exaltation is repeated in various other texts, such as Hebrews 10.12: "when Christ had offered for all time a single sacrifice for sins, he sat down at the right hand of God."[4] There is no distinction here between Resurrection and Ascension, no hint of a two-stage process: Jesus is raised directly to heaven.

The first chapter of Acts is alone in implying that Christ's Ascension was a separate episode that happened sometime after Easter. As Bishop John Shelby Spong says, "The Resurrection-ascension was one act at God's initiative, and before the two aspects were split apart, the word *exaltation* covered both."[5] The Exalted Jesus was sometimes represented as the terrestrial Risen Jesus, sometimes as the celestial Ascended Jesus.

The challenge is more difficult, then, than simply explaining why the early Christians believed that Jesus had been raised from the dead. We have to explain their belief in the Exalted Jesus, a figure who spanned both earth and heaven. What was it that gave the Resurrection of Jesus its celestial dimension, making it more than just another miracle? Why was the Risen Jesus apprehended not just as a revivified mortal, but as a cosmic power?

Failure to explain the binary figure of the Exalted Christ is one of the central problems with all previous theories of the Resurrection. The problem is most obvious in those theories that involve appearances of a flesh-and-blood Jesus. Some claim that Jesus survived the Crucifixion, perhaps being revived in the tomb by the smell of the spices left by Nicodemus,[6] and that he was then seen alive again by his followers. This might explain belief in a simple, Lazarus-style resurrection—at a pinch—but it doesn't even begin to explain how Jesus came to be considered a celestial being. It leads to ludicrous suggestions, such as that Paul developed his faith in Jesus as the "life-giving Spirit" from a meeting with the resuscitated Jesus on the road to Damascus, when his eyes were "dazzled by the glare of the midday sun on Jesus' white robes."[7] As David Friedrich Strauss long ago argued, it is absurd to imagine that a convalescent Jesus, lame and weak from his ordeal, could have convinced his disciples that he had passed through death and come out the other side as its superhuman conqueror.[8]

Traditionalists, who persist in believing that Jesus was miraculously raised in the flesh, have to follow Luke in removing him physically at some point from earth to heaven. To imagine him zooming up through the clouds might have seemed plausible in antiquity, but it takes a peculiarly blind kind of faith to believe in such a rapture today. Sophisticated evangelicals such as Tom Wright, who declares that the Risen Jesus was not simply a physical being composed of flesh, but a "transphysical" being composed of spiritualized flesh, may believe in some sort of divine teleportation, but, unfortunately, we are not told anything about this intriguing process. The slide into pseudo-science is halted by the age-old device of a theological mystery.[9]

It is no easier bringing a purely visionary Jesus down to earth. As far as first-century Jews were concerned, Jesus would not have been the first person to have been assumed into heaven. The Hebrew scriptures tell of two men, Enoch and Elijah, who were taken into heaven before they died, and there was also speculation that Moses had been raised to heaven after his death.[10] These patriarchs might be seen in visions, but that did not mean they had been resurrected, i.e. restored to some form of bodily life. In the story of the Transfiguration, for example, Moses and Elijah are seen briefly on a mountain top, talking with Jesus, but this was never taken to mean that they had been resurrected ahead of him. They could appear momentarily on earth, yet have no part in a new Creation.

Had Jesus been seen in a visionary manner, then, he might have been thought to have been assumed into heaven, but he would have remained as dead (and bodiless) as Moses. On its own, no "vision theory" can explain why Jesus' followers thought he had been resurrected. The only way posthumous visions of Jesus might have prompted belief in the Resurrection is if they had followed the discovery of an empty tomb. Conceivably, the disciples might have interpreted visions of Jesus in light of the fact that his body had vanished and come to the conclusion that God had raised him bodily to heaven. But, besides relying on the doubtful idea of the empty tomb, this type of theory implies a massively improbable coincidence. The historian is left struggling with the idea that Jesus' body was stolen for some reason, a far from common occurrence, after which his followers experienced a unique series of "visions," as recorded in the First Creed.

The way out of all these difficulties lies with the Shroud. Unlike any other solution, the Shroud theory accounts easily for belief in an Exalted Jesus who straddled heaven and earth.

As we have seen, interpreting the Shroud figure as a manifestation of the Risen Jesus would have been fairly straightforward in first-century Judaea, a consequence of viewing the Shroud in light of pre-existing beliefs about people, bodies, images and resurrection. Divining the nature of the manifestation, though, would have been rather more difficult. Was Jesus literally present in the Shroud's image? Was the image itself his new body? Or was it merely a sign—a shadowy double—reflecting his embodiment in some otherwise invisible form? Was he present near his image, like someone standing before a mirror? Or was the Shroud a veil through which he could be seen? Did he exist somehow between the two Shroud figures, front and back? Or was he merely the remote source of the image, separated from it by a physical gulf, like someone seen on TV?

Since the answers to these questions were unknowable, the perceived relationship between Jesus and the figure would have been unstable. His person would have been seen as both within the Shroud and without it, both present and absent. To the extent that he was present, he was resurrected. But, if he was absent from the Shroud, where was he then? As someone restored to life, he could no longer be in Sheol. So he had to be in heaven, as implied by Daniel's prophecy of the risen dead shining like the stars.[11] And that is how he appeared—shining with an inner light. The righteous martyr, it seemed, had been exalted to a place in heaven.

It is important to bear in mind that most of the time the earliest Christians would not have had the Shroud in front of their eyes. The remembered view of the image is very different from the actual view—or, indeed, the view of an illustration. (To get a feel for this, avoid looking at a photo of the Shroud for the rest of this chapter.) Experienced directly, the Shroud figure has a palpable, material presence, which is hard to ignore. Moreover, in front of the thing itself, we tend to think analytically, poring over every incidental detail, registering subtle changes of color and texture, inspecting every part of the cloth and its image. Away from the Shroud, though, we think about it more synthetically, remembering the most salient aspects of the image and uniting them into a coherent idea, an abstract figure. It is this imaginary figure that would have dominated the thoughts of the Shroud's first interpreters. And this figure was, by definition, separate from the Shroud, an object of thought, rather than vision, an ideal and therefore heavenly person.

This interpretation would have been confirmed as soon as Jesus' followers started checking the scriptures, for a number of Hebrew texts describing heavenly characters—texts we know the early Christians came to regard as prophetic—could have been read as referring to the Shroud. To take just one example, the Shroud figure could have been seen as the "one like a son of man" envisioned in Daniel 7.13–14, a celestial, human-like being who approaches the Ancient of Days and is given an everlasting kingdom. Identifying the Shroud figure with such visionary characters, the first Christians could have "discovered" that the Risen Jesus was also a prophesied, heavenly figure.

Theoretically, then, we can see how the Shroud could have inspired the idea of the heavenly, Ascended Jesus, in addition to the Risen Jesus. The belief that Jesus was a celestial person was due to the perception that, as well as being *in* the Shroud's image, he was also *apart* from it, coupled with the conviction that he was mentioned in the Hebrew scriptures. The Resurrection referred to Jesus' presence in the Shroud, while the Ascension referred to his translation to a new plane of existence—heaven—from which he made himself visible via the Shroud. The former located him on earth in his image; the latter located him in heaven at a distance from his image. They were two different ways of talking about the same phenomenon (see Figure 55).

Trafficking between heaven and earth was relatively common in the ancient world. I mentioned above the cases of Enoch, Elijah and Moses, three Jewish patriarchs thought to have made a heavenly ascent (with or without dying first). Similar tales were told among the Greeks, who had fewer qualms about men becoming godlike. An entire class of immortals—the Heroes—were men who had attained semi-divine status by their marvelous deeds. Most famous of all was Hercules, who was supposed to have ascended heavenward from his funeral pyre.[12] Ordinary humans could join the gods, as well. For example, Empedocles, a Sicilian philosopher of the fifth century BC, was celebrated after his death in legends reminiscent of those attached to Jesus. "Little more than a century after his death, stories were already in circulation which told how he had stayed the winds by his magic, how he had restored to life a woman who no longer breathed, and how he then vanished bodily from this mortal world and became a god."[13] There is no evidence that any of these men ascended to heaven via an image, but images could undoubtedly prompt—and be used to exploit— the type of thinking represented by such stories. Nowhere is this more evident than in the funerary art of ancient Egypt.

Among Greeks and Israelites, ascending to the celestial realm was a rare honor; among Egyptians it became a regular aspiration. We have already seen how the anthropoid coffin or mummy-portrait of a deceased Egyptian was designed to serve as a substitute body for his or her *ka* (spiritual double), paralleling the interpretation of the Shroud as the risen body of Jesus. But Egyptian resurrection was not limited to inhabiting a body. Every mummified person assumed a divine aspect: he or she was reborn not simply as his or her entombed self, but also as a god. The tomb-portrait was intended "to serve as a channel for transformation of that individual from a mortal to a divine or celestial form."[14] It is easy to see how the magnificent mask of Tutankhamun (Figure 53) could have been viewed as the face of a god, but the humbler type of mummy-portrait served as a means of divinizing the deceased just as well. The transfiguration of Jesus in the Shroud could have inspired a comparable belief. The spectacularly different impact of the Shroud may be explained very simply by the fact that it was natural, not artificial, and was interpreted in a Jewish, not an Egyptian, context.

Egyptian funerary art supplies an even more intriguing analogy. In certain tombs of the New Kingdom period, including that of Tutankhamun, the deceased was accompanied by a magical item known as an "Osiris bed." A fine example found in the tomb of an official called Maihirpre consists of a wooden stand spread with a linen sheet, bearing a peculiar corn-image of Osiris (Figure 56).[15] The image was formed by molding a silhouette of the god in earth on the sheet, seeding it with grain and watering it before placing it in the tomb. Few texts exist to illuminate the purpose of such beds, but, as the Egyptologist Gwyn Griffiths says, "it is a fair inference . . . that the continued life of the deceased was the aim."[16] As the grain sprouted underground, it embodied the rebirth of Osiris, and, as it did so, it helped to accomplish the rebirth of the tomb's owner, now identified with Osiris. (Recall Paul's likening of resurrection to the germination of a seed.) The corn-image effectively raised Maihirpre into the realm of the gods. As an eerie outline on linen, located in a tomb, and formed, to some extent, naturally, it matches the Shroud in various ways. There is no reason to doubt that the Shroud could have been interpreted similarly, as the transformation of a mortal into an immortal.

In the first century there was one tradition of divine ascent in particular that was common knowledge right across the Roman Empire: the imperial creed of apotheosis, the belief that, after death, the Roman emperor was enthroned among the gods. This creed, which depended heavily on the use of visual imagery, formed the inescapable backdrop to the Christian claim that heaven had recently received a Jewish Messiah.[17]

The Romans derived their belief in imperial apotheosis from the Greeks. Following the example of Alexander the Great, Seleucid and Ptolemaic rulers were regularly deified, so that the whole Hellenistic world was familiar with the concept.[18] The first Roman to be deified after his death was Julius Caesar, the adoptive father of Octavian, the future Augustus. Before his funeral, Caesar's body lay in state in the Roman Forum, hidden from view but represented by a wax effigy. The mob tried to cremate him on the spot and inter his ashes in the Temple of Jupiter, as befitted a god. The Senate managed to thwart this plan, but the popular deification of Caesar could not be checked. Some months later, during the games held in his honor, there appeared the famous comet that was seen by the plebs— and by Octavian—as the soul of Caesar ascending the heavens. Capitalizing on the people's acclamation of his murdered father, Octavian persuaded the Senate to give Caesar formal recognition as a god.[19]

When Augustus himself died in AD 14, his enrolment among the gods was regarded as a matter of course, and his funeral was designed to express this idea. Once again, the body was concealed in a coffin, being represented by a wax effigy displayed above. Two gilded statues of Augustus, one borne on a triumphal chariot, were brought to the Forum as well.[20] After the eulogies were delivered, the body, accompanied by the wax effigy, was carried to the Campus Martius, where Romulus, the legendary founder of Rome, was believed to have ascended to heaven.[21] There it was laid on a pyre and consigned to the flames. Afterward, an official swore on oath that he had seen the form (*effigiem*) of the dead emperor ascending heavenward from the pyre, echoing the ascent of Hercules. This was all the testimony the Senate required to declare formally that Augustus had become a god.

About a decade and a half before Easter, then, Augustus made the same posthumous journey as Jesus, rising into the realm of the divine. The story of the emperor's ascent would have been known throughout the empire, even among Jews, and the Ascension of Jesus would certainly have been viewed in opposition to this pagan precedent. Augustus ascended, to all intents and purposes, in the form of his wax effigy, which disappeared before the eyes of the mourners and was then allegedly seen mounting the heavens. Could Jesus not have emulated him, ascending via his cloth "effigy?" Obviously, the circumstances were completely different, but, as the Egyptian examples show, the imagery of apotheosis could operate in a variety of ways.[22]

Once the ceremonies were over, contact with the deified Augustus was maintained via his portraits, which represented him exalted in the afterlife, as in his earthly life. Due to the likeness of the emperor in his portrait, it was perceived as somehow identical with him.[23] The Shroud could have been viewed similarly, as a likeness through which the absent, celestial Jesus was made manifest. If Romans could look at a gilded colossus and see in it their deified emperor, the followers of Jesus could have looked at the ethereal Shroud figure and seen in it their exalted Messiah. And the fate of his physical body need not have played any part in their thinking, any more than the fate of Augustus's body affected belief in his apotheosis. The flesh was unimportant; images alone could convey you to the stars.

Our hypothesis is now complete. Based on a range of anthropological, archaeological and art-historical evidence, it can reasonably be stated that, if the Shroud was found in Jesus' tomb, it would have caused his followers to believe not only that he had been raised from the dead but also that he had been assumed into heaven. That is to say, it would have prompted belief in his exaltation.

With the help of the Shroud, we can now retell the story of Easter.

PART 5

Easter

18

The Burial and the Myth

The history of the Resurrection begins not on Easter Sunday but on Good Friday, the day of the Crucifixion, with scenes of scarcely imaginable torture—the so-called Passion of Jesus—and the purchase of a fine linen sheet. To understand what happened on Easter morning, when the Risen Christ was first witnessed, we need to understand, first of all, how Jesus died and was laid in the tomb two days earlier.

The Gospels tell us how, on the morning of Good Friday, Jesus was tried by Pontius Pilate and was sentenced to be crucified, how he was then flogged and beaten and crowned with thorns, and finally how he was led out to Golgotha, a slight rise to the northwest of Jerusalem, where his ordeal reached its climax.[1] Essentially the same story is implicit in the Shroud, which documents his sufferings in excruciating detail. There is no point rehearsing those sufferings here. Horrific as it was, there was nothing particularly unusual about the treatment of Jesus. He was just one more victim of the efficient rites of execution practiced by the Roman Empire.

Jesus endured the agony of the cross for about three hours, from noon until 3 p.m., when he eventually gave up the ghost.[2] There is no justification whatsoever for the perennial claim that, somehow, he escaped death, perhaps entering a coma. Three hours of such torture would have been quite sufficient to drain the life from someone as badly beaten as Jesus, and the Shroud, which displays signs of rigor mortis and post-mortem blood flows, is proof positive that he did not survive the cross.

It is the fate of Jesus' body after death that concerns us here. The Gospels all agree that the dead Jesus was laid to rest in a tomb. Although this testimony is sometimes doubted, it is supported by the First Creed and also by the existence of the Shroud. Like Jehohanan, the crucifixion victim whose remains were discovered in an ossuary in 1968, Jesus was buried by sympathizers, not flung into a common grave or left as carrion for wild animals. But, beyond the bare fact of its occurrence, little about his burial is clear. To understand the episode, we need to ask how his body was treated, giving priority to the evidence of the Shroud. Only then will we be ready to decide what happened at the tomb on Easter morning, when the supposed miracle of the Resurrection was discovered.

Once Jesus died, his compatriots would have been concerned to have his body laid in a tomb before sundown, for Jewish law decreed that an executed man should not be hung on a tree overnight.[3] In Jesus' case, the desire to bury him that afternoon would have been particularly urgent, since the next day was a Sabbath, when no work—and hence no funeral—could be performed. In such circumstances, a Jewish deputation would almost certainly have petitioned Pilate for the body, so that the law would not be broken. All the Gospels concur that a petition was made and that the man who made it was a wealthy sympathizer of Jesus named Joseph of Arimathea.

Informed of the Jewish law and disinclined, for once, to provoke needless hostility, Pilate acceded to the request. The order was given to the soldiers guarding the cross to hand Jesus over for burial. The Shroud helps us visualize the scene. First, they checked he was dead by spearing his side. Then they removed the single nail fixing his feet to the *suppedaneum*. Next, they heaved the cross-beam off the top of the *stipes* and dumped it on the ground, with the corpse still attached. Finally, they drew out the nails impaling his wrists, picked up the *patibulum*—to be used for later crucifixions—and headed off back to barracks, leaving the body to be collected by Joseph.

It is difficult to know exactly how Joseph proceeded, but the evidence of the Shroud and the Gospels permits a reasonably confident reconstruction. Mark tells us that, having been granted leave to bury Jesus, Joseph went out and "bought a linen shroud [*sindon*]."[4] This is an explicit reference to the Shroud, which Joseph must have taken with him to Golgotha. He cannot have gone there alone. To carry the body to a tomb, he would have needed the assistance of at least one other man. (This could have been Nicodemus, whom John says assisted at the burial, but John's narrative is untrustworthy at this point, as I shall explain below.)

Before transporting the body, Joseph and his helper, whoever he was, must surely have covered it, partly to veil the upsetting sight of the corpse, partly for the sake of decorum. It is likely that the Shroud was used to wrap the body of Jesus at this stage (cf. Figure 13). The Synoptics (and the *Gospel of Peter*) all mention a *sindon* in connection with Joseph's removal of Jesus' body. In all these texts it is said that the body was wrapped in the linen shroud before being laid in the tomb, implying that Jesus was carried to the tomb in the cloth.[5] I see no reason to doubt that the Shroud was used to transport the body, in conjunction with a simple stretcher or bier. Indeed, this might help explain some of the drips and smudges of blood observable on the cloth, such as those beside the feet and the right elbow.[6]

This would mean that the body of Jesus was washed on Golgotha. As we have seen, the body enfolded in the Shroud was definitely washed, in accordance with Jewish law. It makes sense for this rite to have been performed outside, where the body lay, rather than in a dark, cramped tomb. Had the body been laid unwashed in the Shroud for transport, then uncovered in the tomb, washed, and draped in the cloth once again, we should expect to be able to detect two sets of blood marks—and a lot more blood in general.

The washing of the body is not mentioned in any of the canonical Gospels, but it is recorded in the non-canonical *Gospel of Peter*: "And he took the Lord, *washed him*, wrapped him in linen and brought him into his own sepulchre, called Joseph's Garden."[7] The *Gospel of Peter* also describes another scene omitted by the canonical Gospels: the removal of the nails and the deposition from the cross ("And then they drew the nails from the hands of the Lord and laid him on the earth").[8] In its description of the treatment of the body, then, the *Gospel of Peter* can claim to be more accurate than its New Testament counterparts, suggesting it contains early, well-informed traditions.

Taking account of the Gospel evidence, the Shroud and contemporary Jewish customs, we can reconstruct Joseph's care for the body of Jesus as follows. As the soldiers departed the scene, Joseph and his assistant(s) came up and took possession of the bloody corpse, left lying at the foot of the cross. First of all, they would have broken the rigor mortis in the shoulders and repositioned the hands over the groin, so that they could manoeuvre the body more easily and so that the arms could be contained within the *sovev* (the winding sheet). Then they would have turned the corpse over on its front and washed its back, removing the dirt and blood clots in which it was caked, exposing the marks of the scourge. Next, having placed the *sovev*-covered bier alongside, they would have turned the body over again and laid it on the cloth. They would then have set about washing the front of the body. Taking care to avoid any "unclean" blood ("lifeblood") that had seeped from the body after death, they would have wiped away the grime and sweat and clotted blood everywhere else. The "unclean" blood included the small flow from the spear wound and the fresh dribbles from the hands and feet. As they cleaned the wrists and forearms, which had just been pressed onto the ground, they could not avoid wetting the lifeblood on them, which began to reliquefy and drip down onto the cloth below, mingling with the water. The crown of thorns must have been removed after the head was washed, and the resulting dribbles of blood were left in place.

Given the state of the body, the washing is likely to have taken some time, but the buriers would have worked as quickly as they could, because it was late in the day and Jesus had to be entombed before sunset.[9] The Shroud testifies to the care they took, despite the hurry, cleansing his body being all they could now do for Jesus. Contrary to popular belief, no anointing took place: there is no trace of any ointment on the Shroud, and no Gospel mentions an anointing. Finally, Joseph and his helper(s) draped the other half of the cloth (the half destined to bear the frontal image) over the body, lifted the bier and set off for the tomb.

"Now in the place where he was crucified there was a garden, and in the garden a new tomb where no one had ever been laid. So because of the Jewish day of Preparation, as the tomb was close at hand, they laid Jesus there."[10] This account of the tomb by John is entirely credible. Golgotha was situated beside an old quarry, which was used as a burial-ground and a place for growing fruit and vegetables. The Synoptics tell us that the tomb was hewn out of the rock, which is also perfectly credible: several rock-hewn tombs have been found in the area, cut into the cliffs of the ex-quarry. Matthew states that the sepulchre belonged to Joseph of Arimathea, but this is less likely than John's statement that it was chosen because it was near at hand. It would certainly have been a strange coincidence if Joseph happened to own a tomb nearby.

Is it possible to identify the exact location of the tomb? Christian tradition holds that it is the tomb enshrined in the so-called Edicule at the center of the Church of the Holy Sepulchre in Jerusalem, a tomb excavated in 325–6 when Emperor Constantine set about redeveloping the reputed site of Christ's death, then occupied by a pagan temple. To everyone's amazement, after digging down through layers of infill, the emperor's workmen uncovered an empty tomb, which was immediately hailed as the Holy Sepulchre.[11] Because the Edicule has been almost completely rebuilt since the fourth century, we have no way of knowing whether the identification was based on anything solid, like an inscription, or was simply a convenient guess. Being in the vicinity of Golgotha, the tomb was certainly in the right area, but several other rock-cut tombs of the same period exist nearby, all of them empty, and, for all we know, one these could have been the actual chamber where Jesus was buried.[12]

In any case, the tomb was close by, and the small burial party would not have taken long to reach it. According to the Synoptics, the men were accompanied by some women, including Mary Magdalene, but, if so, they did not take an active part in the burial. They just "followed, and saw the tomb, and how his body was laid."[13] It was up to Joseph and his assistant(s) to fulfil the law. With one of them inside, they would have passed the bier through the low, narrow entrance into the burial chamber, then lifted the body, still loosely enshrouded, onto a broad stone shelf. That was all. The corpse was washed and underground; there was no time to do anything more. The Shroud was left swathed over the body from head and toe, as it had been on the bier. There was no point tying it up, as the women would come to anoint the body after the Sabbath.

Their duty done, the men exited the cave, trundled a blocking stone (or some other obstruction) into place, and, with dusk descending, walked somberly back toward the city. With them may have trailed a group of mournful women, who, thirty-six hours later, would return to the tomb and then leave it again in a state of bewildered excitement.

I said above that John's account of the burial was untrustworthy. We can now see why. His description of the tomb may repeat reliable tradition, but, instead of telling how Joseph wrapped the body of Jesus in a linen shroud, he inserts a fanciful account of a costly funeral:

> Nicodemus also, who had at first come to him by night, came bringing a mixture of myrrh and aloes about a hundred pounds' weight. They took the body of Jesus, and bound it in linen cloths [*othonia*] with the spices, as is the burial custom of the Jews.[14]

This account is clearly incompatible with the reconstruction just achieved on the basis of the Shroud and the brief statements in the Synoptics. Jesus did not receive a full burial, as envisaged by John. His body was not covered in spices and bound in multiple cloths; it was just washed and draped in a linen shroud. The incredible quantity of myrrh and aloes—enough to fill a large coffin—is a clear sign that John's story is fabricated. It is an imaginary scene, representing the kingly style in which Jesus *ought* to have been buried, not the hasty circumstances of his actual burial.[15]

The indications are that John found this story in one of his sources. It may be that whoever originally composed the story knew of the Shroud and intended the "linen cloths" (*othonia*) to refer to it.[16] If so, the reference was lost on John himself, who evidently saw no significance in these cloths. For him, they were just generic elements in a customary burial. Later on, however, John does give a detailed description of another cloth found in the empty tomb, one about which he appears to have specific information. He calls this cloth the *soudarion*. Although it plays no part in his account of the burial, it is worth discussing the *soudarion* in this context, as it evidently relates to the burial cloths.

The *soudarion* comes into the story of Peter and the Beloved Disciple running off to the tomb of Jesus early on Easter morning, having been alerted to the disappearance of the body by Mary Magdalene. Peter enters the tomb first and sees not only the "linen cloths," which were visible from the entrance, but also,

> the napkin [*soudarion*], which had been on [*epi*] his head, not lying with the linen cloths [*othonia*] but rolled up [*entetuligmenon*] in a place by itself.[17]

There are some difficulties of translation here. The Greek word *soudarion*, rendered "napkin" in the RSV translation above, derives from the Latin word *sudarium*, meaning "sweat-cloth." Usually, a *soudarion* would have been about the size of a napkin or hand-towel, but we know of exceptions to this rule, and, if the term was chosen because of its etymology, the cloth could have been any size. John associates the cloth with Jesus' head, but the Greek preposition *epi* can mean "on," "over," or "around," so the precise relationship between his head and the cloth is unclear. Lastly, the word *entetuligmenon* can mean either "rolled up" or "folded up." All this ambiguity means it is difficult to know exactly how John envisaged the *soudarion* in the empty tomb.

A popular idea among Shroud researchers is that he had in mind a bloodstained, towel-sized piece of linen kept since the eighth century in the Spanish city of Oviedo, a relic known as the Sudarium of Oviedo.[18] This relic has recently been the subject of extensive scientific investigation. The investigators claim not only that it was genuinely used to cover the head of a victim of crucifixion, but also that its pattern of bloodstains is consistent with the image of the head on the Shroud of Turin.[19] This claim is difficult to evaluate, since interpreting the Oviedo cloth's bloodstains is far from straightforward, but I see no reason in principle why a cloth used to cover the head of the crucified Jesus should not have survived. If the Shroud was as important as I think it was, any associated cloth would have been of potential interest.[20] However, the provenance of the Oviedo Sudarium is problematic. Legendary histories trace it back only to the year 614, when it was reputedly rescued from Jerusalem, where the Christians were being attacked by a joint force of Persians and Jews.[21] Before the early seventh century, there is no clear trace of the cloth, and an unofficial carbon-dating test may suggest that it came into existence nearer the seventh century than the first (although this result is far from conclusive).[22]

Even if the Sudarium of Oviedo could be proven to be a genuine relic of Jesus, it would still not mean that it was the *soudarion* John mentions. John might well have been thinking of another cloth, and, in fact, a better case can be made for one with a far stronger claim to have been found in the tomb of Jesus—the Shroud itself.[23] A large winding sheet could have been termed a *soudarion*. We know this because a seventh-century bishop called Arculf reported seeing a *soudarion* in Jerusalem, reputed to be the shroud of Christ, which was 8 feet long.[24] From the twelfth century, as interest in the Shroud/Mandylion grew, it was regularly referred to as a *soudarion*, and there is no reason why John could not have referred to it similarly.[25]

Mention of the Mandylion reminds us, though, that the Shroud may not have looked like a large sheet at the time John wrote. What if the Shroud had been transformed by then into the Mandylion? Might the *soudarion* be meant to represent the Shroud in its Mandylion format (minus the framing)? This would certainly help explain the peculiar precision of John's description of the cloth, which fits the Mandylion in several ways. First, the term *soudarion* would have been particularly appropriate for the Mandylion, since, as well as connoting the "sweaty" appearance of the image, it also denoted a cloth of the right apparent size. Second, the association with the head, rather than any other part of the body, makes sense in relation to the image of the Holy Face. Third, the description of the cloth as "folded up" (*entetuligmenon*) fits the reconstruction of the Mandylion as the folded Shroud. For all these reasons—and also for another crucial reason to be explained in due course—the *soudarion* is best interpreted, I think, as an early reference to the Mandylion.

Quite how John imagined the Shroud was used, or how he thought the image came into existence, is difficult to tell. One thing is clear, though: he did not think of it as one of the cloths in which Jesus was buried. His tradition spoke of Jesus being bound in *othonia*, and he is careful to keep these cloths separate from the *soudarion*. Perhaps he thought of it as a cloth used to carry the corpse to the tomb; perhaps he imagined Jesus taking hold of the folded cloth, putting it to his face and projecting onto it a living witness to his Passion;[26] perhaps he did not envisage any scenario at all. John probably gave little or no thought to the *use* of the Shroud. His interest was in its *meaning*, its testimony to the death and Resurrection of Jesus. It was important for him to locate it in the empty tomb, but he probably had no idea how it came to be there.

One final question: if the *soudarion* in John's story of the empty tomb represents the Shroud/Mandylion, why is there no mention of its image? There are two answers to this. First, John's audience would presumably have been aware of the nature of the relic, just as later Christians were aware of the nature of the Mandylion, and did not need to be told that it bore a miraculous imprint. (If I say, "I went to Turin and saw the Shroud," I hardly need mention that the Shroud bears an image.) Secondly, the phenomenon we regard as an image would have been perceived differently in the first century. John himself would have seen it as an angelic double of the Risen Jesus. He clearly felt justified in introducing the cloth into the narrative, but he may have balked at incorporating a reference to the Shroud figure, which would have been difficult to differentiate from the Risen Jesus himself.

Let us return to the scene of the burial.

The entrance is blocked, and the buriers have departed. Nothing moves in the rock-hewn chamber; nothing breathes. In the dark, silent underworld, beyond the bounds of everyday experience, the scarred body of Jesus begins its mysterious migration from flesh to cloth. Gradually, in total obscurity, the linen sheet enveloping the crucified man takes on his ghostly image; two shadowy figures slowly materialize on the inner surface of the Shroud. Still nothing stirs or glimmers in the tomb. The quiet of the grave remains inviolate.

This is how I imagine the immediate afterlife of Jesus, based on the evidence of the Shroud. What occurred to produce the image? Why did the marvelous figures materialize? As yet, no one can say for sure. However, everyone who has studied the Shroud and regards it as authentic agrees that the creation of the image can be described in scientific terms. As Jesus lay in the tomb, something happened to cause the surfaces of some of the linen fibers of the cloth to become discolored in a pattern corresponding to the underlying form of his body.

Many would accept that this could have been a chemical reaction between the Shroud and the decomposing flesh, as argued by Ray Rogers. Others, influenced by their Christian faith, would insist that something supernatural must have happened to produce the Shroud. The majority of sindonologists imagine the body dematerializing in a flash of holy radiance, the image being a visible trace of God's timely reinvention of human flesh. This idea is in tension, of course, with scientific naturalism—miracles, by definition, cannot be explained scientifically—but it is nevertheless conditioned by scientific thinking, as the frequent attempts to describe the supposed miracle in terms of nuclear physics demonstrate. Whether as the result of an ordinary chemical reaction, then, or a burst of supernatural radiation, the Shroud is viewed today through scientific spectacles, as a stain produced by a mysterious process.

This is not how it would have been viewed 2,000 years ago. Any first-century account of the creation of the Shroud would have been very different from the scientific accounts we give today. Bearing in mind the argument of Part 4, it would have involved the appearance in the tomb of an extraordinary being, or beings, enacting the Resurrection (and simultaneous Ascension) of Jesus. The inanimate figures in my account would have been rendered animate; in place of science there would have been myth.

As it happens, an early Christian story fulfilling this prediction does exist, though not in the canonical Gospels, which are silent about the moment of the Resurrection. The story of the "escorted Resurrection-Ascension," as it has been called, is best preserved in the *Gospel of Peter*, which tells of Jesus being fetched from the tomb the night before Easter by a pair of glorious, angelic men.[27] This myth represents a transparent attempt, in my view, to give narrative expression to the Shroud. It could almost have been written to illustrate my argument.

As we have seen, the Shroud could have been viewed in the first century essentially in three different ways: as an angel (or pair of angels); as the Risen Jesus; or as (a sign of) the Ascended Jesus (see Figure 55). As different aspects of the same person—present and absent—the Risen Jesus and the Ascended Jesus would have merged into one another. The angel(s), through whom the Resurrection-Ascension was made manifest, could have been perceived either alone or in company with Jesus. On the basis of this analysis we can say that, if an early Christian myth-maker had wanted to narrate the Resurrection, he would probably have told a story about an angel (or pair of angels) visiting the entombed Jesus and accompanying him as he was raised from the dead and into heaven. This is exactly what we find in the *Gospel of Peter*.

The story goes like this. Following the Crucifixion, Joseph of Arimathea has buried the body of Jesus, and the Jewish elders have engaged some Roman soldiers to guard the tomb, to prevent his disciples from stealing the body and falsely claiming that he had been resurrected.[28] Ironically, the elders and the guards then witness Jesus being resurrected for real.

Now in the night in which the Lord's day dawned, when the soldiers, two by two in every watch, were keeping guard, there rang out a loud voice in heaven, and they saw the heavens opened and two men come down from there in a great brightness and draw nigh to the sepulchre. That stone which had been laid against the entrance to the sepulchre started of itself to roll and gave way to the side, and the sepulchre was opened, and both the young men entered in. When now those soldiers saw this, they awakened the centurion and the elders—for they also were there to assist the watch. And while they were relating what they had seen, they saw again three men come out from the sepulchre, and two of them sustaining the other . . . and the heads of the two reaching to heaven, but that of him who was led of them by the hand over-passing the heavens.[29]

The two men who descend from heaven in a blaze of glory are surely angelic incarnations of the Shroud figures.[30] They are said to enter Jesus' sepulchre, the very place where the Shroud was discovered. When they emerge, they are no longer alone but are accompanied by the Risen Jesus, whom they sustain and lead by the hand. As soon as he exits the tomb, the Risen Jesus merges seamlessly into the Ascended Jesus; while the heads of the two men reach to heaven, Christ's overpasses the heavens, signifying his celestial ascent. This completes the hat-trick of Shroud-inspired motifs.

The connection between the "escorted Resurrection-Ascension" and the Shroud is reinforced by one further incident. As soon as the divine procession disappears, the soldiers and elders get together and discuss what to do. But they are interrupted by another startling apparition:

And while they were still deliberating, the heavens were again seen to open, and a man descended and entered into the sepulchre.[31]

Is this one of the Resurrection-Ascension escorts returning or a new angel altogether? The question is misconceived, since the figures are not individualized. What matters is that he is the equivalent of the previous pair. First, the heavens open, and *two* men come down and enter the tomb; now the heavens open, and *one* man comes down and enters the tomb. The only difference is the number, and this reflects the ambiguity of the Shroud—do the frontal and dorsal images represent one person or two? The reason for altering the number is to prepare for the subsequent tomb-story, in which Mary Magdalene and her female companions encounter a mysterious man sitting in the sepulchre.[32] This forges another link between the Shroud, which must have been found in the sepulchre by the women, and the two men involved in the Resurrection-Ascension.

The story told in the *Gospel of Peter* represents every aspect of the animistic perception of the Shroud, uniting the three key interpretations of the

Shroud figure in one glorious, sacred masque. It is as close a literary analogue of the Shroud hypothesis as we could hope to find. And the match is
especially significant because it is the *only* early Christian account we have
of what happened to Jesus in the tomb. That the *Gospel of Peter* was not
chosen to be part of the New Testament in the fourth century (though it
had its supporters) makes not a whit of difference to its evidentiary value.
It forms part of the same great river of early Christian imagery as flows
through the canonical Gospels. Paying heed to non-canonical works like
the *Gospel of Peter* is essential if we are to achieve a full understanding of
the birth of Christianity.[33]

The nocturnal drama of the *Gospel of Peter* might conceivably be dismissed
as a late, baseless charade, were it without parallel. But it is not. The
Gospel of Peter transmits the fullest version of the "escorted Resurrection-
Ascension" story, but the same basic narrative crops up in a range of other
texts, proving that it was widely known by the late first century.[34] Most
notably, it inspired Luke's tale of the Ascension in Acts.

The Ascension is narrated in the first chapter of Acts, after Luke has
reminded the reader of the Resurrection appearances, said to have taken
place over the course of forty days. This period comes to an end when
Jesus takes his disciples to the Mount of Olives outside Jerusalem and
delivers a valedictory speech, telling them that, once they have received the
Holy Spirit, they will be his witnesses throughout the world:

> And when he had said this, as they were looking on, he was lifted up, and a
> cloud took him out of their sight. And while they were gazing into heaven as
> he went, behold, two men stood by them in white robes, and said "Men of
> Galilee, why do you stand looking into heaven? This Jesus, who was taken
> up from you into heaven, will come in the same way as you saw him go into
> heaven."[35]

The imagery corresponds closely to the *Gospel of Peter* story. At its core
is the figure of the Risen Jesus ascending heavenward, while two angelic
men appear to the startled witnesses. The sequence of events is different—
here, the angelic men make their appearance only after the ascent—but it
is the basic concordance of the imagery that matters. The tale maps onto
the interpretation of the Shroud almost as well as the *Gospel of Peter* narrative (cf. Figure 55). The way in which the two men appear at the very
moment the Risen Christ vanishes from sight is particularly apt, since,
seen as mediating angels, the Shroud figures represent the absent, Ascended
Jesus.[36] The Risen Jesus disappears and is immediately replaced by a pair

of men who speak of his heavenly existence: the text is a perfect match for the split interpretation of the Shroud.

The fact that the "escorted Resurrection-Ascension" is echoed in Acts proves that it was an early, influential story; it was not a marginal tradition, of interest only to "heretics." The earliest Easter narratives were accounts of the historical events of Easter Day, not imaginary descriptions of the Resurrection. Relatively soon, however, someone decided to fill this gap in the Gospel record by consulting the Shroud, the sole "witness" to the Resurrection. The "escorted Resurrection-Ascension" is simply the translation of the Shroud into an appropriate narrative. It is not exactly a historical tradition—as a myth, it can hardly be called historical—but it does reveal how the Resurrection and Ascension were conceived by early Christians.

The core of the narrative is the image of two heavenly men flanking the figure of the Exalted Jesus. This image, which I call the Triple Figure, was at the heart of early Christian myth-making (and possibly also picture-making).[37] Its influence was not confined to stories about Jesus set after his death. The clearest example of its use in another context is the famous tale of the Transfiguration, in which three of the disciples see Jesus gloriously transformed, his face shining "like the sun" and his clothes "white as light," accompanied by two heavenly men (identified as Moses and Elijah).[38] Luke was happy to postpone the occasion of the Resurrection-Ascension by forty days; whoever devised the Transfiguration story decided to shift it earlier instead, employing the same imagery to express the exaltation of Jesus during his earthly ministry (cf. Figure 58).

The popularity of the Triple Figure may have been aided, as we shall see, by its "discovery" in certain passages of scripture, but it was the Shroud that supplied the basis for the imagery. It was in front of the Shroud that, after his death, the followers of Jesus "saw his glory and the two men who stood with him."[39] The settings they gave this idea were superficial; the idea itself was fundamental.

Best preserved in the *Gospel of Peter*, the "escorted Resurrection-Ascension" takes us back, on the wings of the early Christian imagination, to the very moment when Jesus rose from the dead, showing us precisely how the Shroud was understood by its original interpreters. Even now, the Shroud gives rise to some fantastical ideas. The *Gospel of Peter* fairy-tale is comparable to attempts by some sindonologists to envisage the Resurrection as a controlled nuclear reaction, in which Jesus' corpse was transformed into a sort of quantum body, straddling two separate realms of existence.[40]

Modern Shroud researchers cannot help thinking about the Shroud in terms of exotic science, just as the ancients were bound to view it in terms of a cosmic myth.

Moving on, it is time to lay such speculation aside and examine the historical evidence. Christians believe in the Resurrection not because they think anyone witnessed the celestial traffic described in the *Gospel of Peter*, nor because they wager the Shroud was produced by the luminous dematerialization of a human body, but because they have faith in the testimony of Paul and the Easter stories in the Gospels, which speak of what was witnessed in the wake of the supposed miracle. To get to grips with what really happened at Easter, we need to concentrate on this all-important evidence.

19

The Far-from-Empty Tomb

Dawn is breaking over the ancient city of Jerusalem. Quietly, just like any other, a new week is beginning in the capital of Roman-occupied Judaea. Scarcely anything stirs. A little way outside the city walls a small group of women can be seen walking along the track that leads to Golgotha, the place of public execution. They are weeping, and each carries a small jar of ointment in her hands.

After a little, they veer off the track and take a path along the side of the hill, until they reach an area of cultivated ground, where a rocky prominence catches the first, weak rays of the rising sun. At the base of this outcrop is the entrance to a subterranean tomb, visible as a rough rectangle of darkness carved into the rock-face. There is a great round stone alongside, which has evidently been rolled away from its position in front of the cave opening.

When the women see the stone out of place, they stop, startled, and exchange a few words. Tentatively, they approach the tomb. One of them peers in and then enters. The others follow. Inside, instead of the wrapped body of the man whose burial they have come to complete, they find nothing but abandoned burial cloths—the body has vanished! They look around in consternation, wondering what has happened, guessing who might have been there, who might have taken the body of their beloved Jesus. Then, lamenting this latest misfortune, they rush out of the tomb and hasten back along the path to Jerusalem, to tell Peter and the other disciples that the body is no longer where it was laid.

Plus or minus a few details, this is how most of us, nowadays, tell ourselves the story of the women's visit to the tomb on Easter morning, how we rationalize and harmonize the four legendary accounts of the episode found in the Gospels. It is a compelling story, which depends for its appeal on the haunting mystery of the empty tomb and for its plausibility on the lack of any supernatural element. The only problem is that, however compelling it may seem, from the moment the women reach the tomb the story becomes historically unintelligible. For centuries scholars have been trying to account for the supposed fact of the empty tomb and to integrate it into complex theories about the rise of the Resurrection belief, but, for one reason or another, their efforts have all failed. The empty tomb is a "fact" that cannot be made to fit.

What we need is a new explanation of the women's trip to the tomb, one that can reveal what really happened, why the story was originally told, and how it developed into the various stories we know today. The necessary explanation is provided by the Shroud.

To the arguments already given for regarding the tomb-stories as based on a real historical episode we may now add another, based on the Shroud. The very existence of the Shroud is evidence that Jesus' tomb was visited soon after he was buried. For, despite its intended function, the cloth did not remain wrapped around the body; someone removed it after only a short space of time, before the onset of decomposition.[1] The Shroud also reveals that the funerary rites were left incomplete, which suggests that people returned to the sepulchre to complete the burial.

These people, the Gospels tell us, were women. Since burial was a family affair in ancient Judaea, we can be confident that they were relatives of Jesus. It seems that Jesus came from a large family. The Gospels refer to at least two sisters and four brothers, some of whom, at least, were married.[2] There was also his mother, Mary, whom John places at the Crucifixion. Any or all of these women could have attended his burial. Moreover, Jesus is likely to have had a wife. Pious first-century Jews took very seriously God's command to Adam and Eve to "be fruitful and multiply," and it was most unusual for a mature man to remain unmarried. Celibates existed at the time, but there is no evidence that Jesus was one of them. Indeed, it seems that he was followed and executed as a would-be king of Israel,[3] and a celibate king would have been unthinkable.

The Gospels offer us the names of the women who went to the tomb, although their lists are inconsistent. The one name that appears right across the board is Mary Magdalene. She was evidently remembered as the most important member of the group. There are two possible explanations for her prominence. The first is that she subsequently became a dominant personality in the early Church, and so the tomb-stories exaggerate her role in the episode, masking the fact that she was a peripheral figure at the time. The second is that she was indeed the principal member of the burial party. In the latter case, it is likely that she was Jesus' widow. Either way, Mary Magdalene stands out as the most significant female visitor to the tomb.

Piecing together a historical portrait of Mary Magdalene is extremely difficult. Among Gnostic Christians of the late first and second centuries she was revered as a particularly close follower of Jesus. In the *Gospel of Philip*, for instance, she is called his "companion," and it is said that "[Christ loved] her more than [all] the disciples and used to kiss her [often] on her [mouth]."[4] Orthodox Christians, by contrast, came to see her, on little or no evidence, as a reformed prostitute, a misogynistic slander conditioned by their disputes with the Gnostics. There is evidence to suggest that Mary was an influential rival of Peter, a situation which accounts both for her relative obscurity in the canonical Gospels and her later defamation. But, as yet, this rivalry and Mary's role in early Christianity remain obscure.

John is definitely wrong to portray Mary as a lonely soul wandering along to the tomb by herself. His own text testifies to the presence of at least one other woman. When Mary speaks to Peter and the Beloved Disciple she speaks in the first-person plural: "They have taken the Lord out of the tomb, and *we* do not know where they have laid him."[5] Clearly, Mary did not go to the tomb alone in John's source, which he did not edit very carefully. According to all three Synoptic Gospels, Mary Magdalene was accompanied by another Mary. This was almost certainly Jesus' mother, whose attendance at his burial would have been entirely expected.[6] At least one other woman seems to have accompanied them. Mark calls her Salome, while Luke mentions someone called Joanna.[7]

In modern reconstructions of the empty tomb episode Mary Magdalene and her companions are considered the sole protagonists. In each of the four Gospels, however, the women are accosted at or in the tomb by a mysterious, angelic figure (or pair of figures). This overlooked, supernatural protagonist can be identified with the Shroud figure. The tomb-angels are described differently in each of the Gospels, but every detail is explicable in terms of the Shroud.

I am not the first to suggest that the tomb-angels might relate to the Shroud. The Reverend Albert Dreisbach has asked in passing whether John's description of "two angels in white, sitting where the body of Jesus lay, one at the head and one at the feet" might have been inspired by the Shroud.[8] Consider how well the description of the two angels in John's account fits with the two figures lying on the tomb-slab. The angels are said to be

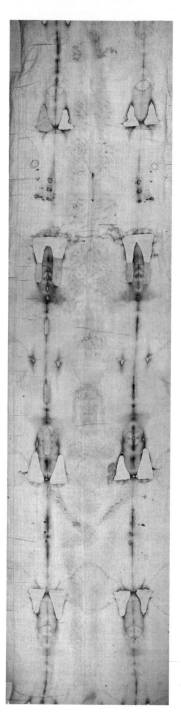

1. The Shroud full-length, as it appeared before the 2002 restoration. The cloth is approximately 14 feet 4 inches long and 3 feet 7 inches wide. Either side of the figures are the parallel scorches and burn holes made in the fire of 1532, patched afterward by Clarissan nuns.

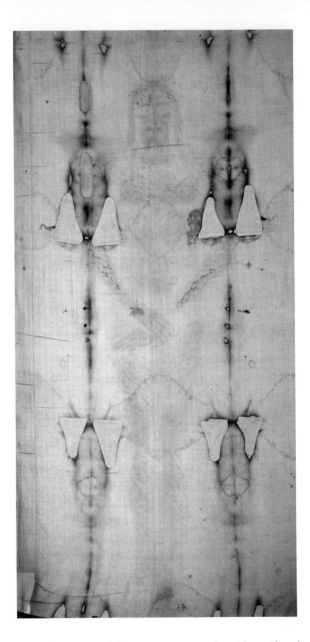

2. Seen vertically, the frontal figure appears to stand upright, as if confronting the viewer. The image is largely undistorted, except for some slight widening of the thighs, due to the fall of the cloth over the legs. Large, diamond-shaped water stains are clearly visible around the knees and chest.

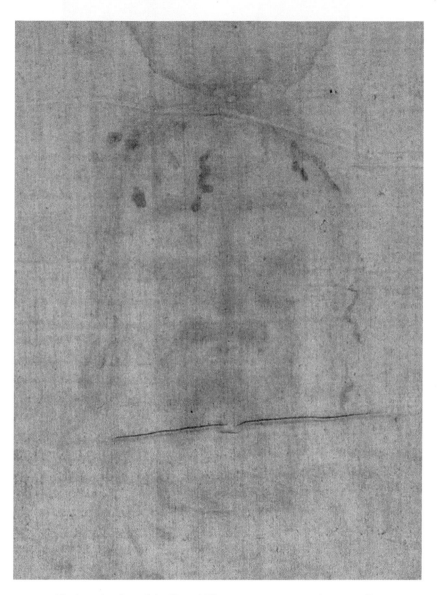

3. The haunting face of the Shroud. The eyes appear open and unnaturally large, the whole visage suffused with inner light. A vertical line cuts through the image on the left, caused by a batch of threads that for some reason did not discolor. Seen in poor light, the bloodstains on the forehead and hair might be mistaken for splashes of water.

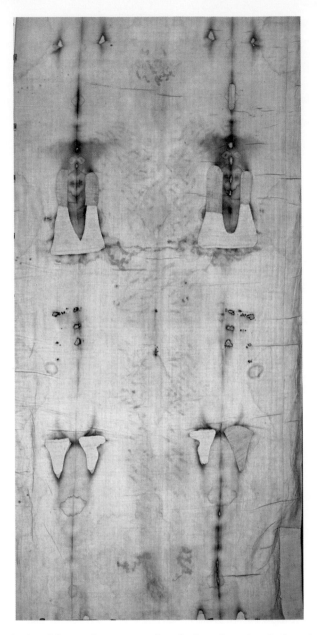

4. The dorsal figure is less arresting than the frontal one, but displays many vivid signs of torture, from the wounds around the scalp to the trails of blood beside the feet. Particularly striking are the marks of flagellation seen all over the body. Note also the symmetrical "poker-holes" either side of the figure.

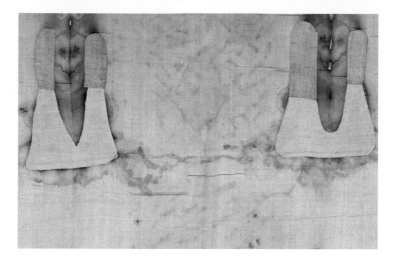

5. Two pools of watery blood stained the cloth either side of the dorsal figure. In the past, these stains have been interpreted by Shroud researchers in terms of the "blood and water" said to have issued from Christ's side as he hung on the Cross (John 19.34). They are much more likely to derive from the washing of the corpse.

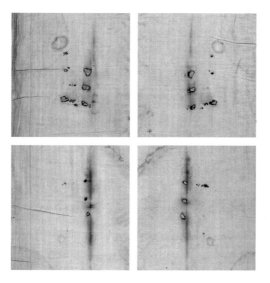

6. The four sets of "poker-holes" either side of the dorsal figure (*top*) and frontal figure (*bottom*). These were made when the cloth was folded in quarters and are possibly the result of an accident involving lumps of burning incense.

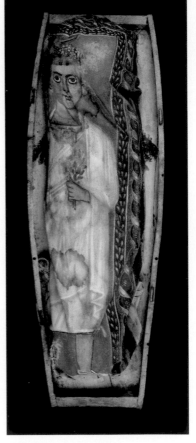

7. A well-preserved linen shroud
from second-century Egypt, bearing
a full-length portrait of a woman.
This is one of many such shrouds
to survive from antiquity. Kept in
the right conditions, linen can
remain intact and pliable over
thousands of years.

8. An Egyptian shroud of the third
century AD, wrapped around the
mummy of a child, whose portrait
it bears. Painted shrouds like this
were a means of ensuring the
survival of the deceased in the next
world. Note the excellent condition
of the linen cloth.

9. A pilgrim's badge made to commemorate the first display of the Shroud at the French village of Lirey in 1355 or 1356, showing the relic held up by two clerics above the Instruments of the Passion and the de Charny coat of arms. Despite the tiny size of the image, the artist has managed to depict the herringbone weave of the cloth.

10. A beautiful depiction of Christ as the "Man of Sorrows," adored by Duke Charles I of Savoy and his wife, Blanche de Montferrat, from the *Très Riches Heures du Duc de Berry*, c.1485. The blood flows and crossed arms of Christ clearly evoke the Shroud, which was acquired by Charles's grandfather, Louis, in 1453.

11. Dated 1516, this painted copy of the Shroud from the church of St Gommaire in Lierre, Belgium, is the earliest to have come down to us. Although delicately painted, it is crude compared to the Shroud-image itself. Significantly, the artist was unable either to comprehend or to reproduce the "negative" quality of the Shroud-image.

12. (*above*) An engraving of the Shroud by Giovanni Testa, made on the occasion of its transferral to Turin in 1578. It was via prints like this that the image of the Shroud was disseminated. As was customary at the time, the figure of Christ has been supplied with a loincloth for the sake of modesty.

13. (*left*) This miniature by Giovanni Battista della Rovere, painted between 1625 and 1630, represents Christ being wrapped in the Shroud at the base of the Cross, in line with the contemporary interpretation of the relic by Jean Jacques Chifflet. Traditionally, the image on the cloth—displayed above by angels—was thought to be a sweat stain produced by the dead body of Christ. It was not associated with Resurrection energy until 1900.

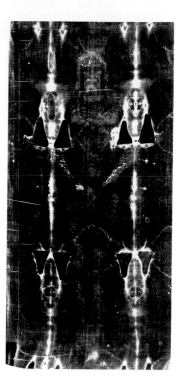

14. Secondo Pia, the man who took the first photograph of the Shroud in 1898. One of the most dramatic moments in the Shroud's history occurred on the night of May 28, 1898, when Pia entered his darkroom and became the first person ever to see the negative view of the Shroud.

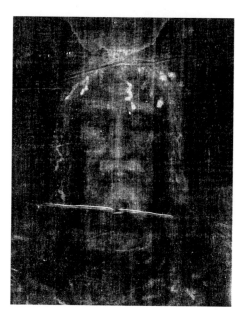

15. (*above*) The frontal figure seen in negative, a view of the Shroud made possible only by the invention of photography in the nineteenth century. The inverted tones, mimicking the effect of light, give a strong impression of relief and make the figure appear far more coherent than it does seen in positive.

16. (*left*) The negative view of the face is now the most familiar image of the Shroud, representing for many the true face of Jesus. It is astonishingly realistic, and shows evident signs of injury: the nose appears slightly disjointed, and there is a conspicuous swelling beneath the right eye. The eyes are revealed to be firmly closed.

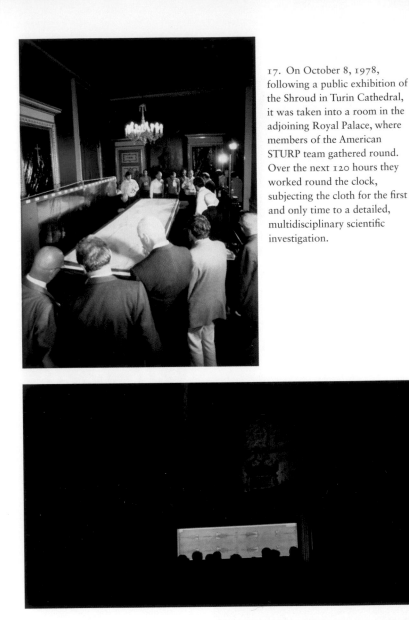

17. On October 8, 1978, following a public exhibition of the Shroud in Turin Cathedral, it was taken into a room in the adjoining Royal Palace, where members of the American STURP team gathered round. Over the next 120 hours they worked round the clock, subjecting the cloth for the first and only time to a detailed, multidisciplinary scientific investigation.

18. The Shroud on display above the high altar of Turin Cathedral, May 2010. The figures on the cloth are plainly visible from the nave. Ahead, pilgrims who have queued for hours to see the relic close-up stand and contemplate it for a few minutes before being moved on.

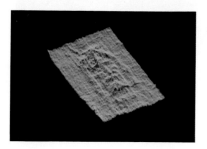

19. The face of the Shroud as seen via a VP-8 Image Analyzer. The undistorted appearance of this image demonstrates that the Shroud encodes information about levels of relief, not of light. If the Shroud-image was in any way "photographic," the face would be distorted in the VP-8. The discovery of this computer transformation has been likened to Secondo Pia's discovery of the photographic negative.

20. In this photomicrograph of an area of the blood-image, taken near the small of the back, deep red particles can be seen on the surfaces of the threads. Samples of this particulate matter have been positively identified as blood.

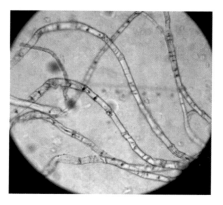

21. This photomicrograph of a body-image area demonstrates the extreme faintness of the image. Although it was taken in the region of the nose, one of the strongest parts of the image, the coloration is barely perceptible. There is no sign of any substance applied to the cloth. The image consists solely of a layer of straw-yellow fibers on the surface of each thread.

22. A photomicrograph of body-image fibers lifted from the Shroud by Ray Rogers in 1978. The straw-yellow color of the body-image is present only on the edges of the fibers, while the medullas are clear. The tape on which the fibers are mounted has yellowed with age, reducing the color contrast.

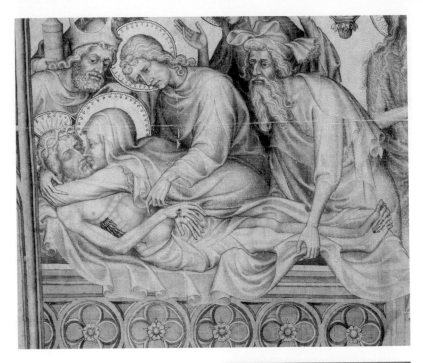

23. (*above*) A late-fourteenth-century depiction of Christ being entombed, a detail from the famous *Parement de Narbonne*. Painted in an extremely refined ink-wash technique on silk, this is perhaps the nearest any fourteenth-century artist came to emulating the Shroud-image.

24. (*right*) This depiction of "The Man of Sorrows" by Naddo Ceccarelli, a pupil of Simone Martini, represents the most naturalistic school of painting in the mid fourteenth century. Naddo's depiction of Christ's wounds and anatomy are noticeably stylized compared with the Shroud-image.

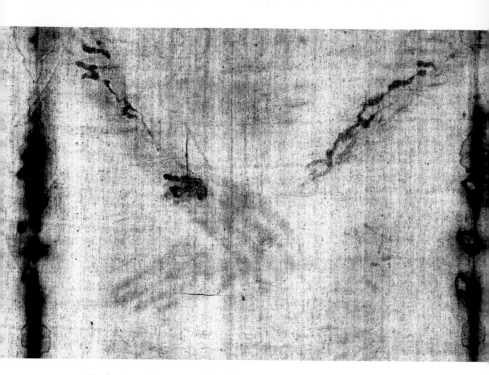

25. The hands and forearms of the Shroud figure. The central bloodstain indicates that a nail penetrated the left wrist, in accordance with anatomical logic, rather than the palm of the hand, as traditionally supposed. The trickles of blood on the forearms are fragmentary, unlike the continuous flows imagined by medieval artists.

26. Having confirmed the death of the Shroud-man, the executioners would have lifted him down from the cross still attached to the *patibulum*. When the nails were extracted from the wrists blood would have dribbled down along the forearms, creating the patterns we see on the Shroud.

27. The feet are covered in bloody smears, consistent with the removal of a nail. The crossing of the feet indicates that a single nail was used, but it is unclear where exactly they were pierced. If the Shroud was a medieval image of the crucified Christ, we should expect the wounds to be more clearly marked.

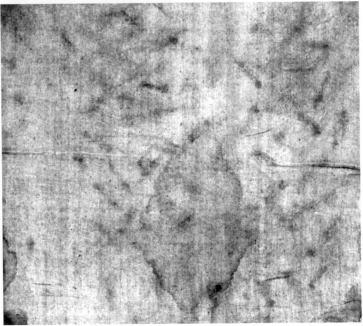

28. The central area of the back is peppered with dumbbell-shaped scourge-marks. For these marks to have been imprinted so precisely the body of the Shroud-man must have been washed and blood clots removed. Only lifeblood—blood that issued after death—would have been left on the body.

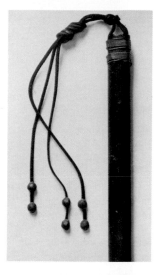

29. This is a reconstruction of a Roman *flagrum* made by Paul Vignon to illustrate the type of weapon used to beat the Shroud-man. The thongs are tipped with small lead weights (*plumbatae*) matching the dumbbell-shaped injuries visible on the Shroud. A *flagrum* similar to this was found in the first-century ruins of Herculaneum but has apparently been lost.

30. The Flagellation of Christ, as conceived by one of the greatest artists of the fourteenth century, Duccio di Buoninsegna. The marks of the whips are represented as dribbles of blood all over the arms and torso, quite unlike the scourge-marks seen on the Shroud.

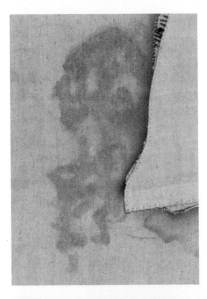

31. This large stain on the right-hand side of the chest shows blood that has oozed out of an elliptical spear wound. The small amount of blood is consistent with the wound having been inflicted after death. There is nothing at all "artistic" about this bloodstain, which differs markedly from medieval depictions of Christ's side wound.

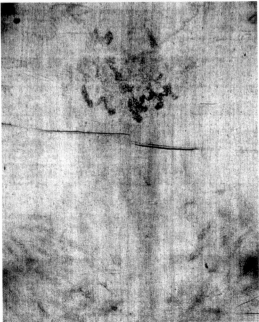

32. The top and back of the Shroud-man's head were evidently covered with small puncture wounds. A number of bloodstains appear to form a ring around the base of the scalp, suggesting something like a crown of thorns. The abrasions on the shoulder blades can also be clearly seen.

33. This painting of Christ by Simone Martini is an underdrawing for a fresco, executed in *sinopia* (red ochre) c.1340. Walter McCrone suggested that Simone, or an artist like him, might have painted the Shroud using a similar technique, but the idea is implausible. Like all medieval artists, Simone represents Christ in an idealized manner, and his brushwork is always evident.

34. Joe Nickell's copy of the Shroud-face (of which this is a negative view) was made by laying a cloth over a bas-relief of Christ's face and dabbing it with iron oxide pigment. This crude image does not bear comparison with the original and is technically very different. It helps demonstrate the sheer improbability of the Shroud-image being a medieval work of art.

35. This replica of the Shroud-image (seen in negative) was produced by Nicholas Allen using a "proto-photographic" technique. Undoubtedly ingenious, it bears a superficial resemblance to the Shroud-image, but its visual structure is very different. Unlike the Shroud, it shows clear signs of directional lighting. And it is extremely doubtful that anyone could have created such an image before the nineteenth century.

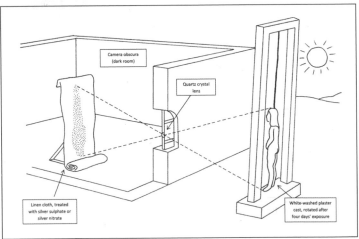

Camera obscura (dark room)

Quartz crystal lens

Linen cloth, treated with silver sulphate or silver nitrate

White-washed plaster cast, rotated after four days' exposure

36. In order to produce his "proto-photographic" copy of the Shroud, Allen hung a sheet of light-sensitized linen inside a large camera obscura fitted with a biconvex lens made of quartz crystal. He then suspended a white plaster cast of a man outside, so that its sunlit image was projected onto the cloth within. After an exposure of eight days, the cloth was imprinted with proto-photographs of the front and back of the plaster cast.

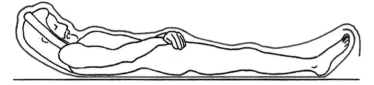

37. Diagram illustrating the manner in which the Shroud enfolded the corpse of the Shroud-man. The draping of the cloth over the toes and shins explains the absence of feet on the frontal figure, while the beard's close proximity to the chest accounts for the apparent lack of a neck. The customary use of a headband to bind up the chin explains the separation of the frontal and dorsal figures.

38. Plant specimens sometimes produce faint imprints on the papers within which they are pressed. In 1942 French pharmacist Jean Volckringer drew attention to these images, arguing that they might shed light on the formation of the Shroud-image. The cause of these "Volckringer patterns" has not yet been definitively established.

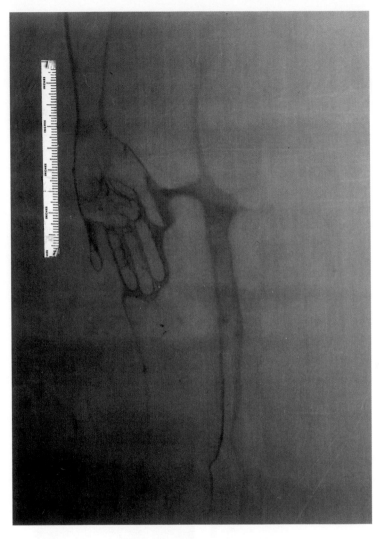

39. In March 1981 staff at the Jospice International hospice in Liverpool discovered this partial imprint of a human figure on the mattress of a man who had just died of pancreatic cancer. The "Jospice imprint," as it is called, is the closest analogy to the Shroud currently known. It is undoubtedly a natural phenomenon, caused by the man's abnormal urine reacting with the nylon material of the mattress cover.

Facsimile of the chemical impression.

Silver medal, belonging to M. Boyer d'Agen, and reputed to be of the XVIth century : Called "Médaille du Campo dei fiori."

Photographic inversion of the chemical impression

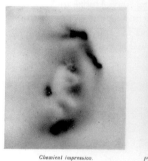

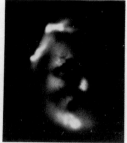

Chemical impression.

Photographic inversion of the chemical impression.

Head of Christ (plaster mould).

IMPRESSIONS PRODUCED BY CHEMICAL ACTION.

40. Plate VIII of Paul Vignon's pioneering study of 1902, *The Shroud of Christ*, illustrating two "vaporographs" created by Vignon and his collaborator, René Colson. These prove that reasonably focused images can be produced by the action of vapours—images, moreover, that convey accurate 3-D information. The photograph (*top center*) appears flat by comparison.

41. In order to test whether a Maillard reaction might have been responsible for the Shroud-image, Ray Rogers and Anna Arnoldi took a piece of linen manufactured and treated according to first-century methods and exposed it to ammonia vapors. Straw-yellow fibers were produced, which had all the characteristics of Shroud body-image fibers.

42. On October 13, 1988, the results of the Shroud carbon-dating test were announced simultaneously in London and Turin. At the press conference held in the British Museum Professor Edward Hall of Oxford University (*left*) informed reporters that the Shroud was a sorry forgery—"Someone just got a bit of linen, faked it up and flogged it." Sitting alongside him were his colleague Dr. Robert Hedges (*right*) and Dr. Michael Tite of the British Museum.

43. Folio 28r of the Pray Codex, a manuscript produced in Hungary between 1192 and 1195, depicts two scenes from the Passion: "The entombment and anointing of Christ" (*top*) and "The three Marys at the tomb" (*bottom*). Both scenes appear to reflect knowledge of the Shroud, knowledge the artist must have acquired in Constantinople.

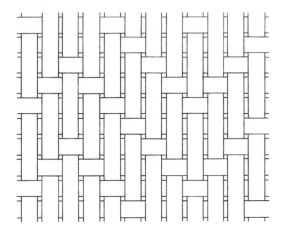

44. The distinctive herringbone weave of the Shroud, technically
known as a three-to-one twill, is created by passing each weft
(horizontal) thread over one warp (vertical) thread and then
under three, in a staggered sequence. Reversing the direction
of the sequence yields the chevron pattern.

45. A detail of the upper rectangle in the scene of "The three Marys at the
tomb," folio 28r of the Pray Codex. The zigzags recall the herringbone weave of
the Shroud. In among them the artist has drawn four tiny circles, arranged in a
"knight's move" pattern, matching the configuration of the Shroud's "poker-
holes." This is good evidence that the Shroud existed in the twelfth century.

46. Throughout the Byzantine Empire the Mandylion was depicted as an image of the disembodied head of Christ set within a horizontal rectangle of cloth, as in this example from a twelfth-century church in Cyprus. The "landscape" format is peculiar for a portrait.

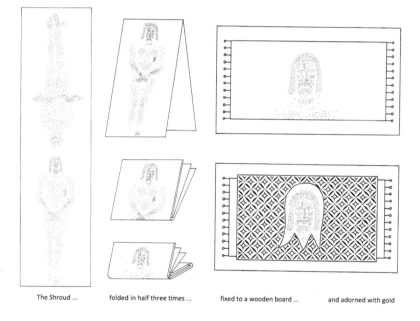

The Shroud ...   folded in half three times ...   fixed to a wooden board ...   and adorned with gold

47. The transformation of the Shroud into the Mandylion (after Ian Wilson). Folded in half three times, the Shroud assumes the appearance of a horizontal towel bearing only a facial image of Jesus, matching the traditional idea of the Mandylion. Arranged thus, it is eight-layered, accounting for the Greek term used of the Mandylion—*tetradiplon* ("four-doubled"). "Fixed to a wooden board and adorned with gold," in the words of one eyewitness, the cloth would have remained generally inaccessible, and the full extent of its image would have been secret.

48. A second-century copy of the famous idol of Artemis worshipped at Ephesus. Pagan images such as this were identified with the gods and goddesses they represented. The practice of idolatry, considered a sin by monotheists, is rooted in animism, a natural human instinct.

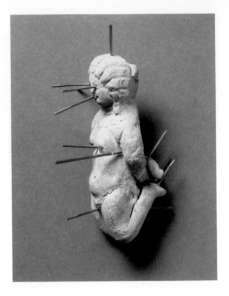

49. This little figurine pierced by needles was created in Egypt, during the third or fourth century AD, to serve a magical purpose, like a voodoo doll. It was equated with a girl called Ptolemais and its treatment was intended to make her fall in love with an admirer, Sarapammon.

50. According to Catholic belief, this modest crucifix from the church of San Damiano outside Assisi was once inhabited by Christ, who spoke from it to St Francis one summer day in 1206. Reports of miracles in which holy persons were temporarily embodied in their images were quite common in medieval Christianity.

XLIII.

The Soul of man.   *Anima hominis.*

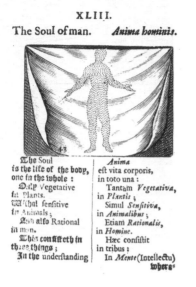

| The Soul is the life of the body, one in the whole : Only Vegetable in Plants. Withal sensitive in Animals ; And also Rational in man. This consisteth in three things ; In the understanding | *Anima* est vita corporis, in toto una : Tantùm *Vegetativa,* in *Plantis* ; Simul *Sensitiva,* in *Animalibus* ; Etiam *Rationalis,* in *Homine.* Hæc consistit in tribus : In *Mente* (Intellectu) where= |

51. A seventeenth-century depiction of the "The Soul of Man," represented as a pale silhouette resting on a white cloth. This image, which is unconnected to the Shroud, illustrates the universal tendency to conceive the soul as a faint, shadowy figure.

52. A detail from the first-century Alexander Mosaic, depicting a battle between Alexander the Great and the Persian emperor, Darius. As he falls to the ground, a stricken soldier glances up and sees his own reflection in a polished shield. This reflected double would have been seen as the man's inner self departing his body at the moment of death.

53. Tutankhamun was buried in a set of coffins, each of them sculpted into a magnificent effigy of the dead pharaoh. The portrait transformed the coffin into a potential body for his spiritual double, or *ka*, which would be reborn as the god Osiris. The image was, in effect, a "spiritual body" for the boy king.

54. An Egyptian mummy of a youth, dating from the late first century AD, fitted with a panel portrait of the young man. Such funerary images, known as "Fayum portraits," began to be made in Egypt at around the same time as the emergence of Christianity. Like the anthropoid coffins of the pharaohs, they were intended to serve as substitute bodies for the spirits of the resurrected dead.

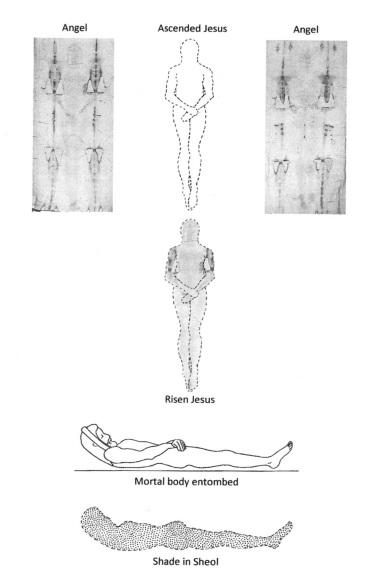

Angel Ascended Jesus Angel

Risen Jesus

Mortal body entombed

Shade in Sheol

55. Diagram representing the first-century conception of the death and
Resurrection-Ascension of Jesus. Initially, when Jesus succumbed to death, his
existence was reduced to that of a shade. On the third day he was raised from
the dead in a new spiritual body, signified by the Shroud. He could then
be viewed either as present in the Shroud-image, the Risen Jesus, or as absent
from it, the Ascended Jesus. In the latter case the Shroud figures were
viewed as independent mediators (angels).

56. This strange object, known as an "Osiris bed," was found in the tomb of Maihirpre, an Egyptian nobleman of the fourteenth century BC. It consists of a bed frame spread with a linen sheet, on which rests an outline figure of the god Osiris. The figure is made of corn, which was left to germinate in the tomb, thereby aiding Maihirpre's rebirth as Osiris.

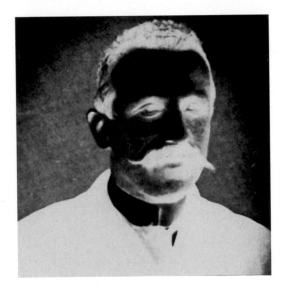

57. It can be difficult to recognize someone via a negative photograph, and the Shroud-face would have presented its first viewers with a similar problem. Although it is not photographic, it inverts the usual tonality of a face in much the same way. Those who knew the Shroud-man would have struggled to see his likeness in it, before experiencing a sudden jolt of recognition.

58. The story of the Transfiguration, depicted here in a fifteenth-century Russian icon, represents Jesus as a radiant, heavenly being, flanked by two attendant figures (Moses and Elijah). The same basic imagery, which I term the Triple Figure, informs the tale of the Ascension in Acts and the "escorted Resurrection-Ascension" in the *Gospel of Peter*.

59. The story of Doubting Thomas, as envisaged by the Revd Albert
Dreisbach, based on a painting by Caravaggio. Dreisbach argues that
this famous story was inspired by an early viewing of the Shroud, seen
as proof of the physical nature of the Resurrection. But what if the
Shroud was seen instead as a sign of spiritual rebirth? Might this clever
montage represent the true character of all the appearances?

seated where Jesus lay, that is, in the very place where his burial cloth would have been.

In Mark and Luke the divine messengers are also situated within the tomb. Luke offers little indication of where precisely the "two men" appeared, saying only that they stood beside the women. Mark, though, specifies that the "young man" was "sitting on the right side" in the tomb. Perhaps this comment, which seems to have been passed on from earlier sources, derives ultimately from some genuine memory of the event. It is impossible now to know.[9] But it is worth emphasizing that Mark agrees with John in stating that the figure was seated in the tomb, reinforcing the connection with the burial cloth.

Only Matthew fails to locate the angel in the tomb, saying instead that "an angel of the Lord" descended from heaven and sat on the entrance stone outside. This version of the story is closely related to the descent of the heavenly men in the *Gospel of Peter*, whom we have already linked to the Shroud. As I have suggested, too, the dazzling whiteness of the bleached cloth and the effect of internal radiance would have impressed the earliest witnesses of the Shroud, and these are precisely the qualities that are ascribed by Matthew to the angel at the tomb: "His appearance was like lightning, and his raiment white as snow."[10] Moreover, the angel is said to have terrified the guards ("for fear of him the guards trembled and became like dead men"),[11] and a few verses later the women depart "with fear and great joy." The experience of coming across the eerie Shroud in a tomb might well have induced a sense of religious dread. So, although Matthew does not specifically record the discovery of a figure in the tomb, his description of the angel and its psychological impact is in line with the Shroud theory.

John and Mark agree with Matthew in saying that the garments of the angels were white. There is little difficulty in seeing these clothes as references to the Shroud. Luke's two men appear "in dazzling apparel."[12] Although this description echoes conventional accounts of angels, it may also reflect the fact that the Shroud figures originally appeared more splendid than they do today—luminescent men within, or behind, a veil of pure white cloth.[13]

The numerical ambiguity of the Shroud figure(s)—does the cloth show two or only one?—explains why there is only one tomb-angel in Mark and Matthew, while in Luke and John there are two.[14] Without the explanation provided by the Shroud, it is hard to see why the writers of John and Luke, working independently, would have bothered to turn a single angel into two, or, alternatively, why Mark and Matthew would have reduced the pair of angels to one.

It is highly significant, too, that the role of the tomb-angels is to proclaim the Resurrection. In Matthew and Mark they state plainly that Jesus is risen and point to the evidence of the empty tomb. Luke's dazzling men make the same point in a rather different way: they remind the women of the prophecy that was spoken to them concerning the Resurrection, opening with a rhetorical question that expresses the foolishness of seeking Jesus' body in the sepulchre. John's angels ask a question that would originally have carried the same force: "Woman, why are you weeping?"—i.e., "Don't you realize that Jesus is alive?"[15]

In all four Gospels, then, the Resurrection is heralded by the angelic figures at the sepulchre. The function of these tomb-angels is neatly encapsulated in the brief reference to them in Luke 24.23, where the two Emmaus disciples tell of the women going to the tomb and seeing "a vision of angels, who said that he was alive." If I am right, and the Shroud did literally reveal the Resurrection, it would have made perfect sense to put a speech proclaiming the Resurrection into the mouths of the Shroud figures.[16]

The different terms used by the Evangelists to denote the tomb-angel(s) suggest slightly different interpretations of the Shroud figure(s). John's "angels" are standard intermediaries between heaven and earth, like the angels who minister to Jesus in the wilderness.[17] Luke's reference to "two men" might initially seem a more modest interpretation, until we remember the "two men" who descend from heaven in a blaze of glory in the *Gospel of Peter*—angels on a par with those seen by Jacob on the celestial ladder.[18] Furthermore, the idea of heavenly "men" delivering a message to earth echoes the well-known tale of the Lord appearing to Abraham in the plains of Mamre to foretell the birth of Isaac. God appeared on that occasion, confusingly, as "three men," later mutating into a pair of angels.[19] Luke may have meant to signal a connection with this episode, one of the most mysterious and impressive appearances of the Lord in the Hebrew Bible. If so, Luke's "men" may actually be higher up the ladder of heavenly glory, as it were, than John's regular angels.

Most exalted of all, perhaps, is Matthew's Angel of the Lord. The account of this figure swooping down from above instantly recalls a variety of stories in the Old Testament in which Yahweh appears in the form of his angel.[20] The Angel of the Lord is no heavenly minion; he is the visible manifestation of the transcendent God. To interpret the Shroud in these terms would have been to imagine standing, like Moses or Hagar, before the very form of Yahweh himself. At least, that is how the phrase would traditionally have been understood by a first-century Jew. Early Christians might have put a different construction on it, once they began to refer to Jesus as "Lord."

By contrast, Mark's "young man" found sitting quietly in the tomb seems fairly mundane—he has often been interpreted as a real person.[21] Why does the author of Mark describe the Shroud in such an understated way? The answer is that it enables him to link the figure with a couple of other youths who appear in his Gospel.[22] Unfortunately, the symbolism of these "young men" is too complex to go into here. For the moment, it is enough to observe that the "young man" in the tomb is Mark's equivalent of the grander tomb-angels in the other Gospels.

The Shroud, then, is the key to understanding the reported sightings of angelic figures at the tomb. This helps prove that the Shroud is authentic, and it also helps prove that the women did go to the sepulchre on Easter morning, just as the Gospels narrate. But what about the supposed disappearance of Jesus' body? Can we make sense of this peculiar report, which has so taxed the minds of believers and skeptics alike?

For the tomb-stories to have been told in the first place, the women must have seen something remarkable when they went to the sepulchre. There are two consistent features of the tomb-stories that might have provided the necessary stimulus: the discovery of an empty tomb and the encounter with the angel(s). In modern scholarship the angels have generally been dismissed as superfluous additions to the story, while the empty tomb has been considered its essential raison d'être. However, now that the angels can be understood as embodiments of a real phenomenon, we can reverse this assessment and dissolve the whole problem of the empty tomb. Originally, the focus of the story about the women's visit to the sepulchre was the encounter with the angel(s), i.e. the discovery of the Shroud, *not* the discovery of an empty tomb. The missing body was added to the story at a later stage. For centuries people have assumed the angels to be legendary and the empty tomb to be historical; in reality it was the other way round.

Why does it help to be able to explain the genesis of the tomb-stories without reference to a missing body? There are two reasons. First, the empty tomb was not a part of the original Christian proclamation: it was not mentioned in the First Creed, and the physical, flesh-and-blood body was irrelevant to Paul's understanding of the Resurrection. Secondly, there is no credible explanation for the supposed disappearance of Jesus' body.[23] The Shroud theory meshes with early Christian testimony and eliminates the need to account for an unlikely circumstance.

If the body stayed in the tomb, how did the idea of its disappearance come about? This is easy to explain. Paul and his fellow apostles, all of whom saw the Shroud, understood the Resurrection in terms of Jesus donning a new, spiritual body which superseded his old, physical body. However, the concept of resurrection was generally understood in antiquity in terms of the physical body being restored to life.[24] Confusion was bound to follow. Unlike the apostles, the great mass of early Christian converts had no direct experience of the Shroud, and many of them, when they heard about the Resurrection, must have assumed it was a physical affair, in line with their preconceptions. They conceived it as the *reanimation* of Jesus' physical body, instead of his *recreation* in a new type of body altogether. (This misunderstanding is documented in 1 Corinthians, written in the mid 50s.) As these second- and third-generation Christians took up the female tomb-story—originally, the story of the women's discovery of the Shroud—they incorporated into it, so to speak, the absent body of Jesus. If Jesus was resurrected, they reasoned, his mortal body must have upped and left the sepulchre. So they made this imagined disappearance the new focus of the tomb-story, the angel(s) being co-opted to point it out. Thus was born the strange legend of the empty tomb.

One of the Gospels contains an intriguing clue that, as originally told, the tomb-story may have assumed the presence of Jesus' body. Consider this literal translation of John 20.12: "and she sees two angels in white, sitting, one at the head and one at the feet, where the body of Jesus lay." Note how the angels are located with respect to parts of Jesus' body. The original word order, followed here, emphasizes the juxtaposition of the angels with the head and the feet of Jesus. This implies that they could be seen beside the body, which makes sense in relation to the Shroud. The verb applied to the corpse, *ekeito* ("lay"), is in the imperfect tense, indicating continuous action in the past. It is compatible either with the body having disappeared prior to Mary's arrival or with its still being in the tomb when she was there. There can be no doubt that John understood it in the former sense, since he thought that the body was missing, but the tradition he inherited seems to have been devised by someone, like Paul, who knew that Jesus' "flesh and blood" played no part in the Resurrection. If so, John 20.12 descends from a very early form of the tomb-story, a sort of narrative fossil preserved beneath layers of Gospel sediment.

It is likely, then, that the body of Jesus remained in the sepulchre. Following the events of Easter morning, it would have been enshrouded once more and left, like any other corpse, to decompose. After a year or so, the bones would have been gathered up and reburied in an ossuary.[25] The

Jerusalem Church presumably honored the site of Jesus' mortal remains, but once his immediate family died, few would have given much thought to Jesus' bones; they were, after all, mere dust, debris left behind by his immortal, spiritual body. Precise knowledge of the place may have been lost during the Jewish War, when the remnant of the Jerusalem Church fled to Pella.[26] It was certainly lost by 135, when Emperor Hadrian built a temple to Venus over the area of Golgotha.

We can now reconstruct the women's visit to the tomb.

It was early morning when Mary Magdalene and her companions approached the sepulchre. The entrance to the tomb was probably closed with a blocking stone, and it must have taken them a few minutes to move this to one side. (The idea that the blocking stone was found mysteriously moved aside is connected to the false idea of heavenly beings entering and exiting the tomb.) Jewish tombs of the period invariably have low, narrow entrances, typically about 27 inches high by 18 inches wide.[27] The women would have had to crouch low to get through, but, once inside the tomb, they would have been able to stand upright. The interior would have been dark, especially at dawn, so they must have brought oil lamps with them to illuminate their work, as well as whatever spices, ointments and cloths were necessary to complete the burial.

Mark's comment that the "young man" was found on the right-hand side of the tomb may indicate the position within the tomb of the enshrouded body of Jesus. The women would have seen it the moment they entered. The lower half of the Shroud, as we have seen, was laid beneath the body, its end wrapped around the feet, while the upper half was draped loosely over the corpse, rejoining the lower half where it overlapped the toes. In order to perform the anointing, the women would have had to have pulled back the top section of the cloth and the end of the lower section covering the feet. As they did so, part of the frontal image, at least, would have been exposed. Their eyes would have been growing used to the dim, lamp-lit interior of the tomb, and they would soon have noticed the strange markings on the pure white linen. Imagine their shock and surprise as they peeled the Shroud back from the body and saw, emerging from the cloth, strange echoes of a human form. Imagine the effect on their frayed nerves of seeing the mysterious Shroud-face, just discernible in the lamplight, hovering inches from the tortured head of Jesus.

Even though the image would have been more distinct then than now (since the fibers of the cloth have yellowed with age, reducing the contrast), it would still have been very faint, and the women must have wondered whether their eyes were deceiving them.

If the body was still in the tomb, as it surely was, we can be sure that they witnessed the image in situ, because only the discovery of the image could explain the irregular removal of the cloth from the sepulchre. If no one had noticed anything unusual about the Shroud, it would have been used, as intended, to wrap up the body. It appears, though, that the women did not remove the Shroud immediately, for it was still there when Peter visited the tomb later that morning (see below, pp. 260–67). This is quite understandable, as they would not have had a substitute cloth with them, and they would have been concerned, too, about its ritual impurity.

For most Shroud aficionados, Mary Magdalene and her companions discovered the first and greatest Christian relic, a material witness to the death, burial and Resurrection of Jesus. But this is an anachronistic interpretation, based on a proclamation that was yet to be made, and it misses the most important point: that the Shroud figure would have been perceived at the time not as an inert, miraculous stain, but as an active participant in the drama.

It is impossible to say exactly how the women would have reacted standing there in the tomb, but in all likelihood they would have experienced the Shroud—consciously or unconsciously—as an other-worldly person, a ghostly visitor from the invisible realm of spirits, shades and demons. At the very least they would have recognized it as a supernatural "sign." They would undoubtedly have been amazed and terrified. Nothing is more likely in these circumstances than that they interrupted the burial and went to tell others of the mysterious figure they had encountered in the burial cloth.

Once the Shroud was removed from the tomb, its interpretation would have followed a more predictable course. Displayed elsewhere, the full extent of the image would have become apparent, and its extraordinary qualities—its "miraculous" origin, its elusive form, its lustrous effect—would certainly have inspired awe in those who witnessed it. We can imagine the cloth stretched out horizontally, as it has been displayed since the fourteenth century, revealing the twin figures head to head, or hung vertically, so that the frontal figure stood upright before the amazed audience. Seen thus, its eerie figures fading in and out of view, the cloth would have seemed like a thin veil separating the material and the spiritual realms. The very faintness of the image would have heightened its emotional impact, a "special effect" that would have made it seem like a waking vision, a sublime revelation of hidden mysteries.

Some witnesses, at least, would soon have started talking about the Shroud figures as spiritual messengers—as angels. And that is how the women's visit to the tomb was generally remembered. It was the "vision of angels" that caused the story of their visit to be told and retold, not any failure to find the body.

In essence, then, the female tomb-stories are reports of a regular funeral expedition interrupted by the discovery of the Shroud. Far from being empty, the sepulchre contained not only the body of Jesus, still lying where it had been placed by Joseph of Arimathea, but also a mysterious apparition in the burial cloth. It was this apparition that startled the women and caused their trip to the tomb to be commemorated in the stories that eventually made their way into the Gospels.

It remains to be seen how the female tomb-stories address the idea of seeing—and being the first to see—the Risen Jesus. This raises a fundamental issue shaping the way the Easter narratives were composed and redacted: the issue of authority. As we are about to see, these sacred stories reflect a bitter first-century battle of the sexes, the unholy ancestor of all current debates about female leadership in the Church.

20

The Appearance to the Women

Who was the first to see the Risen Jesus? If we believe the First Creed, it was Peter, followed by the Twelve and a host of other men. However, Christian writings both inside and outside the New Testament preserve another tradition, one that evidently had broad currency in the first century. According to this tradition, the Risen Christ was first witnessed by Mary Magdalene and her female companions.

This is good news for the Shroud theory, for, if the Risen Christ appeared via the Shroud, the women at the tomb would have been the first to see him. What is more, the female appearance-stories that eventually made it into the Gospels are particularly revealing with regard to the Shroud and Easter. They are not stories, though, of which the male leaders of the first-century Church would necessarily have approved. Indeed, it appears that the women's claim to be the primary witnesses of the Resurrection was deliberately suppressed by the Church hierarchy. That is why there is no mention of Mary Magdalene or any other woman in the First Creed. Fortunately, not all early Christians toed this patriarchal line, and the belief that the Risen Jesus had appeared to the women first was kept alive—and even enshrined in the Gospels.

One of the most famous stories in the New Testament is John's account of the Risen Jesus appearing to Mary Magdalene beside the tomb, a subject known in art by its Latin title *Noli me tangere* ("do not touch me"), the words that Jesus speaks to Mary the moment she recognizes him. More than any other episode in the Gospels, the *Noli me tangere* represents for Christians the mysterious, just-out-of-reach closeness of the Risen Jesus. In a way, I agree, for the *Noli me tangere* is in my opinion one of the oldest tales in the Gospels, containing elements of authentic, eyewitness testimony that bring us almost within touching distance of the original experience of Easter—that is, of the Shroud.

John's story of Mary's emotional encounter with the living form of her dead master begins as a variant of the usual tomb-story.[1] She comes to the tomb while it is still dark, sees the stone taken away from the entrance and rushes off to tell Peter and the Beloved Disciple that the body of Jesus is missing. There follows the story of Peter visiting the tomb in company with the Beloved Disciple, after which Mary's own story recommences:

> But Mary stood weeping outside the tomb, and as she wept she stooped to look into the tomb; and she saw two angels in white, sitting where the body of Jesus had lain, one at the head and one at the feet. They said to her, "Woman, why are you weeping?" She said to them, "Because they have taken away my Lord, and I do not know where they have laid him." Saying this, she turned round and saw Jesus standing, but she did not know that it was Jesus. Jesus said to her, "Woman, why are you weeping? Whom do you seek?" Supposing him to be the gardener, she said to him, "Sir, if you have carried him away, tell me where you have laid him, and I will take him away." Jesus said to her, "Mary." She turned and said to him, "Rabboni!" (which means teacher). Jesus said to her, "Do not hold me, for I have not yet ascended to the Father; but go to my brethren and say to them, I am ascending to my Father and your Father, to my God and your God." Mary Magdalene went and said to the disciples, "I have seen the Lord"; and she told them that he had said these things to her.

The crucial thing to notice in this story is the way in which the Risen Jesus functions as a near-equivalent of the angels in the tomb. Like him, the angels are heralds of the Resurrection, heralds whom Mary fails to recognize as such. They ask her a question designed to trigger new faith—"Woman, why are you weeping?"—but Mary misses its significance and continues to bemoan the disappearance of Jesus' body. She is then confronted by the Risen Jesus himself. Again, she fails to recognize the evidence before her, and again the divine being prompts her to understand, asking exactly the same question as was asked by the angels—"Woman, why are you weeping?" Still she does not realize what has happened, her response echoing the answer she gave the angels. Only when Jesus says her name does she finally see him for who he is.

The Risen Christ in the *Noli me tangere* also echoes the descriptions of the angels in the Synoptic Gospels. In Matthew and Mark, for instance, the angel tells the women to "go [quickly and] tell his disciples," while in John it is the Risen Jesus who tells Mary to "go to my brethren and say to them . . ." Similarly, in Matthew and Luke the women obey the angels and pass on their message to the disciples, while in John Mary obeys the Risen Jesus and passes on *his* message to the disciples.[2] The relationship between the angels in the Synoptic Gospels and the Risen Jesus in John is extraordinarily close, so much so that the portrayals must have a common origin (i.e. an oral or written tradition in which the Resurrection could be revealed to the women either by angels or by the Risen Jesus himself). If the Risen Jesus is the narrative equivalent of the angels, figures we have already identified as literary manifestations of the Shroud figures, then he, too, must be a figure inspired by the Shroud.

Christ's repetition of the angels' question means that the equivalence between the angels and the Risen Jesus is clearly advertised in the *Noli me tangere*. This suggests that the original author of the scene understood the parallel significance of the figures and expected his or her audience to understand it as well. This understanding was lost by the time John incorporated the story into his Gospel, and he repeats it uncomprehendingly.

Another sign that the original author was aware of the Shroud is the portrayal of Mary as initially unable to recognize Jesus, one of the recurrent themes in the Gospel Resurrection stories. The peculiar form of the Shroud would undoubtedly have caused problems of recognition. Like us looking at a poor, negative photo of someone we know (e.g. Figure 57), those who knew Jesus would have struggled to catch his likeness in the smudgy, tonally reversed image on the cloth. Their minds had to make an unprecedented adjustment: they had to learn to see the real, three-dimensional face of Jesus in the odd, spectral stain of the cloth (Figure 3).[3] Once again, the Shroud theory accounts easily for a striking feature of the Gospel Resurrection stories that most other theories do not even address.

The *Noli me tangere*, then, is readily explicable in terms of Mary Magdalene's discovery of the Shroud. The initial sighting of a couple of angels followed by the recognition of Jesus in an unfamiliar guise, all taking place at the sepulchre, is precisely what we should expect in an early narrative about the Shroud's debut appearance.

One further aspect of the *Noli me tangere* is illuminated by the Shroud: the repeated reference to Christ's Ascension. As soon as Mary recognizes Jesus, he tells her not to touch him, on the grounds that he has "not yet ascended to the Father." And he then tells her to tell the disciples not, as might be expected, that he has risen, but that he is ascending to heaven: "go to my brethren and say to them, I am ascending to my Father and your Father, to my God and your God." The implication is that Christ's ascent to heaven is either underway or imminent, occurring, at any rate, *before* his Resurrection appearance to the disciples. This apparent confusion of the Resurrection and the Ascension has caused perplexity in the past, but we can now see that it expresses the dual interpretation of the Shroud figure as both the Risen Jesus and the Ascended Jesus.

As a representation of the combined Resurrection-Ascension, the *Noli me tangere* recalls the tale of the "escorted Resurrection-Ascension" preserved in the *Gospel of Peter*. A detailed comparison of these two texts reveals some intriguing correspondences, pointing to a common source. For instance, the description in the *Gospel of Peter* of a pair of angelic men fetching the Risen Jesus from the tomb finds an echo in John's narrative in the relationship between the tomb-angels and the Risen Jesus, who appear in the same place and speak the same words.[4] Such correspondences imply a deep connection between these two Resurrection-Ascension narratives, a connection going back to the days of the apostles, when the Shroud was still remembered.

The tale of Mary Magdalene's encounter with the Risen Jesus exists in several other versions. The best known is Matthew's, in which the Risen Jesus meets both Mary Magdalene and "the other Mary" as they are running back from the tomb.[5] This account, like John's, is intimately connected to the preceding tomb-story, which ends with the angel addressing the women:

> But the angel said to the women, "Do not be afraid; for I know that you seek Jesus who was crucified. He is not here; for he has risen, as he said. Come, see the place where he lay. Then go quickly and tell his disciples that he has risen from the dead, and behold, he is going before you to Galilee; there you will see him. Lo, I have told you." So they departed quickly from the tomb with fear and great joy, and ran to tell his disciples. And behold, Jesus met them and said, "Hail!" And they came up and took hold of his feet and worshipped him. Then Jesus said to them, "Do not be afraid; go and tell my brethren to go to Galilee; and there they will see me."

Once again, the Risen Christ duplicates the role of the angel. The speeches of the two figures are even more closely related here than they are in John; Jesus repeats parts of the angel's message virtually word for word. This reinforces the argument that the angel at the tomb and the Risen Jesus are just different interpretations of the Shroud figure. Moreover, the fact that two independent narratives share this structural similarity indicates that the shared speech of the angel(s) and the Risen Jesus is a very ancient tradition—Matthew and John are singing, as it were, from the same hymn-sheet.

It is worth noting, additionally, that from the earliest days of the Church Jesus was hailed as "the Lord," so that Matthew's audience could hardly have failed to understand the "angel of the Lord" as the "angel of Christ." The idea of Christ's personal angel announcing his resurrection is especially interesting in light of the remark found in all three Synoptic Gospels that those resurrected "are like angels in heaven."[6] So the Risen Lord not only shares the same speech as his angel, but is also to be imagined as being *like* his angel. The difference between them is purely theoretical—or theological.[7]

In the tradition followed by Matthew and John the Risen Jesus is introduced by his angelic double(s). Another early-Christian writing, the *Epistula Apostolorum*, contains a version of the female tomb-story in which the angels are omitted altogether and the women meet the Risen Jesus directly.

The *Epistula* is a Greek work preserved in Coptic and Ethiopic translations, thought to have been written in the mid second century. Though orthodox opinion holds it to be a pastiche based on the canonical Gospels, in my view it is better understood as an independent composition forming part of the same stream of literary tradition.[8] Its tomb-story reads as follows:

> There went to that place [three] women: Mary, she who belonged to Martha, and Mary [Magd]alene. They took ointment to pour upon his body, weeping and mourning over what had happened. But when they approached the tomb, they looked inside and did not find the body. But as they were mourning and weeping, the Lord appeared to them and said to them, "For whom are you weeping? Now do not weep; I am he whom you seek. But let one of you go to your brothers and say, 'Come, the Master has risen from the dead.'" Martha came and told it to us. We said to her, "What do you want with us, O woman? He who has died is buried, and could it be possible for him to live?" We did not believe her, that the Savior had risen from the dead. Then she went back to the Lord and said to him, "None of them believed me that you are alive." He said, "Let another one of you go to them saying this again to them." Mary came and told us again, and we did not believe her. She returned to the Lord and she also told it to him.[9]

A detailed comparison of this passage and the corresponding passages in the Gospels reveals multiple correspondences, with the Risen Jesus occupying the role played by the angels in the canonical texts. The description of Jesus' sudden appearance in the *Epistula* ("... they looked inside and did not find the body. But as they were mourning and weeping, the Lord appeared to them ...") is virtually identical to that of the mysterious pair of men in Luke ("... when they went in they did not find the body. While they were perplexed about this, behold, two men stood by them . . ."). The statement in the *Epistula* that the Lord appeared to the women "as they were weeping" matches the statement in John that Mary Magdalene saw the angels "as she wept." Jesus' initial speech in the *Epistula* ("I am he whom you seek. But let one of you go to your brothers and say, 'Come, the Master has risen from the dead' ") is closely related to that of the Angel of the Lord in Matthew ("you seek Jesus . . . Then go quickly and tell his disciples that he has risen from the dead").[10] Finally, just as the disciples refuse to believe Martha and Mary that "the Savior had risen from the dead" in the *Epistula*, so they refuse to believe the women's account of the angels at the tomb in Luke.

The *Epistula* thus demonstrates the same equivalence between the angels and the Risen Christ as is found in Matthew and John. But, whereas Matthew and John represent the appearance of the Risen Christ as distinct from, and subsequent to, the angelic appearance, the *Epistula* narrates it *in place of* the angelic appearance, proving beyond doubt that the Risen Jesus and the tomb-angel(s) were interchangeable. The Shroud theory, unlike any other theory, explains how and why this interchangeability arose.

We now have a fix on the Risen Jesus. The *Epistula* locates him at or in the tomb, the very place the Shroud theory would predict for his first appearance. Moreover, if he was originally the other face, as it were, of the mysterious men and angels encountered by the women on Easter morning, then he was definitely first seen inside the tomb—"sitting where the body of Jesus lay," according to the early tradition handed down by John. So we can say not only that the Shroud could and would have inspired talk of a resurrection in first-century Judaea, but also that it was discovered in the very spot where the Risen Jesus was first seen (on the evidence of the Gospels themselves).

Another version of the female appearance-story is found at the beginning of Pseudo-Mark, the collection of Resurrection narratives tacked on to the end of some early manuscripts of Mark:

> Now when he rose early on the first day of the week, he appeared first to Mary Magdalene, from whom he had cast out seven demons. She went and told those who had been with him, as they mourned and wept. But when they heard that he was alive, and had been seen by her, they would not believe it.[11]

Compared with the fulsome narratives of John, Matthew and the *Epistula*, this narrative is sparse, but it is interesting for a couple of reasons. First of all, Pseudo-Mark matches the *Epistula* in omitting any reference to an angel and in having Mary Magdalene meet the Risen Christ directly. Also as in the *Epistula*, she goes and tells the disciples, who refuse to believe her. This basic narrative is also found in Luke 24, except that the Risen Christ is there represented by "two men." This demonstrates yet again that the tomb-angels and the Risen Jesus perform the same role in these stories, implying that they represent the same phenomenon—the Shroud.

The second interesting aspect of Pseudo-Mark's narrative is its portrayal of Mary vis-à-vis the male disciples. Brief though it is, this appearance-story attaches great significance to Mary's experience: its occurrence "early on the first day of the week" is equated with the hour of Christ's rising, and she is explicitly said to have been the first to see the Risen Jesus. When she goes and tells the disciples what she has witnessed, they disbelieve her—characteristically, as it turns out.[12] They are, by implication, relatively faithless. The contrast between the disciples and Mary is stark and pointed. Even if the text simply records what happened, there was no need to focus on the initial disbelief of the disciples. Exactly the same contrast occurs, with greater emphasis, in the *Epistula*, and it is even echoed in Luke.

The women bear witness; the men disbelieve. Something is going on here, besides simple chronicling.

We are beginning to lift the lid not only on the mystery of Easter but also on the motives conditioning its portrayal in the Gospels. This has the potential to upset some major assumptions of New Testament scholarship, for the motives at work are not those we might expect.

Consider the issue of narrating the women's discovery of the Shroud from the point of view of an early Christian story-teller. There were essentially two different ways of referring to the Shroud figure: as the Risen Jesus himself, or as an angelic witness. The first Christian story-tellers could decide which of these two descriptions of the Shroud figure to adopt. Would they make it a story about angels or about the Risen Jesus? They could decide to yoke the two aspects together and tell a story about angels *and* the Risen Jesus,[13] but that, too, was a significant choice. How they decided this basic issue would shape the way the event and its protagonists were remembered.

An important question now arises: if those who narrated the original female tomb-stories were able to choose how to represent the Shroud figure, why did some of them choose to represent it as the Risen Christ? The choice was by no means neutral: it made Mary Magdalene and her female companions the first witnesses of the Risen Jesus. Such a claim would have been highly contentious, for, as we have seen, the First Creed, formulated within a few years of the Crucifixion, gave priority to Peter. Stories about the Risen Christ appearing to a bunch of women at the sepulchre flatly contradicted this authoritative "gospel." So, how come such stories were told?

There is a simple answer: the female appearance-stories, which were deeply embedded in the Gospel sources, deliberately championed the women's role. In other words, they were intended to promote a *matriarchal* agenda, in opposition to the patriarchal views of Peter and his followers.

Once this is realized, the stories suddenly attain a new significance. In all four sources that preserve the female appearance tradition (Matthew, John, the *Epistula* and Pseudo-Mark) the women not only see the Risen Jesus but also announce his resurrection to the male disciples. The women are represented as the original bearers of the "good news," as the informants of the disciples themselves. Moreover, in three of the sources (Matthew, John and the *Epistula*) the women are commissioned to perform this task by the Risen Christ. There is no question of the women neglecting to mention their encounter to the disciples, nor of the disciples learning of the Resurrection before receiving the women's testimony.

The subtlest of the female appearance-stories is John's *Noli me tangere*, a text which is carefully crafted to underscore the authority of Mary Magdalene. To begin with, Mary is marked out as the disciple of the Risen Lord. He calls her by her name, and she responds "Rabboni," meaning teacher, signaling her discipleship. He then instructs her to tell his brethren that he is ascending to heaven. She goes to them immediately and declares that she has seen the Risen/Ascending Jesus. No first-century reader could have failed to appreciate the hierarchical implications of this story. Mary is called to be the special envoy of the Risen Christ, the communicant of hidden knowledge to the inferior male disciples.

The lionization of Mary may also account for the most famous detail in the story, the phrase which gives the scene its traditional name—*Noli me tangere*. Why does Christ tell Mary not to touch him?[14] A significant contrast is being set up between Mary and Doubting Thomas, the skeptical male disciple, whom the Risen Christ invites to "put out [his] hand" to test the Resurrection. While the virtuous female disciple testifies to having seen the Risen Jesus without having touched him, the unworthy male disciple insists on tactile confirmation of the Resurrection.

In the *Noli me tangere* (and also in Pseudo-Mark) Mary Magdalene is presented as a uniquely privileged disciple of the Risen Christ. This is exactly how she is portrayed in certain "heretical" early Christian texts. In the second-century *Gospel of Mary*, for instance, the male disciples are too frightened to go out and preach the gospel until Mary stands up and stiffens their resolve. She is then requested to tell them Christ's secret teachings:

> Peter said to Mary, "Sister, we know that the Savior loved you more than the rest of women. Tell us the words of the Savior which you remember—which you know [but] we do not, nor have we heard them." Mary answered and said, "What is hidden from you, I will proclaim to you." And she began to speak to them these words: "I," she said, "I saw the Lord in a vision and I said to him, 'Lord, I saw you today in a vision.' He answered and said to me, 'Blessed are you, that you did not waver at the sight of me. For where the mind is, there is the treasure.' "[15]

She goes on to reveal what Christ told her about visions, the soul and, presumably, other spiritual matters (unfortunately, most of her speech is missing from the manuscript), inspiring the apostles to begin preaching the gospel. Similarly, in the fourth-century *Pistis Sophia* Mary is the principal interlocutor of the Risen Christ, who calls her "thou blessed one . . . whose heart is more directed to the Kingdom of Heaven than all thy brothers,"[16] while in the third-century *Gospel of Philip* she is the beloved companion of the Savior and is compared with Sophia (Wisdom), the mother of the angels.[17] She is prominent, too, in much earlier works, such as the *Gospel of Thomas*, written in the late first century.[18] Once we are familiar with this "alternative" Christian tradition, the distinction accorded Mary Magdalene in the *Noli me tangere* no longer seems so surprising. The surprise is to recognize this matriarchal passage embedded in one of the canonical Gospels.

The tradition of Mary's apostolic superiority appears to be ancient, then, predating John and probably Matthew, too.[19] The female appearance-story must have been devised in the mid first century to establish her authority in direct opposition to the First Creed.

It is likely that the appearance of the Risen Christ to Mary and her companions at the tomb was commemorated in the Sunday morning ceremony practiced in Bithynia. This early rite, which was apparently established before AD 85,[20] *could* have been instituted by a male hierarchy to commemorate the women's discovery of the Shroud (or the empty tomb), but it is more likely to reflect the matriarchal tradition enshrined in the *Noli me tangere*. The Bithynian ceremony took place "before dawn," matching John's statement that Mary Magdalene went to the sepulchre "while it was still dark,"[21] and, to find out about it, Pliny had to torture a couple of deaconesses, a hint that the services were organized by, perhaps even led by, women. Probably, then, this morning service was a ceremonial equivalent of the female appearance-stories, commemorating, like them, the women's discovery of the Shroud.

Acknowledging the pre-Gospel origins of the female appearance-stories and the depth and antiquity of Mary Magdalene's apostolic reputation leads to one final realization: that Mary was indeed an early Christian teacher. Such stories would not have been told unless she was an influential figure, one who rivalled the male hierarchy of the early Church. The heroine of the "alternative," non-canonical Christian scriptures was no mere figment of the Gnostic imagination. Mary Magdalene was a major apostle, whose important role in the foundation of Christianity was effectively obscured by the male leaders of the early Church.

According to the "feminist" tradition focused on Mary Magdalene, the first appearance of the Risen Christ took place at or in the tomb of Jesus, the very spot where the Shroud was discovered. It occurred, furthermore, when the women went to complete the burial, i.e. when they were engaged in anointing, washing and *enshrouding* the body of Jesus. The location is spot on; the occasion is spot on. And several features of the stories make sense only if those who devised them were familiar with the Shroud. Whoever originally composed the female appearance-stories seems to have known about the discovery of the Shroud on Easter morning.

Given the patriarchal character of first-century Jewish society, it is surprising to find the women's discovery of the Shroud narrated as an encounter with the Risen Christ in any early Christian writings, let alone in the Gospels. The inference must be that there was a strong female input into the composition of the tomb-stories—so much so that the Resurrection narratives in the Gospels became battlegrounds in a virulent war of the sexes.[22]

Solving the Resurrection problem is as much about learning to interpret the motivations of early Christian story-tellers as it is about identifying the likely cause of the Resurrection belief. Recognizing representations of the Shroud in the Gospel narratives is only half the problem; we also have to account for the *manner* of its portrayal. How it is represented in any particular passage appears to depend upon who originally composed the tale, who edited it, and how these different authors felt about the tale's protagonists. Even the briefest of Gospel narratives is potentially a piece of propaganda.

This insight is crucial for understanding the next event described—or, rather, erased—in the Gospel tomb-stories: the appearance to Peter.

21

The Appearance to Peter

As far as Peter and his followers were concerned, the appearance to the women never happened. For them, Peter was the first to see the Risen Jesus. Their point of view is encapsulated in the First Creed, which states that, after rising on the third day, Christ "appeared to Cephas."[1] This claim underscored Peter's initial leadership of the Church.

It is perplexing to discover, then, that nowhere in the Gospels is the appearance to Peter narrated.[2] Luke mentions it in passing but tells us nothing of the circumstances. Otherwise, there is complete silence. What was for the apostolic Church a vital part of the Resurrection witness was apparently of little or no interest to those who composed the Resurrection narratives in the Gospels.

Faced with this silence, many New Testament scholars gloss over the appearance to Peter, preferring to concentrate on the appearances the Evangelists do narrate.[3] Others place a great deal of emphasis on it, some even believing that Peter's experience, whatever it was, sparked the explosion of Resurrection faith, the other apostles being inspired by Peter's example to "see" the Risen Jesus for themselves. But they cannot say where or when this event occurred.[4] It is often said to have taken place in Galilee, days or weeks after the Crucifixion, a conjecture based on the angelic pronouncements in Mark and Matthew, but there is no solid evidence in favor of this location.[5] In short, New Testament scholarship is completely baffled by the report of the appearance to Peter.

The problem disappears, however, if the Shroud is brought into the equation. For although the Gospels fail to narrate an appearance to Peter, two of them, Luke and John, do tell of Peter visiting Jesus' sepulchre on Easter morning (with or without a fellow disciple) and seeing the burial cloths there. If Peter saw the Shroud in the tomb on Easter morning, and if the cloth was understood to manifest the Risen Jesus, then Peter would have been regarded as the first male witness of the Resurrection. The claim of the First Creed can thus be reconciled with the discordant Gospel record.[6]

Given our reconstruction of events so far, the report that Peter went to the tomb on Easter morning should be judged inherently likely. Having discovered a perturbing figure in Jesus' burial cloth, Mary Magdalene and her companions would undoubtedly have interrupted the burial and hurried off to tell their menfolk. The Gospels confirm this scenario, and we may presume that Peter was among those the women found. What would his reaction have been? Skepticism, perhaps, as some of the sources imply—but also, surely, a desire to check their story. So the idea that Peter visited the tomb immediately after the women is entirely plausible. And when he got there, he "found it just as the women had said."[7]

To decide whether or not this was the occasion of the appearance to Peter, we need to determine when and where this appearance took place.

Despite its reticence on the subject, the New Testament provides good evidence that the Risen Jesus was seen by Peter on Easter Day. To begin with, the testimony of the First Creed, that Peter saw the Risen Jesus before the Twelve, can be combined with the evidence of the strong tradition, found in Luke and John (and the *Epistula*), that the appearance to the Twelve took place in Jerusalem late on Easter Day. If this tradition is historical, which it very probably is (see below, pp. 273–5), and if Peter saw the Risen Jesus before the Twelve, then he must have done so earlier that same day, somewhere in the vicinity of Jerusalem.

This is supported by the only explicit reference to the individual appearance to Peter anywhere in the Gospels. In Luke 24.34, just before witnessing the Risen Christ themselves, the Eleven inform the two Emmaus disciples that Jesus has risen and appeared to Peter. Again, this places Peter's experience in or near Jerusalem on Easter Day. The significance of this testimony is slightly compromised by the fact that Luke inserted it into his narrative based on his knowledge of the First Creed.[8] Even so, the reference represents an early record of the event that is compatible with the idea that Peter saw the Risen Jesus when he went to the tomb.

The same chronology can be inferred from the statement in the First Creed that Christ was raised "on the third day." How did the early Christians deduce the time of a miracle that no one witnessed directly? The "prophecy" of Hosea 6.2 ("on the third day he will raise us up") may have been cited in evidence, but the calculation was almost certainly based on the actual course of events.[9] Counting inclusively from Good Friday (in accordance with Jewish custom), the third day was Easter Sunday, when the women went to the tomb. It has been suggested, therefore, that the dating of the Resurrection was determined by the discovery of the "empty tomb," but, as we have seen, the tomb was probably not empty, and the women are omitted from the First Creed. The only option in this context is to understand "on the third day" as a reference to the occasion of the "first" appearance—the appearance to Peter.[10]

So, according to the evidence of the Gospels and the First Creed, the appearance to Peter took place on Easter Day, before the appearance to the Twelve. The only other information we have about Peter during this time is that, having been alerted by the women, he went to Jesus' sepulchre and saw the burial cloths there. If the Shroud theory is correct, this is all the information we need. Seeing the Shroud, Peter would have seen exactly the same phenomenon as was seen by the women—a faint, angelic form emerging from the linen. Later, he and his partisans would remember his inspection of the cloth as the first appearance of the Risen Christ.

This is not how it was remembered, however, in the Gospels. As I have said, two of the Gospels, Luke and John, contain accounts of Peter's visit to the tomb. The briefest of these occurs in Luke's artful tale of the Road to Emmaus.[11] Having told the Risen Jesus (whom they do not recognize) about the women's report of angels at the empty tomb, the Emmaus disciples add, "Some of those who were with us went to the tomb, and found it just as the women had said; but him they did not see." We shall return to the conversation on the Emmaus Road—where all is not as it seems—in a moment.

A slightly more detailed account is included in some early manuscripts of Luke, immediately following the account of the women's abortive trip to the tomb:

> But Peter rose and ran to the tomb; stooping, he saw the linen cloths [othonia] lying by themselves; and he went home wondering at what had happened. (Luke 24.12)

This verse was probably added by an early editor of Luke, but it appears to derive from an ancient source.[12] Its principal interest is the curious focus on the linen cloths. Peter went to the tomb, saw the linen cloths and returned home wondering what had happened: isn't this exactly the sort of report we should expect to have regarding the discovery of the Shroud? Of course, there is no mention of the Shroud figure, but there is a simple reason for this, as we shall see.

A more developed version of the story is found in John. In this famous

tale Peter and the Beloved Disciple are alerted to the disappearance of
Jesus' body by Mary Magdalene, who has seen the stone moved aside from
the tomb but has yet to look inside and see the angels, let alone the Risen
Christ.

> So she ran, and went to Simon Peter and the other disciple, the one whom
> Jesus loved, and said to them, "They have taken the Lord out of the tomb,
> and we do not know where they have laid him." Peter then came out with
> the other disciple, and they went toward the tomb. They both ran, but the
> other disciple outran Peter and reached the tomb first; and stooping to look
> in, he saw the linen cloths [*othonia*] lying there, but he did not go in. Then
> Simon Peter came, following him, and went into the tomb; he saw the linen
> cloths [*othonia*] lying, and the napkin [*soudarion*], which had been on his
> head, not lying with the linen cloths [*othonia*] but rolled up in a place by
> itself. Then the other disciple, who reached the tomb first, also went in,
> and he saw and believed; for as yet they did not know the scripture, that
> he must rise from the dead. Then the disciples went back to their homes.
> (John 20.2–10)

This text contains numerous puzzles. How does Mary know that the body
is missing without having looked into the tomb? Why does the Beloved
Disciple stop at the entrance to the tomb and let Peter catch up and go in
first? What is the strange *soudarion* found lying apart from the other
cloths? If the Beloved Disciple suddenly realized that Jesus had risen from
the dead, why did he and Peter just go back quietly to their homes, apparently without telling anyone?

These puzzles can be solved with the help of the Shroud and the realization that John developed his story from the same narrative source as Luke.

There are three conspicuous differences between John 20.2–10 and
Luke 24.12, all of which indicate that John has heavily modified the
account he inherited. First, whereas John includes the figure of the Beloved
Disciple, Luke does not. Since the Beloved Disciple is a character found
only in John, he may well be an addition to the tale. Second, John places
the story near the beginning of his Resurrection chapter, before Mary
Magdalene sees the angels in the tomb, whereas Luke places it after the
female tomb-story. Luke must preserve the original sequence, since the
interruption of the female tomb-story in John is extremely awkward and
results in Mary reporting the missing body before she has even looked into
the tomb. Originally, the male tomb-story must have followed the *Noli me
tangere*; John has inverted this sequence in order to make the male disciples the first to enter the tomb and the Beloved Disciple the first to believe

in the Resurrection. Third, John introduces into the story a burial cloth not mentioned anywhere else: the intriguing *soudarion*.

Once you strip away the Beloved Disciple and the *soudarion* from John's text and relocate it after the *Noli me tangere*, you end up with a basic narrative that closely resembles Luke 24.12.[13] We can conclude from this that Luke and John both based their versions of the male tomb-story on a common source and that Luke's version is fairly close to the original.

If Luke's account of Peter visiting the tomb is based on a relatively early source, it is likely to reflect eyewitness testimony. This makes it all the more tantalizing in relation to the Shroud. The linen cloths (*othonia*) are the focus of the episode, and it is the sight of these cloths that causes Peter's wonderment. What was so puzzling about them? If they were merely empty, Peter would surely have assumed that someone had taken the body and would have set about trying to recover it.[14] His wandering home meditatively suggests he has seen something much more peculiar. In the past, it has sometimes been imagined that it was the position of the cloths that was perplexing, that their arrangement somehow signaled the miraculous dematerialization of Jesus' body.[15] But this interpretation is obviously dependent on belief in a "transphysical" flesh-and-blood resurrection, for which there is no credible evidence. A far better explanation is that the linen Peter saw was the Shroud and that he went home wondering about its meaning.

This was apparently how John's text was interpreted several centuries later in Spain. One of the most intriguing of all references to Christ's burial cloths is found in a sixth- or seventh-century liturgical text known as the Mozarabic Rite, which tells how "Peter ran with John to the tomb and saw the recent traces [*vestigia*] of the dead and risen man in the linen cloths."[16] This appears to testify to knowledge of an imprint of Jesus' figure on the linen found in his tomb.[17] The Latin word *vestigium*, which means a footprint or, more generally, a visible trace or mark, is an appropriate word to denote the stain on the Shroud. Indeed, in a version of the sixth-century itinerary of Antoninus of Piacenza the very same word, *vestigia*, is used to denote a miraculous image of Christ imprinted on a cloth kept in the Egyptian city of Memphis.[18]

The intention of the Spanish writer, it seems, was to clarify the significance of the linen cloths seen in the tomb by Peter (and by the Beloved Disciple, traditionally identified as John), which is left thoroughly obscure in the Gospels. The disciples were bewildered, we understand, not because the cloths were empty or oddly arranged, but because they saw *vestiges* of Jesus in the linen.[19] That is, they saw his imprint on the Shroud.

The composition of the Mozarabic Rite seems to have been influenced by St. Leander of Seville (d. 599), who lived for a while in Constantinople. He may well have learned of the miraculous *vestigia* on the burial cloth while living in the East, the Shroud/Mandylion having been rediscovered in Edessa a little while earlier. Corroborative evidence that the full-length Shroud-image was witnessed during this period is provided by a sixth-century Georgian manuscript, an apocryphal autobiography of Joseph of Arimathea, in which Joseph describes how he "climbed Holy Golgotha, where the Lord's cross stood, and collected in a headband and a large sheet the precious blood that had flowed from his holy side."[20]

The author of the Mozarabic Rite, then, was probably aware of the recent rediscovery of the Shroud/Mandylion. Ironically, he probably understood the point of the male tomb-story better than either John or Luke. The male tomb-story is thus a classic case of the Gospels transmitting useful information of which the Evangelists themselves were unaware.

Whoever devised the male tomb-story transmitted by Luke and John was not so innocent. He or she must have been fully aware of the "vestiges" of Jesus visible in the Shroud. Why, then, is Peter not said to have encountered the Risen Christ—or even an angel? And why does he go home without telling anyone what he has seen?

To answer these questions we have to understand the original point of the male tomb-story. And to do this, we have to consider it in relation to the tradition of the female appearance-story. As I have explained, John's *Noli me tangere* originally came *before*, not after, the tale of Peter and the Beloved Disciple running to the tomb. So, the story of Peter's uneventful, inconsequential trip to the sepulchre was originally preceded by a memorable account of the Risen Jesus appearing to Mary Magdalene and her female companions. The whole point was the dramatic contrast. Unlike the women, Peter saw nothing and comprehended nothing, and whereas they returned to Jerusalem to announce the Resurrection, he just went quietly home. Peter is being cast in a thoroughly negative light with respect to his female counterparts.

The purpose of the male tomb-story becomes even clearer in light of the Shroud theory. For, if the Risen Christ was seen in the linen, it was not simply a matter of different experiences vouchsafed at the tomb but a moral contrast between the perceptive women, who see the significance of the Shroud immediately (or almost immediately), and the dull-witted Peter, who does not perceive its significance till later. The story is anticlimactic for a reason: it expresses Peter's initial failure to respond to the great sign of the Resurrection. What we have, in fact, is a calculated inversion of the testimony of the First Creed. There, Peter is the first to see the Risen Christ and the women are excluded as witnesses; here, the women are the first to see the Risen Christ and it is Peter who is excluded as a witness. The male tomb-story seems to have been composed as a direct response to the patriarchal "gospel" of the early Church.

A trace of the original, negative purpose of the male tomb-story is detectable in the aforementioned reference to it made by the Emmaus disciple in Luke: "Some of those who were with us went to the tomb, and found it just as the women had said; but him they did not see." The last phrase is crucial, but it does not mean, as is usually assumed, that Jesus' body had vanished. Consider the context: even as they recount the tale of their companions failing to see the Risen Jesus, the Emmaus disciples fail to see the Risen Jesus standing before them! The "appearance" on the road to Emmaus is a story about not seeing the Risen Jesus even though he is present. (It is only in the next scene, the Supper at Emmaus, that the eyes of the two disciples are opened.) This casts the non-appearance to the disciples at the tomb in a new light. It alerts us to the possibility that the men who went to the tomb might have encountered the Risen Christ without realizing it. That is exactly what the male tomb-story implies: Peter saw the linen cloth but not the person therein. He was spiritually blind.

The Emmaus disciples' recitation of the morning's events, finishing with the comment that the disciples did not see Jesus at the tomb, provokes an angry reaction from the (still unrecognized) Risen Jesus: "O foolish men, and slow of heart to believe all that the prophets have spoken! Was it not necessary that the Christ should suffer these things and enter into his glory?"[21] His words are an admonition of the disciples who went to the tomb, just as much as of the Emmaus pair. Why are they all foolish? Because they do not see the Risen Christ in front of them. Why do they not see him? Because they are "slow of heart to believe all that the prophets have spoken." This is a profoundly interesting statement, because it implies that the perception of the Risen Jesus was somehow dependent on faith in the scriptures. It is difficult to see how this can be squared with the traditional notion of a divine revelation, which presumably would have been fully convincing in itself. It is entirely compatible, though, with the Shroud theory, for the Shroud's significance would have been determined, ultimately, via scriptural interpretation. Moreover, the idea of Christ "entering into his glory"—an idea embodied most clearly in the story of the Transfiguration—is an apt description of Jesus' transference into the glorious Shroud figure. The whole Emmaus story is a fable, symbolizing the (alleged) dullness of the disciples in front of the sign of the Risen Jesus.

In all three versions, then, the male tomb-story betrays a surprising anti-Peter agenda. How are we to account for this blatant attack on Peter in the central texts of Christianity? The answer is found in the non-canonical gospels that celebrate Mary Magdalene. For, as well as attesting to the reputation of Mary as a prominent apostle, these texts reflect considerable antagonism between her and Peter.

The rivalry between Mary and Peter is evident in the final "logion" of the first-century *Gospel of Thomas*, in which Peter says to the disciples, "Let Mary leave us, for women are not worthy of life" (meaning eternal life). He is contradicted by Jesus himself, who affirms that "every woman who will make herself male will enter the kingdom of heaven."[22] The fact that the *Gospel of Thomas* ends with this exchange demonstrates the importance of the issue in early Christian debates. A very similar exchange concludes the *Gospel of Mary*. There, having listened to Mary's lengthy recital of Christ's teaching, Peter questions her authority: "Did he really speak with a woman without our knowledge [and] not openly? Are we to turn about and all listen to her? Did he prefer her to us?" Mary defends herself gamely—"Do you think that I thought this up myself in my heart or that I am lying about the Savior?"—and she is backed up by Levi, who rebukes Peter for "contending against the woman like the adversaries."[23] Lastly, in the third-century *Pistis Sophia*, Peter complains about Mary because she speaks too much, prompting her to confess, "I am afraid of Peter because he threatens me and hates our race [i.e. women]."[24]

These literary dramas may reflect the sexual politics of the post-apostolic Church, but the rift between Peter and Mary is almost certainly historical—witness her omission from the First Creed. In any case, the *Gospel of Thomas* proves that Peter was being portrayed as a misogynist by the late first century, when Luke and John were written. That is all the evidence we need to account for his belittlement in the male tomb-story, composed, like the female appearance-stories, by a "feminist" opponent of the First Creed.

As well as the male tomb-story, John knew another tradition about Peter and the burial cloths. This was a tradition that came, apparently, from Edessa, and concerned that mysterious other cloth: the *soudarion*.

As we have seen, John refers, first of all, to the "linen cloths" (*othonia*), a term he inherited from one of his sources. He did not understand that the *othonia* stood in place of the *sindon* (i.e. the Shroud), and so he accorded these "linen cloths" little or no significance. The *soudarion*, however, which he himself introduced into the narrative, is very carefully described, indicating that he had specific information about it and that he deemed it of particular interest.

The significance of the *soudarion* is revealed by analyzing the logic of the story. When the Beloved Disciple arrives at the tomb, he peers in and sees just the *othonia*. This has no effect on him. Soon afterward, Peter arrives, goes in and sees not only the *othonia*, but also the *soudarion*, which evidently cannot be seen from outside—that is why the Evangelist describes it as "not lying with the linen cloths but in a place by itself." The Beloved Disciple then enters as well, and all that is left for him to see is the *soudarion*. Instantly, he sees and believes. What does he believe? That Jesus has been resurrected, as the next verse implies. Moreover, he believes despite being ignorant of the scriptural prophecies that Jesus "must rise from the dead." John is saying, in effect, that the *soudarion* was sufficient *on its own* to prompt faith in the Resurrection.

On the face of it, the idea of a folded sweat-cloth inspiring belief in the Resurrection is profoundly bizarre. Indeed, it would be quite unintelligible, but for the possibility that, by the time John was writing, the Shroud had been transformed into the Mandylion, i.e. folded to the size of a hand-towel and framed so that only the edges of the cloth and the facial image were visible. I have already given several reasons to think that John's *soudarion* is a reference to the Mandylion (see above, p. 231), and its effect on the Beloved Disciple completes the argument. Even in this reduced form the Shroud would have remained a powerful sign of the Resurrection. It was no longer equated with the Risen Jesus himself, but its devotees would still have seen it as representing the Risen Jesus and would have known that it was found in his tomb. It is hardly surprising that someone decided to incorporate a reference to this precious cloth into a Gospel tomb-story.

So the account of Peter entering the tomb and seeing the *soudarion* before anyone else is directly analogous to the First Creed's statement that he was the primary witness of the Risen Christ. They were different ways of saying the same thing: that Peter was the first to see the Shroud.

It is important to emphasize that John was not playing a game with his audience, veiling an appearance of the Risen Christ behind the mundane image of a "sweat-cloth." Rather, he was heir to a tradition about Peter being the first to see the *soudarion*, a tradition which paralleled the belief that Peter was the first to see the Risen Christ. John appears to have been unaware of the claim that Peter saw the Risen Christ before anyone else.

Had he been aware of it, though, he would have been unable to make the connection with Peter's discovery of the *soudarion*, since, like most of his contemporaries, he imagined the Risen Christ to have been a being of flesh and blood. It is only now, with critical hindsight, that we can recognize the underlying unity of the traditions.

In my view, then, the *soudarion* in John 20.7 can be nothing other than an anachronistic description of the Shroud as the Mandylion, the only folded "sweat-cloth" that could ever have inspired faith in the Resurrection.

One major question remains: what did Peter do once he had seen the *soudarion*? Did he remove it from the body immediately, or did he leave it in the tomb, to be retrieved later by someone else? John does not even hint at the fate of the *soudarion* (any more than the Synoptics say what became of the *sindon*). However, a couple of later sources provide evidence that the Shroud was removed from the tomb by Peter himself.[25]

The first of these sources is the legendary *Life of St. Nino*, the apostle of Georgia. Part of this *Life* consists of the saint's "Conjectures," which may well date back to the early fourth century, the time of the apostle herself. In her Conjectures, St. Nino recalls that the *soudarion* "is said to have been found by Peter, who took it and kept it, but we know not if it was ever discovered."[26] This tradition might be dismissed as pure speculation based on the Gospel of John, but there are reasons to take it seriously. It is not known for sure where St. Nino came from, but, whatever her route to the Caucasus, she must have traveled there via eastern Turkey, passing through or near Edessa.[27] It is perfectly plausible that a stream of tradition about the *soudarion* was still current in the region—the same stream of tradition that was tapped earlier by John. Her comment that the *soudarion* was lost at the time of writing also fits in with the later report that, unknown to anyone at the time, the Mandylion was walled up above one of the gateways of Edessa.[28] On balance, then, St. Nino's testimony seems credible.

It is confirmed by an independent source of the mid ninth century, the Syriac *Commentaries on the Gospels* written by Isodad, bishop of Merv, an important trading-center in what is now Turkmenistan, to the north of Iran (ancient Persia).[29] Although he lived five centuries after Nino, Isodad seems to have known rather more than her about the *soudarion*. This is what he says about it in his commentary on John:

> Simon took the *sudara*, and it was for him a crown on his head. And every time that he laid his hands on someone, he put it on his head. He obtained much and frequent aid from it, in the same way that even today the leaders

and the bishops of the Church put turbans on their heads and around the neck in place of that *sudara*.[30]

There are several reasons to take this report seriously. It is clear that Isodad's information is based on a venerable church tradition, and the Nestorian Church to which he belonged had once been well established in Edessa. Moreover, the description of the *soudarion* being used as a "crown" during healing ceremonies ties in with earlier evidence that the Mandylion was used similarly. There is the story, for instance, of the apostle Thaddeus entering King Abgar's audience-hall with the Mandylion placed on his forehead and thereby curing the king of his paralysis.[31] This correspondence is especially significant, since, after its rediscovery in the sixth century, the Mandylion was not officially identified with the *soudarion* found in the tomb, but was regarded instead as a miraculous self-portrait sent to King Abgar by Jesus during his ministry. This means that Isodad's tradition about the *soudarion* cannot have been concocted on the basis of the Abgar legend. It would appear to go back to the time of John, when the Shroud was still identified as the *soudarion*.

We may conclude from the traditions recorded by St. Nino and Isodad of Merv that, at the time the Shroud/Mandylion was sequestered above Edessa's west gate, it was believed to have been taken from Jesus' tomb by Peter. This belief is historically plausible and, as we shall see, it ties in with the evidence of what happened later, on the evening of Easter Day.

The mystery of the appearance to Peter listed in the First Creed can now be laid to rest. What Peter saw was the Shroud in Jesus' tomb on Easter morning. This accounts elegantly for every scrap of information relating to Peter's individual experience at Easter.

Just as interestingly, the discordant records of Peter's first sight of the Shroud provide clear evidence of tensions and disjunctions at the heart of early Christianity. The Shroud was a phenomenon that could be interpreted (and displayed) in different ways, and early Christian authors exploited its ambiguity to the full. It was portrayed variously, depending on the context of the portrayal and the knowledge and prejudices of the author.

To begin with, Peter and his male colleagues represented his initial sight of the Shroud as the first appearance of the Risen Jesus (ignoring the women's prior claim). The First Creed, which promoted this tendentious interpretation of Peter's visit to the tomb, was probably being taught to the apostles within a few years of the Crucifixion. The exclusion of the women from the Creed was justified, no doubt, on the grounds that they were ineligible to serve as public witnesses. But their marginalization was not simply a matter of pragmatism; it reflected the deeply entrenched patriarchal attitudes of the time. And we should not discount the personal element, either. By omitting the women, foremost among them Mary Magdalene, and presenting himself as the primary witness, Peter was clearly establishing his own authority at the expense of theirs.

The women had their revenge. While Paul and the hierarchy of the Jerusalem Church promulgated the First Creed, someone keen to promote the opposing, female point of view composed an influential account of Peter going to the tomb and failing to see the Risen Jesus in the Shroud. While this account was perpetuated in the subsequent Gospel tradition (now surviving in Luke and John), the oral proclamation contained in the First Creed was gradually forgotten. The only Evangelist to cite it was Luke, who inserted it awkwardly into his account of Easter Day. Rather than writing up their own, pro-Peter interpretations of Easter, the Evangelists were engaged in editing traditional narratives that were distinctly antipathetic to Peter.

Meanwhile, the early Christians of Edessa preserved traditions about the *soudarion*, the term by which the Shroud was known after its drastic reinvention as the Mandylion. They told how this cloth had been found by Peter in the tomb on Easter morning and how he had taken it and worn it on his head to achieve miraculous cures. Part of this oral tradition, at least, was known to John, who incorporated it into his retelling of the male tomb-story, and it survived for centuries in churches with links to Edessa. St. Nino of Georgia and Isodad of Merv both knew that Peter had taken the *soudarion* from Jesus' tomb, but neither of them had the remotest idea that this was the occasion of Peter's inaugural encounter with the Risen Christ. Neither, centuries earlier, did John.

Until now, scholars have had no means of bringing order to this confusion of evidence. Only when the linen in the tomb is re-envisaged as the Shroud do all the various pieces of the jigsaw fall into place.

22

The Appearance to the Twelve

Imagine how Peter felt as, emerging from Jesus' tomb, he tucked the Shroud beneath his arm and hurried back along the stony path to Jerusalem. He must have been upset, excited and bewildered, all at the same time. He had just witnessed the crucified body of his beloved leader laid out for burial, cold and dead; but he had also found a mysterious figure staring out from the burial cloth, just as the women had said. Recognizing the figure as a sign, a messenger from beyond the grave, he had decided to remove it from the tomb. Then, as he lifted the body from the cloth, another figure had emerged, this one with its back to him.[1] Two visionary visitants had silently revealed themselves to him in Jesus' tomb.

Now he had them in his hands, rolled up in the cloth, and was carrying them in the direction of the Holy City. What did they mean? His mind must have been whirling. His one fixed idea, surely, would have been to share his discovery with his despondent colleagues, those who, like him, had followed Jesus and were now in mourning. He needed to show the Shroud as soon as possible to the Twelve.

This scenario makes sense in relation to the evidence of the New Testament. The First Creed and the Gospels agree that, after first being seen on Easter morning—whether by Peter or by the women—the Risen Christ appeared to the Twelve.[2] This appearance is remembered in three of the Gospels (Matthew, Luke and John) as the moment of Christianity's foundation, as the occasion when the Risen Christ commissioned his disciples to go out and preach the Kingdom of God. There can be no doubt that it was a hugely significant event. But, once again, New Testament scholarship has been unable to decide the time and place of this appearance, let alone its precise nature. There exists no proper historical understanding of the moment the Church—the community of Christian believers—was conceived. The Shroud, coupled with a fresh, critical view of the Gospel testimony, can help us fill in this historical blank.

Efforts to establish the likely circumstances of the event have been hampered by conflicting evidence. There are two separate traditions in the Gospels regarding the appearance to the Twelve. According to what may be called the Jerusalem Tradition, the Risen Christ appeared to the disciples in Jerusalem on the evening of Easter Day. This tradition is found in the apparently independent narratives of Luke and John and is repeated in other sources, as well. While some scholars consider this tradition historical, most doubt it, presuming that the appearance to the Twelve took place in Galilee, days or even weeks after Easter, as indicated by Mark and Matthew.[3] This "Galilee Tradition" is echoed in the *Gospel of Peter* and John 21. As yet, no one has been able to demonstrate which of the two traditions is historically correct.

Reinterpreting the event as the first display of the Shroud, we may be able, at long last, to establish when and where it took place. Initially, it might seem as if the Jerusalem and Galilee Traditions are equally plausible in relation to the Shroud: the cloth could have been shown to Peter's companions on Easter Day, if they were still in the vicinity of Jerusalem, or it could have been taken to Galilee, to be shown to them there sometime later. But on further consideration, an Easter Day viewing of the Shroud in Jerusalem seems far more likely.

It is sometimes thought that the Twelve fled to Galilee over the Easter weekend, based on Mark's report (repeated by Matthew) that they fled at the moment of his arrest in the Garden of Gethsemane. But this is unlikely. If Peter went to Jesus' tomb on Easter Sunday, he cannot have fled the city three days earlier, and, if he stayed in Jerusalem, the rest of the disciples probably did too. Furthermore, all the Gospels imply the presence of the disciples in Jerusalem on Easter morning, as the recipients of the women's message.[4] That the Twelve stayed in Jerusalem after the Crucifixion and witnessed the Resurrection there is also supported by the opening chapters of Acts, based on traditions separate from those followed in the Gospels.[5]

The flight to Galilee, then, appears to be a figment of the scholarly imagination.[6] When Peter returned to Jerusalem that morning with his peculiar trophy, his colleagues were probably still in the vicinity, lying low. He would have gathered them together as soon as he could and shown them the Shroud. If this reasoning is correct, then it is to the Jerusalem Tradition that we must look for a semi-historical description of the appearance to the Twelve.

Following his dramatic account of the appearance to Mary Magdalene, John provides an oddly stilted report of the appearance to the Twelve.

There is no fuss at all, no surprise, no real emotion. The event is portrayed as a quiet, run-of-the-mill reunion, where Jesus delegates power and authority to his disciples:

> On the evening of that day, the first day of the week, the doors being shut where the disciples were, for fear of the Jews, Jesus came and stood among them and said to them, "Peace be with you." When he had said this, he showed them his hands and his side. Then the disciples were glad when they saw the Lord. Jesus said to them again, "Peace be with you. As the father has sent me, even so I send you." And when he had said this, he breathed on them, and said to them, "Receive the Holy Spirit. If you forgive the sins of any, they are forgiven; if you retain the sins of any, they are retained."[7]

To this serene, uncomplicated story is added a sequel, the famous tale of Doubting Thomas, to be discussed later.

Luke's description of the appearance to the Twelve is much more elaborate than John's. The disciples take a great deal of persuading that their master is raised from the dead, and Jesus' speech covers the fulfillment of prophecy, as well as the future role of the disciples. The action commences while the Emmaus disciples are telling the Eleven "and those who were with them" of their experience on the road and at supper:

> As they were saying this, Jesus himself stood among them. But they were startled and frightened, and supposed that they saw a spirit. And he said to them, "Why are you troubled, and why do questionings rise in your hearts? See my hands and my feet, that it is I myself; handle me and see; for a spirit has not flesh and bones as you see that I have." And while they still disbelieved for joy, and wondered, he said to them, "Have you anything here to eat?" They gave him a piece of broiled fish, and he took it and ate before them.
>
> Then he said to them, "These are my words which I spoke to you, while I was still with you, that everything written about me in the law of Moses and the prophets and the psalms must be fulfilled." Then he opened their minds to understand the scriptures, and said to them, "Thus it is written, that the Christ should suffer and on the third day rise from the dead, and that repentance and forgiveness of sins should be preached in his name to all nations, beginning from Jerusalem. You are witnesses of these things. And behold, I send the promise of my Father upon you; but stay in the city, until you are clothed with power from on high."[8]

Obviously, a great deal of this narrative—including the eating and speaking—is fictional.[9] But there are a number of reasons to suspect that, along with John's narrative, it goes back to an authentic memory of the appearance to the Twelve.

I noted earlier that, although the appearance-stories in the Gospels constitute a jumble of disconnected legends, these twin stories in John and Luke stand out as relatively consistent, like two pieces of a jigsaw that remain attached to one another after the puzzle has been scrambled (and half the pieces lost). Although the texts are linked by a series of agreements, there is no firm evidence that John knew Luke, or vice versa, meaning that their parallel narratives probably descend from the same (very early) written source, or else go back to independent eyewitness testimony (which may, of course, be the same thing).

What is more, the Jerusalem Tradition offers an explanation for the early Christian habit of meeting together on Sunday evenings to "break bread." A perceived encounter with the Risen Christ on the evening of Easter Sunday would explain the origin of this universal ceremony.[10] Since the Lord's Supper appears to have been instituted before AD 33, it cannot have been based on an unfounded legend. The best explanation is that it commemorated the first communal sighting of the Lord, as recorded by John and Luke.[11]

So, the Jerusalem Tradition appears to be historically grounded. But how are we to recognize its historical nucleus? A straightforward method is to identify those elements that the narratives of John and Luke have in common.

Besides stating or implying that the appearance to the Twelve took place in Jerusalem on the evening of Easter Day, the texts share six significant features. First, both the Evangelists describe the event as an indoor gathering.[12] Second, they narrate the appearance of Jesus in exactly the same way, saying simply that Jesus "stood among them."[13] Third, both texts revolve around the Risen Christ displaying his wounds. Fourth, both John and Luke comment that the disciples reacted with joy. Fifth, in both texts the Risen Jesus announces the forgiveness of sins. And sixth, they both introduce the idea of Jesus bestowing the Holy Spirit on the disciples.

The last two motifs, which involve theological reflection, must descend from an earlier telling of the story, implying that John and Luke depend ultimately on a common source. The rest are plainly descriptive and may well reflect the actual experience of the event. Significantly, all four make sense in relation to the Shroud. Indeed, seen in light of the Shroud, they combine to give a vivid impression of the appearance to the Twelve.

The setting, to begin with, is entirely credible. Just two days after the Crucifixion, the Twelve would still have been extremely wary of arrest, and it would have been very risky for them to have been seen together. Yet Peter had an urgent reason to call a meeting—to show them the Shroud. In the circumstances, a night-time gathering behind locked doors is precisely what we should expect. Peter would undoubtedly have ensured tight security for the sake of the Shroud as well.

What about the manner of the appearance? It is often assumed that the description of the Risen Christ suddenly manifesting himself in the room with the disciples implies his ability to pass through solid walls.[14] The Shroud, though, offers a new, realistic way of interpreting the scene. Peter would have brought the cloth to the venue clandestinely, rolled or folded up, and he would have shown it to the assembled company only after the room had been made secure. As the Shroud was unfurled for the first time, the Risen Jesus would literally have appeared in the midst of the Twelve— as the Gospels say, he would have suddenly "stood among them."

At the heart of the Jerusalem Tradition is the inspection of Christ's wounds. This theme, too, may reflect what actually happened when the Twelve first witnessed the Shroud. The blood marks are the most striking feature of the Shroud figure, and they would undoubtedly have drawn attention when the cloth was displayed for the first time. They would have served the same dual purpose as the wounds in the Gospel narratives: to identify the Risen Jesus as one and the same as the mortal Jesus; and to prove not merely his presence but his quasi-corporeal presence—his Resurrection.

Regarding the issue of identity, first of all, it is by no means obvious that the Risen Jesus would have been best recognized via his injuries. If the Twelve had had a communal vision, for instance, they would presumably have recognized Jesus from his face and speech. Similarly, someone resurrected in the flesh would have looked and sounded familiar; his wounds would have been seen as incidental. If, however, what the Twelve witnessed was the Shroud, the traces of Jesus' injuries would have provided a crucial means of identification. The face of the Shroud figure is faint, indistinct and tonally reversed; even those who knew him well could not have been absolutely sure of its likeness to Jesus himself. The figure's wounds, though, are clear and prominent, and they connect the figure indisputably to Jesus: it was Jesus who was crucified and crowned with thorns—not some anonymous ghost. Anxious to decide who their spiritual visitant was, the Twelve would have seen the wounds as crucial signs. Like a sort of supernatural birthmark, they guaranteed the identity of the Risen Jesus.

The second issue was the Shroud figure's mode of being. If this was Jesus, in what state did he now exist? Once again, the blood marks would have helped the Twelve decide. To the naked eye and to the touch the Shroud's body-image appears entirely without substance. It could have been interpreted as a disembodied spirit or as a naked soul, trapped between life and death—or as a reawakened shade, like that of Samuel (see above, p. 206). We can catch an echo of this debate, perhaps, in Luke's startling admission that, when the Risen Christ first appeared to the disciples, they thought he was a spirit. The wounds, though, lent the figure a kind of corporeality. Unlike the body-image, the blood marks are perceptibly "solid," being composed of dried blood, and they must originally have been more substantial than they are today. The wounds, then, were distinctly touchable. This would have aided the diagnosis of resurrection, since resurrection meant not simply a posthumous reappearance, but a return to some form of embodied life. Moreover, the Twelve would have been keenly aware that the blood seen on the figure was lifeblood, preserved after death precisely because it was deemed necessary for any eventual resurrection.

It was primarily the wounds, I believe, that convinced the Twelve that Jesus was not merely visible in the Shroud as a ghost, but that he had been re-clothed in a spiritual body, one consanguine with his mortal body but wholly different in kind.[15]

The Jerusalem Tradition, then, like the female appearance-stories and male tomb-stories, contains several features that support the theory that the Risen Jesus was a figure seen in the Shroud. The sudden appearance behind locked doors, the strange focus on the wounds and the spiritual quality of the Risen Christ all point toward a secret display of the bloodstained burial cloth of Jesus. The Shroud theory also fits in with the likely time and location of the appearance to the Twelve and explains why the Twelve were the next to see the Risen Jesus after Peter. The perfect accord between the Jerusalem Tradition and the Shroud can hardly be a meaningless coincidence. It is yet further proof that the Resurrection was a belief inspired by the Shroud.

The Jerusalem Tradition appears to depend on the eyewitness testimony of someone who was actually present at this momentous, Church-founding event. Who might this hypothetical eyewitness have been? To answer this question, we need to delve, once more, into the sexual politics of the Gospel narratives. We will soon catch echoes of a familiar voice.

The best place to start is with Luke's version of the story, which contains several traces of a critical attitude toward the male disciples. To begin with, they are said to have been frightened when the Risen Christ made his appearance. They may well have been, but to mention their fear in a carefully crafted narrative looks like deliberate detraction. The male disciples are similarly denigrated in the *Gospel of Mary*, being described as too frightened to go out and spread the gospel. Fear was understood as a sign of moral weakness and lack of faith.

Next, Christ's initial question to the disciples represents them as troubled and doubting, indicating that (like Peter at the tomb) they lacked spiritual perception. Worse, they continue to disbelieve even after he shows them his hands and his feet, making them guilty of a further lack of faith. It is only once he has eaten a piece of fish in front of them and, crucially, "opened their minds to understand the scriptures" that the Twelve finally accept the reality of the Risen Jesus. The implicit criticism of the male disciples in this passage recalls their earlier failings: their refusal to believe the women's report of the Resurrection and their failure to see the Risen Christ on the road to Emmaus (and at the tomb), prompting Christ's angry exclamation—"O foolish men!" The whole of Luke's Resurrection chapter appears to be based on a frankly "feminist" tract.

An even more pronounced anti-male agenda is apparent in Pseudo-Mark. The appearance to the Twelve in this text follows the appearances to Mary Magdalene and two unnamed wayfarers and the repeated refusal of the male disciples to believe the testimony of these witnesses:

> Afterward he appeared to the eleven themselves as they sat at table; and he upbraided them for their unbelief and hardness of heart, because they had not believed those who saw him after he had risen.[16]

This text focuses on the disciples' spiritual delinquency to the exclusion of everything else; nothing is said about their joy, or Christ's wounds, or his "flesh and bones," or eating fish. Given what we have learned about the matriarchal agenda underlying the Resurrection narratives, this assault on the reputation of the male disciples should not be too unexpected.

Exactly the same attitude is found in the *Epistula*, which transmits a fascinating, non-canonical version of the Jerusalem Tradition. In this text the Twelve have once again rejected the women's announcement of the Resurrection, prompting the Risen Christ to pay them a visit in person:

> Then the Lord said to Mary and also to her sisters, "Let us go to them." And he came and found us inside, veiled. He called us out. But we thought it was a ghost, and we did not believe it was the Lord. Then [he said] to us, "Come, do not be afraid. I am your master, whom you, Peter, denied three times; and now do you deny again?" But we went to him, doubting in [our] hearts whether

it was possibly he. Then he said to [us], "Why do you still doubt, and are you not believing? I am he who spoke to you concerning my flesh, my death, and my resurrection. That you may know that it is I, put your finger, Peter, in the nail-prints of my hands; and you, Thomas, put your finger in the spear wounds of my side; but you, Andrew, look at my feet and see if they do not touch the ground. For it is written in the Prophet, 'The foot of a ghost or a demon does not join to the ground.'"

But we touched him that we might truly know whether he [had risen] in the flesh, and we fell on our [faces] confessing our sin, that we had been unbelieving. Then the Lord our redeemer said, "Rise up, and I will reveal to you what is above heaven and what is in heaven, and your rest that is in the kingdom of heaven. For my [Father] has given me the power to take up you and those who believe in me."[17]

A more damning indictment of the disciples could hardly be conceived. They are accused of every possible error: misinterpretation, disbelief, fear, denial, doubt, continued disbelief, ignoring Christ's words. In the end they have to touch him and finger his wounds before they will accept the evidence of their eyes. At last, they fall on their faces, confessing their sin. As he raises them up, Christ is referred to pointedly as their redeemer—they are in dire need of redemption.

At the heart of the narrative is the wretched figure of Peter. He is singled out, first of all, by reference to his infamous denial of Jesus in the house of the high priest.[18] Then, ahead of Thomas, he is told to touch Christ's wounds, to assure himself of the reality of the Resurrection. Peter is the polar opposite of Mary Magdalene and the other women, who meet the Risen Jesus and instantly believe.

The anti-male, anti-Peter bias evident in the accounts of the appearance to the Twelve in Luke, Pseudo-Mark and the *Epistula* implies that all these passages go back to a common, "feminist" source. (No such bias is evident in John's version of the tale, but that is due to some rather crude editing on John's behalf, as we shall see.) A matriarchal agenda was fundamental, it seems, to the Gospel descriptions of the appearance to the Twelve.

And so we return to our initial question: if the Jerusalem Tradition is rooted in eyewitness testimony, who might the eyewitness have been? The nature of the testimony leaves little room for doubt: she was a woman. And to have been the source of such a venerable tradition she must have been revered, by some at least, as a major Christian teacher, an eminent apostle. It is hard to avoid the conclusion—remarkable as it may seem—that the Jerusalem Tradition descends from the testimony of the woman whose memory was later systematically blackened by the male leadership of the early Church: Mary Magdalene.

This would explain the attack on Peter in the *Epistula*, an attack that may have been edited out of the canonical versions of the tale. And Mary is surely the most likely source, too, for the connected traditions of the female appearance-story and the male tomb-story, which play out her personal rivalry with Peter. He excluded her from the First Creed; she belittled and castigated him in stories about Easter. It is not an edifying spectacle, but, had Mary not fought her corner so vigorously, her voice would have been lost forever.

An obvious question remains: if Mary is the eyewitness behind these traditions, why does she not feature in the story of the appearance to the Twelve? It is possible that she was excluded from the meeting and that she reconstructed it on the basis of what she heard on the grapevine, her knowledge of the Shroud, and her acquaintance with the Twelve. But it is much more likely, in my view, that she did witness the first display of the Shroud, perhaps even helping Peter introduce it to his male colleagues. That she was present, along with the other women, is suggested by at least two sources. Luke states that the gathering consisted of the disciples "and those who were with them," which is probably a reference to the women, and, as we have just seen, the *Epistula* has the Risen Christ inviting Mary and her sisters to accompany him on his visit to the Twelve. There is evidence, then, that Mary did attend the event, and the compelling realism of the story makes this the best explanation for the origin of the Jerusalem Tradition.

In telling the story of the appearance to the Twelve, Mary may have exaggerated the initial skepticism of the men (and the immediacy of her own faith), but it would be unwise to dismiss this aspect of the tale as pure libel. The Twelve would not have recognized the Shroud as the Risen Jesus instantly, and some would have taken more convincing than others. It is indeed likely that members of the council pawed at the Shroud, trying to determine the nature of the apparition, questioning the idea that it manifested Jesus in a resurrected form. Mary may have witnessed the men's first quizzical examination of the Shroud, representing it later, for her own purposes, as an occasion of discreditable doubt.

If this is the historical basis of the Jerusalem Tradition, it is odd that John, in his version of the tale, makes no mention whatsoever of the disciples' doubt and only hints at the inspection of Christ's wounds. It looks as if he has simply edited out this uncomplimentary part of the tradition, reducing the dramatic encounter to a thoroughly bland reunion—as if Jesus had just returned from a brief trip away. This would also help explain the rather stilted quality of the narrative.

However, John did not discard the polemical, "feminist" material altogether. He recycled it in the form of the famous story of Doubting Thomas:

> Now Thomas, one of the twelve, called the Twin, was not with them when Jesus came. So the other disciples told him, "We have seen the Lord." But he said to them, "Unless I see in his hands the print of the nails, and place my finger in the mark of the nails, and place my hand in his side, I will not believe."
>
> Eight days later, his disciples were again in the house, and Thomas was with them. The doors were shut, but Jesus came and stood among them, and said, "Peace be with you." Then he said to Thomas, "Put your finger here, and see my hands; and put out your hand, and place it in my side; do not be faithless, but believing." Thomas answered him, "My Lord and my God!" Jesus said to him, "Have you believed because you have seen me? Blessed are those who have not seen and yet believe."[19]

This passage is evidently related to the story of the appearance to the Twelve in the *Epistula*, in which the disbelieving Peter and Thomas touch the wounds of the Risen Christ. In fact, John's tale was clearly developed from a version of the Jerusalem Tradition much like that preserved in the *Epistula*, which stands midway between Luke's account of the appearance to the Twelve and the Doubting Thomas story.[20] But rather than preserve the tradition as a single episode, John decided to split it into two: a tame narrative of the appearance to the Twelve on Easter Day, followed by the colorful story of Doubting Thomas. Why?

It is easy to see why John removed the theme of doubt from the story of the Easter Day appearance: he wished to protect—or improve—the reputation of the Twelve. His aim was to dissociate most of the disciples—and especially Peter—from the stigma of disbelief. But why, having removed the burden of doubt from the Twelve, does John then load it onto the unfortunate figure of Thomas? This puzzling decision can be explained, as usual, with the help of the Shroud.

Quite a few researchers have realized that the mysterious tale of Doubting Thomas points in the direction of the Shroud. The Reverend Albert Dreisbach, for example, concludes that John's story was probably based on knowledge of the Shroud and was intended to emphasize the physical nature of the Resurrection, so vividly represented by the wounds (an argument he illustrates with a cleverly retouched Caravaggio, Figure 59). He even speculates that the tradition of the appearance to the Twelve in the First Creed might "somehow be a vestige of a similar appearance of the Shroud . . ."[21] The reason Dreisbach and others have connected the Doubting Thomas story with the Shroud is that Thomas was the reputed founder of Christianity in Edessa, where the Shroud was kept. The Christians of Edessa, the guardians of the Shroud, were known as Thomas Christians. Once this is understood, John's motive in emphasizing the figure of Doubting Thomas becomes apparent. John knew that the Christians of Edessa possessed the cloth of the Risen Christ, the so-called *soudarion*, and he thought their faith in the Resurrection was too dependent on it. The criticism of Thomas is that he believes only because he sees the Risen Christ; his followers, it is implied, believe only because they see the *soudarion*. The proud boast of the Thomas Christians is turned against them: "Blessed are those who have not seen and yet believe."[22]

Like every other Resurrection narrative we have examined, then, John's tale of Doubting Thomas is a polemical description of seeing the Shroud, intended to affect the status and authority of the eyewitnesses concerned. This time, though, it is not a legendary account of a historical event, but an ingenious reinvention of the Jerusalem Tradition, applied to the viewing of the cloth in Edessa at the time John wrote.

It does not follow that John understood the original significance of the Shroud. By the late first century, few Christians outside Edessa were aware of the cloth, and none may have realized that it was, in effect, the Risen Jesus. The source of the Christian proclamation had already been forgotten by then, partly because the Resurrection had been reinterpreted as a physical, flesh-and-blood event, partly because the cloth itself had been transported to a distant land and transformed into the Mandylion. John was one of those who knew of the Shroud, and he understood it to *testify* to the Resurrection. But, as a believer in the empty tomb and the flesh-and-blood Resurrection, he did not understand that it had been the sole sign of the Resurrection and that it revealed Jesus to have been raised in a body composed purely of spirit. John's understanding of the Shroud was similar, in fact, to that of most Shroud aficionados today.

Having reconstructed the events of Easter Day on the basis of our knowledge of the Shroud and of the Gospels themselves, we are left contemplating an extraordinary, matriarchal trilogy underlying the Resurrection narratives: the original female appearance-story, intended to promote the role and status of the women who discovered the Shroud; the original male tomb-story, intended to belittle Peter, one of the leaders of the male hierarchy; and the original story of the appearance to the Twelve, intended to diminish the reputation and authority of this male council. The same muffled but strident voice can be heard in all three parts of the trilogy: the voice of the female opponent—Mary Magdalene.

The Resurrection narratives thus provide a crucial counterweight to the testimony of the First Creed. Neither the Gospels nor the Creed present a rounded, reliable account of Easter, but, taking their evidence together and interpreting it in relation to the Shroud, we can arrive at a balanced understanding of the most influential weekend in world history.

It all began when Jesus' female relatives went to the sepulchre early on Sunday morning to complete his burial. They soon returned with an astonishing tale of encountering an apparition in the tomb, next to the body of Jesus. Peter went off to check their story and found it to be true—an otherworldly figure was indeed visible in the burial cloth. Reckoning that this figure was the bearer of a divine message pertaining to Jesus and his Messianic movement, Peter removed the cloth from the tomb and brought it back to Jerusalem. The Shroud's message needed to be heard urgently, so, as soon as he returned home, excited and shaken, he made contact with his colleagues and arranged a meeting. That evening, after the day's business was done, the Twelve gathered together nervously in the upper room, to be shown the apparition. The women were in attendance. Then, when everyone was present, the Shroud was brought out and held up before the assembled company.

There can never have been a moment like it. The Shroud would have amazed and stupefied the Twelve. Over the course of the evening, examining the cloth and debating with each other, they and their companions would have begun the long process of interpreting the Shroud, trying to agree on the divine message they were meant to hear. We shall eavesdrop on this debate in the next chapter.

One thing they would have sensed immediately, though, as soon as the cloth was unfurled: they were no longer the only persons in the room. They had been joined by someone else, an awe-inspiring, unearthly presence.

The Risen Jesus had entered history.

PART 6

The Birth of the Church

23

In Accordance with the Scriptures

Awaking on the morning of the second day of the week, the day after Easter, the Twelve must have wondered whether the experience of the night before was just a vivid dream. Had they really witnessed an extraordinary apparition of Jesus, bloodied but unbowed, emerging from the linen cloth in which he had been buried? Could their crucified leader really have appeared to them from beyond the grave? Seeking each other out, despite the danger, they would soon have reassured themselves that it was no dream. Jesus had indeed been present among them the previous night. A sign had appeared—a message from God—heralding, no doubt, an imminent twist in the Story of Israel. It was now up to them to interpret the sign and to discover its prophetic meaning.

The situation in Judaea that Passover was tense, particularly so for the followers of Jesus. For twenty years, following the rebellion of AD 6, the nation had been relatively calm, the Roman rulers of the province having accorded the Jews sufficient respect to avert serious unrest. With the arrival of Pontius Pilate, however, everything had changed. As almost his first act, the new prefect had dared to erect imperial idols in the Holy City. Though he spared the protestors in the stadium at Caesarea, it was evident from then on that Pilate held his Jewish subjects in contempt. Judaea was once again under the thumb of an out-and-out tyrant, who threatened the sacred traditions of the Jews and thus their relationship with their God. On top of the continuing oppression of the poor, caused by the imposition of Roman taxes, this was, for some, too much to bear. Resistance became imperative; as in the days of the Maccabees, the nation was crying out for justice and renewal. It is in this context that we should understand the formation of the council of the Twelve, symbolizing the original twelve tribes of Israel, whose restoration would signal the establishment of the Kingdom of God.[1] Until Good Friday, the Twelve looked forward to the redemption of the Promised Land under the leadership of a charismatic descendant of King David.

The day of the Crucifixion saw this hope shattered. In addition to grieving for Jesus, their would-be Messiah, the Twelve must have mourned the
apparent defeat of their cause. It must have seemed as if Yahweh had once
more abandoned his people, leaving them at the mercy of a vicious for-
eigner. That Sabbath must have been one of the most difficult of their lives,
as they struggled to reconcile their faith in Yahweh with the devastating
events of the previous day.

Forty-eight hours later, having seen the Shroud, their mood would have
been transformed. Still grieving, still perplexed by the execution of Jesus,
they were now seized, nevertheless, by an extraordinary sense of excitement, of imminent deliverance. Despite their fears, Yahweh, it seemed, had
not abandoned them: he had given them a sign, a powerful, if confusing,
revelation. Their God had acted. The appearance of the Shroud thus re-
invigorated the followers of Jesus, turning the Crucifixion from a bitter
defeat into a source of inspiration.

But what exactly did the Shroud signify? What was being revealed? Over
the next few days and weeks, as they waited, no doubt, for more spectacular signs to follow, the Twelve and their companions must have deliberated
the meaning of the Shroud. And the way to interpret such a sign in first-
century Judaea, beyond a common-sense appraisal, was to seek references
to it in the scriptures. Among the Dead Sea Scrolls, for instance, are various
texts known as *pesharim* (commentaries), in which contemporary events
are interpreted as the fulfillment of passages of scripture.[2] The arrival of the
Shroud was just the sort of event that the prophets might have predicted.
And the exceptional nature of the sign—a peculiar, unprecedented image—
would have made its interpreters all the more eager for scriptural guidance.
When people want to discover the meaning of images, they invariably try
to interpret them via texts, hoping to substitute definite words for enigmatic marks. It is a risky strategy, and the early Christian interpretation of
the Shroud via the Hebrew scriptures represents, perhaps, the most wayward interpretation of an image in the whole of history.

Wayward or not, it must have been an intensely exciting endeavor. Poring over scrolls in small private libraries, glimpsing references here and
there to the astonishing Shroud figure; meeting together in twos and threes,
excitedly sharing prophecies that spoke, so it seemed, of a resurrected Savior; gathering in their safe house to debate the texts and reacquaint
themselves with the spectacular sign of the Risen Jesus: this is how Jesus'
close followers must have pieced together the essential meaning of the
Shroud. It was a period not of action, but of intense reflection—and anticipation. This time of waiting is represented in Acts as a sort of extended

prayer meeting. Following the Ascension, the Twelve return "to the upper room, where they were staying" in Jerusalem and there devote themselves to prayer, "together with the women and Mary the mother of Jesus, and with his brothers."[3]

That Christianity started with detailed study of the Hebrew scriptures is not merely a conjecture; it is a conclusion based on the evidence of the New Testament itself. There is barely a text in the New Testament that is not rooted in scriptural language and allusions. The earliest text we have, the First Creed, assures us that both the death and Resurrection of Jesus were understood "in accordance with the scriptures," and the early speeches in Acts, put into the mouth of Peter, all emphasize the scriptural basis of the Christian proclamation. Peter tells, for example, how King David, the supposed author of the Book of Psalms, "foresaw and spoke of the resurrection of the Christ" and how Moses prophesied that God would "raise up" a prophet from his people.[4] References such as these support the view that the Shroud was interpreted "in accordance with the scriptures" from the very beginning, before Peter or anyone else stood up in Jerusalem and proclaimed the gospel.

It was during this brief period of study and debate, I believe, that certain core beliefs about Jesus were established, to do with his resurrection, his cosmic identity and his pivotal role in the Jewish drama of salvation.[5]

Christology—the conception of Jesus as an exalted, celestial Messiah—was rooted in the instinctive view of the Shroud as a manifestation of a spiritual presence. There was a natural tendency to see it as a living double of Jesus, and, since it appeared just after his death, it was taken to indicate his transition to a glorious form of post-mortem life. In the context of first-century Jewish ideas, the appearance of such a figure was most easily interpreted as a resurrection, albeit of an unexpected, spiritual kind.

It is important to emphasize that belief in the Resurrection was not spontaneous, but was based on the Jewish expectation of a future resurrection of the righteous dead. This is spelled out by Paul in 1 Corinthians no fewer than three times:

> But if there is no resurrection of the dead, then Christ has not been raised; if Christ has not been raised, then our preaching is in vain and your faith is in vain. We are even found to be misrepresenting God, because we testified of God that he raised Christ, whom he did not raise if it is true that the dead are not raised. For if the dead are not raised, then Christ has not been raised. If Christ has not been raised, your faith is futile and you are still in your sins.[6]

Christian apologists, who assume that the reality of the Risen Christ was self-evident, seem not to notice Paul's repeated assertion that belief in the Resurrection was *dependent* on a prior belief (which is why denying that belief was such a serious matter). If Paul had really been accosted on the road to Damascus by the heavenly Christ, it is hard to see how he could possibly have represented belief in the Risen Christ as conditional upon another belief. But, once it is realized that the Resurrection was an idea inspired by the Shroud, that it was *an interpretation of an image*, Paul's insistence on the link between belief in the general resurrection of the dead and the particular Resurrection of Jesus makes perfect sense. Had the apostles not lived in expectation of a general resurrection, they would not have understood the Shroud as signaling the "first fruits" of a resurrection harvest.

Before Easter, we may be sure, the followers of Jesus were no more fixated on the idea of resurrection than were any other Jews. It would have been for them no more than a vague hope connected with the future emancipation of Israel. After Easter, though, it became, understandably, the central tenet of their faith. In the days immediately following the discovery of the Shroud they probably expected to see resurrected martyrs round every corner and to witness at any moment the spectacular advent of the Kingdom of God. It would not have been obvious at that stage that the raising of Jesus was unique and that the Shroud did not herald the start of a cosmic upheaval. The group must have lived for weeks in a state of feverish excitement, tempered only by growing perplexity, as, day after day, the anticipated events failed to occur.

Meanwhile, they must have scoured the scriptures for passages that spoke of resurrection, hoping to confirm their interpretation of the Shroud. Such passages are actually rather rare, and few seem applicable to the cloth. Ezekiel's famous vision of the resurrection of Israel does not evoke the Shroud in the least, which is why the first Christians never cited it as a prophecy of the Resurrection.[7] (If the Resurrection *had* been considered a flesh-and-blood affair, Ezekiel's vision would presumably have been used regularly as a scriptural "proof.") Other texts, read out of context, seemed to hint at the Easter miracle, but they were hardly convincing or illuminating prophecies.[8]

There were, however, two resurrection scriptures, both much more detailed, that appear to have grabbed the attention of the Shroud's discoverers and fuelled their enthusiasm: the Book of Jonah and chapter 12 of the Book of Daniel.

The story of Jonah, the reluctant prophet, is one of the most familiar in the Old Testament. Called by God to go and preach repentance to the wicked city of Nineveh, Jonah fled his responsibility and boarded a ship to Tarshish instead. Enraged by his disobedience, the Lord whipped up a terrible storm, which threatened to destroy the boat and all on board. In fear of their lives, the mariners sought out Jonah, who was fast asleep below deck, and, discovering that he was the cause of their misfortune, asked him how to appease his God. The prophet told them to throw him into the sea, which, after some hesitation, they did—"and the sea ceased from its raging."[9] Unwilling, however, to consign his prophet to a watery grave, the Lord "appointed a great fish to swallow up Jonah; and Jonah was in the belly of the fish three days and three nights."[10] He was then regurgitated on the coast and told once more to go to Nineveh. This time he obeyed. The people of the city listened to his warnings and repented, and God withheld their punishment.

Jonah's strange deliverance from the sea is presented not as a miraculous evasion of death but as a return from death to life. Jonah describes himself being overwhelmed by the waves and the billows, sinking down into the deep, being imprisoned in the underworld, and finally being resurrected: "The waters closed in over me . . . I went down to the land whose bars closed upon me forever; yet thou didst bring up my life from the Pit, O Lord my God."[11] This was intended as a spiritual allegory, but as far as the early Christians were concerned, the story of Jonah foreshadowed the Resurrection of Jesus and provided a potent means of thinking about the Shroud. We know that they considered it prophetic, because Jonah's importance is emphasized in a Gospel story, in which Jesus lambasts his fellow Jews for sign-seeking: "This generation is an evil generation; it seeks a sign, but no sign shall be given to it except the sign of Jonah."[12] The "sign of Jonah" has long puzzled Christian interpreters.[13] It is best understood as a reference to the Shroud. Just as Jonah was entombed in the fish, so Jesus had been entombed in the Shroud; and just as the fish disgorged the prophet on dry land, restoring him to life, so the Shroud conveyed Jesus to heaven, the sphere from which he reappeared as a resurrected person. Hailed as "something greater than Jonah,"[14] the Shroud, the apostles hoped, would move all Israel to repent, just as Jonah had inspired repentance among the people of Nineveh.

The interest of the Book of Jonah could not compare, however, with the fascination exerted by the Book of Daniel. To the first Christians, baffled and bemused by the discovery of the Shroud, this visionary, psychedelic text must have seemed like a treasure trove of prophetic knowledge. The relevance of the Book of Daniel was assured by the unambiguous resurrection prophecy near its end, a passage that would have resonated strongly with the original perception of the Shroud:

> And many of those who sleep in the dust of the earth shall awake, some to everlasting life, and some to shame and everlasting contempt. And those who are wise shall shine like the brightness of the firmament; and those who turn many to righteousness, like the stars forever and ever.[15]

We can only imagine the awe which must have gripped the founders of the Church when they read these words in the days following Easter. Did the Shroud not represent a literal fulfillment of Daniel's prophecy? Did it not show a righteous martyr, Jesus, glimmering in an ethereal, celestial body, his lamp-like eyes manifesting eternal wakefulness?

Here, surely, was a scriptural key to the Shroud. And Daniel 12 also seemed to reveal what was to come. Israel was entering "a time of trouble, since there never has been since there was a nation," a time that had begun, presumably, with the arrival of Pilate, and would continue until the end, when the righteous would be delivered. The end-times would last "a time, two times, and half a time," or, alternatively, 1,290 days "from the time that the continual burned offering is taken away, and the abomination that makes desolate is set up." During this period, the prophet stated, "many shall purify themselves, and make themselves white, and be refined," a comment that may have influenced the development of the Christian rite of baptism. Finally, after 1,335 days, the Saved would be blessed, and many of the dead would arise—presumably in the same manner as Jesus.

The details were hazy, but the basic outline of the prophecy was clear: a time of unprecedented woe was at hand, during which the righteous were to purify themselves, and at the end of which the promise of the Shroud— the resurrection of the dead—would be fulfilled.

We can now begin to see the full significance of the early-Christian confession that God's raising of Jesus was "promised beforehand through his prophets in the holy scriptures."[16] The prophets, in particular Daniel, not only confirmed the Shroud group in their belief that Jesus had been resurrected, but also began to guide them in their course of action. Easter had been about witnessing the Shroud, apprehending a miracle; the days following, which saw the birth of Christianity, were about coming to terms with the Shroud via the scriptures and deciding how to respond to its message.

Following Easter, the first concern of the Shroud's guardians would have been to determine what had happened to Jesus—and what was about to happen to everyone else. They presumed that Jesus had been resurrected, and it must have been immensely reassuring for them to know that Daniel, at least, had foreseen the type of resurrection they had witnessed. This confirmed their initial interpretation of the Shroud and confirmed also the reliability of Daniel's end-time prophecy, which they could now use as a guide to the present. But, as well as wondering about events, they inevitably began to wonder, too, about the identity of Jesus. Who was this man who had been singled out by God to be the first of the resurrected, ahead of Moses and the prophets and the Maccabean martyrs? They had known Jesus in life as an ordinary mortal, as a friend, leader, relative, husband; now, it seemed, he had to be recognized, despite his ignominious execution, as a major protagonist in the unfolding Story of Israel. And the only way to understand who Jesus had become—or who he had always been, without their realizing it—was to consult the scriptures.

Finding references in the scriptures to the Exalted Jesus—the spirit-person seen in the Shroud—was rather easier than finding prophecies of the Resurrection, since the Hebrew Bible contains numerous obscure, ambiguous figures who can be related to the Shroud in one way or another. We have already seen how Paul identified Jesus with the man created in God's image on the sixth day of Creation, distinguishing him from Adam. Faced with the strange and sudden appearance of the Shroud figure, Paul simply "found" him in a well-known biblical text. The original apostles made similar claims about Jesus. The most important identifications they made—with the Son of Man and with the Suffering Servant—are both explicable as scriptural interpretations of the Shroud.

The title "Son of Man" is applied to Jesus frequently in all four Gospels, but scholars have been at a loss to explain its significance. There is no evidence that it would have meant anything to contemporary Jews, for whom the idiom "son of man" simply meant "man." The title derives, it seems, from a figure seen by the prophet Daniel:

> I saw in the night visions,
> and behold, with the clouds of heaven there came one like a son of man,
> and he came to the Ancient of Days and was presented before him.
> And to him was given dominion and glory and kingdom,
> that all peoples, nations, and languages should serve him;
> his dominion is an everlasting dominion, which shall not pass away,
> and his kingdom one that shall not be destroyed.[17]

Superseding four monstrous beasts, representing "four kings who shall arise out of the earth,"[18] this obscure figure is intended as a personification of victorious Israel. But why was he identified with Jesus?

Consider the text in relation to the Shroud. First of all, Daniel's figure is called "one *like* a son of man," inviting comparison with the human-like Shroud figure. Second, he is exalted in heaven, matching the perception of the Shroud figure as a celestial being. Third, his appearance inaugurates the end of history, the eternal Kingdom of God, which the Shroud was thought to precipitate. The identification of Jesus with the personification of Israel in Daniel 7 depends, therefore, on the Shroud. But this still does not explain why the title "Son of Man" assumed such significance. What was it that made the identification of Jesus with this figure so popular?

Let us return to the resurrection prophecy in Daniel 12. We have already seen how this prophecy helped confirm the initial interpretation of the Shroud, but just as interesting as what it says is who says it. The last three chapters of the Book of Daniel describe a vision granted the prophet on the bank of the River Tigris, consisting of a magnificent, heavenly figure who reveals the future history of Israel:

> I lifted up my eyes and looked, and behold, a man clothed in linen, whose loins were girded with gold of Uphaz. His body was like beryl, his face like the appearance of lightning, his eyes like flaming torches, his arms and legs like the gleam of burnished bronze, and the sound of his words like the noise of a multitude. And I, Daniel, alone saw the vision, for the men who were with me did not see the vision, but a great trembling fell upon them, and they fled to hide themselves. So I was left alone and saw this great vision, and no strength was left in me; my radiant appearance was fearfully changed, and I retained no strength. Then I heard the sound of his words; and when I heard the sound of his words, I fell on my face in a deep sleep with my face to the ground.[19]

Imagine the Twelve reading this text having just witnessed the Shroud, filled with the excitement of seeing a communal vision. They would have had little difficulty identifying the Shroud figure with the person seen by Daniel. He was "clothed in linen"; his gleaming, glistening body, like beryl and burnished bronze, evoked the luminous sheen of the Shroud figure; we know that the face of the Shroud figure was later compared with lightning,[20] and his eyes do indeed seem alight, like flaming torches.

Furthermore, the "man clothed in linen," the counterpart of the heavenly being seen *through* the Shroud, was accompanied by two other figures, like the attendant figures seen *on* the Shroud: "Then I Daniel looked, and behold, two others stood, one on this bank of the stream and one on that bank of the stream."[21] Here, in the scriptures, was an apparent reference to the Triple Figure, the celestial Jesus flanked by two angelic representatives (cf. Figure 55).[22]

For a first-century devotee of the Shroud, there could have been little or no doubt: Daniel, who lived six centuries earlier, had seen the very person revealed in the burial cloth of Jesus. This meant that the celestial Jesus himself had delivered the prophecy of Daniel 12, concerning the end-times and the resurrection of the dead.

But what has this got to do with the "one like a son of man" of Daniel 7? As far as the author of the Book of Daniel was concerned, nothing: the "man clothed in linen" was entirely separate from the personification of Israel. But early Christians, reading the text in light of the Shroud, were bound to identify them. Not only could both figures be connected independently with the Shroud, but they were also referred to in the same way. In Daniel 10, the prophet calls the linen-clad angel "one in the likeness of the sons of men" and "one having the appearance of a man." So the "man clothed in linen" was also "one like a son of man." The emphasis on human *likeness* would have seemed immensely significant to members of the Shroud group, and they may have taken this as proof that the two figures were one and the same.

The title "Son of Man" originally referred, then, to a grand, composite figure, the Messianic ruler of Daniel 7 united with the "man clothed in linen" of Daniel 10–12. This identification transformed Jesus into an ancient heavenly being, one who had appeared long ago to a Hebrew prophet and who would soon be unveiled as God's appointed ruler in Judaea. It was this exalted conception of Jesus that was expressed via the imagery of the Transfiguration.[23]

In one respect, however, this idea differed dramatically from the image of the Shroud: it involved no hint of suffering and death, let alone crucifixion. To understand this aspect of the image the Twelve would have turned, first and foremost, to the Book of Isaiah.

Running like a conspicuous, tangled thread through the intricate tapestry of Second Isaiah (i.e. Isaiah 40–55) are the four songs of the Suffering Servant. This figure is introduced in Isaiah 42 as the "servant" and "chosen" of the Lord, the one who will redeem humanity and establish justice throughout the world. When he reappears later on, however, he is far from triumphant. Though he is eventually vindicated by God and allotted "a portion with the great,"[24] he first has to endure torture and contempt: "I gave my back to the smiters, and my cheeks to those who pulled out the beard; I hid not my face from shame and spitting."[25] He was intended as a personification of long-suffering Israel, but, as we have seen, personifications are easily mistaken for persons, and the first Christians did not hesitate to identify the Servant with Jesus. Once again, they found, to their delight and astonishment, that Jesus had been made known to the prophets and was discoverable in the scriptures.

It was not simply his suffering that connected the Servant with Jesus; significant, too, were his stated role, his exaltation and his appearance. One passage, in particular, must have enthused the Shroud's guardians:

> Behold, my servant shall prosper, he shall be exalted and lifted up, and shall be very high. As many were astonished at him—his appearance was so marred, beyond human semblance, and his form beyond that of the sons of men—so shall he startle many nations; kings shall shut their mouths because of him; for that which has not been told them they shall see, and that which they have not heard they shall understand.[26]

The Servant does not have the form of an ordinary mortal, but resembles humanity; he is *beyond* the "sons of men" (suggestively, Isaiah employs the same phrase as Daniel), "exalted and lifted up," like the Risen Jesus. At the same time his appearance is marred by suffering, just as the Shroud figure is marred by the marks of crucifixion. The rare combination of exaltation and disfigurement, shared by the Servant and the Risen Jesus, would have struck the Shroud's interpreters as particularly significant, and they would have recognized, too, the prophesied astonishment which they themselves felt. Isaiah had to be speaking of Jesus as seen in the Shroud; revelations to kings would surely follow.

The Servant's role as savior of humanity is elaborated in several ways that became fundamental to the Christian view of Jesus. In the first song God says that he has given him "as a covenant to the people, a light to the nations,"[27] providing the scriptural basis for the idea of Christ as a "new covenant" between God and man. Seen in this light, the Shroud would have assumed the awesome significance of the Tablets of the Law received by Moses on Mount Sinai, once kept in the Ark of the Covenant in the Holy of Holies. As a light-bringer, the Servant was "to open the eyes that are blind, to bring out the prisoners from the dungeon, from the prison those who sit in darkness."[28] The latter metaphor was readily interpreted in terms of resurrection (recall Jonah's description of Sheol as a prison). Jesus, then, was to play an active part in raising the dead. He had already prepared the way, for the Servant suffered in order to expiate the sins of Israel: "he was wounded for our transgressions, he was bruised for our iniquities; upon him was the chastisement that made us whole, and with his stripes we are healed."[29] The identification of the Shroud with the Suffering Servant thus gave rise to the notion of Jesus' death as a sacrifice that accomplished the salvation of his people—hence, the First Creed's assertion that "Christ died for our sins in accordance with the scriptures."

It was the Shroud, then, that caused Jesus to be read back into history and forward into the imminent finale of the Story of Israel. By transforming him into an extraordinary, other-worldly figure, both like and unlike a human being, it opened up the possibility of "finding" him in the Hebrew scriptures. The biblical view of the crucified leader of the Twelve did not need years or decades to emerge; it could have been developed by individual members of the Shroud group within days of Easter and crystallized in discussions within weeks. Jesus' posthumous rise may have been truly meteoric.

As the person chosen to establish the Kingdom of God, the Son of Man/ Suffering Servant deserved to be known by the title bestowed on every legitimate king of Israel: the Messiah of the Lord.[30] The prophecies of Daniel and Isaiah were thus important in justifying the acclamation of the crucified Jesus as "*christos*" (the Greek for messiah). But this provocative interpretation of Jesus would have been justified in other ways as well.

Most straightforwardly, the Shroud signaled the vindication of the man crucified by Pilate as a Messianic pretender. If his crucifixion seemed initially to disprove any claim Jesus might have had to be the rightful ruler of Israel, his apparent resurrection overturned that verdict and proved his claim once and for all. The Shroud erased the original shame and meaning of the Crucifixion, declaring Jesus to be that which his executioners denied.[31]

Also significant in the eyes of the Shroud's interpreters would have been the fact that the image looks like a mark produced by a body drenched in ointment. Although, historically, the stain has usually been attributed to sweat, it has been interpreted as an ointment-stain, too, since at least the twelfth century,[32] and, even today, researchers occasionally try to reproduce the image by draping cloths over naked bodies lathered in myrrh and aloes.[33] This perception of the image is significant because of the literal meaning of the Hebrew word *messiah*—"anointed." The Shroud looked like a great sign of anointing, and that made it a seal of divine appointment.

Interpreting the Shroud in these terms, it was via his anointing that the Risen Jesus was made manifest. But if the Shroud indicated an anointing, what sort of "ointment" was believed to be involved? We can rule out a literal interpretation, involving actual oils and spices, because the Shroud is proof that the body of Jesus was not anointed on Good Friday.[34] The Shroud group would have understood the anointing in supernatural terms:

Jesus must have been doused in a divine substance. And it would have been clear to them what that substance was: the Spirit of God.

Often in the Hebrew scriptures God's Spirit was associated with the wind or the breath of life; elsewhere, though, it was conceived in terms of rain or water,[35] and it was also linked to the holy oil with which objects and persons were consecrated.[36] So, Jesus' followers could have thought of God's Spirit as a sort of rarefied liquid, the sort of substance, in other words, that could be used to anoint. Proof that early Christians viewed Jesus as having been spiritually anointed is found in Acts. Just before the Holy Spirit is "poured out" over the first Gentiles to be converted to Christianity, Peter tells them "how God *anointed* Jesus of Nazareth *with the Holy Spirit* and with power."[37]

Jesus was hailed as the Messiah, then, at least in part because the Shroud showed him to have been "immersed" in the Holy Spirit. The Spirit was the medium in which—and agent through which—Jesus was resurrected; it was also the substance in which he was embodied after death, just as flesh was the substance in which he was embodied before death. As Paul puts it, Jesus was "descended from David *according to the flesh* and designated Son of God in power *according to the Spirit of holiness* by his resurrection from the dead."[38]

This helps explain the odd adoption of the title Christ (i.e. Messiah) as a posthumous name for Jesus, both on its own and as a "surname."[39] For God's anointing of Jesus was more than an act of identification: it recreated him as someone whose body was composed of the holy, consecrating Spirit. "Christ" or "Jesus Christ" referred to the spiritually anointed, spiritually embodied Jesus, although it was also used, in retrospect, of the mortal Jesus.

The spiritual interpretation of the Shroud also helped identify Jesus as the Messiah prophesied in the scriptures. It would not have escaped the Twelve's notice that in Isaiah 42.1 God introduces his Servant with the words, "I have put my Spirit upon him," confirming the identification of this Messianic figure with Jesus. But the most significant prophecy, one which had a profound impact on the early Christian imagination, occurs earlier in Isaiah, when the prophet foretells the advent of a Davidic Messiah:

> There shall come forth a shoot from the stump of Jesse, and a branch shall grow out of his roots. And the Spirit of the Lord shall rest upon him, the spirit of wisdom and understanding, the spirit of counsel and might, the spirit of knowledge and the fear of the Lord.[40]

We know that this passage was considered an important prophecy among early Christians, because it is alluded to both by Paul and by John the Seer, the author of Revelation.[41] Jesse was the father of King David, so the "shoot" springing from his "stump" is both a new David and the rightful ruler of Israel. Jesus was a descendant of David, making the prophecy applicable to him, and the statement that "the Spirit of the Lord shall rest upon him" indicated that Isaiah was speaking of the Risen Jesus, anointed by the Spirit.

The imagery used to describe this royal scion would have had further significance. Isaiah calls the "root of Jesse" an ensign—a military standard—who will be "raised" for the entire world.[42] Given the recent furore provoked by Pilate, this would have seemed an appropriate description of the Shroud. God had apparently raised Jesus up in a glorious banner as a direct retort to the idolatrous standards the Romans had dared raise in Jerusalem. Even more suggestive was the metaphor of the Messiah as a "shoot" or "branch." The Shroud literally sprouted from Jesus' flesh, and, as we have seen, Paul used a closely related metaphor—a seedling growing from a seed—to describe the process of resurrection. Isaiah's image of regeneration, then, seemed to anticipate the surprising idea of a *resurrected* Messiah. This redoubled the significance of the prophecy, since no other scripture so much as hinted at such a figure.

Vindicated by his resurrection, announced by the prophets, anointed by the Holy Spirit, the Jesus of the Shroud could hardly have been viewed by those who saw him as anything other than the Messiah. The shocking notion of a crucified Savior of Israel is best explained as a result of meditation on the meaning of the Shroud. And at the heart of the recognition of Jesus as the Messiah was the perception of the Shroud as a spiritual imprint, a holy consecration. All early Christian talk of the descent of the Holy Spirit should be understood, I believe, in light of this realization. The Resurrection is not the only powerful image at the heart of Christianity inspired by the Shroud.

To us, two millennia after the event, all this speculation and interpretation may seem like an abstract intellectual game. But to the Twelve and their associates, confused and bewildered by the Crucifixion and Easter, it would have been an urgent task, like deciphering the coded message of a wartime ally. The Shroud was a secret sign, a revelation from God, and it needed to be "read" as quickly as possible.

The way to read it was, first of all, to use common sense (ancient Jewish common sense) to decide what it was—a manifestation of Jesus alive in a new sort of way—and then, secondly, to look for references to it in the scriptures. Within weeks the Shroud group would have connected it to various texts, confirming Jesus to have been resurrected and revealing him to be a figure of cosmic significance. The Son of Man, the Suffering Servant, the Messiah: Jesus, it seemed, was all of these things and more, an angelic being who was about to revive the nation of Israel and usher in the long-awaited Kingdom of God.

To the Twelve and their companions it must have seemed as though they had been given the key to the scriptures, a final revelation that unlocked the meaning of countless prophecies. But the discovery of every hidden reference took them further and further from mainstream Judaism, in which Israel, not Jesus, was the principal protagonist.

As a cipher the Shroud is unsurpassed. Even modern skeptics may marvel at its ability to mirror mankind's spiritual aspirations and the prophetic imagery of the Hebrew scriptures. The first-century Jews who contemplated the Shroud didn't stand a chance against its overwhelming suggestiveness. They were virtually bound to interpret it as they did, and to separate themselves from their uninitiated compatriots.

The Shroud makes the birth of Christianity seem not inexplicable, but inevitable.

24

The Forgotten Appearances

Days, weeks, months passed, and nothing happened. Despite Yahweh's phenomenal intervention on behalf of Jesus, the Kingdom of God did not follow ineluctably in its wake. Beggars still littered the streets of Jerusalem, concerned not so much with the resurrection of the spirit as with the sustenance of the flesh; the blind and the lame, barred from the Inner Court of the Temple, still gathered by the pools of Siloam and Bethesda, hoping for cures that never came; ordinary citizens got on with their day-to-day business, cowed by the recent display of Roman power. Meanwhile, secure in their opulent homes in the Upper City, Caiaphas and his fellow aristocrats sat back and relaxed, confident that the execution of Jesus had saved the nation (and themselves) from a period of bitter strife.[1] In the Temple— the splendid but unloved Temple of Herod—the priests still offered up the daily sacrifice on behalf of Emperor Tiberius, meekly acknowledging Rome's dominion of the Promised Land.

However thrilling was the revelation of the resurrected Messiah, the Twelve must soon have become frustrated by the failure of the Messianic age to arrive. There were hints in Daniel that they might have to wait a while—"Know therefore and understand that from the going forth of the word to restore and build Jerusalem to the coming of an anointed one, a prince, there shall be seven weeks"[2]—but it would have been difficult to remain patient for long. Some may even have started to doubt the Messianic meaning of the Shroud. For the group to hold together, for faith in the Risen Jesus to continue and flourish, something had to happen. If Yahweh and Jesus remained inactive, the group itself would have to act.

It is at this point that the limitations of the Gospels and Acts as historical records become glaringly apparent. After Easter, early Christian history enters a murky netherworld of pious elaboration and literary invention in which it is difficult to discern even the dim outlines of historical events. The only real light comes from the First Creed.

Following the appearance to the Twelve, the Creed records three further appearances: to "more than five hundred brethren at one time," to James, and to "all the apostles." Each of these events (or series of events) clearly represents an important stage in the formation of the Church. The mass viewing of the Risen Christ by over 500 witnesses must have had a major impact on the movement, and it was evidently regarded as a crucial guarantee of the truth of the gospel—hence Paul's assurance that most of these witnesses were still alive. Just as significant was the appearance to James, the brother of Jesus, who became the revered leader of the Jerusalem Church. And had it not been for the appearances to the apostles, the emissaries of the Church, knowledge of the Risen Jesus would never have been spread abroad. The second half of the First Creed is thus crucial for understanding the initial rise of Christianity. Without it, we would be utterly in the dark.

So, how can we make sense of these forgotten appearances? We need only interpret them as public and private showings of the Shroud. Using historical reasoning and imagination, we can then deduce roughly where, when and why these appearances occurred.

The claim that the Risen Jesus appeared "to over five hundred brethren at one time" is the single most astonishing statement in the whole of the New Testament. Nevertheless, scholars have paid it remarkably little attention. Most acknowledge the potential significance of the report, but, in the absence of any definite description of the appearance, decline to speculate about the circumstances.[3] A few try to link it with this or that Resurrection narrative, despite the fact that the texts themselves provide no encouragement.[4] Still others dismiss it as an apologetic fiction, because it conflicts with their understanding of the Resurrection phenomenon.[5] In short, the claim that the Risen Jesus was seen simultaneously by over 500 people has never been properly assessed; it is one of many historical conundrums that New Testament scholarship sweeps under the carpet.

The majority of Christians, fixated on the Gospels, are either unaware that the problem exists or are happy to leave it in abeyance. Historians, though, are bound to face up to it. Paul and his colleagues were convinced that over 500 of their fellow brethren witnessed a single appearance of the Risen Jesus. What was the occasion they had in mind?

To date, the only real attempts to answer this question have involved equating the More-than-500 appearance with the story of Pentecost.[6] According to Acts 2, the Twelve and their companions were assembled together in a house in Jerusalem on the day of Pentecost (about seven weeks after Easter) when the Holy Spirit came upon them and gave them the power to speak in tongues, so that "devout men from every nation under heaven" could understand them as if they were speaking their own languages.[7] The idea that this unlikely tale represents the historical appearance to more than 500 brethren has little to recommend it. There is nothing in the legend of Pentecost that even hints at a grand, public appearance of the Risen Jesus. Even if the descent of the Holy Spirit can be linked to the Risen Christ, it manifests itself in a private house and lands only on the Twelve and their companions. Equating this scene with the First Creed event is plainly wrong.

The appearance to the More-than-500 must remain, for the moment, a report without a New Testament narrative to match. But we can still work out roughly what happened with the help of the Shroud. If the Risen Christ was seen via the Shroud, his simultaneous appearance to over 500 people is easily explained: following its Easter debut, the Shroud must have been shown to a mass audience. More than 500 people could easily have viewed the Shroud together at the same time, and, since they would all have seen a single objective phenomenon (not 500+ individual hallucinations), their combined testimony would have been extremely impressive (as Paul's comment about them implies).

Anyone who has stood before the cloth in Turin Cathedral, accompanied by several hundred others, has an inkling, I believe, of the kind of experience the More-than-500 must have had. Modern displays of the Shroud effectively re-enact the first Nazarene assembly, the moment when the Church, as a great community of believers, was born.

As a response to the situation in which the Twelve found themselves, a public display of the Shroud would have made sense. As time passed, they would have felt the need to move the situation on, and their initial fear would soon have been replaced by a new-found confidence in the power of God (and Jesus) to protect them. Perhaps they concluded that they themselves were meant to play a part in the inauguration of the Kingdom of God, in "the going forth of the word." Certainly, they would have wanted to share their earth-shattering knowledge of the Resurrection with like-minded comrades. We may assume, I think, that the 500+ brethren were former followers of Jesus, sympathizers who were not part of his inner circle. It is likely that members of this band heard rumors about the Resurrection long before they saw the Risen Jesus for themselves. Whether or not they believed the rumors, they probably pressed to be shown the miraculous cloth. That the Twelve decided to exhibit the Shroud should not surprise us. God had given them an ensign infinitely more glorious than the painted rags and images that adorned the standards of the Roman cohorts; it was time to raise it and show the dejected brethren—and Israel at large—that deliverance was at hand, that the advent of the Messiah was imminent.

Where might this first exhibition of the Shroud have taken place? Some reckon that the appearance to the More-than-500 occurred in Galilee.[8] It is possible that the Twelve and their companions decamped to Galilee, managed to gather together a sizeable band of Galilean brethren, and revealed the Shroud to them in some rural backwater. However, there is no reliable evidence of any of the followers of Jesus fleeing to Galilee soon after the Crucifixion; the Twelve were definitely still in Jerusalem at Easter, and Acts is clear that the early Christians were based in the Holy City until they began to be persecuted. Their persecution was presumably a result, whether delayed or immediate, of their going public about the Risen Jesus, a campaign that would presumably have involved displaying the Shroud to the brethren. In my opinion, then, the appearance to the More-than-500 probably took place in Jerusalem.

We can rule out the idea that the Shroud was displayed in a private house. It would have been impossible to crowd over 500 people into one of the modest dwellings of down-town Jerusalem, and, in any case, the Twelve would hardly have wanted to draw attention to a safe house by holding a mass meeting there. Prudence, convenience and the sheer number of brethren involved implies that the Shroud was displayed in a public place. A synagogue, sanctified by the presence of Torah scrolls, would have provided an appropriate venue and might have been able to accommodate the crowd, but it is unlikely that synagogue officials would have cooperated with the subversive manifestation of an immortal Messiah. Alternatively, there were open spaces in the Lower City, such as the terraces surrounding the Pool of Siloam, where a large crowd could have congregated, but it is difficult to imagine such a significant event being staged on the street.

The longer one thinks about the situation confronting the Twelve, the more likely seems another possibility, one with dramatic implications: the Shroud could have been shown to the brethren in the Temple.

Two considerations weigh in favor of this location. First, the Temple enclosed a vast public space that, especially during the three annual festivals, thronged with Jewish worshippers, whose presence would have afforded some measure of protection from the authorities. Second, the Temple was the symbolic nerve-center of Judaism, the place that was central to the piety and Messianic hopes of first-century Jews. As an object of spiritual awe, on a par with the Ark of the Covenant (see above, p. 294), the Shroud surely had to be delivered to the Temple. And a natural desire to bring the cloth before the presence of Yahweh might have been fuelled by the discovery of Messianic "prophecies" such as Psalm 2.6: "I have set my king on Zion, my holy hill."

We may tentatively conclude, then, that the appearance to the More-than-500—the first ever exhibition of the Shroud—probably took place within the precincts of the Jerusalem Temple. Having agreed on the cloth's significance, the Twelve can hardly have waited more than a few months to raise the banner of Christ—a year at most. A good opportunity would have been afforded by the autumn Feast of Booths, when the city and the Temple would have been teeming with pilgrims. Perhaps it was then, roughly six months after Easter, that the crowd of brethren were presented with the great sign of the Resurrection.

Whenever and wherever it took place, this public display of the Shroud would have been viewed by the governing hierarchy as a highly subversive act. Afterward, the ringleaders would have been in constant danger of arrest, and the Shroud itself would have been under threat. The need for secrecy would have become greater than ever.

As long as no written record of the event can be identified, whatever is said about the appearance to the More-than-500 must remain, to a large extent, speculative. But the scenario envisaged here is perfectly plausible, offering a straightforward means of understanding the First Creed report, and it stands alone as a coherent historical explanation. Rethinking the appearance to the More-than-500 as a display of the Shroud, we can retrieve the event from the historical oblivion to which it has been consigned and appreciate it as a key, Church-founding revelation.

The next appearance was to James. After a mass spectacle this individual viewing might seem rather an anticlimax. Surely, having disclosed himself to one, then twelve, then over 500 followers, the Risen Christ should have proceeded to show himself to thousands and then millions of people, thus ensuring humanity's salvation. Yet, in the context of the present argument, the appearance to James is a logical sequel to the event involving the broad community of brethren.

Long before there was a bishop in Rome, let alone a Catholic pope, the early Church looked to James, the brother of Jesus, as its universal leader.[9] Tradition has it that he was the first "bishop" of Jerusalem, being either elected by his peers or appointed directly by the Risen Christ.[10] It is usually supposed, from a reading of Acts and Paul's letter to the Galatians, that

Peter was the initial leader of the Church and that James took over from him in the mid 30s, but John Painter has argued strongly that Peter was never the official leader of the Nazarenes and that James led them from the beginning.[11] The First Creed, understood in relation to the Shroud, enables us to see the truth of both positions. Peter, it seems, was a sort of caretaker figure, who headed the Shroud group initially but ceded authority to James once the latter was shown the Shroud. In this way James was both appointed by the Risen Jesus and elected by the other leaders of the Church. That Jesus was succeeded by his brother is hardly surprising: dynastic leadership was commonplace in the ancient world, and in the earliest phase of Christianity, certainly up until the end of the first century, members of Jesus' family were dominant.[12]

It may be wondered why, if James was such an important figure, he is now so little known. The answer is simple: he was deliberately marginalized in Acts, the canonical "history" of early Christianity, because his hard-line commitment to the Jewish Torah was an embarrassment to the later Gentile Church.[13] In Paul's letters, our earliest sources, James is mentioned as often as Peter, and his pre-eminence is clear. His pre-eminence is equally clear in non-canonical sources, such as the *Gospel of Thomas*, and in the writings of early Church historians. But in Acts, the text that has determined the traditional view of early Church history, his importance is obscured. History is written by the winners and, after the decimation of Judaea in the Jewish War, the followers of James were very definitely the losers.

The appearance to James was thus hugely significant. It was the moment when the most eminent figure in early Christianity encountered the Risen Christ, ensuring his commitment to the Nazarene cause. If the Shroud theory is correct, it was also almost certainly the occasion when James was recognized as the head of the Church. The circumstances of the event can be reconstructed as follows.

It was probably months after Easter, and the whole of Jerusalem was once again buzzing with news of Jesus, the "King of the Jews" crucified at Passover. Ever since his execution, rumors had been circulating about his supposed resurrection, but few had taken them seriously. Now, over 500 of his former followers were claiming to have seen him alive again, not in the flesh but in a "spiritual body" revealed via his burial cloth. Although no one in Jerusalem had been expecting the resurrection of a lone martyr, the apparition was so well attested that many in the city were convinced. As a consequence of their bold public display of the Shroud, the cloth's guardians found themselves at the head of a significant new party, whose influence probably extended far beyond the rejuvenated band of brethren. After Easter itself, this must have been the most exhilarating moment in the life of the Church.

And yet, the status quo remained unchanged. Despite their efforts, the revolution they anticipated—the glorious arrival of the Kingdom of God— still failed to materialize. Roman troops still tramped as arrogantly as ever through the Promised Land, and, puzzlingly, the Son of Man continued to delay coming "with the clouds of heaven." Nothing changed on the ground, let alone in the sky; there was no cosmic upheaval, no mass resurrection of the dead.

The exciting triumph of the appearance to the More-than-500 must have been followed by a renewed sense of bewilderment and a need to refocus the revolutionary hope of the movement. One obvious way to do this was to elect a new leader. Since Jesus was not yet ready to return and lead them himself, the Nazarenes needed someone to be his earthly representative, someone around whom the brethren could rally. Peter may have shepherded them in the months following Easter, but he could hardly have aspired to take the place of the mortal Jesus. Only one person could: his brother James.

James was probably already a man of substance in Jerusalem. He may have been in touch with the Shroud group, which probably included members of his family, but he is unlikely to have been sympathetic to their views. Of one thing we can be certain: James was not a follower of Jesus before Easter.[14] Had he been, he would surely have been among the Twelve or the More-than-500. This does not necessarily mean that he and Jesus were estranged; brothers can hold differing political and religious views while remaining close. Still, his apparent distance from the Shroud group in the months following Easter suggests there was some tension between them.

The testimony of the More-than-500 and the ensuing furore among the Jerusalem populace must have affected James. We can surmise that he heard what people were saying about Jesus with a mixture of excitement and consternation—excitement because it implied his brother had been favored by God in an extraordinary way, consternation because it revived the memory of his shameful crucifixion. He must have wondered about the sign so many had seen, and, if the followers of Jesus did not come to him first, he may have contacted them, hoping to see the sign for himself. The Shroud group would have welcomed an approach from James. It would have been evident to all that, if he joined the Nazarenes, he would be the new figurehead of the movement. As they accustomed themselves to a second period of waiting, this time at the head of a large party of excitable brethren, the Twelve would have been acutely conscious of the need for a strong, legitimate leader. The rapprochement with James must have seemed like a divine blessing, a necessary part of God's emerging plan.

The process of admitting James into the new sect reached a climax with his being shown the Shroud, the revelation of the Resurrection. James's experience of the cloth, though, would have been quite unlike any of the previous appearances. Those to the women, Peter and the Twelve had been utterly unexpected; that to the crowd of brethren would have been preceded by nothing other than rumor. This time it was different. Before being shown the Shroud, James must have been carefully groomed in the scriptures relating to his risen brother. The occasion itself, representing the investiture of Christ's mortal successor, was of such significance that it must have been conducted with a degree of ceremony. Secrecy would have been essential, given the Messianic nature of the sect. James probably prepared himself by taking a ritual bath beforehand, a customary means of achieving purity and obligatory before entering the inner courts of the Temple, whose sanctity the Shroud would have been felt to equal or surpass. He may well have been ritually anointed, as well. Finally, he would have been ushered into the presence of the Risen Christ.

It must have been a daunting and emotional experience for the young man, to come face to face with his crucified brother, now alive once more, but transformed into a figure of terrifying, celestial splendor. His body was bleeding still, but also gleaming; his face was a powerful, expressionless mask. We do not know how James reacted, but we do know that he left the room convinced that he had seen his resurrected brother. The Nazarenes would have regarded the meeting as a mystical communion that transformed James into a unique representative of Christ.

The location of the ceremony is unknown, although it seems likely that it was a private house somewhere in Jerusalem or its vicinity. Nor do we know when it was held. Perhaps James was shown the Shroud on the first anniversary of Easter; perhaps he was made to wait until the Day of Atonement, six months later, so that his encounter with the Shroud paralleled the passage of the high priest through the veil of the Temple into the Holy of Holies. We do not know, because the appearance to James was deliberately "forgotten" in the official annals of early Christian history.

After the appearance to James and prior to the appearance to Paul, the Risen Christ appeared "to all the apostles." The word "apostle" means an emissary, one "sent out" to convey a message, in this case the gospel of the Risen Christ. Not long after James assumed the leadership of the Church, then, certain Nazarenes were chosen as emissaries of the Risen Lord and were shown the Shroud in preparation for their missions.

The instigation of this campaign should probably be understood as a response to a dramatic change in the fortunes of the new sect. In the wake of the appearance to the More-than-500 and the recruitment of James, the Nazarenes appear to have grown into a large, well-organized assembly, possibly numbering in the thousands. The unity of the assembly seems to have been fostered, from the outset, by the adoption of a communistic rule, the possessions of individual members being sold to support the community and everything being held in common.[15] The growth of this Messianic sect must have alarmed Caiaphas and his colleagues. It was not an organization they could afford to tolerate. At the time of the Shroud's public display, the Nazarenes were apparently perceived as a crew of excitable fantasists; a year or so later they would have been seen as dangerous revolutionaries whose activities posed a serious threat to the regime.

It is likely in these circumstances that the Nazarenes were persecuted, and this is exactly what happened according to Acts. Following the trial and martyrdom of someone called Stephen, an inspired preacher of the gospel, the Church came under attack from the Jerusalem authorities. Spearheading this assault was a young zealot named Saul—the future apostle, Paul.

> And on that day a great persecution arose against the church in Jerusalem; and they were all scattered throughout the region of Judaea and Samaria . . . Saul laid waste the church, and entering house after house, he dragged off men and women and committed them to prison.[16]

Ironically, Paul's attempt to annihilate the Church simply made it stronger. During the period of its exile from Jerusalem, it expanded massively, not only throughout Judaea and Samaria, but also, apparently, in Galilee.[17] The exile and the expansion were intimately related, for it was the "great persecution," I believe, that prompted the appointment of apostles, whose task was to spread the gospel abroad.

There is no reason to think that James and the Twelve sent out any apostles while they were safely ensconced in Jerusalem. Awaiting the Day of the Lord in the Holy City itself, where the cosmic action was bound to be focused, they had no incentive to start proselytizing elsewhere. News would have filtered out to the provinces from the capital, and there were already enough witnesses of the Risen Christ in Jerusalem to inform everyone there of the impending salvation. Everything changed, though, once the Nazarenes were evicted from the city. Their situation now became precarious. As refugees, hounded mercilessly by Paul and his men, their security—and that of the Shroud—was dependent, wherever they went, on local support.

Suddenly, they had an urgent need to make converts. The best way to achieve this was to create apostles, trusted brethren and influential locals, who could bear witness to the reality of the Risen Christ. The men and women entrusted with this duty had to be shown the Shroud. They also had to announce the same gospel as each other, since the consistency of their message would have been crucial to its success. The First Creed, which Paul presents as the universal gospel, was probably devised for this purpose: it was the original Apostles' Creed.

Given the large number of apostles, we should not expect to find their individual initiations narrated in Acts or the Gospels. The only apostle whose story warranted attention was Paul—a very special case. We may guess that the appearances to the apostles were loosely based on the ceremonial appearance to James. Having been schooled in the scriptural proofs of the gospel, the candidates must have ritually purified themselves before being shown the Shroud. In some cases, apostolic initiations may have been linked to baptism. They must have taken place wherever the Shroud was kept on its journey from Jerusalem to Damascus, where Paul became the last of the apostles. One route to Damascus (which need not have been the Shroud's initial destination) would have been via the three regions said to have been evangelized in Acts 9.31—Judaea, Samaria and Galilee—so we can infer that the Shroud traveled north through these regions and that apostles were created en route.

The implication that some of the appearances took place in Galilee is particularly interesting in light of the Galilee Tradition, concerning an appearance to the disciples. Vague and incoherent though it is, this tradition is early and persistent enough to warrant the suspicion that it has a historical basis. Mark's testimony is the vaguest of all. He simply reports the words of the "young man" to the women at the tomb: "But go, tell his disciples and Peter that he is going before you to Galilee; there you will see him, as he told you."[18] Originally, Mark may have gone on to narrate a Galilean appearance to Peter and others, but the text now finishes after the next verse, without narrating any appearances at all.[19] Matthew fulfils the announcement with his story of the Risen Jesus appearing to the Eleven on a mountain in Galilee. It would be unwise to interpret this as an accurate historical record, but it may reflect a widespread belief that the Risen Christ was witnessed in this northern region.

Of greater interest is the story of the appearance by the Sea of Galilee in John 21, which appears to preserve an ancient, allegorical account of viewings of the Shroud.[20] Significantly, this tale is echoed in the *Gospel of Peter*, which ends with an appearance-story that barely gets underway before the manuscript breaks off:

> But I, Simon Peter, and my brother Andrew took our nets and went to the sea. And there was with us Levi, the son of Alphaeus, whom the Lord . . .[21]

Meager as it is, this text provides further evidence that Resurrection appearances were remembered as having happened near the Sea of Galilee. Since the Twelve definitely witnessed the Shroud in Jerusalem, these Galilean appearances should probably be associated with the apostles instead.

Worth noting is the fact that, while Peter is named first in John 21.2 and *Gospel of Peter* 14.60, none of the other names correspond.[22] This suggests that Peter was the dominant figure in the apostolic mission. The same impression is given by Mark, who singles Peter out among those who will see the Risen Jesus in Galilee. He is unlikely to have ferried the Shroud to Galilee alone, but Peter does seem to have led the apostolic campaign to the north. This explains, perhaps, why Paul speaks of Peter, not James, as the leader of "the mission to the circumcised."[23]

With numerous eyewitnesses of the Risen Jesus criss-crossing Galilee and neighboring territories, probably working in pairs to support each other's testimony,[24] it is hardly surprising that the subversive gospel of Christ caught on in the region. Considering the effect of this apostolic campaign on the wider Roman world—and beyond—we can now solve the greatest of all the historical conundrums posed by the birth of Christianity: how a small coterie of Jewish sectarians managed to persuade vast numbers of Jews and Gentiles alike that a crucified revolutionary was the resurrected Savior of the World.

Had the Twelve merely had visions or peculiar feelings about Jesus after his death and tried to interest their compatriots in a scandalous theory about their executed leader, they would have got nowhere. Few would have welcomed their perverse gospel, and the lack of evidence would have been damning. Christianity would soon have fizzled out. But that is not how it began. The reason Christianity succeeded is that it was based on good, solid evidence—misinterpreted, but solid nevertheless. Once they were ejected from Jerusalem, the resourceful founders of the Church made sure that this evidence—a marvelous image on a cloth—was made known to as many people as possible, not directly but via the regulated testimony of numerous eyewitnesses. The testimony of these envoys was convincing, because they all saw the same image and could therefore describe the Risen Jesus in detail without contradicting each other. And they all bore precisely the same message: the "gospel" recited by Paul in 1 Corinthians.

Galilee may have seen the creation of dozens of apostles; others were probably appointed in Samaria and Judaea. If we add to these the Twelve and their companions, the More-than-500, and the crucial figures of James and Paul, we can reckon that there were somewhere in the order of 600 eyewitnesses of the Risen Jesus in the Promised Land—possibly many more. This gave the apostolic Church a tremendously strong core and helps explain how the unlikely creed of the crucified Christ managed to cross the threshold from an isolated cult to a common belief.

The story of the "forgotten appearances" of the Risen Christ—to the More-than-500, to James, and to all the apostles—is the greatest story never told, an extraordinary epic that, thanks to the accidents and biases of early Christian story-telling, has been almost entirely lost to history.

Previously, few have even tried to make sense of these appearances, let alone construe them as parts of a coherent historical narrative. Now, with the help of the Shroud, every appearance listed in the First Creed can be understood naturalistically, as an integral and necessary stage in the development of Christianity. Indeed, the Shroud enables us, for the first time ever, to comprehend the whole of Paul's "gospel" as a succinct history of the birth of the Church. It is a tale of subterfuge and daring, enthusiasm and violence, that only begins to emerge once the Resurrection is recognized as an idea inspired by the Shroud.

We have now traced the history of Christianity's origin from the death and burial of Jesus to the Shroud's arrival in Galilee. This is as far as the First Creed can take us, but it is by no means the end of the story. What happened next was one of the most dramatic incidents in early Christian history. The Shroud, it seems, was taken to Damascus, where it was hunted down by the would-be nemesis of the fledgling Church.

25

The Last of the Apostles

Even with Judaea, Samaria and Galilee teeming with apostles, all bearing witness to the same revelatory figure and proclaiming a single gospel, the success of Christianity was by no means assured. The Nazarenes had been driven from Jerusalem in a vicious pogrom, spearheaded by Paul, and over the next few years the Roman and Jewish authorities continued to harry them wherever they went. At this point Christianity could still have been nipped in the bud. That it was not, that it went on to flourish not only in the Promised Land, but also abroad, among Gentiles as well as Jews, was largely a consequence of the "miraculous" conversion of Paul.

Thankfully, our sources provide a good deal of information about Paul's encounter with the Risen Christ. Not only do we have, in Paul's letters, his own first-hand testimony, but we also have a lengthy account of the episode in Acts. The apostle himself may be "dismayingly discreet," in the words of Jerome Murphy-O'Connor, a leading Paul scholar, and Luke may be misleadingly verbose, but, read carefully, the sources reveal a fair amount about Paul's life-changing epiphany.

The historical background to the conversion of Paul is revealed in a couple of passages written by the apostle himself. First of all, there is the brief account of his experience appended to the First Creed:

> Last of all, as to one untimely born, he appeared also to me. For I am the least of the apostles, unfit to be called an apostle, because I persecuted the Church of God.[1]

Paul's reference to his persecution of the Church indicates that there were plenty of apostles appointed before him, since these missionaries must have helped to establish the churches he persecuted.[2] It also hints at the extraordinary circumstances of his epiphany.

These circumstances are more fully described in Paul's letter to the

Galatians, the opening section of which is a passionate defense of his own apostleship. Concerned to stress his independence from the Jerusalem Church, he insists his gospel is inspired directly by the Risen Christ:

> I want you to know, brothers, that the gospel I preached is not something that man made up. I did not receive it from any man, nor was I taught it; rather, I received it by revelation from Jesus Christ. For you have heard of my previous way of life in Judaism, how intensely I persecuted the church of God and tried to destroy it. I was advancing in Judaism beyond many Jews of my own age and was extremely zealous for the traditions of my fathers. But when God, who set me apart from birth and called me by his grace, was pleased to reveal his Son in me so that I might preach him among the Gentiles, I did not consult any man, nor did I go up to Jerusalem to see those who were apostles before I was, but I went immediately into Arabia and later returned to Damascus.[3]

This autobiographical sketch amounts to a succinct history of the episode. Paul makes no bones about his violent persecution of the Church. His aim, he says, was nothing less than its destruction. He seems to attribute his hostility to his zeal for the traditions of his fathers. This "life in Judaism" came to an end with the all-important "revelation from Jesus Christ," which inaugurated his "life in Christ." The revelation must have occurred in or near Damascus, since Paul says he returned there after going to Arabia.

A similar tale emerges from the narrative of Acts. According to Acts 8.1–3, Paul was the principal enemy of the infant Church, attacking and imprisoning the original believers in Jerusalem and scattering them abroad. Still named Saul, he reappears at the start of Acts 9, preparing to pursue them further afield: "But Saul, still breathing threats and murder against the disciples of the Lord, went to the high priest and asked him for letters to the synagogues at Damascus, so that if he found any belonging to the Way, men or women, he might bring them bound to Jerusalem."[4]

He then journeys to Damascus, and the famous scene of his conversion takes place on the road outside the city. The fact that Acts agrees with Paul on the location of the event proves that Luke's tradition is historically grounded (although it leaps into fiction, as we shall see). It is sometimes doubted that Caiaphas would have given Paul letters to take with him to Damascus, since the city was outside his area of jurisdiction, but the high priest had diplomatic importance and a degree of moral authority over the city's Jewish inhabitants, so the report is credible. Less easy to understand is why Paul wanted to pursue Christians in Damascus. The real battle was nearer to home, in Palestine, where Christianity was flourishing. What was the point of targeting a few outliers far away to the north?[5]

Rather than pursuing a random community of exiled Nazarenes, Paul was surely on the trail of someone—or something—in particular. An obvious target would have been the Shroud. In the course of his anti-Nazarene campaign, Paul would surely have learned of the existence of the sacred cloth, and spies, rumors or interrogation could have alerted him to its presence in Damascus. Determined to destroy the Church, he would have regarded capturing this mysterious "idol" as his ultimate duty, the only means of uprooting the heresy altogether. If Paul knew that the Shroud was in Damascus, he had to follow it there.

Paul left Damascus a changed man—a Christian. Traditionally, his conversion has been attributed to a "vision" he had when he was approaching the city, as described in Acts. Paul's own testimony points to a rather different cause—an encounter with the Shroud.

On only three occasions does Paul unequivocally refer to the moment of his conversion. Two have just been quoted: his self-addition to the First Creed and his account of his God-given "revelation" in Galatians. The other occasion is in 1 Corinthians 9.1: "Am I not an apostle? Have I not seen Jesus our Lord?" Brief as they are, these allusions are extremely valuable, the historical equivalent of red diamonds.[6]

There are many different theories regarding Paul's conversion. The most popular theory is that he had a vision or, as skeptics say, a hallucination. However, Paul's references to the event provide little or no support for this idea, which is based four-square on the unreliable narrative of Acts.[7] Otherwise, it is speculated that Paul had an epileptic fit; that he had a severe migraine; that he was struck by lightning; that he came across a revived, mortal Jesus; and that he didn't really experience anything at all, just came to accept, by God's grace, that he was wrong and his opponents were right.[8] These suggestions are little more than isolated guesses and often depend on a naive reading of the sources. By contrast, the argument that Paul saw the Risen Jesus in the Shroud is part of a much broader theory and does full justice to the literary evidence.

To begin with, Paul's experience was clearly visual. He says nothing about having a fit, or a headache, or a crisis of faith; he says simply that he saw the Risen Christ. The type of vision implied is ordinary eyesight, not a spiritual "seeing." Tellingly, Paul avoids using the usual term for a vision, *optasia*.[9] Instead, when he gives his experience a name in Galatians 1.12, he calls it a "revelation" or an "unveiling" (*apokalupseos*). Like its English translations, the Greek word *apokalupseos* is related to the word for a veil (*kaluptra*). According to the present theory, the Shroud was perceived literally as a veil through which the Risen Jesus made himself apparent. Paul's vocabulary is in perfect accord with the idea that he witnessed the Shroud— not a vision, but a visionary image.

Paul also tells us what he saw: not a flash of heavenly light, as Acts would have it, but an exalted person. He calls this person Christ, Jesus our Lord, Jesus Christ, and God's Son.[10] Clearly, the experience was not straightforward, like meeting a regular person, but the apostle never evinces the least doubt about the subject of his revelation.

Paul was absolutely confident that the appearance to him was of a kind with the other Resurrection appearances, including those to "all the apostles," a group of which he was a member. Having seen the Risen Jesus was one of the marks of an apostle, and other members of the Church evidently acknowledged Paul's apostleship.[11] His apostolic status was confirmed by the three Pillars of the Jerusalem Church, James, Peter and John, since they sanctioned his mission to the Gentiles. Their attitude implies strongly that his witnessing of the Risen Christ was a verifiable, public act, observed by those who were with him at the time.[12] Moreover, failing a divine telegram delivered straight to his consciousness, only the sight and touch of something real could have persuaded the arch-persecutor of the Nazarenes that the Resurrection of Jesus was an inescapable fact. A more ambiguous experience—such as a pang of guilt or a hallucination—might have disturbed and confused him, but it would hardly have given him a cast-iron conviction that he had seen the Risen Christ. So Paul surely witnessed an unmistakable, objective phenomenon. The only plausible candidate for this phenomenon is the Shroud.

We can now make sense of the detailed portrait of the Risen Christ implied by Paul's account of the risen body in 1 Corinthians 15.35–50 (see above, pp. 55–8). No wonder the apostle distinguished so carefully between the weak, dishonorable, mortal body and the powerful, glorious, risen body: he was describing the difference between ordinary flesh and the celestial form seen via the Shroud. No wonder, too, he saw Christ as a second, superior Adam, the harbinger of a new type of humanity. Perceived as a divine revelation, the Shroud not only gave access to the heavenly realm, but also revealed a new order of Creation.[13] At the same time it associated this dawning cosmic transformation with a particular man: Jesus. The metaphor of the risen body as a seedling grown from the seed of the flesh was an obvious one to adopt, because it perfectly expressed the physical relation between the Shroud and the body of Jesus lying in the tomb. (A mere vision would have provided no evidence of the relation between the physical body and the spiritual body.) Finally, Paul would have had no trouble identifying the object of his revelation as Jesus, since others could testify to the origin and likeness of the Shroud.

In short, Paul's extraordinary description of the risen body—detailed, indisputable eyewitness testimony—becomes fully comprehensible once we realize that the Resurrection was a belief generated by the Shroud.

We can also now understand Paul's peculiar comment that God "was pleased to reveal his Son in me."[14] This strange internalization of the experience can be explained via the Shroud. On one level, when Paul saw the Shroud, he met the celestial figure of Jesus, just as Moses met the Angel of the Lord in the Burning Bush—a divine, other-worldly person, who stood outside and beyond him. But on another level, the Shroud was a complex sign which bore upon the salvation of individuals, including Paul himself. One of the fundamental lessons Paul drew from reading Genesis was that the Risen Jesus was the archetype of a new humanity, whose progeny were destined to supersede the line of Adam. He inferred that the Saved (of whom he was one) would share in Christ's spiritual nature, just as mortal humans share in Adam's fleshly nature: "For as in Adam all die, so also in Christ shall all be made alive."[15] On reflection, then, Paul's revelation was not just about meeting the divine other; it was also about recognizing his own share in the body of Christ—God's Son in him.

A dramatic spiritual encounter (whether real or imaginary) could hardly have been confused with subsequent theological reflection. The Shroud, though, could well have been. It signified both a spiritual, archetypal person and the spiritual rebirth of the faithful.[16] So, when Paul pondered the Shroud—as he did, in a sense, every day of his "life in Christ"—he thought not only about the spiritual figure of Christ but also about his own spiritual being. This being was not a future state, but another self that was already alive within him. Paul's view of himself was schizophrenic: he was both an old, outer, physical self, a child of Adam (to be despised), and a new, inner, spiritual self, a child of Christ (to be nurtured).[17]

The conception of this inner, spiritual self was equated with being "born again" while still alive, one of the ideas that set the Nazarene sect apart from mainstream Judaism.[18] According to Paul, the Christian believer becomes a host for the Holy Spirit, the agent of resurrection and the source of eternal life.[19] The Spirit was envisaged as a quasi-physical substance— hence its visibility via the Shroud. In every believer, then, there was a sort of spiritual embryo within the "dead" flesh of the physical body. For early Christians being "born again" was no mere metaphor: it was imagined as a real, numinous process at work in their mortal bodies. They were literally being recreated from within. The believer was pregnant with his or her better self, which would be clothed in a new body on the forthcoming Day of the Lord.[20]

This way of thinking underlies Paul's most startling comment about his conversion experience: that it occurred "as to one untimely born." To be precise, he says that Christ appeared to him "as if to the abortion," envisaging his experience as a traumatic, premature (re)birth.[21] He was totally unprepared for this spiritual parturition, because at the time of the revelation he was rampaging after Christians, trying to destroy the Church. So God, who had set him apart before he was born,[22] acted like a surgeon performing a Caesarean section, presenting him with his spiritual self ahead of time.

It is significant that Paul calls himself "the" abortion, not "an" abortion. He has just introduced himself at the end of the First Creed as the last of the apostles, and he uses the definite article to designate himself with respect to the other members of this group: he is singling himself out as the only one of the apostles to have been "born" ahead of time; he is *the* abortion *among* the apostles. This implies that his peers, by contrast, were ready to witness the Risen Christ.[23] It is hard to see how they could have been prepared for real, visionary encounters, but if the apostolic appearances involved ceremoniously witnessing the Shroud, spiritual preparation would have been taken for granted. Apostolic candidates, selected from among believers, would have been instructed in the scriptures before being shown the revelatory cloth. Paul was not a believer and received no instruction; he just intruded on the Shroud.

Why are Paul's references to his conversion experience so elliptical? One reason, no doubt, is that it involved an emotional convulsion that was intensely painful to recall. Another, I think, is that he had nothing much to say about it, because viewing the Shroud is inherently uneventful. There is nothing dramatic about gazing at a discolored piece of linen—no action, no speaking. Of course, it can be turned into a drama—witness the Resurrection narratives in the Gospels—but it doesn't need to be. It is adequately described as a simple "seeing" or "revelation." Far from being dramatic, then, Paul's conversion experience was quiet and contemplative. What mattered was not the event itself but its timeless significance, and Paul expounded on that in everything he wrote.

To a conventional way of thinking, Paul's testimony is full of difficulties and contradictions: he says that he saw the Risen Christ, yet he fails to describe the encounter in any detail; he is completely confident of his right to be called an apostle, despite his infamous background; he gives a detailed description of the risen body, tied to an account of Jesus as "the last Adam"; and he says he received his gospel through "a revelation of Jesus Christ," which also somehow revealed God's Son within him. Until now, it has been impossible to mold this evidence into a coherent idea of what Paul (and the other apostles) might have seen. But the Shroud makes everything understandable. Presume that Paul saw Jesus in the Shroud, and all the difficulties evaporate.

Several passages in Paul's letters hint at his knowledge of the Shroud, but one, in particular, stands out: in his second letter to the Corinthians Paul returns to the theme of the risen body, describing it in terms that unquestionably evoke the Shroud.[24]

He begins by making the distinction between Christians' outer and inner selves: "Though our outer nature is wasting away, our inner nature is being renewed every day."[25] The former, he says, is visible and transient, the latter invisible and eternal. But what would happen when the physical body died and returned to dust? How could the inner, spiritual nature live on—or live again—after the destruction of its earthly habitation? Paul's answer is that it will be given a spiritual body, the concept set out in his first letter to the Corinthians. Here, though, he describes this future body rather differently:

> For we know that if the earthly tent we live in is destroyed, we have a building from God, a house not made with hands, eternal in the heavens.[26]

The physical body may perish, but the spiritual self planted within each Christian can look forward to a heavenly body "not made by hand" (*acheiropoieton*).

This description is baffling. Why bother stating the obvious, that the celestial bodies of the resurrected will not be manufactured? Saying that something is not handmade only makes sense if it could be handmade or might be confused with something that is handmade. The word *acheiropoietos* ("not made by hand") was clearly coined in opposition to the word *cheiropoietos* ("made by hand"), used in the Septuagint (the ancient Greek translation of the Hebrew Bible) to denote pagan idols and temples.[27] For Paul's audience, then, the word *acheiropoietos* would have connoted the idea of a "non-idol" or "non-pagan temple." But this just deepens the mystery. Why contrast the resurrected body with a pagan image or temple?

All becomes clear when we reflect that, centuries later, the Mandylion (i.e. the folded Shroud) was widely known as an *acheiropoietos*. Other images were called *acheiropoietoi*, too, but the Mandylion appears to have been the original such image, a genuinely "unhandmade" image that spawned numerous copies. When the cloth was rediscovered in the mid sixth century, the Edessans needed to differentiate it from both Christian icons and pagan idols, and the New Testament term *acheiropoietos* fitted the bill perfectly.

Without knowing it, they were repeating the logic of the first-century inventor of the term, who must have had in view exactly the same image—the Shroud. The first Christians would naturally have thought of the Shroud as an *acheiropoietos*, because, as a God-given image, it was opposed in their minds to the graven images (*cheiropoietoi*) worshipped in pagan temples. So, if the Shroud was the sign of the Resurrection, it is hardly surprising that Paul, who thought of the Christian body as a temple for God's Spirit, applied the term to the risen, spiritual body. He was followed by Mark, who refers to the resurrected body of Jesus as a temple "not made with hands."[28] This verges on a literal identification of the Risen Jesus and the Shroud.

Finally, Paul goes on to describe the spirit-body in terms that seal the link:

> Here indeed we groan, and long to put on our heavenly dwelling, so that by putting it on we may not be found naked. For while we are still in this tent, we sigh with anxiety, not that we would be unclothed, but that we would be further clothed, so that what is mortal may be swallowed up by life.[29]

So, the "heavenly dwelling" is envisaged not only as an *acheiropoietos*, but also as a garment covering a naked body. The metaphor is complex, but the source of the imagery is unmistakable: Paul is thinking of the Shroud.[30]

Let us now turn to the well-known account of Paul's conversion in Acts.

> Now as he journeyed he approached Damascus, and suddenly a light from heaven flashed about him. And he fell to the ground and heard a voice saying to him, "Saul, Saul, why do you persecute me?" And he said, "Who are you Lord?" And he said, "I am Jesus, whom you are persecuting; but rise and enter the city, and you will be told what you are to do." The men who were traveling with him stood speechless, hearing the voice but seeing no one. Saul arose from the ground; and when his eyes were opened, he could see nothing; so they led him by the hand and brought him into Damascus. And for three days he was without sight, and neither ate nor drank. (Acts 9.3–9)[31]

Many modern Christians, who find it difficult to believe Luke's tale of the Risen Jesus joining a couple of disciples on the Road to Emmaus, find it easy to believe this account of Paul being accosted from heaven on the road to Damascus. This is just how post-Enlightenment believers imagine an experience of divine revelation—a sudden burst of light from above, with no awkward, physical attributes. It also fuels the skeptical notion that Paul suffered a hallucination, and this idea can be extended via the First Creed to cover the Resurrection appearances in general. So Luke's narrative of the incident on the road to Damascus has become extremely influential, determining how people understand not only the appearance to Paul, but the previous appearances as well. It is the principal prop for the various "vision" theories.

It is important to realize, therefore, that the tale in Acts of a divine ambush on the road to Damascus is no less fanciful than the Emmaus legend. Luke's narrative can be shown to be stitched together from scriptural material, proving that it is largely fictional.

There are clear echoes, first of all, of the story of Moses before the Burning Bush,[32] implying a parallel between Paul's commission to lead the Gentiles to redemption and the calling of Moses, who led the Israelites out of Egypt. The light that flashes around Paul, signaling the heavenly presence, echoes the "flame of fire" in which the Angel of the Lord appears to Moses; Christ calls out, "Saul, Saul," just as the Angel of the Lord calls out, "Moses, Moses"; and the declaration, "I am Jesus," echoes Yahweh's "I am who I am." Any idea that the light and the voice in Acts are historical vanishes the moment these parallels are noticed. Similarly, the idea that Paul fell to the ground before the heavenly apparition is nothing but a literary cliché. The prophet Ezekiel, for instance, repeatedly falls on his face before shining visions of the Lord.[33]

The best known source for the Acts narrative is Daniel 10.5–11, in which the prophet encounters the "man clothed in linen."[34] This passage corresponds to the tale of Paul's conversion in a number of respects. Daniel's angel is characterized by overwhelming brightness ("lightning . . . flaming torches . . . gleam"), recalling the bright light that flashes around Paul; Daniel's companions, like Paul's, fail to see the vision; and both Daniel and Paul fall to the ground before the heavenly presence and are then told to stand up. Clearly, whoever composed the Acts narrative wanted to draw a parallel between Paul's experience and that of Daniel before the man clothed in linen. Part of the reason may have been that Paul's mission to prepare the Jews and the Gentiles for the end-times by proclaiming the Resurrection of Jesus was thought to fulfil Daniel's prophecy of what would happen at the end-times, including the resurrection of the righteous. But this common theme is not really enough to explain the parallel. Daniel's vision is of an angel, not conventionally identified with Christ, and the purposes of the revelations are very different: the apostle is commissioned to preach, whereas the prophet is told to "shut up the words, and seal the book, until the time of end."[35] So, although both visions concern the end-times, it is hard to understand, from the point of view of conventional scholarship, why the story of Paul's encounter with Christ was modelled on Daniel's vision.

From the perspective of the Shroud theory, it is easy. As we have seen, the first Christians understood the man clothed in linen to be one and the same as the Risen Jesus, the man "clothed" in the Shroud. Daniel's vision was a suitable template for an account of the appearance to Paul, because it was thought to represent an earlier appearance of the same celestial figure. So, at the same time as undermining the historicity of the narrative, the very artfulness of Acts 9.3–9 points toward the likely cause of Paul's conversion: a sudden, unanticipated experience of the Shroud.

The Shroud also helps explain the choice of a third scriptural template for the Acts narrative: the story of Heliodorus.[36] Heliodorus was a courtier of King Seleucus of Syria, who was sent to plunder the Jerusalem Temple. On entering the treasury, he was attacked by a terrifying apparition, an angelic rider "of frightening mien," accompanied by two young men, "who stood on either side of him and flogged him continuously, inflicting many blows upon him." The courtier fell to the ground, temporarily blinded, and had to be carried away by his men. Soon afterward, when he was recovering, the young men appeared to him again and instructed him to "report to all people the majestic power of God." Heliodorus obeyed, and returning to Syria, "bore testimony to all concerning the deeds of the supreme God, which he had seen with his own eyes."

The story of the conversion of Heliodorus provided an obvious precedent for the conversion of Paul, and it undoubtedly inspired the denouement of the Damascus road story, in which Paul temporarily loses his sight and has to rely on the help of others.[37] It is only when we reflect on the likely reason for Paul's visit to Damascus, though, that the full significance of the comparison becomes clear. Just as Heliodorus was bent on plundering the Temple in Jerusalem, Paul was intent on robbing the Christians of their sacred treasure, the Shroud. And, just like the Syrian courtier, he was stopped in his tracks by a heavenly manifestation when he was on the very point of accomplishing his evil scheme. It is hardly surprising that an early Christian story-teller decided to model the conversion of Paul on that of Heliodorus.[38]

Paul, then, did not see a bright light, did not fall to the ground, did not hear a voice calling him, did not go blind and did not get led away by his companions: these elements of Luke's story all derive from the scriptures. If we bracket them out, we are left with virtually nothing; the story is little more than a tissue of literary allusions. But while the narrative itself is fictional, the scriptural sources hint at the real character of the event—a disclosure of the Shroud. The original author (not Luke) used the well-known stories of Moses, Daniel and Heliodorus to explain the significance of Paul's epiphany, tying the apostle's experience into the prophetic tradition of ancient Israel. His fiction was meant to express a fundamental truth.

So, the widespread belief that Paul experienced a "heavenly vision" is unjustified. The spectacular audio-visuals of Acts 9 no more prove that the appearances of the Risen Christ were luminous visions than the report in Luke 24 of him walking to Emmaus proves that they were physical meetings. Instead, the scriptural sources of the story indicate that Paul witnessed a relatively down-to-earth apparition, one simultaneously like the Angel of the Lord, the man clothed in linen and the heavenly trio who attacked Heliodorus. The only way of accounting for all these varied analogies is to presume that Paul witnessed the Shroud.

The story of Paul's conversion in Acts may be misleading from a modern point of view, but its original author was evidently well-informed: he knew what really happened to Paul in Damascus. Carefully analyzed, then, the account in Acts 9 can be combined with the evidence of the Shroud and Paul's own words to reconstruct the history of the event.

The story starts with the Shroud in Galilee, where it was taken as a result of Paul's persecution of the Church in Judaea. Sometime prior to 33 the Galilee mission must have come under threat, either from Herod Antipas, the local ruler, or from Paul, and the Shroud was moved on, arriving eventually in Damascus. In all likelihood, the house where it was kept was inside the city, rather than on the outskirts, since that is where the Christian community would have been based. If its guardians thought the cloth was safe in Damascus, however, they were sorely mistaken. For Paul soon learned of its whereabouts, probably from a spy or a captured Christian, and embarked on a mission to seize it. One day in 33, the new Heliodorus marched into the house that served as the Shroud's sanctuary in Damascus and set eyes, at long last, on the source of the Nazarene heresy.

At that moment the whole future of Christianity teetered on a knife-edge. Paul was in a position to strike a body-blow against the Risen Jesus, to rob the Church of its revelatory cloth. He could have taken one glance at the Shroud and dismissed its peculiar markings as a piece of fakery or—worse—a work of magic. He could have bundled it up and delivered it to Caiaphas, or he could have destroyed it on the spot. What would that have said about the power of Christ? If the Church had lost the Shroud to an unrepentant Paul, it might have lost momentum altogether, and faith in the Risen Jesus might have withered away.

But the blow never came. Paul's first glimpse of the Shroud revealed something mysterious, something that caught his attention and stayed his hand. Rather than confiscate the cloth or destroy it, he found himself being drawn in by it, mesmerized by its inexplicable, sublime appearance. The longer he examined it, the more miraculous it must have seemed. But it was not just the quality of the image that snared him. Gazing at the figure's face, he could not escape the feeling that there was someone there in the image, someone looking back at him, perhaps silently judging him.

The poor heresy-hunter must have fought the sensation hard, but he was no match for the Shroud figure, with its unique combination of formal mystery and animistic power. Gradually, Paul succumbed. Against all his expectations, he could see the Risen Jesus before him, as clear (almost) as day. Agonizingly, he began to see himself and his war against the Church in a new light. His moral compass spun round, and the Risen Jesus snatched a remarkable victory from the jaws of defeat.

Such was the "revelation of Jesus Christ" that Paul experienced in Damascus. No blinding light, no haunting voice: just a peculiar stain on a piece of linen. Compared with the spectacular vision of Acts 9, the Shroud may seem disappointingly mundane, but it changed the world none the less. In fact, it is precisely because the Shroud is mundane, as well as marvelous, that it had the capacity to affect first-century people like Paul so dramatically. Being manifestly of the world, it was undeniable. So, like the Beloved Disciple in the tomb, Paul stood over Jesus' burial cloth and "saw and believed."

26

The Move to Edessa

The history of the Resurrection ends with the appearance to Paul, the last official witness of the Risen Jesus; the history of the Shroud carries on, all the way from the first century to the twenty-first. It is not my purpose in this book to trace every twist and turn in the Shroud's tortuous journey from Jerusalem to Turin, but I do need to explain briefly what happened in the years following Paul's conversion, years in which the Shroud passed into relative obscurity and ceased being seen as the material embodiment of the Risen Christ. This crucial alteration in the perception of the cloth was precipitated by its move to the Mesopotamian city of Edessa.

Immediately after his conversion, Acts tells us, Paul stayed in Damascus for three days "without sight, and neither ate nor drank."[1] His blindness may be a symbolic fiction, but the report of his abstinence from food and drink is likely to be historical. Fasting would have been a ready means of expressing his penitence, and it also seems to have been a preparation for baptism.

Paul appears to have joined the local Christian community immediately:

> Now there was a disciple at Damascus named Ananias. The Lord said to him in a vision, "Ananias." And he said, "Here I am, Lord." And the Lord said to him, "Rise and go to the street called Straight, and inquire in the house of Judas for a man of Tarsus named Saul; for behold, he is praying, and he has seen a man named Ananias come in and lay his hands on him so that he might regain his sight."[2]

Knowing Paul's evil reputation, Ananias demurs, but he receives reassurance from the Lord that Paul is "a chosen instrument" to spread the gospel abroad.

So Ananias departed and entered the house. And laying his hands on him he said, "Brother Saul, the Lord Jesus who appeared to you on the road by which you came, has sent me that you may regain your sight and be filled with the Holy Spirit." And immediately something like scales fell from his eyes and he regained his sight. Then he rose and was baptized, and took food and was strengthened.[3]

Apart from the divine intervention, this is a plausible account of Paul's induction into Christianity. It was not enough that he had seen the Shroud and come to believe in the Risen Christ: he also needed to perform the necessary rites of passage, which culminated in baptism. That his three-day fast was in preparation for baptism is implied by the remark that he ate immediately afterward.[4] During this three-day period he must also have received some basic instruction in the new faith, learning the First Creed and the key scriptural prophecies to which it referred.[5] Only then, ritually prepared in body and mind, would he have been ready to be baptized. Ordinarily, all this would have preceded an apostle's exposure to the Shroud. Paul's initiation was topsy-turvy, which is why he saw himself as having been "born" prematurely.

The other local mentioned, besides Ananias, is Judas. Paul is said to be lodging with Judas in a house on "the street called Straight." Remarkably, this street, the east–west high street (*decumanus*) of the Roman city, still exists in modern-day Damascus and is called by the same name in Arabic—an accurate detail that lends credence to the story.[6] Bearing in mind that Paul was a stranger in the city, the most likely person to have hosted him in the immediate aftermath of his conversion was the very person whose household he had just raided. In which case, the house of Judas was probably the Shroud's sanctuary in Damascus and Judas none other than its guardian. Paul, crushed by his experience, seems to have thrown himself on the mercy of his former adversary, who could hardly have refused him hospitality, having witnessed his conversion. Where else would Paul have gone? Who else would have taken him in?

If he was given responsibility for the care of the Shroud, Judas must have been high up in the early Christian hierarchy. Luke lists a second Judas among the Twelve (besides Judas Iscariot), called "Judas of James."[7] This Judas should probably be identified with the supposed author of the New Testament epistle of Jude, called "Judas, brother of James."[8] James, scholars agree, can be none other than James the brother of Jesus, so Judas must have been a brother of Jesus, as well. That one of Jesus' brothers was called Judas is recorded by both Matthew and Mark.[9]

The situation now becomes clear. As a brother of Jesus (and James), Judas would naturally have been regarded as an appropriate person to safeguard the Shroud. Peter, who was apparently the Shroud's custodian in Galilee, must have transferred the cloth to Judas in an effort to put the hounds off the scent. Unfortunately, the ruse failed, suggesting that Paul had good, up-to-date intelligence.[10]

Though now obscure, Judas was evidently a significant figure in the early Church. But however prominent a role he had played previously, it was a decision he took in the days following Paul's arrival in Damascus that would determine the course of history. Presumably in consultation with his fellow Christians, including Ananias and Paul, whose knowledge of the enemy would have been invaluable, Judas decided that the only way to ensure the safety of the Shroud was to send it even further into exile. From the house on Straight Street the cloth of the Risen Christ was to be sent to a distant city-state on the fringes of the Persian Empire.

The first clue we have that the Shroud was taken to Edessa is John's tale of Doubting Thomas. As we have seen, this story is a carefully crafted criticism of the followers of Thomas, the apostle associated with the city of Edessa. Although it is generally supposed that Edessa was not evangelized until the late second century, it is entirely possible that a Christian mission was established there in apostolic times. As G. A. Williamson remarks,

> It would, indeed, be surprising if Christianity, which spread over almost the whole Empire with such remarkable rapidity, should have been withheld from an area so near Palestine, and one where a similar dialect was spoken. Let us not forget that while Edessa is only 180 miles from Antioch, the starting-point of all Paul's journeys, Ephesus is 500, Rome over 1,000 and Spain 2,000.[11]

So, while the legends linking Thomas with Edessa are relatively late, the tradition is by no means incredible, and, importantly, we know of no other location where there might have been Thomas Christians at odds with John's community.

John apparently composed the Doubting Thomas story to belittle a faith he considered too reliant on—and boastful of—the Shroud. We can deduce from this that the cloth was in Edessa at the time John wrote, toward the end of the first century. Following the near-catastrophe of Paul's Damascus raid, there would have been every incentive to move it on again immediately, beyond the furthest reach of the Jerusalem priesthood. Since there is no evidence that the Shroud was ever kept anywhere else in the region, it is reasonable to think that it was taken to Edessa straight from Damascus. This is supported by a late-fourth-century source, the *Doctrine of Addai*, which dates the evangelization of Edessa to around AD 33, the likely year of Paul's conversion.[12]

The New Testament, unfortunately, tells us nothing about Christianity's arrival in Edessa. For information on this episode we have to turn to the legends about the adoption of Christianity by King Abgar, who ruled Edessa from AD 13–50.[13] Having inferred the early evangelization of Edessa from the story of Doubting Thomas, we may take these legends to be rooted in history. Written down relatively late and crammed full of improbabilities, they have to be interpreted very carefully—there are all sorts of ways in which they can mislead us, if we are not on our guard—but the difficulties are hardly greater than those regarding the interpretation of the Gospels, which scholars regularly treat as historical sources.

The earliest known version of the Abgar legend is that recorded by Eusebius toward the beginning of the fourth century.[14] It is a Greek translation of a lengthy document in Syriac, which was available for study, Eusebius tells us, in the Record Office of Edessa. According to this source, Edessa was evangelized at the time of King Abgar by Thaddeus, one of the twelve disciples, in fulfillment of a promise made to Abgar by Jesus himself. Abgar had sent a letter to Jesus while he was still alive, requesting that he come and heal him from a terrible disease. Jesus replied that he was too busy with the work of Salvation, but that, after his Ascension, he would send one of his disciples to "bring life" to him and his city. In the event, Thaddeus was sent to Edessa by "Judas, also known as Thomas," which explains why Thomas was considered the founder of the church in that city.

Strangely, the text makes no mention of any miraculous cloth or image of Christ, which has led some to conclude that no such image existed at this date. But the omission is better explained by the Shroud having been lost and forgotten by then, only to be rediscovered in the mid sixth century. As we have seen, it was probably hidden in a niche above Edessa's west gate.[15]

The second oldest rendition of the Abgar story occurs in the *Doctrine of Addai*. This version is basically the same as that recorded by Eusebius, but it contains a good deal of extra material not found in the earlier work (some invented, some traditional). The hero of the tale, the disciple who brings Christianity to Edessa, is here called Addai (a Syriac corruption of Thaddeus). He is sent to the city by Judas Thomas and arrives soon after the Ascension. Before his arrival, however, we hear of a peculiar incident involving Abgar's messenger to Jesus, a man called Hannan:

When Hannan, the keeper of the archives, saw that Jesus spake thus to him, by virtue of being the king's painter, he took and painted a likeness of Jesus with choice paints, and brought it with him to Abgar the king, his master. And when Abgar the king saw the likeness, he received it with great joy, and placed it with great honor in one of his palatial houses.[16]

The notion of an authentic portrait of Jesus was unusual in the fourth century and probably represents a garbled folk-memory of the Mandylion.[17] The author of the passage cannot have had direct knowledge of the cloth, because he describes the image as having been made with "choice paints," whereas eyewitnesses of the Mandylion were very insistent that, whatever it was, it was not a painting.[18] The *Doctrine of Addai* provides evidence, then, not only that the Shroud came to Edessa in the reign of King Abgar, but also that it was only dimly remembered by the fourth century.

The surest sign that the Abgar legends have a historical basis is that the names of those involved match those of the Damascus apostles mentioned in Acts, who are likely to have been responsible for conveying the Shroud from Damascus to Edessa. "Judas, also known as Thomas," who sends Thaddeus to Edessa, corresponds to Judas, the likely guardian of the Shroud in Damascus. (Thomas is not a real name but the Aramaic for "twin"; it was a nickname Judas acquired, probably due to his close association with the Shroud.)[19] "Hannan," meanwhile, the name of the man who delivers a "likeness of Jesus" to King Abgar in the *Doctrine of Addai*, is the Syriac form of "Ananias"—the name of the apostle who baptized Paul. This double coincidence cannot be ignored: only two Damascus apostles are named in Acts and they both turn up as principal characters in the Abgar legends. Thaddeus may be a third apostle omitted from the Acts narrative or, more probably, a confused double of Judas Thomas.[20] Either way, the transport of the Shroud to Edessa soon after the conversion of Paul—in 33, according to the chronology given in the *Doctrine of Addai*—can now be considered a historical likelihood.

In addition to narrating the story of Doubting Thomas, John tells us of the *soudarion* found in Jesus' tomb. This is best understood, as I have explained, as a reference to the Mandylion, indicating that the Shroud was transformed into the Mandylion sometime during the first century. The reason must have been cultic. Previously, the Shroud would have been kept in a relatively humble chest or jar and would have been seen only occasionally.[21] Framed as the Mandylion, the cloth's facial image was put on permanent display (for those allowed into its presence) and honored by being encased in gold, like many a church icon since. But the full image was lost to view. The creation of the Mandylion thus signals a dramatic shift in the use and perception of the Shroud.

The possibility that the cloth was turned into the Mandylion almost as soon as it arrived in Edessa can be discounted.[22] There are signs, such as John's tale of Doubting Thomas, with its emphasis on witnessing the wounds in Christ's hands and side, that the entire image remained visible for a period of decades. This might be thought to conflict with Paul's statement that the Risen Christ appeared to him "last of all," but the conflict is only apparent. Paul does not say that he was the last person to see the Risen Christ, but that he was *the last of all the apostles* to see the Risen Christ.[23] Witnessing the Shroud was necessary but not sufficient to become an apostle: you also had to be "sent out" by the leaders of the Church—that is what *apostolos* ("envoy") means. Those who were not commissioned to preach by the leaders of the Church were not apostles, even if they had seen the Risen Christ. (The More-than-500, for example, were not apostles.) This helped the Church leaders in Jerusalem control the preaching of the gospel, since the apostles were recognized as authoritative bearers of the one true gospel. That is why Paul insisted on his apostolic status, even though his ideas were in some respects controversial. The title gave him authority in his disputes with opponents.

When the Shroud was taken to Edessa, hundreds of miles north of Jerusalem, it was no longer used to recruit apostles. People there may well have been shown the cloth, but that did not make them envoys of the Church. Unlike those who were shown the Shroud in Judaea, Samaria and Galilee, they were not part of the apostolic campaign led by Peter.[24] The swift conveyance of the Shroud to Edessa thus helps explain the apparent cessation of the Resurrection appearances, as implied by Paul's recitation of the First Creed. It was not that the Risen Christ ceased to be seen immediately after Paul's conversion, but that later witnesses were not appointed apostles.

In time, the fact that no new apostles were being appointed led to a general assumption among Christians everywhere that the Risen Jesus had ceased to manifest himself. He began to be seen by the majority of Christians as a person encountered by the apostles in the past, rather than as a continuing presence on earth. The First Creed, which focused attention on a series of historical appearances, may have fostered this view.

Meanwhile, there arose the mistaken idea that the Resurrection had been a physical, flesh-and-blood revivification. The apostles were powerless to dispel this growing misconception. Paul did his best to explain the original, spiritual conception in his first letter to the Corinthians, but he was fighting a losing battle. With the Shroud out of the way, the memory of the apostolic testimony receding and the number of eyewitnesses decreasing relative to the number of converts, the Christian proclamation inevitably became confused.

The shift from a spiritual understanding of the Resurrection to a fleshly interpretation—clearly visible in the contrast between Paul's testimony and the Gospel stories—is one of the most important developments in the history of Christian thought. It occurred because the idea of the spiritual body, based on the Shroud, was simply too difficult to communicate. It is an idea that is only really comprehensible—or conceivable—in light of the Shroud. This explains the difficulty rank-and-file first-century Christians had in understanding the apostolic view of the Resurrection. The idea of a corpse coming back to life was, by contrast, straightforward and familiar, so that is how converts tended to conceive the Risen Jesus. Gradually, the founders of the Church lost control of the resurrection language they had unleashed. Early Christian story-tellers may even have invented the tradition of the empty tomb by the time Paul wrote 1 Corinthians. And when the Shroud became the Mandylion, permanently hiding Christ's spiritual body from view, the idea of a fleshly resurrection would have become unstoppable.

The effective disappearance of the Shroud in Edessa also helps explain why the references to it in the Gospels are so elliptical. Partly, this is because the original authors of the Easter narratives focused on the animated figure, viewed either as an angel or the Risen Jesus, transforming the cloth into clothing. Partly, it is because later Christians, who repeated the stories, were mostly unaware of the existence of the Shroud and did not realize that the Risen Jesus had been seen in his burial cloth. Hence, the allusions to the cloth in the Synoptic Gospels make it appear quite incidental. Only John had any awareness of the Shroud, but even he misunderstood its relation to the original story. By the end of the first century no one appreciated the full significance of the cloth, that whoever gazed at the *soudarion* was as much a witness of the Risen Jesus as the apostles themselves.

How can this have happened? Reflect that the Shroud could be seen either as a direct manifestation of the Risen Jesus or as an angelic intermediary, representing the Ascended Jesus. What seems to have happened in Edessa is that the angelic interpretation gradually prevailed. By the time John wrote, the image was no longer perceived by anyone as the Risen Jesus. It was viewed, instead, as his angel, his terrestrial avatar.[25]

But why would the Shroud's custodians in Edessa have lost sight of the idea of an encounter with the Risen Jesus, an experience accorded such value in the period immediately following Easter? One reason, no doubt, was that they were not missionaries, intent on spreading the gospel, and had time to dwell on the mysterious signification of the image, on its indeterminate relation to the Risen Christ. At the same time, converts in Edessa, as elsewhere, would have been liable to understand the Resurrection in fleshly terms. Initially, Judas and his companions would have maintained the apostolic understanding of the Shroud, but the cloth would rarely have been seen by anyone else, and the wider community may gradually have become confused about the Resurrection, like Paul's followers in Corinth. The Shroud certainly gave spiritual access to the Risen Jesus—but had not the apostles seen him resurrected in the flesh? Eventually, no one remained in the city to correct this misunderstanding, and even those permitted to see the Shroud began to misconstrue its significance, not realizing that it was all anyone had ever seen of the Risen Jesus.

PART 7

Conclusion

27

The Easter Shroud

We began this book by asking what sparked Christianity, and we can now provide a very simple, if surprising, answer: the Turin Shroud. Finding a peculiar image on the inner surface of his burial cloth, the followers of Jesus became convinced he had been raised from the dead and exalted to heaven. This belief led to the emergence of a new sect within Judaism— Christianity-to-be. The real founder of Christianity was not Peter or Paul or even Jesus, but the Shroud.

I have lived with this realization for seven years now, yet I still find myself wondering occasionally whether it can really be true. The Shroud is an utterly surreal object, dismissed by the world at large as nothing but a medieval folly. Taking it seriously and allowing it to transform your understanding of 2,000 years of human history is a deeply unnerving experience, almost like a religious conversion. Short of joining a cult, it is hard to imagine a more radical departure from the intellectual mainstream.

And what about the 1988 carbon-dating result? This is a question that keeps niggling, even after you have delved into it and discovered how easily the result is undermined. Faith in a scientific verdict supported by popular opinion is difficult to shake off. The temptation to abandon a "heretical" line of thought and simply accept what you have been told— and what everyone else believes—is extremely strong. It is not an impulse that affects only the religious.

Because of the feelings of risk and unreality involved in accepting the Shroud theory, it is vital to be clear about its advantages as a historical explanation. We need to remind ourselves of the key reasons to accept the theory and reassure ourselves that, judged by all standard criteria, it deserves to be believed.

In recent years scholars have emphasized the Jewish context in which Christianity arose. Today, we see Easter as the start of Christianity, but from the perspective of the Resurrection witnesses themselves it heralded the climax of more than a millennium of sacred and not-so-sacred history. It was a turning-point, a happening in the midst of Jewish history, rather than an origin. To have had the impact it did, the Easter phenomenon must have been both spectacularly novel and profoundly Jewish.

The Shroud fits the bill perfectly. As an unprecedented, complex *acheiropoietos* (an image "not made by hand"), it crashed into Jewish history from the outside, as it were, disrupting the regular worldview of its discoverers. But it also represented, in the most paradoxical way imaginable, a Jewish king, and, to be made comprehensible in that time and place, it had to be interpreted in terms of Jewish texts and symbols. The Shroud thus became, for its devotees, a new focus of religious thought, like the Temple, the Land and the Torah. The entire Story of Israel, from Adam and Eve, through Abraham, Moses, Joshua and David, down to Jesus himself, came to be seen through the prism of the Shroud. That is how Christianity could be fully Jewish in origin, yet at the same time diverge so radically from regular Judaism that it eventually went its own, separate way.

Resurrection was a concept already dear to many first-century Jews (manifested, for example, in the preservation of lifeblood when washing a wounded corpse) and was associated, in particular, with martyrdom. As natural animists, the followers of Jesus would have interpreted his reflection in the Shroud as his living re-embodiment, or as a sign thereof, and would have categorized it as a resurrection. Reading the prophets on the subject, especially Jonah and Daniel, they would have been assured that this interpretation was correct. Given the instinctive perception of images as alive and the widespread belief in resurrection among first-century Jews, it is safe to say that the discovery of the Shroud would have been sufficient to prompt belief in the Resurrection.

The history of Easter begins on Good Friday with the entombment of Jesus, an event recorded in the First Creed. The Synoptic Gospels all say that the body was wrapped in a linen sheet, the customary *sovev* (or shroud), and Mark and Luke imply that the burial was left unfinished. The stage was set for the creation of the Shroud-image. A mythical account of its appearance is preserved in the *Gospel of Peter* and is echoed in various other texts, as well, such as the story of the Ascension in Acts.

On the Sunday morning Mary Magdalene and her female companions went to the tomb to complete the burial and discovered the image on the burial cloth. We can be sure that the female tomb-stories are basically historical, because women would not have been made the protagonists in an apologetic fiction. Nor would the Shroud have been preserved if the burial had been completed on Good Friday. We do not have to believe, however, in the unlikely circumstance of an empty tomb. Unattested in the First Creed and unnecessary for belief in the Resurrection, the idea that the body of Jesus disappeared is best understood as a late invention, a motif added to the tomb-stories to comply with the later belief in a flesh-and-blood Resurrection.

As originally told, the stories were about the women meeting with angels and/or the Risen Jesus. The angels recall the Shroud in several ways: their white or bright clothing, their location in or at the tomb, their announcement of the Resurrection, and their numerical ambiguity (one or two?). Tellingly, the angels are interchangeable with the figure of the Risen Christ, as we would expect, if they and the Risen Christ were different aspects or interpretations of the same curious spectacle. Just as suggestive is Mary Magdalene's initial inability to recognize Jesus, a theme echoed in other Resurrection narratives. Catching the likeness of Jesus in the Shroud would have been difficult even for his closest friends and relatives.

The decision to represent the Shroud figure as the Risen Jesus amounts to a significant claim on behalf of the women, chief among them Mary Magdalene: that they were the primary witnesses of the Resurrection. This claim directly contradicts the testimony of the First Creed, which omits to mention an appearance to the women and presents Peter as the first to see the Risen Jesus. This refers to Peter's visit to the tomb soon after the women. Luke and John both tell of Peter witnessing the burial linen, i.e. the Shroud. Recognizing the matriarchal agenda underlying the Resurrection narratives in the Gospels, we can see why this incident is not presented as an appearance-story. Peter is deliberately portrayed as uncomprehending.

The one appearance recorded in both the First Creed and the Gospels is that to the Twelve. This can be reconstructed on the basis of the Jerusalem Tradition, which is not only the best-attested appearance-story but also accounts for the institution of the Lord's Supper, the original form of Sunday worship. The Jerusalem Tradition makes excellent sense in relation to the Shroud. Having removed the Shroud from the sepulchre in the morning, Peter must have shown it to his colleagues at the first available opportunity. The description of the Risen Christ appearing suddenly within the locked chamber, the intense focus on his wounds and the admission in Luke that the witnesses thought he was a spirit all support the contention that he was seen in the Shroud. And the difficulty people would have had in identifying the Shroud figure is reflected in the disciples' initial failure to believe that it was really Jesus (a failing displaced by John onto the figure of Doubting Thomas).

With the help of the Shroud, we can reconstruct the events of Easter Day more confidently than ever before, as the story of the discovery of a certified marvel.

Once Easter is recognized as the moment of the Shroud's discovery, the subsequent course of events seems, in retrospect, almost predictable.

The Shroud would undoubtedly have had a huge psychological impact on the followers of Jesus. To recall Theodor Keim's analogy, it would have been like receiving a "telegram from heaven." As the recipients of such a message, it would have been extraordinary if Mary and Peter and their companions had *not* taken heart and preached about Jesus and the Resurrection. If, after his brutal ordeal at the hands of the Romans, Jesus had been raised from the dead in a glorious, ethereal form, what was there to fear? If they were martyred for the same cause themselves, would God not treat them similarly? The Shroud makes the new-found courage of Jesus' followers after the Crucifixion completely understandable.

Meanwhile, it seems, they started to interpret the cloth "in accordance with the scriptures," leading them to identify Jesus with cosmic figures, such as the Son of Man and the Suffering Servant. A creative reader perusing the Hebrew scriptures with the Shroud in mind can find references to it all over the place—hence many of the "Old Testament" prophecies cited in the New Testament. We do not know when any particular identification was made, but we can be sure the process of scriptural interpretation began almost immediately, since this would have been the only means of understanding the Shroud as a meaningful sign.

Of all the titles posthumously awarded to Jesus, the most significant is the Messiah (or Christ). By rights, a man crucified to death by a Roman governor should never have been hailed subsequently as an all-conquering king. The Shroud turned this symbol of Jewish nationalism on its head. It showed Jesus exalted to a new level of existence, still bearing the marks of his crucifixion and, crucially, the crown of thorns. There could be no clearer sign that the judgment of the world had been overturned, that Jesus' royal status was recognized by Yahweh. The spiritual appearance of the Shroud further bolstered this idea, since it looked as if Jesus had been drenched in the Holy Spirit, conceived as a divine liquid. He had been simultaneously raised and anointed by God.

The Gospel evidence peters out after Easter Day, except for the unreliable Galilee Tradition. The First Creed, however, speaks of a further series of appearances after Easter: to more than 500 brethren, to James, and to all the apostles. Unlike any other Resurrection theory, the Shroud theory can account for these reports easily.

The appearance to the More-than-500 can be understood as a public display of the Shroud to the wider community of Jesus' followers. This must have been the occasion of the first proclamation of the gospel, the inauguration of a new Messianic sect—the Nazarenes—on a collision course with the Jerusalem authorities. The subsequent appearance to James, it seems, was a private ceremony, at which Jesus' brother was initiated into the sect and appointed its new leader by being shown the Shroud. Then, following the expulsion of the Nazarenes from Jerusalem and the outbreak of the "great persecution" led by the youthful Paul, it was decided to create apostles, emissaries who could win support for the Church and warn Israel (and sympathetic Gentiles) of the impending *parousia*. To be effective, these apostles had to be eyewitnesses of the Risen Christ, so they were each shown the Shroud. The Galilee Tradition hints that many of these apostles were initiated in Galilee, where the Shroud was taken for safe keeping, a mission led by Peter.

The "forgotten appearances" of the First Creed can thus be understood as rational steps in an unfolding historical process, rather than ignored as an unlikely series of miracles, hallucinations, or intuitions.

The removal of the Shroud from Jerusalem to Galilee paves the way for the conversion of Paul, the one eyewitness of the Risen Christ whose testimony we still possess. Paul's words suggest strongly that what he saw was the Shroud. In particular, his detailed description of the risen body in 1 Corinthians provides us with an authoritative "photo-fit" of the Risen Jesus that matches the Shroud figure extremely well. Paul's remarks about a visual revelation of God's Son both to him and within him are equally understandable as reflective references to a viewing of the Shroud. The account of Paul's conversion in Acts gives a rather different impression, but, when the narrative is analyzed in terms of its biblical sources, it is easy to see how it grew from an original tale about Paul stumbling on the cloth treasure of the Nazarenes.

The conversion of Paul is the single most striking proof of the reality of the Resurrection phenomenon. Surely, only an "objective vision" as startling and incontestable as the Shroud could have transformed such a rabid inquisitor into a fervent heretic overnight. As a genuine, awe-inspiring marvel, the Shroud has an extraordinary capacity to change people's minds.

The Risen Christ appeared to Paul at Damascus, it seems, because the Shroud had been moved on from Galilee for safety's sake. Following his conversion, it had to be moved on again. The New Testament gives no clue as to where it went, but later Syriac legends imply that it was taken straight to Edessa, then under the rule of King Abgar. Significantly, these legends attribute the evangelization of Edessa to two men, Judas (Thomas) and Ananias, whose names match those of Paul's Damascus associates. And one early text, the *Doctrine of Addai*, implies a date for the episode corresponding to the likely year of Paul's conversion, 33.

The Shroud's flight to Edessa also explains the apparent cessation of the Resurrection appearances. Paul says he was the last apostle to see the Risen Christ, but non-apostles could have viewed the Shroud afterward, without contradicting Paul's testimony. The First Creed was probably devised before 33 and so ends with the appearances to the apostles; any further appearances that took place in Edessa would not have been recorded. In any case, after a while the interpretation of the Shroud changed, as people increasingly imagined the Risen Jesus as a physical being of flesh and blood. The Shroud came to be seen exclusively as an angelic double of the Ascended Jesus. Eventually, the transformation of the Shroud into the Mandylion put paid to any lingering idea of witnessing the Risen Jesus. The *soudarion*, as it was called, could still inspire faith in the Resurrection, but it was now just an iconic sign.

Fortunately for the Church, the disappearance of the Risen Christ did not impede the spread of Christianity. The success of the gospel was founded on the quantity and quality of the eyewitness testimony, based on the Shroud's appearances in the first few years of its existence, a brief, intense period of "revelation." By the time the Shroud was spirited away to Edessa it may have been seen by 600 people or more, who, having all witnessed the same image, were able to give consistent accounts of the Risen Jesus. The reason Christianity became an influential faith, rather than a temporary, irrelevant enthusiasm, was that it involved the proclamation of a real, observable phenomenon by hundreds of credible eyewitnesses. The Shroud makes the rise of Christianity comprehensible, because it provides the necessary, empirical basis for the communal testimony to the Resurrection.

At the same time as enabling us to reconstruct the history of the Resurrection, the Shroud illuminates the way the events came to be told in the Gospels.

The initial proclamation of the gospel was very well organized, all the apostles speaking with same voice—witness the First Creed. Nevertheless, there appear to have been tensions and disagreements from the outset.

Mary Magdalene seems to have fallen out swiftly with Peter and the Twelve over the issue of the Shroud's discovery. They refused to acknowledge her as the first witness of the Resurrection, and, in retaliation, she told the story of Easter Day in a way that boosted her authority and reflected badly on them. Paul's mission to the Gentiles and his abrogation of Jewish law caused further tensions in the following decades. The authority of the Jerusalem Church was far from absolute, and, as its flock expanded, it could not even control its core doctrine.

We can first detect confusion regarding the nature of the Resurrection among Paul's Corinthian followers. Familiar with the concept of physical revival, this is how some of them, at least, interpreted the promise of a future resurrection. They were evidently disturbed when the dead bodies of fellow believers decomposed and, recognizing the impossibility of their ever being reassembled, began denying the future resurrection of the dead. (They did not need to deny the Resurrection of Jesus, since he rose "on the third day," when his body was still intact.) Paul tried to explain to them that they would rise, like Christ, in a completely new, spiritual body, but the idea that resurrection involved returning to life "in the flesh" was deeply entrenched. Gradually, the apostolic understanding of the Resurrection expounded by Paul gave way to the physical interpretation promoted in the Gospels.

The triumph of the false notion of the flesh-and-blood Resurrection was assured by the decimation of the Jerusalem Church in the 60s. First, there was the judicial murder of James in 62, which robbed Jewish Christianity of its figurehead. Then, four years later, the Jewish War erupted, culminating in the sack of Jerusalem in 70. A small band of Christians may have escaped the city, fleeing across the Jordan into the region of the Decapolis, but the hegemony of the Jerusalem Church was at an end.[1] Ecclesiastical authority now devolved to the leaders of the provincial churches established by Paul and the other apostles. Predominantly Gentile, these men and women had little or no understanding of the Resurrection as a new Creation and saw it instead as a revivification. This was the view enshrined in the Gospels.

Only in light of the Shroud is it possible to appreciate the historical complexity of the Resurrection stories in the Gospels. Underlying them all appears to be an original narrative dependent on Mary Magdalene. The Shroud was represented in this tradition as a living, speaking person, a device that has effectively masked its identity ever since. At the same time, the narrative was conceived as a retort to the First Creed, so that the reporting of events is deliberately unbalanced. As this polemical story was disseminated abroad, others felt free to amend it as they wished. Those who believed in a fleshly Resurrection added the disappearance of the corpse to the tomb-stories and introduced physical elements into the appearance-stories—Luke's account of the Risen Jesus eating fish, for example. Those who disliked the negative portrayal of the male disciples edited it accordingly. One writer, John, even managed to turn the original attack on the Twelve into criticism of the Thomas Christians of Edessa, for basing their faith on the Shroud. He had no idea that his own faith rested ultimately on the same piece of cloth.

By the end of the first century, then, the stories told about the Resurrection had become little more than misunderstood legends. We can now trace the development of these legends, peeling back the various layers of distortion and incomprehension. This is as much a part of the Shroud theory as reconstructing the historical events they represent.

There can no longer be any serious doubt that the Shroud provides a viable solution to the age-old puzzle of the Resurrection. It explains the evidence in detail and presents an overall picture—covering the founding events of Christianity and the subsequent distortion of the original gospel—that is fully coherent. Moreover, it has five key virtues that, taken together, ensure it is preferable to any other theory so far proposed.

To begin with, the theory is naturalistic, making it inherently plausible and far simpler than theories that involve, in addition to natural causes, the alleged activity of God. Second, it is based on empirical evidence, unlike other Resurrection theories, which involve purely hypothetical phenomena said to have been witnessed or experienced by the apostles. The argument is also properly theoretical, being rooted in a basic finding of cultural anthropology, that people regularly attribute life and agency to inanimate objects, especially natural, anthropomorphic images such as shadows and reflections. In addition, the theory is extremely elegant, providing a single, integrated explanation for all the tomb-stories and appearance-stories, including the appearance to Paul. Finally, it has tremendous explanatory scope, accounting not only for the key evidence set out in Part 2, but also for the "escorted Resurrection-Ascension" narrated in the *Gospel of Peter*, the basic imagery of the Transfiguration, the recorded rivalry of Mary Magdalene and Peter, the *soudarion* mentioned by John, the identification of Jesus as the Son of Man, and the idea of the descent of the Holy Spirit. No other Resurrection theory can solve additional puzzles like these.

The Shroud theory has another major advantage: it takes account of the

Shroud. This might seem an odd thing to say, but, if the Shroud is an authentic relic of the burial of Jesus, as it would seem to be, it should be recognized as an essential historical source. Until now, it has been considered normal and acceptable for New Testament scholars to ignore the Shroud, but this attitude neither was nor is justified. The Shroud counts against any Resurrection theory that denies the basic historicity of the tomb-stories, since it proves that Jesus received an incomplete burial, that people subsequently visited his tomb and that his body was separated from its winding sheet within a matter of days. It undermines any theory involving body-theft, since thieves are unlikely to have snatched the body while leaving behind the cloth in which it was wrapped. And it disproves the "swoon theory," the idea that Jesus survived the Crucifixion, since the man enfolded in the Shroud was well and truly dead. Virtually all those involved in studying the Resurrection have assumed the relic to be irrelevant, thus blinding themselves to the most important evidence at their disposal.

The only apparent problem with the Shroud theory is the 1988 carbon dating. Skeptics, no doubt, will pin their colors to this rickety mast. I have shown why we should have no faith in this uncorroborated result, although it is impossible, as yet, to determine what might have gone wrong. One badly conducted scientific test proves nothing. As Oxford's Professor Ramsey insists, the 1988 carbon dating was far from definitive and needs to be reassessed in the context of a multidisciplinary research program.[2]

We can be reassured: the Shroud theory really does work.

The challenge that defeated Reimarus and his rationalist successors has finally been met: the birth of Christianity can be integrated, at long last, into a purely secular history of the world. Early Christian belief in the Resurrection can now be thoroughly explained without reference to a super-miracle.

In the early twentieth century the great German theologian Rudolf Bultmann famously argued that it would never be possible to discover what it was that sparked Christianity. This influential view was based, in part, on the sober realization that, given the nature of the written sources, New Testament scholarship was incapable of deducing the true nature of the Resurrection.[3] Bultmann was right about the limitations of New Testament scholarship, but he was wrong to think that the source of the Christian proclamation could never be known. It currently lies in a fire-proof case in Turin Cathedral—an old piece of linen cloth, on which appears the spectral likeness of a crucified man. Far from being a medieval fake, the Shroud of Turin is the very object that, twenty centuries ago, inspired belief in the Resurrection and gave birth to the new religion of Christianity. The Shroud, the most controversial image in the world, is nothing less than the image of the Risen Christ, the alpha and omega of all Christian history.

Timeline

THE HISTORY OF THE SHROUD AT A GLANCE

This timeline represents the history of the Shroud over the course of the last 2,000 years. The reconstruction of the first 1,000 years depends on Ian Wilson's theory that the Shroud and the Mandylion of Edessa were one and the same. Some of the early dates are approximate, the precise chronology having yet to be determined. Major turning-points in the Shroud's career are shown in bold. These events divide the cloth's history into the eight 'chapters' described on the right-hand side. Some major historical events relevant to the history of the Shroud are shown in italics.

2000 —

2010 – Most recent exhibition of the Shroud
2002 – Secret restoration of the Shroud
1988 – Carbon-dating test
1978 – STURP investigation

1931 – Second photographing of the Shroud (Enrie)

1900

1902 – First scientific investigation (Delage and Vignon)
1898 – First photographs taken of the Shroud (Pia)
1861 – Duke Victor Emmanuel II of Savoy accedes to the throne of Italy

THE GREAT ENIGMA
(1898–present): Since being photographed for the first time in 1898, the Shroud has become an object of intense curiosity and scientific scrutiny. It is now much more than just a religious relic.

1800

1700

1694 – Shroud installed in the new Chapel of the Holy Shroud

1600

1598 – Alfonso Paleotto publishes his study of the Shroud
1578 – Shroud transferred permanently to Turin
1532 – Shroud badly damaged in fire at Chambéry
1516 – Francis I of France visits Chambéry; Lierre copy painted

1500 —

1502 – Shroud housed permanently at Chambéry

1453 – Fall of Constantinople to the Turks

THE HOLY SHROUD
(1453–1898): Following the fall of Constantinople to the Turks in 1453, the new owners of the Shroud, the Savoys, are free to promote its cause. The Shroud is gradually accepted as a true relic of Christ's burial, although its provenance is forgotten. Housed in the Holy Chapel at Chambéry, it is almost destroyed in a fire and is later transferred to Turin. During this period the complete image becomes well known, reproduced via paintings and engravings, but the cloth itself is still rarely seen. It is displayed only occasionally to large crowds of pilgrims, to celebrate important state events.

1453 – **Margaret de Charny gives the Shroud to Duke**
Louis I of Savoy
1418 – Shroud given in care to Margaret de Charny and
Humbert de Villersexel

1400

1389 – Shroud displayed again at Lirey;
renewed controversy
1355/6 – **Shroud displayed at Lirey, causing controversy**

A DUBIOUS RELIC
(1355–1453): Over the course
of a century the Shroud's
owners, the de Charnys, try to
establish its reputation.

THE LOOTED TREASURE
(1204–1355): Stolen from
Constantinople in 1204, the
Shroud goes missing for a
century and a half. It
eventually reappears in the
French village of Lirey.

1300

1203–4 – **Fourth Crusade; Shroud seen in Constantinople**
by Robert de Clari

1200

1192–5 – Creation of the Pray Codex
1171 – "Sindon" seen in Constantinople by William of Tyre

THE SECRET SINDON
(944–1204): Extorted from
Edessa by a Byzantine army,
in 944 the Mandylion is
brought to Constantinople,
where it is paraded in
triumph and viewed by
members of the imperial
court. Thereafter, it is kept
hidden away in the Pharos
Chapel. The true nature of
the cloth becomes known to
the city's elite but is kept a
secret; officially, the
Mandylion and the Sindon
are two separate relics.

1100

1092 – Letter mentioning relics of Christ's "burial cloths"
belonging to the Byzantine emperor

1000 –

958 – First mention of the "Sindon" in the Pharos Chapel
944 – **Shroud/Mandylion transferred to Constantinople**

900

THE MANDYLION
(c.550–944): The Shroud is
rediscovered in Edessa, in
the form of the Mandylion,
when the city-walls are rebuilt
in the mid sixth century. It
rapidly becomes one of the
most famous relics in
Christendom, and for nearly
500 years it is Edessa's
principal treasure. It is
associated with the lost
portrait of Christ made for
King Abgar and is generally
understood to be a
miraculous imprint of
Christ's face bestowed on a
linen towel. It is kept locked
away in a shrine, and few
people ever have the
opportunity to see it
unfolded.

800

730 – John Damascene refers to the Mandylion as a
"himation" (cloak)

700

639 – *Muslim conquest of Edessa*

600

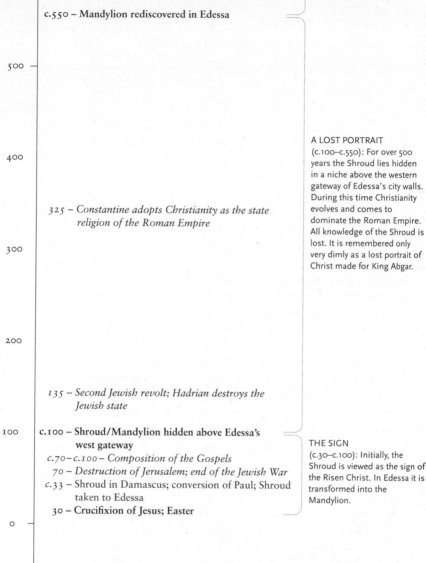

c.550 – Mandylion rediscovered in Edessa

500 –

400

A LOST PORTRAIT
(c.100–c.550): For over 500
years the Shroud lies hidden
in a niche above the western
gateway of Edessa's city walls.
During this time Christianity
evolves and comes to
dominate the Roman Empire.
All knowledge of the Shroud is
lost. It is remembered only
very dimly as a lost portrait of
Christ made for King Abgar.

*325 – Constantine adopts Christianity as the state
religion of the Roman Empire*

300

200

*135 – Second Jewish revolt; Hadrian destroys the
Jewish state*

100 – **c.100 – Shroud/Mandylion hidden above Edessa's
west gateway**
c.70–c.100 – Composition of the Gospels
70 – Destruction of Jerusalem; end of the Jewish War
*c.33 – Shroud in Damascus; conversion of Paul; Shroud
taken to Edessa*
30 – Crucifixion of Jesus; Easter

THE SIGN
(c.30–c.100): Initially, the
Shroud is viewed as the sign of
the Risen Christ. In Edessa it is
transformed into the
Mandylion.

0 –

Acknowledgments

The Shroud of Turin may now be a very public image, but it is also a very intimate relic, the burial cloth of a cruelly executed man. I have barely spoken of the historical Jesus in this book, since the history I describe starts immediately after his death, but all of us, I think, whether Christian or not, should acknowledge the dignity and sacrifice of the person laid to rest in the cloth. First and foremost, the Shroud is his memorial.

The Shroud may have been dismissed by the world at large as a religious fraud, but, fortunately, it has not been without its champions. My own understanding of the cloth rests on more than a century of research conducted by independent-minded scholars and scientists, whose labors have been completely disregarded (and even ridiculed) by the intellectual mainstream. I wish to pay tribute, in particular, to Yves Delage and Paul Vignon, the founders of sindonology; Pierre Barbet, the original "doctor at Calvary"; John Jackson, the leading light of the STURP campaign; Ray Rogers, the most rigorous and insightful of the STURP scientists; and Ian Wilson, the pre-eminent historian of the Shroud. Without the curiosity, dedication and determination of these men—and other men and women like them—we would know virtually nothing about the world's most influential object. Although we have never met, Ian Wilson has kindly provided me with information via e-mail, as have Nicholas Allen and Mark Guscin, both of whom have made significant contributions to the study of the Shroud. And I must also acknowledge the work of John Loken, who was the first to draw attention to the potential significance of the Shroud as a sign of the Risen Jesus.

Like most people, I was entirely ignorant about the Shroud when, in 2002, I joined a postdoctoral study-group at King's College, Cambridge, set up to encourage interdisciplinary approaches in the humanities. The Description Project, as it was called, proved quite a challenge; finding common ground among classicists, anthropologists, historians, art historians and students of literature was far from easy, but our discussions were always lively and thought-provoking, and it was as a direct result of ideas encountered in this forum that I had the crucial insight about the Shroud that led eventually to the writing of this book. I would like to thank Simon

Goldhill, the originator of the Description Project, and my fellow "describers," particularly Soumhya Venkatesan and Andy Merrills, for their stimulating company over the course of four years. I only wish I had been able to discuss the Shroud with them—it would have been the perfect topic for one of our contentious gatherings!

From 2004 to 2006 I held an Early Career Fellowship at King's, funded by the Leverhulme and Newton Trusts. This gave me the opportunity to start thinking seriously about the Shroud, while still pursuing a career as an art historian, and I am extremely grateful to my academic mentors, Joanna Cannon, Paul Binski and Paul Hills, for helping me secure this fellowship. Again, I would have loved to have discussed with them my extra-curricular work on the Shroud, but the need for secrecy dictated otherwise.

Due to the extreme sensitivity of the subject, I knew from the outset that I would have to keep my theory quiet until it was ready to be published. Friends and colleagues were kept in the dark. Over the course of the last seven years, only a handful of people have known of my interest in the Resurrection and the Shroud, and I therefore have relatively few people to thank for their direct involvement in the project. By the same token, I am more indebted than most authors to those upon whom I have relied for advice and help.

At an early stage, when the theory was still relatively unformed, I sought advice from Andrew Chapman, Virginia Brilliant, and Alexander and Graham Greene, all of whom were extremely helpful. Then, in 2006, I had the tremendous good fortune to be put in touch with one of the doyennes of British publishing, Philippa Harrison, at Ed Victor Ltd. It would be difficult to overstate Philippa's importance to this project. Over the course of the last six years, she has guided me through the labyrinthine process of transforming a bright idea into a readable book, encouraged and advised me at every turn, edited innumerable chapter drafts, and kindly volunteered to act as my agent. Rarely can an author have received such invaluable support. My debt to Philippa is immense; it is largely thanks to her that this book has seen the light of day.

I am also fortunate that, when the time came to approach a publisher, Tom Weldon, chief executive of Penguin Books U.K., had the courage and foresight to take on such a difficult, unorthodox project. I am grateful to him and to my editor at Viking, Joel Rickett, whose trusty red pen has greatly improved the rather unwieldy manuscript I handed him last year and who has supervised the book's publication with great skill and consideration. I also thank Brian Tart at Penguin Group (U.S.A.) Inc. for his editorial comments, Trevor Horwood for his meticulous copy-editing of the text and Gesche Ipsen for sourcing the illustrations.

Working alone for years on a deeply controversial topic is not easy, and it would have been impossible without the support of friends and family. To those who have been wondering what on earth I could be doing, thank you for being patient—and I hope it was worth the wait! Finding the words to express my gratitude to my family is difficult. My mother, brother and sister, whose faith in me and my strange ideas has never wavered, gave me the strength to embark on the project in the first place, and their keen interest in it has buoyed me along. Knowing they were behind me made everything so much easier, and I am deeply grateful to all of them for reading and commenting on the manuscript. I also thank my sister for preparing the excellent maps and helping me with the diagrams.

My partner, Mousumi, has been my mainstay throughout. When I first told her of my crazy idea in the summer of 2004, she can hardly have imagined where it would take us or how long and arduous the voyage would be. Yet she never questioned my decision to set sail and has always been there to lend me assistance—and an editor's eye. Without her constant love and support I would have struggled to complete the task; and without her irrepressible sense of humor, undertaking it would have been a lot less fun. I am more grateful to her than I can say.

Notes

1 The Resurrection

1. Tacitus, *Annals*, 15.44 (1996, p. 365).
2. The earliest Christian documents are Paul's letters, written in the 50s, but Paul nowhere discusses the activity of the mortal Jesus. The earliest non-Christian references to Jesus are found in Josephus's *Antiquities of the Jews*, written two generations after the Crucifixion. For these references see below, ch. 5, nn. 10, and 3, respectively.
3. Acts 1.8.
4. Acts 2.32.
5. 1 Corinthians 15.14.
6. Romans 1.4.
7. Matthew 28.17.
8. Matthew 28.13.
9. See Crafer 1913–14, pp. 506–7; Evangeliou 1992.
10. Cited in Hoffmann 1987, p. 86.
11. Tertullian, *The Body of Christ*, 5 (1956, p. 19).
12. It is estimated, for instance, that 70 percent of *The True Doctrine* by Celsus survives in quotation in Origen's counterblast, *Against Celsus* (see Hoffmann 1987, pp. 44–5).
13. On the nineteenth-century "death of God," see Wilson 1999.
14. Reimarus 1970, pp. 239–69. See also Dawes 2000, pp. 54–86.
15. The "swoon theory" was first propounded by Karl Bahrdt, c.1780, followed by Heinrich Paulus and Karl Venturini. For convenient summaries of these writers' reconstructions of the Resurrection episode, see Schweitzer 2000, pp. 41–2, 44–5, 52–3.
16. Strauss 1865, vol. 1, p. 412.
17. See Strauss 1846, vol. 3, pp. 359–74, and, more emphatically, Strauss 1865, vol. 1, pp. 412–29. In the seventeenth century Spinoza held the appearances to be subjective visions inspired by God (see Keim 1883, p. 332). For recent interest in the "subjective vision" theory, see Habermas 2006, p. 83; Habermas 2001.
18. See Keim 1883, vol. 6, p. 364. Volume 6 of the German edition, in which this argument was made, was published in 1873. According to Lüdemann 1994, p. 212 n. 255, the "objective vision" theory was first discussed by Weisse in 1838, although Weisse remained agnostic as to whether the "visions" were objective or subjective.
19. See, e.g., Freeman 2009, pp. 32–4.

20. For surveys of these and other theories, see Wright 2003, pp. 697–706; Habermas and Licona 2004, pp. 81–131; Allison 2005, pp. 201–13, 269–311; Habermas 2006.

21. For early Christianity as a diffuse social movement, see Mack 2001. For the idea of the Resurrection as a Christ-Myth based on pagan precedents, see, e.g., Freke and Gandy 2003; Doherty 2005. The idea of the Christ-Myth goes back to Bruno Bauer in the nineteenth century (see Beilby and Eddy 2010, p. 17).

22. Cf. Lüdemann 1994, p. 14: "It is indeed a shame that as a result of the artificial division into Christian and non-Christian sources, hardly any ancient historian (or even classical philologist), outsiders apart, has adopted any position on the resurrection of Jesus."

23. Thus, for instance, Willi Marxsen held that, although Peter and the disciples evidently experienced something in the wake of Jesus' death, a lack of evidence makes it impossible to know the nature of their experiences (see Marxsen 1970), while Edward Schillebeeckx maintained that the disciples felt an extraordinary sense of grace and forgiveness following the Crucifixion, a spiritual experience that later gave rise to tales of "seeing" the Risen Jesus (see Schillebeeckx 1979, pp. 379–97).

24. See Habermas 2006.

25. Wright 2003, pp. 706–7.

26. Ibid., p. 718. For a succinct critique of Wright's argument, see Allison 2005, pp. 345–50.

27. To date, the fullest counter to Wright's argument of which I am aware is Carrier 2005a. This is in a collection of essays about the Resurrection all written from a rationalist point of view (Price and Lowder 2005). Impressive as it is, this multi-authored volume exemplifies the disjointed nature of the current case against the idea of the Resurrection.

28. Freeman 2009, p. 39. Cf. MacCulloch 2009, p. 95: "Historians are never going to make sense of these reports . . ."

2 The Shroud of Turin

1. The Shroud is currently kept in a fire-proof case in the north transept of the cathedral, while the Royal Chapel is being renovated following a fire in 1997, started by an unknown arsonist (see Wilson 1998, pp. 1–3).

2. John 19.34.

3. See Wilson 1998, pp. 64–6.

4. For the ivory color of the cloth when seen in natural light, see Walsh 1964, p. 6; Wilson 2010, p. 6. For the bleaching of cloth, see Rogers 2008, pp. 18, 35, 99.

5. For the best hypothesis concerning the formation of the Shroud-image, not yet proven, see Chapter 12. For effective criticism of the many attempts to produce artistic replicas of the Shroud-image, see Antonacci 2000, pp. 73–96.

6. I ignore the implausible claim that the Shroud was mocked up in the late fifteenth century by Leonardo da Vinci. For variations on this idea, see, e.g.,

Picknett and Prince 1994 and Haziel 2005. For a useful refutation, see Antonacci 2000, pp. 84–93.

7. For a chronological digest of historical events relevant to the history of the Shroud, see Wilson 1998, pp. 263–313. For the documentation, see Chevalier 1900. An English translation of the report written by Bishop Pierre d'Arcis at the end of 1389 is published in Wilson 1978, pp. 230–35.

8. See below, pp. 181–3, for the testimony of Pierre d'Arcis.

9. For the *Très Riches Heures*, see Lognon and Cazelles 1969. The connection between Jean Colombe's miniature of the "Man of Sorrows" and the Shroud-image is pointed out in Wilson 1998, p. 284.

10. In 1467 Cardinal Francesco della Rovere (later Pope Sixtus IV) wrote that on the Shroud was "the image of Jesus Christ traced in his very blood" (quoted in Wilson 1998, p. 283). Similar statements affirming the authenticity of the Shroud were made by Italian courtiers in 1494 and 1503, reflecting ecclesiastical approval of the relic (see ibid., pp. 285–6).

11. For brief accounts of the 1532 fire, see Wilson 1998, pp. 64–5; Walsh 1964, p. 30.

12. For the Chapel of the Holy Shroud, see Scott 2003.

13. See Chifflet 1624, pp. 145–50, and the comments on his work in Chevalier 1900, pp. 14–17. Chifflet's interpretation enabled the Gospel accounts to be harmonized and other cloth relics, such as the Holy Shroud of Besançon, to be deemed authentic as well.

14. Quoted in Wilson 1998, p. 292.

15. On Pia and the 1898 photography of the cloth, see Walsh 1964, pp. 10–21; Wilson 1978, pp. 13–18.

16. Quoted in Walsh 1964, p. 19.

17. For the claim of Bishop Pierre d'Arcis that the cloth had been found to be "cunningly painted," see Wilson 1978, p. 231. In opposition to d'Arcis, Geoffrey II de Charny maintained that it was genuine and had been generously given to his father, while Margaret de Charny testified that the cloth had been "won" by her grandfather (see Chevalier 1900, pp. 28 and 32 respectively). There is no reason to suppose from their actions that Geoffrey II and his daughter were not sincere in their belief that Geoffrey I had acquired the cloth, rather than commissioned it. For discussion of this evidence, see below, pp. 182–3.

18. Walsh 1964, p. 43.

19. See Delage 1902. For accounts of Delage's intervention, see Walsh 1964, pp. 47–8, 69–83; Wuenschel 1954, pp. 17–28; Wilson 2010, pp. 30–32.

20. See Wuenschel 1954, pp. 25–6; Walsh 1964, pp. 137–9.

21. Quoted and translated in Walsh 1964, pp. 80–81.

22. See Tylor 1903 and Frazer 1913 (first published in 1871 and 1890, respectively).

23. On Barbet, see Walsh 1964, pp. 103–16.

24. For a list of STURP's peer-reviewed publications, see: www.shroud.com/78papers.htm

25. As Belting 1998, p. 9, remarks, "Art historians dislike the Shroud." Attempts to say something meaningful about it are usually highly theoretical, drawing a veil over the embarrassing mystery of its origin.

26. The one art historian who has ventured any suggestion at all as to how the Shroud-image might have been produced artistically was Noemi Gabrielli, who wrote a report on the Shroud as part of the 1973 commission, prior to the STURP investigation. She reckoned that it was a Renaissance print of some sort and attributed it to a great unknown follower of Leonardo da Vinci, an interpretation that forced her to suppose that the present Shroud was substituted for the fourteenth-century Lirey one. This interpretation is untenable for numerous reasons, as will become clear throughout the course of my argument. Nicholas Allen, a South African art historian, has attempted to account for the Shroud as a medieval photograph, an idea I discuss below (see below, pp. 139–42).

27. Quoted in Meacham 2005, p. 99. Fr. Rinaldi, the source of the quote, observed that Ballestrero made this proclamation "almost gleefully."

28. For John Paul II's statement on the theory of evolution, see his Message to the Pontifical Academy of Sciences, delivered October 22, 1996, "Magisterium is concerned with question of evolution for it involves conception of man."

29. The Vatican itself remained silent, allowing headlines like "Vatican concedes Shroud is a fake" to pass unchallenged (headline quoted in Meacham 2005, p. 106).

30. Meacham 2005, p. ii. For a highly critical account of the "conservation" campaign, see ibid., pp. 147–236. For the chief conservator's view of the campaign, see Flury-Lemberg 2003.

31. Translated from a homily delivered in Turin Cathedral and published in a special edition of the local Turinese newspaper, *La Voce del Popolo*, April 10—May 23, 2010, p. 3.

32. Cf. John 19.34.

33. As quoted in Wilson 2010, p. 284, who reports the effect of John Paul's veneration of the Shroud and the words of his homily as follows: "The many photos of the Pope, in simple white, praying on his knees before the Shroud speak louder than any words that he was far from persuaded by the carbon-dating findings. And the words of his homily reinforced this: 'The Shroud is a challenge to our intelligence . . . The mysterious fascination of the Shroud forces questions to be raised about the sacred Linen and the historical life of Jesus . . .'"

34. See Loth 1910, p. 90. See also Chevalier 1900, pp. 50–55.

35. Wilson 1978, p. 211.

3 Judaism before Easter

1. Tacitus, *Histories*, 5.9 (1962–70, vol. 3, p. 191).

2. Pilate's contemporary Philo, the great Jewish philosopher, called him "a man of inflexible, stubborn and cruel disposition" and harked on "his venality, his violence, his thefts, his assaults, his abusive behavior, his frequent executions of untried prisoners, and his endless savage ferocity" (Philo, *Embassy to Caius*, 301–2 (1961, p. 128)). Philo's portrait is borne out by several anecdotes recorded by Josephus.

3. Episodes concerning Pilate are narrated in Josephus's two most important works, *The Jewish War* (written c.75) and *The Antiquities of the Jews* (written c.94). Modern estimates of Josephus's reliability as a historian, particularly regarding the period of Roman rule in Palestine, are relatively favorable, although allowance must be made for the inevitable incursion of his own partisan views. See Bilde 1988, pp. 191–200; Broshi 1982.

4. The episode is narrated in Josephus, *War*, 2.169–74 (1967–79, vol. 2, pp. 389–91); Josephus, *Antiquities*, 18.55–9 (2006, p. 779). For this episode see: Kraeling 1942; Schürer 1973–87, vol. 1, pp. 380–81, 384; Ferguson 2003, p. 416; Bond 1998, pp. 79–84. Kraeling 1942, pp. 272–3, deduces that the troops must have been an infantry cohort, consisting of between 500 and 1,000 men. Gibson 2009, p. 89, argues that the standards were taken to the barracks on the western side of town, not to the Antonia fortress overlooking the Temple.

5. See Kraeling 1942, pp. 269–76. On Roman military standards, see Watson 1969, pp. 127–31. The military standards were regarded, in effect, as deities, and, when the soldiers were in barracks, they were kept in special shrines, before which offerings and sacrifices were made.

6. Josephus, *Antiquities*, 18.59 (2006, p. 779).

7. Finkelstein and Silberman 2001, pp. 1–2. The oldest parts of the Hebrew Bible probably date back to the eighth century BC, but its core seems to have been put together in the late seventh century, in the reign of King Josiah of Judah. The whole saga was then re-edited and finalized in the late fifth century BC. In addition to Finkelstein and Silberman 2001, see Friedman 1988; Lane Fox 1991, esp. pp. 175–200. See also below, n. 10.

8. In the original Hebrew the divine name is written YHWH, which is usually transcribed as Yahweh in English.

9. Genesis 1.31.

10. Genesis 1.26–7; Genesis 2.7. The presence of these two separate accounts of the creation of Man in Genesis is best explained on the basis of the "Documentary Hypothesis," which sees the present text of the Torah as a compilation (made in the fifth century BC) of four source documents (called J, E, D and P). The first narrative of the creation of man belongs to P; the second belongs to J. On the Documentary Hypothesis, see Friedman 1988.

11. Genesis 1.26.

12. Genesis 3.19.

13. Genesis 17.4 and 8.

14. See Exodus 31.18, 40.20. For the Ten Commandments, see Exodus 20.1–17; Deuteronomy 5.6–21. Like the stories of the Creation of Man and the Flood, the Ten Commandments were preserved in two of the four sources that made up the Torah (in this case P and D), hence their dual preservation in slightly different forms (see above, n. 10).

15. Scholars debate exactly when the Israelites became monotheistic, but it seems that from the late seventh century BC, at the latest, there was a party that promoted the worship of Yahweh alone (see Finkelstein and Silberman 2001, pp. 247–9). Monotheism probably emerged as the dominant Hebrew paradigm in

the sixth and fifth centuries BC (see Knight 2008, pp. 28–9). It is uncertain whether the first commandment originally meant Yahweh should be Israel's only god or just principal god (see Lane Fox 1991, pp. 54–5).

16. Exodus 32.

17. In the Deuteronomic version of the Ten Commandments the Sabbath is linked, instead, to God's rescue of the Israelites from bondage (Deuteronomy 5.15).

18. See, for instance, Finkelstein and Silberman 2001, esp. pp. 211–13. The Early Prophets include the books of Joshua, Judges, 1 and 2 Samuel, and 1 and 2 Kings. The books known as 1 and 2 Chronicles cover the same historical period as the books of Samuel and Kings but are even more untrustworthy than these as historical sources (see Lane Fox 1991, pp. 195–7; Friedman 1988, pp. 211–13).

19. 2 Samuel 7.12–13.

20. 1 Kings 8.10–11.

21. 2 Kings 24.14.

22. The Story of Israel up until the Babylonian captivity has been dubbed the "First Bible" or "Primary History" of Israel. As Friedman 1988, p. 232, explains, "The Primary History formed the core around which the rest of the Bible was built . . . The rest of the books of the Hebrew Bible (Old Testament) and the New Testament likewise came to be understood by the communities who preserved them in the context of the central events of the Primary History."

23. On the institution of the synagogue, see Ferguson 2003, pp. 573–82.

24. The so-called Second Isaiah was an anonymous prophet who, according to modern scholars, wrote chapters 40–55 of the Book of Isaiah toward the end of the exile, c.550–540 BC (see, e.g., Lane Fox 1991, p. 97). As far as first-century Jews were concerned, the whole of Isaiah was written by the original prophet, who lived in the eighth century BC.

25. Ezekiel 1.26–8, 6.11 and 16.39–40.

26. Ezekiel 34.23–4. The return of the house of David was also prophesied by Ezekiel's contemporary Jeremiah (Jeremiah 23.5; 33.15–17).

27. On Jewish messianism in the time of Jesus, see Sanders 1992, pp. 295–8; Wright 1992, pp. 307–20. Both Sanders and Wright emphasize that the Messiah was not necessarily expected to be a descendant of David.

28. Ezekiel 37.1–10.

29. Ezekiel 37.11–12.

30. For the formation of the central symbol of Jewish identity, the Torah, which crystallized around texts and traditions that had been around for centuries, see Friedman 1988, pp. 217–33. See also above, n. 7.

31. Daniel 7.13–14.

32. Daniel 12.2–3.

33. According to Nickelsburg 1972, pp. 170–74, the idea of resurrection originated with the idea of the wise man being persecuted and then vindicated, an event that came to be understood as post-mortem.

34. See Wright 2003, pp. 32–45, 85–103; Watson 2005, pp. 104–6. For references to Sheol in the Hebrew scriptures, see Cohn-Sherbok 1996, p. 188.

35. Cf. Genesis 1.1–2.

36. On 2 Maccabees, see Nickelsburg 1981, pp. 118–21.

37. 2 Maccabees 7.11 and 21–3.

38. See Wright 2003, pp. 131–40; Vermes 2008, pp. 47–8. On the Sadducees in general, see Saldarini 2001; Sanders 1992, pp. 317–40; Ferguson 2003, pp. 519–20.

39. See Wright 2003, pp. 190–202; Vermes 2008, pp. 51–4. On the Pharisees in general, see Saldarini 2001; Sanders 1992, pp. 380–451; Ferguson 2003, pp. 514–19.

40. See Wright 2003, pp. 181–9; Vermes 2008, pp. 48–51. On the Essenes in general, see Sanders 1992, pp. 341–79; Ferguson 2003, pp. 521–31.

41. Josephus, *War*, 1.127–58 (1967–79, vol. 2, pp. 61–75).

42. On Antipater, see Schürer 1973–87, vol. 1, pp. 270–77. Idumaea was a region to the south of Judaea, which had been subjugated and Judaized c.125 BC by John Hyrcanus, the greatest of the Hasmonean kings.

43. See Netzer 2006, pp. 119–78. On Herod's Temple, see also Josephus, *Antiquities*, 15.380–425 (2006, pp. 679–84); Sanders 1992, pp. 51–69; Ferguson 2003, pp. 562–5.

44. On Judas the Galilean and his "philosophy," see Josephus, *Antiquities*, 18.4–10, 23–5 (2006, pp. 773–5).

4 The Testimony of Paul

1. Acts tells us that Paul was born in Tarsus, a city of Cilicia (now in southern Turkey), that he was a Roman citizen, a status that gave him certain legal privileges, and that he was a student of the great rabbi Gamaliel I (see Acts 16.37; 21.39; 22.3; 22.25–9). None of these claims can be corroborated. For the argument that Paul was a Roman citizen, see Murphy-O'Connor 1996, pp. 39–41; for a contrary view, see Roetzel 1999, pp. 19–22.

2. See Philippians 3.5 for Paul's "self-confession" as a Pharisee. See also Acts 22.3. See Roetzel 1999, p. 24, for a discussion of Paul's Pharisaic status.

3. Acts 9.1 and Galatians 1.13, respectively.

4. Scholars usually date Paul's conversion around 32–4. For present purposes, nothing much hangs on the precise chronology of Paul's career. Generally, I follow Roetzel 1999, pp. 182–3. As Roetzel says, "it is exceedingly difficult to reconstruct a chronology of Paul's life that inspires confidence." See Galatians 1 for important information provided by Paul himself.

5. Galatians 2.1–10. For discussion of the cause of Paul's second trip to Jerusalem, see Painter 1999, pp. 62–3; Murphy-O'Connor 1996, pp. 132–6. Most scholars equate the meeting described by Paul with that narrated in Acts 15. Paul states that he went up to Jerusalem "in response to a revelation," but, as Murphy-O'Connor argues, this claim was probably motivated by a desire to distance himself from the church of Antioch.

6. On Paul's letters as sources for early Christian history, see, e.g., Barnett 2005, p. 15; Wedderburn 2004, pp. 8–10; Burkett 2002, pp. 292–3.

7. Galatians 2.2. For Paul's contretemps with Peter at Antioch, see Galatians 2.11–14.

8. On 1 Corinthians, see Brown 1997, pp. 511–40; Knight 2008, pp. 180–82.

9. 1 Corinthians 15.13–14.

10. 1 Corinthians 15.1–7. The English term "gospel" translates the Greek *euangelion*, meaning a proclamation of good news. It was a term used in connection with the births of emperors (see Ferguson 2003, p. 46).

11. The second half of 1 Corinthians 15.6, concerning the survival of the More-than-500, must have been added by Paul himself, but the rest of verses 3–7 is undoubtedly a concise oral tradition that the apostle is reciting.

12. See Fuller 1972, pp. 10–14. Price 2005, pp. 73–6, argues that 1 Corinthians 15.3–11 is a post-Pauline interpolation on the grounds that its statement that Paul "received" the gospel as a creedal tradition is contradicted by his avowal in Galatians 1.11–12 that he received his gospel directly from God, not from man. This is unconvincing. Paul is using the word "gospel" in these passages in two different senses: 1) as a codified proclamation of the Christ-event; 2) as a personal interpretation and exposition of the Christ-event. Similarly, we use the word "gospel" today to mean both the core message of Christianity and a type of literary text (cf. Mark 1.1).

13. The translation given above uses the phrase "in these terms" to translate Paul's Greek expression *"tini logo"* ("to the word") in verse 2. The literal sense of this phrase indicates the precision of the verbal tradition Paul is reciting (see Wright 2003, p. 318).

14. Galatians 2.2, 7–9.

15. 1 Corinthians 15.11.

16. See, e.g., Crossan 1993, pp. 391–4.

17. See Philo, *Flaccus*, 83 (2003, p. 69). On Jehohanan, see Zias and Sekeles 1985. Gibson 2009, pp. 110, 132, argues against the idea that executed criminals were generally denied burial in Roman Judaea.

18. For discussion of this issue, see below, pp. 259–60.

19. As Wright 2003, p. 382, says, *ophthe* is "a normal word for ordinary sight." It is a passive form of the verb *horao*—"to see." Paul repeats the word *ophthe* in 1 Corinthians 15.8, and he uses an active form of the same verb (*heoraka*—"I have seen") in 1 Corinthians 9.1. On the use of this word, see also Fuller 1972, pp. 31–2.

20. Lüdemann 1994, p. 48, favors the translation "showed himself to." See also Wright 2003, p. 323.

21. Crucially, in the First Creed the fifth appearance of the Risen Christ to "all the apostles" is differentiated from that to the Twelve. Cf. also 1 Corinthians 9.1; 2 Corinthians 11.13. Knight 2008, p. 287, discusses the pre-Christian use of the term apostle in Judaism. Luke's confusion of the apostles and the Twelve was probably prompted by a desire to restrict Church authority to the supposed heirs of the Twelve.

22. 1 Corinthians 15.8–9.

23. Paul himself called his proclamation "folly" (1 Corinthians 1.21), signaling its opposition to common sense or worldly wisdom. For a helpful exposition of the passage, see Carrier 2005a, pp. 118–54.

24. 1 Corinthians 15.35–49. I place verses 39–41 in square brackets in order to clarify the structure of the argument. It is possible that verses 39–41 were inserted by Paul following his initial composition of the passage, in order to clarify the cosmological basis of the argument. Originally, v. 42 appears to have followed straight on from v. 38.

25. Cf. Wright 2003, pp. 342–3. That Paul regarded the questions as hostile is evident from his intemperate response—"You foolish man!" That these questions are connected to the denial of the future resurrection of the dead is evident from 1 Corinthians 15.12 ("how can some of you say that there is no resurrection of the dead?").

26. This objection was well known in antiquity and was confronted later by St. Augustine. Wright 2003, p. 343 n. 89, agrees that the Corinthians' "objection was not particularly complicated, since it expressed the more or less universal view of pagan antiquity."

27. Technically, Paul's phrase *soma pneumatikon* ("spiritual body") means a body *for* a/the spirit, rather than a body *of* spirit. For clarification of this issue see Wright 2003, pp. 348–52. However, Paul and his fellow apostles did apparently consider the risen body to be composed of spirit, as well as being for a/the spirit (see below, p. 296), so "spiritual body" is an appropriate translation.

28. Paul may be playing here on the regular pagan view that the stars and planets were the bodies of the immortals, especially since many of his Corinthian followers were pagan converts (cf. 1 Corinthians 12.2).

29. On "glory" (*doxa*) in this context, see Wright 2003, pp. 345–6. He makes the point that the word "glory" is not to be taken literally here, but understood in the sense of "honor" or "proper dignity."

30. For this perennial image, associated with pagan corn-gods across the ancient Mediterranean world, see Frazer 1913, part 4, vol. 2, pp. 3–114.

31. Paul's conception of the risen body as a spiritual entity distinct from the mortal body corresponds exactly to the Pharisaic view, as related by Josephus: "Every soul, they maintain, is imperishable, but the soul of the good alone passes into another body; while the souls of the wicked suffer eternal punishment" (Josephus, *War*, 2.163 (1967–79, vol. 2, pp. 385–7)); "All of us, it is true, have mortal bodies composed of perishable matter, but the soul lives forever, immortal; it is a portion of the Deity housed in our bodies . . . [brave] souls, remaining spotless and obedient, are allotted the most holy place in heaven, whence, in the revolution of the ages, they return to find in chaste bodies a new habitation" (Josephus, *War*, 3.372, 374 (1967–79, vol. 2, p. 681)). Riley 1995, p. 21, points out that in this context Paul's argument in 1 Corinthians "must be seen as a possible, even typical, Pharisaic doctrine." We should be aware, however, that Josephus may be describing here a doctrine peculiar to Christian Pharisees. Be that as it may, his testimony helps confirm that many first-century Jews understood the future, risen body to be distinct from the present, mortal body. For Paul's conception of the immortal person as "a portion of God dwelling within our bodies," see below, p. 66.

32. Genesis 3.19.

33. Paul refers to Christ as the "last Adam" because he interprets the two parallel stories of the creation of man in Genesis as two separate events: a) God's creation of the earthly Adam on the second or third day, "when no plant of the field was yet in the earth" (Genesis 2.4–7); b) God's creation of Christ "in his own image" on the sixth day (Genesis 1.26–7). The idea that Genesis describes the creation of two separate Adams was fairly widespread in first-century Judaism, being discussed, for instance, by Philo (see Goff 2009, pp. 119–21, citing Philo, *On Creation*, 134 (2001, p. 82)). Paul insists, contra Philo, that the creation of the physical man precedes that of the spiritual man, matching his conviction that the Resurrection represents the birth of the Second Adam and his own experience of being "born again" spiritually when already alive in the flesh. The implication is that he read the story of Creation in Genesis 1.1–2.3 allegorically, understanding the Resurrection (i.e., the creation of the Second Adam) to mark the sixth cosmic day and the Kingdom of God to be about to begin on the seventh.

34. 1 Corinthians 15.50.

35. A comparable denial of fleshly resurrection can be detected in a pre-Pauline Christian formula. Opening his letter to the Romans, Paul recites an early Christian catechism that contrasts Jesus' resurrected state with his fleshly existence: ". . . the gospel concerning [God's] Son, who was descended from David *according to the flesh* and designated Son of God in power *according to the Spirit of holiness* by his resurrection from the dead, Jesus Christ our Lord . . ." (Romans 1.3–4). As a descendant of David (and thus of Adam), Jesus is said to have lived in the medium of flesh. This medium is then paralleled and contrasted with the Spirit of holiness, in which Jesus was resurrected and designated as the Son of God. Had Jesus been thought to have been resurrected in the flesh, the opposition between flesh and spirit would have been misleading.

36. See above, n. 33.

5 The Impact of Easter

1. Tacitus, *Annals*, 15.44 (1996, p. 365).

2. Wright 1992, p. 360. Mythicists, who doubt the existence of Jesus, combat this pagan corroboration of the Christian story by arguing that Tacitus obtained his information from Gospel-reading Christians (cf. Wells 1982, pp. 16–17; Doherty 2005, p. 202). There are two reasons to doubt this. First, Tacitus refers to Jesus' execution as a setback, indicating that he had no understanding of Christians' positive view of the Crucifixion. Secondly, the information that the "mischief" started in Judaea is unlikely to have been obtained from Gospel-reading Christians, since the Gospels place Christ's ministry in Galilee. From a Roman perspective, though, the trouble began in Jerusalem, with the excitement stirred up by the apostles after the Crucifixion. Leading Romans would have been aware of Christianity from at least the time of its persecution under Nero, and Tacitus was probably tapping an authentically Roman tradition concerning its origins.

3. If Jesus died three days before appearing to Peter, as the Creed implies, he is unlikely to have been crucified before Pilate's time (i.e. before AD 26), because Peter was apparently active into the 50s and 60s. A slightly fuller account of the birth of the Church is found in Josephus, *Antiquities*, 18.63–4 (2006, p. 780), the so-called *Testimonium Flavianum*. Traditionally, this has been viewed as an independent witness to the Christian gospel, but parts of the passage are so sympathetic to Christianity that its authenticity is highly doubtful. Most New Testament scholars now consider it to be at least partially a Christian interpolation, influenced by the Gospels, and thus of limited historical value (see, e.g., Ehrman 1999, pp. 61–2; Crossan 1999, pp. 10–14).

4. Cf. Acts 24.5 and 9.2, respectively. According to Acts 11.26, the followers of Christ were first called Christians in Antioch. Some think this development can be dated to the late 30s or 40s (e.g. Barnett 2005, p. 32), but this is speculative. Whenever the term originated, it is convenient to label the followers of Christ as Christians from the outset.

5. According to Matthew, the name Peter, meaning "rock," was bestowed by Jesus on Simon Barjona in recognition of his importance for the founding of the Church: "you are Peter, and on this rock I will build my Church" (Matthew 16.18; cf. John 1.42). In the Gospels and Acts, Simon is called Peter (or Simon Peter) throughout, although it is uncertain whether, in fact, he received his nickname before or after the Crucifixion. Paul, who first met him in 35, refers to him always as Peter or Cephas.

6. For these episodes, see, respectively: Mark 14.37–41; John 18.10–11; John 18.15–27; John 21.15–17.

7. Acts 9.31–2. For Peter's activity as a missionary, see Painter 1999, pp. 75, 239.

8. See Eusebius, *History of the Church*, 3.1 (1989, p. 65); Jerome, *Illustrious Men*, 1.1–2 (1999, p. 5).

9. See Josephus, *War*, 5.451 (1967–79, vol. 3, p. 341); Brown 1994, pp. 947–8.

10. See Josephus, *Antiquities*, 20.200–203 (2006, p. 877). The reference to "Jesus, who was called Christ" as the brother of James in this passage is the earliest commonly accepted non-Christian reference to Jesus. Some regard this reference as a later interpolation (see, e.g., Wells 1986, p. 11), but without justification in my view.

11. See Josephus, *Antiquities*, 20.200 (2006, p. 877); Galatians 1.19; Matthew 13.55; Mark 6.3; Eusebius, *History of the Church*, 2.23 (1989, p. 59), quoting Hegesippus.

12. For mention of Jesus' sisters, see Matthew 13.56 and Mark 6.3. For the fraternal relationship between Jesus and James, see Painter 1999, pp. 213–20; Bütz 2005, pp. 13–16. The fact that his brother was a prominent figure in first-century Judaea is a clear sign that Jesus was a real person. Those who deny the existence of Jesus have to argue that James was merely the "spiritual" brother of a mythical Jesus (see, e.g., Doherty 2005, pp. 57–8; Wells 1986, p. 21), but this is no more convincing than the theologians' claim that he was a cousin.

13. On the three Pillars, see Eisenman 2002, pp. 140–41.

14. On the Twelve, see Knight 2008, pp. 109–10, 288; Wedderburn 2004, pp. 21–4;

Wells 1986, pp. 122–40. Paul never refers to the Twelve outside the First Creed, and they are conspicuously absent from his account of the Jerusalem Conference (see Galatians 2.1–10). They are present, however, in Luke's account of the Conference in Acts 15 under the misleading title of "the apostles" (see above, p. 54).

15. See Sanders 1985, pp. 103–6; Knight 2008, p. 109; Wedderburn 2004, p. 23. Intriguingly, a similar council of twelve existed at Qumran, together also with a supreme council of three (see Allegro 1964, p. 112).

16. On the apostles, see e.g., Wedderburn 2004, pp. 23–4; Knight 2008, pp. 286–7; Wells 1986, pp. 126–9.

17. See, respectively, 1 Thessalonians 1.1, 2.6; 1 Corinthians 4.6, 9; 1 Corinthians 9.5–6 (cf. Acts 14.14); 2 Corinthians 8.18–23. In Philippians 2.25 Epaphroditus is also called an *apostolos*, but here the term probably means an ordinary messenger.

18. Romans 16.7. On Junia, see Epp 2005.

19. As we shall see, Mary Magdalene may also have been an influential apostle. In later tradition Mary was known as the Apostle to the Apostles (see Haskins 2005, pp. 58–97). On Mary Magdalene, see Haskins 2005; Meyer 2004; Schaberg 2003; de Boer 2004.

20. 1 Corinthians 12.28.

21. Acts 17.13; 19.29.

22. Suetonius, *Life of Claudius*, 24 (1997, p. 228). See Wright 1992, pp. 354–5. The date of the expulsion is usually set at 49, on account of the information in Acts that, when Paul arrived in Corinth (an event fairly securely dated to that year), he found there a man and wife, Aquila and Priscilla, who had "lately come from Italy . . . because Claudius had commanded all the Jews to leave Rome" (Acts 18.1–2).

23. Luke 24.46.

24. Acts 1.8.

25. Fuller 1972, p. 2.

26. See, e.g., the First Creed and Romans 1.1–5. On the catechetical nature of the opening of Paul's letter to the Romans, see, e.g. Hengel 1976, pp. 59–60. Acts, too, has Peter proclaiming Jesus as the Messiah in his earliest sermons (Acts 2.36; 3.18–20).

27. On "the forgiveness of sins" see Wright 1996, pp. 268–74. He summarizes the key point as follows: "From the point of view of a first-century Jew, 'forgiveness of sins' could never simply be a private blessing, though to be sure it was that as well . . . Overarching the situation of the individual was the state of the nation as a whole . . ." (p. 271).

28. Cf. Dunn 2003, p. 209: "It was the claim that Jesus had been crucified *as Messiah*, that crucifixion was at the heart and climax of Jesus' messianic role, which was so offensive." See also Cohn-Sherbok 1996, pp. 191–2, for the inappropriateness of Jesus as a Jewish Messiah.

29. Deuteronomy 21.23. Paul refers to this curse in Galatians 3.13.

30. Tom Wright counts six or seven ways in which the early Christian belief differed

from the traditional Jewish view of resurrection (see Wright 2003, p. 681; Stewart 2006, pp. 18–19, 31).

31. 1 Corinthians 15.16–17.

32. Cf. Cohn-Sherbok 1996, p. 188: "it was not until the early rabbinic period [second century AD] that the doctrine of the general resurrection of the dead became a central feature of Jewish theology."

33. See Wright 2003, p. 681; Stewart 2006, p. 19.

34. Romans 8.10–11. The same notion of spiritual indwelling informs, e.g., Galatians 2.19–20; 1 Thessalonians 5.4–5; 1 Corinthians 6.13–20. This internal, pre-mortem understanding of "resurrection" is clearly expressed in the New Testament epistles (e.g. Romans 8.10: "But if Christ is in you, although your bodies are dead because of sin, your spirits are alive because of righteousness"; Colossians 3.1: "If then you have been raised with Christ, seek the things that are above," and 1 Peter 1.3: "By his great mercy we have been born anew to a living hope through the resurrection of Jesus Christ from the dead"). It is important to note that this new usage was not just metaphorical (as it is conceived today); the early Christians understood baptism into Christ to initiate some sort of metaphysical process, a spiritual transformation that prepared the self for resurrection or transfiguration at the *parousia* (cf. 2 Corinthians 3.18: "And we all, with unveiled face, beholding the glory of the Lord, are being changed into his likeness, from one degree of glory to another").

35. See, e.g., Romans 6.1–11. For the idea of spiritual rebirth, see further below, pp. 315–16.

36. John 3.4.

37. Stewart 2006, p. 18.

38. Acts 20.7 is in one of the "we-passages" and is therefore relatively trustworthy. For evidence of Sunday gatherings in Corinth, see Swinburne 2003, p. 164. Paul refers to the weekly communal meal as "the Lord's supper" (1 Corinthians 11.20). Other explicit statements prescribing the celebration of the Eucharist on Sunday, or "the Lord's Day," are found in the *Didache* and the *First Apology* of Justin (see Swinburne 2003, p. 165). Finally, in Luke the Risen Jesus "breaks bread" and eats fish with his disciples on Easter Sunday, indicating that Luke's community also associated Sunday with a communal, symbolic meal. For this issue, see also Bauckham 1982.

39. Swinburne 2003, pp. 163–4, is surely right to say that, if the distinctive practice of Sunday worship had not been established by the time the original community was dispersed, "we would have heard of disputes about when to celebrate, and some instructions being given from on high (analogous to the way in which disputes about circumcision and eating sacrificial meat were purportedly resolved by the 'Council of Jerusalem' described in Acts 15)." Cf. Bauckham 1982, p. 231: "The very universality of the custom argues its early origin."

40. Pliny the Younger, *Letters*, 10.96 (1963, p. 294).

41. The shift to a new day of worship cannot be explained in terms of the development of a pagan myth about a dying and rising god. As Swinburne 2003, p. 165, says, "There is no plausible origin of the sacredness of Sunday from outside Christianity."

42. Gibbon 1923, vol. 2, p. 2.
43. His theme being the fate of the empire, rather than the birth of Christianity, Gibbon discusses five circumstances that, he argues, favored the new religious institution over the long-term, summarized as follows: "exclusive zeal, the immediate expectation of another world, the claim of miracles, the practice of rigid virtue, and the constitution of the primitive church . . ." (Gibbon 1923, vol. 2, p. 54).
44. For an attempt to liken the birth of the Church to a twentieth-century flying-saucer cult, see Festinger et al. 1956, pp. 23–5. See Wright 2003, pp. 697–701, for effective criticism of Festinger's suggestion.
45. Cf. Acts 4.
46. On the expansion of Christianity in the 30s, see Barnett 2005, pp. 30–32.
47. Freeman 2003, p. 124.
48. See Acts 13.50; 14.5, 19; 19.23–41.
49. Wright 1992, pp. 444–5.

6 The Gospel Stories

1. The Jerusalem Church probably survived in exile at Pella, a city in the Decapolis region to the east of the Jordan. Later sources—Eusebius, *History of the Church*, 3.5 (1989, p. 68); Epiphanius, *Panarion*, 29.7.7–8 (1987–94, vol. 1, p. 118)—report that the Jerusalem Church decamped to this area at the start of the Jewish War. The historicity of this tradition has been challenged (see Brandon 1957, pp. 169–72), but there are good reasons to regard it as historical (see, e.g., Eisenman 2006, pp. 411–12, 510–14).
2. On the breach with Judaism, see Knight 2008, pp. 266–75; Rowland 1985, pp. 299–301.
3. For the emergence of the Christian ministry, see Freeman 2003, pp. 136–42; Knight 2008, pp. 283–94.
4. See below, p. 265, and Lüdemann 2004, pp. 215–19.
5. Cf. Romans 16.1, 3, 7. See Pagels 1980, p. 61.
6. Galatians 3.28.
7. 1 Timothy 2.12. For mention of female ministers, see 1 Timothy 3.8–11, 5.2.
8. Chilton 2005, p. 112.
9. See Pagels 1980, pp. 60–61.
10. See Ehrman 2003.
11. See Ehrman 1999, pp. 41–5; Lane Fox 1991, pp. 126–7. Only one of the Gospels, the fourth, provides any internal evidence regarding its authorship, claiming in its final chapter to have been written by "the disciple whom Jesus loved." The identity of this disciple is uncertain, though; the identification with John is not attested until the mid second century (see Lane Fox 1991, pp. 129, 205).
12. See, e.g., Burkett 2002, pp. 157, 181, 196, 216; Knight 2008, pp. 331–4.
13. On the relationship between John and the Synoptics, see Rowland 1985, p. 326; Robinson 1985; Burkett 2002, pp. 216–19; Knight 2008, p. 333.
14. John 20.1–2, 11–18.

15. She could not have deduced this, of course, simply from the removal of the stone. This illogicality is one sign among many that John has recrafted the Easter stories he inherited. See further below, pp. 244, 261–3, 265–6, 278–80.

16. Mark 16.1–8.

17. Matthew 28.1–10.

18. On the supposed guarding of the tomb, which is definitely unhistorical, see Carrier 2005b, pp. 358–64; Tobin 2009, pp. 538–9.

19. Luke 24.1–11.

20. Wright 2003, p. 589.

21. Women might be called to give evidence in a court of law as and when necessary, but the preference was always for male witnesses, where appropriate. On this complex issue, see, e.g., Wright 2003, pp. 607–8; Schaberg 2003, pp. 227–8, citing Osiek 1993, pp. 103–4. Josephus, *Antiquities*, 4.219 (2006, p. 158) represents the attitude of the average Jewish man in the first century when he reports Moses saying, apropos the regulation of urban magistracies, "let not the testimony of women be admitted, on account of the levity and boldness of their sex . . ."

22. See Origen, *Against Celsus*, 2.59 (1953, p. 112).

23. John 20.2.

24. John 20.7.

25. Luke 24.24.

26. On the issue of the original ending of Mark, see Wright 2003, pp. 617–24; Fuller 1972, pp. 64–8. It is currently disputed whether or not Mark's Gospel originally ended at 16.8. In my opinion it did not.

27. John 20.19–23.

28. John 20.24–9.

29. Matthew 28.16–20.

30. Luke 24.13–35.

31. Luke 24.27.

32. Luke 24.34.

33. Luke 24.36–53.

34. Zahrnt 1963, p. 129.

35. Apologists sometimes offer excuses for the Creed's omission of these witnesses, but their arguments are weak and unconvincing. Richard Swinburne, for instance, avers that, despite being primary witnesses of the Resurrection, the Emmaus disciples were not apostles and so "were not important enough to be official witnesses" (Swinburne 2003, p. 150). One wonders why, if they were so unimportant, the Risen Jesus spent so much time with them and why Luke gave them star billing. Swinburne also claims that "the appearance on the Emmaus road can be regarded simply as an early part of the appearance to the Twelve," because "the appearance to the disciples together included the walkers on the road to Emmaus." This is equally unconvincing: Luke narrates the Emmaus appearance and the appearance to the disciples in Jerusalem as two distinct events, separated by time, place and a vanishing act, and the First Creed lists the appearance to Peter separately from that to the Twelve, although he was present at the evening event, too.

36. Swinburne, harmonizing with gusto, manages "without too much difficulty" to identify both the Doubting Thomas tale and the appearance by the Sea of Galilee (and other stories) with the appearance to "more than five hundred brethren at one time" (see Swinburne 2003, pp. 156–9). This is frankly incredible.

37. As I have explained, Mark did not originally contain any appearance-stories. It is clear, however, from Mark 16.7 that the author of the Gospel did believe in an appearance to the Eleven, at least.

38. Strabo, *Geography*, 10.3.23 (1960–69, vol. 5, p. 119). This passage is cited in a similar context in Mayor 2000, p. 194.

7 The Way Ahead

1. Acts 26.24.

2. One determined apologist manages to deduce from the First Creed, nevertheless, that Paul must have known about an empty tomb and thinks that he probably went to see it when he visited Jerusalem (see Craig 1989, pp. 112–14).

3. There may be one exception to the rule: Matthew's tomb-story appears to echo the story of Daniel in the Lion's Den (see Carrier 2005b, pp. 360–64).

4. Mark 16.12.

5. Matthew 28.17.

6. A direct description of the Resurrection is contained in the non-canonical *Gospel of Peter* (see below, pp. 233–5), but no one believes this to be an eyewitness account of the miracle. For Luke's Ascension narratives, see Luke 24.50–51; Acts 1.6–12.

7. Pliny, *Natural History*, 2.23 (1961–8, vol. 3, p. 237).

8. Cf. Martin 1991, p. 93: "Surely, it is not beyond the realm of possibility that a natural phenomenon, for example, a person who looked like Jesus, could have triggered a collective delusion among Jesus' followers that was fed by wild rumors and speculation." (Cf. Schonfield 1996, pp. 199–207.) Goulder 1996, pp. 52–5, compares the Resurrection appearances with sightings of Bigfoot, although he treats these as hallucinations, rather than illusions.

9. Habermas 2006, pp. 85–6.

10. The partial exception is John Loken, who anticipates my own argument, though he develops it rather differently, in connection with an unnecessary theory about Jesus' body having been stolen by the Jerusalem authorities. See Loken 2006.

11. On the use of comparisons vis-à-vis the origin of Christianity, see Ashton 2000, pp. 6–28; Smith 1990, pp. 36–53. Historical explanation depends, ultimately, on the use of analogies. "Anything truly unique," as Ashton 2000, p. 6, remarks, "would be, strictly speaking, incomprehensible." This is precisely why Christian apologists play down the similarities between the Christian belief in the Resurrection and other, related beliefs: they want Easter to remain incomprehensible, a singular, divine mystery. As Smith 1990, p. 42, observes, it is the attempt to block illuminating comparisons with the Resurrection "that gives the Christian apologetic language of the 'unique' its urgency."

12. For the myth of Pelops, see Gantz 1993, pp. 532–4, 540–45, 646; Burkert 1983, pp. 99–101.

13. The case of Pelops belies Tom Wright's argument that there is no precedent for Christian belief in the "bodily" resurrection of Jesus (see Wright 2003, pp. 32–84). In his wide-ranging survey of pagan beliefs about life after death, Wright overlooks the case of Pelops, though the story is found in several of the Greek and Latin sources he uses.

14. Mayor 2000. For a review of this book, see Naddaf 2003.

15. Mayor 2000, p. 4.

16. See ibid., p. 105.

17. Ibid.: "Once polished and displayed, the bone would inevitably accrue stories to explain its special appearance and origins."

18. Ibid.

8 A Unique Spectacle

1. Wilson 1998, p. 4. Cf. Schwalbe and Rogers 1982, p. 6; Tribbe 1983, p. 142; Zugibe 2005, p. 173.

2. See, e.g., Wilson 1998, p. 75. Cf. Schwalbe and Rogers 1982, p. 6: "the faint image qualities suggest severe technical difficulties with execution."

9 The Cloth Examined

1. Vignon 1902, p. 137.

2. See Jackson et al. 1977, pp. 74–8; Wilson 1978, pp. 197–8. For criticism of this experiment, see Nickell 1998, pp. 88–90.

3. Jackson et al. 1977, p. 78.

4. For the VP-8 Image Analyzer test, see Jackson et al. 1977; Wilson 1978, pp. 198–200; Heller 1983, pp. 38–40; Wilson 1986, pp. 47–9.

5. For the STURP campaign, see Heller 1983; Tribbe 1983, pp. 117–51; Wilson 1986, pp. 47–63; Antonacci 2000, pp. 6–13.

6. See Pellicori 1980; Gilbert and Gilbert 1980; Heller 1983, pp. 138–9; Rogers 2008, pp. 49–51.

7. See Morris et al. 1980; Heller 1983, pp. 135–6; Rogers 2008, pp. 58–9.

8. See Accetta and Baumgart 1980; Rogers 2008, pp. 60–61.

9. For the 1973 tests for blood, see Wilson 1978, pp. 56–60. Translated extracts are given in McCrone 1999, pp. 9–12. Heller 1983, pp. 13–14, is dismissive of the blood tests performed in 1973.

10. See Wilson 1986, p. 56 and color plates 11 and 12.

11. See Antonacci 2000, p. 43; Wilson 1998, p. 86.

12. See Morris et al. 1980, pp. 45–6; Pellicori 1980, p. 1918; Tribbe 1983, pp. 131–2; Rogers 2008, pp. 58–9.

13. Heller and Adler 1981, p. 92. As a twelfth item, they listed "Forensic judgment

of the appearance of the various wound and blood marks," and, in reproducing the list, Heller 1983, p. 216, adds "Positive immunological test for human albumin." See also Rogers 2008, pp. 37–8, who performed an additional (iodine-azide) test, confirming their results.

14. Heller 1983, p. 186.

15. An Italian medical professor, Baima Bollone, who obtained more sizeable samples than those received by Heller and Adler, has claimed to be able to tell not only that the blood was human, but also that it was of the rare type AB (see Bollone 1998, pp. 175–80; Wilson 1998, pp. 89–91; Antonacci 2000, p. 28). Unfortunately, Bollone's results have not been properly published in a science journal. Zugibe 2005, pp. 217–18, queries Bollone's results. For anecdotal evidence regarding further tests of blood samples from the Shroud, including DNA tests, see Wilson 1998, pp. 89–93.

16. Lavoie 1998, p. 97.

17. See, e.g., Barbet 1963, p. 16; Wuenschel 1954, pp. 35–7.

18. See Miller and Pellicori 1981, pp. 75, 76, 82, 85; Tribbe 1983, p. 135; Antonacci 2000, p. 26.

19. See Heller and Adler 1981, p. 90; Tribbe 1983, p. 134; Heller 1983, pp. 185–6; Wilson 1998, p. 88; Antonacci 2000, p. 26.

20. See Jumper et al. 1984, p. 460; Wilson 1986, p. 95; Case 1996, pp. 44–5; Lavoie 1998, p. 59; Antonacci 2000, pp. 41–2. Antonacci notes further that "in the published photomicrographs of the bloodstains, white fibrils appear where the dried blood has broken away from the cloth, suggesting that the bloodstains were transferred to the cloth before the body image was encoded." The formation of the body-image was also blocked by the clear serum haloes, as can be seen from the ultraviolet reflectance photographs of the Shroud (see Rogers 2008, pp. 16, 20).

21. See Lavoie 1998, pp. 90–100.

22. See Zugibe 2005, pp. 142, 214.

23. On the issue of bilirubin, see Heller and Adler 1981, p. 89; Jumper et al. 1984, p. 459; Case 1996, pp. 57–9; Wilson 1998, pp. 88–9; Antonacci 2000, p. 29. For further evidence that old blood can still be red, see Wilson 1998, p. 92. For an alternative explanation for the reddishness of the blood on the Shroud, see below, p. 111.

24. From a lecture given in the Chemistry Department, Queen Mary College, University of London, July 1984 (quoted in Wilson 1986, p. 96).

25. See Jumper et al. 1984, pp. 450–51; Lavoie 1998, pp. 60–61; Wilson 1998, pp. 76–7; Antonacci 2000, p. 36; Rogers 2008, p. 28.

26. See Rogers 2008, p. 29.

27. See Heller and Adler 1981, p. 99; Jumper et al. 1984, p. 451; Tribbe 1983, p. 145; Lavoie 1998, pp. 60–61; Wilson 1998, p. 77; Rogers 2008, pp. 15, 28.

28. See Jumper et al. 1984, p. 451; Antonacci 2000, p. 36; Rogers 2008, p. 15.

29. See Wilson 1986, p. 56; Wilson 1998, p. 76.

30. See Mottern et al. 1980, p. 42; Morris et al. 1980, pp. 45–6; Jumper et al. 1984, p. 453; Tribbe 1983, p. 140; Wilson 1986, p. 56; Rogers 2008, p. 59.

31. See Miller and Pellicori 1981, pp. 75, 84; Rogers 2008, p. 51.

32. See Ghiberti 2002, section 14 and plate 12, and, for the image processing, Fanti and Maggiolo 2004.

33. See Fanti and Maggiolo 2004, p. 492; Zugibe 2005, pp. 187–8; Rogers 2008, p. 4.

34. Rogers 2008, p. 28.

35. See ibid., pp. 31–3.

36. See ibid., pp. 91–3, 99.

37. See Heller 1983, pp. 199–200; Rogers 2008, p. 44.

38. See Heller and Adler 1981, p. 95; Heller 1983, pp. 199–200; Case 1996, pp. 61–3.

39. Rogers 2008, p. 44.

40. Ibid.

41. See Heller 1983, pp. 199–200; Rogers 2008, pp. 44, 51, 99, 101.

42. According to Meacham 2005, p. 133, Rogers retired from the field of sindonology in 1982 "after an altercation with John Jackson."

43. For Raes's examination of the Shroud, see Raes 1976; Wilson 1978, pp. 52–5; McCrone 1999, p. 18.

44. See Wilson 1998, pp. 68–70; Wilson 2010, pp. 74–6; Flury-Lemberg 2001, p. 56.

45. See Flury-Lemberg 2001, pp. 56, 60. Flury-Lemberg's research is helpfully discussed in Wilson 2010, pp. 70–81.

46. See Flury-Lemberg 2001, p. 58.

47. Ibid.

48. See Josephus, *Antiquities*, 3.159–61 (2006, pp. 109–10). This may be of relevance to the interpretation of John 19.23–4, in which the soldiers at the Crucifixion cast lots for the seamless tunic of Jesus (see Brown 1994, p. 957). Sanders 1992, p. 99, notes that the "blue tunic was remarkable partly because it was made of one piece, which implies an extremely wide loom." He presumes, however, that the seamless robe of the high priest was made of wool.

49. On the fabrics used for the Jewish priestly vestments, see Sanders 1992, pp. 94–102.

50. Pliny, *Natural History*, 19.3 (1961–8, vol. 5, pp. 431–3).

51. See Rogers and Arnoldi 2003, p. 108; Zugibe 2005, p. 291; Rogers 2008, p. 18.

52. See Pliny, *Natural History*, 19.18 (1961–8, vol. 5, p. 451); Theophrastus, *Enquiry into Plants*, 9.12.5 (1961, vol. 2, p. 281). Pliny, *Natural History* 19.4, 20.79 (1961–8, vol. 5, p. 435; vol. 6, p. 121) misremembers Theophrastus and attributes the bleaching of linen to a poppy called *heraclion*.

53. See Rogers 2008, p. 39.

54. See ibid., p. 51.

55. See ibid., p. 19. This explanation is favored in Zugibe 2005, p. 216.

56. For this argument, see Rogers 2005; Rogers 2008, pp. 40–43.

57. McCrone 1999, pp. 303–5.

58. See Wilson 1978, p. 63.

59. Frei 1979, p. 198.

60. Ibid.

61. Frei 1983, p. 279 (cf. also p. 282).

62. For useful discussion of Frei's work and its subsequent evaluation, see Wilson 1998, pp. 98–104; Zugibe 2005, pp. 283–9; Wilson 2010, pp. 62–5.

63. Scannerini 1998, p. 218. Nickell 1998, p. 113, argues that, if the pollen data are correct (which he doubts), a medieval forger might have "purchased an *imported* cloth at one of the cloth markets in Troyes (near Lirey)." This argument requires the cloth not only to have been imported from the Near East but also to have traveled via the Anatolian steppes (see Frei 1979, p. 198; Frei 1983, p. 282), coincidentally the same journey as is involved in the most likely reconstruction of the Shroud's pre-European travels. The scenario is not impossible, but it stretches credulity to the limits.

64. Scannerini 1998, p. 223.

65. See Wilson 2010, p. 65.

66. For this research, see Kohlbeck and Nitowski 1986; Wilson 1998, pp. 104–6; Antonacci 2000, p. 109; Zugibe 2005, pp. 311–12; Wilson 2010, pp. 66–8.

67. Kohlbeck and Nitowski 1986, p. 23.

68. See Heller and Adler 1981, p. 86; Heller 1983, p. 126; Wilson 1998, pp. 96–7; McCrone 1999, p. 85; Antonacci 2000, p. 55.

69. See McCrone 1999, p. 85. For criticism of McCrone's painting theory, see below, pp. 135–7. Cormack 1997, p. 121, also considers the pigment particles significant, although he admits (pp. 116–17) that working out how the Shroud-image was made is a "real difficulty."

70. See Wilson 1998, p. 98; Zugibe 2005, pp. 253–4.

71. Wilson 1998, p. 98.

10 The Blood-Image

1. See Delage 1902, pp. 684–5.

2. *Lancet*, April 26, 1902, p. 1201. The writer considers the work of Delage and Vignon as a discovery concerning the potential image-forming properties of dead bodies in general and hails it as "an intensely remarkable and interesting instance of the light which the very latest developments of scientific research may throw on traditions and controversial matters in history."

3. See Antonacci 2000, pp. 15–16. He omits several listed in Wuenschel 1954, p. 34 (Donnet, Romanese, Rodinò and Luna). To combat this army of convinced medics, skeptics put up the lone figure of Dr. Michael Baden, a New York medical examiner, who expressed skepticism regarding the Shroud's authenticity when asked to comment on some photos of it by a journalist (see Nickell 1998, pp. 59–61, 67–70, 75). Baden confessed to being no expert on the subject, and his comments cannot be regarded as a considered judgment.

4. For the *Parement de Narbonne*, see Sterling 1987, pp. 218–25; Nash 2000.

5. For Naddo Ceccarelli, see Chelazzi Dini et al. 1998, pp. 100–103; Bagnoli and Bellosi 1985, pp. 118–20.

6. This perception can be proved by measuring the distance from the wound to the fingertips (see Bucklin 2002, p. 273).

7. The traditional understanding was based on Luke 24.39, John 20.27, Psalms 22.16 and Zechariah 13.6.

8. See Psalms 34.20. For the Destot's space argument, see Barbet 1963, pp. 115–19. Re the "prophecy," see Exodus 12.46, Numbers 9.12, John 19.36.

9. See Zugibe 2005, pp. 72–4.

10. See ibid., pp. 75–9, 81–9. Zugibe is highly critical of Barbet, accusing him of "conducting a single, untenable, invalid experiment using an amputated arm" (Zugibe 2005, p. 67). It has also been suggested that the nail might have been driven into the end of the forearm, between the radius and ulna bones, but Barbet 1963, p. 109, and Zugibe 2005, p. 74, rightly dismiss this idea.

11. See Zugibe 2005, pp. 66, 78–9. Later in his book (p. 255), Zugibe castigates "individuals who pull things out of context in the Bible to prove their point . . ."

12. Zugibe is particularly at fault in this respect and even refers to the testimony of Christian mystics. For example, he appeals to the revelations of St. Brigit as evidence that the feet were fixed in place with two nails, rather than one (ibid., p. 93).

13. See Antonacci 2000, p. 17, citing the opinion of several doctors. This idea is influenced by Barbet's similar analysis of the wrist wound and is related to his idea that, in order to breathe, the Shroud-man must have shifted his body up and down on the cross, altering the angles of his arms and hence the angles of the blood flows (see Barbet 1963, pp. 108–9). This scenario has been challenged, once again, by Zugibe (see Zugibe 2005, pp. 117–18).

14. Zugibe 2005, p. 223.

15. Ibid., pp. 223–4.

16. Bucklin 2002, p. 273. For agreement, see Wilson 1998, p. 37; Antonacci 2000, p. 21.

17. See Vignon 1902, pp. 33–4; Zugibe 2005, pp. 93–5 (discussing the theory of Dr. Gambescia).

18. Vignon 1902, p. 33.

19. Bucklin 1998, p. 100. Other observers agree in calling the scourge marks "dumbbell shaped" (see, e.g., Wilson 1998, p. 42; Zugibe 2005, p. 194).

20. For the *flagrum*, see Vignon 1902, pp. 36, 39; Barbet 1963, p. 46.

21. See Zugibe 2005, p. 19.

22. See Barbet 1963, pp. 45–6 (quoting Plautus); Bucklin 1998, p. 100; Zugibe 2005, p. 22.

23. For other examples, see Wilson 1998, p. 32; Pfeiffer 2000, p. 94. As Wilson comments, "the overriding issue with regard to all such artists' depictions of Jesus' whipping, from whatever period, is that they simply do not bear the slightest serious comparison with the sheer logic of the markings as on the Shroud."

24. See Barbet 1963, p. 98; Antonacci 2000, p. 20.

25. Bucklin 2002, p. 272.

26. See Wilson 1978, pp. 24–5; Antonacci 2000, p. 101. For the *patibulum*, see also Barbet 1963, pp. 40–42, 99; Brown 1994, pp. 912–13, 948; Zugibe 2005, pp. 46–8; Wilson 2010, p. 46.

27. Cf. Zugibe 2005, p. 195: "An image consistent with an abrasion is present in the

region of the right shoulder . . . There is also an image in the region of the left scapula consistent with an abrasion. These abrasions are consistent with injuries sustained while carrying the crosspiece of the cross." For the debate about how the *patibulum* was carried, see Barbet 1963, pp. 41, 99–101; Antonacci 2000, p. 101; Zugibe 2005, pp. 46–8.

28. As Zugibe 2005, p. 219, explains, "even tiny wounds may bleed profusely during heart activity," and the "scourge markings were made many hours prior to removal from the cross, so that encrusted clots would have formed in the wounds, therefore making it difficult to understand how the scourge marks could have left such precise imprints."

29. Ibid., p. 221.

30. See ibid., pp. 215, 221.

31. Ibid., p. 219. This interpretation complies with the fact that no chemical evidence of sweat has been found on the Shroud (p. 220).

32. See Danby 1933, p. 120 (Mishnah, Shabbath 23.5). It is also attested in Acts 9.37. For the statement in the non-canonical *Gospel of Peter* that the body of Jesus was washed, see below, p. 227.

33. Ganzfried 1963, vol. 4, p. 99. For the application of this regulation to the case of the Shroud-man, see Lavoie 1998, pp. 67–75; Wilson 1998, pp. 54–5; Antonacci 2000, pp. 117–18. These writers all assume (incorrectly) that the body wrapped in the Shroud was not washed.

34. It is compatible, for instance, with provisions about "unclean" blood in the Mishnah, discussed in Lavoie 1998, pp. 70–74, for which see Danby 1933, pp. 289–90, 653–4 (Nazir 7.2; Oholoth 3.5).

35. See Ganzfried 1963, vol. 4, p. 100; Leviticus 17.11.

36. Ganzfried 1963, vol. 4, p. 100.

37. Wilson 1998, p. 55 (with reference to Ganzfried 1963, vol. 4, pp. 99–100). Wilson notes that the use of a *sovev* in the case of violent death is also prescribed by the thirteenth-century Jewish scholar Nahmanides.

38. See Wilson 1998, p. 55. Fulbright 2005 states that "long shrouds wrapped under and over the body have in fact been excavated" near Jerusalem and reproduces a Biblical Archaeological Society photograph of just such a burial from Givat ha-Mivtar. Unfortunately, she gives no source for this information.

39. For identification of the wound, see Barbet 1963, pp. 133–4; Bucklin 1998, p. 99; Wilson 1998, p. 37.

40. On the Roman *lancea*, see Bulst 1957, p. 68; Antonacci 2000, pp. 100–101; Wilson 2010, p. 49.

41. For the ancient sources regarding this custom, see Bulst 1957, pp. 50–51; Barbet 1963, pp. 51–2.

42. Joe Nickell, for instance, imagines that such a wound should have produced "a copious flow covering at least the lower side of the body and the thigh" (Nickell 1998, p. 66). Nickell seems to have in mind a wound to a live body, whereas the trickles imprinted on the Shroud evidently seeped from a gash made in a suspended corpse.

43. Bucklin 1998, p. 99.

44. See Barbet 1963, p. 133.

45. For the water stains on the Shroud, see Wilson 2010, pp. 79–83.

46. See Barbet 1963, p. 137; Wilson 1978, p. 29 (quoting Dr. David Willis); Zugibe 2005, p. 196.

47. Following Barbet, many of the Shroud's medical examiners claim that the lance punctured the right atrium of the heart; others suppose that it merely penetrated the right lung and chest cavity. For the various medical opinions about the side wound, see Barbet 1963, pp. 137–8; Zugibe 2005, pp. 139–43. As Zugibe 2005, p. 155, notes, the angle of the blade "depends on how high off the ground the *crucarius* [i.e. the crucifixion victim] was suspended, the height of the soldier who initiated the spear thrust, the place where the soldier was standing (on a hill, mound, etc.), the length of the spear handle, how the spear was held during thrusting, etc.."

48. John 19.34.

49. Bucklin 1998, p. 99. Cf. Wilson 1978, p. 29, quoting Dr. David Willis. In my opinion, the clear patches in the midst of the stain are just gaps between individual trickles of blood (as at the bottom of the stain) or areas that did not transfer because of a depression in the clot. Any clear fluid that came out of the wound would have mixed immediately with the blood (see Zugibe 2005, pp. 142–3).

50. See Wilson 1998, p. 290.

51. See Barbet 1963, pp. 24, 142, 149, 151–2; Bucklin 1970, p. 25. Vignon 1902, p. 20, thought that the stains were connected with the 1532 burn marks.

52. See Wilson 1998, p. 38 (citing the opinion of Dr. Joseph Gambescia); Zugibe 2005, p. 196.

53. STURP's reflectance spectroscopy and microscopic examination in Turin revealed the heels of the Shroud figure to be relatively dirty (see Heller 1983, p. 112). As Heller comments, "What could be more logical than to find dirt on the foot of a man who has walked without shoes? Obviously, no one was crucified wearing shoes or sandals . . . There is not enough dirt to be seen visually, so it follows that no forger would have put it there . . ."

54. Cf. Zugibe 2005, p. 214: "after post-mortem blood flows from a wound, it rarely coagulates, but may dry. Any kind of moisture can reliquefy it."

55. Cf. Ganzfried 1963, vol. 4, pp. 99–100, in which it is stipulated that someone who has died a violent death should be buried not only in his clothes, in case they contain lifeblood, but also with any blood-soaked earth from the spot where he fell.

56. For a useful photograph of a tracing of this dribble laid over the arm of a man lying in the position of the Shroud-man, see Lavoie 1998, p. 83. Lavoie's own theory as to how this dribble formed is different from my own and depends on the nail having been removed from the wrist when the *patibulum* was still on top of the *stipes*, a scenario I consider unlikely.

57. Zugibe 2005, p. 193.

58. Nickell 1998, p. 67. Nickell cites one example in support of his argument, Giovanni da Milano's *Pietà* in the Accademia, Florence (illustrated in Janson 1962, p. 274), which bears no obvious relation to the Shroud-image.

59. Wilson 1998, p. 34.

60. For the "cap" of thorns, see Barbet 1963, pp. 93–7; Bucklin 1998, p. 99; Zugibe 2005, pp. 36–7.

61. Regarding the way in which the blood appears to have dribbled over the hair in places, Zugibe 2005, p. 193 states that in his "forensic reconstruction of the effects of the crown of thorns, the hair would have been saturated with blood and would have been initially dry, exerting an effect similar to that of hair spray . . ." Lavoie argues that the dribbles seen on the frontal locks were actually located on the side of the face, the cloth having been subsequently tautened (see Lavoie 1998, pp. 104–11), but Zugibe's observation makes this hypothesis unnecessary. The matting of the hair may account, too, for the rather solid, prominent appearance of the locks, which would have hung down either side of the head, as it drooped on the cross.

62. Quoted in Lavoie 1998, p. 66.

11 The Body-Image

1. For the "hot statue method," see Ashe 1966; for the "medieval photography" idea, see below, pp. 139–42; for the "shadow shroud theory," see Wilson 2005; for the "acid dabbing method," see the critique by Heimburger and Fanti 2010. For useful reviews of various forgery theories, see Antonacci 2000, pp. 47–59, 73–96; Zugibe 2005, pp. 245–6, 252–62.

2. Quoted in Lavoie 1998, p. 65.

3. See McCrone 1999, pp. 121–2, 287–8. McCrone obtained his knowledge of Simone Martini from the back of a postcard.

4. See Heller and Adler 1981, p. 90; Miller and Pellicori 1981, p. 84; Schwalbe and Rogers 1982, pp. 10–24; Tribbe 1983, p. 144; Jumper et al. 1984, pp. 450–55; Rogers 2008, p. 28.

5. See Schwalbe and Rogers 1982, p. 24; Tribbe 1983, pp. 143–4; Jumper et al. 1984, pp. 454–5.

6. See Schwalbe and Rogers 1982, p. 24; Antonacci 2000, pp. 37–8.

7. See Jumper et al. 1984, p. 453, for a useful summary of the evidence.

8. See Heller and Adler 1981, pp. 97–8; Heller 1983, pp. 148–9, 173–4, 178–80, 194–6; Tribbe 1983, pp. 133–4; Wilson 1986, pp. 89–91; Antonacci 2000, pp. 53–4.

9. See Heller and Adler 1981, pp. 99–100; above, p. 115.

10. Worth noting is the opinion of McCrone formed by Edward Hall, one of the scientists who carried out the 1988 carbon dating of the Shroud. Interviewed by Ian Wilson, Hall stated "very candidly that he was totally unimpressed by McCrone as a scientist and thought he relied far too much on subjective visual assessments from looking through a conventional microscope" (Wilson 1998, p. 198).

11. See Nickell 1998, pp. 100–106. Nickell's "solution" is apparently accepted in Lane Fox 1991, pp. 250–51.

12. See Nickell 1978a; Nickell 1978b.

13. See Nickell 1998, pp. 133–40.

14. See Antonacci 2000, p. 74, for experimental proof of this criticism. For general criticism of Nickell's theory, see Antonacci 2000, pp. 73–6; Zugibe 2005, pp. 255–6.

15. Zugibe 2005, p. 231. Cf. Barbet 1963, p. 91; Bucklin 1970, p. 25.

16. See Zugibe 2005, pp. 179–80, 231; Bucklin 1970, p. 25. Using life-size photographic prints and 3-D imaging, medics have identified various other signs of injury across the face (see Zugibe 2005, pp. 37, 179–80, 230–32). However, I suspect many of these may be artifacts produced by the interaction of the weave and the image-forming mechanism.

17. Nickell 1998, p. 104, admits that his rubbing technique is "not entirely 'mechanical.'"

18. See Picknett and Prince 1994. For a brief refutation of the Leonardo proto-photography theory, see Ware 1997, p. 265.

19. For Allen's theory, see Allen 1993; Allen 1995; Allen 2010. For cogent criticism of Allen's argument, see Wilson 1998, pp. 212–18; Antonacci 2000, pp. 84–93; Zugibe, pp. 261–3. Recently, building on Allen's speculations, Keith Laidler has argued that the Shroud is a photograph produced by the Knights Templar toward the end of the thirteenth century to record the appearance of the embalmed head of Jesus (see Laidler 2000, esp. pp. 163–7).

20. On the nineteenth-century invention of photography in the context of the visual culture of the time, see Crary 1990; Kemp 1990, pp. 167–220.

21. The first records of a lens being used in a camera obscura date from the sixteenth century (see Antonacci 2000, p. 90; Zugibe 2005, p. 262).

22. Antonacci 2000, p. 92. Cf. Ware 1997, p. 264: "[Allen] implicitly assumes, without evidence or justification, the existence of a lens technology that was unknown until several centuries later."

23. Allen 2010, pp. 63–4, suggests weakly that the "proto-photographer" might have worked in a cold climate. As he admits, too, the cadaver would have had to have been painted white (hair and all) to reflect enough sunlight. Ware 1997, p. 264, reckons that, given fourteenth-century lens technology, a more realistic exposure time would have been months, making the task "effectively impossible."

24. X-ray fluorescence spectrometry detected only calcium, strontium and iron (see Morris et al. 1980, pp. 45–6; Heller 1983, p. 136). As noted above, p. 115, particles of silver deriving from the silver chest in which the Shroud was once stored have been found on the cloth, but these are insignificant in this context. For the traces of silver remaining on Allen's replica, see Ware 1997, pp. 264–5.

25. Allen 2010, pp. 16–21, acknowledges that the blood on the Shroud is real. He believes, though, that the scourge marks were achieved with "at least two stamps (which ensured a regular tripartite pattern)" and that elsewhere the blood was trickled and brushed on "with or without an iron based binder" (pp. 137–8). He also avers that the "application of blood was done in accordance with the conventions of the time—that time being the late thirteenth century" (p. 75; cf. p. 94), a statement he does not support with suitable comparisons.

26. See Schwortz 2000: "Allen's image provides the necessary evidence to disqualify photography as the Shroud's image formation process." Schwortz provides a useful critique of Allen's theory. See also Ware 1997, pp. 264–5.

27. That light had nothing to do with the creation of the body-image is proved by the VP-8 Image Analyzer results, which demonstrate that the tonal gradations of the image are determined by cloth-to-body distances, not varying degrees of illumination (see above, p. 101). Fed into a VP-8, Allen's proto-photo produces a horribly distorted image, like any regular photo (see Antonacci 2000, p. 86, Figs 62 and 64).

28. See Piczek 1995; Piczek 1996. Piczek takes no account of the possible effects of rigor mortis. Her analysis leads to the impossible conclusion that "when the image was projected on the Shroud, so to speak, the top half and bottom half of the Shroud, both, have been absolutely straight, more straight than any cloth under normal circumstances could be" (Piczek 1996) and is backed up by a peculiar drawing that neither matches the Shroud figure nor represents an accurate anatomical view—the legs are obviously too long to be foreshortened. For further criticism of Piczek's analysis see Laidler 2000, p. 267.

29. Zugibe 2005, pp. 196–7, explains the representation of the feet in this way, quoting Bulst to the same effect.

30. See Rogers 2008, pp. 43–4.

31. For the rate of decomposition of a dead body, see below, ch. 12, n. 36.

32. Scientific analyses of the Shroud-image support the view that, if the cloth was draped over a man's body, no major distortion should be expected (see Ercoline and Jackson 1982; Latendresse 2005). Incidentally, Latendresse makes the important point that the intensity of the image at any given point is probably governed by the shortest distance from body to cloth; it is unlikely to be an exclusively vertical projection, as assumed by Ercoline and Jackson.

33. For evidence of minor distortions, especially in the region of the face, see Ercoline and Jackson 1982; Latendresse 2005.

34. Allen 2010, p. 64, notes the exaggerated width of the pelvic region, which gives the Shroud figure a "feminine appearance." This is confirmed in Ercoline and Jackson 1982, pp. 577–8; Latendresse 2005.

35. For a summary explanation of rigor mortis, see Zugibe 2005, p. 212.

36. Laidler 2000, p. 185.

37. Zugibe 2005, p. 213, puts it succinctly: "if rigor were not present, there should have been symmetrical images of the legs." And he concludes, therefore, that, when he died, "the man of the Shroud would have been fixed in an attitude of suspension." Cf. Bucklin 1998, p. 99.

38. For this graffito, see Wilson 1984, frontispiece; Brown 1994, pp. 947, 952 n. 37. The feet in this example are splayed apart, but this is irrelevant to the interpretation of the Shroud. Barbet 1963, pp. 43, 64, notes that the first literary reference to a *suppedaneum* occurs in the sixth century and dismisses the idea that one was used in the crucifixion of Jesus as "a product of the artistic imagination." Zugibe 2005, pp. 58, 96, denies that a *suppedaneum* was used for Jesus on the same inadequate grounds.

39. See Schwortz 2000 for discussion of this issue.

40. This is pointed out in Knight and Lomas 1998, pp. 199, 201–2. These authors wrongly deduce from this and other evidence that the Shroud-man was alive and resting in an amply cushioned bed.

41. Cf. Zugibe 2005, p. 213: "the rigor had to be broken at the shoulder joint and slightly at the elbows in order to assume the position present on the Shroud." Incidentally, it is often claimed that the crossing of the hands over the genitals is a sign of medieval prudishness (see, e.g., Nickell 1998, p. 55). There is no substance to this claim. There are plenty of examples of bodies and funerary statues from antiquity that are arranged like this (see, e.g., Wilson 1998, p. 56); it was not a specifically medieval pose. Ancient Jews, in any case, were just as prudish as medieval Europeans, and the Shroud-man's burial was incomplete, meaning that his body would be seen again by others. If he was Jesus, we know historically that his burial was due to be completed by women, which would have made such minimal modesty even more important.

42. See Picknett and Prince 1994; Laidler 2000, pp. 259–69.

43. Cf. Zugibe 2005, p. 179: "there is no discernible neck space due to the raising of the shoulders with the head caught in between them and bent forward." The way the head was bent forward also accounts for the elongated appearance of the neck on the dorsal figure (see ibid., p. 213).

44. See, for instance, Picknett and Prince 1994, pp. 134–8, who measure the lengths of the dorsal and frontal images and then declare that the Shroud-man would have had to have been 2 inches taller at the back than the front, a discrepancy said to indicate that the Shroud is a fake.

45. See Zugibe 2005, pp. 190–91.

46. See, e.g., Antonacci 2000, p. 64.

47. Cf. ibid., p. 177: "using the magnetic lasso tool from the computer program Photoshop, Barrie Schwortz has shown that the sides of the Shroud's facial image are indeed visible in the darker areas on the sides of the face."

48. See Danby 1933, p. 120 (Mishnah, Shabbath 23.5).

49. This figure is derived from the graph correlating image intensity with cloth–body distance in Jackson et al. 1977, p. 77 (cf. Nickell 1998, pp. 92–3).

50. Cf. Bulst 1957, p. 95: "the hair and the beard formed as it were a frame about the face on which the Shroud could rest." The blank areas in between the face and its hairy "frame" are probably due to the cloth having bridged the space between the cheeks and the locks, rather than the inhibiting effect of the headband itself.

12 A Natural Image of Jesus?

1. Josephus, *Antiquities*, 20.102 (2006, p. 867), reports that two sons of Judas the Galilean were crucified under Tiberias Alexander c. AD 46, but there is no evidence they were regarded as messiahs either by the Romans or by the Jewish populace.

2. See Knight and Lomas 1998, pp. 185–215, 314–22.

3. See Straiton 1989. Straiton's idea is partially seconded in Laidler 2000, pp. 203–5, 219–20. For evidence of Muslim crucifixions in medieval times, see Laidler 2000, pp. 197–202; Zugibe 2005, p. 53.

4. The hypothesis cannot be significantly improved by speculating that Christians, rather than Muslims, were responsible. Needless to say, medieval Christians were no more au fait with Jewish burial rites than their Muslims contemporaries. Even if some pious masochist did die on a cross in medieval Europe, his body would hardly have been half-buried like the Shroud-man's. (For an example of non-fatal crucifixion in medieval England, which was condemned as blasphemous, see Binski 2004, p. 201.)

5. Delage 1902, p. 686, reckons the likelihood of the Shroud deriving from the crucifixion of a "Jesus-double" to be in the order of 1 in 10^{10}, a figure not to be taken literally, he says, but as an indication of the implausibility of all the circumstances of the death of Jesus being exactly repeated.

6. See, e.g., Vignon 1902, pp. 134–70; Barbet 1963, pp. 32–5; Volckringer 1991, p. 15.

7. For these suggestions, see Antonacci 2000, pp. 211–36, and Zugibe 2005, pp. 273–4, respectively. (Zugibe reports and criticizes the X-ray hypothesis of Dr. Giles Carter.) For useful reviews of the various radiation theories, see Zugibe 2005, pp. 266–78; Rogers 2008, pp. 77–93.

8. For discussion of the corona discharge hypothesis, see Fanti et al. 2005; Zugibe 2005, pp. 268–73; Rogers 2008, pp. 83–6. The hypothesis originally posited an earthquake as the source of the electrical energy involved, but Fanti et al. 2005 speculate that the corona discharge "could have been a by-product of a particular phenomenon, such as the Resurrection," as do Mary and Alan Whanger 1998, p. 124.

9. See Rogers 2008, pp. 31–3, 56–8, 86–93.

10. Ibid., p. 93. Cf. Jumper et al. 1984, p. 456: "the process that formed the final chemistry took place at lower temperatures (less than 200 °C), because no pyrolitic compounds were found." Miller and Pellicori 1981, p. 84, note that the body-image does not fluoresce under UV light, providing further evidence that it is not a scorch.

11. See Antonacci 2000, pp. 222–32.

12. Rogers 2008, pp. 80–81.

13. Another problem which undermines every radiation hypothesis is the observation of a reverse image in the region of the hair (see above, pp. 106–7). As Rogers 2008, p. 91, asks, "What kind of radiation would penetrate the cloth and color it in the area of the hair and not penetrate the cloth anywhere else?" There is also the fact that the body-image did not form beneath the bloodstains or serum exudations, which X-rays and other forms of radiation would have penetrated easily. Moreover, if X-rays were responsible, emanating from every part of the body, we should expect the image to appear skeletal.

14. See Volckringer 1991. For discussion of Volckringer's work, see Barbet 1963, pp. 33–5; Wilson 1986, pp. 99–100. Dr. Alan Mills has developed a hypothesis involving the release of singlet oxygen to account for both the Volckringer

imprints and the Shroud's body-image (see Mills 1995; Knight and Lomas 1998, pp. 314–22), but his ideas have not yet been confirmed by other scientists.

15. For more on this mattress image, see Wilson 1998, p. 209; Laidler 2000, p. 176.

16. For this experiment and Vignon's perceptive analysis, see Vignon 1902, pp. 154–62.

17. This is such a significant observation that it is worth quoting Vignon's analysis in full: "The sensitive plate recorded even slight gradations, as may be seen in examining the medal. In addition to this the intensity of the emanation decreased so rapidly when the distance increased, that the hollow of the neck, or the slope of the right shoulder, are now *more distinct than in the photograph itself*. Doubtless the photograph gives details which the print made without a lens cannot distinguish, but on the other hand *the photograph is in error with regard to relative relief*. For instance, in the photograph taken through a lens we might think that the right shoulder projects almost as far as the left, and that the chin makes but a very slight projection from the neck. *The chemical impression on the contrary tends rather to exaggerate the variations of the active surface, and on our print, far from perceiving a mere flat representation, we obtain an impression in marked relief*" (Vignon 1902, p. 161, my italics).

18. See, e.g., below, n. 39. Jackson et al. 1982, pp. 569–70, reject the vaporograph theory on the basis of an inadequate experiment that yielded a poorly resolved image, which appeared "somewhat deformed" when processed by the VP-8 Image Analyzer. Their vaporograph (reproduced in Antonacci 2000, p. 62) is much less clear and coherent than the vaporographs created by Vignon and his colleague, René Colson. These earlier images, which Jackson and his colleagues ignore, suggest that vaporographs *may* share the three-dimensional quality of the Shroud-image.

19. Cf. John 19.39–40.

20. See Vignon 1902, pp. 162–70.

21. For the absence of myrrh and aloes on the Shroud, see Rogers 2008, pp. 43–4.

22. See Vignon 1902, p. 155. For discussion and criticism of various contact theories, see Antonacci 2000, pp. 63–8; Zugibe 2005, pp. 248–51; Rogers 2008, p. 94.

23. Rogers and Arnoldi 2003. The same argument is made in Rogers 2008, pp. 29–31, 99–120.

24. See Rogers 2008, p. 109.

25. See ibid., p. 38, and above, pp. 110–11.

26. See Rogers and Arnoldi 2003, p. 108.

27. Rogers 2008, p. 100.

28. Ibid.

29. See Vignon 1902, pp. 163–4. Rogers 2008, p. 31, states without giving a source: "Many shrouds have been observed in archaeological contexts, and some of them show partial images."

30. Rogers and Arnoldi 2003, p. 109; cf. Rogers 2008, p. 105.

31. See Rogers 2008, p. 102.

32. See ibid., pp. 101, 106, 115.

33. See Zugibe 2005, p. 282.

34. Rogers and Arnoldi 2003, p. 112.

35. See Rogers 2008, pp. 108, 118–19. Rogers also notes that the concentration of heavier decomposition molecules, such as putrescine and cadaverine, will diminish rapidly in proportion to the distance from the body, and he observes that this "will be a major factor . . . in calculating the maximum resolution of an image-formation mechanism that involves diffusion" (ibid., p. 115). Although Rogers does not acknowledge any debt to Vignon, he does admit that STURP's dismissal of vapor diffusion as a mechanism involved in forming the image was misleading. While they were right to conclude that the image had nothing to do with diffusion through the cloth, lateral diffusion across the surface of the cloth should not have been excluded as a potential factor. See ibid., p. 112.

36. Mannix 2011, p. 6. Fanti et al. 2005 reject the Maillard reaction hypothesis primarily on the grounds that there are no signs of liquid putrefaction. Rogers 2008, p. 116, cites a recent study by Arpad Vass and others, however, which finds that putrefaction "generally starts between 36 and 72 hours after death." In other words, there could well have been time for the Maillard reaction to occur and for the cloth to have been removed from the body before the body started to putrefy.

37. See, e.g., Rogers 2008, p. 106, who speculates that "such a situation could be explained by the delay in the development of the Maillard reactions' colors at moderate temperatures."

38. Ibid., p. 102.

39. Cf Mills 2009, p. 20, who dismisses the Maillard reaction hypothesis as follows: "It would seem that, as in the related Vignon hypothesis, one might expect a filled silhouette rather than a structured image."

40. Cf. Psalms 16.10.

13 The Carbon-Dating Fiasco

1. Damon et al. 1989, p. 611.

2. On carbon dating and its problems, see Meacham 1986; Antonacci 2000, pp. 155–8.

3. Currie 2004, p. 204.

4. Cf. Meacham 2005, p. 54: "I have excavated, submitted and interpreted around one hundred fifty C-14 samples from Neolithic, Bronze Age and Early Historical sites. Of these dates obtained, about 110 were considered credible, 30 were rejected as unreliable and 10 were problematic."

5. For this example and others, see Antonacci 2000, p. 157; Meacham 1986; Wilson 1998, pp. 192–3. Wilson, p. 192, draws attention to the problematic case of Lindow Man, a "bog body" discovered in the English county of Cheshire, which was carbon dated in 1986, just two years before the Shroud: "Samples from his body were sent to three different British radiocarbon-dating laboratories: Harwell, which dated him to around the fifth century AD; Oxford, which dated him to around the first century AD, and the British Museum, which dated him to the third century BC. Although each laboratory claimed its dating to be accurate to

within a hundred years, in actuality their datings varied between each other by as much as 800 years."

6. Meacham 2005, p. 55.

7. Quoted in Wilson 1998, p. 193.

8. Quoted in Antonacci 2000, p. 171.

9. On the inter-laboratory comparison test, see Burleigh et al. 1986; Gove 1996, pp. 77–81; Antonacci 2000, pp. 174–5.

10. See Burleigh et al. 1986, p. 574.

11. Coghlan 1989.

12. Ibid.

13. Three archaeologists—William Meacham, Roberto Ciarla and Maurizio Tosi— did offer to supervise the carbon-dating operation, but this sensible offer was ignored. See Meacham 2005, p. 83.

14. Gove 1996, p. 14.

15. For the Turin Protocol, see Antonacci 2000, pp. 177–8; Gove 1996, pp. 174–5.

16. See Meacham 2005, p. 75; Gove 1996, p. 153 (who ridicules Meacham's advice).

17. Quoted in Antonacci 2000, p. 177.

18. Even if the threads were unravelled—an option discounted because it would have resulted in too much material being lost in the cleaning process—they could still have been identified by their lineal densities (see Gove 1996, pp. 154, 163).

19. For the objections to the blind-testing charade, see Gove 1996, pp. 154, 163, 168–70; Meacham 2005, pp. 73, 91.

20. Quoted in Gove 1996, p. 252.

21. For detailed accounts of the lead-up to the 1988 carbon-dating test, see Gove 1996, pp. 177–252; Wilson 1998, pp. 179–85; Meacham 2005, pp. 52–90. Needless to say, the difficulties are glossed over entirely in Damon et al. 1989.

22. Cf. Gove 1996, p. 295: "I again thanked providence for ensuring that the carbon-14 results had not been tainted by any involvement by STURP."

23. See Gove 1996, p. 261; Meacham 2005, p. 90; Wilson 2010, p. 87.

24. See Meacham 2005, pp. 92, 96–7; Rogers 2008, pp. 63–76.

25. Quoted in Wilson 1998, p. 7.

26. See Bollone 1998, p. 120.

27. See Wilson 1998, p. 193.

28. Wilson 1998, p. 229, citing Gove et al. 1997.

29. Gove 1996, pp. 160, 291.

30. See Kouznetsov et al. 1996. For criticism of this paper, see Jull et al. 1996.

31. See, e.g., Antonacci 2000, pp. 159–64.

32. See Gove 1996, pp. 308–9; Wilson 1998, pp. 223–31; Garza-Valdes 1998.

33. See Benford and Marino 2002; Benford and Marino 2005.

34. Flury-Lemberg 2007, p. 15. Cf. Flury-Lemberg 2003, p. 60.

35. Rogers 2005, p. 192.

36. See Kersten and Gruber 1994, who report the investigations of the Catholic Counter-Reformation group.

37. See Couzin 2006.

38. Meacham 2005, p. 144. Meacham nevertheless dismisses any idea of a conspiracy

as "patent nonsense," principally because he cannot imagine "who would do such a thing, and why" (p. 117).

39. Speaking in *Shroud of Turin: material evidence*, BBC documentary film, directed by David Rolfe, broadcast March 22, 2008, BBC2.

40. ORAU website: http://c14.arch.ox.ac.uk/embed.php?File=shroud.html (accessed December 28, 2011).

14 The Shroud in the East

1. On the Fourth Crusade and the Sack of Constantinople, see Bartlett 1999, pp. 199–210; Tyerman 2006, pp. 538–54; Herrin 2007, pp. 262–5.

2. See Gibbon 1923, vol. 6, pp. 405–12.

3. My translation after the original French text, for which see de Clari 1924, p. 90. For discussion of this passage see Wilson 1978, pp. 76–7, 145–7; Dembowski 1982; Wilson 1998, pp. 124–5, 142–5; Scavone 2006, p. 12.

4. See Matthew 27.59; Mark 15.46; Luke 23.53. According to Dembowski 1982, p. 15, "*Sydoines* is a masculine singular noun . . . *Sydoine*, or *sidoine*, is a normal rendering of the Latin *syndonis-sindonem* . . ."

5. As Peter Dembowski, an expert on Old French literature, explains, "Before *circa* 1650, *figure* meant what it signified in Latin, i.e. 'figure,' 'outline,' 'form,' etc." (Dembowski 1982, p. 16). Since the *sydoines* was a winding sheet and "rose up straight" so that the *figure* could be seen, it is clear that it manifested an image of Christ's body. Skeptics, misled by the meaning of the word in modern French, have wrongly suggested that Robert's *figure* might refer only to a facial image (see, e.g., Nickell 1998, p. 54).

6. For discussion of the possible route taken by the Shroud from Constantinople to Lirey, see Piana 2007; Wilson 2010, pp. 194–214.

7. Belting 1990, p. 105.

8. Quoted in Lavoie 1998, p. 65.

9. My translation from the original Greek, for which see Dubarle 1985, p. 39 n. 19. For discussion of this passage, see Wilson 1978, p. 144; Dubarle 1985, pp. 37–9; Wilson 1998, p. 145; Scavone 2006, p. 11.

10. Hans Belting has no hesitation in identifying the *sydoines* with the *sindones* (see Belting 1990, p. 105). That Nicholas refers to "sheets" in the plural is not a significant discrepancy. Only a single *sindon* is referred to previously in the Pharos Chapel (see below), and, if the relic was displayed mechanically, as implied by Robert de Clari's description, it may have appeared like a pair of sheets. Green 1969, p. 329, notes that in the eighth century John Damascene also uses the plural to refer to Christ's shroud (*sindonas*).

11. For rare fourteenth-century depictions of Christ naked, see Steinberg 1983, pp. 131–3.

12. *Aperilepton* may have been an accepted theological term for Christ (see Dubarle 1985, p. 39 n. 20). If so, the question is why this strange term was adopted by theologians in the first place. After all, in the Middle Ages bodies were defined by

their outlines, which guaranteed their correct depiction. The term itself could have been inspired by the un-outlined image on the Shroud. Whether directly or indirectly, then, Nicholas's description of the body wrapped by the Sindon as *aperilepton* may reflect the strangely ethereal Shroud-image. See also Dubarle 1985, p. 42, where he discusses the term *aperigraptos*, meaning roughly the same thing.

13. See Riant 1878, p. 216; Wilson 1998, p. 271.

14. For this source, see Riant 1878, p. 208; Joranson 1950; Wilson 1978, p. 143; Scavone 2006, pp. 7–9.

15. See Mazzucchi 1983; Wilson 1998, pp. 268–9; Scavone 2006, p. 5. Wilson translates the phrase as "God-bearing," while Scavone translates it as "the *sindon* which God wore."

16. On the Pray Codex see Berkovits 1969, pp. 19–20; Dubarle 1985, pp. 44–6; Bongert 1995, pp. 98–101; Lejeune 1995, pp. 104–9; Dubarle 1998, pp. 47–57; Dubarle 2000.

17. Cf. John 19.39–40.

18. Cf. Mark 16.5–6.

19. See Wilson 1978, p. 137.

20. Cited in Dubarle 2000, p. 183.

21. See Dubarle 1985, p. 44; Dubarle 2000, p. 183.

22. See Dubarle 1985, p. 45; Dubarle 2000, pp. 185–6. The Shroud's unusual weave also caught the attention of the artist who designed the 1355 pilgrim badge (Figure 9).

23. Cf. Dubarle 1985, p. 45.

24. This correspondence is first noted in Dubarle 1998, p. 51. Dubarle credits the observation to a Dr. Y. Cartigny. The fifth circle in the lower rectangle may reflect the scattered damage around the four main poker-holes.

25. For crosses on liturgical garments as symbols of Christ's wounds and Crucifixion, see Marriott 1886, p. 173; Norris 1949, p. 32. See also Hill 1993 for the cross as the symbolic body of Christ.

26. For the *polystaurion*, see Walter 1982, pp. 13–16; Woodfin 2004, p. 297.

27. The celebrant of the Lord's Supper has represented Christ ever since the first century. The symbolism of priestly garments is complex and changeable. In the fourth century, Pope Sylvester ordained that the officiating priest should wear linen, recalling the linen in which Jesus was buried (see Marriott 1886, pp. 107–8). From the eighth century a bishop's outer garments were understood as a symbol of Christ's body (see Woodfin 2004, p. 297), while a fifteenth-century patriarch of Thessalonica interpreted the *polystaurion* as signifying the robe worn by Christ during his Passion (see Marriott 1886, p. 173). Ideas of this sort provide the context for the *polystaurion*-like representation of the Shroud in the Pray Codex.

28. Wilson 1978, pp. 230–31.

29. The first to discuss the d'Arcis Memorandum of 1389 was Canon Lalore in an article of 1877, which is quoted extensively in Chevalier 1899, pp. 9–13. More recent authors who set store by d'Arcis's claim that the relic was "a work of

human skill" are Nickell 1998, pp. 12–17; Lane Fox 1991, p. 250 (whose account of the Lirey affair is reliant on Nickell).

30. On the story of the controversies over archaeopteryx, in some ways a mirror-image of the Shroud-controversy, see Chambers 2002.

31. See Chevalier 1900, pp. xv, xxiii, respectively.

32. See Nickell 1998, pp. 15–16, for the argument that the silence of the de Charnys helps prove the Shroud a fake.

33. See Chevalier 1900, pp. xvii, xviii.

34. In 1205 Theodore Angelos, a nephew of one of the recently deposed Byzantine emperors, wrote to Pope Innocent III requesting help in recovering, among other things, "the linen in which our Lord Jesus Christ was wrapped after his death," then known to be in Athens (see Piana 2007, p. 45; Scavone 2006, p. 15; Wilson 2010, pp. 211–14). Similar diplomatic pressure could easily have been applied in 1389.

35. Chevalier 1900, p. 28.

36. For this skeptical argument, see, e.g., Nickell 1998, pp. 12, 21, 41–8.

37. Meacham 1983, p. 309.

38. For the early history of the Portland Vase, see Walker 2004, pp. 17–18; Painter and Whitehouse 1990, pp. 24–7. It has, in fact, been argued that the vase was made in the sixteenth century (see Eisenberg 2003), but the argument has not won acceptance and depends not on the lack of provenance, but on a dubious iconographic analysis.

39. See above, p. 17.

40. For Wilson's Mandylion theory, see Wilson 1978, pp. 92–147; Drews 1984, pp. 31–75; Kersten and Gruber 1994, pp. 102–90; Wilson 1998, pp. 149–75; Antonacci 2000, pp. 122–54; Wilson 2010, pp. 111–88.

41. Examples include the Madonna of Guadalupe (see Freedberg 1989, pp. 110–11), the Lateran *Acheropita* (see Belting 1994, pp. 64–8; Zaninotto 2000) and the Holy Face of Lucca (see Webb 1986; Manselli et al. 1984).

42. See Runciman 1931; Cameron 1981.

43. Transcribed and translated in Guscin 2009, pp. 7–69. A translation is also provided in Wilson 1978, pp. 235–51.

44. Guscin 2009, p. 11.

45. Thus, for example, the eighth-century patriarch Germanus of Constantinople refers to the image as "the impression of Christ's sweat-soaked face" (quoted in Wilson 1978, pp. 94–5). For explicit denials in the sources that the image was produced with paint, see Guscin 2009, pp. 75, 131, 205. For further instances of the image being interpreted as a sweat stain, see Guscin 2009, pp. 25, 29 and 153.

46. Luke 22.44.

47. See Guscin 2009, pp. 25, 77, 85.

48. Similarly, a text of c.800 speaks of the Mandylion as "a blood-stained image of the Lord" (see Wilson 1998, p. 269; Kersten and Gruber 1994, p. 165).

49. Quoted in Guscin 2009, p. 180. Wilson 1978, p. 95, and Runciman 1931, p. 250, agree that Symeon's testimony implies the image was "extremely blurred."

50. See Wolf 1998, p. 169, for the origin of this legend.

51. These references occur in the seventh-century *Acts of Thaddeus* (see Guscin 2009, p. 146), the eighth-century *Nouthesia Gerontos* (see Guscin 2009, p. 154), the ninth-century *Epistola Abgari* (see Ragusa 1989, pp. 35, 50 n. 3), and the tenth-century *Vita Alexius* (see Wilson 1998, p. 269).

52. See Guscin 2009, pp. 90, 94, 112.

53. See Matthew 27.35; Mark 15.24; Luke 23.34; John 19.23. For John Damascene's account of the Mandylion, see Guscin 2009, p. 152. Similarly, the Mandylion was termed a *peplos* ("robe") by Leo the Deacon, writing in the late tenth century (see Wilson 1998, p. 152; Drews 1984, p. 39). Even the term "Mandylion" itself, adopted in the eighth or ninth century, may hint that the cloth was relatively large, if, as Guscin 2009, p. 179, argues, "it derives from the Latin *mantilium*, a general word for a (large) cloth." (See Guscin 2009, p. 205, for further comments on the etymology of the word.) In English, the word "mantle" has the same etymology, as does the obsolete word "mandylion," used of an outer garment, such as that worn by a knight over his armor.

54. See Guscin 2009, pp. 95, 146. For discussion of the term *tetradiplon*, see Wilson 1978, pp. 99–100; Drews 1984, pp. 36–41; Wilson 1998, pp. 152–3; Fulbright 2005; Wilson 2010, pp. 140–41. Cameron 1981, p. 22 n. 35, admits that the term *tetradiplon* "would indeed seem to support the idea that the cloth in question was 'folded in four,'" but denies this is significant, because Christ is said only to have wiped his face on the cloth. This is irrelevant, though. See also below, ch. 18, n. 26.

55. According to the tenth-century *Narratio*, the cloth was "fixed to a wooden board and adorned with the gold that can still be seen" (Guscin 2009, p. 33). For a basic reconstruction of the Mandylion, see Wilson 1998, p. 153.

56. Before its transfer to Constantinople, the cloth may have been removed from its frame only once, when it was found in Edessa in the 550s. For the likely date of the Mandylion's discovery in Edessa, see Cameron 1981, pp. 5–10. For evidence that knowledge of its full image was known to a few in the early seventh century, see below, pp. 262–3. For the religious awe with which the Mandylion was regarded in Edessa, making public scrutiny of the relic impossible, see the account in the *Narratio* (Guscin 2009, pp. 64–5).

57. Others apparently interpreted the blood marks as drops of water, since "in even a moderately subdued light it is virtually impossible to distinguish a color difference between 'body' and 'blood' stains on the Shroud" (Wilson 1978, p. 102), yielding the idea that Christ washed his face before drying it on the cloth.

58. Quoted in Guscin 2009, p. 207. Similarly, in his *Historia Ecclesiastica* of c.1130 Ordericus Vitalis tells how the Mandylion displays "the form and size of the Lord's body to all who look on it" (quoted in Guscin 2009, p. 206). A full-body imprint is also specified in an anonymous Latin sermon of c.1130 (see Wilson 1998, p. 270) and in the *Otia Imperialis* of Gervase of Tilbury, written c.1211 (see Guscin 2009, pp. 206–7). It is also hinted at in the two Greek texts that refer to the cloth as the *tetradiplon*: both of these tell how King Abgar asked his messenger to record in a drawing Christ's "whole bodily appearance" (see Guscin 2009, pp. 90–91, 94–5, 146), implying that this wish was seen to be fulfilled in the hidden folds of the Mandylion.

59. The continuing denial by skeptics that the Mandylion was in any way Shroud-like is founded on the widespread aversion to any suggestion that the Shroud might predate the thirteenth century, but almost as important is a methodological error committed by historians of the relic. Both Steven Runciman and Averil Cameron, the most influential writers on the topic, proceed from the assumption that the earliest references to the relic provide the best evidence for its appearance (see Runciman 1931; Cameron 1981). This assumption is based on the historical principle of privileging earlier sources over later ones, which is appropriate for the study of events, for which earlier sources are closer to eyewitness testimony and therefore generally more reliable, but not for the study of objects, which, unlike events, endure over time, meaning that for them the best eyewitness testimony may well be contained in later sources. In the case of the Mandylion, the testimony of those who saw the image in Constantinople in 944 should be privileged over descriptions given by earlier writers, who may be repeating hearsay.

60. See Guscin 2009, pp. 30–37. Wilson has attempted to reconstruct the early history of the Mandylion on the basis of this legend (see Wilson 1978, pp. 112–18; Wilson 1998, pp. 161–75; Wilson 2010, pp. 127–34). Although I agree with his basic contention that the relic was walled up above the western gate of the city, I believe the circumstances of its sequestration and discovery need to be rethought.

15 The Animated Shroud

1. *Shroud of Christ?*, TV documentary aired on Channel 4, April 7, 2004.
2. Cf. Freedberg 1989, pp. 436–7, who connects the "moment" at which such aesthetic contemplation became prominent in Europe with Roger de Piles.
3. On animism and anthropomorphism, see Guthrie 1993; Guthrie 2002.
4. As the art theorist Tom Mitchell puts it, "the phenomenon of the living image or animated icon is an anthropological universal, a feature of the fundamental ontology of images as such" (Mitchell 2005, p. 11).
5. Guthrie 2002 argues that, historically, animism may even have been an important cause of religious beliefs.
6. On the statues of Jagannath and his relatives in Puri, see Gell 1998, pp. 144–9.
7. It is also this that gives the devotees access to the "soul" of the god. As Gell 1998, pp. 135–6, comments, "Eyes are, of all body orifices, those which signify 'interiority' (i.e. the possession of mind and intentionality) most immediately." It is important to note that the eyes of the Shroud figure appear to be wide open.
8. Acts 19.23–41.
9. Acts 19.35.
10. On ancient pagan images "not made by hand," see Freedberg 1989, pp. 33–7, 66–74; Belting 1994, pp. 55–6; McBeath and Gheorghe 2005. The most famous *diopetes* was the Palladium, a wooden image of Pallas Athene kept in the temple of Vesta in Rome, for which see McBeath and Gheorghe 2004. Idols such as the Palladium were not only thought to embody the divine being they represented,

but were also thought to be celestial in themselves, bodies as heavenly as the divine persons they contained. It may seem clear to us that such statues were, in reality, of human manufacture, but the ancient belief in their divine origin was undoubtedly sincere. Christians, too, have traditionally identified certain man-made images as of divine origin (e.g. the Madonna of Guadalupe, for which see above, ch. 14, n. 41), and such identifications are still being made—witness the recent rise of the cult of the Veil of Manopello, an obviously painted image that has started to attract attention as "another Shroud" (see Gaeta 2005).

11. Freedberg 1989, pp. 34-5, quotes Pausanias and comments on his words, as follows: "'Its appearance,' he recalls, 'suggested something of the divine'—even though (or perhaps because) it was 'outlandish and not like the customary Greek gods.'... There was nothing to stop the Methymnan fishermen from throwing away the object they found in their nets, but it looked like a god." For the original story, see Pausanias, *Description of Greece*, 10.19.3 (1965-9, vol. 4, pp. 471-3).

12. See Freedberg 1989, p. 265.

13. This is a major theme in Freedberg 1989.

14. Brilliant 1991, p. 7. He later describes his book as an attempt to "analyze the magical effect which portrait images have on the viewer" (p. 20).

15. It is not just images that are treated animistically. Alfred Gell brilliantly describes the "vehicular animism" that characterizes our attitudes toward our cars (Gell 1998, pp. 18-19). See also Guthrie 1993, pp. 60-61, 119-20. It is undoubtedly the case, however, that anthropomorphic images engage our animistic attention in a unique way (cf. Freedberg 1989, p. 73: "The anthropomorphization of an image makes its animate quality both more palpable and more terrifying"). Our proclivity to regard things animistically and anthropomorphically is closely related to our propensity to see intentionality in inanimate systems, a propensity Daniel Dennett has labelled the "intentional stance" (Dennett 1987).

16. Guthrie 1993, p. 54. There may be more to animism than this (see Gell 1998, pp. 121-33), but there is no need here for an in-depth discussion of its causes and modes of expression.

17. Cf. Guthrie 1993, p. 3: "Scanning the world for human and human-like things and events, we find apparent instances everywhere. We later judge many of these interpretations mistaken, but those that are correct more than justify the strategy. Because betting on the most significant interpretations is deeply rooted, anthropomorphism is spontaneous, plausible, and even compelling."

18. See Numbers 21.6-9; 2 Kings 18.4. On the Brazen Serpent as a magical image "integrated into the religious value system of the Bible," see Schäfer 1997, p. 30.

19. 2 Maccabees 12.40. On this episode, see Bohak 2008, pp. 119-21. Schäfer 1997, pp. 33-4, notes the strong "correlation between magic and idolatry" in both biblical and rabbinic Judaism.

20. On Jewish magical practices in antiquity, see Segal 1987, pp. 79-108; Bohak 2008, pp. 70-142; Schäfer 1997. According to Bohak 2008, p. 68, "the supposed incompatibility between magic and monotheism is nothing but a hoax"; while Schäfer 1997, p. 33, argues that in biblical and later Judaism, "magic is regarded as part of, and not opposed to religion." For Jewish practice and belief in magic

in the context of the debate about Christian origins, see, for instance, Smith 1973, pp. 217–37; Sanders 1993, pp. 135–54.

21. Contra, for instance, Wilson 1978, p. 112, who assumes that the Shroud would have been understood to break the second commandment.

22. Cf. Dunn 2003, p. 253, citing the examples of Enoch, Elijah, Ezra, Baruch and Moses: "Jewish monotheistic faith could accommodate the idea of one highly exalted [i.e. raised to celestial glory], without (apparently) any thought that Jewish monotheism was compromised or would have to be rethought."

23. On this topic, see Ferguson 2003, pp. 507–11; Freedberg 1989, pp. 55–6; Gibson 2009, pp. 85–6, 139.

24. Referring to the excavated paintings, Goodman 1987, p. 16 n. 28, notes that "opinion clearly differed on the permissibility of animal representation." Gibson 2009, p. 86, observes that they are "of such good quality that they might have looked respectable in any Roman town house, even at Pompeii." For the Herodian images, see Josephus, *War*, 5.180–81 (1967–79, vol. 3, p. 253); Josephus, *Antiquities*, 15.395, 416 (2006, pp. 681, 683).

25. See Numbers 21.4–9; Exodus 25.18–22; 1 Kings 6.23–8, 8.6–7.

26. See Genesis 16.7–14 (appearance to Hagar); Exodus 3.1–6 (appearance to Moses); Exodus 13.21–2 (leading the Israelites); Genesis 28.12 (Jacob's ladder); Genesis 18 (three divine men). For further instances of the Lord appearing in the guise of a "man," see Genesis 32.24–30; Joshua 5.13–15.

27. See, e.g., Wright 1992, p. 258; Dunn 1989, pp. 150–51.

28. Cf. Dunn 1989, p. 129: "One of the major features of late pre-Christian and non-Christian Judaism is the tremendous development of language which can readily be understood as denoting intermediate beings between God and man."

29. On the *Book of Enoch*, see Nickelsburg 1981, pp. 46–55. Parts of this work date back to the third century BC.

30. Vanderkam 1989, pp. 7–8. The original story in the Book of Genesis, written centuries earlier, does not mention the creation of a single angel.

31. Charles 1908, p. 38.

32. Tobit 12.15.

33. For white linen as a sign of "special purity" in connection with the Jewish priesthood, see Sanders 1992, pp. 96–101.

34. See Dunn 1989, pp. 152–3, with references to the relevant scrolls.

35. Cf. Wilson 1978, pp. 112–13, who suggests that the disciples would have been very anxious about the Shroud's contravention of the purity laws.

36. Matthew 28.1–4.

16 The Risen Jesus

1. See below, p. 250 and ch. 20, n. 3.

2. Cf. Freedberg 1989, p. 276: "When we see the resembling image, we elide it with the living prototype it represents . . ."

3. This argument has been made previously in Loken 2006, pp. 107–42. Remarkably,

it was anticipated by nineteenth-century German scholars, meditating on the disciples' discovery of the burial cloths (presumed to be unmarked). Regarding belief in the Resurrection, Strauss 1846, vol. 3, p. 367, observes, "The first impetus to this opinion, it has been conjectured, was given by the circumstance that on the second morning after the burial his grave was found empty, the linen clothes which lay in it being taken first for angels and then for an appearance of the risen Jesus himself . . ." See also Keim 1883, p. 326.

4. Celano 1997, pp. 147–8. This story is typical of the sort of miracle that many Christians believe happen occasionally: see Freedberg 1989, pp. 283–316.

5. On the persistence of "body–mind" dualism, see Humphrey 1999.

6. Humphrey 1999, p. 3, cites census data from the 1980s revealing that 88 percent of Americans and 61 percent of Europeans then believed in a soul and that 71 percent of Americans and 43 percent of Europeans believed in the survival of the soul after death.

7. See Watson 2005, pp. 102–6.

8. Homer, *Odyssey*, 11.476 (1962, p. 180). As Gregory Riley notes, in Homer and other ancient Greek authors, souls are conceived as mere images (*eidola*) of people (Riley 1995, pp. 48–50). Furthermore, "the dead retained not only their appearance (*eidolon*), but, in appropriate instances, even the marks (*stigma*) of the implements which caused their demise . . . the dead retained their *stigmata* as an essential characteristic of their *eidola*" (ibid., pp. 50–51). This is extremely suggestive in relation to the Shroud-image, which bears the marks of Jesus' torture and crucifixion.

9. Vermes 2008, pp. 20–21.

10. 1 Samuel 28.3–25. For the meaning of 'elohim, see Wright 2003, pp. 93–4.

11. Genesis 2.7, 3.19.

12. 2 Corinthians 4.7.

13. See Plato, *Republic*, 10.620 (1974, p. 454). On belief in reincarnation in the ancient world, see Wright 2003, pp. 77–9; Burkert 1985, pp. 298–301; Dodds 1951, pp. 150–56; Watson 2005, pp. 105, 116.

14. See Freedberg 1989, pp. 278–9; Tylor 1903, vol. 2, p. 176.

15. Freedberg 1989, pp. 276–8, argues that belief in metempsychosis is not an adequate explanation for the widespread confusion of people and their portraits, on the basis that the phenomenon depends on a deep cognitive identification of the person with the image, not a cultural theory about "souls" and their abilities. I accept Freedberg's analysis of the phenomenon, but, wherever the person is thought to be constituted in part by an inextinguishable "soul," metempsychosis may be regarded as an available rationalization of the instinctive identification of image and prototype.

16. The only possible evidence of Jewish belief in metempsychosis is found in the Gospels, in the report that Herod Antipas suspected Jesus of being John the Baptist raised from the dead: "At that time Herod the tetrarch heard about the fame of Jesus; he said to his servants, 'This is John the Baptist, he has been raised from the dead; that is why these powers are at work in him' " (Matthew 14.1–2; cf. Mark 6.14–16; Luke 9.7–9). The original significance of this saying is hard to discern, but it has been argued that it reflects a belief that the "powers" of a dead

man could take up residence in another (see Harvey 1994, p. 69). However, Wright 2003, p. 413 n. 44, takes issue with this interpretation.

17. Cf. Wedderburn 1999, p. 69: "to claim that someone had risen from the dead was compatible with a considerable variety of descriptions of what an encounter with that person would be like." On the interchangeability of reincarnation and resurrection, see Tylor 1903, vol. 2, pp. 19–20.

18. See Foucault 2002, pp. 19–50, for a classic account of this premodern "episteme."

19. See, e.g., Frazer 1913, part 1, vol. 1, pp. 207–14, part 2, pp. 77–100; Von Negelein 1902.

20. Frazer 1913, part 1, vol. 1, pp. 211, 213.

21. Later on, there was tremendous interest in miraculous impressions among early Christians. In the church at Lydda, for example, there was a column that supposedly bore the imprint of the Virgin, who had once leaned against it, while in North Africa there was a cloth relic reputed to bear an imprint of St. Stephen (see Belting 1994, pp. 57, 49, respectively). On the religious fascination with footprints and other bodily imprints, see Gibson 2005, pp. 167–70, and Dubabin 1990, pp. 85–9, who cites examples of imprints understood to signify "the presence of the divinity appearing to his or her worshippers" (p. 86).

22. See Frazer 1913, part 2, pp. 77–92, for the general equation of shadow and soul. On evidence for this belief among ancient Jews, see Van der Horst 1977; Van der Horst 1979, pp. 33–5. Having considered a number of biblical and rabbinic texts, Van der Horst 1979, p. 35, concludes that they leave "no doubt that this conception of the shadow as an influential force was also found in Judea during the Hellenistic-Roman period." On medieval Jewish beliefs about shadows, see Trachtenberg 1939, pp. 214–15. Van der Horst 1979, pp. 35–6, suggests similar ideas may also be found in Gnostic texts such as *The Hypostasis of the Archons* (for which see Robinson 1990, pp. 161–9, esp. pp. 165, 167).

23. Acts 5.15. On this, see Van der Horst 1977; Van der Horst 1979, p. 30; Stoichita 1997, p. 55. Even the presence and power of God could be conceived in terms of a shadow, cf. the announcement made by the angel Gabriel to the Virgin Mary in Luke 1.35: "The Holy Spirit will come upon you, and the power of the Most High will *overshadow* you . . ." On Luke 1.35, see Van der Horst 1977, pp. 211–12. Cf. also Sanders 1992, p. 72: "In first-century Palestine it was generally accepted that corpse-impurity could also be contracted by 'overshadowing' the corpse or by being 'overshadowed' by the corpse."

24. James 1924, p. 185. That this text may reflect awareness of the Shroud, as Dreisbach 2001 argues, is supported by the strong association of Thomas with Edessa.

25. On ancient mirrors, see Melchior-Bonnet 2001, pp. 9–13; Gregory 1997, pp. 47–9, 56–60.

26. See Gregory 1997, p. 48.

27. Melchior-Bonnet 2001, p. 102.

28. See ibid., pp. 283–4 n. 2; cf. Frazer 1913, part 2, pp. 94–6.

29. See Mack 1994, pp. 153–4. I find this interpretation of the motif more persuasive than Ada Cohen's suggestion that the reflection was meant by the artist as

a comment upon the illusionistic power of his art (see Cohen 1997, pp. 162–4). See also Taylor 2008, pp. 140–43.

30. Gregory 1997, p. 57. On mirrors as spiritual doubles, see also Goldberg 1985, pp. 3–7. On the use of mirrors in Jewish magic, see Trachtenberg 1939, pp. 43, 128, 185, 215, 219, 302 n. 56.

31. 1 Corinthians 13.12.

32. See Seaford 1984. As Seaford points out, "this does not mean that Paul had direct knowledge of the mysteries" (p. 120).

33. A brilliant depiction of just such an initiation, which depends on the idea of reflection, is found on one of the walls of the Villa of the Mysteries in Pompeii. On the interpretation of this scene, see Taylor 2008, pp. 128–33.

34. Mark 5.29–30. Cf. Matthew 9.20–22; Luke 8.43–8. Cf. also Matthew 14.36; Acts 19.12. See Frazer 1913, part 1, vol. 1, pp. 205–7, for further examples of clothing embodying an absent person.

35. Tylor 1903, vol. 2, p. 152, reports a traditional ceremony in China which involved "enticing into a sick man's coat the departing spirit which has already left his body." Analogously, the Shroud could have been seen as a "coat" in which Jesus' spirit had been caught.

36. See Taylor 2000, p. 10.

37. On the Fayum portraits, see Doxiadis 1995; Bierbrier 1997; Walker 2000. The reason for the invention of this new type of funerary art is still unknown. It might possibly be worth considering a link between the Fayum portraits and early Egyptian awareness of the Shroud (thinking which need not be recognizably Christian or Jewish). The chronological coincidence is certainly striking. It is worth noting that, according to Doxiadis 1995, p. 39, "Jews and Christians, as members of the Hellenized population that had largely adopted the Egyptian way of death, are probably among those portrayed, though we have no concrete evidence at this stage."

38. Mack 1994, p. 178. Doxiadis 1995, p. 45, calls them suggestively "the visual incarnation of their subjects."

39. Judaea always had close links with Egypt, and there was a particularly large and important population of Jews in Alexandria with close ties to the mother country: one has only to think of the Alexandrians who debated with Stephen in Jerusalem (Acts 6.9) and the Egyptian would-be messiah routed by Felix (Josephus, *War*, 2.261–3 (1967–79, vol. 2, p. 425)).

40. It should be noted that the shade itself was probably not conceived as entirely incorporeal: "the prevailing philosophic outlook of the time held that the soul was a kind of finely particled material 'body' " (Riley 1995, p. 56; cf. Tylor 1903, vol. 1, pp. 429, 453–7, 501). To be resurrected, however, it needed to be clothed in a new body created by God.

17 The Ascended Jesus

1. Acts 9.3–6. Cf. Acts 22.6–11; 26.12–18. For an analysis of this fictional episode, see below, pp. 318–21.

2. John 11.1–44 and Acts 9.36–42, respectively.

3. Philippians 2.8–10. The "name which is above every name" is presumably "Lord" (*kyrios*), the title that signals Christ's universal dominion (see Dunn 2003, p. 246). As Dunn explains (p. 245), the confession of Christ's Lordship was "the public expression of belief that 'God raised him from the dead,'" because "the resurrection was understood as the decisive event in his becoming Lord." On the Resurrection as the moment of Christ's assumption of eschatological glory, see Newman 1997.

4. Cf. Hebrews 12.2; Romans 8.34; Ephesians 1.20; 1 Peter 3.21–2. We even find this imagery, somewhat surprisingly, in Acts, inherited from one of Luke's sources. Delivering his first sermon on the day of Pentecost, Peter explicitly identifies the Resurrection with Christ's exaltation in heaven: "This Jesus God raised up, and of that we are all witnesses. Being therefore exalted at the right hand of God . . ." (Acts 2.32–3; cf. Acts 5.30–31). The idea here, unquestionably, is that Jesus was raised directly from the grave to the right hand of God—and that the apostles were witnesses of this extraordinary fact. It is worth noting that Luke 23.43 and Luke 16.22 imply direct ascent to heaven after death as well.

5. Spong 1991, p. 224. Cf. Barker 1996, p. 5: "elsewhere in the New Testament resurrection and ascension are not distinguished"; Dunn 2003, p. 265: "The resurrection was itself the exaltation which installed Jesus into his new status [as Lord]. Within the New Testament, Paul is not alone in this; it is only Acts 1 which offers a different schema." The one possible exception to this rule is 1 Timothy 3.16, a late, pseudo-Pauline letter.

6. John 19.39–40.

7. Graves and Podro 1953, p. 805.

8. See above, p. 7.

9. For the idea of "transphysicality" see Wright 2003, pp. 477–8. Wright notes the historical problem created by this notion: "If Jesus really was alive again in (what we would call) a physical body of some sort . . . and if after a short while this physical body ceased to be present (without the body being in a tomb anywhere), then some kind of explanation for the new state of affairs is called for" (Wright 2003, p. 654). Nowhere, though, does he say how or why the "transphysical" Jesus ceased to be present.

10. Of Enoch it is simply said that "he walked with God; he was not, for God took him" (Genesis 5.24). Elijah was separated from his servant, Elisha, by a fiery chariot and taken up to heaven in a whirlwind (2 Kings 2.11). This well-known story may have helped legitimize the idea of Jesus' ascent in the minds of the first Christians, especially as Jesus was sometimes associated with Elijah (cf. Mark 6.15.) For the idea of the assumption of Moses into heaven, which is not narrated in the Bible, see Dunn 1989, p. 17; Wright 2003, p. 95.

11. Daniel 12.3.

12. On the death and ascent of Hercules, see Diodorus Siculus, 4.38.4–5 (1961–70, vol. 2, p. 467); Burkert 1985, pp. 209–10. It was also sometimes thought that the gods themselves were former kings who had been immortalized, a belief known as Euhemerism.

13. Dodds 1951, p. 145.

14. Corcoran 1997, p. 50.

15. See Griffiths 1980, pp. 167–9.

16. Ibid., pp. 167–8. Behind the idea lay the belief "that the principle of death and rebirth in nature provided some impetus affecting the view of human death" (Griffiths 1980, p. 170).

17. On the cult and apotheosis of Roman emperors, see Ferguson 2003, pp. 207–12; MacCormack 1981, pp. 94–106; Price 1987. Kreitzer 1990 draws attention to the relevance of the idea of imperial apotheosis to the development of Christology, concluding that the Roman belief "must take its proper place in any attempt to trace the development of New Testament Christological thought" (p. 217). New Testament scholars continue to ignore the parallel on the dubious grounds that "it fulfilled a primarily political rather than religious function" (Dunn 2003, p. 247). For the absence of any meaningful distinction between the political and religious in this context, see Gradel 2002, pp. 27–53. See also below, n. 22.

18. For the cult of Alexander, see Ferguson 2003, pp. 204–5.

19. On the funeral and *consecratio* of Julius Caesar, see Price 1987, pp. 71–2.

20. On the funeral of Augustus, see Cassius Dio, *Roman History*, 56.34–42 (1961–70, vol. 7, pp. 74–99); Suetonius, *Life of Augustus*, 100 (1997, pp. 122–3); Price 1987, pp. 73–82.

21. For the myth of the ascent of Romulus, see Livy, 1.16.2–8 (1967–8, vol. 1, pp. 57–61).

22. It might be thought that there was a fundamental difference between the two cases, the apotheosis of the Roman emperor being a transparently political doctrine, designed to enhance the power of the ruling dynasty, whereas the Ascension of Jesus was a spontaneous belief, generated by purely religious experiences; the pagan idea was an insincerely held fiction, whereas the Christian idea was a genuine article of faith. However, this would be to misunderstand the imperial creed. The concept may have served the political aims of the Roman emperors, but that did not prevent their subjects taking it seriously—that is, regarding it religiously. As Price 1987, p. 80, explains, "the political context and political arguments about the merits of divinizing a particular emperor were important, but so too was the expectation that the apotheosis was real. The former emperor actually did ascend to heaven and his successor established a cult because he believed in him." And so did the people. The creed had begun, after all, with the Roman plebs witnessing a strange heavenly phenomenon—a comet—and hailing it as the divine Caesar.

23. The relationship between the emperor and his image is explained by the fourth-century writer Athanasius of Alexandria as follows: "In the image there is the idea and form of the emperor . . . The emperor's likeness is unchanged in the image, so that who sees the image sees the emperor in it, and again who sees the emperor, recognizes him to be the one in the image . . . The image might well say, 'I and the emperor are one. I am in him and he is in me'" (quoted in Freedberg 1989, p. 392). Cf. Belting 1994, p. 103: "The imperial cult of images equated the person represented with the portrait. This identification led to granting the images almost all the honors and rights due to the emperor himself."

18 The Burial and the Myth

1. For the identification of the site of Golgotha, see Biddle 1999, pp. 53–70; Gibson 2009, pp. 116–22.

2. The approximate timeframe is supplied by Matthew 27.45–50; Mark 15.33–9; Luke 23.44–7; John 19.14–17.

3. See Deuteronomy 21.22–3. That this rule was applied to victims of crucifixion is made clear by Josephus: "malefactors who have been sentenced to crucifixion are taken down and buried before sunset" (Josephus, *War*, 4.317 (1967–79, vol. 3, p. 93)).

4. Mark 15.46.

5. E.g. Matthew 27.59–60: "And Joseph took the body, and wrapped it in a clean linen shroud, and laid it in his own new tomb, which he had hewn in the rock." That the body was wrapped in the cloth before entering the tomb is explicit in the *Gospel of Peter* 6.24. The enshrouding of bodies in a single linen sheet is attested in the Talmud (see Brown 1994, p. 1245).

6. Bennett 2001, pp. 26, 128, is adamant that the Shroud could not have been used to transport the body, but her opinion is based on the view, since disproved by Zugibe, that the body of Jesus was not washed. She posits the use of two separate sheets, one to transport the body, another—the Shroud—to bury it. This would have been quite unnecessary. For a description of a Jewish funeral procession of the period, see Luke 7.11–17.

7. *Gospel of Peter* 6.24. On the *Gospel of Peter*, see Foster 2010; Foster 2007; Ehrman 2003, pp. 13–28; Crossan 1988. An early, first-century date for the core of the *Gospel of Peter* has been championed by Crossan. For a summary of general opinion and arguments in favor of a second-century date, see Foster 2010, pp. 169–72.

8. *Gospel of Peter* 6.21. In Mark 15.46 and Luke 23.53 it is said that Joseph of Arimathea took Jesus down from the cross. This is extremely unlikely. The Roman soldiers would have had the necessary *furcillae* (forked poles) to lift the *patibulum* off the *stipes*, and they would have been sure to recover the *patibulum* and the nails. NB The *Gospel of Peter* is inaccurate in attributing the Crucifixion of Jesus to the Jews, rather than the Romans.

9. Cf. Luke 23.54.

10. John 19.41–2.

11. For the discovery of the Holy Sepulchre, see Brown 1994, p. 1282; Biddle 1999, pp. 65–6; Gibson 2009, pp. 149–54.

12. For these other tombs near Golgotha, see Biddle 1999, pp. 56, 66; Gibson 2009, pp. 120 (Fig. 10), 121, 129, 151, 154. As Gibson observes repeatedly, the contents of all these tombs would have been removed in 44, when Jerusalem was extended by Herod Agrippa to include the area around Golgotha. So they would all have been empty when rediscovered. If the tomb of Jesus contained any remains in 44, they would have been reburied elsewhere. This might conceivably have helped fuel the legend of the empty tomb (for which see below, pp. 243–5). It may

also have a bearing on the vexed issue of the Talpiot tomb (for which see below, ch. 19, n. 25).

13. Luke 23.55; cf. Matthew 27.61; Mark 15.47.

14. John 19.39–40.

15. See Brown 1994, pp. 1260–64.

16. Signs that vv. 39–40 are an insertion derived from another source are: a) that, if they are omitted, John's narrative is essentially very close to the Synoptics' (see Brown 1994, pp. 1271–2); b) that the beginning of v. 40 ("They took the body of Jesus") repeats the action at the end of v. 38 ("So he came and took away his body"). For evidence that the *othonia* in Luke 24.12 were originally meant to represent the Shroud, see below, pp. 260–63. The use of the plural is not a bar to the identification, since both Nicholas Mesarites and John Damascene refer to the Shroud in the plural, as well (see above, pp. 176–7 and ch. 14, n. 10). Robinson 1985, p. 291, notes that *othonia* "is almost certainly to be understood not as a diminutive but as a generic term meaning linen cloths or clothes, here, grave-clothes." Fulbright 2005 agrees.

17. John 20.7.

18. On the Sudarium of Oviedo, see Bennett 2001; Guscin 1998; Guscin 2004.

19. See Bennett 2001, pp. 84–9.

20. The Shroud-image precludes the possibility that the Oviedo cloth was a burial cloth. The use of a cloth to cover the face of a corpse may be attested in the Mishnah (see Fulbright 2005), but it would only have been necessary in the case of a normally clothed corpse, not a naked one enveloped in a *sovev*.

21. For the history of the Sudarium of Oviedo, see Bennett 2001, pp. 20–37; Guscin 1998, pp. 9–20. For the 614 siege of Jerusalem, see Bennett 2001, pp. 29–30.

22. For the carbon dating of the Sudarium of Oviedo, see Bennett 2001, pp. 78–83; Guscin 1998, pp. 76–88. Bennett is understandably skeptical of the results so far obtained, which are certainly not definitive. More serious, in my view, is the historical silence regarding the relic before the seventh century.

23. That the *soudarion* might represent the Shroud has been suggested previously (see Wilson 1978, pp. 42–3) but has never been properly argued.

24. See Wilson 1978, pp. 75–6; Wilson 2010, pp. 147–9. (Arculf refers to the cloth as a *sudarium*, the Latin equivalent of *soudarion*.) Cf. also Meacham 1983, p. 288: "In the vernacular Aramaic, *soudara* included larger cloths . . ."

25. The Shroud is referred to as a *sudarium* by, among others, William of Malmesbury c.1150 (see Riant 1878, p. 211); Nicholas Soemundarson in 1157 (see Riant 1878, p. 214); Emperor Baldwin II of Constantinople in 1247 (see Riant 1878, p. 135); King Charles VI of France in 1389 (see Chevalier 1900, Appendix, p. I).

26. This might seem illogical to us, but it was apparently believed by Ordericus Vitalis, who imagined Christ wiping his face on the Mandylion and thereby bestowing on it an image of his entire body (see above, ch. 14, n. 58).

27. The theme of the "escorted Resurrection-Ascension" (a phrase which usefully reflects the triple interpretation of Shroud-image) has been discussed by John Dominic Crossan (see Crossan 1988, pp. 337–62).

28. Cf. Matthew 27.62–6. For the fictional story of the guarding of the tomb, see above, ch. 6, n. 18.

29. *Gospel of Peter* 9.35–10.40.

30. Angels are sometimes called simply "men" in the Hebrew scriptures (e.g. Genesis 18.2; Genesis 32.24).

31. *Gospel of Peter* 11.44.

32. *Gospel of Peter* 13.55.

33. On the Resurrection in Gnostic literature, see Franzmann 1996, pp. 156–9. The idea that works outside the canon might contain valuable information about Christian origins is one that many New Testament scholars either play down or dismiss out of hand. This prejudice has ensured that (with the possible exception of the *Gospel of Thomas*) non-canonical texts such as the *Gospel of Peter* have not been seriously and fairly assessed as historical sources, potentially on a par with the narratives of the New Testament. This may be a very significant mistake—almost as significant as ignoring the Shroud.

34. These texts include an early Latin translation of the Gospel of Mark (Codex Bobiensis), the Ascension of Isaiah and the Report of Pilate (see Crossan 1988, pp. 341–5, 355).

35. Acts 1.9–11.

36. It has been suggested previously that the pair of men at the Ascension might be modelled on figures in Jewish apocalyptic literature (see, e.g., Crossan 1988, p. 346), but there is no potential source that definitely predates Acts.

37. I suspect that the misinterpretation and reinterpretation of primitive Christian art may lie behind the imagery of certain narratives in the Gospels. This possibility has been raised previously in Graves and Podro 1953, pp. xiv–xv.

38. Matthew 17.1–13; Mark 9.1–13; Luke 9.28–36.

39. Luke 9.32.

40. See, e.g., Antonacci 2000, p. 224.

19 The Far-from-Empty Tomb

1. See Rogers 2008, pp. 107, 110 and 116, for the argument that the cloth was removed from the body before the onset of decomposition, which would have begun 36–72 hours after death.

2. Mark 6.3; Matthew 13.55–6. Paul provides proof that Jesus' brothers were married (1 Corinthians 9.5).

3. The evidence for this is twofold: a) Jesus was supported by a council of Twelve, representing the twelve tribes of Israel (see 1 Corinthians 15.5); b) the Romans crucified him as a would-be king, witness Matthew 27.29, 37; Mark 15.17, 26; Luke 23.38; John 19.2–3, 19–22; and the wounds of the crown of thorns visible on the Shroud. Arguments that Jesus would have been celibate for religious reasons are tenuous, being founded on the unreliable evidence of the Gospels.

4. Quoted in Pagels 1980, p. 64. For the reputation of Mary Magdalene among Gnostics, see Lüdemann 2004, p. 214.

5. John 20.2.

6. Cf. Tabor 2006, pp. 78–80.

7. Mark 16.1; Luke 24.10. Customarily, burial involved communal lamentation, so Luke may be right to imply that the group numbered five or more (although public lamentation was banned in cases of execution).

8. John 20.12. Dreisbach 1997 asks: "Could this be the very first reference to the ventral and dorsal images of the Man of the Shroud?" See also Loken 2006, pp. 110, 122, 131, 138.

9. It might be thought that Mark's information tallies significantly with the archaeological evidence of the Edicule in the Church of the Holy Sepulchre in Jerusalem, thought by many to be the very tomb in which Jesus was laid. The Edicule consists now of a small room with a single couch on the right-hand side. However, as Martin Biddle has shown, the present form of the Edicule was determined many centuries later, under the influence of Mark's description (see Biddle 1999, pp. 55, 117).

10. Matthew 28.3. Significantly, the angel here is described as the virtual twin of Jesus in Matthew's account of the Transfiguration: "And he was transfigured before them, and his face shone like the sun, and his garments became white as light" (Matthew 17.2). For the Transfiguration, see above, p. 236. Cf. also Revelation 1.12–16, which describes a similar figure.

11. Cf. also Matthew 17.6, in which the disciples fall on their faces in awe at the Transfiguration, a passage connected also to Daniel 10, in which the prophet Daniel falls on his face before the "man clothed in linen" (see below, pp. 292–3).

12. Luke 24.4.

13. See Lee 2004, pp. 16, 71, for the traditional imagery of bright clothing associated with celestial beings. It is worth noting, too, that fine linen is associated with angels throughout the Book of Revelation and that in Revelation 15.6 they are said to be clothed in "pure bright linen." Intriguingly, a related angelic visitation described in the apocryphal *Gospel of Barnabas* (an enigmatic text preserved in a late medieval Italian version) involves an explicit veiling of the angels' resplendent bodies behind linen (see Ragg and Ragg 1907, p. 485). The context and function of this angelophany is very similar to the appearance of the tomb-angels.

14. This ambiguity is felt repeatedly in modern discussions of the Shroud. Interestingly, the corresponding discrepancy in the number of angels was picked up by Celsus (see Hoffmann 1987, p. 90).

15. John 20.13. This same criticism is implicit in the opening questions of the "young man" the women find sitting in the tomb in the *Gospel of Peter* 56: "Wherefore are ye come? Whom seek ye? Not him that was crucified? He is risen and gone. But if ye believe not . . ."

16. One early third-century Gnostic text, the so-called *Tripartite Tractate*, actually describes the transfer of life from Jesus' mortal body to the angels, precisely paralleling the present interpretation of the Shroud-image: "and when he was in the tomb as a dead man the [angels] thought that he was alive, [receiving] life from the one who had died" (Robinson 1990, p. 101). The angelic figures here are essentially Jesus redivivus, just like the Shroud figures.

17. See Matthew 4.11.
18. Genesis 28.12.
19. Genesis 18.2, 19.1.
20. See above, p. 201.
21. See, e.g., Morison 1958, pp. 158–65; Schonfield 1996, pp. 199–205.
22. On these youths, see, for instance, Fowler 1998; Haren 1998; Guscin 2006.
23. For the various attempts to account for the supposed disappearance of Jesus' body, see Habermas and Licona 2004, pp. 93–103; Allison 2005, pp. 201–4; Carrier 2005b.
24. On the regular understanding of the concept of resurrection in the ancient world, see Wright 2003, pp. 32–206.
25. This raises the intriguing possibility that the ossuary of Jesus, having been reinterred in a tomb outside Agrippa's wall, might be found by archaeologists (see above, ch. 18, n. 12). In fact, it has recently been claimed that the ossuary of Jesus has already been found in a tomb in East Talpiot, a suburb of Jerusalem (see Tabor 2006, pp. 22–33; Jacobovici and Pellegrino 2007; Feuerverger 2008). There is strong opposition to this claim, for obvious reasons, but it is by no means impossible, and the statistical analysis of the epigraphic evidence by Feuerverger is thought-provoking. The Talpiot tomb can hardly be the tomb in which Jesus was laid on Good Friday, but it could be that in which his remains were reburied after 44, along with other members of his family.
26. See above, ch. 6, n. 1.
27. See Kloner and Boaz 2007, p. 52.

20 The Appearance to the Women

1. John 20.1–19.
2. Furthermore, in Matthew and Mark the tomb-angel tells the women, "you seek Jesus," whereas in John the Risen Jesus asks Mary, "Whom do you seek?" Cf. the similar question in Luke 24.5: "Why do you seek the living among the dead?"
3. Allen 1995, p. 34 n. 4, observes that, after staring intently at the "negative" Shroud-image for a while, it is possible to see a "positive" after-image upon turning away. The face of Jesus could have been "revealed" to Mary and others in this way.
4. That is to say, John 20.3–17 echoes the imagery of the Triple Figure. Furthermore, the opening words of the Risen Jesus to Mary in John 20.15 ("Woman, why are you weeping? Whom do you seek?") are closely paralleled by the opening words of the tomb-angel to Mary and her companions in Gospel of Peter 56 ("Wherefore are ye come? Whom seek ye?"); and just as Jesus concludes his speech in John 20.17 by declaring his Ascension ("I am ascending to my Father and your Father, to my God and your God"), so the tomb-angel announces the Ascension at the end of his speech in Gospel of Peter 56 ("he is risen and is gone thither whence he was sent"). John and the Gospel of Peter also share a Resurrection story set on the Sea of Galilee (see below, p. 309).

5. Matthew 28.1–10.

6. Mark 12.25. Cf. Matthew 22.30; Luke 20.36.

7. Matthew's female appearance-story contains one other point of interest: the statement that, approaching the Risen Jesus, the women "took hold of his feet and worshipped him." As Richard Carrier has observed, the image of the women worshipping at Christ's feet alludes to Psalm 132, one of the Psalms of Ascent, in which the Psalmist exhorts Israel to find a tabernacle for the Lord, to go to the tabernacle and to "worship at his footstool" (see Carrier 2005a, pp. 189–90). In support of the connection Carrier points out, pp. 229–30 n. 361, that, although "worship" is a strong Matthean theme, "in nine other verses that use the motif, 'feet' are never mentioned . . . Their insertion here is therefore a marker." The moment we substitute the Shroud for the Risen Christ, the allusion becomes meaningful. Being both the cloth in which Jesus was enveloped when he was raised and the terrestrial "residence" of the Risen Christ, the Shroud could easily have been seen as the "tent" of the resurrected Jesus, an idea echoed in several of Paul's letters (e.g. 2 Corinthians 5.1–4—see below, pp. 317–18).

8. On the *Epistula Apostolorum*, see Fuller 1972, pp. 192–4; Crossan 1988, pp. 234–6; Hills 2009. Regarding the doctrine of the Resurrection, it presents, in Tom Wright's words, "a theological position very like that of the New Testament, the other Apostolic Fathers and the Apologists" (Wright 2003, p. 499). Nowhere, however, does its Easter story plainly copy the canonical Gospels, and it differs from them markedly in terms of content.

9. Quoted in Fuller 1972, p. 192. I have followed the Coptic version here, rather than the Ethiopic.

10. Jesus' words in *Epistula* 10—"For whom are you weeping? . . . I am he whom you seek. But let one of you go to your brothers and say . . ."—are also clearly echoed in the speech Jesus makes to Mary Magdalene in John 20.15, 17— "Woman, why are you weeping? Whom do you seek? . . . Go to my brethren and say . . ." These coincidences are further signs of a shared literary or oral heritage.

11. Mark 16.9–11. For Pseudo-Mark, see Fuller 1972, pp. 155–7. This "longer ending" of Mark is considered canonical, although most scholars are now agreed that it was added to the Gospel sometime in the second century.

12. Cf. Mark 16.13–14.

13. Cf. John 20.11–17.

14. The reason given in the text—"for I have not yet ascended to the Father"—is redactional, in my opinion. It does not make sense (why would it have been legitimate to touch Jesus after his Ascension?) and seems to have been concocted on the basis of the next verse. For previous explanations of this passage, see, e.g., Wright 2003, p. 666; Fuller 1972, pp. 138–9.

15. Robinson 1990, p. 525. For the *Gospel of Mary*, see, besides Robinson 1990, King 2003.

16. Schmidt 1978, p. 53.

17. See Robinson 1990, p. 148.

18. For the *Gospel of Thomas*, see Robinson 1990, pp. 124–38. Mary features also

in the late-first-century *Sophia of Jesus Christ* and the c.100 *Dialogue of the Saviour* (for which, see Robinson 1990, pp. 220–43; 244–55, respectively). In the latter she is singled out for praise, being said to understand completely and to "make clear the abundance of the revealer" (p. 252). Mention should also be made of the *First Apocalypse of James* (ibid., pp. 260–68), in which Mary is one of several women praised for their spiritual perception.

19. Brown 1979, p. 154, suggests that the pre-eminent Mary Magdalene of Gnostic tradition might have been inspired by her portrayal in John. However, the belief in her apostolic authority was already widespread by the time John compiled his Gospel. The texts cited in n. 18 above are all more-or-less contemporary with John, and the other three versions of the female appearance-story (those in Matthew, Pseudo-Mark and the *Epistula*), all of which testify implicitly to her pre-eminent role, are of approximately the same date or earlier.

20. Pliny's letter was written c.110. Some of those he interrogated claimed to have abandoned Christianity twenty-five years previously, implying that the ceremonies in which they partook were established before 85.

21. John 20.1.

22. For a thoughtful analysis of the potential female contribution to the development of the Passion-Resurrection narratives, see Crossan 1999, pp. 527–73. Crossan observes, based on cross-cultural anthropological studies, that "female lament poetry is a direct social protest against oppressive male institutions, whether political and economic or religious and theological" (p. 541) and believes that "there is *some* very basic connection between female lament tradition and the development of the passion-resurrection story" (p. 528).

21 The Appearance to Peter

1. 1 Corinthians 15.5.

2. Lüdemann 1994, p. 89, puts it more forcibly: "it is astounding that there is no detailed report of the first appearance of Jesus to Peter in the New Testament . . ."

3. See, for instance, Wright 2003, p. 324, who manages only a couple of sentences on the appearance to Peter, merely noting its double attestation in 1 Corinthians 15.5 and Luke 24.34.

4. See, e.g. Marxsen 1970, pp. 79–97; Lüdemann 1994, pp. 84–100, 174–5.

5. See, e.g., Fuller 1972, p. 35; Lüdemann 1994, p. 174. This argument not only depends on the questionable assumption that Mark 16.7 is the earliest and most reliable evidence at hand, but also involves explaining away the contrary chronological indications of Luke 24.34 and 1 Corinthians 15.4–5.

6. Hitherto, New Testament scholars have made just as heavy weather of the male tomb-stories as they have of the appearance to Peter—unsurprisingly, if they are two sides of the same coin. Skeptics have generally tried to dismiss the male tomb-stories as Gospel fictions, asserting, for instance, that Luke 24.12 and Luke 24.24 are merely "embellishments" of the female tomb-story told by Mark (see, e.g., Carrier 2005a, p. 165). Theologians, meanwhile, have tended to focus on

John's idea that the Beloved Disciple inferred the Resurrection on the basis of seeing the burial cloths and, taking the story literally, have tried to imagine how the cloths' arrangement might have testified to such a miracle (on these interpretations, see, e.g., Robinson 1985, p. 293).

7. Luke 24.24.

8. Several clues indicate that Luke 24.34 is an interpolation. First, it is inserted awkwardly into the surrounding text, interrupting the natural flow of the story; as Reginald Fuller says, "Its effect is to take the wind out of the sails of the Emmaus disciples" (Fuller 1972, p. 112; cf. Marxsen 1970, pp. 51–2). Secondly, it is the only occasion in Luke when Peter is referred to as Simon, which implies that Luke inherited the formula. Thirdly, as Fuller points out, it reproduces almost verbatim the corresponding clauses of the First Creed: "he was raised . . . and that he appeared to Cephas . . ."

9. It is unlikely that the idea of a third-day Resurrection derived from Hosea 6.2, because, as Fuller 1972, p. 24, says, "there is no unequivocal evidence anywhere for the use of Hosea 6.2 among the *testimonia* or proof texts in the early Christian community."

10. For discussion of this issue, see Fuller 1972, pp. 23–7; Lüdemann 1994, p. 47; Wright 2003, p. 322. Of course, the time of the Resurrection could have been determined by the early morning appearance to the women. This is the implication, for instance, of Pseudo-Mark's statement that Christ appeared to Mary Magdalene "when he rose early on the first day of the week" (Mark 16.9). But it is unlikely that the chronology indicated in the First Creed depends on an appearance that it does not acknowledge.

11. Luke 24.13–27.

12. For discussion of this issue, see Fuller 1972, pp. 101–3; Lüdemann 1994, pp. 138–9.

13. The Gospel of John was not written all at once; it is a layered text, containing material composed and edited at different times (see Ashton 2007). We have already come across one clear example of this editing process: the redrafting of the female tomb-story to exclude Mary Magdalene's companions, an alteration betrayed by the careless retention of the first-person plural in Mary's speech in John 20.2 (see above, p. 240). On John as a redrafted Gospel, see, besides Ashton 2007, Fortna 1989; Bultmann 1971, pp. 6–7.

14. Cf. John 20.2, 15.

15. See, e.g., Maier 1991, pp. 184–5; Swinburne 2003, pp. 182–3. As Robinson 1979, p. 270, points out, however, "dematerialization is . . . a distinctively twentieth-century way of envisaging the relationship between flesh and spirit, matter and energy." First-century Jews would have thought in terms of "waking up" and "coming out."

16. My translation. The original Latin is quoted in Green 1969, p. 329 n. 12: "ad monumentum Petrus cum Johanne cuccurrit, recentiaque in linteaminibus defuncti et resurgentis vestigia cernit."

17. This has long been argued by sindonologists. See, for instance, Wilson 1978, pp. 74–5.

18. See Bulst 1957, p. 113 n. 10, pp. 125–6 n. 91. In connection with this Egyptian

image, mention should also be made of the contemporary "cloth imprint of St. Stephen in North Africa" (see above, ch. 16, n. 21).

19. It has been suggested, in opposition, that the *vestigia* should be understood figuratively, as indicating "merely the wrapped state of the cloths as though still enfolding the absent body" (Green 1969, p. 329 n. 12). This is unlikely, not only because "vestigia . . . in linteaminibus" can hardly refer to the "state of the cloths," but also because the idea of the body dematerializing in the tomb is modern, not ancient or medieval (see above, n. 15).

20. Wilson 1998, p. 171, citing Dan Scavone. The precise vocabulary used to describe the cloths is unclear to me, as the original Georgian text has not been published, but the "head-band" and "large sheet" appear to correspond to the *soudarion* and *sindon*, respectively. The full text has been translated into German (see Harnack 1901), from which Scavone's translation is taken.

21. Luke 24.25–6.

22. Robinson 1990, p. 138.

23. Ibid., pp. 526–7.

24. Quoted in Lüdemann 2004, p. 219. See ibid., pp. 215–22, for the issue of Mary's rivalry with Peter. See also King 2003, pp. 172–3.

25. Other Christian writings of the second, fourth and fifth centuries claim that the *othonia* were taken by Pilate and his wife or by Joseph of Arimathea (see Green 1969, pp. 328–9). These reports are definitely fictional.

26. Quoted in Green 1969, p. 329. See also Guscin 2004, pp. 19–22, for St. Nino's reference to the *soudarion*. The manuscript of the *Life of St. Nino* dates to the thirteenth century, but according to Green 1969, p. 329 n. 11, "St. Nino's conjectures seem to belong to the least suspect part of her legendary life . . . it may be a fourth or a fifth century witness to the Petrine tradition."

27. The sources differ on her place of origin: she is said variously to have come from Cappadocia, Jerusalem, Rome, Constantinople and Gaul.

28. See above, p. 188.

29. For Isodad of Merv, see Bennett 2001, pp. 23–4; Green 1969, p. 329; Guscin 2004, pp. 22–4.

30. Quoted in Bennett 2001, p. 24.

31. As told in the *Narratio de imagine edessena* (see Guscin 2009, p. 27).

22 The Appearance to the Twelve

1. Cf. Exodus 33.23, in which Moses is promised a view of God's back.

2. I leave the Emmaus pair out of consideration, since the story is fictional (see above, p. 81). I refer to the Twelve, rather than the Eleven, because that is how they are styled in the First Creed. Apparently, they were officially known as the Twelve, however many of them there actually were at the time.

3. For the judgment that the Jerusalem Tradition is historical, see, e.g., Swinburne 2003, p. 156. For championing of the Galilee Tradition, see, e.g., Fuller 1972, pp. 34–5; Lüdemann 1994, p. 174; O'Collins 1980, pp. 22–3, 36–8.

4. Cf. O'Collins 1980, p. 36: "Obviously Mark's account of the arrest in Gethsemane . . . does not necessarily indicate a flight back to Galilee. In fact, both the Galilee (Mark and Matthew) and Jerusalem (Luke and John 20) traditions agree in supposing that at least up to the Easter Day itself Jesus' disciples were still in Jerusalem . . ." For the flight of the disciples, see Mark 14.50; Matthew 26.56.

5. On the use of sources in Acts, see Brown 1997, pp. 316–18.

6. Cf. Fuller 1972, p. 34: "the assumption that after the disciples forsook Jesus and fled, they immediately made their way to Galilee . . . has been stigmatized by M. Albertz as a 'Legende der Kritik.' "

7. John 20.19–23.

8. Luke 24.33, 36–49.

9. Note that the attention-grabbing references to the Risen Jesus eating and displaying his "flesh and bones" are peculiar to Luke, being absent from the corresponding narratives in John, Pseudo-Mark and the *Epistula*. This reinforces the suspicion that they have been added to the story by Luke for apologetic purposes.

10. See above, pp. 67–8. John introduces the appearance as taking place "in the evening on that day, the first day of the week" (John 20.19), emphasizing the temporal connection with the Lord's Supper, while Luke's narrative, with its broiled fish, implies a communal meal. In a corresponding passage, Pseudo-Mark records that the Risen Jesus appeared to the Eleven "as they were sitting at table" (Mark 16.14).

11. It might be argued, instead, that the Gospel stories were inspired by the weekly service, but that would leave the origin of the Sunday ritual unexplained. It could also be argued, of course, that the stories inspired the Sunday ritual, but that would imply an extremely early date for the stories, certainly prior to 55, the date of 1 Corinthians, in which Paul speaks of the Lord's Supper and hints at gatherings on the first day of the week, and probably prior to 33, when Christian congregations were already dispersed (see above, p. 67).

12. The parallel narratives in Pseudo-Mark and the *Epistula* both locate the action indoors, as well, supporting the view that the interior setting is authentic.

13. In Greek: "*este eis to meson*" (John 20.19); "*este en meso auton*" (Luke 24.36).

14. See, e.g., Wright 2003, p. 605.

15. Of course, they would also have been able to understand the blood marks as stains caused by the wounds in Jesus' flesh touching the cloth, but this rational understanding of the blood marks would not have prevented them being seen also as belonging to the animated Shroud figure. Similarly, a rational understanding of the artistic practices involved in making idols does not prevent the animistic perception of such images.

16. Mark 16.14.

17. *Epistula Apostolorum* 11–12.

18. See Mark 14.66–72; Matthew 26.69–75; Luke 22.54–62; John 18.15–27.

19. John 20.24–9.

20. That the Doubting Thomas episode was created by John out of the Jerusalem Tradition is strongly argued in Riley 1995, pp. 69–99 (though without reference to the *Epistula*).

21. See Dreisbach 2001; cf. also Loken 2006, p. 126 n. 12. As a committed Christian, Dreisbach does not pursue this line of thought and continues to interpret the Resurrection itself as a spiritual event witnessed in a visionary manner. Loken suggests that the story of Doubting Thomas "may partly be based on a second showing of the shroud image, or on the disciples' changing attitude toward that image."

22. For an interesting interpretation of the Doubting Thomas story that similarly emphasizes the tension between Thomas and Johannine Christians, see Riley 1995, pp. 100–26. (Cf. also Pagels 2003, pp. 30–73.) New Testament scholars frequently try to put a positive "spin" on the story of Doubting Thomas, pointing out that the disciple is not actually said to have touched Christ's wounds, despite the invitation to do so, and that he is the first to confess Jesus as "my Lord and my God" (see, e.g., Wright 2003, pp. 664, 668, 677–8). These aspects of the story, though, are probably accidents resulting from John's dismemberment of his source narrative, in which Thomas was one of several disciples who touched Christ's wounds and confessed him as their Lord and God (cf. *Epistula* 11–12, which probably reflects the source more accurately). John can hardly mean Thomas to be seen in a good light, since he ends with Christ's withering criticism of him—the moral of the story.

23 In Accordance with the Scriptures

1. For the symbolism of the twelve tribes, see Sanders 1993, pp. 184–5.
2. For the relevant Scrolls, see Vermes 1995, pp. 320–23, 333–56. On *pesharim*, see Eisenman 2002, pp. 80–81, 85; Painter 1999, p. 231.
3. Acts 1.12–14.
4. Acts 2.31, 3.22.
5. Needless to say, early Christians would have continued to reflect on the meaning of the Shroud in relation to the scriptures as long as the cloth was known and remembered, so it is impossible to say precisely when the prophetic status of any particular text was first discerned. Some of the "prophecies" I discuss here may only have been adduced later on, and the Shroud's interpreters were undoubtedly interested in others I omit to mention. Knowing the precise course of the Shroud's exegesis, though, is not important; what matters is recognizing its potential speed and eventual outcome.
6. 1 Corinthians 15.13–17.
7. Ezekiel 37.1–10—quoted above, p. 39.
8. E.g. Hosea 6.2: "After two days he will revive us; on the third day he will raise us up" (alluded to in First Creed—see above, p. 53); Psalms 16.10: "For thou dost not give me up to Sheol, or let thy godly one see the Pit" (cited by Peter in Acts 2.31).
9. Jonah 1.15.
10. Jonah 1.17.
11. Jonah 2.5–6. The story of Jonah appears to have been constructed around the

psalm Jonah speaks from the belly of the whale (Jonah 2.2–9), which describes spiritual alienation from God in terms of drowning at sea and being caged in Sheol. To this imagery the author of the Book of Jonah added the representation of Sheol as a great fish.

12. Luke 11.29. Cf. Matthew 12.39, 16.4. The story of Jonah also inspired the Gospel stories of the stilling of the storm (Matthew 8.23–7; Mark 4.35–41; Luke 8.22–5) and the walking on the water (Matthew 14.22–33; Mark 6.45–52; John 6.15–21). In both cases, Jesus is revealed to be "something greater than Jonah" (Luke 11.32).

13. The difficulties begin with Matthew, who sees it as an allusion to the "three days and three nights" that Jesus spent in the tomb: "For as Jonah was three days and three nights in the belly of the whale, so will the Son of Man be three days and three nights in the heart of the earth" (Matthew 12.40). The original association of the Jonah story with Jesus can hardly have depended on this supposed parallel, since Jesus did not spend "three days and three nights in the heart of the earth." Matthew's version of the saying does indicate, however, that the Jonah association was connected to the Resurrection. Luke hints at a better interpretation, although the words he puts into Jesus' mouth are slightly ambiguous: "For as Jonah became a sign to the men of Nineveh, so will the Son of Man be to this generation" (Luke 11.30). The use of the future tense implies that this is a reference to the Resurrection, rather than the climax of Jesus' earthly career. This implies that the "sign of Jonah" was the Shroud, the sign that Jesus had been delivered from the watery abyss of death. For helpful comments on the "sign of Jonah," see Wright 2003, pp. 432–3.

14. Luke 11.32. Cf. Matthew 12.41. See also Matthew 12.6, 42.

15. Daniel 12.2–3.

16. Romans 1.2.

17. Daniel 7.13–14.

18. Daniel 7.17.

19. Daniel 10.5–9.

20. Cf. Matthew 28.3.

21. Daniel 12.5.

22. Further references to the Triple Figure could have been detected in 2 Maccabees 3.24–6, for which see below, p. 320; Genesis 18.2.

23. Significantly, Matthew's version of the Transfiguration incorporates a clear allusion to Daniel 10.9–12 (see Matthew 17.7), thus demonstrating that the figure of the man clothed in linen was associated with the idea of the Son of Man.

24. Isaiah 53.12.

25. Isaiah 50.6. Cf. Isaiah 53.3–6: "He was despised and rejected by men; a man of sorrows, and acquainted with grief; as one from whom men hide their faces he was despised, and we esteemed him not."

26. Isaiah 52.13–15.

27. Isaiah 42.6.

28. Isaiah 42.7.

29. Isaiah 53.5.

30. See above, pp. 38–9.

31. In case there was any doubt, one of the songs of the Suffering Servant confirmed his guiltlessness: "I know that I shall not be put to shame; he who vindicates me is near . . . Behold the Lord God helps me; who will declare me guilty?" (Isaiah 50.7–9).

32. The Pray Codex of 1192–5 implies that the Shroud-image was connected with the anointing of Christ's body, since it pairs the scene containing the representation of the Shroud with the unusual scene of the Anointing (see above, pp. 178–81).

33. See, e.g., Kersten and Gruber 1994, pp. 297–300.

34. See above, p. 154 and ch. 12, n. 21. The anointing was to be done by the women who went to the tomb on Easter morning.

35. Cf. Isaiah 44.3–4.

36. See Exodus 30.22–33. In 1 Samuel 16.13, for instance, David is apparently consecrated by the Spirit working through the oil: "Then Samuel took the horn of oil, and anointed him in the midst of his brothers; the Spirit of the Lord came mightily upon David from that day forward."

37. Acts 10.38. This phrase probably preserves a very ancient Christian formula: note the similarity of expression in Acts 1.8 (cf. John 20.22) and especially Romans 1.4. Of course, Luke thought Jesus was anointed at his baptism, but the action of the Spirit was originally associated with the Resurrection (cf. Romans 1.4), which came to be symbolized by his baptism. (For the intimate association of resurrection and baptism, see Barker 1996, pp. 27–55.) Looking for a specific prophecy of the descent of the Spirit, the Shroud group could have turned to Isaiah 61.1: "The Spirit of the Lord God is upon me, because the Lord has anointed me to bring good tidings to the afflicted"—a prophecy quoted, in fact, in Luke 4.18. Also relevant is Joel 2.28–9, in which God foretells a time when he will "pour out" his Spirit on all flesh, a prophecy quoted in Acts 2.17.

38. Romans 1.3–4.

39. This usage is found throughout the Gospels and Epistles: e.g. Matthew 1.1; Mark 1.1; John 1.17; Acts 4.10; Romans 1.1; 1 Peter 1.1; 1 John 1.3; Revelation 1.1.

40. Isaiah 11.1–2.

41. See Romans 15.12; Revelation 5.5. As if to confirm Isaiah's words, Daniel also foretold the coming of "an anointed one, a prince" (Daniel 9.25–6).

42. Isaiah 11.10–12.

24 The Forgotten Appearances

1. The sentiment expressed by Caiaphas in John 11.50 (cf. John 18.14) is surely historical: "It is expedient . . . that one man should die for the people, and that the whole nation should not perish."

2. Daniel 9.25.

3. See, e.g., Perkins 1984, p. 89; Barnett 2005, p. 18.

4. Richard Swinburne, willing to countenance "minor errors and a very small amount of theologizing" in the Gospel accounts, suggests that it might be reflected in several of the Resurrection narratives (see above, ch. 6, n. 35). More typical is Tom Wright's circumspect comment that it is "likely that the appearance to the 500 was an occasion like that reported in Matthew 28.16–20 (though Matthew only mentions the Eleven there)" (Wright 2003, p. 325).

5. See, e.g., Price 2005, pp. 80–81, who judges "the very notion of a resurrection appearance to 500 at one time to be a late piece of apocrypha, reminiscent of the extravagances of the Acts of Pilate."

6. See, e.g., Gilmour 1961; Fuller 1972, p. 36; Lüdemann 1994, pp. 100–108.

7. To the non-devout it was just babble, as Acts 2.13 makes clear: "But others mocking said, 'They are filled with new wine.' " The accusation of drunkenness may have been common among unbelievers who heard early Christians "speaking in tongues," and Luke may have meant to defend the practice against this slur.

8. This is what both Wright and Swinburne have in mind (see above, n. 4).

9. "One of the most difficult problems to be dealt with by a contemporary historian, in search of the role of James, is the bias of the modern reader . . . The treatment of James in the New Testament is already one-sided and tendentious. In the early centuries we find tradition that corrects this bias and tradition that extends it. In the long run the tradition that extended the bias triumphed, and the modern reader interprets the evidence of the New Testament from this point of view" (Painter 1999, pp. 270–71). See also below, n. 13.

10. See ibid., p. 155.

11. See ibid., pp. 42–4.

12. Cf. ibid., p. 151: "the important issue for leadership was membership in the family of Jesus." For the dynastic character of early Christian leadership, see Bütz 2005, pp. 115–22.

13. Cf. Painter 1999, p. 56: "[Luke] sought to minimize the role of James because he was aware that James represented a hard-line position on the place of circumcision and the keeping of the law, a position that Luke himself did not wish to maintain." Painter discusses other reasons for the historical sidelining of James as well (ibid., pp. 269–76).

14. Traditionally, New Testament scholars have doubted that James was a follower of Jesus during his lifetime on the basis of Mark 3.31–5; cf. Matthew 12.46–50; Luke 8.19–21; John 7.3–5. Recently, several scholars have concluded that this Gospel evidence is ambiguous and that James probably was a close follower of his brother (see Painter 1999, pp. 11–41; Bütz 2005, pp. 20–47). While I agree that the Gospel evidence is inconclusive, I consider the evidence of the First Creed, read in light of the Shroud theory, to count decisively against this new interpretation.

15. For the size of the early Jerusalem Church, see Acts 2.41, 4.4, 6.7; for its communistic rule, see Acts 2.44–5, 4.32–5.11.

16. Acts 8.1, 3. It is stated in Acts 8.1 that the "apostles" (by which Luke means the Twelve—see above, p. 54) were exempted from this persecution and allowed to remain in Jerusalem. This is totally implausible, not least because Paul himself

testifies that as a youth he attempted to destroy the church (Galatians 1.13). The statement probably reflects Luke's belief that the leadership of the Church maintained a constant presence in the Holy City.

17. Acts 9.31.

18. Mark 16.7.

19. If Mark did originally conclude with a Galilean appearance-story, it is likely to have been set beside the Sea of Galilee, echoing John 21.1–11 and the fragmentary story that ends the *Gospel of Peter*.

20. The allegory turns on the idea of "fishing for men" (cf. Matthew 4.19; Mark 1.17). It has yet to be properly explicated.

21. *Gospel of Peter* 14.60.

22. Peter is also pre-eminent in Luke 5.1–11, another version of the same story.

23. Galatians 2.8.

24. Cf. Mark 6.7; Luke 10.1.

25 The Last of the Apostles

1. 1 Corinthians 15.8–9.

2. Cf. Galatians 1.22–3.

3. Galatians 1.11–17. The translation here is from the New International Version of the Bible. For Paul's use of the word "gospel" here, see above, ch. 4, n. 12. See also below, ch. 26, n. 5.

4. Acts 9.1–2.

5. The reason for Paul's trip to Damascus is an issue conventional scholarship has never adequately explained. For discussion, see Murphy-O'Connor 1996, pp. 69–70.

6. Other phrases and passages in Paul's letters are sometimes taken as allusions to his Damascus experience (2 Corinthians 4.6, 12.1–4; Philippians 3.8), but, since their relevance is not immediately clear, we can here leave them out of account. On the interpretation of these passages, see e.g., Lüdemann 1994, pp. 53–4; Wright 2003, pp. 384–8.

7. As Wright 2003, p. 376, rightly comments: "What seems to have happened is that mainstream critical scholarship has forgotten its much-trumpeted principle of reading Paul's own letters as primary evidence and the accounts in Acts as secondary."

8. For the epilepsy theory, see Landsborough 1987; Dewhurst and Beard 2003, pp. 83–4. For the migraine theory, see Göbel et al. 1995. For the lightning theory, see Bullock 1994. For the mistaken identity theory, see, e.g., Kersten and Gruber 1994, pp. 338–9; Thiering 1992, p. 139; Graves and Podro 1953, pp. 804–6. Regarding the final suggestion, Schillebeeckx 1979, p. 378, interprets Paul's conversion as "a faith-motivated experience in response to an eschatological disclosure, expressed in a Christological affirmation of Jesus as the risen One." For a clear refutation of this view, see Wright 2003, pp. 701–6.

9. The words Paul uses are *ophthe* and *heoraka*, both forms of the verb *horao*, the

plain meaning of which is "to see" (see above, ch. 4, n. 19). As Tom Wright observes, "Paul intends a 'seeing' which is something quite different from the manifold spiritual experiences, the 'seeing' with the eye of the heart, which many Christians in most periods of history have experienced . . . This was, for him, a one-off, initiatory 'seeing,' which constituted him as an apostle but would not be repeated" (Wright 2003, p. 382). Cf. Fuller 1972, p. 32: "[Paul] distinguishes [his experience] clearly from the kind of visionary experience to which he alludes in 2 Corinthians 12:2–4." Fuller also notes, p. 33, that Acts 26.19 is the only occasion in the New Testament when a Resurrection appearance is called a "vision," an instance "to be set to the account of the author of Luke-Acts."

10. These are the subjects of the verb in 1 Corinthians 15.3, 1 Corinthians 9.1, Galatians 1.12, and Galatians 1.15–16, respectively. When Paul refers to Jesus as God's Son, he means to express his uniquely close relationship to God, established via the Resurrection; he does not consider Christ an aspect of God himself (an idea that arose later), but a second "power" in heaven. For the development of the idea of Jesus' divinity, see Dunn 1989. The earliest unambiguous expression of Jesus' divinity is probably John 1.1–18.

11. That is why he could afford to declare himself "unfit to be called an apostle" in 1 Corinthians 15.9: the Corinthians knew that being an apostle depended primarily on the gift of a special revelation, rather than personal fitness.

12. Cf. Wright 2003, p. 383: "it is noteworthy that [1 Corinthians] 15.1–11 as a whole clearly speaks of a *public event* for which there is *evidence* in the form of *witnesses* who *saw something and can be interrogated*."

13. Paul stresses the idea of new creation on several occasions: e.g., 2 Corinthians 5.17; Galatians 6.15.

14. The Greek phrase *en emoi*—"in me"—is usually translated, for convenience, "to me." This translation may be "grammatically possible" (Marxsen 1970, p. 102), but the regular reading, "in me," is supported by Paul's expansion of the idea slightly later in the same letter: "I have been crucified with Christ; it is no longer I who live, but it is Christ who lives in me" (Galatians 2.20). The apostle is evidently reflecting here on his conversion experience, which he understood as a spiritual death and rebirth. For a helpful discussion of this passage, see Barcley 1999, pp. 23–6.

15. 1 Corinthians 15.22.

16. Operating thus, the Shroud would have been a sign whose complex functioning approximated that of the written Gospels, which both represent the person of (the Risen) Jesus and communicate spiritual values and insights. Regarding Paul's dual means of expressing his experience, it has been argued that he moved from the language of Galatians to that of 1 Corinthians, i.e. that he received a non-visual "revelation" that was later spoken about, and possibly perceived, as the "seeing" of a divine figure (see, e.g., Marxsen 1970, pp. 105–6). This idea is not only highly speculative but is also at odds with the very early formulation of the First Creed.

17. See Romans 7.14–25 for a vivid description of Paul's inner conflict.

18. See above, p. 66. Baptism was an important sign of entry into this new life, which is why Paul speaks of being "baptized into Christ" (Romans 6.3; Galatians 3.27; cf. 1 Corinthians 12.12–13). On Paul's understanding of baptism, see Dunn 2003, pp. 442–59; above, ch. 5, n. 34.

19. See Romans 8.11, quoted above, p. 66.

20. See above, ch. 4, n. 31, for the parallel "Pharisaic" belief reported by Josephus.

21. The Greek word used, *ektroma*, means "an untimely birth, due either to miscarriage or, more normally, abortion" (Wright 2003, p. 327). Paul may even be insulting himself, since the word *ektroma* could be used as a term of abuse (see Wright 2003, p. 327; Fuller 1972, p. 43).

22. See Galatians 1.15.

23. For alternative explanations, see Wright 2003, pp. 328–9, who suggests that Paul means to compare himself to Miriam in Numbers 12.12, and Fuller 1972, p. 43, who favors the idea that Paul was known as "the abortion" by his opponents.

24. See also Romans 8.29; 2 Corinthians 4.4–6; Galatians 3.27; Philippians 3.20–21; Ephesians 4.24; Colossians 1.15, 3.9–10.

25. 2 Corinthians 4.16.

26. 2 Corinthians 5.1.

27. See Légasse 1997, pp. 33–4, 129 n. 46. See also the Septuagint version of, e.g., Leviticus 26.1; Isaiah 2.18.

28. See Mark 14.58. The word *acheiropoietos* is also used in Hebrews 9.11, 9.24, and Colossians 2.11. In each case it is connected with the idea of the Resurrection. For Paul's view of the Christian body as a temple, see 1 Corinthians 3.16–17; 2 Corinthians 6.16 (cf. John 2.18–21).

29. 2 Corinthians 5.2–4.

30. It might be supposed that the reference to clothing in this passage alludes to the rite of baptism, which involved being draped in a linen cloth (cf. Smith 1973, pp. 176, 216). But this just begs the question: why would the baptismal cloth have been associated with eternal life and a body "not made with hands?" Rather than explaining Paul's imagery, baptism should be seen as a parallel, ritual expression of the same profound idea: spiritual rebirth, as revealed by the Shroud.

31. Luke repeats the story on two further occasions (Acts 22.6–11 and 26.12–19), but Acts 9.3–9 appears closest to Luke's source. There are significant discrepancies between Luke's three versions of the story. In the passage just quoted, for instance, it is said that Paul's companions "heard the voice," while in Acts 22.9 it is said that they "did not hear the voice." Meanwhile, those aspects of the accounts that are consistent are not corroborated by Paul's own testimony. Luke tells us repeatedly that Paul saw a shining light and heard a voice, but the apostle himself says nothing of either. (As Wright 2003, p. 383, observes, light is conspicuous by its absence in Paul's accounts of the Risen Christ.) Most seriously, Paul is adamant that he saw the Risen Jesus, but Luke omits to mention this essential point. A visible manifestation is implied, however, by Christ's words to Paul in Acts 26.16: "But rise and stand upon your feet; for I have appeared to you for this purpose, to appoint you to serve and bear witness to the things in which you have seen me and to those in which I will appear to

you . . ." These words probably derive from Luke's source, having been excised in Acts 9 but retained here. The mysterious "things" in which Christ says he has appeared and will appear to Paul may well have referred originally to the Shroud. There are further hints in Acts 9 that Paul did see Jesus, but these traces of an appearance merely emphasize Christ's invisibility in Luke's descriptions of the epiphany. It seems that Luke edited out the figure of Christ from an inherited account of the "vision" without removing all the dependent references. His reasons had to do with his belief that the Risen Jesus was a flesh-and-blood figure, who appeared only to the Eleven and a few of their companions before ascending to heaven. In Luke's view, Paul's conversion took place after the Ascension, so he could not have seen the Risen Jesus on earth. Cf. also Ashton 2000, p. 83 n. 17: "Luke nowhere states that Paul actually *saw* Jesus, which may have something to do with his sense that to have *seen* the risen Jesus was an indispensable condition of true apostleship: for Luke (barring Acts 14:4, 6) there were only twelve apostles, and Paul was not one of them." Furthermore, he could not be allowed to see the Ascended Jesus in a vision, because that might suggest the appearances to the Eleven were visionary, too, undermining belief in a flesh-and-blood resurrection. Hence, the bizarre invention of an invisible vision: Paul is struck down by a burst of celestial light, but Christ, the subject of the revelation, is unseen.

32. Exodus 3.

33. See Ezekiel 1.28, 3.23, 43.3. See Wright 2003, p. 396 n. 65, for further parallels.

34. Quoted above, p. 292.

35. Daniel 12.4.

36. 2 Maccabees 3. See Wright 2003, pp. 390–91. The following quotations from 2 Maccabees 3 are from the NRSV translation.

37. The commission given to Heliodorus in 2 Maccabees 3.34 may also inform Christ's speech in Acts 26.16–18, in which Paul is commissioned to bear witness to what he has seen among the Gentiles, just as Heliodorus is told to testify to God's power "to all people." On Acts 26.16, see above, n. 31.

38. A well-informed early Christian reading 2 Maccabees could not have failed to notice the rapport between the description of the divine beings who waylaid Heliodorus and the figures seen in the Shroud, the figures that waylaid Paul. Admittedly, the Shroud-man was not a horseman, but he did possess a "frightening mien," and he was attended by two glorious young men. Like Daniel's vision of the man clothed in linen, flanked by two sidekicks, the story of Heliodorus provides a scriptural parallel to the Triple Figure seen in the Shroud. It is possible that the two "splendidly dressed" youths of 2 Maccabees 26 influenced Luke's description of the two men "in dazzling apparel" in the empty tomb (Luke 24.4). Furthermore, the scene of the young men flogging the courtier to within an inch of his life is eerily echoed—and inverted—in the marks of flagellation that crisscross the bodies of the Shroud figures.

26 The Move to Edessa

1. Acts 9.9.

2. Acts 9.10–12.

3. Acts 9.17–19.

4. The three-day period of the fast also echoes the idea of the Resurrection occurring "on the third day." This suggests that early baptismal ceremonies might regularly have been preceded by a three-day fast, the whole rite symbolizing Christ's Crucifixion, death and Resurrection over the course of three days (Friday to Sunday).

5. This might be thought to conflict with Paul's avowal in Galatians 1.16 that, following his conversion, he "did not confer with flesh and blood." However, in this passage (Galatians 1.11–17) Paul has in mind not the basic form of the gospel, which was common to all the apostles, himself included (cf. 1 Corinthians 15.11), but his own idiosyncratic doctrine, which he considered inspired by God, via the "revelation of Jesus Christ" and personal meditation on the scriptures. See above, ch. 4, n. 12.

6. See Maier 1991, p. 252.

7. Luke 6.16; cf. Acts 1.13. The mention in John 14.22 of "Judas (not Iscariot)" is presumably a reference to this same Judas.

8. Jude 1.1.

9. See Mark 6.3; Matthew 13.55. For the authorship of the epistle of Jude, see Brown 1997, pp. 748–50, 756–8; Burkett 2002, p. 446.

10. Interestingly in the Pseudo-Clementine *Recognitions* it is said that Paul "was hastening to Damascus chiefly on this account, because he believed that Peter had fled thither" (Jones 1995, p. 108). This is plausible and is compatible with the idea that Paul was pursuing the Shroud, which was apparently in Peter's possession in Galilee. It may be regarded as certain that Peter was not in Damascus when Paul arrived in the city, because he is not mentioned in Acts 9 and because Paul says that he met him some years later (Galatians 1.18).

11. Quoted in Guscin 2009, p. 158. See ibid., pp. 157–9, for the debate about the early evangelization of Edessa.

12. For the *Doctrine of Addai*, see Phillips 1876. The narrative of the *Doctrine* commences in October during the "343rd year of the kingdom of the Greeks [i.e. the Seleucid era]," corresponding to the 33rd year of the Common Era, i.e. AD 32. A good deal of action and journeying precedes the city's evangelization, implying that this took place the next year. Eusebius, *History of the Church*, 1.13 (1989, p. 34), places the evangelization of Edessa in the year 340 of the Seleucid era, i.e. AD 30, which confirms that it took place around this time, but conflicts slightly with my chronology of the Resurrection appearances. The round figure, however, may indicate that Eusebius is giving an approximate date from memory.

13. For Abgar V, see Segal 1970, pp. 12, 62–5, 72–6.

14. Eusebius, *History of the Church*, 1.13 (1989, pp. 30–34).

15. See above, p. 188; ch. 14, n. 60.

16. Phillips 1876, p. 5.

17. The idea of the existence of an authentic portrait of Christ was not entirely absent before the sixth century. The Gnostic sect of the Carpocratians claimed to possess images based on a portrait of Jesus produced by Pilate (see Drews 1984, pp. 76–96). The supposed authorship of this prototype suggests that these images showed Jesus during or after his Passion (echoing the Shroud).

18. See above, p. 185.

19. John always translates the word "Thomas" into Greek—*didymos*—to ensure his readers are aware of its meaning. It is unlikely that Judas was an actual twin, let alone the twin brother of Jesus, as implied in the third-century *Book of Thomas the Contender* (for which see Robinson 1990, p. 201). He may have engaged in magical practices in which he identified with Jesus via the Shroud, whose twin images were spiritual twins of Jesus. For the possibility that magical rituals formed a part of early Christian practice, see Smith 1978.

20. See Eisenman 2002, p. 142. "Judas of James" is listed as one of the twelve disciples in Luke 6.16 but is replaced by "Thaddeus" in Matthew 10.3 and Mark 3.18.

21. For evidence that the Shroud was originally kept in a jar, see Guerreschi and Salcito 2002; Guerreschi and Salcito 2005.

22. See Wilson 1978, pp. 113–14, for this argument.

23. For three reasons, I think, the phrase "and last of all," with which Paul begins his personal addendum to the First Creed, should be understood to refer specifically to his place among the apostles: 1) it picks up the reference to "all" the apostles in the previous verse; 2) it anticipates his remark in v. 9 that he is "the least of the apostles"; 3) it helps explain his reference to himself in v. 8 as "*the* abortion" (for this issue, see above, p. 316). This leaves open the possibility that other non-apostles saw the Risen Christ after him.

24. Paul, who saw the Shroud in Damascus, was an exception (as he was in many ways). He probably received his commission three years after his conversion, when he met Peter and James in Jerusalem (Galatians 1.18–19).

25. There are reasons to think that the Shroud is represented by the Johannine figures of the Paraclete and the Angel of Revelation, both of which are angelic doubles of Jesus, but these identifications are too complex to be discussed here.

27 The Easter Shroud

1. See above, ch. 6, n. 1.

2. See above, pp. 171–2. Strictly speaking, with regard to the argument about Easter, the carbon dating is irrelevant. Whatever its date, the Shroud is evidence that, if you crucify a man in the manner recorded of Jesus in the Gospels, wash his body in conformity with Jewish custom, wrap it in a winding sheet manufactured in accordance with first-century textile techniques and then remove it within the space of a few days, you can create on the cloth a nebulous, anthropomorphic imprint. So, even if it is insisted that the Shroud itself must be medieval, it can legitimately be argued that an exactly similar cloth could have been found in the

tomb of Jesus. This may seem pedantic, but it exposes the futility of trying to use the carbon dating as an argument against the Shroud theory.

3. Bultmann's skepticism regarding the historical investigation of New Testament narratives is summed up in this famous sentence: "I do indeed think that we can now know almost nothing concerning the life and personality of Jesus, since the early Christian sources show no interest in either, are moreover fragmentary and often legendary; other sources about Jesus do not exist" (Bultmann 1935, p. 8). Regarding the Resurrection, he wrote as follows: "If the event of Easter Day is in any sense an historical event . . . , it is nothing else than the rise of faith in the risen Lord . . . All that historical criticism can establish is the fact that the first disciples came to believe in the resurrection. The historian can perhaps to some extent account for that faith from the personal intimacy which the disciples had enjoyed with Jesus during his earthly life, and so reduce the resurrection appearances to a series of subjective visions. But the historical problem is scarcely relevant to Christian belief in the resurrection" (Bultmann 1953, p. 42).

References

All biblical quotations are from the Revised Standard Version unless otherwise stated in the notes.

Ancient sources

Cassius Dio, *Roman History*
(Cassius Dio, *Dio's Roman History*, trans. E. Cary, 9 vols, London, 1961–70)

Diodorus Siculus
(*Diodorus Siculus*, trans. C. Oldfather et al., 12 vols, London, 1961–70)

Epiphanius, *Panarion*
(Epiphanius, *The Panarion of Epiphanius of Salamis*, trans. F. Williams, 2 vols, Leiden, 1987–94)

Eusebius, *History of the Church*
(Eusebius, *The History of the Church from Christ to Constantine*, trans. G. Williamson, ed. A. Louth, London, 1989)

Homer, *Odyssey*
(Homer, *The Odyssey*, trans. R. Fitzgerald, London, 1962)

Jerome, *Illustrious Men*
(Jerome, *On Illustrious Men*, trans. T. Halton, Washington, 1999)

Josephus, *Antiquities*
(Josephus, *Jewish Antiquities*, trans. W. Whiston, Ware, 2006)

Josephus, *War*
(*Josephus*, trans. H. Thackery, 9 vols, London, 1967–79)

Livy
(*Livy*, trans. B. Foster, 14 vols, London, 1967–8)

Origen, *Against Celsus*
(Origen, *Contra Celsum*, trans. H. Chadwick, Cambridge, 1953)

Pausanias, *Description of Greece*
(Pausanias, *Description of Greece*, trans. and ed. W. Jones, 4 vols, London, 1965–9)

Philo, *Embassy to Caius*
(Philo of Alexandria, *Legatio ad Gaium*, trans. and ed. E. Smallwood, Leiden, 1961)

Philo, *Flaccus*
(Philo of Alexandria, *Philo's Flaccus: the first pogrom*, trans. and ed. P. W. van der Horst, Leiden, 2003)

Philo, *On Creation*
(Philo of Alexandria, *On the Creation of the Cosmos According to Moses*, trans. and ed. D. Runia, Leiden, 2001)

Plato, *Republic*
(Plato, *The Republic*, trans. D. Lee, 2nd edn, Harmondsworth, 1974)

Pliny the Elder, *Natural History*
(Pliny the Elder, *Natural History*, trans. H. Rackham, 10 vols, London, 1961–8)

Pliny the Younger, *Letters*
(Pliny the Younger, *The Letters of Pliny the Younger*, ed. B. Radice, Harmondsworth, 1963)

Strabo, *Geography*
(Strabo, *The Geography of Strabo*, trans. H. Jones, 8 vols, London, 1960–69)

Suetonius, *Life of Augustus*, *Life of Claudius*
(Suetonius, *Lives of the Twelve Caesars*, Ware, 1997)

Tacitus, *Annals*
(Tacitus, *The Annals of Imperial Rome*, trans. M. Grant, rev. edn, London, 1996)

Tacitus, *Histories*
(*Tacitus*, trans. M. Hutton et al., 5 vols, London, 1962–70)

Tertullian, *The Body of Christ*
(Tertullian, *Tertullian's Treatise on the Incarnation*, trans. and ed. E. Evans, London, 1956)

Theophrastus, *Enquiry into Plants*
(Theophrastus, *Enquiry into Plants*, trans. and ed. A. Hort, 2 vols, London, 1961)

Modern sources

Accetta, J. S. and J. S. Baumgart, 1980, "Infrared reflectance spectroscopy and thermographic investigations of the Shroud of Turin," *Applied Optics*, 19/12, pp. 1921–9

Allegro, J., 1964, *The Dead Sea Scrolls: a reappraisal*, 2nd edn, London

Allen, N., 1993, "Is the Shroud of Turin the first recorded photograph?," *South African Journal of Art History*, 11, pp. 23–32

——, 1995, "Verification of the nature and causes of the photo-negative images on the Shroud of Lirey-Chambéry-Turin," *De Arte*, pp. 21–35

——, 2010, *The Holy Shroud and the Crystal Lens*, 2nd edn, Port Elizabeth

Allison, D., 2005, *Resurrecting Jesus: the earliest Christian tradition and its interpreters*, New York

Antonacci, M., 2000, *The Resurrection of the Shroud: new scientific, medical and archaeological evidence*, New York

Ashe, G., 1966, "What sort of picture?," *Sindon*, pp. 15–19

Ashton, J., 2000, *The Religion of Paul the Apostle*, London

——, 2007, *Understanding the Fourth Gospel*, 2nd edn, Oxford

Bagnoli, A. and B. Bellosi (eds), 1985, *Simone Martini e "chompagni"* (exhibition catalogue, Siena, Pinacoteca nazionale, March 27—October 31, 1985), Florence

Barbet, P., 1963, *A Doctor at Calvary*, trans. the Earl of Wicklow, New York

Barcley, W. B., 1999, *Christ in You: a study in Paul's theology and ethics*, Oxford

Barker, M., 1996, *The Risen Lord: the Jesus of history as the Christ of faith*, Edinburgh

Barnett, P., 2005, *The Birth of Christianity: the first twenty years*, Cambridge

Bartlett, W. B., 1999, *God Wills It! An illustrated history of the Crusades*, Stroud

Bauckham, R. J., 1982, "The Lord's Day," in *From Sabbath to Lord's Day: a biblical, historical, and theological investigation*, ed. D. A. Carson, Grand Rapids, pp. 221–50

Beilby, J. and P. Eddy (eds), 2010, *The Historical Jesus: five views*, London

Belting, H., 1990, *The Image and its Public in the Middle Ages: form and function of early paintings of the Passion*, trans. M. Bartusis and R. Meyer, New York

——, 1994, *Likeness and Presence: a history of the image before the era of art*, trans. E. Jephcott, London

——, 1998, "In search of Christ's body. Image or imprint?," in *The Holy Face and the Paradox of Representation*, ed. H. L. Kessler and G. Wolf, Bologna, pp. 1–11

Benford, S. and J. Marino, 2002, "Historical support for a 16th-century restoration in the Shroud C-14 sample area," www.shroud.com/pdfs/histsupt.pdf (accessed January 15, 2012)

——, 2005, "New historical evidence explaining the 'invisible patch' in the 1988 C-14 sample area of the Turin Shroud," www.shroud.com/pdfs/benfordmarino.pdf (accessed January 15, 2012)

Bennett, J., 2001, *Sacred Blood, Sacred Image: the Sudarium of Oviedo*, Littleton, CO

Berkovits, I., 1969, *Illuminated Manuscripts in Hungary, XI–XVI Centuries*, trans. Z. Horn, Budapest

Biddle, M., 1999, *The Tomb of Christ*, Stroud

Bierbrier, M. (ed.), 1997, *Portraits and Masks: burial customs in Roman Egypt*, London

Bilde, P., 1988, *Flavius Josephus between Jerusalem and Rome: his life, his works and their importance*, Sheffield

Binski, P., 2004, *Becket's Crown: art and imagination in Gothic England 1170–1300*, London

Bohak, G., 2008, *Ancient Jewish Magic: a history*, Cambridge

Bollone, B., 1998, *Sindone: la prova*, Milan

Bond, H., 1998, *Pontius Pilate in History and Interpretation*, Cambridge

Bongert, Y., 1995, "L'iconographie du Christ et le Linceul de Turin," in *L'identification scientifique de l'homme du Linceul, Jesus de Nazareth. Actes du Symposium Scientifique International, Rome (1993)*, ed. A. Upinsky, Paris, pp. 93–101

Brandon, S. G. F., 1957, *The Fall of Jerusalem and the Christian Church: a study of the effects of the Jewish overthrow of A.D. 70 on Christianity*, London

Brilliant, R., 1991, *Portraiture*, London

Broshi, M., 1982, "The credibility of Josephus," *Journal of Jewish Studies*, 33, pp. 379–84

Brown, R., 1979, *The Community of the Beloved Disciple*, London

——, 1994, *The Death of the Messiah*, London

——, 1997, *An Introduction to the New Testament*, New York

Bucklin, R., 1970, "Legal and medical aspects of the trial and death of Christ," in *Medicine, Science and the Law*, 10, pp. 14–26

——, 1998, "An autopsy on the man of the Shroud," in *Non fait de main d'homme. Actes du troisième symposium scientifique international du CIELT (Nice 1997)*, Paris, pp. 99–101

——, 2002, "The Shroud of Turin: a pathologist's viewpoint," in *The Shroud of Turin: unraveling the mystery. Proceedings of the 1998 Dallas Symposium*, ed. A. Adler, Alexander, NC, pp. 271–6

Bullock, J. D., 1994, "Was Saint Paul struck blind and converted by lightning?," *Survey of Ophthalmology*, 39/2, pp. 151–60

Bulst, W., 1957, *The Shroud of Turin*, trans. S. McKenna and J. Galvin, Milwaukee

Bultmann, R., 1935, *Jesus and the Word*, trans. L. Smith and E. Huntress, London

——, 1953, "New Testament and mythology," in *Kerygma and Myth*, ed. H. Bartsch, trans. R. Fuller, London

——, 1971, *The Gospel of John: a commentary*, trans. G. Beasley-Murray, Oxford

Burkert, W., 1983, *Homo necans: the anthropology of ancient Greek sacrificial ritual and myth*, trans. P. Bing, London

——, 1985, *Greek Religion*, trans. J. Raffan, Oxford

Burkett, D., 2002, *An Introduction to the New Testament and the Origins of Christianity*, Cambridge

Burleigh, R. et al., 1986, "An intercomparison of some AMS and Small Gas Counter Laboratories," *Radiocarbon*, 28, pp. 571–7

Bütz, J., 2005, *The Brother of Jesus and the Lost Teachings of Christianity*, Rochester, VT

Cameron, A., 1981, "The Skeptic and the Shroud" (inaugural lecture at King's College, London, April 1980), in A. Cameron, *Continuity and Change in Sixth-century Byzantium*, London, chapter V

Carrier, R., 2005a, "The spiritual body of Christ and the legend of the empty tomb," in *The Empty Tomb: Jesus beyond the grave*, ed. R. M. Price and J. J. Lowder, New York, pp. 105–231

——, 2005b, "The plausibility of theft," in *The Empty Tomb: Jesus beyond the grave*, ed. R. M. Price and J. J. Lowder, New York, pp. 349–68

Case, T., 1996, *The Shroud of Turin and the C-14 Dating Fiasco: a scientific detective story*, Cincinnati

Celano, T. da, 1997, *The Life of St. Francis of Assisi and the Treatise of Miracles*, trans. C. Bolton, Assisi

Chambers, P., 2002, *Bones of Contention: the archaeopteryx scandals*, London

Charles, R. H. (trans. and ed.), 1908, *The Testaments of the Twelve Patriarchs*, London

Chelazzi Dini, G. et al., 1998, *Five Centuries of Sienese Painting*, trans. C. Warr, London

Chevalier, U., 1899, *Le Saint Suaire de Turin: est-il l'original ou une copie?* Chambéry

——, 1900, *Étude critique sur l'origine du St. Suaire de Lirey-Chambéry-Turin*, Paris

Chifflet, J. J., 1624, *De linteis sepulchralibus Christi Servatoris crisis historica*, Antwerp

Chilton, B., 2005, *Mary Magdalene: a biography*, New York

Coghlan, A., 1989, "Unexpected errors affect dating techniques," *New Scientist*, September 30, p. 26

Cohen, A., 1997, *The Alexander Mosaic: stories of victory and defeat*, Cambridge

Cohn-Sherbok, D., 1996, "The Resurrection of Jesus: a Jewish view," in *Resurrection Reconsidered*, ed. G. D'Costa, Oxford, pp. 184–200

Corcoran, L., 1997, "Mysticism and the mummy portraits," in *Portraits and Masks: burial customs in Roman Egypt*, ed. M. Bierbrier, London, pp. 45–53

Cormack, R., 1997, *Painting the Soul: icons, death masks and shrouds*, London

Couzin, J., 2006, "Breakdown of the year: scientific fraud," *Science*, 314, p. 1853

Crafer, T. W., 1913–14, "The work of Porphyry against the Christians, and its reconstruction," *Journal of Theological Studies*, 15, pp. 360–95, 481–512

Craig, W. L., 1989, *Assessing the New Testament Evidence for the Historicity of the Resurrection of Jesus*, Studies in the Bible and Early Christianity 16, Lewiston, NY

Crary, J., 1990, *Techniques of the Observer: on vision and modernity in the nineteenth century*, London

Crossan, J. D., 1988, *The Cross that Spoke: the origins of the Passion narrative*, London

——, 1993, *The Historical Jesus: the life of a Mediterranean Jewish peasant*, Edinburgh

——, 1999, *The Birth of Christianity: discovering what happened in the years immediately after the execution of Jesus*, New York

Currie, L. A., 2004, "The remarkable metrological history of radiocarbon dating [II]," *Journal of Research of the National Institute of Standards and Technology*, 109/2, pp. 185–217

Damon, P. E. et al., 1989, "Radiocarbon dating of the Shroud of Turin," *Nature*, 337, pp. 611–15

Danby, H. (trans.), 1933, *The Mishnah*, Oxford

Dawes, G. (ed.), 2000, *The Historical Jesus Quest: landmarks in the search for the Jesus of history*, 2nd edn, Louisville

De Boer, E., 2004, *The Gospel of Mary: beyond a Gnostic and a biblical Mary Magdalene*, London

De Clari, R., 1924, *La conquête de Constantinople*, ed. P. Lauer, Paris

Delage, Y., 1902, "Le linceul de Turin," *Revue scientifique*, 4th ser., 17, pp. 683–7

Dembowski, P., 1982, "Sindon in the old French chronicle of Robert de Clari," *Shroud Spectrum International*, 1/2, pp. 13–18

Dennett, D., 1987, *The Intentional Stance*, Cambridge, MA

Dewhurst, K. and A. W. Beard, 2003, "Sudden religious conversions in temporal lobe epilepsy," *Epilepsy and Behavior*, 4, pp. 78–87

Dodds, E. R., 1951, *The Greeks and the Irrational*, London

Doherty, E., 2005, *The Jesus Puzzle: did Christianity begin with a mythical Christ?* Ottawa

Doxiadis, E., 1995, *The Mysterious Fayum Portraits*, London

Dreisbach, A., 1997, "The Shroud of Turin: its ecumenical implications," www.shroud.com/dreisbc2.htm (accessed January 15, 2012)

——, 2001, "Thomas and the cenacle reconsidered," www.shroud.com/pdfs/dreisbc3.pdf (accessed January 15, 2012)

Drews, R., 1984, *In Search of the Shroud of Turin: new light on its history and origins*, Totowa, NJ

Dubabin, K. M. D., 1990, "Ipsa deae vestigia . . . footprints divine and human in Graeco-Roman monuments," *Journal of Roman Archaeology*, 3, pp. 85–109

Dubarle, A., 1985, *Histoire ancienne du Linceul de Turin*, vol. 1, Paris

——, 1998, *Histoire ancienne du Linceul de Turin*, vol. 2, Paris

——, 2000, "L'icona del 'Manoscritto Pray,'" in *Le icone di Cristo e la Sindone: un modello per l'arte cristiana*, ed. F. Cavazzuti and L. Coppini, Milan, pp. 181–8

Dunn, J., 1989, *Christology in the Making*, 2nd edn, London

——, 2003, *The Theology of Paul the Apostle*, 2nd edn, London

Ehrman, B., 1999, *Jesus: apocalyptic prophet of the new millennium*, Oxford

——, 2003, *Lost Christianities: the battles for scripture and the faiths we never knew*, Oxford

Eisenberg, J., 2003, "The Portland Vase: a glass masterwork of the later Renaissance?," *Minerva*, 14/5, pp. 37–41

Eisenman, R., 2002, *James the Brother of Jesus*, London

——, 2006, *The New Testament Code: the cup of the Lord, the Damascus Covenant, and the blood of Christ*, London

Epp, E. J., 2005, *Junia: the first woman apostle*, Minneapolis

Ercoline, W. and J. Jackson, 1982, "Examination of the Turin Shroud for image distortions," *IEEE 1982 Proceedings of the International Conference on Cybernetics and Society (Seattle 28–October 30, 1982)*, New York, pp. 576–9

Evangeliou, C., 1992, "Plotinus's anti-Gnostic polemic and Porphyry's *Against the Christians*," in *Neoplatonism and Gnosticism*, ed. R. T. Wallis, New York, pp. 111–28

Fanti, G. and R. Maggiolo, 2004, "The double superficiality of the frontal image of the Turin Shroud," *Journal of Optics A: Pure and Applied Optics*, 6, pp. 491–503

Fanti, G. et al., 2005, "Body image formation hypotheses based on corona discharge," www.dim.unipd.it/fanti/corona.pdf (accessed January 15, 2012)

Ferguson, E., 2003, *Backgrounds of Early Christianity*, 3rd edn, Cambridge

Festinger, L. et al., 1956, *When Prophecy Fails*, Minneapolis

Feuerverger, A., 2008, "Statistical analysis of an archaeological find," *Annals of Applied Statistics*, 2/1, pp. 3–54

Finkelstein, I. and N. A. Silberman, 2001, *The Bible Unearthed: archaeology's new vision of ancient Israel and the origin of its sacred texts*, London

Flury-Lemberg, M., 2001, "The linen cloth of the Turin Shroud: some observations on its technical aspects," *Sindon* (new series), 16, pp. 55–76

——, 2003, *Sindone 2002*, Turin

——, 2007, "The invisible mending of the Shroud, the theory and the reality," *BSTS Shroud Newsletter*, 65, pp. 10–27

Fortna, R., 1989, *The Fourth Gospel and its Predecessor: from narrative source to present Gospel*, Edinburgh

Foster, P., 2007, "The so-called Gospel of Peter: the current state of research," *Expository Times*, 118, pp. 318–25

——, 2010, *The Gospel of Peter: introduction, critical edition and commentary*, Leiden

Foucault, M., 2002, *The Order of Things: an archaeology of the human sciences*, 3rd edn, London

Fowler, M., 1998, "Identification of the Bethany Youth in the Secret Gospel of Mark with other figures found in Mark and John," *Journal of Higher Criticism*, 5/1, pp. 3–22

Franzmann, M., 1996, *Jesus in the Nag Hammadi Writings*, Edinburgh

Frazer, J. G., 1913, *The Golden Bough: a study in magic and religion*, 3rd edn, 8 parts, London (repro. 1980)

Freedberg, D., 1989, *The Power of Images: studies in the history and theory of response*, London

Freeman, C., 2003, *The Closing of the Western Mind*, London

——, 2009, *A New History of Early Christianity*, London

Frei, M., 1979, "Il passato della Sindone alla luce della palinologia," in *La Sindone e la scienza. Atti del II congresso internazionale di Sindonologia (Turin 1978)*, ed. P. Coero-Borga, Turin, pp. 191–200

——, 1983, "Identificazione e classificazione dei nuovi pollini della Sindone," in *La Sindone: scienza e fede. Atti del II convegno nazionale di Sindonologia (Bologna 1981)*, ed. L. Coppini and F. Cavazzuti, Bologna, pp. 277–84

Freke, T. and P. Gandy, 2003, *The Jesus Mysteries: was the original Jesus a pagan god?* 2nd edn, London

Friedman, R., 1988, *Who Wrote the Bible?* London

Fulbright, D., 2005, "'A clean cloth": what Greek word usage tells us about the burial wrappings of Jesus," *BSTS Shroud Newsletter*, 62, n.p.

Fuller, R., 1972, *The Formation of the Resurrection Narratives*, London

Gaeta, S., 2005, *L'altra Sindone: la vera storia del volto di Gesù*, Milan

Gantz, T., 1993, *Early Greek Myth: a guide to literary and artistic sources*, Baltimore

Ganzfried, S., 1963, *Code of Jewish Law (Kitzur Shulchan Aruch)*, 4 vols, trans. H. E. Goldin, rev. edn, New York

Garza-Valdes, L., 1998, *The DNA of God*, New York

Gell, A., 1998, *Art and Agency: an anthropological theory*, Oxford

Ghiberti, G., 2002, *Sindone, le immagine 2002: Shroud images*, Turin

Gibbon, E., 1923, *The Decline and Fall of the Roman Empire*, 6th edn, 7 vols, London

Gibson, S., 2005, *The Cave of John the Baptist*, London

———, 2009, *The Final Days of Jesus: the archaeological evidence*, New York

Gilbert, R. and M. Gilbert, 1980, "Ultraviolet-visible reflectance and fluorescence spectra of the Shroud of Turin," *Applied Optics*, 19/12, pp. 1930–36

Gilmour, S. M., 1961, "The Christophany to more than five hundred brethren," *Journal of Biblical Literature*, 80, pp. 248–52

Göbel, H. et al., 1995, "Headache classification and the Bible: was St. Paul's thorn in the flesh migraine?," *Cephalalgia: an international journal of headache*, 15/3, pp. 180–81

Goff, M., 2009, "Genesis 1–3 and conceptions of humankind in 4QInstruction, Philo and Paul," in *Early Christian Literature and Intertextuality*, vol. 2: *Exegetical Studies*, ed. C. Evans and H. Zacharias, London, pp. 114–25

Goldberg, B., 1985, *The Mirror and Man*, Charlottesville

Goodman, M., 1987, *The Ruling Class of Judaea: the origins of the Jewish revolt against Rome A.D. 66–70*, Cambridge

Goulder, M., 1996, "The baseless fabric of a vision," in *Resurrection Reconsidered*, ed. G. D'Costa, Oxford, pp. 48–61

Gove, H., 1996, *Relic, Icon or Hoax? Carbon dating the Turin Shroud*, Bristol

Gove, H. et al., 1997, "A problematic source of organic contamination of linen," *Nuclear Instruments and Methods in Physics Research—Section B*, 123, pp. 504–7

Gradel, I., 2002, *Emperor Worship and Roman Religion*, Oxford

Graves, R. and J. Podro, 1953, *The Nazarene Gospel Restored*, London

Green, M., 1969, "Enshrouded in silence: in search of the first millennium of the Holy Shroud," *Ampleforth Journal*, 74/3, pp. 320–45

Gregory, R., 1997, *Mirrors in Mind*, London

Griffiths, J. G., 1980, *The Origins of Osiris and His Cult. Studies in the history of religions (supplements to* Numen*)*, 40, Leiden

Guerreschi, A. and M. Salcito, 2002, "Photographic and computer studies concerning the burn and water stains visible on the Shroud and their historical consequences," www.shroud.com/pdfs/aldo3.pdf (accessed January 16, 2012)

———, 2005, "Further studies on the scorches and the watermarks," www.shroud.com/pdfs/aldo4.pdf (accessed January 16, 2012)

Guscin, M., 1998, *The Oviedo Cloth*, Cambridge

——, 2004, *The History of the Sudarium of Oviedo: how it came from Jerusalem to northern Spain in the seventh century A.D.*, New York

——, 2006, "Further possibilities for the interpretation of Mark 14.51–52," *BSTS Shroud Newsletter*, 64, pp. 53–6

——, 2009, *The Image of Edessa*, Leiden

Guthrie, S., 1993, *Faces in the Clouds*, Oxford

——, 2002, "Animal animism: evolutionary roots of religious cognition," in *Current Approaches in the Cognitive Science of Religion*, ed. I. Pyysiäinen and V. Anttonen, London, pp. 38–67

Habermas, G., 2001, "Explaining away Jesus' Resurrection: the recent revival of hallucination theories," *Christian Research Journal*, 23/4, pp. 26–31, 47–9

——, 2006, "Mapping the recent trend toward the bodily Resurrection appearances of Jesus in light of other prominent critical positions," in *The Resurrection of Jesus: John Dominic Crossan and N. T. Wright in dialogue*, ed. R. Stewart, London, pp. 78–92

Habermas, G. and M. Licona, 2004, *The Case for the Resurrection of Jesus*, Grand Rapids

Haren, M. J., 1998, "The naked young man: a historian's hypothesis on Mark 14.51–52," *Biblica*, 79, pp. 525–31

Harnack, A., 1901, "Ein in georgischer Sprache überliefertes Apokryphon des Josef von Arimathia," in *Sitzungberichte der Königlich preussischen Akademie der Wissenschaften*, 17, pp. 920–31

Harvey, A., 1994, "'They discussed among themselves what this "rising from the dead" could mean' (Mark 9.10)," in *Resurrection: essays in honor of Leslie Houldon*, ed. S. Barton and G. Stanton, London, pp. 69–78

Haskins, S., 2005, *Mary Magdalen: the essential history*, London

Haziel, V., 2005, *La Passione secondo Leonardo: il genio di Vinci e la Sindone di Torino*, Milan

Heimburger, T. and G. Fanti, 2010, "Scientific comparison between the Turin Shroud and the first handmade whole copy," www.acheiropoietos.info/proceedings/HeimburgerWeb.pdf (accessed January 16, 2012)

Heller, J. H., 1983, *Report on the Shroud of Turin*, Boston

Heller, J. H. and A. D. Adler, 1981, "A chemical investigation of the Shroud of Turin," *Canadian Society of Forensic Sciences Journal*, 14/3, pp. 81–103

Hengel, M., 1976, *The Son of God: the origin of Christology and the history of Jewish-Hellenistic religion*, Philadelphia

Herrin, J., 2007, *Byzantium: the surprising life of a medieval empire*, London

Hill, T., 1993, "The cross as symbolic body: an Anglo-Latin liturgical analogue to the *Dream of the Rood*," *Neophilologus*, 77/2, pp. 297–301

Hills, J. (trans and ed.), 2009, *The Epistle of the Apostles*, Santa Rosa, CA

Hoffmann, R., 1987, *Celsus on the True Doctrine*, Oxford

Humphrey, N., 1999, *Leaps of Faith: science, miracles and the search for supernatural consolation*, 2nd edn, New York

Jackson, J. et al., 1977, "The three dimensional image on Jesus' burial cloth,"

Proceedings of the 1977 United States Conference of Research on the Shroud of Turin, March 23–24 (1977), Albuquerque, New Mexico, New York, pp. 74–94

————, 1982, "Three dimensional characteristic of the Shroud image," in *IEEE 1982 Proceedings of the International Conference on Cybernetics and Society (Seattle 28–October 30, 1982)*, New York, pp. 559–75

Jacobovici, S. and C. Pellegrino, 2007, *The Jesus Tomb: the discovery that will change history forever*, London

James, M. R. (trans.), 1924, *The Apocryphal New Testament*, Oxford

Janson, H. W., 1962, *A History of Art: a survey of the visual arts from the dawn of history to the present day*, London

Jones, F., 1995, *An Ancient Jewish Christian Source on the History of Christianity: pseudo-Clementine* Recognitions 1.27–71, Atlanta

Joranson, E., 1950, "The problem of the spurious letter of Emperor Alexius to the Count of Flanders," *American Historical Review*, 55, pp. 811–32

Jull, A. J. T. et al., 1996, "Factors affecting the apparent radiocarbon age of textiles: a comment on 'Effects of fires and biofraction of carbon isotopes on results of radiocarbon dating of old textiles: the Shroud of Turin,' by D. A. Kouznetsov et al.," *Journal of Archaeological Science*, 23, pp. 157–60

Jumper, E. et al., 1984, "A comprehensive examination of the various stains and images on the Shroud of Turin," *Advances in Chemistry Series 205: Archaeological Chemistry—III*, ed. J. Lambert, Washington, DC, pp. 447–76

Keim, T., 1883, *The History of Jesus of Nazareth*, 6 vols, trans. E. Geldart and A. Ransom, London

Kemp, M., 1990, *The Science of Art: optical themes in western art from Brunelleschi to Seurat*, London

Kersten, H. and E. Gruber, 1994, *The Jesus Conspiracy: the Turin Shroud and the truth about the Resurrection*, trans., Shaftesbury

King, K., 2003, *The Gospel of Mary of Magdala: Jesus and the first woman apostle*, Santa Rosa, CA

Kloner, A. and Z. Boaz, 2007, *The Necropolis of Jerusalem in the Second Temple Period*, Leuven

Knight, C. and R. Lomas, 1998, *The Second Messiah: Templars, the Turin Shroud and the great secret of freemasonry*, London

Knight, J., 2008, *Christian Origins*, London

Kohlbeck, J. A. and E. L. Nitowski, 1986, "New evidence may explain image on Shroud of Turin," *Biblical Archaeology Review*, 12/4, pp. 18–29

Kouznetsov, D. et al., 1996, "Effects of fires and biofraction of carbon isotopes on results of radiocarbon dating of old textiles: the Shroud of Turin," *Journal of Archaeological Science*, 23, pp. 109–21

Kraeling, C. H., 1942, "The episode of the Roman standards at Jerusalem," *The Harvard Theological Review*, 35/4, pp. 263–89

Kreitzer, L., 1990, "Apotheosis of the Roman emperor," *Biblical Archaeologist*, 53, pp. 210–17

Laidler, K., 2000, *The Divine Deception: the Church, the Shroud and the creation of a holy fraud*, London

Landsborough, D., 1987, "St. Paul and temporal lobe epilepsy," *Journal of Neurology, Neurosurgery, and Psychiatry*, 50, pp. 659–64

Lane Fox, R., 1991, *The Unauthorized Version: truth and fiction in the Bible*, London

Latendresse, M., 2005, "The Turin Shroud was not flattened before the images formed and no major image distortions necessarily occur from a real body," www.sindonology.org/papers/latendresse2005a.pdf (accessed January 16, 2012)

Lavoie, G., 1998, *Unlocking the Secrets of the Shroud*, Allen, TX

Lee, D., 2004, *Transfiguration*, London

Légasse, S., 1997, *The Trial of Jesus*, trans. J. Bowden, London

Lejeune, J., 1995, "Étude topologique des Suaires de Turin, de Lier et de Pray," in *L'identification scientifique de l'homme du Linceul Jesus de Nazareth. Actes du Symposium Scientifique International (Rome, 1993)*, ed. A. Upinsky, Paris, pp. 104–9

Lognon, J. and R. Cazelles, 1969, *Les Très Riches Heures du Duc de Berry*, London

Loken, J., 2006, *The Shroud was the Resurrection: the body theft, the Shroud in the tomb, and the image that inspired a myth*, Ann Arbor

Loth, A., 1910, *La photographie du Saint Suaire de Turin*, Paris

Lüdemann, G., 1994, *The Resurrection of Jesus*, trans. J. Bowden, London

——, 2004, *The Resurrection of Christ: a historical enquiry*, New York

McBeath, A. and A. D. Gheorghe, 2004, "Meteor beliefs project: the Palladium in ancient and early Medieval sources," *WGN, the Journal of the International Meteor Organization*, 32/4, pp. 117–21

——, 2005, "Meteor beliefs project: meteorite worship in the ancient Greek and Roman worlds," *WGN, the Journal of the International Meteor Organization*, 33/5, pp. 135–44

MacCormack, S., 1981, *Art and Ceremony in Late Antiquity*, Berkeley

MacCulloch, D., 2009, *A History of Christianity: the first three thousand years*, London

Mack, B., 2001, *The Christian Myth: origins, logic and legacy*, London

Mack, J. (ed.), 1994, *Masks: the art of expression*, London

Maier, P., 1991, *In the Fullness of Time: a historian looks at Christmas, Easter and the early Church*, New York

Mannix, D., 2011, "Shroud image formation: some notes on the mechanism proposed by Rogers and Arnoldi," *BSTS Shroud Newsletter*, 74, pp. 2–6

Manselli, R. et al., 1984, *Lucca, il Volto Santo e la civiltà medioevale. Atti, convegno internazionale di studi (Lucca, Palazzo Pubblico 21–23 ott. 1982)*, Lucca

Marriott, W., 1886, *Vestiarum Christianum: the origin and gradual development of the dress of the holy ministry in the Church*, Oxford

Martin, M., 1991, *The Case against Christianity*, Philadelphia

Marxsen, W., 1970, *The Resurrection of Jesus of Nazareth*, trans. M. Kohl, London

Mayor, A., 2000, *The First Fossil Hunters: paleontology in Greek and Roman times*, Oxford

Mazzucchi, C., 1983, "La testimonianza più antica dell'esistenza di una sindone a Costantinopoli," *Aevum*, 57, pp. 227–31

McCrone, W. C., 1999, *Judgment Day for the Shroud of Turin*, New York

Meacham, W., 1983, "The authentification of the Turin Shroud: an issue in archaeological epistemology," *Current Anthropology*, 24/3, pp. 283–311

———, 1986, "Radiocarbon measurement and the age of the Turin Shroud," www.shroud.com/meacham.htm (accessed January 15, 2012)

———, 2005, *The Rape of the Turin Shroud: how Christianity's most precious relic was wrongly condemned, and violated*, n.p.

Melchior-Bonnet, S., 2001, *The Mirror: a history*, trans. K. Jewett, London

Meyer, M., 2004, *The Gospels of Mary: the secret tradition of Mary Magdalene*, New York

Miller, V. and S. Pellicori, 1981, "Ultraviolet fluorescence photography of the Shroud of Turin," *Journal of Biological Photography*, 49/3, pp. 71–85

———, 2009, "Hypotheses for image formation on the Turin Shroud," *BSTS Shroud Newsletter*, 69, pp. 16–22

Mills, A., 1995, "Image formation on the Shroud of Turin: the reactive oxygen intermediates hypothesis," *Interdisciplinary Science Reviews*, 20/4, pp. 319–27

Mitchell, W. J. T., 2005, *What Do Pictures Want? The lives and loves of images*, Chicago

Morison, F., 1958, *Who Moved the Stone?* 2nd edn, London

Morris, R. A. et al., 1980, "X-ray fluorescence investigation of the Shroud of Turin," *X-ray Spectrometry*, 9/2, pp. 40–47

Mottern, R. W. et al., 1980, "Radiographic examination of the Shroud of Turin—a preliminary report," *Materials Evaluation*, 38/12, pp. 39–44

Murphy-O'Connor, J., 1996, *Paul: a critical life*, Oxford

Naddaf, G., 2003, "The bones of giants," *Classical Review* (new series), 53, pp. 195–7

Nash, S., 2000, "The *Parement de Narbonne*: context and technique," in *The Fabric of Images: European paintings on textile supports in the fourteenth and fifteenth centuries*, ed. C. Villers, London, pp. 77–87

Netzer, E., 2006, *The Architecture of Herod, the Great Builder*, Tübingen

Newman, C., 1997, "Resurrection as glory: divine presence and Christian origins," in *The Resurrection*, ed. S. Davis et al., Oxford, pp. 59–89

Nickell, J., 1978a, "The Shroud of Turin unmasked," *The Humanist*, Jan.–Feb., pp. 20–22

———, 1978b, "The Shroud of Turin—solved!," *The Humanist*, Nov.–Dec., pp. 30–32

———, 1998, *Inquest on the Shroud of Turin*, New York

Nickelsburg, G. W. E., 1972, *Resurrection, Immortality and Eternal Life in Intertestamental Judaism*, Harvard Theological Studies 26, London

———, 1981, *Jewish Literature between the Bible and the Mishnah*, London

Norris, H., 1949, *Church Vestments: their origin and development*, London

O'Collins, G., 1980, *The Easter Jesus*, 2nd edn, London

Osiek, C., 1993, "The women at the tomb: what are they doing there?," *Ex auditu*, 9, pp. 97–107

Pagels, E., 1980, *The Gnostic Gospels*, London

———, 2003, *Beyond Belief: the secret gospel of Thomas*, London

Painter, J., 1999, *James: the brother of Jesus in history and tradition*, Edinburgh

Painter, K. and D. Whitehouse, 1990, "The history of the Portland Vase," *Journal of Glass Studies*, 32, pp. 24–84

Pellicori, S., 1980, "Spectral properties of the Shroud of Turin," *Applied Optics*, 19/12, pp. 1913–20

Perkins, P., 1984, *Resurrection: New Testament witness and contemporary reflection*, London

Pfeiffer, H., 2000, "Le piaghe di Cristo nell'arte e la Sindone," in *Le icone di Cristo e la Sindone: un modello per l'arte cristiana*, ed. F. Cavazzuti and L. Coppini, Milan, pp. 89–104

Phillips, G., (trans. and ed.), 1876, *The Doctrine of Addai, the Apostle*, London

Piana, A., 2007, *Sindone: gli anni perduti*, Milan

Picknett, L. and C. Prince, 1994, *Turin Shroud: In Whose Image? The shocking truth unveiled*, London

Piczek, I., 1995, "Is the Shroud a painting?," www.shroud.com/piczek.htm (accessed April 17, 2011)

——, 1996, "Alice in Wonderland and the Shroud of Turin," www.shroud.com/piczek2.htm (accessed April 17, 2011)

Price, R. M., 2005, "Apocryphal apparitions: 1 Corinthians 15:3–11 as a post-Pauline interpolation," in *The Empty Tomb: Jesus beyond the grave*, ed. R. M. Price and J. J. Lowder, New York, pp. 69–104

Price, R. M. and J. J. Lowder (eds), 2005, *The Empty Tomb: Jesus beyond the grave*, New York

Price, S. R. F., 1987, "From noble funerals to Divine Cult: the consecration of Roman emperors," in *Rituals of Royalty: power and ceremonial in traditional societies*, ed. D. Cannadine and S. Price, Cambridge, pp. 56–105

Raes, G., 1976, "Appendix B—Rapport d'Analise," *La S. Sindone (Rivista diocesana torinese)*, January, pp. 79–83

Ragg, L. and L. Ragg (trans.), 1907, *The Gospel of Barnabas*, Oxford

Ragusa, I., 1989, "The iconography of the Abgar cycle in Paris Ms. Lat. 2688 and its relationship to Byzantine cycles," *Miniatura*, 2, pp. 35–51

Reimarus, H. S., 1970, *Fragments*, ed. C. Talbert, trans. R. Fraser, Philadelphia

Riant, Paul, 1878, *Exuviae sacrae constantinopolitanae*, vol. 2, Geneva

Riley, G., 1995, *Resurrection Reconsidered: Thomas and John in controversy*, Minneapolis

Robinson, J., 1979, "The Shroud and the New Testament," in *La Sindone e la scienza. Atti del II congresso internazionale di Sindonologia (Turin 1978)*, ed. P. Coero-Borga, Turin, pp. 265–88

——, 1985, *The Priority of John*, London

Robinson, J. (ed.), 1990, *The Nag Hammadi Library*, New York

Roetzel, C., 1999, *Paul: the man and the myth*, Edinburgh

Rogers, R., 2005, "Studies on the radiocarbon sample from the Shroud of Turin," *Thermochimica Acta*, 425, pp. 189–94

——, 2008, *A Chemist's Perspective on the Shroud of Turin*, Florissant, CO

Rogers, R. and A. Arnoldi, 2003, "The Shroud of Turin: an amino-carbonyl reaction

(Maillard reaction) may explain the image formation," *Melanoidins*, 4, pp. 106–13 (www.shroud.com/pdfs/rogers7.pdf)

Rowland, C., 1985, *Christian Origins: an account of the setting and character of the most important Messianic sect of Judaism*, London

Runciman, S., 1931, "Some remarks on the image of Edessa," *Cambridge Historical Journal*, 3, pp. 238–52

Saldarini, A., 2001, *Pharisees, Scribes and Sadducees in Palestinian Society*, 2nd edn, Cambridge

Sanders, E., 1985, *Jesus and Judaism*, London

———, 1992, *Judaism: practice and belief, 63 BCE–66 CE*, London

———, 1993, *The Historical Figure of Jesus*, London

Scannerini, S., 1998, "Tracce botaniche sulla Sindone," in *Sindone: cento anni di ricerca*, ed. B. Barberis and G. M. Zaccone, Rome

Scavone, D., 2006, "Acheiropoietos Jesus images in Constantinople: the documentary evidence," www.shroudstory.com/scavone/scavone1.htm (accessed June 9, 2011)

Schaberg, M., 2003, *The Resurrection of Mary Magdalene: legends, apocrypha, and the Christian Testament*, London

Schäfer, P., 1997, "Magic and religion in ancient Judaism," in *Envisioning Magic: a Princeton seminar and symposium*, ed. P. Schäfer and H. Kippenberg, Leiden, pp. 19–43

Schillebeeckx, E., 1979, *Jesus: an experiment in Christology*, New York

Schmidt, C. (ed.), 1978, *Pistis Sophia*, trans. V. Macdermot, Leiden

Schonfield, H., 1996, *The Passover Plot*, 3rd edn, Shaftesbury

Schürer, E., 1973–87, *The History of the Jewish People in the Age of Jesus Christ (175 B.C.—A. D. 135)*, rev. and ed. G. Vermes et al., 3 vols, Edinburgh

Schwalbe, L. A. and R. N. Rogers, 1982, "Physics and chemistry of the Shroud of Turin: a summary of the 1978 investigation," *Analytica Chimica Acta*, 135, pp. 3–49

Schweitzer, A., 2000, *The Quest of the Historical Jesus*, trans. and ed. J. Bowden, London

Schwortz, B., 2000, "Is the Shroud of Turin a medieval photograph? A critical examination of the theory," www.shroud.com/pdfs/orvieto.pdf (accessed June 9, 2011)

Scott, J. B., 2003, *Architecture for the Shroud: relic and ritual in Turin*, Chicago

Seaford, R., 1984, "1 Corinthians 13.12," *Journal of Theological Studies* (new series), 35, pp. 117–20

Segal, A., 1987, *The Other Judaisms of Late Antiquity*, Atlanta

Segal, J. B., 1970, *Edessa "The Blessed City,"* Oxford

Smith, J. Z., 1990, *Drudgery Divine: on the comparison of early Christianities and the religions of late antiquity*, London

Smith, M., 1973, *Clement of Alexandria and a Secret Gospel of Mark*, Cambridge, MA

———, 1978, *Jesus the Magician*, Wellingborough

Spong, J. S., 1991, *Rescuing the Bible from Fundamentalism*, New York

Steinberg, L., 1983, *The Sexuality of Christ in Renaissance Art and Modern Oblivion*, London

Sterling, C., 1987, *La peinture médiévale à Paris 1300–1500*, vol. 1, Paris

Stewart, R. (ed.), 2006, *The Resurrection of Jesus: John Dominic Crossan and N. T. Wright in dialogue*, London

Stoichita, V., 1997, *A Short History of the Shadow*, London

Straiton, M., 1989, "The man in the Shroud: a 13th-century crucifixion action-replay," *Catholic Medical Quarterly*, 40, pp. 135–43

Strauss, D. F., 1846, *The Life of Jesus Critically Examined*, 4th edn, 3 vols, London

——, 1865, *A New Life of Jesus*, 2 vols, London

Swinburne, R., 2003, *The Resurrection of God Incarnate*, Oxford

Tabor, J., 2006, *The Jesus Dynasty: the hidden history of Jesus, his royal family, and the birth of Christianity*, London

Taylor, J., 2000, "Before the portraits: burial practices in Pharaonic Egypt," in *Ancient Faces: mummy portraits from Roman Egypt*, ed. S. Walker, 2nd edn, London, pp. 9–13

Taylor, R., 2008, *The Moral Mirror of Roman Art*, Cambridge

Thiering, B., 1992, *Jesus the Man: a new interpretation from the Dead Sea Scrolls*, London

Tobin, P., 2009, *The Rejection of Pascal's Wager: a skeptic's guide to the Bible and the historical Jesus*, Gamlingay

Trachtenberg, J., 1939, *Jewish Magic and Superstition: a study in folk religion*, New York

Tribbe, F., 1983, *Portrait of Jesus? The illustrated story of the Shroud of Turin*, New York

Tyerman, C., 2006, *God's War: a new history of the Crusades*, London

Tylor, E., 1903, *Primitive Culture: researches into the development of mythology, philosophy, religion, art, and custom*, 4th edn, 2 vols, London

Van der Horst, P. W., 1977, "Peter's shadow," *New Testament Studies*, 23, pp. 204–13

——, 1979, "Der Schatten im Hellenistischen Volksglauben," in *Studies in Hellenistic religions*, ed. M. J. Vermaseren, Leiden, pp. 27–36

Vanderkam, J. (ed.), 1989, *The Book of Jubilees*, Louvain

Vermes, G., 1995, *The Dead Sea Scrolls in English*, 4th edn, Sheffield

——, 2008, *The Resurrection*, London

Vignon, P., 1902, *The Shroud of Christ*, London

——, 1939, *Le Saint Suaire de Turin devant la science, l'archéologie, l'histoire, l'iconographie, la logique*, 2nd edn, Paris

Volckringer, J., 1991, *The Holy Shroud: science confronts the imprints*, trans. V. Harper, ed. R. Morgan, Manly, NSW

Von Negelein, J., 1902, "Bild, Spiegel und Schatten im Volksglauben," *Archiv für Religionwissenschaft*, 5, pp. 1–37

Walker, S., 2000, *Ancient Faces: mummy portraits from Roman Egypt*, 2nd edn, London

——, 2004, *The Portland Vase*, London

Walsh, J., 1964, *The Shroud*, London

Walter, C., 1982, *Art and Ritual of the Byzantine Church*, London

Ware, M., 1997, "On proto-photography and the Shroud of Turin," *History of Photography*, 21/4, pp. 261–9

Watson, G. R., 1969, *The Roman Soldier*, London

Watson, P., 2005, *Ideas: a history from fire to Freud*, London

Webb, D. M., 1986, "The Holy Face of Lucca," in *Anglo-Norman Studies*, IX: *Proceedings of the Battle Conference*, ed. R. A. Brown, Wolfeboro, pp. 227–37

Wedderburn, A. J. M., 1999, *Beyond Resurrection*, London

——, 2004, *A History of the First Christians*, London

Wells, G. A., 1982, *The Historical Evidence for Jesus*, Buffalo

——, 1986, *Did Jesus Exist?* rev. edn, London

Whanger, M. and A. Whanger, 1998, *The Shroud of Turin: an adventure of discovery*, Franklin, TN

Wilson, A. N., 1999, *God's Funeral*, London

Wilson, I., 1978, *The Turin Shroud*, London

——, 1984, *Jesus: the evidence*, London

——, 1986, *The Evidence of the Shroud*, London

——, 1998, *The Blood and the Shroud*, London

——, 2010, *The Shroud: the 2000-year-old mystery solved*, London

Wilson, N. D., 2005, "Father Brown fakes the Shroud," www.booksandculture.com/articles/2005/marapr/3.22.html (accessed January 15, 2012)

Wolf, G., 1998, "From Mandylion to Veronica: picturing the 'disembodied' face and disseminating the true image of Christ in the Latin West," in *The Holy Face and the Paradox of Representation*, ed. H. Kessler and G. Wolf, Bologna, pp. 153–79

Woodfin, W., 2004, "Liturgical textiles," in *Byzantium: faith and power* (exhibition catalogue, Metropolitan Museum of Art), ed. H. C. Evans, New York

Wright, N. T., 1992, *The New Testament and the People of God* (*Christian Origins and the Question of God*, vol. 1), London

——, 1996, *Jesus and the Victory of God* (*Christian Origins and the Question of God*, vol. 2), London

——, 2003, *The Resurrection of the Son of God* (*Christian Origins and the Question of God*, vol. 3), London

Wuenschel, E. A., 1954, *Self-portrait of Christ: the Holy Shroud of Turin*, New York

Zahrnt, H., 1963, *The Historical Jesus*, trans. J. Bowden, London

Zaninotto, G., 2000, "L'Acheropita del Ss. Salvatore nel Sancta Sanctorum del Laterano," in *Le icone di Cristo e la Sindone: un modello per l'arte cristiana*, ed. F. Cavazzuti and L. Coppini, Milan, pp. 164–80

Zias, J. and E. Sekeles, 1985, "The crucified man from Giv'at ha-Mivtar: a reappraisal," *Israel Exploration Journal*, 35, pp. 22–7

Zugibe, F., 2005, *The Crucifixion of Jesus: a forensic enquiry*, New York

Index